THE
VINEYARD
BIBLE

THE
VINEYARD
BIBLE

A CENTRAL NARRATIVE
AND INDEX

Edited by Avery Brooke; Assistant Editors: Eleanor Allen,
Katheryne M. Fincke, Elizabeth Moynahan, Rose E. Hoover

THE SEABURY PRESS · NEW YORK

1980
The Seabury Press
815 Second Avenue · New York, N.Y. 10017

Library of Congress Cataloging in Publication Data
Bible. English. Authorized. Selections. 1980.
The Vineyard Bible.

Quotations from the King James Version.
Includes index.
1. Brooke, Avery. II. Title.
BS391.2.B74   220.5′203   79-27593
ISBN 0-8164-0144-6

Concerning the use of this book:

The narrative index is made up of quotations from the King James version of the Bible. These lines are often abridged or paraphrased. If you wish to refer to the exact verse in the Bible, please use the *key word index* in the back of the book.

Contents

Introduction   xi

Old Testament
EARLIEST BIBLICAL STORIES   1

1 · Creation and the Garden of Eden   3
2 · After Eden   5
3 · Abraham and Sarah, Isaac and Rebekah   7
4 · Jacob and Esau, Rachel and Leah   10
5 · Joseph and His Brothers: The Move to Egypt   12
6 · Moses and the Children of Israel in Egypt   13
7 · Moses and the Children of Israel
       in the Wilderness   16

STORIES FROM THE HISTORICAL BOOKS   25

8 · Across the Jordan: Israel under the Judges   27
9 · Israel under Saul, David and Solomon   32
10 · The Divided Kingdom:
       Early Prophets, Elijah and Elisha   39
11 · Defeat of Jerusalem: Exile and Return   45

PSALMS, POETRY, PROVERBS, AND WISDOM   47

12 · Job   49
13 · Psalms   55
14 · Proverbs   69
15 · Ecclesiastes   74
16 · The Song of Songs, which is Solomon's   77

ISAIAH   79

17 · Isaiah's Vision of Judah and Jerusalem   81
18 · All Nations   85
19 · Warning and Hope for God's Rebellious People   88
20 · A Message of Comfort   91

OTHER PROPHETS   97

21 · Jeremiah and Lamentations   99
22 · Ezekiel   105
23 · Daniel   110
24 · Hosea and Joel   114
25 · Amos and Obadiah   118
26 · Jonah, Micah and Nahum   120
27 · Habakkuk, Zephaniah and Haggai   123
28 · Zechariah and Malachi   125

New Testament
THE LIFE OF CHRIST   129

29 · The Birth of Christ and Preparation
        for his Ministry   131
30 · Early Ministry in Galilee   136
31 · Teaching and Healing   143
32 · Some Stories Told Only by Luke   149
33 · In the Midst of his Ministry   154
34 · Shadows of Things to Come   160
35 · Some Stories Told Only by John   165
36 · Jesus in Jerusalem   169
37 · Teachings on the End of the World   172
38 · Death and Resurrection   175
39 · The Acts of the Apostles   189

40 · Paul's Letter to Rome   199
41 · Paul's Letters to the Corinthians   205
42 · Letters to Galatia and Ephesus   213
43 · Letters to Philippi, Colossa, and Thessalonica   218
44 · Paul Writes to Timothy, Titus, and Philemon   223
45 · A Letter to the Hebrews   228
46 · Letters from James and Peter   232
47 · Letters from John and Jude   237
48 · The Revelation of John for the
         Seven Churches in Asia   240

Gazetteer   249

Key Word Index   263

Acknowledgments

To compile a volume such as THE VINEYARD BIBLE necessitates making thousands of choices. We wished to include those lines and stories which are most apt to be carried in peoples' hearts as teachers, talismans, and revealers of the greatest truths. These were difficult choices to make and the diverse backgrounds of the editors of this book have been a tremendous help in the process of selection. Kay Fincke's background was in music, Eleanor Allen's in speech and drama, and Elizabeth Moynahan's in art history. Rose Hoover is a Baptist minister, and my own primary interest is writing about and teaching prayer. To this basic group of five, we added the insights of Harriet Corrigan whose research on the use of psalms was invaluable, Shelley Burtt who came to us as a seventeen-year-old apprentice and later went on to Harvard where she is now a senior and president of "The Harvard Independent," and Janet Brown whose trained legal mind, coupled with her Biblical knowledge, helped us to avoid many an error or inconsistency. These seven editors worked with me at different times over a six-year period, and our common love of the Bible increased as we worked. All of us owe thanks to Joan Frank for her support and encouragement during this long task. A book such as this needs an incredible amount of painstaking typing. Throughout years of work on many versions of the same material, she retained her patience, accuracy and enthusiasm, and encouraged us all.

Avery Brooke

Introduction

Christians and non-Christians alike either know, or hope, that the Bible contains words of great meaning, wisdom, and love that may help them in the living of their lives. *But where are those words when they need them?* The Bible is a long and complex book, indeed it is a collection of books. Those fortunate enough to be really familiar with the Bible find the needed words and stories springing to mind and, if only partially remembered, they know the Bible well enough to be able to find the desired passage with little difficulty. Unfortunately, most people, including many Christians, are not that comfortable and practically familiar with the Bible. It is for these people that this book has been compiled.

The major portion of *The Vineyard Bible* is a narrative index. The most familiar lines—the very core of the Bible—have been arranged so that they may be read in sequence, revealing as much as is possible in a short space, of the content, beauty, and truth of the original passages from which they were taken. Underneath each line, or group of lines, their location in the Bible is indicated so that those who wish to refer to the original may do so.

Beyond the focus on individual lines and passages, the narrative index is designed for reading as well as reference. When read as one would read any other sequential material, the whole panorama of the Bible becomes clear and the essential oneness of this group of diverse books is revealed. To aid the reader gain this larger perspective, we have interwoven those books of the Bible where the same stories have been told in different versions. (The Gospels in the New Testament and the historical books in the Old Testament.)

The Vineyard Bible also contains an alphabetical *key word index* which is unusually extensive. In addition to referring to page numbers in the book, the *key word index* refers to chapter and verse in the Bible itself.

A *gazetteer* has been included primarily for travelers to the Mediterranean and the Near East. The Bible has imprinted many places in our minds and hearts, and although the truth of the stories associated with these places is beyond time and place, nonetheless it is moving to be able to find the pertinent Biblical passages associated with a town or an area that is identifiable today. To stand, for instance, in the ruins of King Solomon's stables, to see the horse troughs from which his horses drank, and to read simultaneously of this great and wise king enhances both the place and the stories. To realize that in Capernaum today one can see the foundation of a house that in all likelihood was Peter's and then go back to your hotel and read of Peter and his home town is awesome. For convenience, we have included modern place names as well as Biblical ones.

The Vineyard Bible is based on the *King James Version.* We have paraphrased as needed for clarity or abridgement. Believing that the constant interruption of elipses would spoil the readability, we have only used them to indicate that an important section has been left out for reasons of space. A few portions of the Bible—such as the Beatitudes—cannot be properly abridged and we have given only an indication, a reminder, and the citation as we did not wish to include the whole section verbatim for reasons of length. Our most frequent abridgments have been of passages, of stories, or of whole chapters. What sometimes appears to be a paragraph is often a collection of scattered lines that seemed to us to convey the sense and feeling of the whole.

If you search the shelves of libraries and book stores today, you are unlikely to find anything similar to *The Vineyard Bible.* It is not a dictionary, concordance, or commentary. It simply introduces the Bible by presenting the very heart of the Bible itself.

Avery Brooke

Abbreviations

	Used in Text	Used in Index
Genesis	Gen.	Gen.
Exodus	Ex.	Ex.
Leviticus	Lev.	Lev.
Numbers	Num.	Num.
Deuteronomy	Deut.	Deut.
Joshua	Josh.	Josh.
Judges	Judges	Jg.
Ruth	Ruth	Ruth
I Samuel	I Sam.	I Sam.
II Samuel	II Sam.	II Sam.
I Kings	I Kings	I Kg.
II Kings	II Kings	II Kg.
I Chronicles	I Chron.	I Chr.
II Chronicles	II Chron.	II Chr.
Ezra	Ezra	Ezra
Nehemiah	Neh.	Neh.
Esther	Esther	Est.
Job	Job	Job
Psalms	Psalm	Ps.
Proverbs	Prov.	Prov.
Ecclesiastes	Eccles.	Ec.
Song of Solomon	Song	Song
Isaiah	Isaiah	Isa.
Jeremiah	Jer.	Jer.
Lamentations	Lament.	Lam.
Ezekial	Ezek.	Ezek.
Daniel	Dan.	Dan.
Hosea	Hosea	Hos.
Joel	Joel	Joel
Amos	Amos	Amos
Obadiah	Obad.	Obad.
Jonah	Jonah	Jonah
Micah	Micah	Micah

Nahum	Nahum	Nahum
Habakkuk	Hab.	Hab.
Zephaniah	Zeph.	Zeph.
Haggai	Hagg.	Hagg.
Zechariah	Zech.	Zech.
Malachi	Mal.	Mal.
Matthew	Matt.	Matt.
Mark	Mark	Mk.
Luke	Luke	Lk.
John	John	Jn.
Acts of the Apostles	Acts	Acts
Romans	Rom.	Rom.
I Corinthians	I Cor.	I Cor.
II Corinthians	II Cor.	II Cor.
Galatians	Gal.	Gal.
Ephesians	Eph.	Eph.
Phillipians	Phil.	Phil.
Colossians	Col.	Col.
I Thessalonians	I Thess.	I Th.
II Thessalonians	II Thess.	II Th.
I Timothy	I Tim.	I Tim.
II Timothy	II Tim.	II Tim.
Titus	Titus	Tit.
Philemon	Philem.	Philem.
Hebrews	Heb.	Heb.
James	Jas.	Jas.
I Peter	I Peter	I Pet.
II Peter	II Peter	II Pet.
I John	I John	I Jn.
II John	(not cited)	
III John	III John	III Jn.
Jude	Jude	Jude
Revelation	Rev.	Rev.

Old Testament

EARLIEST BIBLICAL STORIES

Creation and the
Garden of Eden

THE CREATION OF THE WORLD
Gen. 1—2:3

SECOND ACCOUNT OF CREATION
Gen. 2:4–25

IN THE BEGINNING GOD CREATED THE HEAVEN
AND THE EARTH
The earth was without form, and void
Darkness was upon the face of the deep
The spirit of God moved upon the face of the waters
Gen. 1:1–2

GOD SAID, LET THERE BE LIGHT:
AND THERE WAS LIGHT
God divided the light from the darkness
God called the light Day and the darkness he called Night
Gen. 1:3–5

GOD CREATED THE EARTH AND THE SEAS
Let the waters be gathered together, let the dry land
    appear
God called the dry land, Earth, the waters called he Seas
And God saw that it was good
Gen. 1:9–10

LET THE EARTH BRING FORTH GRASS
Herb yielding seed and fruit tree yielding fruit
And God saw that it was good
Gen. 1:11–12

LET THE WATERS BRING FORTH LIVING CREATURES
Let birds fly above the earth
And God created great whales

Let the earth bring forth cattle and creeping things
And God saw that it was good
Gen. 1:20–25

THE CREATION OF ADAM AND EVE
So God created man in his own image
Let them have dominion over all the earth
And God blessed them and said be fruitful and multiply
Gen. 1:26–31

AND IT WAS VERY GOOD
God saw everything he had made and it was very good
Thus the heavens and the earth were finished
God rested on the seventh day from all his work
God blessed the seventh day and sanctified it
Gen. 1:31—2:3

SECOND ACCOUNT OF THE CREATION OF ADAM AND EVE
God formed man of the dust from the ground
And breathed into his nostrils the breath of life
Man became a living soul
It is not good that the man should be alone
The Lord made a woman from Adam's rib
They were both naked and unashamed
Bone of my bones, flesh of my flesh
A man cleaves to his wife and they shall be one flesh
Gen. 2:7–25

THE LORD PLANTED A GARDEN EASTWARD IN EDEN
Every tree that is pleasant to the sight
    and good for food
The tree of life in the midst of the garden
And the tree of knowledge of good and evil
God put man in the garden to till and keep it
Of every tree you may freely eat
But of the tree of the knowledge of good and evil you
    shall not eat
Gen. 2:8–17

Adam gave names to all the cattle, birds and beasts
Gen. 2:19–20

TEMPTATION AND DISOBEDIENCE OF ADAM AND EVE
The serpent was more subtle than any beast
God told them not to eat the fruit of the tree
The serpent said: When you eat you will be like gods
Knowing good and evil
Eve ate the forbidden fruit and gave some to Adam
Gen. 3:1–6

THEIR EYES WERE OPENED
AND THEY KNEW THEY WERE NAKED
They sewed fig leaves together and made aprons
They heard the voice of the Lord and hid
Who told you that you were naked? Have you eaten
    of the tree?
The woman gave me fruit
The serpent beguiled me
Gen. 3:7–13

THE JUDGMENT OF GOD
In sorrow shalt thou bring forth children
In the sweat of your face you shall eat bread
Dust you are and to dust you shall return
And God sent them forth from the garden
Gen. 3:14–24

After Eden

CAIN ROSE UP AGAINST ABEL AND KILLED HIM
Where is Abel your brother?
Am I my brother's keeper?
You shall be a fugitive and a wanderer on the earth
My punishment is more than I can bear
The Lord put a mark on Cain to protect him
Gen. 4:8–15

Jubal was the father of all those who play the harp
    and the organ
Gen. 4:21

The days of Methuselah were nine hundred
    and sixty-nine years
Gen. 5:27

GOD TELLS NOAH HE WILL DESTROY ALL FLESH
God saw the wickedness of man was great
It repented the Lord that he had made man
And the Lord said: I will destroy man
But Noah found favor in the eyes of the Lord
Noah begat three sons, Shem, Ham, and Japheth
Gen. 6:5–13

NOAH'S ARK
Make yourself an ark of gopher wood
You shall come into the ark, you, your wife, your sons,
    and their wives
Bring two of every living thing, male and female
Take with you every sort of food for you and them
Thus did Noah as God commanded
Gen. 6:14–22

THE FLOOD
The fountains of the great deep burst forth
The windows of heaven were opened
The rain was upon the earth forty days and forty nights
The waters prevailed one hundred and fifty days
Gen. 7:4–24

THE FLOOD RECEDES
The Ark rested on Mount Ararat
Noah sent forth a dove
The second time the dove brought an olive leaf
Noah went forth and his sons and his wife . . .
And Noah builded an altar to the Lord
Gen. 8

THE RAINBOW: GOD'S COVENANT WITH NOAH
Never again will I kill every living creature
While the earth remaineth, seed time and harvest . . .
    shall not cease
I establish my covenant with you
My bow in the cloud shall be a token
Gen. 8:21—9:17

THE TOWER OF BABEL
The whole earth was of one language
Let us build a tower whose top will reach unto heaven
God said: Now nothing they propose will be impossible
The Lord did therefore confound the language
    and scatter them abroad
Gen. 11:1–9

Abraham (Abram) and Sarah (Sarai); Isaac and Rebekah

THE CALL OF ABRAM
Go to a land that I will show you
I will make of thee a great nation
Into the land of Canaan they came
Unto thy seed will I give this land
Gen. 12:1–8

ABRAM WENT DOWN INTO EGYPT
FOR THERE WAS A FAMINE
Abram pretended Sarai was his sister
Pharaoh said: Why did you not tell me
    she was your wife?
Gen. 12:10–20

ABRAM AND LOT
Let there be no strife between me and thee
If thou take the left hand then I take the right

7

Lot chose the plain of Jordan
Abram dwelled in the land of Canaan
God said: I will make your seed as the dust of the earth
Abram dwelt by the oaks of Mamre at Hebron
Abram rescued Lot from captivity
Melchizedek brought forth bread and wine
    and blessed Abram
Gen. 13—14:20

ABRAM'S VISION AND COVENANT
Fear not Abram, I am thy shield
And thy exceeding great reward
Unto thy seed have I given this land
Gen. 15

SARAI'S BARRENNESS
Sarai bare Abram no children
Sarai took Hagar her maid and gave her to Abram
Hagar conceived a son, Ishmael
He will be a wild man, his hand will be against every man
Gen. 16

GOD'S COVENANT WITH ABRAM
Thy name shall be Abraham, father of many nations
I will give unto thee and to thy seed . . .
    all the land of Canaan
Every man child among you shall be circumcised
Gen. 17:1–14

AS FOR SARAI THY WIFE, SARAH SHALL BE HER NAME
She shall be a mother of nations
Abraham laughed for they were old
Sarah thy wife shall bear thee a son . . . Isaac
I will establish my covenant with him
Sarah laughed within herself
Gen. 17:15—18:16

SODOM AND GOMORRAH
Abraham: Wilt thou destroy the righteous with the wicked?
The Lord: For the sake of ten I will not destroy the city
Escape for thy life, look not behind thee
The Lord rained on Sodom and Gomorrah brimstone
    and fire
Lot's wife looked back and became a pillar of salt
Gen. 18:16—19:26

THE BIRTH OF ISAAC
Sarah bare Abraham a son in his old age
Gen. 21:1–7

ABRAHAM SENT HAGAR AND ISHMAEL AWAY
Let me not see the death of the child
God heard the voice of the lad
Gen. 21:9–21

THE SACRIFICE OF ISAAC
Take now thy son, thy only son, and offer him
    as a burnt offering
Isaac: Where is the lamb for a burnt offering?
God will provide himself a lamb
Abraham bound his son and laid him on the altar
The angel of the Lord called:
Lay not your hand upon the lad
For now I know you fear the Lord
Abraham looked up and beheld a ram in the thicket
Gen. 22:1–18

ABRAHAM SENT HIS SERVANT
TO FIND A WIFE FOR ISAAC
Go unto my country, to my kindred
The servant found Rebekah at the well
Isaac took Rebekah, she became his wife and he loved her
Gen. 24

Jacob (Israel) and Esau, Rachel and Leah

REBEKAH GIVES BIRTH TO JACOB AND ESAU
Two nations are in thy womb
The elder shall serve the younger
The first born, Esau, had skin like a hairy garment
The second born, Jacob, took hold of Esau's heel
Gen. 25:21–26

ESAU SELLS HIS BIRTHRIGHT TO JACOB
FOR POTTAGE
Gen. 25:27–34

JACOB STEALS ESAU'S BLESSING FROM ISAAC
Isaac was old and his eyes were dim
Rebekah disguised Jacob in Esau's clothes
She put skins of goats upon his hands
Isaac: The voice is Jacob's but the hands are Esau's
Isaac blessed Jacob—thinking him Esau
Esau cried, bless me, even me also
Gen. 27:1–40

JACOB FLEES FROM ESAU
Esau hated Jacob because of the blessing
He said in his heart: I will slay my brother Jacob
Rebekah told Jacob to flee to her brother Laban
Tarry with him until thy brother's fury turn
Gen. 27:41—28:10

JACOB'S LADDER
Jacob dreamed of a ladder reaching to heaven
The land whereon thou liest will I give to thee
Thy seed shall be as the dust of the earth
Behold I am with you and will keep you

Jacob called the place Bethel
Of all that thou shalt give me, I will give a tenth
    unto thee
Gen. 28:10–22

RACHEL AND LEAH
Rachel came to the well with her father's sheep
Jacob moved the stone from the well's mouth
He told Rachel that he was Rebekah's son
Laban said surely thou art my bone and flesh
And Jacob abode with him
Jacob loved Rachel and served seven years for her
In the evening Laban took Leah to Jacob
Did I not serve with thee for Rachel?
Thou shalt serve another seven years for Rachel
Gen. 29:1–28

The Lord watch between me and thee when we are absent
    one from another
Gen. 31:49

JACOB'S AND ESAU'S RECONCILIATION
Deliver me I pray thee from the hand of my brother Esau
Esau ran to meet him and embraced him
Jacob built a house and booths in Succoth
Gen. 32:3–21; 33:1–20

JACOB WRESTLES WITH AN ANGEL
Jacob was alone and a man wrestled with him
Until the breaking of the day
He touched the hollow of his thigh
Jacob cried I will not let thee go, except thou bless me
Gen. 32:22–32

Thy name shall be called no more Jacob, but Israel
Gen. 32:28

Joseph and His Brothers:
The Move to Egypt

ISRAEL LOVED JOSEPH MORE THAN ALL HIS CHILDREN
He made him a coat of many colors
His brothers stripped him of his coat of many colors
They cast him into a pit in Dothan
Gen. 37:3–36

JOSEPH WAS SOLD TO POTIPHAR,
AN OFFICER OF PHARAOH
Potiphar's wife cast her eyes upon Joseph
Joseph's master put him into prison
Gen. 37:36; 39:1–23

JOSEPH INTERPRETED THE DREAMS
OF PHARAOH'S BUTLER AND BAKER
Gen. 40

JOSEPH INTERPRETED PHARAOH'S DREAMS
Pharaoh dreamed of seven fat cows and seven thin
Seven ears of corn, rank and good, and seven thin ears
There will be seven years of plenty
        and seven years of famine
Gen. 41:1–36

PHARAOH SET JOSEPH OVER ALL THE LAND OF EGYPT
In the years of plenty Joseph laid up food
Joseph gathered corn as the sand of the sea
Famine was over all the earth
But in Egypt there was bread
Gen. 41:38–57

JOSEPH'S BROTHERS CAME TO EGYPT TO BUY CORN
Joseph knew his brothers but they knew him not
Joseph turned away and wept
I am Joseph your brother whom you sold into Egypt

God did send me before you to preserve life
You shall bring my father to the land of Goshen
And you shall eat the fat of the land
Gen. 42—45

ISRAEL BLESSED JOSEPH'S SONS
Let my name be named on them
God shall bring you into the land of your fathers
Gen. 48

THE TWELVE TRIBES OF ISRAEL
Reuben . . . unstable as water thou shalt not excel
Judah is a lion's whelp
Gen. 49

Moses and the Children
of Israel in Egypt

THERE AROSE A NEW KING OVER EGYPT
WHO KNEW NOT JOSEPH
The children of Israel were fruitful
    and increased abundantly
Behold, the children of Israel are mightier than we
They built for Pharaoh treasure cities,
    Pithom and Raamses
Ex. 1:1–14

THE BIRTH OF MOSES
Pharaoh decreed the death of all Hebrew sons
Moses' mother took for him an ark of bulrushes
And laid it in the reeds by the river's brink
The daughter of Pharaoh came down to wash
And she had compassion
This is one of the Hebrews' children

The child grew and became her son
She called him Moses
Ex. 1:15—2:10

WHEN MOSES WAS GROWN
Moses saw his brothers' burdens
He saw an Egyptian beating an Hebrew
And slew the Egyptian and hid him in the sand
Moses fled to the land of Midian
Ex. 2:11–15

I have been a stranger in a strange land
Ex. 2:22

MOSES AND THE BURNING BUSH
The bush burned with fire and was not consumed
God called to Moses from the midst of the bush
The place on which you stand is holy ground
Moses hid his face, afraid to look upon God
The Lord said: I have seen the affliction of my people
I am come to deliver them out of Egypt
To a land flowing with milk and honey
I will send thee unto Pharaoh
Ex. 3:1–10

MOSES ARGUED WITH GOD
Who am I that I should go unto Pharaoh?
They will not believe me
I am slow of speech and of a slow tongue
God promised to teach Moses what to say
Ex. 3:11—4:17

MOSES ASKED GOD'S NAME
I AM THAT I AM
Ex. 3:13–15

LET MY PEOPLE GO
Moses told Pharaoh thus saith the Lord
Who is the Lord, that I should obey his voice?
Aaron's rod became a serpent
Ex. 5:1—7:10

THE PLAGUES OF EGYPT
The Lord hardened Pharaoh's heart
The rivers of Egypt turned to blood
The frogs came up and covered the land
All the dust of the land became lice
There came a grievous swarm of flies
All the cattle of Egypt died
Ashes became a boil upon man and beast
The Lord rained hail upon the land
And the locusts went up over all the land
Darkness over the land of Egypt,
       darkness which may be felt
Ex. 7—10

IT IS THE LORD'S PASSOVER
I will bring one more plague on Pharaoh
All the firstborn of Egypt shall die
Take a lamb without blemish and slaughter it
Strike the blood on the lintels and door posts
Eat in haste with unleavened bread, the bread of affliction
I will pass through Egypt and smite the firstborn
When I see the blood I will pass over you
This day shall be a memorial
And you shall keep it a feast
Seven days shall you eat unleavened bread, the bread of
       affliction
The Lord brought the children of Israel out of Egypt
Ex. 11—12; cf. Lev. 23:5–8; Deut. 16:1–8

Moses and the Children of Israel in the Wilderness

THE LORD DID BRING THE CHILDREN OF ISRAEL
OUT OF EGYPT
Sanctify unto me all the firstborn
Remember this day in which ye came out from Egypt . . .
The Lord went before them by day in a pillar of cloud
By night in a pillar of fire
Ex. 12:51—13

CROSSING THE RED SEA
Pharaoh pursued the children of Israel with chariots
The Lord said: Lift up thy rod and divide the sea
Israel passed through walls of water on dry ground
Moses stretched forth his hand and the sea returned
Waters covered the chariots and horses
        and all the host of Pharaoh
Ex. 14

MOSES' SONG OF VICTORY
The horse and his rider hath he thrown into the sea
The Lord is my strength and song
He is become my salvation
The Lord is a man of war: the Lord is his name
Thy right hand is become glorious in power
Thou sentest forth thy wrath
Which consumed them as stubble
Miriam and all the women went out
        with timbrels and dances
Ex. 15:1–21

MANNA IN THE WILDERNESS
Would to God we had died in the land of Egypt
We sat by the fleshpots and ate bread to the full
Ye have brought us into this wilderness
To kill us with hunger

Ye shall eat flesh and know that I am the Lord your God
At even the quails came up and covered the camp
Behold I will rain bread from heaven for you
In the morning manna covered the ground
It was like coriander seed and honey
Ex. 16; Num. 11:6–9, 31

GIVE US WATER THAT WE MAY DRINK
Moses smote the rock and water came forth abundantly
You shall not bring this congregation
    into the land I have given them
Ex. 17:2–7; Num. 20:7–13

THE FORCES OF JOSHUA FOUGHT WITH AMALEK
Aaron and Hur held up Moses' hands and Israel
    prevailed
Ex. 17:8–16

JETHRO'S COUNSEL TO MOSES
Thou shalt teach them ordinances and laws
Thou shalt provide able men as rulers and judges
They shall bear the burden with thee
Ex. 18

GOD APPEARED TO MOSES ON MOUNT SINAI
Moses went up unto God and the Lord called unto him
If you keep my covenant you will be a holy nation
Mount Sinai was wrapped in smoke, the Lord descended
    upon it in fire
I am the Lord your God
Ex. 19 (Ex. 20—34)

THE TEN COMMANDMENTS
Thou shalt have no other gods before me
Thou shalt not make any graven image
    nor bow down to them
Thou shalt not take the name of the Lord in vain

Remember the sabbath, to keep it holy
Honor thy Father and thy Mother
Thou shalt not kill
Thou shalt not commit adultery
Thou shalt not steal
Thou shalt not bear false witness against thy neighbor
Thou shalt not covet . . .
Ex. 20:1–17; Deut. 5

The Lord wrote the commandments
    on two tables of stone
Ex. 24:12; 31:18; 32:16

Eye for eye, tooth for tooth . . .
Ex. 21:24; Matt. 5:38

THE WORSHIP OF THE GOLDEN CALF
While Moses was on Sinai Aaron made a golden calf
God warned Moses: It is a stiffnecked people
On his return Moses' anger waxed hot
He cast the tablets out of his hands
Who is on the Lord's side? let him come unto me
Ex. 32

SHOW ME THY GLORY
Thou canst not see my face: for no man shall see me
    and live
I will put thee in a crack of the rock
And cover thee with my hand while I pass by
Ex. 33:18–23

THE ARK AND THE TABERNACLE
The Israelites constructed the ark and the tabernacle
Moses put the testimony into the ark
And the ark into the tabernacle
Ex. 35—40; Num. 9:15–23

LAWS CONCERNING SACRIFICE
Lev. 1—7

THE CONSECRATION OF AARON AND HIS SONS
Lev. 8—10

THE SERVICE OF THE LEVITES
Num. 8:6–26; I Chron. 23:24–32

LAWS CONCERNING CLEAN AND UNCLEAN
Swine is unclean to you. Of their flesh shall ye not eat
Lev. 11—18; Deut. 14:3–21

THE DAY OF ATONEMENT
The tenth day of the seventh month . . .
Aaron shall sacrifice two goats
One shall be a sin offering to the Lord
The other shall go for a scapegoat into the wilderness
He will be an atonement for the iniquities of Israel
Ex. 30:10; Lev. 16, 23:26–32; Num. 29:7–11

THE SABBATH
God blessed the seventh day and sanctified it
You shall work six days but the seventh is the sabbath
Gen. 2:3; Ex. 20:8–11, 23:12; Lev. 23:3; Deut. 5:12–15

THE LORD BLESS THEE AND KEEP THEE
The Lord make his face shine upon thee
    and be gracious unto thee
The Lord lift up his countenance upon thee
    and give thee peace
Num. 6:24–26

TWELVE SPIES SENT TO CANAAN
Moses sent them to spy out the land
It floweth with milk and honey
They are stronger than we
Would God we had died in this wilderness!
The Lord said: How long will this people provoke me?
Your children shall wander in the wilderness forty years
Num. 13—14:37

19

THE DEATH OF AARON
The Lord spoke to Moses and Aaron at Mount Hor
Aaron shall be gathered unto his people
He shall not enter the land
Aaron died on top of Mount Hor
Num. 20:22–29

BALAAM'S ASS
Balaam rose in the morning and saddled his ass
God's anger was kindled because he went
The ass saw the angel of the Lord standing in the way
And the Lord opened the mouth of the ass . . .
Balaam said: I have sinned
For I knew not what stood in the way
Num. 22:21–35

Let me die the death of the righteous
Num. 23:10

God is not a man, that he should lie
Num. 23:19

What hath God wrought!
Num. 23:23

How goodly are thy tents, O Jacob . . .
Num. 24:5

THE CALLING OF JOSHUA
God told Moses to go to Mount Abarim
To see the chosen land
When thou hast seen it, thou also shalt be gathered
     unto thy people
Let the Lord set a man over the congregation
Take thee Joshua a man in whom is the spirit
Num. 27:12–23

Be sure your sin will find you out
Num. 32:23

THE SONG OF MOSES
He is the Rock, his work is perfect
For all his ways are judgment: a God of truth
He kept him as the apple of his eye
Deut. 32:1–43

THE BLESSING OF MOSES
As thy days, so shall thy strength be
Underneath are the everlasting arms
Deut. 33

MOSES DIED IN THE LAND OF MOAB
No man knows of his sepulchre unto this day
There arose not a prophet since in Israel
        like unto Moses
Deut. 34:5–12

PASSOVER
The fourteenth day of the first month
        is the Lord's passover
On the fifteenth day is the feast of unleavened bread
I will pass over you and the plague shall not be upon you
Ex. 12, 23:15; Lev. 23:5–8; Num. 28:16–17; Deut. 16:1–8

FEAST OF WEEKS
Fifty days after passover shall be the feast of weeks
The feast of harvest, the firstfruits of thy labors
Ex. 23:16; Lev. 23:9–22; Deut. 16:9–12

ROSH HASHANAH
On the first day of the seventh month
Ye shall have an holy convocation
It is a day of blowing the trumpets
Lev. 23:23–25; Num. 29:1–6

YOM KIPPUR
On the tenth day of the seventh month
There shall be a day of atonement
And ye shall afflict your souls
Lev. 23:26–32; Num. 29:7–11

THE FEAST OF TABERNACLES
SHALL BE FOR SEVEN DAYS
On the fifteenth day of the seventh month
All that are Israelites born shall dwell in booths
Ex. 23:16; Lev. 23:33–36, 39–44; Num. 29:12–34; Deut. 16:13–15

THE LORD THY GOD SHALL KEEP UNTO THEE
THE COVENANT
Thou shalt be blessed above all people
Thou shalt keep the commandments of the Lord
The Lord thy God bringeth thee into a good land
A land wherein thou shalt eat bread without scarceness
Deut. 7—11

Man doth not live by bread only
But by every word . . . of the Lord
Deut. 8:3

A dreamer of dreams
Deut. 13:1

The wife of thy bosom
Deut. 13:6

The poor shall never cease out of the land
Deut. 15:11

MOSES CALLED THE NATION
TO A NEW COMMITMENT TO GOD
If you do all his commandments, God will bless you
But if thou wilt not hearken, cursed shalt thou be

And thou shalt become an astonishment
A proverb . . . among all nations
I have set before you life and death, blessing
    and cursing
Therefore choose life
That both thou and thy seed may live
Deut. 27—30

The secret things belong unto the Lord our God
Deut. 29:29

In the morning thou shalt say:
Would God it were evening!
Deut. 28:67

THE SUMMARY OF THE LAW
Hear O Israel: The Lord our God is one Lord
You shall love the Lord your God with all your heart . . .
And these words shall be in thine heart
Thou shalt teach them diligently unto thine children . . .
Thou shalt bind them for a sign upon thine hand . . .
The Lord your God has chosen you to be a special people
Thou shalt love thy neighbor as thyself
Lev. 19:18; Deut. 6—7; cf. Matt. 19:19, 22:37—39; cf. Mark 12:29—33

Old Testament

STORIES

FROM THE

HISTORICAL
BOOKS

Across the Jordan:
Israel under the Judges

JOSHUA BECAME THE LEADER OF ISRAEL
The Lord instructed him to cross the Jordan into Canaan
Be strong and of a good courage
Be not afraid neither be thou dismayed
Deut. 34:9; Josh. 1:1–9

RAHAB AND THE SPIES
Joshua sent spies to view the land, especially Jericho
A harlot named Rahab gave them shelter and hid them
She let them down by a cord through the window
And they promised protection to her and her family
Josh. 2

CROSSING THE JORDAN
Behold the ark of the covenant passeth over before you
The Israelites passed over on dry ground
Until all the people were passed clean over Jordan
They set up twelve stones from the Jordan in Gilgal
        as a sign
Josh. 3:11–17

THE DESTRUCTION OF JERICHO
Six days the Israelites circled the city blowing trumpets
On the seventh day Joshua said to the people: Shout
The people raised a great shout
And the wall fell down flat
They utterly destroyed all that was in the city
But Joshua saved Rahab, the harlot, alive
His fame was noised throughout all the country
Josh. 6

Mighty men of valor
Josh. 6:2

27

THE ISRAELITES CONQUERED THE KINGDOM OF AI
Josh. 7—8

THE DECEIT OF THE GIBEONITES
Joshua was tricked into a treaty
Let them be hewers of wood and drawers of water
Josh. 9

THE AMORITE KINGS WERE VANQUISHED
The sun stood still and the moon stayed
Until the people had avenged themselves
    against their enemies
Josh. 10:12–43

THE DIVISION OF THE LAND AMONG
THE TRIBES OF ISRAEL
Josh. 13—22

JOSHUA WAS OLD AND STRICKEN IN YEARS
I am going the way of all the earth
Josh. 13:1, 23:14

ISRAEL FORSOOK THE LORD
There arose another generation who did not know
    the Lord
The Lord raised up judges to save them
Judges 2:10–23

They shall be as thorns in your sides
Judges 2:3

DEBORAH AND BARAK
Deborah, a prophetess, was judge of Israel
She told Barak the Lord would deliver Israel
Barak summoned ten thousand men to subdue Sisera
Jael, Heber's wife, killed Sisera with a tent peg
Judges 4

SONG OF DEBORAH
I Deborah arose, I arose a mother in Israel
The stars in their courses fought against Sisera
Judges 5

She brought forth butter in a lordly dish
Judges 5:25

Why tarry the wheels of his chariots?
Judges 5:28

THE ANGEL OF THE LORD CAME TO GIDEON
Thou shalt save Israel from the hand of the Midianites
Gideon destroyed the altar of Baal
Gideon asked for a sign that Israel would be saved
Dew on a fleece of wool as a sign from the Lord
Judges 6:11–40

GIDEON AND THE MIDIANITES
The Lord said: The people are too many
Lest Israel say: Mine own hand hath saved me
The people are yet too many
Set aside those that lap the water as a dog
Take only those that cup their hand to their mouth
By those three hundred will I save you
Gideon put a trumpet in every man's hand
Blow the trumpets and say:
The sword of the Lord, and of Gideon
And all the host ran and cried and fled
Judges 7

For as the man is, so is his strength
Judges 8:21

Say now Shibboleth and he said Sibboleth
Judges 12:6

THE BIRTH OF SAMSON
An angel appeared to Manoah's wife:
The child shall be a Nazarite unto God
She bore a son and called him Samson
Judges 13:2–25

SAMSON'S RIDDLE
There was a swarm of bees and honey
    in the carcass of the lion
He said: Out of the eater came forth meat
And out of the strong came forth sweetness
Judges 14:5–19

SAMSON'S REVENGE ON THE PHILISTINES
Samson burned the corn and vineyards
    of the Philistines
He smote them hip and thigh with a great slaughter
The men of Judah bound him
To deliver him to the Philistines
The cords became as flax that was burnt with fire
With the jawbone of an ass have I slain a thousand men
Judges 15

SAMSON AND DELILAH
Tell me, I pray thee, wherein thy great strength lieth
If I be shaven then my strength will go
The Philistines be upon thee, Samson
The Philistines put out his eyes
Strengthen me, I pray thee, only this once, O God . . .
Samson grasped the two pillars of the house
    and pulled it down
So the dead which he slew at his death
Were more than he slew in his life
Judges 16

From Dan even to Beersheba
Judges 20:1

All the people arose as one man
Judges 20:8

IN THOSE DAYS THERE WAS NO KING IN ISRAEL
Every man did that which was right in his own eyes
Judges 21:25

RUTH AND NAOMI
Entreat me not to leave thee
Whither thou goest, I will go
Thy people shall be my people, and thy God my God
So they went to Bethlehem
And Ruth gleaned in the field of Boaz
Boaz took Ruth and she became his wife
Ruth bore a son, Obed, father of Jesse, father of David
Ruth

HANNAH PRAYED FOR A SON
AND PROMISED HIM TO THE LORD
Eli, the priest, thought she was drunk
No my lord, I am a woman of sorrowful spirit
She bore a son and named him Samuel
When he was weaned, she took him to Eli in the temple
As long as he lives he shall be lent to the Lord
I Sam. 1

HANNAH'S SONG OF THANKSGIVING TO THE LORD
I Sam. 2:1–10

In the flower of their age
I Sam. 2:33

ELI AND SAMUEL
The child ministered unto the Lord before Eli
Samuel grew in the presence of the Lord
The Lord called Samuel: and he answered, Here am I
Speak, Lord, for thy servant heareth
I Sam. 2:11–26, 3:1–21

Be strong and quit yourselves like men
I Sam. 4:9

THE ARK OF THE COVENANT
CAPTURED BY THE PHILISTINES
And the word of Samuel came to all Israel
The glory is departed from Israel
    for the ark of God is taken
The Philistines returned the ark to Israel
The Israelites solemnly repented
    and subdued the Philistines
And Samuel judged Israel all the days of his life
I Sam. 4—7

Israel under Saul, David, and Solomon

ISRAEL ASKED SAMUEL FOR A KING
I Sam. 8

SAUL ANOINTED KING BY SAMUEL
When Samuel saw Saul, the Lord said: Behold the man . . .
Is Saul also among the prophets?
All the people shouted: God save the king
I Sam. 9—10

The Lord sought a man after his own heart
I Sam. 13:14

Every man's sword was against his fellow
I Sam. 14:20

JONATHAN (SAUL'S SON) AND THE HONEYCOMB
I Sam. 14:24–33

THE LORD REPENTED MAKING SAUL KING
He sent Samuel to Jesse:
I have provided me a king among his sons
For the Lord seeth not as man seeth
Man looks on outward appearance
The Lord looks on the heart
Jesse made seven sons pass before Samuel
The Lord hath not chosen these
Samuel anointed David, the youngest,
    in anticipation of his reign
The spirit of the Lord came upon David
    from that day forward
I Sam. 15:35—16:13

AN EVIL SPIRIT TROUBLED KING SAUL
David's music refreshed Saul
I Sam. 16:14–23

DAVID AND GOLIATH
There came out of the Philistine's camp a champion,
    Goliath
David said: Let no man's heart fail because of him
Your servant will go and fight with this Philistine
Go and the Lord be with thee
He chose five smooth stones out of the brook
David prevailed over the Philistine with a sling
    and a stone
I Sam. 17

I know thy pride and the naughtiness of thine heart
I Sam. 17:28

THE FRIENDSHIP BETWEEN DAVID AND JONATHAN
The soul of Jonathan was knit with the soul of David
Jonathan loved him as he loved his own soul
I Sam. 18:1–5

SAUL, JEALOUS OF DAVID, SOUGHT TO KILL HIM
Saul hath slain his thousands,
    and David his ten thousands
I Sam. 18:6–12 (22—24, 26—27, 29)

JONATHAN SAVED DAVID FROM SAUL'S ANGER
I Sam. 19—20

DAVID THE OUTLAW
I Sam. 21—26

Wickedness proceedeth from the wicked
I Sam. 24:13

Bound in the bundle of life with the Lord thy God
I Sam. 25:29

I have played the fool
I Sam. 26:21

SAUL AND THE WITCH OF ENDOR
I Sam. 28

THE DEATH OF KING SAUL AND HIS SONS
Saul took a sword and fell upon it
An Amelekite took Saul's crown and bracelet to David
I Sam. 31; II Sam. 1; I Chron. 10

DAVID'S LAMENT ON THE DEATHS
OF SAUL AND JONATHAN
Tell it not in Gath . . .
In their death they were not divided
They were swifter than eagles, stronger than lions
How are the mighty fallen . . .
Thy love to me was wonderful, passing the love of women
II Sam. 1:17–27

Know ye not that there is a prince fallen this day?
II Sam. 3:38

DAVID MADE KING OVER ALL ISRAEL
II Sam. 5:1–5; I Chron. 11:1–3

JERUSALEM—THE CITY OF DAVID
David and all Israel went to Jerusalem
He built houses in the city of David
David brought the ark of God into the city of David
David danced before the Lord with all his might
II Sam. 6; I Chron. 11—16:6

DAVID'S PSALM OF THANKSGIVING
Give thanks unto the Lord, call upon his name
For great is the Lord, and greatly to be praised
For his mercy endureth for ever
I Chron. 16:7–36

THE HOUSE OF DAVID
I will raise up your son after you and . . .
    establish his kingdom
Thy throne shall be established for ever and ever
II Sam. 7; I Chron. 17

DAVID AND BATHSHEBA
David took Bathsheba, wife of Uriah,
    and she conceived a child
Set ye Uriah in the forefront of the hottest battle
When the mourning was past she became his wife
What David had done displeased the Lord
II Sam. 11

NATHAN TOLD DAVID A PARABLE
There were two men, one rich, one poor
The poor man had nothing, save one little ewe lamb
The rich man took the poor man's lamb
Nathan said to David thou art the man
David said I have sinned against the Lord
II Sam. 12:1–15

THE DEATH OF DAVID'S CHILD
David besought God for the child
On the seventh day the child died
While the child was yet alive I fasted and wept
Now he is dead . . . can I bring him back again?
I shall go to him, but he shall not return to me
II Sam. 12:15–23

For we must needs die
And are as water spilt on the ground . . .
II Sam. 14:14

ABSALOM'S TREACHERY AND DEATH
Absalom stole the hearts of the men of Israel
David was forced to fight Absalom
Deal gently for my sake with Absalom
Absalom's head caught fast in an oak as he rode his mule
Joab and ten young men slew Absalom
Would God I had died for thee, O Absalom,
     my son, my son!
II Sam. 15:13—19:8

DAVID'S VICTORY SONG
The Lord is my rock, and my fortress, and my deliverer
In him will I trust: he is my shield
My high tower, my refuge, my savior
The waves of death compassed me
I cried to my God and my cry did enter his ears
The Lord thundered from heaven
He delivered me from them that hate me
For thou art my lamp, O Lord:
And the Lord will lighten my darkness
II Sam. 22

David the son of Jesse . . . the sweet psalmist of Israel
II Sam. 23:1

The men that went in jeopardy of their lives
II Sam. 23:17

DAVID'S CHARGE TO SOLOMON
The Lord has chosen you to build the temple:
Be strong and do it
David gave to Solomon the pattern
    of the house of the Lord
The palace is not for man, but for the Lord God
For all things come of thee
And of thine own have we given thee
Our days on the earth are as a shadow
I Chron. 22, 28—29:1–19

THE ANOINTING OF SOLOMON
David said to Bathsheba: Solomon thy son
    shall reign after me
And Zadok the priest anointed Solomon
David slept with his fathers
He died in a good old age, full of days . . .
I Kings 1—2:12; I Chron. 29:22–28

SOLOMON ASKED GOD FOR WISDOM
I am but a little child:
I know not how to go out or come in
Give thy servant a wise and an understanding heart
I Kings 3:3–15; II Chron. 1:7–12

SOLOMON AND THE TWO MOTHERS
The living child is mine, the dead child yours
King Solomon said: Bring me a sword
Divide the living child in two
O my Lord give her the living child . . .
Solomon said: give the living child to the first woman,
    she is its mother
I Kings 3:16–28

SOLOMON'S RICHES AND WISDOM
Judah and Israel dwelt safely
Every man under his vine . . .
Forty thousand stalls of horses for his chariots
He spake three thousand proverbs
All came to hear the wisdom of Solomon
I Kings 4:25–34

As the sand which is by the sea in multitude
I Kings 4:20

THE BUILDING OF THE TEMPLE
Solomon built the temple in Jerusalem on Mount Moriah
He asked King Hiram of Tyre to hew cedars of Lebanon
They quarried costly stones to lay the foundation
Solomon overlaid the temple with gold
Two cherubims overlaid with gold were set
    in the sanctuary
I Kings 5—7; II Chron. 2—4

THE ARK OF THE COVENANT WAS BROUGHT
TO THE TEMPLE
I Kings 8:1–13; II Chron. 5:2—6:11

SOLOMON'S PRAYER OF DEDICATION
I Kings 8:14–61; II Chron. 6:3–42

A proverb and a byword among all people
I Kings 9:7

SOLOMON AND THE QUEEN OF SHEBA
The Queen of Sheba came to test Solomon
    with hard questions
Thy wisdom and prosperity exceedeth thy fame
Solomon's navy brought gold, silver, ivory, apes,
    and peacocks
I Kings 10:1–23; II Chron. 9:1–22

SOLOMON'S APOSTASY
King Solomon loved many strange women
His wives turned away his heart after other gods
The Lord said: I will surely rend the kingdom from thee
I will rend it out of the hand of thy son
I Kings 11:1–13

The Divided Kingdom:
Early Prophets Elijah and Elisha

THE KINGDOM SPLITS IN TWO
Rehoboam succeeded Solomon as King of Judah
Jeroboam ruled as King of Israel
There was civil war throughout their reigns
I Kings 12–14; II Chron. 10–12

My father hath chastised you with whips but I . . .
    with scorpions
I Kings 12:11

To your tents, O Israel
I Kings 12:16

AHAB OF ISRAEL
Ahab and his wife, Jezebel, worshiped Baal
Elijah prophesied drought
I Kings 16:28—17:1

ELIJAH FED BY RAVENS
The Lord commanded Elijah to flee
Hide thyself by the brook Cherith
Thou shalt drink of the brook
I have commanded the ravens to feed thee
I Kings 17:2–7

ELIJAH DWELT WITH A POOR WIDOW

An handful of meal in a barrel, and a little oil
    in a cruse
And the barrel of meal wasted not
Neither did the cruse . . . fail
The son of the widow fell sick and died
Elijah cried unto the Lord:
Let this child's soul come into him again
See, thy son liveth
I Kings 17:8–24

OBADIAH AGAINST JEZEBEL

Jezebel slew the prophets of the Lord
Obadiah took a hundred and hid them by fifty in a cave
I Kings 18:1–16

ELIJAH CHALLENGED THE PROPHETS OF BAAL

Ahab sent all Israel and the prophets of Baal
    to Mount Carmel
Elijah said: How long halt ye between two opinions?
The God that answereth by fire, let him be God
They cried: O Baal hear us. But there was no answer
Elijah mocked: Either he is talking,
    or he is pursuing . . .
Elijah cried: Hear me O Lord!
Then the fire of the Lord fell
I Kings 18:17–40

ELIJAH PRAYED FOR RAIN

Elijah went up to the top of Mount Carmel
He cast himself down upon the earth
He said to his servant: look toward the sea
There ariseth a little cloud out of the sea,
    like a man's hand
Elijah told Ahab: Get thee down that the rain
    stop thee not
The heaven was black with clouds

And there was a great rain
And he girded up his loins, and ran before Ahab
I Kings 18:4–46

THE CALL OF ELISHA
Elijah fled from Jezebel
Stand upon the mount before the Lord
A great wind rent the mountains . . .
After the wind an earthquake
The Lord was not in the earthquake . . .
After the fire a still small voice
Elijah cast his mantle upon Elisha
I Kings 19

NABOTH'S VINEYARD
Ahab spake: Give me thy vineyard
Naboth: The Lord forbid it
Jezebel had Naboth stoned to death
Ahab rose up to take possession of the vineyard
I Kings 21:1–16

ELIJAH PROPHESIES TO AHAB
The dogs shall lick thy blood
Ahab said: hast thou found me, O mine enemy?
And the dogs shall eat Jezebel by the wall of Jezreel
There was not like unto Ahab for wickedness
I Kings 21:17–25

MICAIAH'S PROPHECY
Shall I go against Ramoth-gilead to battle or forbear?
The Lord shall deliver it into the hand of the king
I saw all Israel scattered upon the hills
As sheep without a shepherd
The King said: Feed him with bread of affliction . . .
I Kings 22:1–40; II Chron. 18

THE REIGN OF JEHOSHAPHAT OF JUDAH
Jehoshaphat made peace with the king of Israel
His heart was lifted up in the ways of the Lord
The Ammonites came against Jehoshaphat to battle
O Judah and Jerusalem: fear not . . .
For the Lord will be with you
Praise the Lord for his mercy endureth forever
I Kings 22:41–50; II Chron. 17—20

KING AHAZIAH AND ELIJAH
Is it not because there is not a God in Israel
That ye go to inquire of Baalzebub?
I Kings 22:51; II Kings 1; II Chron. 22:1–9

ELISHA INHERITED ELIJAH'S MANTLE
Let a double portion of thy spirit be upon me
Elijah went up by a whirlwind into heaven
He took the mantle of Elijah that fell from him
II Kings 2:1–15

ELISHA AND THE WIDOW'S OIL
II Kings 4:1–7

ELISHA AND THE SHUNAMMITE WOMAN
When Elisha was come into the house
Behold the child was dead and laid upon his bed
Elisha prayed unto the Lord
Elisha stretched himself upon the child
And the flesh waxed warm
II Kings 4:8–37

There is death in the pot
II Kings 4:40

NAAMAN CURED OF LEPROSY BY ELISHA
Naaman, captain to the king of Syria, was a great man
    but a leper

Go and wash in Jordan seven times and thou
    shalt be clean
There is no God in all the earth but in Israel
II Kings 5

THE FLOATING AXE-HEAD
As one was felling a beam, the axe-head fell
    into the water
Elisha cast a stick in and the iron did swim
II Kings 6:1–7

Is thy servant a dog, that he should do this great thing?
II Kings 8:13

THE KINGS OF ISRAEL AND JUDAH
TO THE FALL OF SAMARIA
II Kings 8:16–17

JEHU WAS ANOINTED KING OF ISRAEL
Jehu conspired against Joram, son of Ahab and Jezebel
What hast thou to do with peace? turn thee behind me
The driving is like the driving of Jehu
    for he driveth furiously
Jehu smote Joram dead
And cast him in the field of Naboth
Jezebel painted her face and looked out at a window
All the house of Ahab and the prophets of Baal
    were slain
II Kings 9—10

ATHALIAH (JEZEBEL'S DAUGHTER) QUEEN OF JUDAH
Athaliah destroyed all the royal family
But Joash, son of Ahaziah, was saved
Jehoiada, the priest, anointed Joash
He made a covenant with the Lord
Queen Athaliah was slain and Joash ruled over Judah
II Kings 11:1–20; II Chron. 22:10–23

THE REIGN OF JOASH (JEHOASH) OF JUDAH
They repaired the house of the Lord
II Kings 11:21—12:21; II Chron. 24

THE DEATH OF ELISHA
Elisha was fallen sick of his sickness whereof he died
Joash, king of Israel, came down and wept
O my father, my father! The chariot of Israel!
II Kings 13:14–21

UZZIAH (AZARIAH) THE LEPER KING
II Kings 15:1–7; II Chron. 26

SAMARIA FALLS TO ASSYRIA
The King of Assyria took Samaria
And carried Israel away into exile
Israel did secretly those things
That were not right against the Lord
II Kings 17

THE KINGS OF JUDAH TO THE FALL OF JERUSALEM
II Kings 18—25; II Chron. 10—36

HEZEKIAH'S REIGN
He kept the Lord's commandments and he prospered
Assyrian emissaries harangued the people of Judah
Isaiah said: Be not afraid of the words
    which thou hast heard
That which thou hast prayed to me . . . I have heard
Out of Jerusalem shall go forth a remnant
Set thine house in order
II Kings 18—20; II Chron. 29—32

HEZEKIAH'S PASSOVER
There assembled at Jerusalem much people
    to keep the feast
So there was great joy in Jerusalem

Since the time of Solomon there was not the like
    in Jerusalem
II Chron. 30

JOSIAH, KING OF JUDAH
Josiah did that which was right in the sight of the Lord
The book of the law was found in the temple
Josiah purged the land of pagan worship
He made a covenant with God and celebrated the
    passover
I Kings 13:1–3; II Kings 22—23:28; II Chron. 34—35

I will wipe Jerusalem as a man wipeth a dish . . .
II Kings 21:13

Defeat of Jerusalem:
Exile and Return

THE BABYLONIAN CAPTIVITY
Nebuchadnezzar came up against Jerusalem
And did besiege it
He carried away all Jerusalem to Babylon
And burnt the house of the Lord
II Kings 24:10–16, 25:1–21; II Chron. 36:5–21; Jer. 39

THE PROCLAMATION OF CYRUS, KING OF PERSIA
The Lord God hath charged me to build him an house
    in Jerusalem
II Chron. 36:22–23; Ezra 1:1–4; Isaiah 44:26–28, 45:1–13

RETURN TO JERUSALEM
Jerusalem lieth waste
And the gates thereof are burned with fire
God will prosper us
We his servants will arise and build
Ezra 1, 2, 7—10; Neh. 1, 2, 7:6–73

REBUILDING OF THE TEMPLE
The foundation of the house of the Lord was laid
The work on the house of God ceased
Darius decreed that the work resume
And the temple was finished
Ezra 3—6

REBUILDING THE WALLS OF JERUSALEM
So the wall was finished
They perceived that this work was wrought of our God
Neh. 3—6, 12:27–47

THE RENEWAL OF THE COVENANT
Ezra read the book of the law to the people
Israel stood and confessed their sins
A God ready to pardon, gracious and merciful,
      slow to anger . . .
They entered into an oath to walk in God's law
Neh. 8—10

ESTHER: A JEWISH QUEEN OF PERSIA
The king dethroned Queen Vashti
He loved Esther and laid the royal crown upon her head
Esther 1—2:1—17

A PLOT AGAINST THE JEWS
Haman sought to destroy all the Jews
Mordecai: The man whom the king delighted to honor
Rent his clothes, and put on sackcloth with ashes
Esther interceded with the king
They hanged Haman on the gallows prepared for
      Mordecai
Esther 2:19—7

THE FEAST OF PURIM
The Jews smote all their enemies
They established two days of feasting and gladness
These days of Purim should not fail from among the Jews
Esther 9

46

Old Testament

PSALMS,
POETRY,
PROVERBS,
AND
WISDOM

Job

JOB FEARED GOD AND SHUNNED EVIL
He was a perfect and upright man
Rich in family and possessions
Job 1:1–5

SATAN'S CHALLENGE
The Lord asked Satan: Whence comest thou?
From going to and fro in the earth
    and from walking up and down
The Lord said: Have you considered my servant, Job?
Satan said: Doth Job fear God for nought?
Touch his possessions and he will curse you
The Lord said: All that he has is in your power
Job 1:6–12

JOB LOST ALL THAT HE HAD
Naked came I out of my mother's womb
    and naked shall I return
The Lord gave and the Lord hath taken away
Blessed be the name of the Lord
Job 1:7–22

SATAN TESTS JOB A SECOND TIME
Touch his bone and his flesh and he will curse you
Satan smote Job with sore boils from head to toe
Job's wife said: Curse God and die
In all this Job did not sin
Job 2:1–10

JOB'S THREE SILENT FRIENDS:
ELIPHAZ, BILDAD, AND ZOPHAR
His friends came to mourn with him and comfort him
None spake a word unto him
They saw that his grief was very great
Job 2:11–13

JOB'S COMPLAINT TO GOD
Let the day perish wherein I was born
Why died I not from the womb?
In death the wicked cease from troubling
And the weary be at rest
Wherefore is light given to him that is in misery
And life unto the bitter in soul?
Job 3

ELIPHAZ SPEAKS OF CONFIDENCE IN GOD
Who ever perished being innocent?
They that plow iniquity and sow wickedness
    reap the same
Fear came upon me and trembling
Unto God would I commit my cause
He taketh the wise in their own craftiness
Thou shalt be in league with the stones of the field
And the beasts of the field shall be at peace with thee
Thou shalt come to thy grave in a full age
    like a shock of corn
Job 4—5

Shall mortal man be more just than God?
Job 4:17

Man is born unto trouble as the sparks fly upward
Job 5:7

JOB'S RESPONSE
Oh that my grief were thoroughly weighed
And my calamity laid in the balances together!
That God would grant me the thing that I long for!
What is my strength that I should hope?
My days are swifter than a weaver's shuttle
I would not live alway:
Let me alone, for my days are vanity
Job 6—7

BILDAD'S FIRST SPEECH CONCERNING GOD'S JUSTICE
Doth God pervert judgment?
Doth the Almighty pervert justice?
We are but of yesterday and know nothing
Our days upon earth are a shadow
Behold God will not cast away a perfect man
Neither will he help the evil doers
Job 8

JOB'S REPLY
I will speak in the bitterness of my soul
I will say unto God, Do not condemn me
I am full of confusion:
Therefore see thou mine affliction
O that I had given up the ghost and no eye had seen me!
Job 9—10

The land of darkness and the shadow of death
Job 10:21

ZOPHAR'S SPEECH
Canst thou by searching find out God?
If iniquity be in thine hand put it far away
And thine age shall be clearer than the noonday
Job 11

JOB'S RESPONSE
No doubt wisdom will die with you
The just upright man is laughed to scorn
But now ask the beasts and they shall teach thee . . .
God discovereth deep things out of darkness:
And bringeth out to light the shadow of death
Man that is born of woman is of few days
        and full of trouble
Yea, man giveth up the ghost and where is he?
If a man die shall he live again?
Job 12—14

With the ancient is wisdom, in length of days
    understanding
Job 12:12

ELIPHAZ REPROVED JOB
Should a wise man utter vain knowledge
And fill his belly with the east wind?
Thine own mouth condemneth thee and not I
The wicked man travaileth with pain all his days
For he stretcheth out his hand against God
Job 15

JOB'S REPLY
Miserable comforters are ye all
Mine eye poureth out tears unto God
My days are past, my purposes are broken off
I have said to corruption: Thou art my father
Job 16—17

BILDAD ANSWERED
His own counsel shall cast him down
It shall bring him to the king of terrors
Job 18

JOB'S FAITH IN EXTREMITY
How long will ye vex my soul?
Know now that God hath overthrown me
My bone cleaveth to my skin and to my flesh
I am escaped with the skin of my teeth
Oh that my words were now written!
Graven with an iron pen and lead in the rock for ever!
I know that my redeemer liveth
    and in my flesh shall I see God
Job 19

Seeing the root of the matter is found in me
Job 19:28

ZOPHAR'S RESPONSE
The triumphing of the wicked is short
Though wickedness be sweet in his mouth . . .
Job 20

JOB REPLIES
Suffer me that I may speak, and after, mock on
Why should not my spirit be troubled?
Shall any teach God knowledge?
Job 21

ELIPHAZ'S SPEECH
Is it any pleasure to the Almighty
    that thou art righteous?
Acquaint now thyself with him and be at peace
Job 22

JOB REPLIES
Oh that I knew where I might find him!
I would order my cause before him
When he hath tried me I shall come forth as gold
Job 23

BILDAD'S LAST SPEECH
Yea, the stars are not pure in his sight
How much less man which is a worm?
Job 25

HYMN TO WISDOM
But where shall wisdom be found?
The price of wisdom is above rubies
Behold, the fear of the Lord, that is wisdom
And to depart from evil is understanding
Job 28

The land of the living
Job 28:13

JOB RECALLS THE PAST
As I was in the days of my youth
When my children were about me
I caused the widow's heart to sing for joy
I was eyes to the blind, and feet was I to the lame
They waited for me as for the rain
Now I am a brother to dragons and a companion to owls
Job 29—30

ELIHU'S WRATH KINDLED AGAINST JOB
He justified himself rather than God
Great men are not always wise
Far be it from God that he should do wickedness
For he will not lay upon man more than right
Job 32—34

One among a thousand
Job 33:23

He multiplieth words without knowledge
Job 35:16

Fair weather cometh out of the north
Job 37:22

GOD ANSWERS JOB OUT OF THE WHIRLWIND
Who is this that darkeneth counsel
    by words without knowledge?
Gird up thy loins like a man for I will demand of thee
Where wast thou when I laid the foundations
    of the earth?
When the morning stars sang together?
Hast thou entered into the springs of the sea?
Hath the rain a father?
Or who hath begotten the drops of dew?
Canst thou bind the sweet influences of Pleiades . . .?
Who hath given understanding to the heart?

Who can number the clouds in wisdom?
Hast thou given the horse strength?
Job 38—40:2

JOB ANSWERS GOD IN HUMILITY
Behold I am vile; what shall I answer thee?
Job 40:4

Behold now behemoth . . . he eateth grass like an ox
Job 40:15

Canst thou draw out leviathan with an hook?
Job 41:1

JOB'S RESPONSE TO GOD
I have heard of thee by the hearing of the ear:
But now mine eye seeth thee
Job 42:1–5

GOD REBUKES THE FRIENDS
AND RESTORES JOB'S FORTUNE
The Lord blessed the latter end of Job
      more than his beginning
Job 42:7–17

The Psalms

Blessed is the man that walketh not
      in the counsel of the ungodly
But his delight is in the law of the Lord . . .
And he shall be like a tree planted by the rivers . . .
The ungodly are not so: but are like the chaff . . .
Psalm 1:1–4

WHY DO THE HEATHEN RAGE
And the people imagine a vain thing

Blessed are all they that put their trust in him
Psalm 2

Lord, lift up the light of thy countenance upon us
I will both lay me down in peace, and sleep
Psalm 4:6, 8

OUT OF THE MOUTH OF BABES AND SUCKLINGS
What is man, that thou art mindful of him?
Thou has made him a little lower than the angels . . .
How excellent is thy name in all the earth!
Psalm 8

How long wilt thou forget me, O Lord?
Psalm 13:1

The fool hath said in his heart: There is no God
There is none that doeth good, no, not one
Psalm 14:1, 3; 53:1, 3

Lord, who shall abide in thy tabernacle?
Who shall dwell in thy holy hill?
Psalm 15:1

The lines are fallen unto me in pleasant places
My reins also instruct me in the night seasons
I shall not be moved
Psalm 16:6–8

Keep me as the apple of the eye, hide me
      under thy wings
Psalm 17:8

I WILL LOVE THEE, O LORD, MY STRENGTH
The sorrows of death compassed me
The floods of ungodly men made me afraid
Psalm 18

THE HEAVENS DECLARE THE GLORY OF GOD
The firmament sheweth his handiwork
Day unto day uttereth speech . . .

In them hath he set a tabernacle for the sun
The law of the Lord is perfect . . .
More to be desired are they than gold, sweeter than honey
Cleanse thou me from secret faults
Let the words of my mouth . . . be acceptable in thy sight
Psalm 19

MY GOD, MY GOD, WHY HAST THOU FORSAKEN ME?
All they that see me laugh me to scorn . . .
I am poured out like water
And all my bones are out of joint
They pierced my hands and my feet
They part my garments among them
All the ends of the world shall remember
     and turn unto the Lord
Psalm 22

THE LORD IS MY SHEPHERD; I SHALL NOT WANT
He maketh me to lie down in green pastures . . .
He restoreth my soul
Though I walk through the valley
     of the shadow of death . . .
Thou preparest a table before me
In the presence of mine enemies
Surely goodness and mercy shall follow me
     all the days of my life
Psalm 23

THE EARTH IS THE LORD'S,
AND THE FULNESS THEREOF
For he hath founded it upon the seas
Who shall ascend into the hill of the Lord?
He that hath clean hands, and a pure heart
Lift up your heads, O ye gates
Who is this King of glory?
The Lord of hosts, he is the King of glory
Psalm 24

Lord, I have loved the habitation of thy house
Psalm 26:8

THE LORD IS MY LIGHT AND MY SALVATION:
WHOM SHALL I FEAR?
Though an host should encamp against me
In this will I be confident
Teach me thy way, O Lord, and lead me in a plain path
Psalm 27

The Lord is my strength and my shield
Psalm 28:7

Worship the Lord in the beauty of holiness
Psalm 29:2

Weeping may endure for a night
But joy cometh in the morning
Psalm 30:5

Into thine hand I commit my spirit . . .
I am forgotten as a dead man out of mind
My times are in thy hand
Psalm 31:5, 12, 15

Sing unto him a new song
Psalm 33:3

O taste and see that the Lord is good
Keep thy tongue from evil
And thy lips from speaking guile
Depart from evil, and do good; seek peace, and pursue it
Psalm 34:8, 13–14

Rescue my soul from their destructions,
    my darling from the lions
Psalm 35:17

The meek shall inherit the earth
The wicked in great power . . . like a green bay tree
Psalm 37:11, 35

I WILL KEEP MY MOUTH WITH A BRIDLE
I held my peace even from good
Lord, make me to know mine end,
    and the measure of my days
Every man at his best state is altogether vanity
He heapeth up riches and knoweth not
    who shall gather them
For I am a stranger with thee, and a sojourner
O spare me, that I may recover strength
    before I go hence
Psalm 39

I WAITED PATIENTLY FOR THE LORD;
AND HE HEARD MY CRY
He brought me out of an horrible pit
And set my feet upon a rock
Psalm 40

AS THE HART PANTETH AFTER THE WATER BROOKS
My soul thirsteth for God, for the living God
My tears have been my meat day and night
Why art thou cast down, O my soul?
Why art thou disquieted in me?
Deep calleth unto deep at the noise of thy waterspouts
Psalm 42

O send out thy light and thy truth: let them lead me
Psalm 43:3

We are counted as sheep for the slaughter
Psalm 44:22

My tongue is the pen of a ready writer
Psalm 45:1

GOD IS OUR REFUGE AND STRENGTH,
A VERY PRESENT HELP
Therefore will not we fear, though the earth be removed
There is a river, the streams whereof
Shall make glad the city of God
God is in the midst of her; she shall not be moved
Be still, and know that I am God
The Lord of hosts is with us; the God of Jacob
    is our refuge
Psalm 46

Man that is in honor, and understandeth not
Is like the beasts that perish
Psalm 49:20

Every beast of the forest is mine
And the cattle upon a thousand hills
Psalm 50:10

HAVE MERCY UPON ME, O GOD,
ACCORDING TO THY LOVING-KINDNESS
I acknowledge my transgressions
And my sin is ever before me
I was shapen in iniquity
And in sin did my mother conceive me
Purge me with hyssop, and I shall be clean
Wash me, and I shall be whiter than snow
Create in me a clean heart, O God
And take not thy holy Spirit from me
Open thou my lips
And my mouth shall show forth thy praise
A broken and a contrite heart, O God,
    thou wilt not despise
Psalm 51

We took sweet counsel together
The words of his mouth were smoother than butter . . .
Psalm 55:14, 21

They are like the deaf adder that stoppeth her ear
Which will not hearken to the voice of charmers
Psalm 58:4–5

Lead me to the rock that is higher than I
Psalm 61:2

He only is my rock and my salvation
Psalm 62:6

My soul thirsteth for thee in a dry and thirsty land
Psalm 63:1

Thou crownest the year with thy goodness
Psalm 65:11

Make a joyful noise unto God, all ye lands
We went through fire and through water
Psalm 66:1, 12

God be merciful unto us, and bless us
And cause his face to shine upon us
That thy way may be known . . . thy saving health
    among all nations
Psalm 67:1–2

God setteth the solitary in families
Psalm 68:6

SAVE ME, O GOD; FOR THE WATERS ARE COME IN
UNTO MY SOUL
I sink in deep mire, where there is no standing
I am weary of my crying
For the zeal of thine house hath eaten me up
They gave me gall for my meat
And in my thirst . . . vinegar
Psalm 69

Cast me not off in the time of old age
Psalm 71:9

A stubborn and rebellious generation
Psalm 78:8

HOW AMIABLE ARE THY TABERNACLES,
O LORD OF HOSTS!
Yea, the sparrow hath found an house,
       and the swallow a nest
Blessed are they that dwell in thy house
They go from strength to strength
A day in thy courts is better than a thousand
I had rather be a doorkeeper in the house of my God
Than to dwell in the tents of wickedness
Psalm 84

Mercy and truth are met together
Righteousness and peace have kissed each other
Psalm 85:10

Glorious things are spoken of thee, O city of God
Psalm 87:3

Lord, why castest thou off my soul?
Why hidest thou thy face from me?
Psalm 88:14

LORD, THOU HAS BEEN OUR DWELLING PLACE
IN ALL GENERATIONS
Before the mountains were brought forth
Or thou hadst formed the earth, thou art God
Thou turnest man to destruction; and sayest:
Return ye children of men
For a thousand years in thy sight are but as yesterday
They are like grass which groweth up
In the morning it flourisheth, and groweth up
In the evening it is cut down, and withereth
We spend our years as a tale that is told

The days of our years are threescore years and ten
So teach us to number our days
Psalm 90

HE THAT DWELLETH IN THE SECRET PLACE
OF THE MOST HIGH
Surely he shall deliver thee from the snare
    of the fowler
Thou shalt not be afraid for the terror by night . . .
Nor for the pestilence that walketh in darkness
A thousand shall fall at thy side
He shall give his angels charge over thee
Thou shalt tread upon the lion and adder
Psalm 91

IT IS A GOOD THING TO GIVE THANKS
UNTO THE LORD
To show forth thy loving-kindness in the morning
Upon an instrument of ten strings, and upon the psaltery
For thou, Lord, hast made me glad through thy work
The righteous shall flourish like the palm tree
Psalm 92

O COME, LET US SING UNTO THE LORD
For the Lord is a great God, A great King above all gods
The sea is his, and he made it
And his hands formed the dry land
O come, let us worship and bow down
We are the people of his pasture
And the sheep of his hand
Psalm 95

SING UNTO THE LORD, ALL THE EARTH
Give unto the Lord the glory due unto his name
O worship the Lord in the beauty of holiness
Psalm 96

The Lord reigneth; let the earth rejoice
Psalm 97:1

O SING UNTO THE LORD A NEW SONG
Let the sea roar, and the fulness thereof
Let the floods clap their hands
Let the hills be joyful together
Psalm 98

MAKE A JOYFUL NOISE UNTO THE LORD,
ALL YE LANDS
Serve the Lord with gladness
Know ye that the Lord he is God
Enter into his gates with thanksgiving
For the Lord is good; his mercy is everlasting
Psalm 100

My days are consumed like smoke
I am like a pelican of the wilderness;
        an owl of the desert
I watch, and am as a sparrow alone upon the house top
Psalm 102:3, 6–7

BLESS THE LORD, O MY SOUL
Bless the Lord, O my soul
And forget not all his benefits
The Lord is merciful and gracious, slow to anger . . .
As far as the east is from the west
So far hath he removed our transgressions from us
For he knoweth our frame; he remembereth
        that we are dust
As for man, his days are as grass: as a flower
        of the field . . .
For the wind passeth over it, and it is gone
Psalm 103

O LORD, HOW MANIFOLD ARE THY WORKS
Who coverest thyself with light as with a garment
Who maketh his angels spirits; his ministers
      a flaming fire
 And wine to gladden the heart of man . . .
The trees are full of sap, the cedars of Lebanon
How manifold are thy works!
The earth is full of thy riches
So is this great and wide sea:
There go the ships. There is that leviathan
These wait all upon thee
That thou mayest give them their meat in due season
Psalm 104

Such as sit in darkness and in the shadow of death
They that go down to the sea in ships
They reel to and fro, and stagger like a drunken man
Psalm 107:10, 23, 27

The Lord said unto my Lord:
Sit thou at my right hand, until I make thine enemies
      thy footstool
Thou hast the dew of thy youth
The Lord hath sworn, and will not repent
Psalm 110:1, 3–4

The fear of the Lord is the beginning of wisdom
Psalm 111:10

From the rising of the sun
Unto the going down of the same
The Lord's name is to be praised
Psalm 113:3

The mountains skipped like rams
And the little hills like lambs
Psalm 114:4

They have mouths, but they speak not
Eyes have they, but they see not
They have ears, but they hear not
Psalm 115:5–6; Psalm 135:16–17

I said in my haste, All men are liars
I will take the cup of salvation
And call upon the name of the Lord
Precious in the sight of the Lord is the death
    of his saints
Psalm 116:11, 13, 15

The stone which the builders refused
Is become the headstone of the corner
This is the day which the Lord hath made
Blessed be he that cometh in the name of the Lord
Psalm 118:22, 24, 26

Thy word is a lamp unto my feet, a light unto my path
Psalm 119:105

I WILL LIFT UP MINE EYES UNTO THE HILLS,
FROM WHENCE COMETH MY HELP
He will not suffer thy foot to be moved
He that keepeth thee will not slumber
The sun shall not smite thee by day
Nor the moon by night
The Lord shall preserve thy going out and thy coming in
Psalm 121

I was glad when they said unto me
Let us go into the house of the Lord
Psalm 122:1

They that sow in tears shall reap in joy
He that goeth forth and weepeth, bearing precious seed
Shall come again with rejoicing, bringing his sheaves
Psalm 126:5–6

EXCEPT THE LORD BUILD THE HOUSE,
THEY LABOR IN VAIN
He giveth his beloved sleep
Lo, children are an heritage of the Lord
Happy is the man that hath his quiver full of them
Psalm 127

Thy wife shall be as a fruitful vine
    by the sides of thine house
Psalm 128:3

OUT OF THE DEPTHS HAVE I CRIED
UNTO THEE, O LORD
My soul waiteth for the Lord
More than they that watch for the morning
Psalm 130

I WILL NOT GIVE SLEEP TO MINE EYES,
OR SLUMBER TO MINE EYELIDS
Until I find out a place for the Lord
The Lord hath sworn unto David:
The fruit of the body will I set upon thy throne
Psalm 132

How good and how pleasant for brethren
    to dwell together in unity!
Psalm 133:1

FOR HIS MERCY ENDURETH FOR EVER
Psalm 136

BY THE RIVERS OF BABYLON WE SAT DOWN AND WEPT
We hanged our harps upon the willows
How shall we sing the Lord's song in a strange land?
Psalm 137

O LORD, THOU HAST SEARCHED ME, AND KNOWN ME
Thou knowest my downsitting and mine uprising
Whither shall I go from the Spirit?

Or whither shall I flee?
If I ascend up into heaven, thou art there
If I take the wings of the morning
And dwell in the uttermost parts of the sea
Even there shall thy hand lead me and thy right hand
     hold me
I will praise thee; for I am fearfully
     and wonderfully made
Search me, O God, and know my heart
Try me, and know my thoughts
Psalm 139

They have sharpened their tongues like a serpent
Psalm 140:3

Let my prayer be set forth before thee as incense
Set a watch, O Lord, before my mouth
Keep the door of my lips
Psalm 141:2–3

The Lord is gracious, full of compassion, slow to anger
Psalm 145:8

Put not your trust in princes, nor in the son of man . . .
Psalm 146:3

He telleth the number of the stars
He calleth them all by their names
Psalm 147:4

PRAISE YE HIM, ALL HIS ANGELS
Praise ye him, sun and moon
Praise him, all ye stars of light
Ye dragons, and all deeps
Fire, and hail; snow, and vapors
Fruitful trees, and all cedars . . .
Psalm 148

PRAISE HIM WITH THE SOUND OF THE TRUMPET
Praise him with the timbrel and dance
Let everything that hath breath praise the Lord
Psalm 150

Proverbs

To give subtilty to the simple,
    to the young man knowledge
Prov. 1:4

My son, if sinners entice thee, consent thou not
Prov. 1:10

Wisdom crieth without; she uttereth her voice
    in the streets
Prov. 1:20

Trust in the Lord with all thine heart . . . he shall direct
    thy paths
Prov. 3:5–6

Her ways are ways of pleasantness
And all her paths are peace
Prov. 3:17

Wisdom is the principal thing; therefore get wisdom
Prov. 4:7

Keep thy heart with all diligence
For out of it are the issues of life
Prov. 4:23

The lips of a loose woman drip honey . . .
But her end is bitter as wormwood,
    sharp as a two-edged sword
Prov. 5:3–4

Go to the ant, thou sluggard
Consider her ways and be wise
Prov. 6:6

Yet a little sleep, a little slumber,
A little folding of the hands to sleep
Prov. 6:10

Can a man take fire in his bosom,
    and his clothes not be burned?
Prov. 6:27

Come, let us take our fill of love until the morning
Prov. 7:18

He goeth after her straightway
As an ox goeth to the slaughter
Prov. 7:22

Wisdom is better than rubies
Prov. 8:11

Reprove not a scorner, lest he hate thee
Rebuke a wise man, and he will love thee
Prov. 9:8

Stolen waters are sweet
And bread eaten in secret is pleasant
Prov. 9:17

A wise son maketh a glad father
A foolish son is the heaviness of his mother
Prov. 10:1

Hatred stirreth up strifes; but love covereth all sins
Prov. 10:12

In the multitude of counsellors there is safety
Prov. 11:14; 15:22

He that trusteth in his riches shall fall
Prov. 11:28

A virtuous woman is a crown to her husband
Prov. 12:4

The way of a fool is right in his own eyes
Prov. 12:15

Hope deferred maketh the heart sick
Prov. 13:12

The desire accomplished is sweet to the soul
Prov. 13:19

He that spareth his rod hateth his son
He that loveth him chasteneth him
Prov. 13:24

Fools make a mock at sin
Prov. 14:9

In all labor is profit: but talk tends only to penury
Prov. 14:23

A soft answer turneth away wrath
Prov. 15:1

A merry heart maketh a cheerful countenance
Prov. 15:13

Better is a dinner of herbs where love is
Than a stalled ox and hatred therewith
Prov. 15:17

A word spoken in due season, how good is it!
Prov. 15:23

Before honor is humility
Prov. 15:33, 18:12

Pride goeth before destruction
And an haughty spirit before a fall
Prov. 16:18

The hoary head is a crown of glory
Prov. 16:31

Whoso mocketh the poor reproacheth his Maker
Prov. 17:5

A friend loveth at all times
Prov. 17:17

A merry heart doeth good like a medicine
Prov. 17:22

Even a fool, when he holdeth his peace, is counted wise
Prov. 17:28

A wounded spirit who can bear?
Prov. 18:14

Whoso findeth a wife findeth a good thing
Prov. 18:22

There is a friend that sticketh closer than a brother
Prov. 18:24

Wealth maketh many friends
Prov. 19:4

Wine is a mocker, strong drink is raging
Prov. 20:1

Even a child is known by his doings
Prov. 20:11

Meddle not with him that flattereth with his lips
Prov. 20:19

It is better to dwell in a corner of the housetop
Than with a brawling woman in a wide house
Prov. 21:9, 25:24

A good name is rather to be chosen than great riches
Prov. 22:1

Train up a child in the way he should go:
When he is old, he will not depart from it
Prov. 22:6

The borrower is servant to the lender
Prov. 22:7

Remove not the ancient landmark
Prov. 22:28

As he thinketh in his heart, so is he
Prov. 23:7

Despise not thy mother when she is old
Prov. 23:22

A word fitly spoken is like apples of gold
    in pictures of silver
Prov. 25:11

Heap coals of fire upon his head
Prov. 25:22

As cold waters to a thirsty soul
So is good news from a far country
Prov. 25:25

As a dog returneth to his vomit
So a fool returneth to his folly
Prov. 26:11

Boast not thyself of tomorrow
For thou knowest not what a day may bring forth
Prov. 27:1

Let another man praise thee, and not thine own mouth
Prov. 27:2

To the hungry soul every bitter thing is sweet
Prov. 27:7

Better is a neighbor that is near than a brother far off
Prov. 27:10

He that maketh haste to be rich shall not be innocent
Prov. 28:20

Where there is no vision, the people perish
Prov. 29:18

The way of a man with a maid
Prov. 30:19

Who can find a virtuous woman?
Her price is far above rubies . . .
Prov. 31:10–31

Ecclesiastes

VANITY OF VANITIES, ALL IS VANITY
What profit hath a man of all his labor under the sun?
One generation passeth away and another generation
    cometh
All the rivers run into the sea; yet the sea is not full
The eye is not satisfied with seeing,
    nor the ear with hearing
There is no new thing under the sun
There is no remembrance of former things
That which is crooked cannot be made straight
In much wisdom is much grief
Eccles. 1

Wisdom excelleth folly, as far as light excelleth
    darkness
Eccles. 2:13

How dieth the wise man? as the fool
Eccles. 2:16

TO EVERY THING THERE IS A SEASON
And a time to every purpose under the heaven
A time to be born and a time to die . . .
A time to love and a time to hate
A time of war and a time of peace
Eccles. 3:1–8

I praised the dead which are already dead
    more than the living
Eccles. 4:2

Better is an handful with quietness than both hands full
    with vexation
Eccles. 4:6

A threefold cord is not quickly broken
Eccles. 4:12

Better is a poor and a wise child
    than an old and foolish king
Eccles. 4:13

BE NOT RASH WITH THY MOUTH
God is in heaven and thou on earth:
    therefore let thy words be few
Better is it that thou shouldst not vow . . .
Eccles. 5:1–7

The sleep of a laboring man is sweet whether he eat little
    or much
Eccles. 5:12

As he came forth of his mother's womb,
    naked shall he return
Eccles. 5:15

A good name is better than precious ointment
Eccles. 7:1

It is better to go to the house of mourning
    than the house of feasting
Eccles. 7:2

Better is the end of a thing than the beginning thereof
Eccles. 7:8

Be not righteous over much
Eccles. 7:16

WISDOM STRENGTHENETH THE WISE
There is not a just man that doeth good and sinneth not
I find more bitter than death the woman whose heart
    is snares
God hath made man upright
Eccles. 7:17–29

A man hath no better thing . . . than to eat, drink,
    and be merry
Eccles. 8:15

ALL THINGS COME ALIKE TO ALL
For to him that is joined to all the living there is hope
For a living dog is better than a dead lion
For the living know that they shall die
But the dead know not anything
Whatsoever thy hand findeth to do, do it with thy might
The race is not to the swift nor the battle to the strong
Wisdom is better than weapons of war
Eccles. 9

A feast is made for laughter and wine maketh merry . . .
Eccles. 10:19

A bird of the air shall carry the voice
Eccles. 10:20

Cast thy bread upon the waters . . .
Eccles. 11:1

Rejoice, O young man, in thy youth
Eccles. 11:9

REMEMBER NOW THY CREATOR
IN THE DAYS OF THY YOUTH
In the day when the keepers of the house tremble
The grasshopper shall be a burden
And desire shall fail
Of making many books there is no end
And much study is a weariness of the flesh
Let us hear the conclusion of the whole matter
Fear God and keep his commandments
This is the whole duty of man
Eccles. 12

The Song of Songs, which is Solomon's

I AM BLACK, BUT COMELY
Thy love is better than wine
I am the rose of Sharon, and the lily of the valleys
As the apple tree among the trees of the wood
So is my beloved among the sons
His banner over me was love
Stay me with flagons, comfort me with apples
For I am sick with love
Song 1:1—2:5

THE VOICE OF THE TURTLE
Rise up, my love, my fair one, and come away
For, lo, the winter is past, the rain is over and gone
The flowers appear on the earth
And the voice of the turtle is heard in our land
Song 2:10–12

The little foxes, that spoil the vines
Song 2:15

My beloved is mine, and I am his
He feedeth among the lilies
Until the day break, and the shadows flee away
Song 2:16–17

By night on my bed I sought him . . .
Song 3:1

BEHOLD THOU ART FAIR, MY LOVE
Thou hast doves' eyes within thy locks
Thy lips are like a thread of scarlet
And thy speech is comely
Thy two breasts are like two young roes

Thou art all fair, my love; there is no spot in thee
A garden inclosed is my sister, my spouse
Song 4:1–12

RETURN O SHULAMITE
Who is she that looketh forth as the morning
Fair as the moon and terrible as an army with banners?
Return, return, O Shulamite, that we may look upon thee
Song 6:10–13

HOW FAIR AND HOW PLEASANT ART THOU, O LOVE
Thy navel is like a round goblet
Thy belly is like an heap of wheat set about with lilies
Thy neck is as a tower of ivory
Song 7:2–6

I am my beloved's, and his desire is toward me
Song 7:10

Set me as a seal upon thine heart for love is strong
      as death
Jealousy is cruel as the grave
Many waters cannot quench love
Song 8:6–7

Make haste, my beloved, and be thou like to a roe
Or to a young hart upon the mountains
Song 8:14

Old Testament

ISAIAH

Isaiah's Vision of Judah and Jerusalem

HEAR, O HEAVENS
I have nourished and brought up children
And they have rebelled against me
The ox knoweth his owner and the ass his master's crib
But Israel doth not know, my people doth not consider
The whole head is sick, and the whole heart faint
Except the Lord had left us a small remnant
We should have been as Sodom and Gomorrah
Isaiah 1:1–10

As a lodge in a garden of cucumbers, a besieged city
Isaiah 1:8

TO WHAT PURPOSE ARE YOUR SACRIFICES?
Bring no more vain oblations
Incense is an abomination unto me
Your new moons and your feasts my soul hateth
When ye spread forth your hands, I will hide mine eyes
Yea, when ye make many prayers, I will not hear
Your hands are full of blood
Isaiah 1:11–15

CEASE TO DO EVIL
Learn to do well; relieve the oppressed . . .
Come now, and let us reason together:
Though your sins be as scarlet,
     they shall be as white as snow
If you be willing and obedient,
     you shall eat the good of the land
But if you refuse you shall be devoured with the sword
How is the faithful city become an harlot!
Isaiah 1:16–21

IN THE LAST DAYS
The mountain of the Lord's house shall be exalted
    above the hills
And all nations shall flow unto it
He will teach us of his ways
And we will walk in his paths:
He shall judge among the nations
And they shall beat their swords into plowshares . . .
Nation shall not lift up sword against nation
Neither shall they learn war any more
Isaiah 2:1–5

ENTER INTO THE ROCK
Hide thee in the dust
For everyone that is lifted up shall be brought low:
And the cedars of Lebanon, every high tower
Every fenced wall, all the ships of Tarshish
The loftiness of man shall be made low
Isaiah 2:10–22

What mean ye that ye grind the faces of the poor?
Isaiah 3:15

THE DAUGHTERS OF ZION ARE HAUGHTY
They walk with stretched forth necks and wanton eyes
Walking and mincing as they go
And making a tinkling with their feet
The Lord will take away the bravery of their ornaments
Instead of sweet smell there shall be stink
Isaiah 3:16–26

In that day seven women shall take hold of one man
Isaiah 4:1

THE LORD'S VINEYARD
My well-beloved hath a vineyard in a fruitful hill . . .
And it brought forth wild grapes
What could have been done more that I have not done?

I will break down the wall and lay it waste
For the vineyard of the Lord is the house of Israel
The men of Judah his pleasant plant
He looked for judgment, but behold oppression
For righteousness, but behold a cry
Woe unto them that join house to house . . .
Woe to those who rise up early in the morning
     to follow strong drink
Woe unto them that draw iniquity with cords of vanity
And sin as it were with a cart rope
Woe unto them that call evil good and good evil
Isaiah 5

IN THE YEAR THAT KING UZZIAH DIED
I saw the Lord sitting upon a throne, high and lifted up
Above it stood the seraphims: each one had six wings . . .
Holy, holy, holy, is the Lord of hosts:
The whole earth is full of his glory
Isaiah 6:1–4

WOE IS ME!
Because I am a man of unclean lips
One of the seraphims flew unto me,
     with a live coal in his hand
And he laid it upon my mouth and said:
Thine iniquity is taken away, thy sin purged
I heard the Lord: Whom shall I send
     and who will go for us?
I said: Here am I. Send me
And he said: Go and tell this people . . .
Lord how long? Until the cities be wasted
The land utterly desolate
Isaiah 6

THE LORD'S SIGN TO THE HOUSE OF DAVID
Behold, a virgin shall conceive and bear a son
And shall call his name Immanuel
Isaiah 7:13–14

A STONE OF STUMBLING
The Lord shall be a sanctuary
But a stone of stumbling and a rock of offence
To both the houses of Israel
Isaiah 8:14

UNTO US A SON IS GIVEN
The people that walked in darkness have seen
    a great light
They that dwell in the land of the shadow of death
Upon them hath the light shined
For unto us a child is born, unto us a son is given
And the government shall be upon his shoulder
And his name shall be called Wonderful, Counselor
The mighty God, The everlasting Father, The Prince
    of Peace
Of the increase of his government and peace
    there shall be no end
Isaiah 9:6–7

For all this his anger is not turned away
But his hand is stretched out still
Isaiah 9:12, 17, 21, 10:4

O ASSYRIAN, THE ROD OF MINE ANGER
I will send him against an hypocritical nation
To take the spoil and to tread them down
Like the mire of the streets
The light of Israel shall be for a fire, his Holy One
    for a flame
And shall consume the glory of his forest
    and his fruitful field
Isaiah 10:5–19

THE STEM OF JESSE
There shall come forth a rod out of the stem of Jesse
And a Branch shall grow out of his roots:

The spirit of the Lord shall rest upon him . . .
With righteousness shall he judge the poor
And with the breath of his lips shall he slay the wicked
Isaiah 11:1–5

THE PEACEABLE KINGDOM
The wolf also shall dwell with the lamb
And the leopard shall lie down with the kid . . .
And a little child shall lead them
The lion shall eat straw like the ox
The suckling child shall play on the hole of the asp
They shall not hurt or destroy in all my holy mountain:
For the earth shall be full of the knowledge of the Lord
As the waters cover the sea
Isaiah 11:6–9

AN ENSIGN FOR THE NATIONS
The Lord shall assemble the outcasts of Israel
And gather Judah from the four corners of the earth
Isaiah 11:10–16

All Nations

BABYLON SHALL FALL
The day of the Lord cometh, cruel with wrath
        and fierce anger
Every one that is found shall be thrust through
Their children also shall be dashed to pieces
        before their eyes
The wild beasts shall cry in their desolate houses
And dragons in their pleasant palaces
Isaiah 13

THE FALL OF LUCIFER
How art thou fallen from heaven, O Lucifer,
        son of the morning!

How art thou cut down to the ground
For thou hast said in thine heart:
I will ascend into heaven
I will exalt my throne above the stars of God
I will be like the most High
Yet thou shalt be brought down to hell
Is this the man that made the earth to tremble?
Isaiah 14:12–16

THE DOWNFALL OF THE ASSYRIANS
I will break the Assyrian in my land
And tread him underfoot
Then shall his burden depart from their shoulders
Isaiah 14:25

DAMASCUS SHALL BE A RUINOUS HEAP
The nations shall rush like the rushing of many waters
But God shall rebuke them and they shall flee far off
They shall be chased as the chaff of the mountains
Like a rolling thing before the whirlwind
Isaiah 17

THE BURDEN OF EGYPT
The Lord rideth upon a swift cloud
And shall come into Egypt:
I will set the Egyptians against the Egyptians
They shall fight everyone against his brother
City against city, kingdom against kingdom
And the spirit of Egypt shall fail in the midst thereof
Isaiah 19

Babylon is fallen, is fallen . . .
Isaiah 21:9

Watchman, what of the night?
Isaiah 21:11

Let us eat and drink: for tomorrow we shall die
Isaiah 22:13

I will fasten him as a nail in a sure place
Isaiah 22:23

THE FALL OF TYRE
Howl, ye ships of Tarshish
For your strength is laid waste
Isaiah 23:14

THE EARTH IS UTTERLY BROKEN DOWN
The Lord maketh the earth empty
And scattereth the inhabitants
And it shall be, as with the people, so with the priest
As with the maid so with her mistress
The earth mourneth and fadeth away
All joy is darkened, the mirth of the land is gone
Isaiah 24

O LORD, THOU ART MY GOD
I will praise thy name for thou hast done
    wonderful things
Thy counsels of old are faithfulness and truth
Thou hast been a strength to the poor . . .
A refuge from the storm, a shadow from the heat
Isaiah 25:1–5

A feast of fat things, a feast of wines on the lees
Isaiah 25:6

He will swallow up death in victory
The Lord God will wipe away tears from all faces
Isaiah 25:8

BECAUSE HE TRUSTETH IN THEE
Thou wilt keep him in perfect peace
Whose mind is stayed on thee

Trust ye in the Lord for ever:
For in the Lord JEHOVAH is everlasting strength
In the way of thy judgments, O Lord,
      have we waited for thee
The desire of our soul is to thy name
      and remembrance of thee
Lord, thou wilt ordain peace for us
For thou also hast wrought all our works in us
Isaiah 26

Awake and sing, ye that dwell in dust
Isaiah 26:19

Hide thyself as it were for a little moment
Until the indignation be overpast
Isaiah 26:20

Even leviathan that crooked serpent
Isaiah 27:1

Israel shall blossom and bud
And fill the face of the world with fruit
Isaiah 27:6

Warning and Hope for God's Rebellious People

WHOM SHALL HE TEACH KNOWLEDGE?
Whom shall he make to understand doctrine?
For precept must be upon precept, line upon line,
Here a little and there a little
Ye have said: We have made a covenant with death
And with hell are we at agreement
We have made lies our refuge, under falsehood
      have we hid
Isaiah 28

It shall be a vexation only to understand the report
Isaiah 28:19

Stay yourselves and wonder, cry ye out and cry:
They are drunken but not with wine
They stagger but not with strong drink
Isaiah 29:9

Their strength is to sit still
Isaiah 30:7

WOE TO THE REBELLIOUS CHILDREN
Go write it before them in a table and note it in a book
That it may be for the time to come for ever and ever:
That this is a rebellious people
Children that will not hear the law of the Lord
Isaiah 30:8–9

RETURNING AND REST
In returning and rest shall ye be saved
In quietness and in confidence shall be your strength
But ye said: No, we will flee upon horses
Therefore will the Lord wait
Blessed are all they that wait for him
Though the Lord gave you the bread of adversity
And the water of affliction
Yet thine eyes shall see thy teacher
Thine ears shall hear a word behind thee saying:
This is the way, walk ye in it
Isaiah 30:15–21

THE SHADOW OF A GREAT ROCK
Behold, a king shall reign in righteousness
And princes shall rule in judgment
And a man shall be as an hiding place from the wind
As rivers of water in a dry place
As the shadow of a great rock in a weary land
Isaiah 32:1–2

IT IS THE DAY OF THE LORD'S VENGEANCE
Streams shall be turned into pitch
And the dust thereof into brimstone
From generation to generation it shall lie waste
None shall pass through it for ever and ever
Thorns shall come up in her palaces
Nettles and brambles in the fortresses
It shall be an habitation of dragons and a court for owls
Isaiah 34

THE LAME MAN LEAPS AS AN HART
The desert shall rejoice and blossom as the rose
Strengthen ye the weak hands and confirm
        the feeble knees
Say to them that are of a fearful heart:
Be strong, fear not: behold, your God will come . . .
Then the eyes of the blind shall be opened . . .
Then shall the lame man leap as an hart . . .
The parched ground shall become a pool
And the thirsty land springs of water
The ransomed of the Lord shall return
And sorrow and sighing shall flee away
Isaiah 35

Thou trusteth in the staff of this broken reed
Isaiah 36:6

INCLINE THINE EAR, O LORD
Open thine eyes, O Lord, and see
The kings of Assyria have laid waste all the nations
And have cast their gods into the fire:
For they were no gods, but the work of men's hands
Now therefore, O Lord our God, save us from his hand
That all the kingdoms of the earth
May know that thou art the Lord
Isaiah 37:17–20

HEZEKIAH'S ILLNESS
In those days was Hezekiah sick unto death
Isaiah said: Set thine house in order
For thou shalt die
Hezekiah turned his face toward the wall and prayed:
Remember now, O Lord, I beseech thee
How I have walked before thee in truth
And have done that which is good in thy sight
And Hezekiah wept
The Lord said: I have heard thy prayer
    and seen thy tears
Behold, I will add unto thy days fifteen years
And I will deliver thee out of the hand
    of the king of Assyria
Isaiah 38:1-8

I shall go softly in the bitterness of my soul
Isaiah 38:15

A Message of Comfort

COMFORT YE, COMFORT YE MY PEOPLE
Speak ye comfortably to Jerusalem and cry unto her:
Her warfare is accomplished, her iniquity pardoned . . .
Prepare ye the way of the Lord
Make straight in the desert a highway for our God
Every valley shall be exalted and every mountain made low
The crooked shall be made straight
    and the rough places plain:
And the glory of the Lord shall be revealed . . .
All flesh is grass and goodliness
    as the flower of the field:
The grass withereth, the flower fadeth . . .
But the word of our God shall stand for ever
Isaiah 40:1-8

LIFT UP THY VOICE WITH STRENGTH
Say unto the cities of Judah: Behold your God!
He shall feed his flock like a shepherd
He shall gather the lambs with his arm
Who hath measured the waters in the hollow of his hand
Weighed the mountains in scales
And the hills in a balance?
Who hath directed the Spirit of the Lord
    or hath taught him
And showed to him the way of understanding?
Behold the nations are as a drop of a bucket
All nations before him are as nothing
Isaiah 40:9–17

TO WHOM WILL YE LIKEN GOD?
What likeness will ye compare unto him?
Have ye not known? Have ye not heard?
Hath it not been told you from the beginning?
It is he that sitteth upon the circle of the earth . . .
That stretcheth out the heavens as a curtain
And spreadeth them out as a tent to dwell in:
Lift up your eyes and behold
Who hath created these things
Isaiah 40:18–26

RUN AND NOT BE WEARY
The everlasting God fainteth not, neither is weary
They that wait upon the Lord shall renew their strength
They shall mount up with wings as eagles
They shall run and not be weary, walk, and not faint
Isaiah 40:28–31

THOU, ISRAEL, ART MY SERVANT
I have chosen thee and not cast thee away
Fear thou not for I am with thee
Be not dismayed for I am thy God
I will strengthen thee and uphold thee
Isaiah 41:8–10

A BRUISED REED

Behold my servant, mine elect, in whom my soul
 delighteth
I have put my spirit upon him
A bruised reed shall he not break . . .
Isaiah 42:1–3

A LIGHT TO THE GENTILES

I the Lord have called thee in righteousness
And will hold thine hand and will keep thee
And give thee for a covenant of the people
For a light of the Gentiles
To open blind eyes, to bring out prisoners from prison
Isaiah 42:6–7

Shall the clay say to him that fashions it,
 what makest thou?
Isaiah 45:9

O that thou hadst hearkened to my commandments!
Then had thy peace been as a river
And thy righteousness as the waves of the sea
Isaiah 48:18

There is no peace unto the wicked
Isaiah 48:22

THE GARDEN OF THE LORD

The Lord shall comfort Zion
He will comfort all her waste places
He will make her wilderness like Eden
Her desert like the garden of the Lord
Joy and gladness shall be found therein
Thanksgiving and the voice of melody
Sorrow and mourning shall flee away
Isaiah 51:1–11

THE CUP OF TREMBLING
I have taken out of thine hand the cup of trembling
Even the dregs of the cup of my fury
Thou shalt no more drink it again
Isaiah 51:17–22

How beautiful are the feet of him
    that bringeth good tidings . . .
Isaiah 52:7

They shall see eye to eye
Isaiah 52:8

A MAN OF SORROWS
He is despised and rejected of men . . .
And acquainted with grief
Surely he hath borne our griefs and carried our sorrows
All we like sheep have gone astray
And the Lord hath laid on him the iniquity of us all
He is brought as a lamb to the slaughter
Isaiah 53

Everyone that thirsteth, come ye to the waters
Isaiah 55:1

Seek ye the Lord while he may be found
Call ye upon him while he is near
Isaiah 55:6

AN EVERLASTING SIGN
My thoughts are not your thoughts
Neither are your ways my ways
For as the heavens are higher than the earth
So are my ways higher than your ways . . .
For ye shall go out with joy and be led forth with peace
Instead of the thorn shall come up the fir tree

And instead of the brier shall come up the myrtle tree
And it shall be for an everlasting sign
    that shall not be cut off
Isaiah 55:8–13

Peace to him that is far off and to him that is near
Isaiah 57:19

A FAST ACCEPTABLE TO THE LORD
Is not this the fast that I have chosen?
To loose the bands of wickedness
To undo the heavy burdens . . .
Is it not to deal thy bread to the hungry?
When thou seest the naked, that thou cover him?
Then shall thy light break forth as the morning
And thine health shall spring forth speedily
Then shalt thou call and the Lord shall answer
Thy light shall rise in obscurity
And thy darkness be as the noonday
And the Lord shall guide thee continually
Isaiah 58

They make haste to shed innocent blood . . .
The way of peace they know not
Isaiah 59:7–8

THE SPIRIT OF THE LORD IS UPON ME
He hath sent me to bind up the broken hearted
To proclaim liberty to the captives
To proclaim the acceptable year of the Lord . . .
To comfort all that mourn
To give them beauty for ashes
And the oil of joy for mourning
The garment of praise for the spirit of heaviness
Isaiah 61:1–3

I have trodden the winepress alone . . .
Isaiah 63:3

In all their affliction he was afflicted
And the angel of his presence saved them
Isaiah 63:9

All our righteousness are as filthy rags
And we all do fade as a leaf
Isaiah 64:6

I am holier than thou
Isaiah 65:5

For, behold, I create new heavens and a new earth
Isaiah 65:17

THEY SHALL PLANT VINEYARDS
They shall build houses and inhabit them
They shall plant vineyards, and eat the fruit of them
They shall not build and another inhabit
They shall not plant and another eat
Isaiah 65:21–22

Before they call, I will answer
While they are yet speaking, I will hear
Isaiah 65:24

As one whom his mother comforteth, so will I comfort you
Isaiah 66:13

Old Testament

OTHER
PROPHETS

Jeremiah and Lamentations

JEREMIAH'S CALL TO BE GOD'S PROPHET
Before thou camest forth out of the womb
I ordained thee a prophet unto the nations
Lord God, I cannot speak for I am a child
Say not I am a child:
Whatsoever I command thee thou shalt speak
Behold I have put my words in thy mouth
Jer. 1

THE JUDGMENT OF GOD
Ye defiled my land and made mine heritage an
    abomination
O Jerusalem, wash thine heart from wickedness
For my people is foolish, they have not known me
To do good they have no knowledge
The whole land shall be desolate yet will I not make
    a full end
Jer. 2—4

THY CHILDREN HAVE FORSAKEN ME
When I had fed them they then committed adultery
They were as fed horses in the morning:
Every one neighed after his neighbor's wife
Hear now this, foolish people . . . which have eyes
    and see not . . .
This people hath a revolting and a rebellious heart
Jer. 5

GOD'S DECLARATION OF WAR
They shall thoroughly glean the remnant of Israel
    as a vine
Saying, Peace, peace when there is no peace
Stand ye in the ways, and see, and ask for the old paths
But they said, we will not walk therein
Jer. 6

AMEND YOUR WAYS AND YOUR DOINGS
Opress not the stranger, the fatherless, the widow . . .
Is this house, which is called by my name, become
    a den of robbers?
Obey my voice and I will be your God
Truth is perished and is cut off from their mouth
The harvest is past, the summer is ended,
    and we are not saved
Is there no balm in Gilead?
Jer. 7—8

THINE HABITATION IS IN THE MIDST OF DECEIT
Oh that I had in the wilderness
A lodging place of wayfaring men
I will make Jerusalem heaps, and a den of dragons
I will feed them . . . with wormwood . . .
For a voice of wailing is heard out of Zion
Jer. 9; cf. 23:15

Give glory to the Lord your God before he cause
    darkness
Jer. 13:16

Can the Ethiopian change his skin or the leopard
    his spots?
Jer. 13:23

I am weary with repenting
Jer. 15:6

Her sun is gone down while it was yet day
Jer. 15:9

A man of strife and a man of contention
Jer. 15:10

TRUST IN GOD
The sin of Judah is written with a pen of iron
It is graven upon the table of their heart
Cursed be the man that trusteth in man
And whose heart departeth from the Lord
Blessed is the man that trusteth in the Lord
The heart is deceitful above all things: who can know it?
I the Lord search the heart
Jer. 17:1–10

As the partridge sitteth on eggs . . .
Jer. 17:11

Thou art my hope in the day of evil
Jer. 17:17

As the clay in the potter's hand so are ye in mine hand
Jer. 18:6

JEREMIAH PROPHESIES TO ZEDEKIAH OF JUDAH
I will deliver Zedekiah to Nebuchadrezzar of Babylon
I set before you the way of life and the way of death
I will punish you according to the fruit of your doings
Jer. 21

O earth, earth, earth, hear the word of the Lord
Jer. 22:29

I WILL RAISE UNTO DAVID A RIGHTEOUS BRANCH
In his days Judah shall be saved and Israel dwell safely
This is his name *The Lord Our Righteousness*
Jer. 23:1–8

AGAINST FALSE PROPHETS
I have not sent these prophets, yet they prophesied
They are prophets of the deceit of their own heart
I am against the prophets . . . that steal my words
Jer. 23:9–40

GOD'S PROMISE OF ISRAEL'S RETURN
FROM CAPTIVITY
Ye shall seek me and find me
And I will turn away your captivity
I will heal thee of thy wounds
And ye shall be my people and I will be your God
Jer. 29—30

THE RESTORATION OF ISRAEL
O Lord, save thy people, the remnant of Israel
He that scattered Israel will gather him
I will turn their mourning into joy
Jer. 31:1–30

A voice was heard in Ramah, lamentation
    and bitter weeping:
Rachel weeping for her children
Jer. 31:15

Fathers have eaten a sour grape
And children's teeth are set on edge
Jer. 31:29; cf. Ezek. 18:2–3

A NEW COVENANT WITH THE HOUSE OF ISRAEL
I will put my law in their inward parts
And write it in their hearts
Jer. 31:31–34

With my whole heart and with my whole soul
Jer. 32:41

BARUCH READS THE PROPHECIES OF JEREMIAH
Baruch wrote from the mouth of Jeremiah
    all the words of the Lord
Jeremiah commanded Baruch to read them
    in the house of the Lord
King Jehoiakim cut it with his penknife

And cast it in the fire until all the roll was consumed
The Lord said to Jeremiah: Take thee another roll
Jehoiakim shall have none
    to sit upon the throne of David
Jer. 36

JERUSALEM DESTROYED BY BABYLON
Nebuchadnezzar slew the sons of Zedekiah
    before his eyes
He put out Zedekiah's eyes and took him to Babylon
    in chains
But the poor were given vineyards and fields
And Jeremiah was spared and dwelt among the people
Jer. 39—40

ISRAEL IS A SCATTERED SHEEP
First the king of Assyria hath devoured him
And last this Nebuchadrezzar king of Babylon
Behold I will punish the king of Babylon
As I have punished the king of Assyria
And I will bring Israel again to his habitation
Jer. 50:1-33

THEIR REDEEMER IS STRONG
The Lord of hosts is his name
The Lord hath brought forth our righteousness
He hath made the earth by his power
He hath established the world by his wisdom
And hath stretched out the heaven by his understanding
Jer. 50:34—51:15

GOD'S JUDGMENT AGAINST BABYLON
Babylon shall become heaps, a dwelling place for dragons
I will bring them down like lambs to the slaughter
The broad walls of Babylon shall be utterly broken
And her high gates shall be burned with fire
Jer. 51:16-64

THE FATE OF JERUSALEM
How doth the city sit solitary that was full of people!
She weepeth sore in the night
And her tears are on her cheeks:
Among all her lovers she hath none to comfort her
All her gates are desolate . . . and she is in bitterness
The Lord hath afflicted her
For the multitude of her transgressions
Is it nothing to you, all ye that pass by?
Behold and see if there be any sorrow
    like unto my sorrow
Lament. 1

THE LORD WAS AS AN ENEMY
He hath swallowed up Israel
He hath swallowed up her palaces
He hath destroyed his strongholds
And increased in the daughter of Judah
    mourning and lamentation
The law is no more
Her prophets also find no vision from the Lord
The Lord hath fulfilled his word
He hath thrown down and hath not pitied
Lament. 2:5–17

CRY OUT IN THE NIGHT
Pour out thine heart, lift up thy hands to the Lord
For the life of thy young children
That faint for hunger in the top of every street
Lament. 2:19

THE ANGUISH OF JEREMIAH
I am the man that hath seen affliction
    by the rod of his wrath
He hath set me in dark places as they that be dead of old
He hath inclosed my ways with hewn stone
He hath made my paths crooked and pulled me in pieces
Lament. 3:1–21

CONCERNING THE MERCY OF GOD
It is of the Lord's mercies that we are not consumed
Because his compassions fail not
They are new every morning
The Lord is my portion: Therefore will I hope in him
It is good for a man that he bear the yoke in his youth
The Lord will not cast us off for ever
He will have compassion
According to the multitude of his mercies
For he doth not afflict willingly
    nor grieve the children of men
Let us search and try our ways
    and turn again to the Lord
Let us lift up our heart with our hands unto God
Lament. 3:18–41

Ezekiel

As I was among the captives by the river of Chebar
The heavens were opened and I saw visions of God
Ezek. 1:1

THE VISION OF FOUR CHERUBIM
A whirlwind came out of the north,
    a great cloud and a fire
With the likeness of four living creatures
Each with the face of a man, a lion, an ox, and an eagle
Two wings of every one were joined one to another
Ezek. 1:4–14

THE VISION OF FOUR WHEELS
There was a wheel beside each living creature
Their appearance was as a wheel in the middle of a wheel
Their rings were full of eyes
The spirit of the living creature was in the wheels
Ezek. 1:15–25

GOD IN GLORY
Above the firmament was the likeness of a throne
On the throne was a likeness of a man
I saw the appearance of fire round about within it
The likeness of the glory of the Lord
I fell upon my face
Ezek. 1:26–28

SON OF MAN HEAR WHAT I SAY
I send thee to the children of Israel
To a rebellious nation . . . impudent children
    and stiffhearted
Whether they hear or forbear
They shall know a prophet has been among them
Be not afraid of their words nor dismayed at their looks
But thou, son of man, hear what I say
A hand gave Ezekiel a roll of a book
There was written therein lamentations and mourning
    and woe
Ezek. 2—3:14

A WATCHMAN UNTO ISRAEL
So the Spirit lifted me up, and took me away
I went in bitterness in the heat of my spirit
But the hand of the Lord was strong upon me
I have made thee a watchman unto Israel
He that heareth let him hear
Ezek. 3:14–27

THIS IS JERUSALEM
I have set it in the midst of the nations
She hath changed my judgments into wickedness
Therefore thus saith the Lord God:
Behold, I, even I, am against thee
The whole remnant of thee will I scatter to the winds
And make the land desolate
Ezek. 5—6

BEHOLD THE DAY, BEHOLD, IT IS COME
An end is come upon the four corners of the land
Mine eye shall not spare thee
I will recompense thee according to thy ways
The rod hath blossomed, pride hath budded
Violence is risen up into a rod of wickedness
All knees shall be weak as water
They shall gird themselves with sackcloth
     and horror shall cover them
Ezek. 7

A VISION OF JERUSALEM'S IDOLATRY
The spirit lifted me up between the earth and the heaven
Son of man dig now in the wall . . .
I beheld a door and he said: Go in
Behold the wicked abominations that they do here
Creeping things, abominable beasts and all the idols
     of Israel
Neither will I have pity though they cry in mine ears
Ezek. 8

CHERUBIMS AND A SAPPHIRE THRONE
Ezek. 10—11

EZEKIEL PROPHESIES TO THOSE IN CAPTIVITY
I have set thee for a sign
And they shall know that I am the Lord
Eat bread with quaking and drink water with trembling
There is a proverb: The days are prolonged
     and every vision faileth
This proberb shall cease, the days are at hand
Ezek. 12

As is the mother, so is her daughter
Ezek. 16:44

THE PARABLE OF THE EAGLES AND THE VINE
A great eagle with great wings . . . came unto Lebanon
And took the highest branch of the cedar

He planted the seed of the land
It grew and became a spreading vine
There was a second eagle
And the vine did bend its roots toward him
The Lord said: I will take a branch of the cedar
    and plant it
It will bear fruit and be a goodly cedar
Ezek. 17

THE JUSTNESS OF GOD
Therefore I will judge you, O house of Israel
Make you a new heart and a new spirit
Ezek. 18

A LAMENTATION FOR THE PRINCES OF ISRAEL
What is thy mother? A lioness
She brought up one of her whelps
The nations also heard of him; he was taken in their pit
They brought him with chains unto the land of Egypt
Ezek. 19

FIRE AND SWORD
Say to the forest of the south:
I will kindle a fire in thee
It shall devour every green tree and every dry tree
Say to Israel: I will draw forth my sword
    out of his sheath
And will cut off from thee the righteous and the wicked
Ezek. 20:45—21:32

GOD'S REVENGE ON FOREIGN NATIONS
Behold I am against thee O Tyre
I shall make thee a desolate city
Set thy face against Sidon
I will send into her pestilence
And blood into her streets
The land of Egypt shall be desolate and waste
Ezek. 25—32

108

THE FALL OF JERUSALEM
The city is smitten
For I will lay the land most desolate
And the pomp of her strength shall cease
Ezek. 33:21–33

WOE BE TO THE SHEPHERDS OF ISRAEL
I will seek out my sheep and will deliver them
I will feed my flock
I will set up one shepherd over them
I the Lord will be their God
Ezek. 34

THE VALLEY OF DRY BONES
Son of man can these bones live?
O ye dry bones hear the word of the Lord
The bones came together bone to bone
They lived and stood up upon their feet
Son of man these bones are the whole house of Israel
I shall place you in your own land
Ezek. 37

THE ARMY OF GOG
Set thy face against Gog, the land of Magog
Thou shalt come up against my people of Israel
Every man's sword shall be against his brother
Ezek. 38—39

THE VISION OF THE TEMPLE
There was a man whose appearance was like brass
With a line of flax and a measuring reed
He brought me to the temple and measured the posts
Show the house to the house of Israel
O princes of Israel: remove violence . . .
        and execute judgment
This land shall fall unto you for inheritance
Ezek. 40—48

The Book of Daniel

DANIEL AT THE PALACE OF NEBUCHADNEZZAR
In the third year of the reign of Jehoiakim
Nebuchadnezzar king of Babylon came
    and besieged Jerusalem
And the Lord gave Jehoiakim into his hand
Daniel, Hananiah, Mishael, and Azariah
    were brought to the palace
They received new names: Belteshazzar and Shadrach,
    Meshach and Abednego
Dan. 1:1–7

THE KING'S MEAT
Daniel would not defile himself with the king's meat
Prove thy servants I beseech thee for ten days
With pulse to eat and water to drink
After ten days their countenances were fairer and fatter
Dan. 1:8–16

NEBUCHADNEZZAR'S DREAM
Nebuchadnezzar dreamed dreams, wherewith his spirit
    was troubled
Magicians, astrologers, and sorcerers
    came to interpret the dream
None can show it to the king except the gods
The king was furious and commanded that all the wise
    men be destroyed
The secret of the dream was revealed to Daniel
Bring me before the king and I will interpret his dream
Thou, O king, sawest a great image of gold, silver,
    and brass
His feet part of iron, part of clay
Then was the iron, clay, brass, silver, and gold
    broken to pieces
And became like the chaff of the summer threshing floors

Thou, O king, art a king of kings, but God
Shall set up a kingdom which shall never be destroyed
Dan. 2

THE FIERY FURNACE
Nebuchadnezzar set up a golden image
All were commanded to fall down and worship it
Whoso falleth not down
Shall be cast into a fiery furnace
Nebuchadnezzar in rage called Shadrach, Meshach,
    and Abednego
Do not ye serve my gods nor worship the golden image?
Our God whom we serve is able to deliver us
    from the fiery furnace
Shadrach, Meshach, and Abednego fell down bound into
    the furnace
Nebuchadnezzar called them forth
Not a hair of their head was singed
Dan. 3

NEBUCHADNEZZAR'S MADNESS
Nebuchadnezzar was driven from men and did eat grass
    like an ox
Dan. 4

THE HANDWRITING ON THE WALL
Belshazzar the king made a great feast
They drank out of golden vessels
    from the temple in Jerusalem
And praised the gods of gold and silver, of brass, iron,
    wood, and stone
The fingers of a man's hand wrote upon the wall
All the wise men of the king came
But could not read the writing
Now let Daniel be called and he will interpret
MENE: God hath numbered thy kingdom and finished it
TEKEL: Thou art weighed in the balances
    and found wanting

PERES: Thy kingdom is divided
That night Belshazzar was slain and Darius became king
Dan. 5

IN THE LION'S DEN
Darius signed a decree that no man should petition
     any God or man
But Daniel was found making supplication to his God
The law of the Medes and the Persians altereth not
They brought Daniel and cast him into the den of lions
The king said: Thy God will deliver thee
The king rose very early in the morning
     and went unto the den of lions
O Daniel, servant of the living God
Is thy God able to deliver thee?
My God hath sent his angel and shut the lions' mouths
No manner of hurt was on him
Because he believed in his God
Dan. 6

DANIEL'S VISION OF THE FOUR BEASTS
Four great beasts came up from the sea . . .
The Ancient of days did sit, whose garment
     was white as snow
I saw in the night visions: one like the Son of man
His dominion is an everlasting dominion
Which shall not pass away
Dan. 7

THE VISION OF THE RAM AND THE GOAT
Daniel lifted up his eyes and saw a ram with two horns
Behold, an he goat ran unto him in the fury of his power
He cast him to the ground and stamped on him
A voice said: Gabriel, make this man
     to understand the vision
The two horns of the ram are the kings of Media
     and Persia
The goat is the king of Greece

112

In the latter time of their kingdom a king shall arise
A king of fierce countenance,
    understanding dark sentences
His power shall be great
And he will destroy the mighty and the holy
Dan. 8

DANIEL'S CONFESSION
We have sinned and have committed iniquity
Neither have we hearkened unto thy servants the prophets
To the Lord our God belong mercies and forgiveness
Let thy fury be turned away from thy city Jerusalem
O my God, incline thine ear and hear
Behold our desolations
Dan. 9:3–19

THE GIFT OF GABRIEL
Daniel: I am come to give thee skill and understanding
I am come to show thee for thou art greatly beloved
Dan. 9:20–27

A VISION OF A MAN
His face had the appearance of lightning
His eyes as lamps of fire
O Daniel, greatly beloved
Understand the words that I speak
I am come to make thee understand
    what shall befall thy people
Fear not, peace be unto thee, be strong
Dan. 10

THE COURSE OF FUTURE HISTORY
Dan. 11

THE TIME OF THE END
At that time Michael, who guards thy people, shall arise
There shall be a time of trouble such as never was

At that time thy people shall be delivered
Many of them that sleep in the dust shall awake
Some to everlasting life and some to shame and contempt
Many shall run to and fro and knowledge
    shall be increased
How long shall it be to the end of these wonders?
The words are closed up and sealed
    till the time of the end
Blessed is he that waiteth
Dan. 12

Hosea and Joel

Ye are the sons of the living God
Hosea 1:10

HOSEA AND GOMER
The Lord said to Hosea: Take thee a wife of whoredoms
For the land hath committed great whoredom
So he went and took Gomer
Hosea 1

ISRAEL THE FAITHLESS WIFE
I will not have mercy upon her children
I will hedge up her way with thorns . . .
I will also cause all her mirth to cease
I will destroy her vines and her fig trees
Hosea 2:1–13

FAITHLESS WIFE RESTORED
I will bring her into the wilderness
    and speak comfortably
I will betroth thee unto me in faithfulness
And thou shalt know the Lord
I will say unto them that were not my people:

Thou art my people
And they shall say: Thou art my God
Hosea 2:14–23

WARNING TO JUDAH
There is no truth, mercy, nor knowledge of God
My people are destroyed for lack of knowledge
Like people, like priest
They sinned against me
Therefore will I change their glory into shame
Whoredom and wine take away the heart
Though thou, Israel, play the harlot, yet let not Judah
    offend
Hosea 4

THE JUDGMENT OF GOD
Hear this, O priests, and hearken, ye house of Israel
Give ye ear, O house of the king
For judgment is toward you
I will pour out my wrath upon them like water
I will go till they acknowledge their offence
    and seek my face
Hosea 5

HE WILL RAISE US UP
Come let us return unto the Lord
For he hath torn and he will heal
He hath smitten and he will bind us up
In the third day he will raise us up
And we shall live in his sight
He shall come as the latter and the former rain
    unto the earth
Hosea 6:1–3

I DESIRED MERCY AND NOT SACRIFICE
Your goodness is as a morning cloud
And as the early dew it goeth away

I desired mercy and not sacrifice
And the knowledge of God more than burnt offerings
Hosea 6:4–6

They have sown the wind
And they shall reap the whirlwind
Hosea 8:7

God will cast them away and they shall be wanderers
    among the nations
Hosea 9:17

Ye have plowed wickedness, ye have reaped iniquity
Hosea 10:13

I drew them with bands of love
Hosea 11:4

THE REDEMPTION OF GOD
I will ransom them from the power of the grave
I will redeem them from death
O death, I will be thy plagues
O grave, I will be thy destruction
Hosea 13:14

THE WORD OF THE LORD TO JOEL
Sanctify a fast, call a solemn assembly
And cry unto the Lord
The seed is rotten under the clods
The barns are broken, the corn withered
Joel 1

BLOW A TRUMPET IN ZION
Sound an alarm in my holy mountain
Let all the inhabitants of the land tremble
For the day of the Lord cometh for it is nigh at hand
All faces shall gather blackness
The earth shall quake before them

The sun and the moon shall be dark
And the stars shall withdraw their shining
Joel 2:1–11

TURN TO ME WITH ALL YOUR HEART
Rend your heart and not your garments
And turn unto the Lord your God:
For he is gracious and merciful, slow to anger
And of great kindness and repenteth him of the evil
Let the priests weep between the porch and the altar
Let them say: Spare thy people, O Lord
Joel 2:12–17

FEAR NOT O LAND
Be glad and rejoice. The Lord will do great things
Ye shall know that I am the Lord your God and none else
I will pour out my spirit upon all flesh
Your sons and daughters shall prophesy
Your old men shall dream dreams, your young men
        see visions
Whosoever shall call on the name of the Lord
        shall be delivered
Joel 2:18–32

PREPARE WAR
Wake up the mighty men
Beat your plowshares into swords
And your pruninghooks into spears
Joel 3:9–10

Multitudes, multitudes in the valley of decision
For the day of the Lord is near
Joel 3:14

Amos and Obadiah

THE LORD WILL ROAR FROM ZION
And the habitations of the shepherds shall mourn
I brought you up from the land of Egypt
And led you forty years through the wilderness
And I raised up of your sons for prophets
But you commanded the prophets saying: Prophesy not
Therefore the flight shall perish from the swift
Neither shall the mighty deliver himself
The courageous shall flee away naked
Amos 1—2

They sold the righteous for silver
And the poor for a pair of shoes
Amos 2:6, cf. 8:6

O CHILDREN OF ISRAEL
You only have I known of all the families of the earth
Therefore I will punish you for all your iniquities
Can two walk together, except they be agreed?
An adversary there shall be even round about the land
He shall bring down thy strength from thee
And thy palaces shall be spoiled
I will smite the winter house with the summer house
The great houses shall have an end
Amos 3

PREPARE TO MEET THY GOD
He that forms the mountains and creates the wind
And declares to man his thought
That makes the morning darkness
The Lord, the God of hosts, is his name
Amos 4:12–13

SEEK YE ME, AND YE SHALL LIVE
Seek him that makes the seven stars and Orion
And turns the shadow of death into morning
Amos 5:4–8

I DESPISE YOUR FEAST DAYS
I take no delight in your solemn rituals
I will not accept your burnt offerings
Take away the noise of your songs
But let judgment run down as waters
And righteousness as a mighty stream
Amos 5:21–24

THE PLUMBLINE
The Lord stood on a wall made by a plumbline
With a plumbline in his hand
I will set a plumbline in the midst of Israel
And will not again pass by them
Amos 7:7–8

The mountains shall drop sweet wine
And all the hills shall melt
Amos 9:13

I have made thee small among the heathen
The pride of thine heart hath deceived thee
Obad. v. 2–3

THE DAY OF THE LORD IS NEAR
As thou hast done, it shall be done unto thee:
Thy reward shall return upon thine own head
Obad. v. 15

Jonah, Micah, and Nahum

ARISE, GO TO NINEVEH
Cry against it for their wickedness is come up before me
But Jonah rose to flee from the presence of the Lord
He went down to Joppa and found a ship
     going to Tarshish
The Lord sent out a mighty tempest and the mariners
     were afraid
Let us cast lots that we may know for whose cause
     this evil is upon us
So they cast lots and the lot fell upon Jonah
What shall we do unto thee that the sea may be calm?
Take me up and cast me forth into the sea
So they took up Jonah and cast him forth into the sea
And the sea ceased from raging
Jonah 1:1–15

JONAH AND THE WHALE
The Lord had prepared a great fish to swallow up Jonah
And Jonah was in the belly of the fish three days
     and three nights
Jonah prayed unto the Lord out of the fish's belly
Out of the belly of hell cried I
And thou heardest my voice
In the midst of the seas, the floods compassed me about
All thy billows and thy waves passed over me
When my soul fainted, I remembered the Lord
The Lord spake unto the fish and it vomited out Jonah
     upon dry land
Jonah 1:17—2

JONAH'S PROPHECY TO NINEVEH
The Lord said to Jonah a second time: Arise, go unto
     Nineveh
Preach unto it the preaching I bid thee:
Yet forty days and Nineveh shall be overthrown

The people of Nineveh believed God
   and proclaimed a fast
And God saw that they turned from their evil way
And God repented of the evil that he had said
   he would do unto them
Jonah 3

JONAH'S ANGER AT GOD'S CHANGE OF HEART
It displeased Jonah and he was very angry
It is better for me to die than to live
The Lord said: Doest thou well to be angry?
Jonah went out of the city and sat in a booth
And the Lord God prepared a gourd to come over Jonah
   to shade him
But God prepared a worm, and it smote the gourd which
   withered
The Lord said: Thou hast had pity on the gourd
Should not I spare Nineveh?
Jonah 4

THE WORD OF THE LORD TO MICAH
The Lord will come down and tread upon the high places
The mountains will melt as wax before the fire
Therefore I will go stripped and naked
I will make a wailing like the dragons
And mourning as the owls
Micah 1

Truly I am full of power by the spirit of the Lord
To declare to Jacob his transgression
And to Israel his sin
Micah 3:8

THE REIGN OF THE LORD
In the last days it shall come to pass
That the mountain of the house of the Lord shall be
   established
It shall be exalted above the hills

Nations shall say: Come let us go
    to the mountain of the Lord
We will walk in his paths
They shall beat their swords into plowshares
Neither shall they learn war anymore
They shall sit every man under his vine
    and under his fig tree
And none shall make them afraid
Micah 4:1–4

THOU BETHLEHEM
Out of thee shall come forth one who is to be the ruler
    in Israel
Now shall he be great unto the ends of the earth
Micah 5:2–4

What doth the Lord require of thee, but to do justly
To love mercy, and to walk humbly with thy God?
Micah 6:8

I WILL WAIT FOR THE GOD OF MY SALVATION
My God will hear me
Rejoice not against me, O mine enemy
When I fall, I shall arise
When I sit in darkness
The Lord shall be a light unto me
Micah 7:7–8

THE POWER OF THE LORD
The Lord is slow to anger and great in power
And will not at all acquit the wicked
The Lord hath his way in the whirlwind and the storm
And the clouds are the dust of his feet
Who can stand before his indignation?
Who can abide the fierceness of his anger?
The Lord is good, a stronghold in the day of trouble
He knoweth them that trust in him
Nahum 1

THE DESTRUCTION OF NINEVEH
She is empty, and void, and waste
And the heart melteth and the knees smite together
Much pain is in all loins and the faces gather blackness
Woe to the bloody city!
The noise of a whip and the rattling of the wheels
The prancing horses and jumping chariots
There is a multitude of slain
They stumble upon their corpses
Nineveh is laid waste. Who will bemoan her?
Nahum 2—3

Habakkuk, Zephaniah, and Haggai

O Lord, how long shall I cry and thou wilt not hear!
Hab. 1:2

HABAKKUK'S PROPHECY
Write the vision and make it plain upon tablets
That he may run that readeth it
Because thou hast spoiled many nations
The remnant of the people shall spoil thee
For the stone shall cry out of the wall
Woe to him that buildeth a town with blood
Hab. 2:2–12

The earth shall be filled with knowledge of the glory
    of the Lord
As the waters cover the sea
Hab. 2:14

The Lord is in his holy temple
Let all the earth keep silence before him
Hab. 2:20

PRAYER OF HABAKKUK

O Lord I have heard thy speech and was afraid
O Lord revive thy work in the midst of the years
In wrath remember mercy
I will rejoice in the Lord
I will joy in the God of my salvation
Hab. 3

THE WORD OF THE LORD TO ZEPHANIAH

The day of the Lord is at hand
There shall be a cry from the fish gate, howling
    from the second quarter
And a great crashing from the hills
I will search Jerusalem with candles
And punish the men that say in their heart:
The Lord will not do good nor evil
The day of the Lord is a day of wrath
I will bring distress upon men
That they shall walk like blind men
Because they have sinned against the Lord
Their blood shall be poured out as dust
And their flesh as the dung
Zeph. 1

THE FATE OF NINEVEH

This is the rejoicing city that dwelt carelessly
That said in her heart, I am, and there is none beside me
How is she become a desolation
Everyone that passeth by her shall hiss
Zeph. 2:15

CONDEMNATION OF JERUSALEM

She obeyed not the voice. She received not correction
She trusted not in the Lord. She drew not near to her God
Her judges are evening wolves, they gnaw not the bones
    till the morrow

Her prophets are light and treacherous persons
Her priests have polluted the sanctuary, done violence
    to the law
Zeph. 3:1–7

THE FAITHFUL REMNANT
I will leave an afflicted and poor people
And they shall trust in the name of the Lord
Zeph. 3:12–13

THE WORD OF THE LORD TO HAGGAI
Go up to the mountain and build the house
And I will take pleasure in it, saith the Lord
The Lord stirred up the spirit of the remnant
And they came and worked in the house of the Lord
Be strong ye people and work
For I am with you, saith the Lord
Hagg. 1—2

Zechariah and Malachi

THE WORD OF THE LORD TO ZECHARIAH
The Lord hath been sore displeased with your fathers
Your fathers, where are they?
And the prophets, do they live forever?
Zech. 1:1–5

ZECHARIAH'S VISION
A man riding upon a red horse stood among
    the myrtle trees
Behind him red horses, speckled, and white
We have walked to and fro through the earth
And behold all the earth sitteth still and is at rest
I am returned to Jerusalem with mercies
My house shall be built in it
And the Lord shall yet comfort Zion
Zech. 1:8–21

SING AND REJOICE
I have spread you abroad as the four winds of the heaven
Lo, I come, and I will dwell in the midst of thee
Zech. 2

Behold, I will bring forth my servant the *Branch*
Zech. 3:8, cf. 6:12–13

Not by might, nor by power, but by my spirit
    saith the Lord of hosts
Zech. 4:6

For who hath despised the day of small things?
Zech. 4:10

SPEAK EVERY MAN THE TRUTH
Show mercy and compassion every man to his brother
Oppress not the widow and the fatherless
Let none of you imagine evil against his brother
Zech. 7:8–14, 8:16–17

We will go with you: for we have heard
    that God is with you
Zech. 8:23

THE MESSIANIC PROPHECY
Rejoice greatly, O daughter of Zion!
Shout O daughter of Jerusalem!
Behold, thy King cometh unto thee
He is just and having salvation
Lowly and riding upon an ass . . .
And he shall speak peace unto the heathen
Turn ye to the stronghold, ye prisoners of hope
Zech. 9:9–12

So they weighed for my price thirty pieces of silver
Zech. 11:12

What are these wounds in thine hands?
Those with which I was wounded
    in the house of my friends
Zech. 13:6

FROM THE RISING OF THE SUN
Even unto the going down of the same
My name shall be great among the Gentiles
Mal. 1:11

HAVE WE NOT ALL ONE FATHER?
Hath not one God created us?
Why do we deal treacherously
    every man against his brother?
Mal. 2:10

I WILL SEND MY MESSENGER
And he shall prepare the way before me
But who may abide the day of his coming?
Who shall stand when he appeareth?
For I am the Lord, I change not
Mal. 3:1–6

BEHOLD THE DAY COMETH
The Sun of righteousness shall arise
With healing in his wings
Behold, I will send you Elijah the prophet
Before the coming of the great
    and dreadful day of the Lord
He shall turn the heart of the fathers to the children
And the heart of the children to their fathers
Mal. 4:1–6

THE LIFE

OF

CHRIST

The Birth of Christ
and Preparation for His Ministry

THE WORD WAS GOD
In the beginning was the Word
And the Word was with God, and the Word was God
In him was life and the life was the light of men
The light shineth in darkness
And the darkness has not overcome it
He is the true light which lighteth every man
That cometh into the world
John 1:1–9

THE WORD WAS MADE FLESH
He was in the world and the world knew him not
But to as many as received him gave he power
    to become sons of God
And the word was made flesh and dwelt among us
John 1:10–14

JOHN THE BAPTIST WHO PREPARED THE WAY
The angel Gabriel appeared to Zacharias
Thy wife, Elisabeth, shall bear thee a son
Thou shalt call his name John
To make ready a people prepared for the Lord
Luke 1:5–25

THE ANNUNCIATION
The angel Gabriel was sent from God to Mary
Blessed art thou among women
She was troubled at his saying
Fear not, Mary, for thou hast found favor with God
Thou shalt bring forth a son and call his name Jesus
How shall this be, seeing I know not a man?
The Holy Ghost shall come upon thee
The child to be born shall be called the Son of God

Mary said: Behold the handmaid of the Lord
Be it unto me according to thy word
Luke 1:26–38

THE MAGNIFICAT: THE SONG OF MARY
Mary visited her cousin Elisabeth
Elisabeth said: Blessed art thou among women
Mary said: My soul doth magnify the Lord
My spirit hath rejoiced in God my Saviour
He hath regarded the low estate of his handmaiden
Luke 1:39–56

MARY WAS FOUND WITH CHILD OF THE HOLY GHOST
Joseph did not want to shame her
The angel said: Joseph, fear not to take Mary as
      your wife
They shall call him Emmanuel, meaning God with us
Joseph took Mary as his wife but knew her not
Matt. 1:18–25

THE SONG OF ZACHARIAS ON THE BIRTH OF JOHN
Thou, child, shalt be called the prophet of the Highest
Thou shalt go before the face of the Lord
      to prepare his ways
The dayspring from on high hath visited us
To give light to them that sit in darkness
To guide our feet in the way of peace
Luke 1:67–79

THE BIRTH OF JESUS
Joseph went from Nazareth to Bethlehem to be taxed
With Mary who was great with child
She brought forth her firstborn son
And wrapped him in swaddling clothes
And laid him in a manger
Because there was no room for them in the inn
Luke 2:1–7

GOOD TIDINGS OF GREAT JOY
There were shepherds abiding in the field
Keeping watch over their flock by night
And the angel of the Lord came upon them
And they were sore afraid
Fear not for, behold, I bring you good tidings
        of great joy
A Saviour is born which is Christ the Lord
You will find the babe wrapped in swaddling clothes
        lying in a manger
Glory to God in the highest and on earth peace,
        good will toward men
Luke 2:8–14

THE SHEPHERDS CAME WITH HASTE TO BETHLEHEM
They found Mary, Joseph, and the babe lying
        in a manger
They made known abroad the saying concerning
        this child
All that heard it wondered at those things
But Mary pondered them in her heart
Luke 2:15–20

THE CIRCUMCISION
When eight days old he was circumcised and called Jesus
Luke 2:21

THE PRESENTATION OF JESUS IN THE TEMPLE
There was a man in Jerusalem named Simeon,
        just and devout
The Spirit revealed to him that he would see Christ
        before he died
He took Jesus up in his arms and blessed God:
Lord now lettest thou thy servant depart in peace
For mine eyes have seen thy salvation
Anna, a prophetess, gave thanks likewise unto the Lord
Luke 2:22–39

THE VISIT OF THE WISE MEN (MAGI, KINGS)

There came wise men from the east to Jerusalem, saying:
Where is he that is born King of the Jews?
We have seen his star in the east
And are come to worship him
The star went before them and stood over the young child
The wise men fell down and worshiped him
And presented gifts of gold, frankincense, and myrrh
Matt. 2:1–2, 9–11

THE SLAUGHTER OF THE INNOCENTS

When Jesus was born in Bethlehem, Herod was king
He told the wise men: Go and search for the young child
That I may come and worship him also
Being warned in a dream, the wise men did not return
Herod slew all the children two years old and under
Fulfilling the prophecy: Rachel
      weeping for her children
Matt. 2:1–8, 16–18

THE FLIGHT OF THE HOLY FAMILY INTO EGYPT

The angel of the Lord appeared to Joseph in a dream
Take the young child and his mother and flee into Egypt
They lived there until the death of Herod
Joseph, Mary, and the child returned to Israel
      and dwelt in Nazareth
Fulfilling the prophecy: He shall be called a Nazarene
Matt. 2:13–15, 19–23

JESUS AS A BOY IN JERUSALEM AT PASSOVER

The child grew, and waxed strong in spirit
When he was twelve years old they went to Jerusalem
      for the feast
And the child, Jesus, tarried behind in Jerusalem
And Joseph and Mary knew not of it
After three days they found him in the temple
Son, why hast thou thus dealt with us?
Wist ye not that I must be about my Father's business

His mother kept all these sayings in her heart
And Jesus increased in wisdom and stature,
 and in favor with God and man
Luke 2:40–52

THE MINISTRY OF JOHN THE BAPTIST
There was a man sent from God whose name was John
To bear witness of the Light that all men might believe
Repent ye for the kingdom of heaven is at hand
The voice of one crying in the wilderness:
Prepare ye the way of the Lord, make his paths straight
Many were baptized in the Jordan, confessing their sins
John wore camel's hair and a leather girdle
And his food was locusts and wild honey
Matt. 3:1–6; Mark 1:1–6; Luke 3:1–6; John 1:6–7

JOHN SPEAKS OF JESUS
He that cometh after me is preferred before me
Whose shoes I am not worthy to unloose
I have baptized you with water:
He shall baptize you with the Holy Spirit and with fire
Matt. 3:11–12; Mark 1:7–8; Luke 3:15–18; John 1:15–28

THE BAPTISM OF JESUS
Jesus came from Nazareth
And was baptized by John in the Jordan
The heavens opened and he saw the spirit of God
 descending like a dove
This is my beloved Son in whom I am well pleased
John said: Behold the Lamb of God
Matt. 3:13–17; Mark 1:9–11; Luke 3:21–22; cf. John 1:29–34

THE TEMPTATION
Jesus was led by the Spirit into the wilderness
He was in the wilderness forty days tempted by Satan
He had fasted forty days and nights and he hungered
The devil said: Command these stones be made bread
Man shall not live by bread alone

The devil set him on a pinnacle of the temple:
Cast thyself down
Jesus said: Thou shalt not tempt the Lord thy God
The devil offered Jesus the kingdoms of the world
Jesus said: Get thee hence, Satan
Thou shalt worship the Lord thy God
And him only shalt thou serve
Matt. 4:1–11; Mark 1:12–13; Luke 4:1–13

Early Ministry in Galilee

JOHN AGAIN SPEAKS OF JESUS
The next day, looking upon Jesus, John again said:
Behold the Lamb of God!
One who heard John speak was Andrew
Andrew said to Simon Peter: We have found the Messiah
John 1:35–42

THE CALL OF THE FIRST DISCIPLES
Jesus, walking by the Sea of Galilee,
        saw two brothers
Simon, called Peter, and Andrew, his brother
Casting a net into the sea, for they were fishermen
Follow me and I will make you fishers of men
They straightway left their nets and followed him
Going on he saw two other brothers, James and John
Mending their nets with Zebedee their father
He called them and immediately they left
        and followed him
Matt. 4:18–22; Mark 1:16–20

FISHERS OF MEN
Jesus said to Simon: Let down your nets for a catch
Master, we toiled all night and took nothing
They drew in a great multitude of fishes in their nets

Simon Peter said: Depart from me
    for I am a sinful man, O Lord
Jesus said: Fear not, from henceforth
    thou shalt catch men
Luke 5:1–11; cf. John 21:1–14

CAN ANY GOOD THING COME OUT OF NAZARETH?
The day following Jesus findeth Philip
Philip tells Nathanael: We have found him
Nathanael: Can any good thing come out of Nazareth?
Philip saith unto him: Come and see
Jesus saith of him: Behold an Israelite
    in whom is no guile!
Nathanael answered: Rabbi, thou art the Son of God
John 1:43–51

MINISTRY IN GALILEE
He went about all Galilee
Preaching in their synagogues
And healing all manner of sickness
Matt. 4:23–25; Mark 1:39; Luke 4:44

THE MARRIAGE IN CANA
There was a marriage in Cana of Galilee
When they wanted more wine Jesus' mother said:
    they have no wine
Woman what have I to do with thee?
Mine hour is not yet come
Jesus said: Fill the waterpots with water
Bear them unto the governor of the feast
The governor of the feast called the bridegroom:
Thou hast kept the good wine until now
John 2:1–11

JESUS IN THE SYNAGOGUE AT CAPERNAUM
They were astonished at his teaching
For he taught them as one that had authority

There was in their synagogue a man with
    an unclean spirit
Who cried out: What have we to do with thee?
Jesus rebuked him saying: Hold thy peace
    and come out of him
The unclean spirit cried with a loud voice and came out
The fame of Jesus spread abroad throughout Galilee
Matt. 7:28–29; Mark 1:21–28; Luke 4:31–37

PETER'S MOTHER-IN-LAW HEALED
Matt. 8:14–15; Mark 1:29–31; Luke 4:38–39

THE SERMON ON THE MOUNT
Seeing the multitudes, he went up on the mountain
And he opened his mouth and taught them
Matt. 5:1–2

THE BEATITUDES
Blessed are the poor in spirit
For theirs is the kingdom of heaven . . .
Rejoice and be glad, for great is your reward in heaven
Matt. 5:3–12; Luke 6:20–23

THE SALT OF THE EARTH
Ye are the salt of the earth
But if the salt has lost its savor
It is good for nothing but to be cast out
And trodden under foot of men
Matt. 5:13; Luke 14:34–35; cf. Mark 9:49–50

YE ARE THE LIGHT OF THE WORLD
A city set on a hill cannot be hid
Neither do men put a candle under a bushel
Let your light so shine before men
That they see your good works and glorify your Father
Matt. 5:14–16; Mark 4:21–22; Luke 8:16–17; 11:33

JESUS' WORDS ON THE LAW
Think not that I am come to destroy the law
    or the prophets:
I am not come to destroy but to fulfill
It is easier for heaven and earth to pass away
Than for one jot or tittle of the law to pass away
Matt. 5:17–20; Luke 16:17

ANGER AND RECONCILIATION
Ye have heard: Thou shalt not kill, but I say:
Whosoever is angry with his brother without cause
Shall be in danger of judgment
Whosoever shall say, Thou fool
Shall be in danger of hell fire
If thy brother have ought against thee
Leave thy gift before the altar
First be reconciled to thy brother
Then come and offer thy gift
Matt. 5:21–26

ADULTERY
Ye have heard: Thou shalt not commit adultery
But I say: Whosoever looketh on a woman to lust after her
Hath committed adultery with her already in his heart
Matt. 5:27–28

If thy right hand offend thee, cut it off . . .
Matt. 5:30, 18:8–9; Mark 9:43–48

DIVORCE
Whosoever putteth away his wife, except for unchastity
And marrieth another committeth adultery
Matt. 5:31–32, 19:9; Mark 10:11–12; Luke 16:18

SWEARING
Swear not at all
Neither by heaven for it is God's throne
Nor by the earth for it is his footstool

Neither by Jerusalem for it is the city
     of the great King
But let your communication be: Yea, yea; Nay, nay
Matt. 5:33–37

AN EYE FOR AN EYE
Ye have heard: an eye for an eye and a tooth for a tooth
But I say unto you that ye resist not evil
Whosoever shall smite thee on thy right cheek
     turn him the other
If any man take away thy coat, let him have thy cloak also
Whosoever shall compel thee to go a mile, go with him
     twain
Matt. 5:38–42; Luke 6:29–30

LOVE YOUR ENEMIES
Bless them that curse you. Do good to them that hate you
Pray for them which despitefully use you
For your Father maketh his sun to rise on the evil
     and the good
And sendeth rain on the just and on the unjust
Be ye therefore perfect as your Father which is in heaven
Matt. 5:43–48; Luke 6:27–28, 32–36

GIVE CHARITY SECRETLY
When you give alms, do not sound a trumpet
But let not thy left hand know what thy right hand doeth
Thy Father which seeth in secret shall reward thee openly
Matt. 6:1–4

OUR FATHER (THE LORD'S PRAYER)
When thou prayest enter into thy closet
And pray to thy Father which is in secret
For your Father knoweth what things ye have need of
His disciples said unto him: Lord, teach us to pray
Our Father which art in heaven . . .
Matt. 6:5–15; Mark cf. 11:25–26; Luke 11:1–4

FASTING
When ye fast be not as the hypocrites
    of a sad countenance
Anoint thine head and wash thy face
    so as not to appear fasting
Matt. 6:16–18

WHERE YOUR TREASURE IS
Lay not up treasures upon earth
Where moth and rust doth corrupt
And thieves break through . . .
But lay up for yourselves treasures in heaven
For where your treasure is
There will your heart be also
Matt. 6:19–21; Luke 12:33–34

THE SOUND EYE
The light of the body is the eye
If thine eye be single, thy whole body shall be full of light
If the light that is in thee be darkness
How great is that darkness!
Matt. 6:22–23; Luke 11:34–36

YOU CANNOT SERVE GOD AND MAMMON
He who is faithful in very little
Is faithful also in much
No man can serve two masters
For he will hate the one and love the other
Matt. 6:24; Luke 16:10–13

TAKE NO THOUGHT ABOUT YOUR LIFE
Consider the lilies of the field. They toil not . . .
Even Solomon in all his glory
Was not arrayed like one of these
Seek ye first the Kingdom of God
And all these things shall be added unto you
Take therefore no thought for the morrow
Sufficient unto the day is the evil thereof
Matt. 6:25–34; Luke 12:22–31

JUDGE NOT THAT YE BE NOT JUDGED
For with what judgment ye judge, ye shall be judged
Forgive and ye shall be forgiven
Why beholdest thou the mote that is in thy brother's eye
But considerest not the beam that is in thine own eye?
Matt. 7:1-5; Luke 6:37-42

Do not cast your pearls before swine
Matt. 7:6

ASK AND IT SHALL BE GIVEN YOU
Seek and ye shall find
Knock and it shall be opened unto you
Matt. 7:7-11; Luke 11:9-13

THE GOLDEN RULE
As ye would that men should do to you,
    do ye also to them
Matt. 7:12; Luke 6:31

ENTER THE NARROW GATE
For wide is the gate that leadeth to destruction
Strait is the gate and narrow the way leading into life
Matt. 7:13-14; Luke 13:23-24

FALSE PROPHETS
Beware of false prophets
Which come to you in sheep's clothing
By their fruits ye shall know them
Matt. 7:15-20; Luke 6:43-45

WHY CALL YE ME, LORD?
Not everyone that saith Lord, Lord,
    shall enter the kingdom
Why call ye me, Lord, Lord, and do not
    the things which I say?
Depart from me ye that work iniquity
Matt. 7:21-23; Luke 6:46; 13:27

142

HOUSES ON ROCK AND ON SAND
Whosoever heareth these sayings of mine and doeth them
Is like a man which built his house upon a rock
The rain descended and the floods came
    and it fell not
But every one that heareth these sayings
    and doeth them not
Shall be like a foolish man
Which built his house on the sand
And the rain descended, and the floods came, and it fell
Matt. 7:24–27; Luke 6:47–49

Teaching and Healing

A LEPER IS HEALED
Lord, if thou wilt, thou canst make me clean
Jesus, moved with compassion, touched him, saying:
Be thou clean
And immediately his leprosy was cleansed
Jesus saith: See thou tell no man
Matt. 8:1–4; Mark 1:40–45; Luke 5:12–16

THE CENTURION'S SERVANT
In Capernaum a centurion asked Jesus to heal
    his dying servant
Jesus said: I will come and heal him
Lord, I am not worthy that thou should come
    under my roof
Speak the word only and my servant shall be healed
Jesus said: I have not found so great faith,
    no, not in Israel
Go thy way as thou hast believed so be it done unto thee
Matt. 8:5–13; Luke 7:1–10

THE NATURE OF DISCIPLESHIP
Master, I will follow thee
Foxes have holes . . . the Son of man has nowhere
   to lay his head
One disciple said: Let me first go and bury my father
Jesus said: Follow me and let the dead bury their dead
Matt. 8:18–22; Luke 9:57–62

STILLING THE STORM
Jesus went into a ship with his disciples
   and a storm arose
Master, Master, carest thou not that we perish?
O ye of little faith!
He arose and rebuked the wind and the raging water
They marveled: What manner of man is this?
That even winds and sea obey him
Matt. 8:23–27; Mark 4:35–41; Luke 8:22–25

THE GADARENE SWINE
Jesus asked: What is thy name?
He answered: My name is Legion: for we are many
The devils went into a herd of swine
Which ran into the sea and drowned
Matt. 8:28–34; Mark 5:1–20; Luke 8:26–39

TAKE UP THY BED AND WALK
They brought a man who was paralyzed to Jesus
But could not get near because of the multitude
So they let him down through the roof on his bed
Jesus said: My son, thy sins are forgiven thee
The scribes and Pharisees said: Who can forgive sins,
   but God alone?
Jesus said: Arise, and take up thy bed and walk
And immediately he rose and departed glorifying God
They were amazed: We have seen strange things today
Matt. 9:1–8; Mark 2:1–12; Luke 5:17–26

THE CALLING OF MATTHEW (LEVI)
Jesus saw Matthew sitting in the tax office
Jesus said: Follow me. And he rose and followed him
Matt. 9:9; Mark 2:14; Luke 5:27–28

WHY EATETH YOUR MASTER WITH SINNERS?
Those who are well have no need of a physician
I am not come to call the righteous but sinners
Matt. 9:10–13; Mark 2:15–17; Luke 5:29–32

NEW WINE
Jesus was asked: Why do your disciples not fast?
Can the wedding guests mourn
While the bridegroom is with them?
No man putteth a piece of new cloth on an old garment
Neither do men put new wine into old bottles
Matt. 9:14–17; Mark 2:18–22; Luke 5:33–39

JAIRUS' DAUGHTER
AND THE WOMAN WITH AN ISSUE OF BLOOD
A ruler named Jairus said to Jesus:
My daughter is even now dead
Come lay your hand on her and she will live
On the way a woman with a hemorrhage
    touched the hem of his garment
Jesus said: Thy faith hath made thee whole
At Jairus' house Jesus said: The maid is not dead
    but sleepeth
Matt. 9:18–26; Mark 5:21–43; Luke 8:40–56

THE HEALING OF TWO BLIND MEN
According to your faith be it done unto you
Matt. 9:27–31; 20:29–34

HE MAKES THE DUMB TO SPEAK
But the Pharisees said he casts out devils
    by the prince of devils
Matt. 9:32–34, 12:22–24; Luke 11:14–15; cf. Mark 3:22

A HOUSE DIVIDED

If a house be divided against itself
　　that house cannot stand
If Satan also is divided, how will his kingdom stand?
He that is not with me is against me
Matt. 12:25–30; Mark 3:23–27; 9:40; Luke 11:17–23

THE TWELVE DISCIPLES

When he saw the multitudes, he was moved with
　　compassion
They were like sheep having no shepherd
Jesus said: The harvest is plenteous
　　but the laborers few
When he called his twelve disciples, he gave them power . . .
The names of the twelve apostles are these . . .
Matt. 9:36—10:4; Mark 3:13–19; 6:34; Luke 6:13–16

THE DISCIPLES SENT FORTH

Go to the lost sheep of the house of Israel
Preach saying, the kingdom of heaven is at hand
Heal the sick, cleanse the lepers, raise the dead . . .
Freely ye have received, freely give
Take nothing for your journey, no staff, no bread,
　　no money . . .
Whosoever shall not receive you . . . shake off the dust
　　of your feet
I send you forth as sheep in the midst of wolves:
Be ye therefore wise as serpents, harmless as doves
Matt. 10:5–16; Mark 6:7–11; Luke 9:1–6

Peace be to this house
Matt. 10:13; Luke 10:5

BEWARE OF MEN

They will deliver you up to the councils
And will scourge you in their synagogues
But take no thought how or what ye shall speak:
For it is not ye that speak but the Holy Spirit

Brother shall deliver up brother to death
The children shall rise up against their parents
Ye shall be hated of all men for my name's sake
But he that endureth to the end shall be saved
Fear not them which kill the body
Fear him which is able to destroy both soul and body
Matt. 10:17–28, 24:9, 13; Mark 13:9–13; Luke 12:4–12, 21:12–17

The disciple is not above his master
Matt. 10:24; Luke 6:40

What I tell you in darkness, that speak ye in light
Matt. 10:27; Luke 12:3

GOD'S CONCERN FOR US
Are not two sparrows sold for a farthing?
One of them shall not fall on the ground
      without your Father's will
The very hairs of your head are all numbered
Fear ye not, ye are of more value than many sparrows
Matt. 10:29–33; Luke 12:6–7

NOT PEACE BUT A SWORD
I am come to set a man against his father . . .
A man's foes shall be they of his own household
He that loveth father or mother more than me
      is not worthy of me
Matt. 10:34–37; Luke 12:51–53, 14:26

TAKE UP YOUR CROSS
He that takes not his cross to follow after me
Is not worthy of me
He that loses his life for my sake shall find it
What shall it profit a man if he gain the whole world
And lose his own soul?
He that receives me, receives him that sent me
Matt. 10:38–40, 16:24–26; Mark 8:34–36; Luke 9:23–25, 14:27

JOHN IN PRISON
John sent two of his disciples to Jesus
Art thou he that should come?
Jesus said: Go tell John what you hear and see
The blind receive their sight, the lame walk
Matt. 11:2–6; Luke 7:18–23

JESUS SPEAKS OF JOHN
What went ye into the wilderness to see?
A reed shaken with the wind?
A man clothed in soft raiment?
To see a prophet? Yea, and more than a prophet
This is he of whom it is written
Behold I send my messenger who shall prepare thy way
Matt. 11:7–10; Luke 7:24–27

YE HAVE NOT DANCED
Like children in the marketplace calling to their fellows:
We piped and ye have not danced
We mourned and ye have not lamented
John came neither eating nor drinking
And they say: He hath a devil
The Son of man came eating and drinking
And they say: Behold a glutton and winebibber
A friend of publicans and sinners
Matt. 11:16–19; Luke 7:31–34

THE FATHER AND I ARE ONE
Thou hast hid these things from the wise
And revealed them unto babes
All things are delivered unto me of my Father
No man hath seen God at any time; the Son
    hath declared him
No man knoweth the Son but the Father
The Son can do nothing of himself
    but what he seeth the Father do
All men should honor the Son

Even as they honor the Father
He that hath seen me hath seen the Father
Matt. 11:25–27; Luke 10:21–22; John 1:18, 5:17–23, 10:30, 38;
   14:7–20

REST IN THE LORD
Come unto me, all ye that labor and are heavy laden
Take my yoke upon you and learn of me
For my yoke is easy and my burden light
Matt. 11:28–30

EARS OF CORN ON THE SABBATH
As Jesus and his disciples went through the corn
   on the sabbath
They began to pluck the ears of corn and to eat
Some asked: Why are you doing what is not lawful
   on the sabbath?
Jesus said: The sabbath was made for man
   and not man for the sabbath
Matt. 12:1–8; Mark 2:23–28; Luke 6:1–5

A MAN WITH A WITHERED HAND
Is it lawful to heal on the sabbath?
The man stretched forth his hand and it was whole
Matt. 12:9–14; Mark 3:1–6; Luke 6:6–11

When he had sent the multitudes away
He went up into a mountain to pray
Matt. 14:23; Mark 6:46; Luke 6:12

Some Stories Told Only by Luke

THE GOOD SAMARITAN
And who is my neighbor?
A man fell among thieves and was left half dead

A passing Samaritan had compassion on him
Go and do likewise
Luke 10:29–37

MARY AND MARTHA
Mary sat at Jesus' feet and listened
Martha cumbered with much serving complained:
Do you not care that I serve alone?
Jesus said: Martha, Martha, thou art troubled
     about many things
One thing is needful and Mary hath chosen the good part
Luke 10:38–42

THE PARABLE OF A FRIEND IN NEED
Which of you shall go to a friend at midnight and say:
Lend me three loaves for a friend of mine is come
And I have nothing to set before him?
And he shall answer: Trouble me not. I cannot rise . . .
Though he will not rise because he is a friend
He will rise in answer to persistent demands
Luke 11:5–8

THE PARABLE OF THE RICH FOOL
A rich man had no room to store his crops
And he said I will build greater barns
God said: Fool! This night thy soul shall
     be required of thee
So is he that layeth up treasure for himself . . .
Luke 12:13–21

To whom much is given, of him will much be required
Luke 12:48

THE FIG TREE WITHOUT FIGS
A certain man had a fig tree planted in his vineyard
He came and sought fruit and found none
He told his dresser of the vineyard: Cut it down

The dresser said: Let it alone this year
    till I shall dig around it . . .
If it bear not after that, thou shalt cut it down
Luke 13:6–9

THE WOMAN WITH A SPIRIT OF INFIRMITY
Luke 13:10–17

THE HEALING OF A MAN WITH DROPSY
Luke 14:1–6

PARABLE ON HUMILITY
When thou art bidden by any one to a wedding feast
Sit not down in a place of honor
Lest a more important man arrive
And the host will say: Give your place to this man
For every one who exalts himself will be humbled
And he who humbles himself will be exalted
Luke 14:7–11

INVITE THOSE IN NEED
When you give a dinner call not your friends
    or rich neighbors
But invite the poor, the maimed, the lame and the blind:
And thou shalt be blessed because they cannot repay you
Luke 14:12–14

COUNTING THE COST
Which of you intending to build a tower
    does not count the cost?
Lest he is not able to finish it and all begin to mock
Or what king going to war does not plan his strategy?
Likewise he who does not forsake all he has
    cannot be my disciple
Luke 14:28–33

THE LOST COIN

What woman having ten pieces of silver
 if she lose one piece
Doth not light a candle and sweep the house
 till she find it
And calleth her friends and neighbors, saying:
Rejoice with me for I have found the piece
 which I had lost
Luke 15:8–10

THE PRODIGAL SON

A man had two sons: the younger went into a far country
And wasted his substance with riotous living
There arose a famine and he tended swine
And would willingly have eaten the husks
That the swine ate, but no man gave unto him
My father's servants have bread and I perish with hunger
He arose and came to his father
Who had compassion and ran and kissed him
Father, I have sinned against heaven and in thy sight . . .
His father said: Bring the fatted calf
Let us eat and be merry
For this my son was dead and is alive again
Luke 15:11–24

THE PRODIGAL SON'S BROTHER

The elder son was angry: These many years
 have I served thee
Thou never gavest me a kid to make merry
 with my friends
But for thy son who devoured thy living with harlots
Thou hast killed the fatted calf
Son, thou art ever with me and all that I have is thine
Luke 15:25–32

THE UNJUST STEWARD
Luke 16:1–8

THE PARABLE OF LAZARUS AND THE RICH MAN
A beggar named Lazarus lay at the rich man's gate
Desiring to be fed with the crumbs from the table
The beggar died and was carried by angels
     into Abraham's bosom
The rich man died and from hell saw Lazarus
Father Abraham, have mercy and send Lazarus
     to comfort me
In life you received good things
     and Lazarus evil things
Now he is comforted and you are tormented
Between us there is a great gulf
The rich man begged Abraham to warn his brothers
Abraham said: They have Moses and the prophets
Luke 16:19–31

THE MASTER AND HIS SERVANT
Which of you will say to a servant:
Go and sit down to meat?
And will not rather say: Serve me till I have eaten?
Doth he thank that servant for his obedience?
When ye shall have done all things which are commanded
You say we are unprofitable servants: We have done
     our duty
Luke 17:7–10

THE HEALING OF TEN LEPERS
Arise, go thy way: thy faith hath made thee whole
One of them turned back and glorified God
Were not ten cleansed? Where are the nine?
Luke 17:11–19

The kingdom of God is within you
Luke 17:21

THE PARABLE OF THE UNJUST JUDGE
There was a judge which feared not God neither
     regarded man

A widow came and said: Avenge me of mine adversary
He thought: I will avenge her
Lest by her coming she weary me
Shall not God likewise avenge his own
     who cry day and night?
Luke 18:1–8

THE PARABLE OF THE PUBLICAN AND THE PHARISEE
Two men went up into the temple to pray
The Pharisee said: I thank thee
     that I am not as other men . . .
The publican said: God be merciful to me a sinner!
This man went down to his house justified
     rather than the other
For he that humbleth himself shall be exalted
Luke 18:9–14

ZACCHAEUS IN THE SYCAMORE TREE
Jesus entered Jericho and was passing through
A rich tax collector named Zacchaeus sought to see him
Being short of stature he ran and climbed a sycamore tree
Jesus said: Zacchaeus, come down
Today I must abide at thy house
All murmured that he was gone to be the guest of a sinner
Zacchaeus said: Behold, Lord, I give half my goods
     to the poor
Jesus said: This day is salvation come to this house
The Son of man is come to seek and to save
     that which was lost
Luke 19:1–10

In the Midst of His Ministry

Woe unto you when all men shall speak well of you!
Luke 6:26

THE SON OF THE WIDOW OF NAIN
There was a dead man carried out, an only son
Jesus had compassion and said: Young man arise
He that was dead sat up and began to speak
They glorified God: A great prophet has risen among us
Luke 7:11–17

SHE WASHED HIS FEET WITH TEARS
Jesus went into the Pharisee's house and sat down
    at the table
A woman of the city who was a sinner
Came with an alabaster box of ointment
Washed his feet with tears
And anointed them with the ointment
Her sins, which are many, are forgiven:
    for she loved much
To whom little is forgiven, the same loveth little
Thy faith hath saved thee: go in peace
Luke 7:36–50; cf. Matt. 26:6–13; cf. Mark 14:3–9; cf. John 12:1–8

Whosoever speaketh against the Holy Spirit
Will not be forgiven
Matt. 12:32; Mark 3:29; Luke 12:10

A SIGN FROM HEAVEN
Master we would see a sign from thee
Jesus said: Can ye not discern the signs of the times?
A wicked and adulterous generation seeketh a sign
There shall be no sign given but the sign of Jonas
Matt. 12:38–42, 16:1–4; Mark 8:11–13; Luke 11:16, 29–32, 12:54–56

THE EMPTY HOUSE AND THE WICKED SPIRITS
An unclean spirit will return to an empty house
With seven spirits more wicked than he
Matt. 12:43–45; Luke 11:24–26

JESUS' MOTHER AND BROTHERS
Your mother and brothers are outside asking for you
They could not reach him for the crowd
Who are my mother and brothers?
My mother and brothers are those who hear
      the word of God and do it
Matt. 12:46–50; Mark 3:31–35; Luke 8:19–21

THE PARABLE OF THE SOWER
A great multitude gathered on the shore
And Jesus taught them from a boat:
A sower went forth to sow
Some seeds fell upon a rock
Some among thorns, some on good ground
He who hath ears to hear, let him hear
It is given unto you to know the mysteries
      of the kingdom of heaven
Matt. 13:1–23; Mark 4:1–20; Luke 8:4–15

THE SEED GROWING SECRETLY
First the blade, then the ear
After that the full corn in the ear
When the grain is ripe . . . the harvest has come
Mark 4:26–28

THE PARABLE OF THE WEEDS
An enemy sowed weeds among the wheat:
Let both grow until the harvest
Then burn the weeds but gather the wheat into my barn
He who sows the good seed is the Son of man
The good seed are the children of the kingdom
The weeds are the children of the wicked one
The harvest is the end of the world
Matt. 13:24–30, 36–43

THE PARABLE OF THE MUSTARD SEED
The kingdom of heaven is like a mustard seed
The smallest of all seeds
When it is grown it becomes a tree
Matt. 13:31–32; Mark 4:30–32; Luke 13:18–19

THE PARABLE OF THE LEAVEN
The kingdom of heaven is like leaven
A woman hid it in three measures of meal
Till the whole was leavened
Matt. 13:33; Luke 13:20–21

THE PARABLE OF THE TREASURE
The kingdom of heaven is like a treasure hid in a field
When a man finds it, he sells all and buys the field
Matt. 13:44

THE PARABLE OF THE PEARL OF GREAT PRICE
The kingdom of heaven is like a merchant
    seeking goodly pearls
Who found a pearl of great price
And sold all that he had and bought it
Matt. 13:45–46

The kingdom of heaven is like a net
Which gathered all kinds of fish
They sorted good from bad and cast the bad away
Matt. 13:47–50

A PROPHET IS NOT WITHOUT HONOR
Jesus read in the synagogue: The Spirit of the Lord
    is upon me . . .
He has sent me to preach . . . the acceptable year
    of the Lord
They took offense at him but Jesus said:
A prophet is not without honor
    except in his own country . . .
Matt. 13:54–58; Mark 6:1–6; Luke 4:16–30; John 4:44; Isaiah 61:1–2

THE IMPRISONMENT AND BEHEADING
OF JOHN THE BAPTIST
Herod had bound John in prison for Herodias' sake
For John said: It is not lawful
    to have thy brother's wife
The daughter of Herodias danced and pleased Herod
Who said: Ask of me whatsoever thou wilt
And she answered: The head of John the Baptist
The executioner brought his head on a platter
Matt. 14:1–12; Mark 6:14–29

THE FEEDING OF THE FIVE THOUSAND
We have here but five loaves and two fishes
What are they among so many?
Jesus took them, blessed them, and gave to the disciples
And the multitude did eat and were filled
Jesus said: Gather the fragments that nothing be lost
Matt. 14:13–21; Mark 6:30–44; Luke 9:10–17; John 6:1–14

JESUS WALKING ON THE WATER
There arose a storm and Jesus went to them
    walking on the water:
Be of good cheer. It is I: be not afraid
Jesus said to Peter: Come
And Peter walked on the water
He became afraid and beginning to sink cried:
Lord, save me
O thou of little faith, wherefore didst thou doubt?
The disciples said: Of a truth, thou art the Son of God
Matt. 14:22–33; Mark 6:45–52; John 6:15–21

WHAT DEFILES A MAN
Why do your disciples disobey the tradition?
For they do not wash their hands before they eat
Jesus said: You hypocrites!
Well did Isaiah prophesy of you:
This people honors me with their lips
But their heart is far from me . . .

Not what goes into the mouth defiles a man
But what comes out of the mouth
To eat with unwashed hands does not defile a man
Matt. 15:1–20; Mark 7:1–23

If the blind lead the blind, both shall
        fall into the ditch
Matt. 15:14

THE GREEK WOMAN'S DAUGHTER
My daughter is grievously vexed with a devil
Jesus said: I am not sent but to the lost sheep
        of Israel
It is not meet to take the children's bread
        and cast it to the dogs
Yet the dogs eat of the crumbs
        that fall from their master's table
O woman, great is thy faith:
Be it unto thee even as thou wilt
Her daughter was made whole from that hour
Matt. 15:21–28; Mark 7:24–30

HEALING OF A DEAF AND DUMB MAN
They brought to Jesus one who was deaf
And had an impediment in speech
Jesus put his fingers into his ear, spit,
        and touched his tongue
Straightway his ears were opened and he spoke clearly
He maketh both the deaf to hear and the dumb to speak
Mark 7:31–37

SEVEN LOAVES AND SEVERAL FISHES
Jesus said: I have compassion on the multitude
I will not send them away fasting
He took the loaves and fishes, gave thanks,
        and brake them
They did all eat and were filled
Matt. 15:32–39; Mark 8:1–10

THE LEAVEN OF THE PHARISEES
The leaven of the Pharisees is hypocrisy
Matt. 16:5–12; Mark 8:14–21; Luke 12:1

THE BLIND MAN OF BETHSAIDA
I see men as trees walking
He was restored and saw every man clearly
Mark 8:22–26

Shadows of Things to Come

THE JEWS SOUGHT TO KILL HIM
Jesus said: My time is not yet come
He went up into the temple and taught
How has this man knowledge having never studied?
My doctrine is not mine but his that sent me
If any man thirst, let him come unto me
Many people said: This is the Prophet
Others said: This is the Christ
Some would have arrested him
But no man laid hands on him
The officers said: Never man spake like this man
John 7

Judge not according to appearance
John 7:24

WHOM DO MEN SAY THAT I AM?
Peter said: Thou art the Christ,
    the Son of the living God
Jesus said: Thou art Peter. Upon this rock
    I will build my church
I will give unto thee the keys of the kingdom
Matt. 16:13–20; Mark 8:27–30; Luke 9:18–21

Get thee behind me, Satan!
Matt. 16:23; Mark 8:33

PREDICTION OF THINGS TO COME
The Son of man must suffer many things
He shall be betrayed into the hands of men
They shall kill him and the third day he shall be raised
Matt. 16:21, 17:22-23, 20:18-19, 28; Mark 8:31, 9:30-32, 10:32-34;
    Luke 9:22, 43-45, 18:31-34

THE TRANSFIGURATION
Jesus, Peter, John, and James went up a mountain to pray
Jesus' countenance was altered and his raiment
    became white
Moses and Elijah appeared in glory to talk with Jesus
Peter said: Let us make three tabernacles
There came a cloud and a voice saying:
This is my beloved Son
Matt. 17:1-8; Mark 9:2-8; Luke 9:28-36

ELIJAH IS COME ALREADY
Why do the scribes say Elijah must come first?
Elijah is come already and they knew him not
The disciples understood that he spoke
    of John the Baptist
Matt. 17:10-13; Mark 9:11-13

THE HEALING OF AN EPILEPTIC BOY
Lord have mercy on my son
For thy disciples could not cure him
O faithless and perverse generation . . . bring him to me
All things are possible to him that believeth
The boy's father said: Lord I believe,
    help thou mine unbelief!
Jesus rebuked the devil and he departed out of him
The child was cured from that very hour
If you had faith as a grain of mustard seed
You could say to this mountain:
Move hence to yonder place

Nothing shall be impossible unto you
Whatsoever ye ask in prayer, believing, ye shall receive
Matt. 17:14–21; Mark 9:14–29; Luke 9:37–43; cf. Luke 17:6

A CHILD IN THE MIDST
Jesus set a child in the midst of them
Except ye be converted and become as little children
Ye shall not enter the kingdom of heaven
Whosoever shall humble himself as this little child
The same is greatest in the kingdom of heaven
Whosoever shall offend one of these little ones
It were better that a millstone were hanged about his neck
And that he were drowned in the depths of the sea
He that is least among you, the same shall be great
Matt. 18:1–6; Mark 9:33–42; Luke 9:46–48

THE LOST SHEEP
What man of you having an hundred sheep
    if he lose one of them
Doth he not leave the ninety and nine in the wilderness
And go after that which is lost until he find it?
And when he hath found it, he layeth it on his shoulders
Rejoice with me for I have found my sheep which was lost
Likewise joy shall be in heaven
Over one sinner that repenteth
Matt. 18:12–14; Luke 15:1–7

ON FORGIVENESS
How often shall I forgive my brother? Seven times?
Not seven times but seventy times seven
Matt. 18:15–22; Luke 17:3–4

For where two or three are gathered together in my name
There am I in the midst of them
Matt. 18:20

THE PARABLE OF THE UNMERCIFUL SERVANT
The kingdom of heaven is like a king
    whose servant owed him money

Master, have patience with me and I will pay thee all
The master was moved with compassion and
    forgave the debt
The servant was owed money by a fellow servant
    who also begged patience
But he would not be patient, and cast him into prison
Then the master was wroth: O thou wicked servant
And delivered him to the tormentors
So shall my heavenly Father do to you
If you forgive not your brother's trespasses
Matt. 18:23–35

ON MARRIAGE
A man shall leave father and mother
And cleave to his wife
They are no longer two but one flesh
What God hath joined together let not man put asunder
Matt. 19:4–6; Mark 10:6–9

SUFFER LITTLE CHILDREN
They brought young children to him
And his disciples rebuked those that brought them
But when Jesus saw it, he was much displeased and said:
Suffer the little children to come unto me
    and forbid them not:
For of such is the kingdom of God
Matt. 19:13–15; Mark 10:13–16; Luke 18:15–17

THE RICH YOUNG MAN
Good Master, what shall I do to have eternal life?
Why callest thou me good?
None is good, save one, that is, God
If thou wilt enter into life keep the commandments
These have I kept from my youth up
If thou would be perfect
Go and sell what thou hast and give to the poor

The young man went away sorrowful,
    for he had great possessions
Matt. 19:16–22; Mark 10:17–22; Luke 18:18–24

THROUGH THE EYE OF A NEEDLE
Jesus said: It will be hard for a rich man
    to enter the kingdom
It is easier for a camel
    to go through the eye of a needle
His disciples were amazed: Who then can be saved?
With God all things are possible
    Peter said: We have forsaken all
What shall we have therefore?
Ye shall sit upon twelve thrones . . .
Every one that hath forsaken houses, or brethren . . .
    shall receive an hundredfold . . .
Matt. 19:23–29; Mark 10:23–30; Luke 18:24–30

THE PARABLE OF THE LABORERS IN THE VINEYARD
The kingdom of heaven is like a householder
Who hired laborers for his vineyard at a penny a day
Throughout the day he hired other laborers
In the evening they all received a penny
The first grumbled: These last worked only one hour
Is it not lawful to do what I choose with what is mine?
So the last will be first, and the first last
For many are called but few are chosen
Matt. 20:1–16; Mark 10:31

ON THY RIGHT HAND
Grant that my two sons may sit
One on thy right hand and the other on the left . . .
Jesus said: Ye know not what ye ask
Are ye able to drink of the cup I drink of . . . ?
To sit on my right hand and left is not mine to give
The Son of man came not to be ministered unto
    but to minister

He came to give his life a ransom for many
Whosoever will be chief among you let him be
     your servant
Matt. 20:20–28; Mark 10:35–45; cf. Matt. 23:11

THE HEALING OF BARTIMAEUS
As Jesus was leaving Jericho, blind Bartimaeus
     sat by the highway
He cried: Jesus, thou son of David, have mercy on me!
Jesus asked: What wilt thou that I should do?
And immediately he received his sight and followed Jesus
Mark 10:46–52; Luke 18:35–43; cf. Matt. 20:29–34

Whatsoever ye ask in prayer, believing, ye shall receive
Matt. 21:21; Mark 11:24

Some Stories Told only by John

JESUS AND NICODEMUS
Except a man be born again,
     he cannot see the kingdom of God
How can a man be born when he is old?
That which is born of the flesh is flesh
And that which is born of the Spirit is spirit
The wind bloweth where it listeth . . .
How can these things be?
If ye believe not earthly things, how shall ye believe
     heavenly things?
John 3:1–15

FOR GOD SO LOVED THE WORLD
For God so loved the world
That he gave his only begotten Son
That whosoever believeth in him should not perish
But have everlasting life
Light is come into the world and men loved darkness . . .
John 3:16–21

JOHN THE BAPTIST SPEAKS OF JESUS
I am not the Christ but am sent before him
He must increase but I must decrease
The Father loves the Son
And has given all things into his hand
He that believes in the Son has everlasting life
John 3:25–36

JESUS AND THE SAMARITAN WOMAN
Jesus said to her: Give me to drink
Whosoever drinks of the water I shall give,
    shall never thirst
For it will be a well of water
    springing up into everlasting life
God is Spirit: They that worship him
    worship in spirit and in truth
John 4:5–42

My meat is to do the will of him that sent me
John 4:34

Look on the fields, for they are white to harvest
John 4:35

THE NOBLEMAN'S SON
He besought Jesus to heal his son
For he was at the point of death
Except ye see signs and wonders, ye will not believe
Sir, come down ere my child die
Jesus said unto him: Go thy way, thy son liveth
The nobleman believed, and his whole house
John 4:45–54

THE POOL OF BETHESDA
A man was there who had had an infirmity
    thirty-eight years
Jesus said: Will thou be made whole?
Rise, take up thy bed and walk

The Jews sought to slay Jesus
    for healing on the sabbath
John 5:1–16

THE WITNESS OF JOHN THE BAPTIST
John bare witness unto the truth
He was a burning and a shining light
Ye were willing for a season to rejoice in his light
John 5:33, 35

HAD YOU BELIEVED MOSES
Search the scriptures:
In them you think you have eternal life
They testify of me yet you will not come to me
Had you believed Moses, you would have believed me
John 5:39–47

I AM THE BREAD OF LIFE
Our fathers did eat manna in the desert
My Father gives you the true bread from heaven
I am the bread of life:
He that comes to me shall never hunger
He that believes in me shall never thirst
He that believes in me has everlasting life
It is the Spirit that quickens
We believe that you are that Christ,
    the Son of the living God
John 6:22–69

THE WOMAN TAKEN IN ADULTERY
He that is without sin among you
Let him cast the first stone
Convicted by their own conscience they all left
Jesus asked: Woman, has no man condemned you?
She said: No man, Lord
Neither do I condemn thee: go and sin no more
John 8:3–11

THE TRUTH SHALL MAKE YOU FREE
He that followeth me shall not walk in darkness . . .
I judge no man and yet if I judge, my judgment is true
Whither I go, ye cannot come
I am not of this world
Ye shall know the truth, and the truth
    shall make you free
Whosoever committeth sin is the servant of sin
He that is of God heareth God's words
Before Abraham was, I am
John 8:12-59, 9:5, 12:46

THE HEALING OF A MAN BORN BLIND
Jesus said: I must work the works of him that sent me
The night cometh, when no man can work
I am the light of the world
He told the blind man: Go, wash in the pool of Siloam
The blind man said: Whereas I was blind, now I see
John 9:1-41

THE GOOD SHEPHERD
He that enters in by the door
    is the shepherd of the sheep
I am the door. I am come that they might have life
And have it more abundantly
The good shepherd gives his life for the sheep
I know my sheep and am known of mine
As the Father knoweth me, even so know I the Father
Other sheep I have which are not of this fold
John 10:1-18

THE RAISING OF LAZARUS
A certain man named Lazarus of Bethany was sick
His sisters, Mary and Martha, sent for Jesus
When Jesus came Lazarus had lain in the grave four days
Martha said: Whatsoever thou wilt ask of God,
    God will give it thee
Jesus said: Thy brother shall rise again

I am the resurrection and the life
He that believeth in me, though he were dead,
    yet shall he live
Whosoever liveth and believeth in me shall never die
He cried with a loud voice: Lazarus, come forth
John 11:1–44

Jesus wept
John 11:35

Jesus in Jerusalem

DEPARTURE FROM GALILEE
Get thee out and depart for Herod will kill thee
Tell that fox I cast out devils
    and do cures today and tomorrow
The third day I shall be perfected
Nevertheless I must walk today and tomorrow
For it cannot be that a prophet perish out of Jerusalem
Luke 13:31–33

THE ENTRY INTO JERUSALEM
When they were come to the Mount of Olives, Jesus said:
Go into the village and you shall find a colt
They brought the colt and set him thereon
A very great multitude spread their garments in the way
Others cut down branches and spread them on the way
The multitudes that went before cried, saying: Hosanna!
Blessed is he that comes in the name of the Lord!
Matt. 21:1–11; Mark 11:1–10; Luke 19:28–38; John 12:12–15

PREDICTION OF THE DESTRUCTION OF JERUSALEM
He beheld the city and wept
They shall not leave one stone upon another
Because thou knewest not the time of thy visitation
Luke 19:41–44

CASTING OUT THE MONEYCHANGERS
Jesus cast out all them that sold and bought
    in the temple

And overthrew the tables of the moneychangers
My house shall be called the house of prayer
But ye have made it a den of thieves
Matt. 21:12–13; Mark 11:15–18; Luke 19:45–48; John 2:13–17

THE AUTHORITY OF JESUS
The chief priests asked: Who gave thee this authority?
Jesus said: If you answer one thing I will tell you
The baptism of John, was it from heaven or of men?
If we say from heaven he will say:
    Why believed ye him not?
But if we say of men, all the people will stone us
They answered: We cannot tell whence it was
Jesus said: Neither tell I you by what authority
    I do these things
Matt. 21:23–27; Mark 11:27–33; Luke 20:1–8

THE PARABLE OF THE TWO SONS
The father told the first son: Go work in my vineyard
The son said: I will not
But afterwards he repented and went
The second son said: I go, sir, and went not
Which of the two did the will of his father?
Matt. 21:28–32

THE PARABLE OF THE WICKED TENANTS
A man planted a vineyard and let it out to vinegrowers
He sent his servants for the fruit and they were killed
He sent his son who was also killed
The owner will destroy the workers
And give the vineyard to others
Matt. 21:33–46; Mark 12:1–12; Luke 20:9–19

The stone which the builders rejected
Is become the head of the corner
Matt. 21:42; Mark 12:10; Luke 20:17

THE GREAT BANQUET
A man made a great supper and sent his servant to say:
Come, for all things are now ready
And they all with one consent began to make excuse
Then the master was angry and said to the servant:
Go into the streets and bring the poor, maimed,
    and blind . . .
Go to the highways and hedges and compel all to come
None of those men which were bidden
    shall taste of my supper
Luke 14:16–24; cf. Matt. 22:1–14

THE MARRIAGE FEAST
The kingdom of heaven is like a king
    who gave a marriage feast
None of the guests came
And he sent his servants to find others
One came without a wedding garment
And was cast into outer darkness
There shall be weeping and gnashing of teeth
For many are called but few are chosen
Matt. 22:1–14; cf. Luke 14:16–24

THE TRIBUTE TO CAESAR
Is it lawful to give tribute unto Caesar or not?
Render unto Caesar the things which are Caesar's
And unto God the things that are God's
Matt. 22:15–22; Mark 12:13–17; Luke 20:20–26

CONCERNING THE RESURRECTION
I am the God of Abraham, Isaac, and Jacob
God is not the God of the dead but of the living
Matt. 22:23–33; Mark 12:18–27; Luke 20:27–40

THE GREAT COMMANDMENTS
Hear O Israel: The Lord our God is one Lord
Thou shalt love the Lord thy God with all thy heart . . .
Thou shalt love thy neighbor as thyself

On these two commandments
    hang all the law and the prophets
Matt. 22:34–40; Mark 12:28–34; Luke 10:25–28; Lev. 19:18; Deut.
  6:4–5

QUESTION CONCERNING DAVID'S SON
What think ye of Christ? whose son is He?
The Pharisees said: The son of David
If David then call him Lord, how is he his son?
Matt. 22:41–46; Mark 12:35–37; Luke 20:41–44

WHITED SEPULCHRES
Woe to you, scribes and Pharisees, hypocrites
For ye make clean the outside of the cup
But within you are full of extortion and wickedness
You are like whited sepulchres which appear beautiful
But are full of dead men's bones and uncleanness
Matt. 23:1–33; cf. Mark 12:38–40; cf. Luke 11:37–52

O JERUSALEM, JERUSALEM
Thou that killest the prophets
How often would I have gathered thy children
As a hen gathereth her chickens under her wings
Matt. 23:37–39; Luke 13:34–35

THE WIDOW'S MITE
Mark 12:41–44; Luke 21:1–4

PREDICTION OF THE DESTRUCTION OF THE TEMPLE
There shall not be left here one stone upon another . . .
Matt. 24:1–2; Mark 13:1–2; Luke 21:5–6

Teachings on the End of the World

THE APOCALYPSE
Matt. 24:3–36; Mark 13:3–37; Luke 21:8–36

SIGNS OF CHRIST'S COMING
What shall be the sign of thy coming?
Take heed that no man deceive you
Many shall come in my name, saying, I am Christ
Ye shall hear of wars and rumors of war
For nation shall rise against nation
    and kingdom against kingdom
All these are the beginning of sorrows
Matt. 24; Mark 13:3-8, 21-23; Luke 21:7-36

THE SUFFERING OF THE DISCIPLES
Then shall they deliver you up to be afflicted
Ye shall be hated of all nations for my name's sake
Whoever kills you will think he does God a service
Many false prophets shall arise
Because iniquity shall abound,
    the love of many shall wax cold
He that shall endure unto the end shall be saved
The gospel shall be preached in all the world
And then shall the end come
Matt. 24:9-14; Mark 13:9-13; Luke 21:12-19; cf. John 16:2-6

THE DAY OF WRATH
When ye see the abomination of desolation
    spoken of by Daniel
Flee to the mountains:
Let him on the house top not come down
Let him in the field not turn back again
And woe to them that are with child
There shall arise false Christs and false prophets
The sun shall be darkened, the moon not give light,
    the stars fall
Upon the earth distress of nations
Men's hearts failing them for fear
They shall see the Son of man coming with power
    and glory
He shall send angels with a great sound of a trumpet
They shall gather his elect from the four winds
Matt. 24:15-31; Mark 13:14-27; Luke 21:20-28

THE LEAVES OF THE FIG TREE
When the branch puts forth leaves, you know
    summer is near
When the powers of heaven are shaken,
    the kingdom of God is near
Matt. 24:32–33; Mark 13:28–29; Luke 21:29–31

Heaven and earth shall pass away
But my words shall not pass away
Matt. 24:35; Mark 13:31; Luke 21:33

LEST COMING SUDDENLY
If the goodman of the house knew
    when the thief was coming
He would have been awake
Watch therefore:
For you know not what hour your Lord comes
Lest coming suddenly he find you sleeping
Matt. 24:42–44; Mark 13:34–37; Luke 12:39–40

Two men will be in the field, one is taken and one left
Matt. 24:40; Luke 17:36

THE PARABLE OF THE FAITHFUL SERVANT
The master will come unexpectedly
And reward the faithful servant but punish the wicked
There shall be weeping and gnashing of teeth
Matt. 24:45–51; Luke 12:42–48

THE PARABLE OF THE WISE AND FOOLISH VIRGINS
The kingdom of heaven is like ten virgins
Five did not get oil for their lamps and five did
When the bridegroom came, five were not ready
Watch therefore for you know neither the day nor hour
Matt. 25:1–13

THE PARABLE OF THE TALENTS
A man entrusted his goods to his servants
To one he gave five talents, another two, another one

He returned and settled accounts with them
The first said: Master, here are five talents
    and five talents more
Well done, good and faithful servant . . .
The third said: I was afraid,
    and hid my talent in the earth
Thou wicked and slothful servant
Unto every one that hath shall be given
But from him that hath not shall be taken away
Even that which he hath
Matt. 25:14–30; Luke 19:11–27

THE LAST JUDGMENT
The Son of man shall come in his glory
Before him shall be gathered all nations:
He shall separate them as a shepherd divideth sheep
    from goats
Come, ye blessed of my Father
Inherit the kingdom prepared for you
For I was hungry and ye gave me meat, I was thirsty . . .
Lord, when did we see thee hungry?
Inasmuch as ye have done it unto one
    of the least of these
Ye have done it unto me
To those others he will say:
Depart from me into everlasting fire
Matt. 25:31–46

Death and Resurrection

NOW IS MY SOUL TROUBLED
The hour is come that the Son of man should be glorified
Unless a grain of wheat fall into the ground and die . . .
If it die, it bringeth forth much fruit
He that loveth his life shall lose it

If any man serve me, let him follow me
Father save me from this hour . . .
John 12:23–27

CHILDREN OF LIGHT
Yet a little while is the light with you
Walk while you have the light
Lest darkness come upon you
While ye have light, believe in the light
That ye may be the children of light
He that believeth on me, believeth on him that sent me
John 12:35–36, 44–50

If I be lifted up, I will draw all men to me
John 12:32

They loved the praise of men more than the praise
    of God
John 12:43

CONSPIRACY OF THE CHIEF PRIESTS AND SCRIBES
Jesus said unto his disciples
After two days is the feast of the Passover
The Son of man is betrayed to be crucified
The chief priests and scribes sought how to kill him
Matt. 26:1–5; Mark 14:1–2; Luke 22:1–2

THE ANOINTING AT BETHANY
A woman with an alabaster box of ointment came to Jesus
And poured it on his head as he sat at meat
His disciples were indignant:
To what purpose is this waste?
It might have been sold for much and given to the poor
Jesus said: Ye have the poor always with you
But me ye have not always: She did it for my burial
Matt. 26:6–13; Mark 14:3–9; cf. Luke 7:36–50; cf. John 12:1–8

JUDAS' BETRAYAL
They covenanted with him for thirty pieces of silver
He that dips his hand with me in the dish shall betray me
Judas said: Master, is it I?
Jesus said: Thou hast said
That thou doest, do quickly
Matt. 26:14–25; Mark 14:10–21; Luke 22:3–6, 21–23; John 13:1, 21–30

THE INSTITUTION OF THE LORD'S SUPPER
And as they were eating
Jesus took bread and blessed it and brake it
Take, eat. This is my body
He took the cup and gave thanks: Drink ye all of it
This is my blood of the new testament
        which is shed for many . . .
Do this in remembrance of me
I will not drink henceforth the fruit of the vine
Until I drink it new with you in my Father's kingdom
Matt. 26:26–29; Mark 14:22–25; Luke 22:14–20; I Cor. 11:23–25

Having loved his own, he loved them unto the end
John 13:1

The Father had given all things into his hands
He was come from God and went to God
John 13:3

THE WASHING OF THE DISCIPLES' FEET
Jesus took a towel, girded himself, and began to wash
        the disciples' feet
Peter said: Thou shalt never wash my feet
Jesus said: If I wash thee not,
        thou hast no part with me
Lord, not my feet only, but also my hands and my head
If I have washed your feet ye also ought to wash
        one another's feet
The servant is not greater than his lord
John 13:4–20

LOVE ONE ANOTHER
Little children, yet a little while I am with you
A new commandment I give unto you:
That ye love one another
As I have loved you, that ye also love one another
By this shall all men know that ye are my disciples
John 13:33–35

LET NOT YOUR HEART BE TROUBLED
Ye believe in God, believe also in me
In my Father's house are many mansions . . .
I go to prepare a place for you . . .
I will come again that where I am, there ye may be also
Whither I go you know and the way you know
John 14:1–4

LORD, HOW CAN WE KNOW THE WAY?
I am the way, the truth, and the life
No one comes to the Father but by me
He that hath seen me hath seen the Father
Believe me that I am in the Father
Whatsoever ye shall ask in my name, that will I do
If ye love me, keep my commandments
John 14:5–15

THE SPIRIT OF TRUTH
The Father shall give you another Comforter
    even the Spirit of truth
I will not leave you comfortless
The Holy Spirit shall teach you all things
Peace I leave with you, my peace I give unto you
John 14:16–31, 15:26

I AM THE TRUE VINE
Abide in me and I in you
I am the vine, ye are the branches
As the Father has loved me, so I have loved you
John 15:1–10

Greater love hath no man than this
That he lay down his life for his friends
John 15:13

You have not chosen me, but I have chosen you
John 15:16

None of you asketh me: Whither goest thou? (Quo vadis?)
John 16:5

JOY FOLLOWS SORROW
Because I have said these things,
    sorrow hath filled your heart
It is expedient for you that I go away
When the Spirit of truth is come
He will guide you into all truth
Ye shall weep and lament, but your sorrow
    shall be turned into joy
I will see you again and your heart will rejoice
Ask and ye shall receive that your joy may be full
Be of good cheer: I have overcome the world
John 16:6–33

After they had sung an hymn, they went out
    to the Mount of Olives
Matt. 26:30; Mark 14:26; Luke 22:39

ON THE MOUNT OF OLIVES
Peter said: Lord, whither goest thou?
Whither I go thou canst not follow
But thou shalt follow me afterwards
After I am risen, I will go before you to Galilee
Peter said: I am ready to go with thee into prison
    and to death
Jesus said: The cock shall not crow
    till thou hast denied me thrice
Matt. 26:30–35; Mark 14:26–31; Luke 22:31–34, 39; John 13:36–38

JESUS PRAYS FOR HIS DISCIPLES
As thou hast sent me into the world
So have I also sent them
Neither pray I for these alone
But for them which shall believe on me
    through their word
That they all may be one
John 17:18-21

IN THE GARDEN OF GETHSEMANE
Jesus said: My soul is exceeding sorrowful,
    even unto death
Tarry ye here and watch with me
He fell on his face and prayed:
O my Father, if it be possible, let this cup pass from me
Nevertheless not my will, but thine, be done
He came to the disciples and found them asleep
Jesus said: Could ye not watch with me one hour?
The spirit is indeed willing, but the flesh is weak
Let us be going. He that betrays me is at hand
Matt. 26:36-46; Mark 14:32-42; Luke 22:40-46

THE ARREST OF JESUS
Judas came with a band with swords and staves
He came up to Jesus and said: Hail, Master!
And kissed him
One of Jesus' friends cut off the ear of a servant
    of the high priest
Jesus said: All who take the sword
    will perish by the sword
And he touched his ear and healed him
Then all the disciples forsook him and fled
Matt. 26:47-56; Mark 14:43-50; Luke 22:47-53; John 18:1-11

PETER'S DENIAL
Peter followed him afar off unto the high priest's
A maid said: This man also was with him
Woman, I know him not

They said to Peter: Thou art also of them
Peter said: Man, I am not
Another said: This fellow also was with him
Peter denied it
While he was speaking, the cock crowed
And he went out and wept bitterly
Matt. 26:58, 69–75; Mark 14: 54, 66–72; Luke 22:54–62; John
    18:15–18, 25–27

IN THE HOUSE OF THE HIGH PRIEST
The priests and council sought false witness against Jesus
That they might put him to death but they found none
The high priest asked: Are you the Christ,
    the Son of God?
Jesus said: Thou hast said. If I tell you,
    you will not believe
He hath spoken blasphemy
What further witness do we need?
They spat in his face, blindfolded him, and struck him
Saying: Prophesy! Who is it that struck you
Matt. 26:57–68; Mark 14:53–65; Luke 22:54–71; John 18:19–24

JESUS DELIVERED TO PILATE, THE GOVERNOR
Matt. 27:1–2; Mark 15:1; Luke 23:1; John 18:28–29

THE DEATH OF JUDAS
I have sinned in betraying innocent blood
He threw down the pieces of silver and hanged himself
The priests took the silver and bought the potter's field to
    bury strangers
Matt. 27:3–10; Acts 1:18–19

JESUS BEFORE PILATE
Pilate asked Jesus: Art thou the King of the Jews?
Jesus said: Thou sayest. My kingdom is
    not of this world
For this cause came I into the world: To bear witness
    to the truth

Pilate asked: What is truth?
I find in him no fault at all
Matt. 27:11–14; Mark 15:2–5; Luke 23:2–5; John 18:28–38

JESUS BEFORE HEROD
Luke 23:6–11

THE DEATH SENTENCE
At the Passover the governor
    was wont to release a prisoner
They had then a notable prisoner called Barabbas
Pilate said to the people:
Whom will ye that I release unto you?
They said: Barabbas! Now Barabbas was a robber
What shall I do then with Jesus which is called Christ?
The multitude cried: Let him be crucified!
Pilate washed his hands: I am innocent of the blood
    of this just man
The people said: His blood be on us and on our children
When he had scourged Jesus, he delivered him
    to be crucified
Matt. 27:15–26; Mark 15:6–15; Luke 23:13–25; John 18:39–40,
    19:1–16

THE MOCKING OF JESUS
The soldiers stripped him and put on a purple robe
And plaited a crown of thorns and put it upon his head
Pilate said: Behold the man!
They bowed the knee and said: Hail, King of the Jews!
They spat upon him and smote him on the head
And led him away to crucify him
Matt. 27:27–31; Mark 15:16–20; John 19:2–5

THE CRUCIFIXION
They compelled Simon of Cyrene to bear his cross
And brought him to a place called Golgotha
They crucified him and parted his garments, casting lots
Father, forgive them for they know not what they do

They put up a sign: *THIS IS JESUS THE KING OF THE JEWS*
There were two thieves crucified with him
One said: If thou be the Son of God,
    save yourself and us
The other said: Remember me
    when you come into your kingdom
Jesus said: Today you will be with me in Paradise
Matt. 27:32–44; Mark 15:21–32; Luke 23:26–43; John 19:17–24

THE DEATH ON THE CROSS
Jesus saw his mother and the disciple he loved
And said: Woman, behold thy son!
And to the disciple: Behold thy mother!
There was a darkness over all the earth
Jesus cried out: My God, my God, why hast thou forsaken me?
He said: I thirst. They gave him vinegar to drink
Father, into thy hands I commend my spirit
Jesus said: It is finished
The sun was darkened and the veil of the temple was rent
One of the soldiers pierced his side with a spear
A centurion glorified God: Truly this was the Son of God
Matt. 27:45–56; Mark 15:33–41; Luke 23:44–49; John 19:25–37

THE BURIAL OF JESUS
Joseph of Arimathea went to Pilate
And begged the body of Jesus
Wrapped it in a clean linen cloth
And laid it in his own new tomb
Matt. 27:57–61; Mark 15:42–47; Luke 23:50–56; John 19:38–42

THE EMPTY TOMB
At dawn Mary Magdalene and the other Mary
    went to the tomb
The angel said: Fear not, for I know you seek Jesus
Why seek ye the living among the dead?
Tell his disciples that he is risen from the dead
And they departed quickly with fear and great joy
Matt. 28:1–8; Mark 16:1–8; Luke 24:1–11; John 20:1–10

THE FIRST APPEARANCE OF THE RISEN CHRIST
Jesus appeared to Mary Magdalene and she knew him not
Jesus said: Woman, why weepest thou? whom seekest
   thou?
Sir, if thou have borne him hence,
      where hast thou laid him?
Jesus said: Mary. She turned and said:
      Rabboni! (Teacher)
Touch me not for I am not yet ascended to my Father
Mary Magdalene came and told the disciples
      she had seen the Lord
Mark 16:9–11; John 20:11–18; cf. Matt. 28:9–10

THE ROAD TO EMMAUS
Two of them went that same day to a village
      called Emmaus
Jesus himself came near and went with them
      but they knew him not
They said to Jesus: Abide with us:
      for it is toward evening
As Jesus sat with them he took bread,
      blessed it, and brake it
And their eyes were opened and they knew him
      and he vanished
They returned to Jerusalem and told the disciples:
The Lord is risen indeed!
And how he was known to them in breaking of bread
Mark 16:12–13; Luke 24:13–35

JESUS' APPEARANCE TO THE DISCIPLES
Jesus himself stood in the midst of them and said:
Peace be unto you!
Behold my hands and my feet that it is I myself
He breathed on them and said: Receive the Holy Spirit
Preach the gospel to every creature
If you forgive anyone's sins, they stand forgiven
Mark 16:14–18; Luke 24:36–49; John 20:19–23

ON A MOUNTAIN IN GALILEE
The eleven disciples went away
    unto a mountain in Galilee
And when they saw Jesus they worshiped him
Jesus said: All power is given unto me in heaven
    and in earth
Go ye therefore, teach all nations and baptize them
In the name of the Father and of the Son
    and of the Holy Ghost
Teaching them to observe all things that I have
    commanded
And, lo, I am with you always even
    unto the end of the world
Matt. 28:16–20

DOUBTING THOMAS
Except I see the prints of the nails, I will not believe
Jesus said to Thomas: Behold my hands
Reach thy hand and thrust it into my side
Be not faithless but believing
Thomas said: My Lord and my God!
Jesus said: Blessed are they that have not seen, yet
    believe
John 20:24–29

ON THE SEA OF TIBERIAS
The disciples were fishing all night but caught nothing
In the morning Jesus stood on the shore
    but they knew him not
He told them to cast the net
    on the right side of the ship
They were not able to draw it in
    for the multitude of fish
The disciple whom Jesus loved said to Peter:
It is the Lord
The other disciples came in a little ship
As soon as they were come to land,
    they saw a fire of coals

And fish laid thereon
Jesus said: Come and dine
He took bread and gave it to them with the fish
John 21:1–14; cf. Luke 5:1–11

FEED MY LAMBS
Peter said: Lord thou knowest that I love thee
Jesus said: Feed my lambs
A second time Jesus said: Lovest thou me?
Feed my sheep
He said unto him the third time: Lovest thou me?
Peter said: Lord, thou knowest all things . . .
Jesus said: Feed my sheep
John 21:15–17

THE ASCENSION
While he blessed them, he was carried up into heaven
Mark 16:19–20; Luke 24:50–51; Acts 1:1–14

New Testament

BEGINNINGS
OF THE
CHURCH

The Acts of the Apostles

AFTER JESUS' ASCENSION
They returned to Jerusalem from the mount called Olivet
When they were come in, they went into an upper room
And all continued in prayer and supplication
Acts 1:12–14

THE CALLING OF MATTHIAS
Acts 1:23–26

ON THE DAY OF PENTECOST
They were all with one accord in one place
Suddenly there came a sound from heaven
    as of a mighty wind
There appeared unto them cloven tongues like as of fire
Which rested upon each of them
And they were all filled with the Holy Spirit
And began to speak with other tongues as the Spirit
    gave them utterance
When this was noised abroad, devout Jews of
    every nation asked:
How hear we every man in our own tongue?
And they were amazed and said: What does this mean?
Others mocking said: These men are full of new wine
Acts 2:1–13

PETER'S SERMON
These are not drunken as ye suppose
This is that which was spoken by the prophet Joel
I will pour out of my Spirit upon all flesh:
And your sons and your daughters shall prophesy
Your young men shall see visions
And your old men dream dreams
I will show wonders in heaven above
And signs in the earth beneath

The sun shall be turned into darkness
 and the moon into blood
Whosoever shall call on the name of the Lord
 shall be saved
This Jesus hath God raised up
 whereof we all are witnesses
God hath made that same Jesus both Lord and Christ
Acts 2:14–36

THE HEALING OF THE LAME MAN
Silver and gold have I none
But such as I have, give I thee:
In the name of Jesus Christ rise up and walk
And he, leaping up, stood and walked
And entered the temple with Peter and John,
 praising God
By what power or by what name have ye done this?
Peter said: By the name of Jesus Christ of Nazareth
They commanded them not to teach in the name of Jesus
But with great power gave the apostles witness
 of the resurrection
And great grace was upon them all
Acts 3—4

ANANIAS AND SAPPHIRA
Acts 5:1–11

THE APOSTLES IN PRISON
By the hands of the apostles
 were many signs and wonders wrought
Insomuch that they brought the sick into the streets
That the shadow of Peter might fall on them
The high priest and Sadducees
 were filled with indignation
And put them in the common prison
Acts 5:12–18

THE ESCAPE FROM PRISON
An angel of the Lord opened the prison doors
      and brought them forth
Go speak to the people the words of this life
One said: Behold, the men you put in prison
      are teaching in the temple
Peter and the apostles said: We ought to obey God not men
We are his witnesses and so is also the Holy Spirit
Gamaliel said: If this idea be of men,
      it will come to nought
If it be of God, ye cannot overthrow it
Acts 5:19–42

THE FIRST DEACONS
Brethren, choose seven men of honest report
When they had prayed, they laid their hands on them
And Stephen did great wonders among the people
Acts 6:1–8

THE MARTYRDOM OF STEPHEN
Certain of the synagogue disputed with Stephen
And set up false witnesses: We have heard him
      blaspheme
They cast Stephen out and stoned him
And they laid down their clothes at Saul's feet
And Stephen cried: Lord Jesus, receive my spirit
Acts 6:9—8:2

EARLY PERSECUTION OF THE CHURCH:
THE SPREAD OF THE GOSPEL
There was a great persecution against the church
Saul made havoc of the church,
      committing men and women to prison
They that were scattered abroad
      went everywhere preaching the word
Acts 8:1–8

SIMON THE MAGICIAN
Simon offered to buy the power of the laying on of hands
Peter said: Thy money perish with thee
Thou hast thought that the gift of God may be purchased
Thy heart is not right in the sight of God
Thou art in the gall of bitterness
    and in the bond of iniquity
Simon said: Pray to the Lord for me
Acts 8:9–24

THE ETHIOPIAN EUNUCH
Philip opened his mouth and preached unto him Jesus
The eunuch said: I believe that Jesus Christ
    is the Son of God
Philip baptized the eunuch who went on his way rejoicing
Acts 8:26–40

THE CONVERSION OF SAUL:
ON THE ROAD TO DAMASCUS
Saul, yet breathing out threatenings and slaughter . . .
As he journeyed, he came near Damascus
Suddenly there shined round about him a light
    from heaven:
He fell to the earth and heard a voice:
Saul, Saul, why persecutest thou me?
He said: Who art thou, Lord?
I am Jesus whom thou persecutest
Lord, what wilt thou have me do?
Arise and go into the city and it shall be told thee
He was three days without sight
    and neither did eat nor drink
Acts 9:1–9, cf. 22:6–11, cf. 26:12–18

SAUL AND ANANIAS
The Lord said to Ananias: Arise, go into the street
    called Straight
And inquire for one called Saul to restore his sight

Ananias entered the house
    and putting his hands on him said:
The Lord hath sent me that thou mightest receive thy sight
Immediately the scales fell from his eyes
    and he received sight
And he arose and was baptized
Acts 9:10–18

SAUL'S FIRST PREACHING
He preached Christ in the synagogues
And confounded the Jews of Damascus
    who took counsel to kill him
But the disciples took him by night
And let him down by the wall in a basket
Acts 9:20–25

SAUL AND THE DISCIPLES IN JERUSALEM
Acts 9:26–31

TABITHA (DORCAS) RESTORED TO LIFE
Acts 9:36–42

CORNELIUS THE CENTURION
An angel of God came to Cornelius and said:
Send men to Joppa to Simon whose surname is Peter
As they went on their journey
Peter went up upon the house top to pray
He fell into a trance, saw heaven opened
    and a great sheet descending
Wherein were all manner of fourfooted beasts
    and fowls of the air
There came a voice: Rise, Peter; kill, and eat
Not so, Lord. I have never eaten any thing unclean
    or common
What God hath cleansed, that call not thou common
Peter came to Caesarea and Cornelius fell down
    and worshiped him

Peter said: Stand up. I myself also am a man
God hath shown me that I should not call
    any man common
Cornelius said: We are all here present before God
    to hear all things
While Peter spake the Holy Spirit fell on all which heard
    the word
Acts 10

And the disciples were called Christians first
    at Antioch
Acts 11:26

PETER FREED FROM PRISON BY AN ANGEL
Acts 12:1–19

THE JOURNEYS OF BARNABUS AND PAUL
Cyprus, Perga, Pisidian Antioch, Iconium, Lystra,
    and Derbe
Acts 13—14

A HEALING IN LYSTRA
There sat a man, a cripple from his mother's womb
Paul said: Stand upright on thy feet
And he leaped up and walked
The people said: The gods are come down to us
    in the likeness of men
They called Barnabus, Jupiter and Paul, Mercury
But the apostles replied: We also are men of
    like passions with you
Acts 14:8–18

THE CONFERENCE AT JERUSALEM
Some taught: Except ye be circumcised ye cannot be saved
Paul and Barnabas had dissension with them
The apostles and elders came together
    to consider this matter

And when there had been much disputing
Peter said: God put no difference between us and them
The apostles and elders sent letters to the Gentiles
It seemed good to us, being assembled with one accord
To send chosen men with our beloved Barnabas and Paul
Acts 15:1–35

PAUL AND BARNABUS ARGUE AND PART
Acts 15:36–41

PAUL REVISITS CHURCHES IN SYRIA AND CILICIA
Acts 15:36–41

TIMOTHY JOINS PAUL
Acts 16:1–5

PAUL TAKES THE GOSPEL TO EUROPE
Paul visits Troas, Neapolis, Philippi, Thessalonica, Beroea,
    Athens, and Corinth
Acts 16:6—18:28

COME TO MACEDONIA
A vision appeared to Paul: a man of Macedonia who said:
Come over into Macedonia and help us
Therefore Paul went to Philippi via Samothrace
    and Neapolis
He baptized Lydia a seller of purple and
    all her household
Acts 16:9–15

PAUL AND SILAS IN PRISON
The Romans beat Paul and Silas and cast them in prison
But they prayed and sang praises to God
And a great earthquake freed the prisoners
The jailkeeper, trembling, asked them:
What must I do to be saved?
Paul said: Believe on the Lord Jesus Christ
    and thou shalt be saved
Acts 16:19–40

PAUL AT ATHENS
Ye men of Athens, I perceive that ye are
        too superstitious
I found an altar with the inscription:
To the unknown God
Whom ye ignorantly worship I declare unto you
God that made the world . . . dwelleth not in temples
        made with hands
He hath made of one blood all nations of men
        for to dwell on the earth
For in him we live and move and have our being
Acts 17:16–34

Certain lewd fellows of the baser sort
Acts 17:5

Your blood will be upon your own heads
From henceforth I will go unto the Gentiles
Acts 18:6

An eloquent man and mighty in the scriptures
Acts 18:24

PAUL TRAVELS FROM EPHESUS TO JERUSALEM
Via Philippi, Troas, Assos, Mitylene (Lesbos), Chios,
        Samos, Trogylium, Miletus, Cos, Rhodes, Patara,
        Tyre, Ptolemais, Caesarea
Acts 19—21:15

PAUL AT EPHESUS
Have you received the Holy Spirit?
When Paul had laid his hands upon them:
The Holy Spirit came upon them
God wrought special miracles by the hands of Paul
So mightily grew the word of God and prevailed
But some cried: Great is Diana of the Ephesians!
Acts 19

Eutychus fell asleep as Paul preached
Acts 20:9–12

For it is more blessed to give than to receive
Acts 20:35

PAUL IN JERUSALEM
I am ready to die at Jerusalem
For the name of the Lord Jesus
The Jews of Asia stirred up the people
The chief captain commanded him to be bound in chains
Paul said: I am a Jew of Tarsus,
    a citizen of no mean city
The chief captain said: With a great sum
    obtained I this freedom
Paul said: I was free born
To the Jews Paul said: I am a Pharisee,
    the son of a Pharisee
Acts 21:15—23:22

IN CUSTODY IN CAESAREA
Paul told Felix the governor:
I have a conscience void of offence toward God
    and toward men
And he spoke to Felix of faith in Christ
Felix trembled and said: Go thy way for this time
When I have a convenient season, I will call for thee
Acts 23:15—24:25

PAUL'S DEFENSE
Unto the Jews have I done no wrong I appeal unto
    Caesar
I stand and am judged for the hope
Of the promise made by God to our fathers
That Christ should suffer and rise from the dead
Paul, thou art beside thyself
Much learning doth make thee mad
I am not mad but speak forth the words of truth and
    soberness
Agrippa said: Almost thou persuadest me
    to be a Christian

This man might have been set at liberty
If he had not appealed to Caesar
Acts 25—26

PAUL SAILS FROM JERUSALEM TO ROME
Via Sidon, Myra, Lasea (Crete), Malta, Syracuse (Sicily),
   Rhegium, Puteoli, Forum of Appius, Three Taverns
Acts 27—28

SHIPWRECKED ON THE WAY TO ROME
There arose a tempestuous wind
No small tempest lay on us
All hope was taken away
An angel said: Fear not, Paul
They ran the ship aground
And they escaped all safe to land
The island was called Melita (Malta)
Acts 27:14—28:1

A POISONOUS VIPER
Paul gathered a bundle of sticks
And laid them on the fire
A poisonous viper fastened on his hand
He shook off the beast and felt no harm
Acts 28:3–6

PAUL IN ROME
Paul dwelt . . . two years in his own hired house
Preaching the kingdom of God
And teaching those things which concern Jesus Christ
No man forbidding him
Acts 28:16–31

Paul's Letter to Rome

PAUL, A SERVANT OF JESUS CHRIST
To all that be in Rome, beloved of God,
    called to be saints:
Grace to you and peace from God our Father
    and the Lord Jesus Christ
I long to see you that I may impart some spiritual gift
So I am ready to preach the gospel
    to you that are at Rome
Rom. 1:1–15

THE GOSPEL OF CHRIST
It is the power of God unto salvation
    to every one that believeth
To the Jew first and also to the Greek
As it is written: The just shall live by faith
Rom. 1:16–17

THE SINS OF THE PAGAN WORLD
The wrath of God is revealed against all ungodliness
When they knew God, they glorified him not as God
Professing themselves to be wise they became fools
They changed the truth of God into a lie
And worshiped and served the creature
    more than the Creator
Rom. 1:18–32

THEREFORE THOU ART INEXCUSABLE, O MAN
For wherein thou judgest another, thou condemnest
    thyself
But we are sure that the judgment of God
    is according to truth . . .
God will render to every man according to his deeds
But glory, honor, and peace to every man
    that worketh good
To the Jew first and also to the Gentile

For there is no respect of persons with God
Not the hearers of the law are just before God
But the doers of the law shall be justified
Rom. 2

A law unto themselves
Rom. 2:14

JUSTIFICATION BY FAITH
There is none that doeth good, no, not one
By the law is the knowledge of sin
All have sinned and come short of the glory of God
A man is justified by faith without the deeds of the law
While we were yet sinners, Christ died for us
Rom. 3:9—5:11

Let God be true but every man a liar
Rom. 3:4

Where no law is, there is no transgression
Rom. 4:15

Who against hope believed in hope
Rom. 4:18

SIN AND DISOBEDIENCE IN ADAM
By one man sin entered into the world and death by sin
So death passed upon all men for that all have sinned
For as by one man's disobedience many were made sinners
So by the obedience of one shall many be made righteous
Where sin abounded, grace did much more abound
Rom. 5:12–21

NEW LIFE IN CHRIST
Shall we continue in sin that grace may abound?
God forbid

Knowing that Christ being raised from the dead
    dieth no more
Death hath no more dominion over him
For in that he died, he died unto sin once:
But in that he liveth, he liveth unto God
Sin shall not have dominion over you
For the wages of sin is death
But the gift of God is eternal life
    through Jesus Christ
Rom. 6

We should serve in newness of spirit
    not in oldness of the letter
Rom. 7:6

For the good that I would I do not:
But the evil which I would not, that I do
Rom. 7:19

O wretched man that I am!
Who shall deliver me from this body of death?
Rom. 7:24

There is therefore now no condemnation
To them which are in Christ Jesus
Rom. 8:1

THE LIFE OF THE SPIRIT
To be carnally minded is death
To be spiritually minded is life and peace
For as many as are led by the Spirit of God
    they are sons of God
You have received the Spirit of adoption whereby we cry:
Abba, Father!
We are the children of God and if children, then heirs
Heirs of God and joint heirs with Christ
Rom. 8:1–17

CHRISTIAN HOPE
The sufferings of this present time cannot be compared
With the glory which shall be revealed in us
The whole creation groaneth and travaileth in pain
Ourselves also which have the firstfruits of the Spirit
We are saved by hope: but hope that is seen is not hope
The Spirit itself maketh intercession for us
With groanings which cannot be uttered
Rom. 8:18–26

IF GOD BE FOR US
All things work together for good to them that love God
If God be for us, who can be against us?
Who shall separate us from the love of Christ?
Neither death, nor life, nor angels, nor principalities . . .
Nor height, nor depth, nor any other creature
Shall separate us from the love of God . . .
Rom. 8:28–39

We are more than conquerors through him that loved us
Rom. 8:37

Hath not the potter power over the clay . . . ?
Rom. 9:21

HOW SHALL THEY HEAR?
Whosoever shall call upon the name of the Lord
      shall be saved
How shall they call on him in whom they have
      not believed?
How shall they believe in him of whom they have
      not heard?
How shall they hear without a preacher?
How shall they preach except they be sent?
Rom. 10:13–15

All day long I have held out my hands
      to a disobedient people
Rom. 10:21

GLORY TO GOD
O the depth of the riches of the wisdom
    and knowledge of God!
How unsearchable are his judgments
And his ways past finding out
For who hath known the mind of the Lord
From him, through him, and to him are all things
Rom. 11:33–36

THE CHRISTIAN LIFE
Present your bodies a living sacrifice,
    holy, acceptable to God
And be not conformed to this world but be
    ye transformed
I say to every man not to think of himself more highly
    than he ought
So we, being many, are one body in Christ . . .
Having gifts differing according to the grace that is given
Rom. 12:1–8

PAUL'S ADMONITIONS
Let love be without dissimulation
Abhor that which is evil; hold to that which is good
Be kindly affectioned one to another with brotherly love
Be patient in tribulation, constant in prayer
Bless them which persecute you, bless and curse not
Rejoice with them that do rejoice
    and weep with them that weep
Be of the same mind one toward another
Be not wise in your own conceits
Rom. 12:9–16

OVERCOME EVIL WITH GOOD
Recompense to no man evil for evil
If it be possible, live peaceably with all men
Vengeance is mine. I will repay saith the Lord
If thine enemy hunger, feed him . . .

In so doing thou shalt heap coals of fire on his head
Be not overcome of evil, but overcome evil with good
Rom. 12:17–21

Render therefore to all their dues
Owe no man anything
Rom. 13:7–8

THE ARMOR OF LIGHT
The night is far spent, the day is at hand:
Let us therefore cast off the works of darkness
Let us put on the armor of light
Let us walk honestly as in the day,
    not in strife and envying
But put ye on the Lord Jesus Christ . . .
Rom. 13:12–14

WHETHER WE LIVE OR DIE
Let every man be fully persuaded in his own mind
For none of us liveth to himself
    and no man dieth to himself
Whether we live therefore or die we are the Lord's
Rom. 14:5–8

Let us therefore follow after the things
    which make for peace
Rom. 14:19

We then that are strong
Ought to bear the infirmities of the weak
Rom. 15:1

Now the God of hope fill you with all joy and peace
    in believing
Rom. 15:13

Salute one another with an holy kiss
Rom. 16:16

Paul's Letters to the Corinthians

WE PREACH CHRIST CRUCIFIED
I beseech you that there be no divisions among you
We preach Christ crucified
Unto the Jews a stumblingblock, unto the Greeks
     foolishness
God has chosen the foolish things to confound the wise
I Cor. 1

THE WISDOM AND POWER OF GOD
I was with you in weakness and in much fear
     and trembling
That your faith might not be in the wisdom of men
But in the power of God
We speak the wisdom of God in a mystery,
     even the hidden wisdom . . .
Eye hath not seen, nor ear heard . . .
The things which God hath prepared for them that love him
God hath revealed them unto us by his Spirit
For who hath known the mind of the Lord
     that he may instruct him?
But we have the mind of Christ
I Cor. 2

I have fed you with milk and not with meat
I Cor. 3:2

CHRIST THE ONE FOUNDATION
I have planted, Apollos watered, but God gave the increase
We are laborers together with God
According to the grace of God, I have laid the foundation
Let every man take heed how he buildeth thereupon
For other foundation can no man lay than Jesus Christ
Every man's work shall be made manifest
     and the fire shall try it

You are the temple of God and the Spirit of God
    dwelleth in you
Let no man glory in men:
You are Christ's and Christ is God's
I Cor. 3

The wisdom of this world is foolishness with God
I Cor. 3:19

FOOLS FOR CHRIST
Ministers of Christ and stewards of the mysteries of God
It is required in stewards that a man be found faithful
Judge nothing before the time until the Lord come
We are made a spectacle unto the world,
    to angels, and to men
We are fools for Christ's sake but you are wise in Christ
I Cor. 4

Absent in body but present in spirit
I Cor. 5:3

A little leaven leavens the whole lump
I Cor. 5:6

Christ our passover is sacrificed for us:
Therefore let us keep the feast . . .
I Cor. 5:7–8

All things are lawful for me
But all things are not expedient
I Cor. 6:12, 10:23

YOUR BODY IS A TEMPLE OF THE HOLY SPIRIT
Ye are bought with a price
Glorify God in your body and in your spirit
I Cor. 6:18–20

ADMONITIONS ON MARRIAGE
Let every man have his own wife, every woman
        her own husband
It is better to marry than to burn
Let not the wife depart from her husband
Let not the husband put away his wife
I Cor. 7

Knowledge puffs up but love instructs
I Cor. 8:1

If meat makes my brother to offend, I will eat no flesh
I Cor. 8:13

ALL THINGS TO ALL MEN
Though I be free from all men yet am I servant unto all
Unto the Jews I became as a Jew
I am made all things to all men that I might save some
I Cor. 9

They which run in a race, run all,
        but one receiveth the prize
I Cor. 9:24

Wherefore let him that thinketh he standeth take heed
        lest he fall
I Cor. 10:12

God will not suffer you to be tempted
        above that ye are able
But will with the temptation make a way to escape . . .
I Cor. 10:13

You cannot drink the cup of the Lord and the cup of
        devils
I Cor. 10:21

For the earth is the Lord's and the fulness thereof
I Cor. 10:26

Whatsoever ye do, do all to the glory of God
I Cor. 10:31

CONCERNING COMMUNION
The Lord Jesus the night he was betrayed took bread:
And when he had given thanks, he brake it
Take, eat: this is my body which is broken for you:
This do in remembrance of me
After the same manner, also he took the cup
This cup is the new testament in my blood:
This do ye, as oft as ye drink it, in remembrance of me
I Cor. 11:23–26; cf. Matt. 20:26–29; cf. Mark 14:22–25; cf. Luke
    22:15–20

SPIRITUAL GIFTS
There are diversities of gifts but the same Spirit
For to one is given by the Spirit the word of wisdom . . .
To another faith by the same Spirit . . .
As the body is one, and all the members of that body one
So also is Christ
For by one Spirit are we all baptized into one body
Now ye are the body of Christ and members in particular
I Cor. 12

CONCERNING LOVE
Though I speak with the tongues of men and of angels
    and have not love
I am become as sounding brass or a tinkling cymbal
Love never faileth . . .
We know in part and we prophesy in part
When I was a child, I spake as a child . . .
When I became a man, I put away childish things
For now we see through a glass, darkly;
        but then face to face

Now abideth faith, hope, love, these three
But the greatest of these is love
I Cor. 13

PROPHECY AND SPEAKING IN TONGUES
He that speaks in an unknown tongue speaks not to men
      but to God
But he that prophesies speaks to men
      for their edification
Greater is he that prophesies than he that
      speaks with tongues
Except he interprets
Be not children in understanding
God is not the author of confusion but of peace
Let all things be done decently and in order
I Cor. 14

CONCERNING RESURRECTION
Christ died for our sins according to the scriptures
He was buried and he rose again the third day
If Christ be not risen, then is our preaching vain
And if Christ be not raised, your faith is vain
As in Adam all die, in Christ shall all be made alive
The last enemy that shall be destroyed is death
I Cor. 15:1–26

By the grace of God I am what I am
Yet not I, but the grace of God which was with me
I Cor. 15:10

If I have fought with beasts at Ephesus
What advantage it me if the dead rise not?
Let us eat and drink for tomorrow we die
I Cor. 15:32

HOW ARE THE DEAD RAISED UP?
The body is sown in corruption.
It is raised in incorruption

Sown a natural body and raised a spiritual body
Flesh and blood cannot inherit the kingdom of God
We shall not all sleep but we shall all be changed
In a moment, in the twinkling of an eye,
    at the last trump:
For the trumpet shall sound and the dead shall be raised
Death is swallowed up in victory
O death where is thy sting?
O grave, where is thy victory?
Thanks be to God which giveth us the victory
Through our Lord Jesus Christ
Therefore be ye steadfast,
    abounding in the work of the Lord
I Cor. 15:35–58

Watch ye, stand fast in the faith
I Cor. 16:13

THE GOD OF ALL COMFORT
Blessed be God, the Father of mercies
Who comforteth us in all our tribulation
That we may be able to comfort
For as the sufferings of Christ abound in us
So our consolation also abounds by Christ
Who has put his seal upon us
And given us the promise of the Spirit in our hearts
II Cor. 1

YOU ARE WRITTEN IN OUR HEARTS
Not on monuments of stone but on the pages of the
    human heart
God also hath made us able ministers of the new
    testament
Not of the letter but of the spirit:
For the letter killeth but the spirit giveth life
We use great plainness of speech
Where the Spirit of the Lord is, there is liberty
II Cor. 3

WE FAINT NOT
We preach not ourselves but Christ Jesus the Lord
We have this treasure in earthen vessels
We are troubled on every side yet not distressed
Our light affliction worketh for us an eternal weight
    of glory
While we look not at the things which are seen
For the things which are seen are temporal
But the things which are not seen are eternal
II Cor. 4

We have a building of God, an house not made with hands
II Cor. 5:1

For we walk by faith not by sight
II Cor. 5:7

To be absent from the body and present with the Lord
II Cor. 5:8

OLD THINGS ARE PASSED AWAY
The love of Christ constrains us
If any man be in Christ, he is a new creature:
Old things are passed away. All things are become new
All things are of God who hath reconciled us to himself
    by Christ
God was in Christ, reconciling the world unto himself
Now then we are ambassadors for Christ . . .
He hath made him to be sin for us, who knew no sin
II Cor. 5:14–21

WORKERS TOGETHER WITH HIM
Receive not the grace of God in vain
Now is the accepted time. Now is the day of salvation
In stripes, in imprisonments, in tumults . . .
By pureness, by knowledge, by longsuffering . . .
By honor and dishonor, by evil report and good report

Dying, behold we live, as chastened and not killed
As sorrowful yet alway rejoicing, as poor,
     yet making many rich
Having nothing, and yet possessing all things
II Cor. 6

The sorrow of the world worketh death
II Cor. 7:10

ON ALMSGIVING
He which soweth sparingly shall reap also sparingly
Every man according as he purposeth in his heart,
     so let him give
For God loveth a cheerful giver
God is able to make all grace abound toward you
Thanks be to God for his unspeakable gift
II Cor. 9

Though I be rude in speech
II Cor. 11:6

Satan himself is transformed into an angel of light
II Cor. 11:14

For ye suffer fools gladly seeing ye yourselves are wise
II Cor. 11:19

PAUL'S SUFFERINGS
In labors more abundant, in stripes above measure
In journeyings often, in perils of waters,
     in perils of robbers . . .
In weariness and painfulness . . . in hunger and thirst . . .
Besides those things, the care of all the churches
II Cor. 11:21–33

I speak as a fool
II Cor. 11:23

Who is weak and I am not weak? If I must glory
I will glory of the things which concern my infirmities
II Cor. 11:29-30

PAUL'S VISION
Caught up to the third heaven
Whether in the body or out, I cannot tell
II Cor. 12:1-5

MY STRENGTH IS MADE PERFECT IN WEAKNESS
There was given to me a thorn in the flesh
Lest I should be exalted above measure
I besought the Lord thrice that it might depart from me
And he said: My grace is sufficient for thee
Most gladly therefore will I rather glory
     in my infirmities
For when I am weak, then am I strong
II Cor. 12:7-10

For we can do nothing against the truth, but for the truth
II Cor. 13:8

The grace of the Lord Jesus Christ, the love of God
And the communion of the Holy Spirit be with you all
II Cor. 13:14

Letters to Galatia and Ephesus

Paul, an apostle not of men, but by Jesus Christ
Unto the churches of Galatia, grace be to you
And peace from God the Father
     and from our Lord Jesus Christ
Gal. 1:1-3

THE TRUE GOSPEL
The gospel which was preached of me is not after man
But by the revelation of Jesus Christ
Gal. 1:9–12

James, Cephas, and John gave to me and Barnabus
The right hands of fellowship
Gal. 2:9

DEAD TO THE LAW
I through the law am dead to the law that I might live
    unto God
I am crucified with Christ: nevertheless I live
Yet not I, but Christ liveth in me
Gal. 2:19–20

O FOOLISH GALATIANS
Received ye the Spirit by works of the law
Or by the hearing of faith?
No man is justified by law in the sight of God
The just shall live by faith
Gal. 3:1–11

YOU ARE ALL ONE
There is neither Jew nor Greek, bond nor free,
    male nor female:
For you are all one in Christ Jesus
Gal. 3:26–29

THE ADOPTION OF SONS
God sent forth his Son to redeem them
    that were under the law
That we might receive the adoption of sons
Because you are sons God has sent forth
    the Spirit of his Son
Into your hearts, crying Abba, Father
Thou art no more a servant, but a son
How turn ye again to the weak and beggarly elements?
Gal. 4:1–9

Am I become your enemy, because I tell you the truth?
Gal. 4:16

THE FRUIT OF THE SPIRIT
Stand fast therefore in the liberty
      wherewith Christ hath made us free
Whosoever are justified by the law, ye are fallen from grace
Ye have been called unto liberty . . . by love
      to serve one another
Walk in the Spirit and ye shall not fulfill the lust
      of the flesh
For the flesh lusteth against the Spirit, and the Spirit
      against the flesh
The fruit of the Spirit is love, joy, peace . . .
Gal. 5

DO GOOD UNTO ALL MEN
Bear one another's burdens
And so fulfill the law of Christ
Be not deceived, God is not mocked:
Whatsoever a man soweth, that shall he also reap
Let us not be weary in well doing
As we have therefore opportunity,
      let us do good unto all men
God forbid that I should glory
Save in the cross of Christ
Gal. 6

To the saints which are at Ephesus
Eph. 1:1

THE GRACE OF GOD
God, who is rich in mercy, hath quickened us
      together with Christ
By grace are ye saved through faith and that
      not of yourselves
Not of works, lest any man should boast

We are his workmanship, created in Christ Jesus
    unto good works
He hath broken down the partition between us
Ye are built upon the foundation of the apostles
    and prophets
Jesus Christ being the chief corner stone
Eph. 2

ROOTED AND GROUNDED IN LOVE
I, Paul, the prisoner of Jesus Christ for you Gentiles
Was made a minister according to the gift
    of the grace of God
That I should preach the unsearchable riches of Christ
To be strengthened with might by his Spirit
    in the inner man
That Christ may dwell in your hearts by faith
Being rooted and grounded in love
You may know the love of Christ
That you might be filled with all the fulness of God
Eph. 3

Walk worthy of the vocation wherewith ye are called
Eph. 4:1

UNTO EVERY ONE OF US
There is one body, and one Spirit
One hope of your calling
One Lord, one faith, one baptism
One God and Father of all, who is above all
    and through all
Unto every one of us is given grace
    according to the gift of Christ
He led captivity captive and gave gifts to men
He gave some apostles, some prophets, some evangelists
For the perfecting of the saints, the work of the ministry
Eph. 4:4–13

216

Be no more children, tossed to and fro
And carried about with every wind of doctrine
But speaking the truth in love
Eph. 4:14–15

BE RENEWED IN THE SPIRIT OF YOUR MIND
Put on the new man created in righteousness and holiness
We are members one of another
Be ye angry and sin not
Let not the sun go down on your wrath
Be ye kind one to another, tenderhearted, forgiving . . .
Eph. 4:23–32

THE NEW LIFE IN CHRIST
Walk in love as Christ also hath loved us
And hath given himself for us an offering
    and sacrifice to God
Walk as children of light
Have no fellowship with the works of darkness
Be filled with the Spirit, speaking to yourselves
In psalms and hymns and spiritual songs
Singing and making melody in your heart to the Lord
Giving thanks always for all things unto God
Eph. 5:1–20

CHRISTIAN MARRIAGE
Husbands, love your wives even as Christ loved the church
And the wife see that she reverence her husband
He that loveth his wife loveth himself
For no man ever yet hated his own flesh but cherisheth it
For this cause shall a man leave his father and mother
And be joined unto his wife: they two shall be one flesh
Eph. 5:21–33

PARENTS AND CHILDREN
Children, obey your parents. Honor thy father
    and mother

Fathers, provoke not your children to wrath
Bring them up in the nurture and admonition of the Lord
Eph. 6:1–4; cf. Col. 3:20–21

BE STRONG IN THE LORD
Put on the whole armor of God
To stand against the wiles of the devil
For we wrestle not against flesh and blood
But against principalities, powers, rulers of darkness
Stand therefore, your loins girt about with truth
Having on the breastplate of righteousness . . .
Take the shield of faith and the helmet of salvation
And the sword of the Spirit which is the word of God
Watching with all perseverance and supplication
     for all saints
Eph. 6:10–18

I am an ambassador in bonds
Eph. 6:20

Letters to Philippi, Colossae, and Thessalonica

For to me to live is Christ, and to die is gain
Phil. 1:21

THE EXAMPLE OF CHRIST
Let this mind be in you which was also in Christ Jesus
Christ took upon him the form of a servant . . .
He humbled himself and became obedient
     unto death even of the cross
God hath exalted him and given him a name above
     every name
That at the name of Jesus every knee should bow . . .
That every tongue should confess
     that Jesus Christ is Lord

Work out your own salvation with fear and trembling
For it is God which worketh in you . . .
Phil. 2

What things were gain to me
Those I counted loss for Christ
Phil. 3:7

Forgetting those things which are behind,
    and reaching forth
I press toward the mark
    for the prize of God in Christ Jesus
Phil. 3:13–14

Whose end is destruction, whose God is their belly . . .
Phil. 3:19

REJOICE IN THE LORD ALWAY
And again I say: Rejoice! Let your moderation be known
    unto all men
The Lord is at hand. Be careful for nothing
But in everything by prayer and supplication
Let your requests be made known unto God
And the peace of God which passeth all understanding
Shall keep your hearts and minds through Christ Jesus
Phil. 4:4–7

Whatsoever things are true . . . think on these things
Phil. 4:8

I have learned, in whatsoever state I am,
    therewith to be content
Phil. 4:11

I can do all things through Christ which strengtheneth me
Phil. 4:13

God shall supply all your need
Phil. 4:19

TO THE SAINTS AND FAITHFUL AT COLOSSAE
We give thanks to God praying always for you
Who hath delivered us from the power of darkness
And translated us into the kingdom of his dear Son
Who is the image of the invisible God
Col. 1:1–15

HE IS BEFORE ALL THINGS
For by him were all things created, visible and invisible
Whether thrones, dominions, principalities, or powers
He is before all things and by him all things consist
Col. 1:16–17

LET NO ONE DELUDE YOU
I say lest any man should beguile you with enticing words
Though I be absent in the flesh
Yet am I with you in the spirit
As ye have received Christ Jesus so walk ye in him
Beware lest any man spoil you
        through philosophy and vain deceit
Ye are complete in him which is the head of all
Col. 2

A shadow of things to come
Col. 2:17

Touch not, taste not, handle not
Col. 2:21

SEEK THOSE THINGS WHICH ARE ABOVE
Set your affection on things above, not on the earth
For you are dead and your life is hid with Christ in God
There is neither Greek nor Jew,
        circumcision nor uncircumsion. . .
Christ is all and in all

Put on therefore compassion, kindness, lowliness,
    meekness, long suffering
Forgiving one another even as Christ forgave you
Above all put on love which is the bond of perfectness
Let the peace of God rule in your hearts and be thankful
Whatsoever you do in word or deed,
    do all in the name of the Lord
Col. 3

Fathers, provoke not your children to anger
Lest they be discouraged
Col. 3:21

Whatsoever you do, do it heartily, as to the Lord
Col. 3:23

Let your speech be always with grace,
    seasoned with salt
Col. 4:6

Luke, the beloved physician
Col. 4:14

Take heed to the ministry which you have received
    in the Lord
Col. 4:17

TO THE CHURCH OF THE THESSALONIANS
Grace be unto you and peace from God our Father
We remember without ceasing your work of faith
    and labor of love
We were gentle with you as a nurse cherishes her children
I Thess. 1—2

Lest our labor be in vain
I Thess. 3:5

The Lord make you to increase and abound in love
I Thess. 3:12

God hath not called us unto uncleanness but unto holiness
I Thess. 4:7

Study to be quiet and to do your own business
I Thess. 4:11

THE SECOND COMING
If we believe that Jesus died and rose again
Even so them which sleep in Jesus will God bring with him
The Lord himself shall descend from heaven with a shout
With the voice of the archangel and with trump of God
The dead in Christ shall rise first
I Thess. 4:14–18

THE CHILDREN OF LIGHT
The day of the Lord cometh like a thief in the night
But you brethren are not in darkness
Let us watch and be sober
Putting on the breastplate of faith and love . . .
See that none render evil for evil unto any man
Rejoice evermore. Pray without ceasing
In every thing give thanks . . . hold fast that which is good
And the very God of peace sanctify you wholly
I Thess. 5

BELOVED OF THE LORD
God has from the beginning chosen you to salvation
Through sanctification of the Spirit
    and belief of the truth
Therefore stand fast and hold the traditions

Our Lord hath given us everlasting consolation
    and good hope
Comfort your hearts and stablish you
    in every good word and work
II Thess. 2

The Lord direct your hearts into the love of God
II Thess. 3:5

Be not weary in well doing
II Thess. 3:13

Letters to Timothy, Titus, and Philemon

Unto Timothy, my own son in the faith
I Tim. 1:2

TEACH NO OTHER DOCTRINE
Do not give heed to fables and endless genealogies
Some having swerved have turned aside
    unto vain jangling
Desiring to be teachers of the law
Understanding neither what they say
    nor whereof they affirm
We know that the law is good, if a man use it lawfully
The law is not made for a righteous man but for
    the lawless
According to the glorious gospel of the blessed God
I Tim. 1:4–14

Christ Jesus came into the world to save sinners
    of whom I am the chief
I Tim. 1:15

Unto the King eternal, immortal, invisible . . .
I Tim. 1:17

A RANSOM FOR ALL
Prayers, intercessions, and giving of thanks
    be made for all men
For kings and for all that are in authority
That we may lead a quiet and peaceable life
    in all godliness
This is good and acceptable in the sight of God
Who will have all men to be saved and to know the truth
For there is one God and one mediator,
    the man Christ Jesus
Who gave himself a ransom for all
I Tim. 2:1-6

PAUL'S ATTITUDE TOWARD WOMEN
Let the women learn in silence with all subjection
I Tim. 2:9-15

CONCERNING BISHOPS
A bishop must be blameless, vigilant, sober,
    of good behavior
One that ruleth well his own house
For if a man know not how to rule his own house
How shall he take care of the church of God?
I Tim. 3:1-7

CONCERNING DEACONS
Likewise must the deacons be grave, not given to
    much wine
Holding the mystery of the faith in a pure conscience
I Tim. 3:8-13

Not greedy of filthy lucre
I Tim. 3:3, 8

The house of God which is the church of the living God
The pillar and ground of the truth
I Tim. 3:15

God was manifest in the flesh, justified in the Spirit
Seen of angels, preached unto the Gentiles . . .
I Tim. 3:16

Speaking lies in hypocrisy
Their conscience seared with a hot iron
I Tim. 4:2

Every creature of God is good and nothing to be refused
I Tim. 4:4

INSTRUCTIONS FOR TIMOTHY
Refuse profane and old wives' fables and exercise thyself
    unto godliness
Let no man despise thy youth
But be thou an example of the believers
Neglect not the gift that is in thee
Rebuke not an elder but entreat him as a Father
Use a little wine for thy stomach's sake
I Tim. 4:7—5:23

WE BROUGHT NOTHING INTO THIS WORLD
It is certain we can carry nothing out
Having food and raiment let us be content
They that will be rich fall into temptation
For the love of money is the root of all evil
But thou, O man of God, flee these things
Fight the good fight of faith, lay hold on eternal life
I Tim. 6:7–12

King of Kings, Lord of Lords
I Tim. 6:15

Be rich in good works
I Tim. 6:18

Avoid profane and vain babblings and oppositions
Of science, falsely so called
I Tim. 6:20

THE GIFT OF GOD
Stir up the gift of God which is in thee
By the putting on of my hands
God hath not given us the spirit of fear
But of power, and of love, and of a sound mind
II Tim. 1:6–7

A WORKMAN THAT NEED NOT BE ASHAMED
Be strong in the grace that is in Christ Jesus
Endure hardness as a good soldier of Jesus Christ
Shun profane and vain babblings
The Lord give thee understanding in all things
For if we be dead with him, we shall also live with him:
If we suffer, we shall also reign with him
If we deny him, he also will deny us
II Tim. 2

The word of God is not bound
II Tim. 2:9

The Lord knoweth them that are his
II Tim. 2:19

Flee also youthful lusts
II Tim. 2:22

Having a form of godliness but denying the power thereof
II Tim. 3:5

All that will live godly in Christ Jesus
    shall suffer persecution
II Tim. 3:12

HOLY SCRIPTURES
From a child thou hast known the holy scriptures
Which are able to make thee wise . . .
All scripture is given by inspiration of God
II Tim. 3:15–17

I CHARGE THEE
Preach the word. Be instant in season, out of season
Do the work of an evangelist
I have fought a good fight, I have finished my course
I have kept the faith
II Tim. 4:1–8

The Lord reward him according to his works
II Tim. 4:14

I was delivered out of the mouth of the lion
II Tim. 4:17

To Titus mine own son after the common faith
Grace, mercy, and peace . . .
Titus 1:4

CONCERNING ELDERS (BISHOPS)
Ordain elders in every city
If any be blameless, the husband of one wife
Having faithful children not accused of riot or unruly
For a bishop must be blameless
Not selfwilled, not soon angry . . .
But a lover of hospitality, of good men
Holding fast the faithful word
Titus 1:5–9

Unto the pure all things are pure
Titus 1:15

Let no man despise thee
Titus 2:15

FROM A ROMAN PRISON
Paul, a prisoner of Jesus Christ
And Timothy our brother unto Philemon
Our dearly beloved and fellow laborer
I make mention of thee always in my prayers
Philemon v. 1–4

PLEA FOR A RUNAWAY SLAVE
I beseech thee for my son Onesimus
Not now as a servant but a beloved brother
If thou count me a partner, receive him as myself
If he hath wronged thee, I will repay
Philemon v. 10–21

A Letter to the Hebrews

THE BRIGHTNESS OF HIS GLORY
God, who at sundry times and in divers manners
Spake in time past unto the fathers by the prophets
Hath in these last days spoken unto us by his Son
Who being the brightness of his glory
      and the image of his person
Sat down on the right hand of the Majesty on high
Heb. 1:1–3

Who makest his angels spirits
      and his ministers a flame of fire
Heb. 1:7

How shall we escape if we neglect so great salvation
Heb. 2:3

WHAT IS MAN THAT THOU ART MINDFUL OF HIM?
Or the son of man that thou visitest him?
Thou madest him a little lower than the angels
Thou crownedst him with glory and honor
And set him over the works of thy hands
Thou hast put all things in subjection under his feet
But we see not yet all things put under him
Heb. 2:6–8

A LITTLE LOWER THAN THE ANGELS
We see Jesus who was made a little lower than the angels
That he by the grace of God
  should taste death for everyman
And deliver them who through fear of death
  were in bondage
In all things to be made like his brethren
To make reconciliation for the sins of the people
For in that he hath suffered, being tempted
He is able to succor them that are tempted
Heb. 2:9–18

JESUS AND MOSES
This man was counted worthy of more glory than Moses
He who has builded the house has more honor
  than the house
And he that built all things is God
Heb. 3

LET US LABOR
We which have believed do enter into rest
And God did rest the seventh day from all his works
Let us labor therefore to enter into that rest
Lest any man fall after the same example of unbelief
For the word of God is quick and powerful
Sharper than any two-edged sword . . .
A discerner of the thoughts and intents of the heart
Heb. 4:1–13

JESUS THE HIGH PRIEST
We have a great high priest, Jesus the Son of God
Tempted like as we are, yet without sin
Let us therefore come boldly unto the throne of grace
And find grace to help in time of need
Christ glorified not himself but he that said:
Thou art my Son, today have I begotten thee

Thou art a priest for ever
    after the order of Melchizedek
Heb. 4:14—5:10

Strong meat belongeth to them that are of full age . . .
Heb. 5:14

They crucify to themselves the Son of God afresh
Heb. 6:6

God is not unrighteous to forget your work and labor of
    love
Heb. 6:10

An anchor of the soul, sure and steadfast
Heb. 6:19

A NEW COVENANT
This is the covenant that I will make
    with the house of Israel
I will put my laws into their minds
And write them on their hearts
And I will be their God and they shall be my people
All shall know me from the least of them to the greatest
I will be merciful to their unrighteousness
Their sins and their iniquities will I remember no more
Heb. 8

THE NEW TESTAMENT
Where a testament is,
    there must be the death of the testator
Without shedding of blood is no remission
For Christ is not entered into the holy places
    made with hands
But into heaven itself
    to appear in the presence of God for us

So Christ was once offered to bear the sins of many
And we are sanctified through the offering
    of the body of Christ
Heb. 9

It is a fearful thing
To fall into the hands of the living God
Heb. 10:31

FAITH IN GOD
Now the just shall live by faith
Faith is the substance of things hoped for
The evidence of things not seen
By faith Abel . . .
Heb. 10:38—11:40

They were strangers and pilgrims on the earth
Heb. 11:13

A CLOUD OF WITNESSES
Seeing we are compassed about
    with so great a cloud of witnesses
Let us lay aside every weight and sin which doth beset us
And let us run with patience the race that is set before us
Looking unto Jesus the author and finisher of our faith
Who for the joy that was set before him endured the cross
For whom the Lord loveth he chasteneth
For what son is he whom the father chasteneth not?
Heb. 12:1–11

MAKE STRAIGHT PATHS FOR YOUR FEET
Follow peace with all men and holiness
Looking diligently lest any man fail of the grace of God
Lest any root of bitterness springing up trouble you
Heb. 12:12–15

Come unto mount Sion, the heavenly Jerusalem
And to the spirits of just men made perfect
Heb. 12:22–23

Our God is a consuming fire
Heb. 12:29

Let brotherly love continue
Entertain strangers for thereby have some
     entertained angels unawares
Heb. 13:1–2

The Lord is my helper and I will not fear what man shall
     do unto me
Heb. 13:6

Jesus Christ the same yesterday, today, and for ever
Heb. 13:8

For here we have no continuing city but seek one to come
Heb. 13:14

To do good and to communicate, forget not:
For with such sacrifices God is well pleased
Heb. 13:16

The God of peace make you perfect in every good work
Heb. 13:21

Letters from James and Peter

COUNT IT JOY WHEN YE FALL INTO TEMPTATION
Let patience have her perfect work
That ye may be perfect and entire, wanting nothing

If any of you lack wisdom let him ask of God
Blessed is the man that endureth temptation
When he is tried, he shall receive the crown of life
Jas. 1:1–16

A double minded man is unstable in all his ways
Jas. 1:8

Every perfect gift is from above
    and cometh from the Father
With whom there is no variableness,
    nor shadow of turning
Jas. 1:17

Let every man be swift to hear, slow to speak,
    slow to wrath
For the wrath of man worketh not the righteousness of God
Jas. 1:19–20

DOERS OF THE WORD
Be ye doers of the word not hearers only
Deceiving your own selves
Who looks into the perfect law of liberty
    and continues therein
This man shall be blessed
Pure religion is to visit the fatherless and widows . . .
And to keep oneself unspotted from the world
Jas. 1:22–27

SHOW NO PARTIALITY
Hath not God chosen the poor of this world?
But ye have despised the poor
If ye have respect to persons, ye commit sin
Jas. 2:1–9

FAITH WITHOUT WORKS
Though a man say he hath faith but not works
Can faith save him?

If a brother or sister be naked and destitute
And you say: Depart in peace, and give them nothing
What doth it profit?
As the body without the spirit is dead
So faith without works is dead also
Jas. 2:14–26

ON CONTROLLING OUR TONGUES
The tongue is a little member and boasteth great things
Behold, how great a matter a little fire kindleth!
The tongue is a fire, a world of iniquity
It defileth the whole body
It is an unruly evil, full of poison
Out of the same mouth proceedeth blessing and cursing
Jas. 3

Ye receive not, because ye ask amiss
Jas. 4:3

DRAW NIGH TO GOD
God resisteth the proud but giveth grace to the humble
Submit yourselves therefore to God
Resist the devil and he will flee from you
Draw nigh to God and he will draw nigh to you
Humble yourselves in the sight of the Lord
And he shall lift you up
Jas. 4:6–10

WHAT IS YOUR LIFE?
It is a vapor that appears a little time
And then vanishes away
Jas. 4:14

If the Lord will, we shall live
Jas. 4:15

YOU RICH MEN
Weep and howl for your miseries that shall come upon you
Your riches are corrupted and your garments motheaten
You have heaped treasure together for the last days
You have lived in pleasure on the earth and been wanton
Jas. 5:1–6

Ye have heard of the patience of Job
Jas. 5:11

THE EFFECTIVENESS OF PRAYER
Is any among you afflicted? Let him pray
The prayer of faith shall save the sick
If he have committed sins, they shall be forgiven him
Confess your faults one to another
Pray one for another, that you may be healed
The fervent prayer of a righteous man availeth much
Jas. 5:12–20

PETER TO SCATTERED STRANGERS
Blessed be the God and Father of our Lord Jesus Christ!
By his great mercy we have been born anew to
    a living hope
Whom having not seen, ye love
Yet believing ye rejoice with joy unspeakable
    and full of glory
Wherefore gird up your mind, be sober and hope
    to the end
Be holy in all manner of conversation
Because it is written: Be ye holy for I am holy
I Peter 1:1–22

ALL FLESH IS AS GRASS
And all the glory of man as the flower of grass
The grass withereth and the flower falleth away
But the word of the Lord endureth for ever
I Peter 1:24–25

A stone of stumbling and a rock of offence
I Peter 2:8

YOU ARE THE PEOPLE OF GOD
A chosen generation, a royal priesthood, an holy nation
Abstain from fleshly lusts which war against the soul
With well doing ye may put to silence the ignorance of
        foolish men
Honor all men. Love the brotherhood
Fear God. Honor the king
I Peter 2:9–17

CONCERNING SUFFERING
What glory is it if you are beaten for your faults
And take it patiently?
But if you do well and suffer for it . . .
This is acceptable with God
Christ also suffered for us leaving us an example
For you were as sheep going astray
But now are returned to the Shepherd
        and Bishop of your souls
I Peter 2:20–25

The ornament of a meek and quiet spirit
I Peter 3:4

Giving honor unto the wife, as unto the weaker vessel
I Peter 3:7

BE OF ONE MIND
Having compassion one of another
Not rendering evil for evil but contrariwise blessing
It is better that ye suffer for well doing
        than for evil doing
I Peter 3:8–17

Charity shall cover the multitude of sins
I Peter 4:8

If any man suffer as a Christian, let him not be ashamed
I Peter 4:16

You shall receive a crown of glory that fadeth not away
I Peter 5:4

AS A ROARING LION
Be sober, be vigilant
Because your adversary the devil as a roaring lion
Walketh about seeking whom he may devour
I Peter 5:8

And the day star arise in your hearts
II Peter 1:19

The dog is turned to his own vomit again
II Peter 2:22

One day is with the Lord as a thousand years . . .
II Peter 3:8

The day of the Lord will come as a thief in the night
II Peter 3:10

Letters from John and Jude

GOD IS LIGHT
We write that your joy may be full
God is light and in him is no darkness at all

If we walk in the light, we have fellowship
     one with another
And the blood of Jesus Christ his Son
     cleanseth us from all sin
If we say we have no sin, we deceive ourselves
And the truth is not in us
If we confess our sins, he is faithful
     and just to forgive us
If any man sin, we have an advocate with the Father,
     Jesus Christ
He is the propitiation for our sins, and not for ours only
But also for the sins of the whole world
I John 1:4—2:2

LOVE NOT THE WORLD
Love not the things that are in the world
The world passeth away and the lust thereof:
But he that doeth the will of God abideth for ever
I John 2:15–17

He is antichrist that denieth the Father and the Son
I John 2:22

Marvel not, my brethren, if the world hate you
I John 3:13

BOWELS OF COMPASSION
Who has this world's goods and sees his brother in need
And shutteth up his bowels of compassion
How dwelleth the love of God in him?
Let us not love in word, but in deed and truth
I John 3:17–18

GOD IS LOVE
Beloved, let us love one another: for love is of God
He that loveth not knoweth not God: for God is love
Herein is love, not that we loved God,
     but that he loved us

God sent his only begotten Son into the world
    that we might live
If we love one another, God dwells in us
He that dwells in love, dwells in God and God in him
We love him because he first loved us
There is no fear in love: perfect love casteth out fear
I John 4

There are three that bear record in heaven:
The Father, the Word, and the Holy Spirit
    and these three are one
I John 5:7

He that has the Son has life
I John 5:12

He that doeth good is of God
He that doeth evil hath not seen God
III John v. 11

Jude, the servant of Jesus Christ
And brother of James . . .
Jude v. 1

THE BLACKNESS OF DARKNESS
Raging waves of the sea, foaming out their shame
Wandering stars, to whom is reserved
The blackness of darkness forever
Jude v. 13

Keep yourselves in the love of God
And of some have compassion, making a difference
Jude vv. 21, 22

The Revelation of John
for the Seven Churches in Asia

I AM ALPHA AND OMEGA
The beginning and the end
Which is and which was and which is to come,
     the Almighty
Rev. 1:8

JOHN ON PATMOS
I was in the Spirit and heard behind me a great voice:
What thou seest write in a book
And send it to the seven churches of Asia
Rev. 1:9–11

JOHN'S VISION OF THE SON OF MAN
I saw seven golden candlesticks
And in the midst one like unto the Son of man
His head and his hairs were white as snow
His feet like fine brass
And his voice as the sound of many waters
He had in his right hand seven stars
When I saw him I fell at his feet as dead
Fear not, I am the first and the last
I am he that liveth and was dead
And behold, I am alive for ever more
And have the keys of hell and of death
Rev. 1:12–20

TO THE CHURCH OF EPHESUS
I know thy works, thy labor, and thy patience
I have somewhat against thee:
Thou hast left thy first love
Remember therefore from whence thou art fallen,
     and repent
To him that overcometh will I give to eat
     of the tree of life
Rev. 2:1–7

TO THE CHURCH OF SMYRNA
Be thou faithful unto death
And I will give thee a crown of life
Rev. 2:8–11

TO THE CHURCH IN PERGAMOS (PERGAMUM)
Repent or I will come unto thee quickly
And fight against them with the sword of my mouth
Rev. 2:12–17

TO THE CHURCH IN THYATIRA
He that overcometh, to him will I give
    power over the nations
And he shall rule them with a rod of iron
And I will give him the morning star
Rev. 2:18–29

TO THE CHURCH IN SARDIS
He that overcometh will be clothed in white raiment
I will not blot out his name from the book of life
Rev. 3:1–6

TO THE CHURCH IN PHILADELPHIA
I have set before thee an open door
And no man can shut it for thou hast kept my word
Behold, I come quickly: hold fast that which thou hast
He that overcometh will I make a pillar
    in the temple of God
Rev. 3:7–13

TO THE CHURCH IN LAODICEA
I know thy works that thou art neither cold nor hot:
Because thou art lukewarm
I will spew thee out of my mouth

Behold I stand at the door and knock:
    if any open the door
I will come in and sup with him and he with me
Rev. 3:14–22

THE VISION OF THE THRONE
A throne was set in heaven and one sat on the throne
There was a rainbow about the throne
I saw four and twenty elders sitting around the throne
There were seven lamps which are the seven spirits of God
Before the throne there was a sea of glass
        like unto crystal
Rev. 4:1–6

THE VISION OF THE BEASTS
And around the throne were four beasts full of eyes
The first beast was like a lion
The second beast like a calf
The third beast had a face as a man
The fourth was like an eagle
They rest not day and night: saying Holy, holy, holy
Lord God Almighty which was, and is, and is to come
Thou art worthy, O Lord, to receive glory and honor . . .
For thou hast created all things
And for thy pleasure they are created
Rev. 4:6–11

THE SEVEN SEALS
I saw a book sealed with seven seals
I wept much because no man was found worthy
        to open and read it
Lo, in the midst of the elders
Stood a Lamb as it had been slain
And he came and took the book
And they sang a new song, saying:
Thou art worthy to take the book and open the seals
For thou wast slain and hast redeemed us to God
Worthy is the Lamb that was slain

Blessing, honor, glory, and power be unto him
    that sitteth upon the throne
And unto the Lamb for ever and ever. Amen
Rev. 5

FOUR HORSEMEN OF THE APOCALYPSE
I saw a white horse and he that sat on him had a bow
    and a crown
He went forth conquering and to conquer
There came out another horse that was red
Power was given the rider to take peace from the earth
I beheld a black horse and he that sat on him
Had a pair of balances in his hand
Behold a pale horse:
His rider was death and Hell followed him
Men said to the mountains, fall on us and hide us
The great day of his wrath has come:
Who shall be able to stand?
Rev. 6

HURT NOT THE EARTH
I saw four angels on the four corners of the earth
Holding the four winds of the earth
Another angel, having the seal of God, cried with a loud voice
Hurt not the earth, neither the sea, nor the trees
Till we have sealed the servants of our God
    on their foreheads
Rev. 7:1–3

THE PEOPLE OF GOD
There were sealed an hundred and forty four thousand
    of the children of Israel
Then I beheld a multitude of all nations and kindreds
These are they which came out of great tribulation
And have washed their robes in the blood of the Lamb
They shall hunger no more neither thirst any more

The Lamb which is in the midst of the throne
    shall feed them
And God shall wipe away all tears from their eyes
Rev. 7:4–17

DESTRUCTION AND DEVASTATION
When he had opened the seventh seal
There was silence in heaven
Seven angels began sounding seven trumpets
A great star fell from heaven, burning like a lamp
The name of the star was Wormwood
Rev. 8

The bottomless pit
Rev. 9:1

I saw a mighty angel: in his hand a little book
He set his right foot on the sea and his left foot on earth
Rev. 10:1–2

THE SEVENTH TRUMPET
The seventh angel sounded the trumpet
    and there were voices:
The kingdoms of this world
    are become the kingdoms of our Lord . . .
Rev. 11:15–19

THE WOMAN AND THE DRAGON
There appeared a great wonder in heaven:
A woman clothed with the sun, and the moon
    under her feet
A great red dragon having seven heads and ten horns
And there was war in heaven:
Michael and his angels fought against the dragon
The great dragon was cast out,
    that old serpent called the Devil
And Satan which deceiveth the whole world
    was cast out into the earth

I heard a voice saying: Now is come salvation and strength
The kingdom of God and the power of Christ
Rev. 12

THE VISION OF THE TWO BEASTS
I saw a beast rise up out of the sea having seven heads
He had power to make war with the saints
    and to overcome them
I beheld another beast coming up out of the earth
He exerciseth all the power of the first beast before him
And deceiveth them that dwell on earth
Rev. 13

THOSE WHICH FOLLOW THE LAMB
Lo, a Lamb stood on Mount Sion
With him an hundred forty and four thousand
These are they which follow the Lamb
These were redeemed from among men
    being the firstfruits unto God
They are without fault before the throne of God
Fear God and give glory to him
For the honor of judgment is come!
Babylon is fallen, is fallen, that great city . . .
Blessed are the dead which die in the Lord
That they may rest from their labors
Rev. 14

THE SEVEN LAST PLAGUES
Seven angels came out of the temple
    having the seven plagues
One of the four beasts gave the seven angels
    seven golden vials
Full of the wrath of God who liveth for ever and ever
Rev. 15—16

Great and marvelous are thy works, Lord God Almighty
Rev. 15:3

ARMAGEDDON
And he gathered them into a place called Armageddon
Rev. 16:16

THE WHORE OF BABYLON
I saw a woman sit upon a scarlet colored beast
Upon her forehead was a name written:
Babylon the Great, Mother of Harlots and Abominations
    of the Earth
Babylon the great is fallen, is fallen
Her sins have reached heaven
And God hath remembered her iniquities
Rev. 17—18

THE MARRIAGE OF THE LAMB
Alleluia: for the Lord God omnipotent reigneth!
Let us be glad and rejoice:
For the marriage of the Lamb is come
His wife is ready arrayed in the fine linen
    of the righteousness of saints
Rev. 19:6–10

KING OF KINGS AND LORD OF LORDS
I saw heaven opened and behold a white horse
He that sat upon him was called Faithful and True
His name is called The Word of God
Rev. 19:11–16

THE DEFEAT OF SATAN
I saw an angel come down from heaven
With the key of the bottomless pit
He laid hold of the Devil and bound him a thousand
    years
And cast him into the bottomless pit
That he should deceive the nations no more
Rev. 20:1–3

THE FINAL JUDGMENT

I saw the dead stand before God and their books were
    opened:
And another book was opened which is the book of life
And the dead were judged out of those books
Rev. 20:11–15

THE NEW JERUSALEM

I saw a new heaven and a new earth . . .
And the holy city, new Jerusalem, coming down
    from God
A voice cried: Behold the tabernacle of God is with men
And they shall be his people and God shall be with them
God shall wipe away all tears from their eyes
There shall be no more death, neither sorrow nor crying . . .
For the former things are passed away and I make all
    things new
He that overcometh shall inherit all things
Rev. 21

THE WATER OF LIFE

He showed me a pure river of water of life,
    clear as crystal
On either side of the river was the tree of life
There shall be no night there
The Lord God giveth light
I am Alpha and Omega, the beginning and the end
The first and the last
And the Spirit and the bride say, Come
And let him that heareth say, Come
Whosoever will, let him take the water of life freely
Rev. 22

Surely I come quickly. Amen. Even so, come, Lord Jesus
Rev. 22:20

Gazetteer

Abarim: The name of a mountainous region, southwest of Amman, in modern Jordan. From Mt. Nebo (Pisgah), its principal peak, Moses viewed the land of Canaan (Num. 27:12-23), p. 20.

Ai: A city (kingdom) conquered by the Israelites. Some believe that the ruins of Ai are at el-Tell, two miles east of Bethel (Josh. 7—8), p. 28.

Aijalon: The Valley of Aijalon is about fifteen miles west of Jerusalem. Here "the sun stood still" while Joshua fought (Josh. 10:12-43), p. 28.

Ammon: Ammon is now modern Amman, the capital of Jordan. Ammonite kings battled Jehosophat (I Kings 22:41-50; II Chron. 17—20), p. 42.

Amorites: See Amurru

Amurru: The Amorites inhabited the land of Amurru which lay in the Syro-Arabian desert east of Damascus. There were Amorites living in Canaan when the Israelites arrived, and some sources identify the Amorites with the Canaanites. Joshua fought the Amorite kings (Josh. 10:12-43), p. 28.

Antioch of Pisidia: Partially excavated ruins reveal a formerly magnificent city. It was two miles east of modern Yalvac in central Turkey. Paul and Barnabus visited here, and the Christian community of Antioch was probably the recipient of Paul's letter to the Galations (Acts 13:13-48), p. 194.

Antioch of Syria: Now the modern city of Antakya, Turkey, it was a major center for the early church and the base from which Paul and Barnabus journeyed. Excavations have been conducted, but very little is visible from apostolic times (Acts 11:26), p. 194.

Ararat: There are several possible sites for the traditional resting place for Noah's ark. The most traditional is in Armenia on the Turkish-Russian border (Gen. 8), p. 6.

Arimathea: The location of Arimathea is thought to have been about twenty miles east of Tel Aviv.

Joseph of Arimathea laid Jesus' body in his tomb (Matt. 27:57-61: Mark 15:42-47; Luke 23:50-56; John 19:38-42), p. 183.

Armageddon: Traditional site of the last great war between good and evil. Most scholars identify Armageddon with Mt. Megiddo and the plain below, sometimes called Esdraelon or Jezreel. Megiddo is one of the most impressive sites in modern Israel. Excavations disclose human habitation as early as 4000 B.C. Here Deborah prophesied and Sisera was defeated (Judges 4—5). The horse stalls of Solomon's stables and a 165-foot-long water shaft are still visible (Rev. 16:16), p. 246.

Ashdod: Now south of Tel Aviv, Ashdod was a Philistine strong-hold in Old Testament times. The Philistines captured the Ark of the Covenant and took it to Ashdod (I Sam. 4—7), p. 32.

Ashkelon or **Ashgelon:** A former Philistine town, Ashkelon is now two cities: Migdal, the old settlement, and Ashkelon-by-the-Sea. Ashkelon is on the coast south of Tel Aviv. Here Samson slew thirty men (Judges 14:5-19), p. 30.

Assos: Paul visited Assos, a seaport on the west coast of modern Turkey known today as Behramkoy. There are extensive archeological excavations (Acts 20:13-14), p. 196.

Assyria: A powerful enemy of ancient Israel, Assyria lies today within the borders of present day Iraq (II Kings 17) (Isa. 14:25) (Isa. 38:1-8), pp. 44, 86, 91.

Athens: Here, on Mars' Hill, Paul preached his sermon to the Greeks, identifying the unknown God (Acts 17:16-34), p. 196.

Babylon: The capital city of the Babylonian empire whose king, Nebuchadnezzar, took Jerusalem captive. The fall of Babylon was prophesied by Isaiah, Jeremiah, and in Revelation. The ruins are near Baghdad in Iraq and include the throne room of King Nebuchadnezzar (II Kings 24:10-16; 25:1-21; II Chron. 36:5—

Babylon: (continued)
21; Jer. 39) (Isa. 13) (Jer. 51:16–64) (Dan. 1:1–7) (Rev. 14) (Rev. 17—18), pp. 45, 85, 103, 110, 245, 246.

Beersheba: The southernmost town of Old Testament Israel (from Dan to Beersheba). It is in the Negev region of modern Israel. Here one can see the well believed to have been used by Abraham (Gen. 21:9–21) (Judges 20:1), p. 30.

Berea: See *Beroea.*

Beroea: A city in northern Greece visited by Paul when he took the Gospel to Europe (Acts 17:10–14), p. 195.

Bethabara: Mentioned by John as the site of Jesus' baptism, Bethabara is called Bethany in some translations, but this is not the Bethany on the Mount of Olives on the Jordan River near Jericho (Matt. 3; Mark 1:1–11; Luke 3:1–22; John 1:6–7) (John 1:29–34), p. 135.

Bethany: A village on the east slope of the Mount of Olives, Bethany was the home of Mary, Martha, and Lazarus. (For site of Jesus' baptism, see Bethabara.) Here the woman with an alabaster box anointed Jesus, and here he ascended into heaven (John 11:1–44) (Matt. 26:6–13; Mark 14:3–9) (Mark 16:19–20; Luke 24:50–51; Acts 1:1–14), p. 176.

Bethel: The town where Jacob had his dream of a ladder reaching to heaven. It is about twelve miles north of Jerusalem and is today called Beitin (Gen. 28:10–22), p. 11.

Bethesda, Pool of: A pool in Jerusalem which may be seen today near the Sheep Gate. Here Jesus healed a man who had an infirmity for thirty-eight years (John 5:1–16), p. 166.

Bethlehem: The birthplace of Jesus is now a suburb of Jerusalem. One can visit the Church of the Nativity and other sites. Bethlehem is where Ruth and Naomi settled, and Ruth gleaned in the field of Boaz (Ruth) (Micah 5:2–4) (Luke 2:1–7) (Luke 2:15–20), pp. 31, 122, 133.

Bethphage: Jesus sent his disciples to Bethphage to fetch the colt for his entry to Jerusalem. Some identify Bethphage with the village of Abu Dis, southeast of Bethany (Matt. 21:1–11; Mark 11:1–10; Luke 19:28–38; John 12:12–15), p. 169.

Bethsaida: Hometown of Peter, Andrew, and Philip, Bethsaida is on the north shore of the Sea of Galilee and near the area where Jesus fed the four thousand. Here Jesus restored a blind man's sight. Traces of an aqueduct, a Roman road, and a town wall are visible (John 1:44) (Mark 8:22–26) (Matt. 15:32–39; Mark 8: 1–10), p. 160.

Caesarea: The ruins of Caesarea are on the Mediterranean between Tel Aviv and Haifa. Most obvious is the Crusader City, but one may also see the older Roman amphitheatre where early Christians were martyred. This city figured importantly in New Testament and later Christian times and was the residence of the Roman procurators including Pontius Pilate. It was the home of Cornelius the centurion, where Peter preached and was visited by Paul on his trip from Ephesus to Jerusalem. Paul was later imprisoned here (Acts 10) (Acts 21) (Acts 23:15–24:25), pp. 193, 196, 197.

Caesarea Philippi: Today this village is known as Baniyas and is on the northern border of Israel and Syria. There are few remains of the ancient city (Matt. 16:13–20; Mark 8:27–30; Luke 9:18–21), p. 160.

Calvary: See Golgotha.

Cana: Today called Kfar Kanna, it is four miles from Nazareth. (Some sources say Khirbet Qana, the ruins of an ancient village nine miles from Nazareth, is really the biblical Cana.) Here Jesus performed his first miracle by turning water into wine. He also healed a nobleman's son. Cana is the traditional home of Nathanael (John 2:1–11) (John 4:45–54), p. 137.

Canaan: Canaan was the country occupied by the Canaanites in pre-Israelite times. It consisted of the land between the Jordan River and the Mediterranean. Abram (Abraham) was told by God to go to Canaan, and he dwelt there. After the Exodus from Egypt, Moses sent men to spy out the land, and Joshua led Israel back into Canaan (Gen. 12:1–8) (Gen. 13—14:20) (Num. 13—14:37) (Deut. 34; Josh. 1:9), pp. 7, 8, 19.

Capernaum: Capernaum is a town on the Sea of Galilee where Jesus taught and healed. Among its ruins are the foundations of St. Peter's house. A second century synagogue rests on the site of an older one where it is likely that Jesus taught (Matt. 7:28–29; Mark 1:21–28; Luke 4:31–37) (Matt. 8:5–13; Luke 7:1–10) (John 4:45–54), pp. 137, 143.

Cappadocia: A former Roman province in what is now eastern Turkey. Cappadocians were among those at Pentecost and were recipients of Peter's letters (Acts 2:9) (I Pet. 1:1), pp. 189, 232.

Carmel: Mt. Carmel is on the Mediterranean Sea near the modern port of Haifa. Here Elijah challenged the prophets of Baal (I Kings 18:17–40), p. 40.

Chebar River: Along the banks of this canal in Babylonia lived most of the exiled people of Judah. It was east of the city of Nippur (Ezek. 1:1), p. 105.

Cherith: The location of the brook where Elijah hid and was fed by ravens is not certain. It is possibly modern Wadi Yabis, east of the Jordan (I Kings 17:2–7), p. 39.

Chios: An island in the east central region of the Aegean Sea. The chief city, also formerly called Chios, is today's Scio. Chios was visited by Paul on his trip from Ephesus to Jerusalem (Acts 20:15), p. 196.

Cilicia: Cilicia is now part of southern Turkey. Paul came from Tarsus, which was the capital of Cilicia. Most of the towns visited by Paul and Barnabus are now covered by new settlements, but some ruins are visible (Acts 13—14) (Acts 15:36–41), p. 195.

Colossae: The city of Colossae is located in what is now southwest Turkey (the Phrygian District of Paul's time). Ruins of the city and its acropolis are visible. The church of Colossae received the letter to the Colossians (Col. 1—4), p. 220.

Corinth: A city in Greece visited by Paul when he took the Gospel to Europe and to whom he wrote the letters to the Corinthians. Many Roman ruins survive, and one can see the agora where Paul was brought before the tribunal (Acts 18) (I & II Cor.), pp. 195, 205.

Cos: An island in the Aegean Sea visited by Paul on his trip from Ephesus to Jerusalem (Acts 21:1), p. 196.

Cyprus: An island in the Mediterranean about forty miles off the coast of Turkey, Cyprus was the home of Barnabus and was also visited by Paul and Mark (Acts 13—14) (Acts 15:39).

Cyrene: Cyrene is in Libya on the north coast of Africa. Simon of Cyrene carried Jesus' cross (Matt. 27:32–44; Mark 15:21–32; Luke 23:26–43; John 19:17–24), p. 194.

Damascus: Damascus is the present capital of Syria. It was the home of Naaman the leper who was cured by Elisha. Isaiah prophesied that the city would become a ruinous heap. Saul (Paul) was converted on the way to Damascus (II Kings 5) (Is. 17) (Acts 9:1–25), pp. 86, 192.

Dan: Near the headwaters of the Jordan, Dan is the northernmost town of biblical Israel. The ruins of Tel Dan include a crosscut through seven levels of settlement (Josh. 19:40–48) (Judges 20:1) (I Kings 12:25–30), p. 30.

Dead Sea: The salt lake at the mouth of the Jordan River, the lowest place (1,286 feet below sea level) on earth. It was part of the southern border of Israel when it was divided among the tribes (Josh. 15:5), p. 28.

Derbe: A city in southern Turkey, probably on the site of present-day Kerti Huyuk, Derbe was visited by

Derbe: (*continued*)
Paul and Barnabus and later revisited by Paul (Acts 14:6) (Acts 16:1) (Acts 20:4).

Dothan: A town in Israel fifteen miles north of Shechem. Today's Tel Dotha has archeological findings from 3000 B.C. Joseph's brothers cast him into a pit in Dothan and sold him into slavery (Gen. 37:3–36), p. 194.

Dura: The plain where King Nebuchadnezzar set up a golden image for all to worship. Its exact location is not known today, but it was near the city of Babylon (Dan. 3), p. 111.

Edom: The area south of the Dead Sea occupied by Esau's descendants. Two well-known Edomites were Job and King Herod (Gen. 32:3–21; 33:1–20) (Obad.).

Emmaus: Now called Amwas, it lies west of Jerusalem. Jesus appeared to two disciples on the road to Emmaus (Mark 16:12–13; Luke 24:13–35), p. 184.

Endor: South of Mt. Tabor, Endor was the home of a witch consulted by King Saul (I Sam. 28), p. 34.

Ephesus: Ephesus now lies in western Turkey. It is an important biblical and historical site and has been extensively excavated and restored. Among the buildings now visible are the temple of Diana and the theatre where Paul spoke. Tradition says that the Apostle John and the Virgin Mary spent their last years in Ephesus and were buried here. Paul's letter to the Ephesians was to the church at Ephesus, and it was one of Revelation's seven churches in Asia (Acts 19) (Acts 20:17–36) (Eph.) (Rev. 2:1–7), pp. 196, 209, 215, 240.

Esdraelon: See Armageddon and Jezreel.

Ethiopia: Called Cush in the Old Testament, Ethiopia was the land along the Nile from Aswan to Kartoum. Philip baptized an eunuch from Ethiopia (Acts 8:26–40), p. 192.

Forum of Appius: Here Paul was greeted by members of the church on his way to Rome. It was a station on the Appian Way (the Roman road from Rome to Brundisium) (Acts 28:15), p. 198.

Gadara: Probably Gerasa on the northeast shore of the Sea of Galilee. Here steep cliffs line the water's edge. Jesus commanded devils to enter a herd of Gadarene swine (Matt. 8:28–34; Mark 5:1–20; Luke 8:26–39), p. 144.

Galatia: Paul founded churches in this former Roman province in what is now central Turkey. Pisidia was a region of Galatia, and the Christians of Pisidian Antioch probably were the recipients of Paul's letter to the Galatians (Acts 16:6; 18:23) (Gal.).

Galilee: A region west, north, and south of the Sea of Galilee. Biblical sites in Galilee include Cana, Migdal, Nazareth, Mt. Hermon, Tiberias, Mount of Beatitudes, Capernaum, Jezreel Valley, and Megiddo. Galilee figures largely in stories of Jesus' ministry. See particularly (Matt. 4:18–25; 7:28–29; 8:14–15; Mark 1:16–31, 39; Luke 5:1–11; 4:31–39, 44; John 1—2:11; 21:1–14) (Luke 13:31–33) (Matt. 28:16–20), p. 213.

Galilee, Sea of: Located in the northeast of present-day Israel, the Sea of Galilee is often mentioned in the Gospels. It is also called the Sea of Tiberias, Chinnereth, or Gennesaret (Matt. 4:18–22; Mark 1:16–20; Luke 5:1–11) (John 21:1–14), pp. 136, 137, 169.

Gath: A city of old Philistia and the home of Goliath. David did not want Saul's death known in Gath. Its exact location is not known, but it could have been located at Tel es-Safi at the mouth of the valley of Elah (I Sam. 17:4) (II Sam. 1:17–27), p. 34.

Gaza: Samson pulled down the pillars of the house in this Philistine town which is now in southern Israel near the Mediterranean (Judges 16), p. 30.

Gehenna: The place south of Jerusalem known as the city's garbage dump and the Valley of Hinnom.

Gehenna is translated as "hell" in the New Testament (Matt. 5:30; 18:8–9; Mark 9:43–48).

Gerizim: The mountain where Moses called the nation to a new commitment to God is near the town of Nablus. According to Samaritan tradition, this is where Abraham offered Isaac as a sacrifice (Gen. 22:1–18) (Deut. 27:12).

Gethsemane: A garden on the Mount of Olives at Jerusalem. Ancient olive trees grow there today. Here, prior to his arrest, Jesus prayed while the disciples slept (Matt. 26:36–46; Mark 14:32–42; Luke 22:40–46) (Matt. 26:47–56; Mark 14:43–50; Luke 22:47–53; John 18:2–11), p. 180.

Gibeon: A city six miles northwest of Jerusalem, known today as el-Jib. Archeological remains include the pool of Gibeon with seventy-nine steps cut into the rock. The Gibeonites tricked Joshua into a treaty and saved their city. Here Solomon asked for wisdom (Josh. 9) (I Kings 3:3–15; II Chron. 1:7–12), p. 28, 37.

Gilead: A region east of the Jordan where strong trees grew that were noted for their medicinal balm. The prophet Elijah was from the region of Gilead (Jer. 7—8), p. 100.

Gilgal: The campsite near Jericho where the Israelites set up twelve stones (for the twelve tribes) after crossing the Jordan into Canaan (Josh. 3:11—4:20), p. 27.

Golgotha: Also known as Calvary and the Hill of the Skull, Golgotha was the place of Jesus' crucifixion. Two places in modern Jerusalem are associated with Golgotha. The most traditional is marked by the Church of the Holy Sepulchre. Gordon's Calvary is another favored location (Matt. 27:32–44; Mark 15:21–32; Luke 23:26–43; John 19:17–24), p. 182.

Gomorrah: A town believed to have been at the southern end of the Dead Sea, it is now under water. The Lord rained fire and brimstone on Sodom and Gomorrah (Gen. 18:16—19:26), pp. 9, 81.

Goshen: A region of Egypt in the eastern part of the Nile Delta. Here Joseph's father, Jacob, came to live, and the Israelites stayed from the time of Joseph until the Exodus (Gen. 42—45).

Haran: On the first stage of his journey to Canaan from Ur, Abraham journeyed to Haran. Later, he sent his servant to Haran (Nahor) to find a wife for his son Isaac, and there Jacob met Rachel at the well. Today spelled Harran, it lies in eastern Turkey (Gen. 27:41—28:5; 29:1–28), pp. 9, 26.

Hazor: Israel's largest archeological site, Hazor is north of the Sea of Galilee. Key battles against the Canaanites were fought here by Joshua, Deborah, and Barak (Josh. 2) (Judges 4), pp. 27, 28.

Hebron: The city of Hebron is twenty-four miles from Jerusalem. Today, the Cave of Machpelah, also known as the Tomb of the Patriarchs containing the tombs of Abraham, Isaac, Joseph, and their wives, is Hebron's main attraction. Abram dwelt by the oaks of Mamre at Hebron. Hebron was David's first capital and the place of Absalom's rebellion (Gen. 13—14:20) (II Sam. 15:13—19:8).

Hinnom: See *Gehenna.*

Hor: Tradition says that the mountain where Aaron died is Jebel Haran. It lies south of the Dead Sea and north of Petra (ancient capital of Edom, the rose-red city carved from the living rock). Other authorities prefer Jebel Madeirah (Num. 20:22–29), p. 20.

Horeb: See *Sinai.*

Iconium: Part of the old province of Galatia, now modern Konya in Turkey, it was visited by Barnabus and Paul (Acts 14:1–7), p. 194.

Israel: The land of Israel reached its greatest extension under Kings David and Solomon when it extended north to the Euphrates River and south below Mt. Sinai. Then it split in two and was called Judah in

Israel: (*continued*)
the south and Israel or Samaria in the north.

Jaffa: See *Joppa.*

Jericho: The excavations of Jericho are located six miles north of the Dead Sea (less than an hour's drive from Jerusalem). Here Rahab the harlot hid the Israelite spies, and Joshua and the Israelites had their first great victory. In Jericho Jesus found Zaccheus in the sycamore tree, and he healed blind Bartimaeus as he left the city. The story of the Good Samaritan takes place on the road between Jerusalem and Jericho (Josh. 2) (Josh. 6) (Luke 10:29–37) (Luke 19:1–10) (Matt. 20:29–34; Mark 10:46–52; Luke 18:35–43), pp. 27, 154, 165.

Jerusalem: The chief city of Israel, sacred to Jews, Christians, and Moslems, it is also called the City of David, the City of Zion, and the Holy City. It was the capital of Israel under David and Solomon and of the kingdom of Judah after the split (II Sam. 6; I Chron. 11:4–25; 12—16:7) Solomon built the temple on Mt. Moriah (I Kings 5—7; II Chron. 2—4) Jerusalem's defeat, exile and return (II Kings 24:10–16; 25:1–21; II Chron. 36:5–23; Ez. 1—10; Neh. 1—8; 12:27–47) Prophecies about Jerusalem (II Kings 18—20; 21; II Chron. 29—32) (Isa. 1—12) (Jer. 2—4; 9) (Jer. 39—40) (Lam. I) (Ezek. 5—6; 8) (Zeph. 3:1–7) (Zech. 9:9–12) Presentation of the infant Jesus in the temple (Luke 2:22–39) Wise men inquire of Herod (Matt. 2:1–12) Jesus as a boy stayed behind in the temple (Luke 2:40–52) Jesus entered Jerusalem on a colt and predicted its destruction (Matt. 21:1–11); Mark 11:1–10; Luke 19:28–38, 41–44; John 12:12–19) Fate of Jerusalem lamented by Jesus (Matt. 23:37–39; Luke 13:34–35) Jesus' death and resurrection (Matt. 26–28; Mark 14–16; Luke 22–24; John 12–20) The disciples returned to Jerusalem after the Ascension (Acts 1:12–14) Saul (Paul)

met with the disciples after his conversion (Acts 9:26–31) At a conference in Jerusalem, the apostles and elders agree to reach out to the Gentiles (Acts 15:1–35) Paul put in chains (Acts 21:15—23:22) Description of the new Jerusalem (Rev. 21). *See complete index listings.*

Jezreel: A town and a valley in northern Israel. Place of Naboth's vineyard and where Jezebel died. See also Armageddon (I Kings 21:1–16) (II Kings 9:30–37), p. 41.

Joppa: The harbor city of Jaffa is adjacent to Tel Aviv and built on the ruins of old Joppa. Local excavations are housed in the Archeological Museum. Here Jonah fled, Peter restored Tabitha to life and had his vision about clean and unclean animals. This site is memorialized by the Monastery of St. Peter (Jonah 1:1–15) (Acts 9:36–42; 10), pp. 120, 193.

Jordan River: The chief river of Israel, flowing through the entire country from its source at the northern border to its outlet in the Dead Sea. It was crossed by Joshua and the Israelites when they entered Canaan. Here Naaman washed seven times and was cured of leprosy. John baptized Jesus in the Jordan (see Bethabara) (Deut. 34:9; Josh. 1:1–9; 3:11–4) (II Kings 5) (Matt. 3:1–6; Mark 1:1–6; Luke 3:1–6; John 1:6–7) (Matt. 3:13–17; Mark 1:9–11; Luke 3:21–22; John 1:29–34), pp. 8, 27, 43, 135.

Judah: One of the original tribes of Israel, it occupied the territory between Jerusalem and Hebron. When the united kingdom split after Solomon's reign, Judah became the Southern kingdom, Samaria the Northern (I Kings 12—14; II Chron. 10—12) (II Kings 18—25; II Chron. 10—36), pp. 38, 44.

Judea: See *Judah.*

Kidron: The valley and brook (dry except after heavy rain) between Jerusalem and the Mount of Olives, it is known today as Wadi Sitti Maryam. Some say this was where Eze-kiel had his vision of the dry bones. David crossed the valley fleeing Ab-salom, and Jesus crossed it to Geth-semane (Ezek. 37) (II Sam. 15:23) (John 18:1), pp. 36, 106.

Laodicea: The ruins of Laodicea are near modern Denizli in western Tur-key. Paul's letter to the Colossians was also to be taken to the church at Laodicea, and Revelation described the church in Laodicea as "luke-warm" (Rev. 3:14–22), p. 241.

Lasea: Lasea was a small city on the southern coast of Crete. Its ruins are believed to be near Fair Havens. Paul passed by here on his way to Rome as a prisoner (Acts 27:7–12).

Lebanon: The country and mountain range north of Israel, famous for the cedars used in building the temple (I Kings 5:6) (Ezek. 17), pp. 38, 107.

Lystra: The mound of ancient Lystra and foundations of a small Byzantine church are visible today near Konya in Turkey. Lystra was Timothy's hometown and was visited by Barna-bus and Paul who were likened to gods after Paul had healed a cripple (Acts 13—14), p. 194.

Macedonia: Paul, in a dream, was asked to visit Macedonia, now an area in northern Greece. See also Philippi, Thessalonica, and Berea (Acts 16:9–15), p. 195.

Magdala: Today called el-Mejdel and located on the west shore of the Sea of Galilee, Magdala was the home of Mary Magdalene (Matt. 28:1–10; Mark 16:1–11; Luke 24:1–11; John 20:1–18), pp. 183, 184.

Magog: The land from which Gog came. A symbolic land for those who challenge the rule of God (Ezek. 38—39), p. 109.

Malta: An island sixty miles south of Sicily where Paul was shipwrecked on his way to Rome. St. Paul's Bay, the traditional place of the shipwreck, is the entrance to the city of Valetta (Acts 27:39—28:10), p. 198.

Mamre: See *Hebron.*

Mars' Hill: See *Athens.*

Megiddo: See Armageddon.

Melita: See *Malta.*

Midian: The Midianites lived in what is now northwest Saudi Arabia on the eastern shore of the Gulf of Aqa-bah. Moses fled to Midian after kill-ing an Egyptian. Later, Gideon led the Israelites in a successful battle against the Midianites (Ex. 2:11–15) (Judges 6:11–40; 7), p. 14.

Miletus: Miletus was visited by Paul. Its ruins, called Palatia, are near Ephesus in Turkey (Acts 20:13–38), p. 196.

Mitylene: The chief city of the island of Lesbos, off the east coast of Tur-key, Mitylene was visited by Paul on his trip from Ephesus to Jerusalem (Acts 20:14), p. 196.

Moab: Moses died in the land of Moab, a country east of the Dead Sea; it was also the home of Ruth (Deut. 34:5–12), p. 21.

Moriah: Traditionally the place where Abraham went to offer Isaac, Mt. Moriah is the site in Jerusalem where Solomon built the temple. It is now sheltered by the Muslin "Dome of the Rock" (Gen. 22:1–18) (I Kings 5—7; II Chron. 2—4), p. 38.

Mount of Beatitudes: The traditional site of the Sermon on the Mount on the northwest shore of the Sea of Galilee near Capernaum (Matt. 5:1–2), p. 138.

Mount of Olives: On the eastern slopes of Jerusalem, here Jesus wept over Jerusalem and went with his disciples to the Garden of Gethsem-ane (Matt. 26:30–35; Mark 14:26–31; Luke 22:31–34, 39; John 13:36–38) (Acts 1:12–14), p. 179.

Nain: Today called Nein, it is a small village in Galilee about five miles from Nazareth. Ruins of the old town are still visible. Here Jesus raised from death the son of the widow of Nain (Luke 7:11–17), p. 155.

Nazareth: The home of Joseph, Mary, and Jesus is today a city in northern Israel. Churches memorial-ize the sites where the angel Gabriel

Nazareth: (continued)
appeared to Mary, Joseph had his carpenter's shop, and the Holy Family worshiped (Luke 1:26–38) (Luke 2:1–7) (Matt. 2:13–15, 19–23) (John 1:43–51), pp. 132, 134, 137.

Neapolis: Now called Kavalla and in Greece, Neapolis was in Macedonia and was the port of Philippi (ten miles away) and the first place in Europe visited by Paul (Acts 16:11), p. 195.

Nebo: See *Abarim*.

Negev: The arid region in southern Israel that merges with Sinai. Abraham's wanderings took place here, and here Hagar was helped by an angel. From the Negev spies were sent into Canaan (Gen. 12:1–9; 13:1–3) (Gen. 16:1–15) (Gen. 21:9–21) (Num. 13—14:37), pp. 8, 9, 19.

Ninevah: Former capital of the Assyrian empire, Ninevah's ruins are across the Tigris River from modern Mosul in Iraq. Jonah was reluctant to prophesy against Ninevah's destruction and also relucatant to prophesy its salvation. Nahum and Zephaniah also prophesied against Ninevah (Jonah) (Nahum 2—3) (Zeph. 2:15), pp. 120, 121, 123, 124.

Olivet: See *Mount of Olives*.

Patara: A seaport town opposite the island of Rhodes, Patara was visited by Paul on his trip from Ephesus to Jerusalem. Patara is now the modern village of Gelemish in Turkey. Ruins of the old town remain (Acts 21:1), p. 196.

Patmos: An island in the Aegean Sea off the coast of Turkey, Patmos is where John had his vision and wrote the book of Revelation. The Monastery of St. John is located near the traditional cave of revelation (Rev. 1:9–11), p. 240.

Perga: A leading city of ancient Pamphylia, Perga was visited by Barnabus and Paul. The extensive ruins of Perga are near the modern village of Murtuna on the Turkish coast. There is an acropolis and a walled lower city with a magnificent city gate (Acts 13:13–14), p. 194.

Pergamum or **Pergamos:** Now Bergama in western Turkey, Pergamum is fifteen miles inland from the Aegean. It was probably the most spectacular city of Asia Minor and was one of Revelation's seven churches in Asia. Much of the old city may be seen today (Rev. 2:12–17), p. 241.

Persia: In Old Testament times the Persian Empire, at its height, stretched from India to the Aegean Sea and to Egypt. In modern times it is usually considered synonymous with Iran. King Cyrus of Persia let the Israelites return from exile and rebuild Jerusalem and the temple. This work was completed under King Darius. Esther was the Queen of Persia (II Chron. 6:22–23; Ez. 1—10; Neh. 1—2; 7:6–73; Isa. 44:26–28; 45:1–13; Jer. 37—39) (Est. 1–2:18), pp. 45, 112.

Philadelphia: One of the seven churches in Revelation, Philadelphia is now the town of Alasehir in Turkey. It was, and still is, a small town in good farming country. Some ruins are visible (Rev. 3:7–13), p. 241.

Philippi: A former Roman colony in northern Greece, Philippi was the first place in Europe where Paul established a church. He later visited here on his trip from Ephesus to Jerusalem and sent the church his letter to the Philippians (Acts 16:12–40) (Acts 20:6) (Phil.), pp. 195, 196, 218.

Philistia: The area in Israel between Joppa and Gaza along the Mediterranean that became part of Israel under King David. Samson fought the Philistines. The Philistines captured and returned the Ark of the Covenant. David killed the Philistine giant, Goliath (Judges 15—16) (I Sam. 4—7) (I Sam. 17), pp. 30, 32, 33.

Phoenicia: A country on the east coast of the Mediterranean roughly equivalent to modern Lebanon. Its chief towns were Tyre and Sidon. Here Jesus healed the Greek woman's daughter. Paul passed through Phoenicia, preaching, on his way to the conference at Jerusalem

(Matt. 15:21–28; Mark 7:24–30)
(Acts 15:3), pp. 159, 194.

Pisgah: See *Abarim.*

Pithom: A treasure city built by the children of Israel for Pharoah, the exact site of Pithom has not been established. It was probably either Tel el-Ratabah or Tel el-Maskhutah in the east delta of Egypt (Ex. 1:1–14), p. 13.

Ptolemais: Present day Acre (Akko) on the coast of northern Israel, Ptolemais was visited by Paul on his trip from Ephesus to Jerusalem. Excavations and the old walled city may be seen today (Acts 21:7), p. 196.

Puteoli: Modern Pozzuoli in Italy, Puteoli is on the Bay of Naples. It was visited by Paul on his way to Rome. Ruins include the market hall, temple of Augustus, and an amphitheatre (Acts 28:13), p. 198.

Raamses: A treasure city of Pharoah built by the children of Israel. Scholars do not agree on the precise location of this royal residence city. It was somewhere in the Egyptian Delta (Ex. 1:1–14), p. 13.

Ramah: There are several Ramahs in Israel. Samuel's Ramah is probably modern Rentis. Rachel wept for her children in the Ramah now known as er-Ram, a village five miles north of Jerusalem (I Sam. 1:19) (Jer. 31:15) (Matt. 2:18), p. 102.

Ramoth-gilead: Ramoth-gilead is now Tel-Ramith near the Syrian border of Israel. Here Micaiah prophesied King Ahab would die. Ahab died in battle here, and Jehu was anointed king (I Kings 22:1–40; II Chron. 18) (II Kings 9), p. 41.

Red Sea: Moses parted the water of the Red Sea for the Israelites to escape Pharoah. The Red Sea crossing could have been at the southern extension of Lake Menzaleh (Ex. 14), p. 16.

Rhegium: Modern Reggio is on the southern tip of Italy. Paul stopped here on his way to Rome (Acts 28:13), p. 198.

Rhodes: A Greek island and city in the Aegean Sea, Rhodes was visited by Paul on his trip from Ephesus to Jerusalem. The city built here during the Crusades still exists (Acts 21:1), p. 196.

Rome: Paul was a prisoner in Rome for two years and, according to tradition, both Peter and Paul were martyred in Rome. Paul wrote a letter to "all that be in Rome" and to Philemon from a Roman prison (Rom.) (Philem.), pp. 198, 199.

Samaria: Samaria was both a city and a region. The city was the capital of the Northern Kingdom when Israel divided into two kingdoms. Today the city is known as Sebaste and is about forty miles north of Jerusalem. Extensive excavations include the ruins of Ahab's palace, examples of Israelite masonry, temples, walls, streets, and tombs. Here Elisha cured Naaman, the good Samaritan had compassion, and Jesus asked a Samaritan woman for water (II Kings 5; 8:16–17) (Luke 10:29–37) (John 4:5–42), p. 44.

Samos: An island and a city in the Aegean Sea, just off the coast of Turkey near Ephesus. Samos was visited by Paul on his trip from Ephesus to Jerusalem (Acts 20:15), p. 196.

Sardis: One of the seven churches in Revelation, Sardis was the capital of the ancient kingdom of Lydia in what is now western Turkey. One may still see the temple of Artemis, the gymnasium, and an early synagogue (Rev. 3:1–6), p. 241.

Sharon: The coastal plain from Joppa to south of Mt. Carmel. The rose of Sharon in the Song of Solomon is a type of crocus (Song 2:1).

Sheba: Sheba was a kingdom in Arabia whose queen visited King Solomon (I Kings 10:1–23; II Chron. 9:1–22), p. 38.

Shechem: Known today as Nablus, Shechem is well excavated. Besides a temple, walls, etc., one can see Jacob's well where Jesus talked with the Samaritan woman. Abraham passed through Shechem when he entered Canaan, and here Jacob's brothers pastured sheep (Gen. 12:6)

Shechem: (continued)
(Gen. 37:3–36) (I Kings 12) (John 4:5–42), pp. 7, 10, 166.

Shiloh: Today known as Seilun, nine miles north of Bethel, Shiloh was the town where Eli was priest, Hannah made her vow, and Samuel spent his youth (I Sam. 1—3), pp. 31–32.

Shunem: Now the town of Solem, it overlooks the Valley of Jezreel where Elisha raised the Shunammite woman's son to life (II Kings 4:8–37).

Sidon: A Phoenician seaport city between Tyre and Beirut, Sidon is now Saida in Lebanon. Sidon was the home of Jezebel and was prophesied against by Ezekiel. Jesus taught in Sidon, and Paul sailed by the port on his way to Rome (Ezek. 25—32) (Matt. 15:21–28); Mark 7:24–30) (Acts 27:3), pp. 108, 198.

Siloam: A pool in Jerusalem and, with aqueducts, part of the biblical city's water works. The blind man washed in the pool of Siloam and could see (John 9:1–41), p. 168.

Sinai: The mountain where Moses received the Ten Commandments. Thirteen mountains claim to be the Old Testament Sinai. Tradition locates it at the southern tip of the Sinai peninsula, and most likely it is Jebel Musa, with Ras-es-Safsaf giving it good competition. The Monastery of St. Catherine is on Jebel Musa (Ex. 19—34), pp. 17, 18.

Smyrna: Modern Izmir in Turkey, Smyrna was one of the seven churches of Asia in Revelation. Smyrna has been a busy commercial center from biblical times to the present. The Roman forum and aqueducts are still standing (Rev. 2:8–11), p. 241.

Sodom: The Lord rained fire and brimstone on Sodom. No trace of the city can be found today, which may be under the waters of the southern end of the Dead Sea. Tradition says Lot's wife turned into a pillar of salt when she turned back to see Sodom burn and connects this story with Jebel Usdum (Mt. of Sodom), a mountain of crystalline salt (Gen. 18:16—19:26), p. 241.

Succoth: Succoth was a city north of the Dead Sea on the east side of the Jordan River. Today the site of Succoth has been identified as Tel Deir'Alla. Jacob built a house and booths in Succoth after reconciling with his brother Esau, and Jews still commemorate this today (Gen. 32:3–21; 33:1–20), p. 11.

Sychar: See *Shechem*.

Syracuse: A city on the east coast of the island of Sicily where Paul stayed on his way to Rome. The ruins of ancient Syracuse include the temple of Athena (which became a Christian cathedral in the seventh century), the Greek theatre, the amphitheatre, and Christian catacombs of the third and fourth centuries (Acts 28:12), p. 198.

Syria: In the Old Testament, Syria was the Aramean land whose capital was Damascus. In the New Testament it was part of the same Roman province as Palestine. Naaman, captain to the King of Syria, was cured of leprosy. Paul visited churches in Syria (II Kings 5) (Acts 13—16:5), p. 195.

Tabgha: The traditional site of the miracle of the feeding of the five thousand, Tabgha is near Capernaum (Matt. 14:13–21; Mark 6:39–44; Luke 9:10–17; John 6:1–14), p. 158.

Tabor: A mountain seven miles east of Nazareth, it is now called Jebel-el-Tur. Here Barak gathered his forces to fight Sisera. Traditionally known as the mountain where the Transfiguration occurred, it is marked by a Greek monastery and a Franciscan basilica (Judges 4) (Matt. 17:1–8; Mark 9:2–8; Luke 9:28–36), pp. 28, 161.

Tarshish: Tarshish was a seaport, probably on the coast of Spain near Gibraltar. Whatever its original place, it came to symbolize a distant paradise. The most famous ships of early Bible days were the ships of Tarshish. Jonah boarded a ship to Tarshish (Isa. 2:10–22) (Isa. 23:14) (Jonah 1:1–15), pp. 82, 87, 120.

Tarsus: The hometown of Paul, Tarsus is located in what is now southern Turkey (Acts 22:3), p. 197.

Tekoa: Known today as Tequ, the unexcavated ruins of Tekoa are five miles south of Bethlehem. The prophet Amos was from Tekoa (Amos 1:1).

Thessalonica: The city visited by Paul when he took the Gospel to Europe is modern Thessalonika in Greece. The Thessalonians were recipients of letters from Paul. Parts of the old city wall and the Via Egnatia (probably the road traveled by Paul) are still standing (Acts 17:1–9) (I & II Thess.).

Three Taverns: A station on the Appian Way, thirty miles from Rome, which was visited by Paul on his way to that city (Acts 28:15), pp. 195, 221.

Thyatira: Nothing remains of ancient Thyatira (now Akhisar) in western Turkey. It was the home of Lydia, seller of purple, who met Paul in Greece and became a Christian. Thyatira was one of the seven churches of Revelation (Acts 16:14) (Rev. 2:18–29), pp. 195, 241.

Troas: A port in northwest Turkey, south of ancient Troy, Troas was visited twice by Paul (Acts 16:8–11) (Acts 20:5–12), pp. 195, 196.

Trogylium: A promontory on the west shore of Turkey near the island of Samos. "St. Paul's Bay" is an anchorage just outside Trogylium. Here Paul stopped on his journey from Ephesus to Jerusalem (Acts 20:15), p. 196.

Tyre: Tyre today is a small town called Sur, twenty-five miles south of Sidon in Lebanon. It was the home of King Hiram who provided the cedars of Lebanon for Solomon to build the temple. Jezebel was the daughter of the king of Tyre and Sidon. Tyre was prophesied against by Isaiah and Ezekial and visited both by Paul and Jesus (I Kings 5—7; II Chron. 3—4) (I Kings 16:28—17:1) (Isa. 23:14) (Ezek. 25–32) (Matt. 15:21–28; Mark 7:24–30) (Acts 21:3–7), pp. 38, 87, 108, 196.

Ur: Abraham's home city is known today as al-Muqayyer in Iraq. Extensive ruins include private houses and a large ziggurat (Gen. 15:7), p. 8.

Zion: Originally the fortified hill of pre-Israelite Jerusalem, Zion became a symbol for Jerusalem as the city of God's temple. Isaiah, Joel, and Amos prophesied about Zion. It is identified as the heavenly Jerusalem and the place for those who follow the Lamb (Isa. 3:16–26) (Isa. 51:1–11) (Joel 2:1–11) (Amos 1—2) (Heb. 12:22) (Rev. 14), pp. 82, 93, 100, 116, 118, 122, 125, 126.

Key Word Index

Aaron: A. and Hur held up Moses' hands, p. 17, (Ex. 17:11, 12)

A. died on top of Mount Hor, p. 20, (Num. 20:28)

A. made a golden calf, p. 18, (Ex. 32:3–4)

A.'s rod became a serpent, p. 15, (Ex. 7:10)

A. shall be gathered unto his people, p. 20, (Num. 20:24)

A. shall sacrifice, p. 19, (Lev. 16:5)

consecration of A. and his sons, p. 19, (Lev. 8—10)

Moses and A. at Mount Hor, p. 20, (Num. 20:23)

the death of A., p. 20, (Num. 20:22–29)

Abarim: God told Moses to go to Mount A., p. 20, (Num. 27:12)

Abba: crying A., Father, p. 214, (Gal. 4:6)

whereby we cry: A., Father, p. 201, (Rom. 8:15)

Abednego: Belteshazzar and Shadrach, Meshach and A., p. 110, (Dan. 1:7)

Abel: Cain rose up against A., p. 5, (Gen. 4:8)

Where is A. your brother?, p. 5, (Gen. 4:9)

Abide: a. in me and I in you, p. 178, (Jn. 15:4)

A. with us, p. 184, (Lk. 24:29)

Abomination: incense is an a., p. 81, (Isa. 1:13)

when ye see the a. of desolation, p. 173, (Matt. 24:15; Mk. 13:14; cf. Lk. 21:20)

Abominations: the wicked a. that they do there, p. 107, (Ezek. 8:9)

Abraham: (See Abram)

A. beheld a ram in the thicket, p. 9, (Gen. 22:13)

A. bound his son, p. 9, (Gen. 22:9)

A., father of many nations, p. 8, (Gen. 17:5)

A. laughed for they were old, p. 8, (Gen. 17:17)

A. sent Hagar and Ishmael away, p. 9, (Gen. 21:9–21)

before A. was, I am, p. 168, (Jn. 8:58)

carried by angels into A.'s bosom, p. 153, (Lk. 16:22)

Sarah bare A. a son, p. 9, (Gen. 21:7)

the God of A., Isaac and Jacob, p. 171, (Matt. 22:32; Mk. 12:26; Lk. 20:37)

Abram: (See also Abraham)

A. and Lot, p. 7, (Gen. 13—14:20)

A. dwelled in the land of Canaan, p. 8, (Gen. 13:12)

A. dwelt by the oaks of Mamre, p. 8, (Gen. 13:18)

A. pretended Sarai was his sister, p. 7, (Gen. 12:13)

A. rescued Lot, p. 8, (Gen. 14:16)

A.'s vision and covenant, p. 8, (Gen. 15)

A. went down into Egypt, p. 7. (Gen. 12:10)

call of A., p. 7, (Gen. 12:1–8)

fear not A., I am thy shield, p. 8, (Gen. 15:1)

God's covenant with A., p. 8, (Gen. 17:1–19)

Melchizedek . . . blessed A., p. 8, (Gen. 14:19)

Sarai bare A. no children, p. 8, (Gen. 16:1)

Sarai gave Hagar her maid to A., p. 8, (Gen. 16:1–2)

Absalom: A.'s head caught fast in an oak, p. 36, (II Sam. 18:9)

A. stole the hearts, p. 36, (II Sam. 15:13)

A.'s treachery and death, p. 36, (II Sam. 15:13—19:8)

David was forced to fight A., p. 36, (II Sam. 15:13—19:8)

deal gently . . with A., p. 36, (II Sam. 18:5)

Joab . . . slew A., p. 36, (II Sam. 18:14–15)

O A., my son, my son, p. 36, (II Sam. 18:33)

Absent: a. from the body and present with the Lord, p. 211, (II Cor. 5:8)

a. in body but present in spirit, p. 206, (I Cor. 5:3)

a. one from another, p. 11, (Gen. 31:49)

though I be a. in the flesh, p. 220, (Col. 2:5)

Abstain: a. from fleshy lusts, p. 236, (I. Pet. 2:11)

Abundantly: and have [life] more a., p. 168, (Jn. 10:10)

According: be it unto me a. to thy word, p. 132, (Lk. 1:38)

Acquainted: and a. with grief, p. 94, (Isa. 53:3)

Adam: a woman from A.'s rib, p. 4, (Gen. 2:22)

A. gave names to all the . . . beasts, p. 5, (Gen. 2:20)

as in A. all die, p. 209, (I Cor. 15:22)

Second account of the creation of A. and Eve, p. 4, (Gen. 2:7–25)

temptation and disobedience of A. and Eve, p. 5, (Gen. 3:1–6)

the creation of A. and Eve, p. 4, (Gen. 1:26–31)

Added: all these things shall be a., p. 141, (Matt. 6:33; Lk. 12:31)

Adder: the deaf a. that stoppeth her ear, p. 61, (Ps. 58:4)

tread upon the lion and a., p. 63, (Ps. 91:13)

Adoption: receive the a. of sons, p. 214, (Gal. 4:5)

you have received the Spirit of a., p. 201, (Rom. 8:15)

Adultery: and marrieth another committeth a., p. 139, (Matt. 5:32; 19:9: Mark 10:11–12; Luke 16:18)

hath committed a. . . . in his heart, p. 139, (Matt. 5:28)

shall not commit a., p. 139, (Matt. 5:27)

thou shalt not commit a., p. 18, (Ex. 20:14)

when I had fed them they then committed a., p. 99, (Jer. 5:7)

woman taken in a., p. 167, (Jn. 8:3)

Adversary: an a. there shall be round about the land, p. 118, (Amos 3:11)

Advocate: if any man sin, we have an a., p. 238, (I John 2:1)

Affection: set your a. on things above, p. 220, (Col. 3:2)

Affectioned: be kindly a. one to another, p. 203, (Rom. 12:10)

Afflict: he doth not a. willingly, p. 105, (Lam. 3:33)

ye shall a. your souls, p. 22, (Lev. 23:27; Num. 29:7)

Afflicted: deliver you up to be a., p.

173, (Matt. 24:9; Mk. 13:9; Lk. 21:12)

I will have an a. and poor people, p. 125, (Zeph. 3:12)

in all their affliction he was a., p. 96, (Isa. 63:9)

a. by the rod of his wrath, p. 104, (Lam. 3:1)

bread of adversity, and water of a., p. 89, (Isa. 30:20)

feed him with bread of a., p. 41, (I Kg. 22:27; II Chr. 18:26)

in all their a., p. 96, (Isa. 63:9)

our light a. worketh . . . glory, p. 211, (II Cor. 4:17)

see thou mine a., p. 51, (Job 10:15)

the a. of my people, p. 14, (Ex. 3:7)

Afraid: a. and beginning to sink, p. 158, (Matt. 14:30)

a. to look upon God, p. 14, (Ex 3:6)

be not a., p. 27, (Josh. 1:9)

be not a. of the words, p. 44, (I Kg. 19:6)

be not a. of their words, p. 106, (Ezek. 2:6)

I have heard thy speech and was a., p. 124, (Hab. 3:2)

I was a., and hid my talent, p. 175, (Matt. 25:25; cf. Lk. 19:20)

it is I: be not a., p. 158, (Matt. 14:27; Mk. 6:50; Jn. 6:20)

none shall make them a., p. 122, (Micah 4:4)

not be a. for the terror by night, p. 63, (Ps. 91:5)

they were sore a., p. 133, (Lk. 2:9)

ungodly men made me a., p. 56, (Ps. 18:4)

Against: I have somewhat a. thee, p. 240, (Rev. 2:4)

Age: in the flower of their a., p. 31, (I Sam. 2:33)

thine a. shall be clearer than noonday, p. 51, (Job 11:17)

Agrippa: A.: . . . persuadest me to be a Christian, p. 197, (Acts 26:28)

Ahab: A. and Jezebel worshipped Baal, p. 39, (I Kg. 16:31)

A.: Give me thy vineyard, p. 41, (I Kg. 21:2)

A. King of Israel, p. 39, (I Kg. 16:28—17:1)

A. sent Israel and the prophets of Baal . . . , p. 40, (I Kg. 18:20)

A. took possession of the vineyard, p. 41, (I Kg. 21:16)

all the house of A. . . . were slain, p. 43, (II Kg. 10:25)

Elijah prophesies to A., p. 41, (I Kg. 21:17-25)

not like unto A. for wickedness, p. 41, (I Kg. 21:25)

ran before A., p. 41, (I Kg. 18:46)

Ahaziah: King A. and Elijah, p. 42, (I Kg. 22:51; II Kg. 1; II Chron. 22:1-9)

Ai: Israelites conquered the kingdom of A., p. 28, (Josh. 7—8)

Alabaster: a. box of ointment, p. 176, (Matt. 26:7; Mk. 14:3)

with an a. box of ointment, p. 155, (Lk. 7:37)

Alarm: sound an a. in my holy mountain, p. 116, (Joel 2:1)

Alive: I am a. for evermore, p. 240, (Rev. 1:18)

while the child was yet a., p. 36, (II Sam. 12:22)

All: a. that I have is thine, p. 152, (Lk. 15:31)

a. things are of God, p. 211, (II Cor. 5:18)

a. things come alike to a., p. 76, (Ec. 9:2)

a. things come of thee, p. 37, (I Chr. 29:14)

a. things to all men, p. 207, (I Cor. 9:22)

I will draw a. men to me, p. 176, (Jn. 12:32)

Almighty: I sit any pleasure to the A., p. 53, (Job 22:3)

Alms: when you give a., p. 140, (Matt. 6:2)

Alone: that the man should be a., p. 4, (Gen. 2:18)

trodden the winepress a., p. 96, (Isa. 63:3)

Alpha: I am A. and Omega, p. 247, (Rev. 22:13)

I am A. and Omega, the beginning and the end, p. 240, (Rev. 1:8)

Altar: Gideon destroyed the a. of Baal, p. 29, (Jg. 6:25,27)

laid him on the a., p. 9, (Gen. 22:9)

leave thy gift before the a., p. 139, (Matt. 5:24)

Noah builded an a., p. 6, (Gen. 8:20)

weep between the porch and the a., p. 117, (Joel 2:17)

Amalek: Joshua fought with A., p. 17, (Ex. 17:8-16)

Amazed: they were all a., p. 144, (Mk. 2:12; Lk. 5:26)

Ambassador: I am an a. in bonds, p. 218, (Eph. 6:20)

Ambassadors: we are a. for Christ, p. 211, (II Cor. 5:20)

Amelekite: an A. took Saul's crown to David, p. 34, (II Sam. 1:10)

Amend: a. your ways and your doings, p. 100, (Jer. 7:3)

Amiss: receive not, because you ask a., p. 234, (Jas. 4:3)

Ammonites: the A. came against Jehoshaphat, p. 42, (II Chr. 20:1)

Amorite: the A. kings were vanquished, p. 28, (Josh. 10:12-43)

Ananias: A. and Sapphira, p. 190, (Acts 5:1-11)

A. . . . . putting his hands on him, p. 193, (Acts 9:17)

Saul and A., p. 192, (Acts 9:10-18)

Anchor: an a. of the soul, sure and steadfast, p. 230, (Heb. 6:19)

Ancient: the A. of days did sit, p. 112, (Dan. 7:9)

with the a. is wisdom, p. 52, (Job 12:12)

Andrew: A., his brother, p. 136, (Matt. 4:18; Mk. 1:16)

one who heard John speak was A., p. 136, (Jn. 1:40)

Angel: a. appeared to Manoah's wife, p. 30, (Jg. 13:2-3)

an a.: Fear not Paul, p. 198, (Acts 27:23-24)

An a. of God came to Cornelius, p. 193, (Acts 10:3)

an a. of the Lord opened, p. 191, (Acts 5:19)

a., having the seal of God, p. 243, (Rev. 7:2)

a. of the Lord came to Gideon, p. 29, (Jg. 6:11)

Jacob wrestles with an a., p. 11, (Gen. 32:24)

Angel: (continued)

my God hath sent his a. . . . , p.
112, (Dan. 6:22)

Peter freed from prison by an a., p.
194, (Acts 12:1–19)

the a. . . . appeared to Joseph, p.
134, (Matt. 2:13)

the a. Gabriel, p. 131, (Lk. 1:11, 19)

the a. of his presence, p. 96, (Isa.
63:9)

the a. of the Lord came upon them,
p. 137, (Lk. 2:9)

the a. said: . . . I know you seek
Jesus, p. 183, (Matt. 28:5; Mk.
16:6)

the ass saw the a. of the Lord, p. 20,
(Num. 22:23)

transformed into an a. of light, p.
212, (II Cor. 11:14)

Angels: a little lower than the a., p.
56, (Ps. 8:5)

a little lower than the a., p. 228,
(Heb. 2:7,9)

a. with a great sound of a trumpet,
p. 173, (Matt. 24:31)

carried by a. into Abraham's bosom,
p. 153, (Lk. 16:22)

four a. on the four corners, p. 243,
(Rev. 7:1)

his a. charge over thee, p. 63, (Ps.
91:11)

Michael and his a. fought the
dragon, p. 244, (Rev. 12:7)

praise ye him, all his a., p. 68, (Ps.
148:2)

seen of a., preached unto Gentiles, p.
225, (I Tim. 3:16)

seven a. . . . having the seven
plagues, p. 245, (Rev. 15:6)

seven a. sounding seven trumpets, p.
244, (Rev. 8:6)

some have entertained a. unawares,
p. 232, (Heb. 13:2)

who makest him a. spirits, p. 228,
(Heb. 1:7)

who maketh his a. spirits, p. 65, (Ps.
104:4)

Anger: a. and reconciliation, p. 139,
(Matt. 5:21–26)

God's a. was kindled, p. 20, (Num.
22:22)

gracious and merciful, slow to a., p.
46, (Neh. 9:17)

his a. is not turned away, p. 84, (Isa.
9:12, 17, 21; 10:4)

merciful and gracious, slow to a., p.
64, (Ps. 103:8)

Moses' a. waxed hot, p. 18, (Ex.
32:19)

O. Assyrian, the rod of mine a., p.
84, (Isa. 10:5)

saved David from Saul's a., p. 34, (I
Sam. 19—20)

slow to a., p. 117, (Joel 2:13)

the Lord is slow to a., p. 12, (Nahum
1:3)

who can abide the fierceness of his
a.?, p. 122, (Nahum 1:6)

Angry: be ye a. and sin not, p. 217,
(Eph. 4:26)

doest thou well to be a.?, p. 121, (Jonah 4:4)

it displeased Jonah and he was a., p.
121, (Jonah 4:1)

the elder son was a., p. 152, (Lk.
15:28)

whosoever is a. with his brother, p.
139, (Matt. 5:22)

Anna: A., a prophetess, gave thanks,
p. 133, (Lk. 2:36, 38)

Annunciation: the a., p. 131, (Lk.
1:26–38)

Anoint: a. thine head and wash thy
face, p. 141, (Matt. 6:17)

Anointed: Zadok the priest a. Solomon, p. 37, (I Kg 1:39)

Anointing: the a. at Bethany, p. 176,
(Matt. 26:6–13; Mk. 14:3–9; cf.
Lk. 7:36–50; Jn. 12:1–8)

the a. of Solomon, p. 37, (I Kg. 1–
2:12; I Chr. 29:22–25)

Answer: before they call, I will a., p.
96, (Isa. 65:24)

Ant: to the a., thou sluggard, p. 69,
(Prov. 6:6)

Antichrist: a. that denieth the Father,
p. 238, (I John 2:22)

Apes: ivory, a. and peacocks, p. 38, (I
Kg. 10:22; II Chr. 9:21)

Apocalypse: four horsemen of the a.,
p. 243, (Rev. 6)

the a., p. 172, (Matt. 24:3–36; Mk.
13:3–57; Lk. 21:7–36)

Apollos: I have planted, A. watered,
p. 205, (I Cor. 3:6)

Apostasy: Solomon's a., p. 39, (I Kg.
11:1–13)

Apostle: (see also Disciple) Paul, an a.
not of men, p. 213, (Gal. 1:1)

Apostles: built upon the foundation

of the a. . . . , p. 260, (Eph. 2:20)

by the hands of the a., p. 190, (Acts 5:12)

Peter and the other a., p. 191, (Acts 5:29)

some a., some prophets . . . , p. 216, (Eph. 4:11)

the a. and elders came together, p. 194, (Acts 15:6)

the a. and elders sent letters, p. 195, (Acts 15:23)

the a. in prison, p. 190, (Acts 5:12–18)

the names of the twelve a., p. 146, (Matt. 10:2–4; Mk. 3:16–19; Lk. 6:13–16)

with great power gave the a., p. 190, (Acts 4:33)

Appear: to a. in the presence of God for us, p. 230, (Heb. 9:24)

Appearance: man looks on outward a., p. 33, (I Sam. 16:7)

Appius: Paul stops at Forum of A., p. 198, (Acts 28:15)

Apple: as the a. tree, p. 77, (Song 2:3)

keep me as the a. of the eye, p. 56, (Ps. 17:8)

the a. of his eye, p. 21, (Deut. 32:10)

Apples: comfort me with a., p. 77, (Song 2:5)

Like a. of gold, p. 73, (Prov. 25:11)

Aprons: and made a., p. 5, (Gen. 3:7)

Ararat: Ark rested on Mount A., p. 6, (Gen. 8:4)

Archangel: with the voice of the a., p. 222, (I Th. 4:16)

Argue: Paul and Barnabus a., p. 195, (Acts 15:36–41)

Arise: A., and take up thy bed, p. 144, (Mk. 2:9, 11; Lk. 5:24)

when I fall, I shall a., p. 122, (Micah 7:8)

Ark: an a. of bulrushes, p. 13, (Ex. 2:3)

an a. of gopher wood, p. 6, (Gen. 6:14)

a . . . captured by the Philistines, p. 32, (I Sam. 4—7)

a. of the covenant was brought to the temple, p. 38, (I Kg. 8:1–13; II Chr. 5:2—6:11)

A. rested on Mount Ararat, p. 6, (Gen. 8:4)

behold the a. of the covenant, p. 27, (Josh. 3:11)

constructed the a. and the tabernacle, p. 18, (Ex. 35:10–12)

David brought the a. of God into the city, p. 35, (II Sam. 6:12)

Moses put the testimony into the a., p. 18, (Ex. 40:20)

Noah's a., p. 6, (Gen. 6:14–22)

put the a. into the tabernacle, p. 18, (Ex. 40:21)

returned the a. to Israel, p. 32, (I Sam. 6:21)

the a. and the tabernacle, p. 18, (Ex. 35:4–40)

the a. of God is taken, p. 32, (I Sam. 4:22)

You shall come into the a., p. 6, (Gen. 6:18)

Armageddon: gathered them into a place called A., p. 246, (Rev. 16:16)

Armor: let us put on the a. of light, p. 204, (Rom. 13:12)

put on the whole a. of God, p. 218, (Eph. 6:11)

Arms: the everlasting a., p. 21, (Deut. 33:27)

Army: terrible as an a. with banners, p. 78, (Song 6:10)

Arrest: the a. of Jesus, p. 180, (Matt. 26:47–56; Mk. 14:43–52; Lk. 22:47–53; Jn. 18:2–11)

Arrested: would have a. him, p. 160, (Jn. 7:44)

Ascension: after Jesus' a., p. 189, (Acts 1:12–14)

the a., p. 186, (Mk. 16:19; Lk. 24:51; Acts 1:1–14)

Ashamed: workman that need not be a., p. 226, (II Tim. 2:15)

Ashes: give them beauty for a., p. 95, (Isa. 61:3)

put on sackcloth with a., p. 46, (Est. 4:1)

Asia: the Jews of A., p. 197, (Acts 21:27)

Ask: a. and it shall be given you, p. 142, (Matt. 7:7; Lk. 11:9)

a. and ye shall receive, p. 179, (Jn. 16:24)

a. of me whatsoever thou wilt, p. 158, (Matt. 14:7; Mk. 6:22–23)

whatsoever ye a. in my name, p. 178, (Jn. 14:13–14)

Asleep: Etuychus fell a., p. 196, (Acts 20:9)

Asp: child shall play on the hole of the a., p. 85, (Isa. 11:8)

Ass: Balaam's a., p. 20, (Num. 22:21–35)

Balaam saddled his a., p. 20, (Num. 22:21)

lowly and riding upon an a., p. 126, (Zech. 9:9)

the a. saw the angel of the Lord, p. 20, (Num. 22:23)

the Lord opened the mouth of the a., p. 20, (Num. 22:28)

with the jawbone of an a., p. 30, (Jg. 15:16)

Assembled: a. with one accord, p. 195, (Acts 15:25)

Assos: Paul travels via A., p. 196, (Acts 20:13)

Assyria: deliver thee from the king of A., p. 91, (Isa. 38:6)

punished the king of A., p. 103, (Jer. 50:18)

Samaria falls to A., p. 44, (II Kg. 17)

the king of A. hath devoured him, p. 103, (Jer. 50:17)

the kings of A. have laid waste, p. 90, (Isa. 37:18)

Assyrian: A. emissaries harangued the people, p. 44, (II Kg. 18:17–37)

I will break the A., p. 86, (Isa. 14:25)

O A., the rod of mine anger, p. 84, (Isa. 10:5)

Assyrians: the downfall of the A., p. 86, (Isa. 14:25)

Astonishment: become an a., a proverb, p. 23, (Deut. 28:37)

Athaliah: A. destroyed all the royal family, p. 43, (II Kg. 11:1; II Chr. 22:10)

A., Queen of Judah, p. 43, (II Kg. 11:1–20; II Chr. 22:10—23:21)

Queen A. was slain, p. 43, (II Kg. 11:20; II Chr. 23:21)

Athens: Paul at A., p. 196, (Acts 17:16–34)

Paul visits A., p. 195, (Acts 17:15)

ye men of A., p. 196, (Acts 17:22)

Atonement: a day of a., p. 22, (Lev. 23:27; cf. Num. 29:11)

a. for the iniquities of Israel, p. 19, (Lev. 16:10, 21)

the day of a., p. 19, (Lev. 23:27)

Author: the a. and finisher of our faith, p. 231, (Heb. 12:2)

Authority: for all that are in a., p. 224, (I Tim. 2:2)

neither tell I you by what a., p. 170, (Matt. 21:27; Mk. 11:33; Lk. 20:8)

priests: Who gave thee a.?, p. 170, (Matt. 21:23; Mk. 11:28; Lk. 20:2)

taught them as one that had a., p. 137, (Matt. 7:29; Mk. 1:22; cf. Lk. 4:32)

the a. of Jesus, p. 170, (Matt. 21:23–27; Mk. 11:27–33; Lk. 20:1–8)

Avenge: a. his own who cry day and night, p. 154, (Lk. 18:7)

a. me of mine adversary, p. 154, (Lk. 18:3)

Awake: a. and sing, p. 88, (Isa. 26:19)

many that sleep shall a., p. 114, (Dan. 12:2)

Axe-head: the floating a., p. 43, (II Kg. 6)

Azariah: Daniel, Hananiah, Mishael and A., p. 110, (Dan. 1:6)

Uzziah (A.) the leper king, p. 44, (II Kg. 15:1–7; II Chr. 26)

Baal: Ahab and Jezebel worshipped B., p. 39, (I Kg. 16:31)

Elijah and the prophets of B., p. 40, (I Kg. 18:17–40)

Gideon destroyed the altar of B., p. 29, (Jg. 6:25, 27)

sent the prophets of B. to Mount Carmel, p. 40, (I Kg. 18:20)

the prophets of B. were slain, p. 43, (II Kg. 10, 25—28)

they cried: O B. hear us, p. 40, (I Kg. 18:26)

Baalzebub: sendest to inquire of B.?, p. 42, (II Kg. 1:6)

Babblings: avoid profane and vain b. and oppositions, p. 225, (I Tim. 6:20)

Babe: they found Mary, Joseph, and the b., p. 133, (Lk. 2:16)

you will find the b. wrapped in swaddling clothes, p. 133, (Lk. 2:12)

Babel: the tower of B., p. 7, (Gen. 11:1–9)

Babes: out of the mouth of b., p. 56, (Ps. 8:2)

revealed them unto b., p. 148, (Matt. 11:25; Lk. 10:21)

Babylon: B. is fallen, is fallen, p. 86, (Isa. 21:9)

B. is fallen, is fallen, p. 245, (Rev. 14:8)

B. shall become heaps, p. 103, (Jer. 51:37)

B. shall fall, p. 85, (Isa. 13)

B. the great is fallen, p. 246, (Rev. 18:2)

B. the Great, Mother of Harlots, p. 246, (Rev. 17:5)

by the rivers of B., p. 67, (Ps. 137:1)

carried away all Jerusalem to B., p. 45, (II Kg. 24:14–15; Jer. 39:9)

deliver Zedekiah to Nebuchadrezzar of B., p. 101, (Jer. 21:7)

God's judgment against B., p. 103, (Jer. 51:16–64)

he took him in chains to B., p. 103, (Jer. 39:7)

I will punish the king of B., p. 103, (Jer. 50:18)

Jerusalem destroyed by B., p. 103, (Jer. 39—40)

Nebuchadnezzar king of B., p. 110, (Dan. 1:1)

the broad walls of B., p. 103, (Jer. 51:58)

this Nebuchadrezzar king of B., p. 103, (Jer. 50:17)

Babylonian: the B. Captivity, p. 45, (II Kg. 24:10–16; 25:1–21; II Chr. 36:5–21; Jer. 37—39)

Bad: and cast the b. away, p. 157, (Matt. 13:48)

Baker: Pharaoh's butler and b., p. 12. (Gen. 40)

Balaam: B.'s ass, p. 20, (Num. 22:21–35)

B . . . saddled his ass, p. 20, (Num. 22:21)

Balances: a pair of b. in his hand, p. 243, (Rev. 6:5)

calamity laid in the b., p. 50, (Job 6:2)

Balm: no b. in Gilead, p. 100, (Jer. 8:22)

Bands: loose the b. of wickedness, p. 95, (Isa. 58:6)

Banner: his b. over me was love, p. 77, (Song 2:4)

Banners: terrible as an army with b., p. 78, (Song 6:10)

Banquet: the great b., p. 171, (Lk. 14:15–24; cf. Matt. 22:1–14)

Baptism: b. of John, was it from heaven, p. 170, (Matt. 21:25; Mk. 11:30; Lk. 20:4)

one Lord, one faith, one b., p. 216, (Eph. 4:5)

the b. of Jesus, p. 135, (Matt. 3:13–17; Mk. 1:9–11; Lk. 3:21–22; cf. Jn. 1:29–34)

Baptist: the ministry of John the B., p. 135, (Matt. 3:1–6; Mk. 1:1–6; Lk. 3:1–6; Jn. 1:6–7)

Baptize: he shall b. you with the Holy Spirit, p. 135, (Matt. 3:11; Mk. 1:8; Lk. 3:16; Jn. 1:33)

teach all nations and b. them, p. 185, (Matt. 28:19; cf. Mk. 16:15–16)

Baptized: b. by John in the Jordan, p. 135, (Matt. 3:13; Mk. 1:9; Lk. 3:21)

by one Spirit are we all b., p. 208, (I Cor. 12:13)

he arose and was b., p. 193, (Acts 9:18)

he b. Lydia a seller of purple, p. 195, (Acts 16:14, 15)

I have b. you with water, p. 135, (Matt. 3:11; Mk. 1:8; Lk. 3:16; Jn. 1:26, 33)

many were b. in the Jordan, p. 135, (Matt. 3:6; Mk. 1:5; cf. Lk. 3:3)

Philip b. the eunuch, p. 192, (Acts 8:38)

Barabbas: a notable prisoner called B., p. 182, (Matt. 27:16; Mk. 15:7)

they said: B.! Now B. was a robber, p. 182, (Jn. 18:40; cf. Matt. 27:21; Mk. 15:11; Lk. 23:18)

Barak: B. summoned ten thousand, p. 28, (Jg. 4:14)

Deborah and B., p. 28, (Jg. 4)

Barnabus: James, Cephas and John gave to me and B., p. 214, (Gal. 2:9)

journeys of B. and Paul, p. 194. (Acts 13—14)

Paul and B. argue, p. 195, (Acts 15:36–41)

Paul and B. had dissension with them, p. 194, (Acts 15:2)

they called B., Jupiter, p. 194, (Acts 14:12)

Barnabus: (continued)
with our beloved B. and Paul, p. 195, (Acts 15:25)

Barns: I will build greater b., p. 150, (Lk. 12:18)

the b. are broken, p. 116, (Joel 1:17)

Bartimaeus: blind B. sat by the highway, p. 165, (Mk. 10:46; cf. Matt. 20:30; Lk. 18:35)

Baruch: B. reads the prophecies, p. 102, (Jer. 36—38)

B. wrote from the mouth of Jeremiah, p. 102, (Jer. 36:4)

Jeremiah commanded B. to read, p. 102, (Jer. 36:8)

Basket: down by the wall in a b., p. 193, (Acts 9:25)

Bathsheba: David and B., p. 35, (II Sam. 11)

David said to B., Solomon, thy son, shall reign, p. 37, (I Kg. 1:30)

David took B., wife of Uriah, p. 35, (II Sam. 11:3–5)

Battle: in the forefront of the hottest b., p. 35, (II Sam. 11:15)

nor the b. to the strong, p. 76, (Ec. 9:11)

Beam: the b. that is in thine own eye, p. 142, (Matt. 7:3; Lk. 6:41)

Bear: if it b. not, . . . cut it down, p. 151, (Lk. 13:9)

Beast: a b. rise up out of the sea, p. 245, (Rev. 13:1)

b. coming up out of the earth, p. 245, (Rev. 13:11)

every b. of the forest is mine, p. 60, (Ps. 50:10)

he shook off the b., p. 198, (Acts 28:5)

the first b. was like a lion, p. 242, (Rev. 4:7)

the second b. like a calf, p. 242, (Rev. 4:7)

the third b. had a face as a man, p. 242, (Rev. 4:7)

Beasts: Adam gave names to all the . . . b., p. 5, (Gen. 2:20)

all manner of fourfooted b. and fowls, p. 193, (Acts 10:12)

fought with b. at Ephesus, p. 209, (I Cor. 15:32)

four b. full of eyes, p. 242, (Rev. 4:6)

great b. came up from the sea, p. 112, (Dan. 7:3)

like the b. that perish, p. 60, (Ps. 49:20)

now ask the b., p. 51, (Job 12:7)

the b. of the field, p. 50, (Job 5:23)

the wild b. shall cry, p. 85, (Isa. 13:22)

Beatitudes: the b., p. 138, (Matt. 5:3–12; Lk. 6:20–23)

Beautiful: how b. are the feet of him . . . , p. 94, (Isa. 52:7)

Beauty: give them b. for ashes, p. 95, (Isa. 61:3)

in the b. of holiness, p. 58, (Ps. 29:2)

worship the Lord in the b. of holiness, p. 63, (Ps. 96:9)

Bed: take up thy b. and walk, p. 144, (Mk. 2:9, 11; cf. Lk. 5:24)

take up thy b. and walk, p. 144, (Matt. 9:1–8; Mk. 2:1–12; Lk. 5:17–26)

take up thy b. and walk, p. 166, (Jn. 5:8)

Beersheba: from Dan even to B., p. 30, (Jg. 20:1)

Bees: a swarm of b. and honey, p. 30, (Jg. 14:8)

Beggar: a b. named Lazarus, p. 153, (Lk. 16:20)

Beggarly: to the weak and b. elements?, p. 214, (Gal. 4:9)

Beginning: better is the end . . . than the b., p. 75, (Ec. 7:8)

I am Alpha and Omega, the b. and the end, p. 240, (Rev. 1:8)

in the b. God created, p. 3, (Gen. 1:1)

in the b. was the word, p. 131, (Jn. 1:1)

the b. and the end, p. 247, (Rev. 22:13)

these are the b. of sorrows, p. 173, (Matt. 24:8; Mk. 13:8)

told you from the b., p. 92, (Isa. 40:21)

Begotten: today have I b. thee, p. 229, (Heb. 5:5)

Beguile: lest any man should b. you, p. 220, (Col. 2:4)

Beheading: imprisonment and b. of John the Baptist, p. 158, (Matt. 14:1–12; Mk. 6:14–29)

Behemoth: behold now b., p. 55, (Job 40:15)

Behold: b. I stand at the door and knock, p. 242, (Rev. 3:20)

b. the man, p. 32, (I Sam. 9:17)

Being: live and move and have our b., p. 196, (Acts 17:28)

Believe: b. in him of whom they have not heard?, p. 202, (Rom. 10:14)

b. on the Lord Jesus Christ, p. 195, (Acts 16:31)

except I see . . . I will not b., p. 185, (Jn. 20:25)

I b.: help thou mine unbelief, p. 161, (Mk. 9:24)

if ye b. not earthly things, p. 165, (Jn. 3:12)

that all men might b., p. 135, (Jn. 1:7)

the eunuch said: I b., p. 192, (Acts 8:37)

they that have not seen yet b., p. 185, (Jn. 20:29)

they will not b. me, p. 14, (Ex. 4:1)

which shall b. on me through their word, p. 180, (Jn. 17:20)

ye b. in God, b. also in me, p. 178, (Jn. 14:1)

Believed: as thou hast b. so be it done, p. 143, (Matt. 8:13)

call on him in whom they have not b.?, p. 202, (Rom. 10:14)

Nineveh b. God and proclaimed a fast, p. 121, (Jonah 3:5)

no manner of hurt because he b. in his God, p. 112, (Dan. 6:23)

the nobleman b., p. 166, (Jn. 4:53)

why b. ye him not, p. 170, (Matt. 21:25; Mk. 11:31; Lk. 20:5)

Believes: he that b. in me, p. 167, (Jn. 6:35)

he that b. in me, p. 167, (Jn. 6:47)

he that b. in the Son, p. 166, (Jn. 3:36)

Believeth: are possible to him that b., p. 161, (Mk. 9:23)

b. in me shall never die, p. 169, (Jn. 11:26)

he that b. in me, though he were dead, p. 169, (Jn. 11:25)

he that b. on me, p. 176, (Jn. 12:44)

salvation to every one that b., p. 199, (Rom. 1:16)

whosoever b. in him should not perish, p. 165, (Jn. 3:16)

Believing: be not faithless but b., p. 185, (Jn. 20:27)

fill you with all joy and peace in b., p. 204, (Rom. 15:13)

Belly: his b. with the east wind, p. 52, (Job 15:2)

out of the b. of hell cried I, p. 120, (Jonah 2:2)

thy b. is like an heap of wheat, p. 78, (Song 7:2)

whose God is their b., p. 219, (Phil. 3:19)

Beloved: for thou art greatly b., p. 113, (Dan. 9:23)

I am my b.'s, p. 78, (Song 7:10)

my b. among the sons, p. 77, (Song 2:3)

Belshazzar: B. the king made a great feast, p. 111, (Dan. 5:1)

B. was slain and Darius became King, p. 112, (Dan. 5:30, 31)

Belteshazzar: B. and Shadrach, Meshach and Abednego, p. 110, (Dan. 1:7)

Bemoan: who will b. her?, p. 123, (Nahum 3:7)

Beroea: Paul visits B., p. 195, (Acts 17:10)

Bethany: the anointing at B., p. 176, (Matt. 26:6–13; Mk. 14:3–9; cf. Lk. 7:36–50; Jn. 12:1–8)

Bethel: Jacob called the place B., p. 11, (Gen. 28:19)

Bethesda: the pool of B., p. 166, (Jn. 5:1–16)

Bethlehem: B. out of thee . . . one who is to be the ruler in Israel, p. 122, (Micah 5:2)

shepherds came with haste to B., p. 133, (Lk. 2:15–16)

they went to B., p. 31, (Ruth 1:19)

to B. to be taxed, p. 132, (Lk. 2:4, 5)

when Jesus was born in B., p. 134, (Matt. 2:1)

Bethsaida: the blind man of B., p. 160, (Mk. 8:22–26)

Betray: that dips his hand . . . shall b. me, p. 177, (Matt. 26:23; Mk. 14:20; cf. Jn. 13:26; Lk. 22:21)

Betrayal: Judas' b., p. 177, (Matt. 26:14–25; Mk. 14:10–21; Lk. 22:3–13; 21—23; Jn. 13:21–30)

Betrayed: be b. into the hands of men, p. 161, (Matt. 17:22;

Betrayed: *(continued)*
    20:18; Mk. 9:31; 10:33; Lk.
    9:44; 18:32)
Jesus the night he was b. took bread,
    p. 208, (I Cor. 11:23)
the Son of man is b., p. 176, (Matt.
    26:2)
Betraying: sinned in b. innocent
    blood, p. 181, (Matt. 27:4)
Betrays: he that b. me is at hand, p.
    180, (Matt. 26:46; Mk. 14:42)
Betroth: b. thee unto me in faithful-
    ness, p. 114, (Hos. 2:20)
Beware: b. lest any man spoil you
    through philosophy, p. 220,
    (Col. 2:8)
b. of men, p. 146, (Matt. 10:17–28;
    24:9, 13; Mk. 13:9–13; Lk. 12:4–
    12; 21:12–17)
Bidden: none of those men which
    were b., p. 171, (Lk. 14:24)
Bildad: B. answered, p. 52, (Job
    18:1)
B.'s first speech, p. 51, (Job 8)
B.'s last speech, p. 53, (Job 25)
Eliphaz, B., and Zophar, p. 49, (Job
    2:11)
Billows: thy b. and thy waves passed
    over, p. 120, (Jonah 2:3)
Bind: b. the . . . Pleiades . . . ?, p.
    54, (Job 38:31)
b. them for a sign, p. 23, (Deut. 6:8)
hath smitten and he will b. us up, p.
    115, (Hos. 6:1)
to b. up the broken-hearted, p. 95,
    (Isa. 61:1)
Bird: a b. of the air, p. 76, (Ec.
    10:20)
Birds: let b. fly above, p. 3, (Gen.
    1:20)
Birth: Rebekah gives b., p. 10, (Gen.
    25:21–26)
the b. of Jesus, p. 132, (Lk. 2:1–7)
the b. of John, p. 132, (Lk. 1:67–79)
the b. of Moses, p. 13, (Ex. 1:15–22;
    2:1–10)
Birthright: Esau sells his b. to Jacob,
    p. 10, (Gen. 25:27–34)
Bishop: a b. must be blameless, p.
    224, (I Tim. 3:2; Tit. 1:7)
Shepherd and B. of your souls, p.
    236, (I Pet. 2:25)
Bishops: concerning b. (elders), p.
    224, (I Tim. 3:1–7; Tit. 1:5–9)

Bitter: b. as wormwood, p. 69, (Prov.
    5:4)
every b. thing is sweet, p. 73, (Prov.
    27:7)
life unto the b. in soul, p. 50, (Job
    3:20)
more b. than death the woman
    . . . , p. 75, (Ec. 7:26)
Bitterness: the b. of my soul, p. 51,
    (Job 10:1)
go softly in the b. of my soul, p. 91,
    (Isa. 38:15)
in b. in the heat of my spirit, p. 106,
    (Ezek. 3:14)
in the gall of b., p. 192, (Acts 8:23)
lest any root of b. springing up, p.
    231, (Heb. 12:15)
Black: I am b., but comely, p. 77,
    (Song 1:5)
Blackness: the b. of darkness forever,
    p. 239, (Jude v. 13)
Blade: first the b., then the ear, p.
    156, (Mk. 4:28)
Blaspheme: we have heard him b., p.
    191, (Acts 6:11)
Blasphemy: he hath spoken b., p.
    181, (Matt. 26:65; Mk. 14:64: cf.
    Lk. 22:71)
Bless: b. the Lord, O my soul, p. 64,
    (Ps. 103:1–2)
b. them that curse you, p. 140, (Matt.
    5:44; Lk. 6:28)
b. them which persecute you, p. 203,
    (Rom. 12:14)
Esau cried, b. me, p. 10, (Gen. 27:34)
except thou b. me, p. 11, (Gen.
    32:26)
God be merciful unto us, and b. us,
    p. 61, (Ps. 67:1)
God will b. you, p. 22, (Deut. 28:2)
the Lord b. thee and keep thee, p.
    19, (Num. 6:24)
Blessed: b. above all people, p. 22,
    (Deut. 7:14)
b . . . among women, p. 131, (Lk.
    1:28)
b. are the poor, p. 138, (Matt. 5:3;
    Lk. 6:20)
b. art thou among women, p. 132,
    (Lk. 1:42)
b. be God the Father of mercies, p.
    210, (II Cor. 1:3)
b. be he that cometh in the name
    . . . , p. 66, (Ps. 118:26)

b. is he that waiteth, p. 114, (Dan. 12:12)
b. is the man that trusteth in the Lord, p. 101, (Jer. 17:7)
come, you b. of my Father, p. 175, (Matt. 25:34)
God b. the seventh day, p. 4, (Gen. 2:3)
Hosanna! B. is he that comes, p. 169, (Matt. 21:9; Mk. 11:9; Lk. 19:38; Jn. 12:13)
Isaac b. Jacob, p. 10, (Gen. 27:23)
Israel b. Joseph's sons, p. 13, (Gen. 48)
Jesus b. them and gave, p. 158, (Matt. 14:19; Mk. 6:41; Lk. 9:16; Jn. 6:11)
Job b. the name, p. 49, (Job 1:21)
Lord b. the latter end of Job, p. 55, (Job 42:12)
thou shalt be b. because they cannot repay, p. 151, (Lk. 14:14)
Blessing: b., honor, glory and power be unto him, p. 243, (Rev. 5:13)
life and death, b. and cursing, p. 23, (Deut. 30:19)
steals Esau's b. from Isaac, p. 10, (Gen. 27:1–40)
the b. of Moses, p. 21, (Deut. 33:25–27)
Blind: a b. man lead a b. man, p. 142, (Matt. 15:14; Lk. 6:39)
b. Bartimaeus sat by the highway, p. 165, (Mk. 10:46; cf. Matt. 20:30; Lk. 18:35)
eyes of the b. shall be opened, p. 90, (Isa. 35:5)
eyes to the b., p. 54, (Job 29:15)
healing of two b. men, p. 145, (Matt. 9:27–31)
if the b. lead the b., p. 159, (Matt. 15:14)
the b. man of Bethsaida, p. 160, (Mk. 8:22–26)
the b. receive their sight, p. 148, (Matt. 11:5; Lk. 7:22)
the healing of a man born b., p. 168, (Jn. 9)
they shall walk like b. men, p. 124, (Zeph. 1:17)
to open b. eyes, p. 93, (Isa. 42:7)
whereas I was b., now I see, p. 168, (Jn. 9:25)

Blindfolded: b. him and struck him, p. 181, (Mk. 14:65; Lk. 22:64)
Blood: and b. into her streets, p. 108, (Ezek. 28:23)
b. on the lintels and door posts, p. 15, (Ex. 12:7)
b. shall be poured out as dust, p. 124, (Zeph. 1:17)
b. will be upon your own heads, p. 196, (Acts 18:6)
hands are full of b., p. 81, (Isa. 1:15)
he hath made of one b., p. 196, (Acts 17:26)
his b. be on us and on our children, p. 182, (Matt. 27:25)
make haste to shed innocent b., p. 95, (Isa. 59:7)
that buildeth a town with b., p. 123, (Hab. 2:12)
the b. of Jesus Christ cleanseth us, p. 238, (I John 1:7)
the new testament in my b., p. 208, (I Cor. 11:25)
this is my b. of the new testament, p. 177, (Matt. 26:28; Mk. 14:24; Lk. 22:20; I Cor. 11:25)
washed their robes in the b. of the Lamb, p. 243, (Rev. 7:14)
when I see the b. I will pass, p. 15, (Ex. 12:13)
without shedding of b. is no remission, p. 230, (Heb. 9:22)
woman with an issue of b., p. 145, (Matt. 9:18–26; Mk. 5:21–43; Lk. 8:40–56)
Bloody: woe to the b. city, p. 123, (Nahum 3:1)
Blot: I will not b. out his name, p. 241, (Rev. 3:5)
Boast: b. not . . . of tomorrow, p. 73, (Prov. 27:1)
not of works, lest any man b., p. 215, (Eph. 2:9)
Boat: Jesus taught them from a b., p. 156, (Matt. 13:2–3; Mk. 4:1–2)
Boaz: B. took Ruth, p. 31, (Ruth 4:13)
Ruth gleaned in the field of B., p. 31, (Ruth 2:3)
Body: all the members of that one b. one, p. 208, (I Cor. 12:12)
and raised a spiritual b., p. 210, (I Cor. 15:44)

Body: (continued)

as the b. is one, p. 208, (I Cor. 12:12)

baptized into one b., p. 208, (I Cor. 12:13)

begged the b. of Jesus, p. 183, (Matt. 27:58; Mk. 15:43; Lk. 23:52; Jn. 19:38)

b. is a temple of the Holy Spirit, p. 206, (I Cor. 6:19)

fruit of thy b. , . . . upon thy throne, p. 67, (Ps. 132:11)

in the b. or out, I cannot tell, p. 213, (II Cor. 12:3)

my b. which is broken for you, p. 208, (I Cor. 11:24)

now ye are the b. of Christ, p. 208, (I Cor. 12:27)

sanctified through . . . the b. of Christ, p. 231, (Heb. 10:10)

take, eat. This is my b., p. 177. (Matt. 26:26; Mk. 14:22; cf. Lk. 22:19; I Cor. 11:24)

the b. is sown in corruption, p. 209, (I Cor. 15:42)

the b. without the spirit is dead, p. 234, (Jas. 2:26)

we, being many, are one b. in Christ, p. 203, (Rom. 12:5)

Boil: a b. upon man and beast, p. 15, (Ex. 9:10)

Boils: b. from head to toe, p. 49, (Job 2:7)

Boldly: come b. unto the throne of grace, p. 229, (Heb. 4:16)

Bond: in the b. of iniquity, p. 192, (Acts 8:23)

neither b. nor free, p. 214, (Gal. 3:28)

Bondage: who through fear of death were in b., p. 229, (Heb. 2:15)

Bone: b. of my bones, p. 4, (Gen. 2:23)

my b. cleveth to my skin, p. 52, (Job 19:20)

thou art my b. and flesh, p. 11, (Gen. 29:14)

touch his b. and his flesh, p. 49, (Job 2:5)

Bones: all my b. are out of joint, p. 57, (Ps. 22:14)

full of dead men's b. and uncleanness, p. 172, (Matt. 23:27)

son of man can these b. live?, p. 109, (Ezek. 37:3)

the b. came together bone to bone, p. 109, (Ezek. 37:7)

these b. are the whole house of Israel, p. 109, (Ezek. 37:11)

ye dry b. hear the word of the Lord, p. 109, (Ezek. 37:4)

Book: a b. sealed with seven seals, p. 242, (Rev. 5:1)

a hand gave Ezekiel a b., p. 106, (Ezek. 2:9)

another b. was opened which is the b. of life, p. 247, (Rev. 20:12)

Ezra read the b. of the law, p. 46, (Neh. 8:1–3)

in his hand a little b., p. 244, (Rev. 10:2)

not blot his name from the b. of life, p. 241, (Rev. 3:5)

note it in a b., p. 89, (Isa. 30:8)

the b. of the law was found, p. 45, (II Kg. 22:8; II Chr. 34:14)

thou art worthy to take the b., p. 242, (Rev. 5:9)

Books: of making many b. there is no end, p. 76, (Ec. 12:12)

their b. were opened, p. 247, (Rev. 20:12)

were judged out of those b., p. 247, (Rev. 20:12)

Booth: Jonah . . . sat in a b., p. 121, (Jonah 4:5)

Booths: b. in Succoth, p. 11, (Gen. 33:17)

Israelites . . . shall dwell in b., p. 22, (Lev. 23:42)

Born: a child is b., . . . a son is given, p. 84, (Isa. 9:6)

a Saviour is b., p. 133, (Lk. 2:11)

a time to be b., p. 74, (Ec. 3:2)

except a man be b. again, p. 165, (Jn. 3:3)

how can a man be b. when he is old?, p. 165, (Jn. 3:4)

man that is b. of woman, p. 51, (Job 14:1)

that which is b. of the flesh, p. 165, (Jn. 3:6)

that which is b. of the Spirit, p. 165, (Jn. 3:6)

Borrower: the b. is servant, p. 72, (Prov. 22:7)

Bosom: the wife of thy b., p. 22, (Deut. 13:6)

Bought: sold all he had and b. it, p. 157, (Matt. 13:46) ye are b. with a price, p. 206, (I Cor. 6:20)

Bound: b. in chains, p. 197, (Acts 21:33)

b. in the bundle of life, p. 34, (I Sam. 25:29)

the men of Judah b. him, p. 30, (Jg. 15:13)

Bow: my b. in the cloud, p. 7, (Gen. 9:13)

Bowels: shutteth up his b. of compassion, p. 238, (I John 3:17)

Byword: a proverb and a b., p. 38, (I Kg. 9:7)

Brambles: nettles and b. in the fortresses, p. 90, (Isa. 34:13)

Branch: a B. shall grow out of his roots, p. 84, (Isa. 11:1)

bring forth my servant the b., p. 126, (Zech. 3:8; cf. 6:12–13)

will raise unto David a righteous b., p. 101, (Jer. 23:5)

Branches: cut down b . . . and spread them, p. 169, (Matt. 21:8; Mk. 11: 8; Jn. 12:13)

Brass: a man whose appearance was like b., p. 109, (Ezek. 40:3)

Brawling: a b. woman in a wide house, p. 72, (Prov. 21:9; 25:24)

Bread: as Jesus sat with them he took b., p. 184, (Lk. 24:30)

ate b. to the full, p. 16, (Ex. 16:3)

b. eaten in secret, p. 70, (Prov. 9:17)

b. of adversity, and water of affliction, p. 89, (Isa. 30:20)

b. of affliction, p. 15, (Deut. 16:3)

b. without scarceness, p. 22, (Deut. 8:9)

cast thy b. upon the waters, p. 76, (Ec. 11:1)

command these stones be made b., p. 135, (Matt. 4:3; Lk. 4:3)

deal thy b. to the hungry, p. 95, (Isa. 58:7)

eat b. with quaking, p. 107, (Ezek. 12:18)

feast of unleavened b., p. 21, (Ex. 23:15; Lev. 23:6)

feed him with b. of affliction, p. 41, (I Kg. 22:27; II Chr. 18:26)

I am the b. of life, p. 167, (Jn. 6:35)

I will rain b. from heaven, p. 17, (Ex. 16:4)

Jesus the night he was betrayed took b., p. 208, (I Cor. 11:23)

Jesus took b. and blessed it, p. 177, (Matt. 26:26; Mk. 14:22; Lk. 22:19; I Cor. 11:23–24)

known of them in breaking of b., p. 184, (Lk. 24:35)

man doth not live by b. only, p. 22, (Deut. 8:3)

no staff, no b., no money, p. 146, (Matt. 10:10; Mk. 6:8; Lk. 9:3)

not live by b. alone, p. 135, (Matt. 4:4; Lk. 4:4)

the true b. from heaven, p. 167, (Jn. 6:32)

took b. and gave it to them with the fish, p. 186, (Jn. 21:13)

Breastplate: having on the b. of righteousness, p. 218, (Eph. 6:14)

the b. of faith and love, p. 222, (I Th. 5:8)

Breasts: two b. are like two young roes, p. 77, (Song 4:5)

Breath: b. of his lips shall he slay the wicked, p. 85, (Isa. 11:4)

the b. of life, p. 4, (Gen. 2:7)

Brethren: for b. to dwell together in unity, p. 67, (Ps. 133:1)

to be made like his b., p. 229, (Heb. 2:17)

Bride: the Spirit and the b. say, Come, p. 247, (Rev. 22:17)

Bridegroom: the b. is with them, p. 145, (Matt. 9:15; Mk. 2:19; Lk. 5:34)

when the b. came, p. 174, (Matt. 25:10)

Bridle: keep my mouth with a b., p. 59, (Ps. 39:1)

Brier: instead of the b., p. 95, (Isa. 55:13)

Brightness: the b. of his glory, p. 228, (Heb. 1:3)

Brimstone: on Sodom and Gomorrah b. and fire, p. 9, (Gen. 19:24)

the dust thereof into b., p. 90, (Isa. 34:9)

Broken: a b. and a contrite heart, p. 60, (Ps. 51:17)

Broken-hearted: to bind up the b., p. 95, (Isa. 61:1)

Brook: hide by the b. Cherith, p. 39, (I Kg. 17:3)

Brother: a b. far off, p. 73, (Prov. 27:10)

a b. to dragons, p. 54, (Job 30:29)

am I my b.'s keeper?, p. 5, (Gen. 4:9)

Brother: (*continued*)

be reconciled to thy b., p. 139, (Matt. 5:24)

b. deliver up b. to death, p. 147, (Matt. 10:21; Mk. 13:12)

b. or sister be naked and destitute, p. 234 (Jas. 2:15)

every man against his b., p. 127, (Mal. 2:10)

every man's sword against his b., p. 109, (Ezek. 38:21)

every man to his b., p. 126, (Zech. 7:9)

fight everyone against his b., p. 86, (Isa. 19:2)

imagine evil against his b., p. 126, (Zech. 7:10)

the prodigal son's b., p. 152, (Lk. 15:25–32)

thy b. have ought against thee, p. 139, (Matt. 5:23)

to have thy b.'s wife, p. 158, (Matt. 14:4; Mk. 6:18)

your b. whom ye sold, p. 12, (Gen. 45:4)

Brothers: his b. stripped him of his coat, p. 12, (Gen. 37:23)

Jesus . . . saw two b., p. 136, (Matt. 4:18; Mk. 1:16)

Joseph knew his b., p. 12, (Gen. 42:8)

Moses saw his b.' burdens, p. 14, (Ex. 2:11)

two other b., James and John, p. 136, (Matt. 4:21; Mk. 1:19; Lk. 5:10)

your mother and b. are outside, p. 156, (Matt. 12:47; Mk. 3:32; Lk. 8:20)

Bucket: a drop of a b., p. 92, (Isa. 40:15)

Build: b. houses and inhabit the, p. 96, (Isa. 65:21)

chosen you to b. the temple, p. 37, (I Chr. 28:10)

except the Lord b. the house, p. 67, (Ps. 127:1)

his servants will arise and b., p. 45, (Neh. 2:20)

intending to b. a tower, p. 151, (Lk. 14:28)

not b. and another inhabit, p. 96, (Isa. 65:22)

Builders: the stone which the b. refused, p. 66, (Ps. 118:22)

the stone which the b. rejected, p. 170, (Matt. 21:42; Mk. 12:10; Lk. 20:17)

Buildeth: take heed how he b. thereupon, p. 205, (I Cor. 3:10)

that b. a town with blood, p. 123, (Hab. 2:12)

Building: the b. of the temple, p. 38, (I Kg. 5—7; II Chr. 2—4)

Built: he b. houses in the city, p. 35, (I Chr. 15:1)

he that b. all things is God, p. 229, (Heb. 3:4)

Bulrushes: an ark of b., p. 13, (Ex. 2:3)

Bundle: bound in the b. of life, p. 34, (I Sam. 25:29)

Burden: and my b. light, p. 149, (Matt. 11:30)

bear the b. with thee, p. 17, (Ex. 18:22)

b. depart from their shoulders, p. 86, (Isa. 14:25)

the b. of Egypt, p. 86, (Isa. 19:1)

Burdens: bear one another's b., p. 215, (Gal. 6:2)

Moses saw his brothers' b., p. 14, (Ex. 2:11)

undo the heavy b., p. 95, (Isa. 58:6)

Burial: she did it for my b., p. 176, (Matt. 26:12; Mk. 14:8; Jn. 12:7)

the b. of Jesus, p. 183, (Matt. 27:57–61; Mk. 15:42–47; Lk. 23:50–56; Jn. 19:38–42)

Burn: b. the weeds but gather the wheat, p. 156, (Matt. 13:30)

Burned: his clothes not be b., p. 70, (Prov. 6:27)

the bush b. with fire, p. 14, (Ex. 3:2)

Burning: Moses and the b. bush, p. 14, (Ex. 3:1–10)

Burnt: b. the house of the Lord, p. 45, (II Kg. 25:9; II Chr. 36:19)

more than b. offerings, p. 116, (Hos. 6:6)

will not accept your b. offerings, p. 119, (Amos 5:22)

Bury: let me first go and b., p. 144, (Matt. 8:21; Lk. 9:59)

Bush: from the midst of the b., p. 14, (Ex. 3:4)

the b. burned with fire, p. 14, (Ex. 3:2)

Bushel: put a candle under a b., p.

138, (Matt. 5:15; Mk. 4:21; Lk. 8:16; 11:33)

Butler: Pharaoh's b. and baker, p. 12, (Gen. 40)

Butter: b. in a lordly dish, p. 29, (Jg. 5:25)

words . . . were smoother than b., p. 61, (Ps. 55:21)

Buys: sells all and b. the field, p. 157, (Matt. 13:44)

Caesar: appealed to C., p. 198, (Acts 26:32)

I appeal unto C., p. 197, (Acts 25:11)

lawful to give tribute unto C.?, p. 171, (Matt. 22:17; Mk. 12:14; Lk. 20:22)

unto C. the things which are Caesar's, p. 171, (Matt. 22:21; Mk. 12:17; Lk. 20:25)

Caesarea: in custody in C., p. 197, (Acts 23:15–35; 24)

Paul travels via C., p. 196, (Acts 21:8)

Peter came to C., p. 193, (Acts 10:24)

Cain: C. rose up against Abel, p. 5, (Gen. 4:8)

the Lord put a mark on C., p. 5, (Gen. 4:15)

Calamity: c. laid in the balances, p. 50, (Job 6:2)

Calf: Aaron made a golden c., p. 18, (Ex. 32:3–4)

bring the fatted c., p. 152, (Lk. 15:23)

the second beast like a c., p. 242, (Rev. 4:7)

Call: before they c., I will answer, p. 96, (Isa. 65:24)

c. on the name of the Lord, p. 190, (Acts 2:21)

c. upon him while he is near, p. 94, (Isa. 55:6)

the c. of Elisha, p. 41, (I Kg. 19)

Called: many are c. but few are chosen, p. 164, 171, (Matt. 20:16; 22:14)

Calling: the c. of Matthew (Levi), p. 145, (Matt. 9:9; Mk. 2:14; Lk. 5:27, 28)

the c. of Matthias, p. 189, (Acts 1:23–26)

Camel: a c. to go through the eye of a needle, p. 164, (Matt. 19:24; Mk. 10:25; Lk. 18:25)

John wore c.'s hair, p. 135, (Matt. 3:4; Mk. 1:6)

Cana: the marriage in C., p. 137, (Jn. 2:1–11)

Canaan: Abram dwelled in the land of C., p. 8, (Gen. 13:12)

all the land of C., p. 8, (Gen. 17:8)

into the land of C., p. 7, (Gen. 12:5)

twelve spies sent to C., p. 19, (Num. 13—14:37)

Candle: put a c. under a bushel, p. 138, (Matt. 5:15; Mk. 4:21; Lk. 8:16; 11:33)

Candles: search Jerusalem with c., p. 124, (Zeph. 1:12)

Candlesticks: I saw seven golden c., p. 240, (Rev. 1:12)

Capernaum: in C. a centurion, p. 143, (Matt. 8:5; Lk. 7:1–2)

the synagogue at C., p. 137, (Matt. 7:28–29; Mk. 1:21–28; Lk. 4:31–37)

Captives: as I was among the c., p. 105, (Ezek. 1:1)

proclaim liberty to the c., p. 95, (Isa. 61:1)

Captivity: Ezekiel prophesies to those in c., p. 107, (Ezek. 12)

he led c. captive, p. 216, (Eph. 4:8)

Israel's return from c., p. 102, (Jer. 29–30)

the Babylonian c., p. 45, (II Kg. 24:10–16; 25:1–21; II Chr. 36:5–21; Jer. 37–39)

turn away your c., p. 102, (Jer. 29:14)

Carcase: in the c. of the lion, p. 30, (Jg. 14:8)

Care: the c. of all the churches, p. 212, (II Cor. 11:28)

Carelessly: the rejoicing city that dwelt c., p. 124, (Zeph. 2:15)

Carmel: Elijah went up . . . Mount C., p. 40, (I Kg. 18:42)

prophets of Baal to Mount C., p. 40, (I Kg. 18:20)

Carnally: to be c. minded is death, p. 201, (Rom 8:6)

Cast: and c. the bad away, p. 157, (Matt. 13:48)

c. him into a pit in Dothan, p. 12, (Gen. 37:17, 24)

c. him into the bottomless pit, p. 246, (Rev. 20:3)

Cast: (*continued*)
c. himself down upon the earth, p. 40, (I Kg. 18:42)
c. into outer darkness, p. 171, (Matt. 22:13)
c. me forth into the sea, p. 120, (Jonah 1:12)
c. off the works of darkness, p. 204, (Rom. 13:12)
c. out into the earth, p. 244, (Rev. 12:9)
c. thy bread upon the waters, p. 76, (Ec. 11:1)
c. thyself down, p. 136, (Matt. 4:6; Lk. 4:9)
good for nothing but to be c. out, p. 138, (Matt. 5:13)
let him c. the first stone, p. 167, (Jn. 8:7)
let us c. lots that we may know, p. 120, (Jonah 1:7)
not c. away a perfect man, p. 51, (Job 8:20)
not c. thee away, p. 92, (Isa. 41:9)
The Lord will not c. us off for ever, p. 105, (Lam. 3:31)
took up Jonah and c. him into the sea, p. 120, (Jonah 1:15)
why art thou c. down, O my soul?, p. 59, (Ps. 42:5)
Casting: c. out the moneychangers, p. 170, (Matt. 21:12–13; Mk. 11:15–19; Lk. 19:45–48; Jn. 2:13–17)
parted his garments, c. lots, p. 182, (Matt. 27:35; Mk. 15:24; Lk. 23:33–34; Jn. 19:18, 23–24)
Catch: fear not, . . . thou shalt c. men, p. 137, (Lk. 5:10)
Cattle: c. and creeping things, p. 4, (Gen. 1:24)
the c. of Egypt died, p. 15, (Ex. 9:6)
the c. upon a thousand hills, p. 60, (Ps. 50:10)
Cause: order my c. before him, p. 53, (Job 23:4)
Cave: Obadiah hid them in a c., p. 40, (I Kg. 18:4)
Cease: c. to do evil, p. 81, (Isa. 1:16)
Cedar: a branch of the c. and plant it, p. 108, (Ezek. 17:22)
bear fruit and be a goodly c., p. 108, (Ezek. 17:23)
took the highest branch of the c., p. 107, (Ezek. 17:3)

Cedars: c. of Lebanon, p. 38, 65, 82, (I Kg. 5:1–10; II Chr. 2:3–16; Ps. 104:16: Isa. 2:13)
Centurion: c.'s servant, p. 143, (Matt. 8:5–13; Lk. 7:1–10)
Cornelius the c., p. 193, (Acts 10:1–33)
Cephas: James, C. and John gave to me and Barnabus, p. 214, (Gal. 2:9)
Chaff: c. of the summer threshing floors, p. 110, (Dan. 2:35)
the c. of the mountains, p. 86, (Isa. 17:13)
the ungodly are like the c., p. 55, (Ps. 1:4)
Chains: bound in c., p. 197, (Acts 21:33)
with c. unto the land of Egypt, p. 108, (Ezek. 19:4)
Change: I am the Lord, I c. not, p. 127, (Mal. 3:6)
Changed: all be c . . . at the last trump, p. 210, (I Cor. 15:52)
Chariot: the c. of Israel, and the horsemen, p. 42, (II Kg. 2:12)
Chariots: prancing horses and jumping c., p. 123, (Nahum 3:2)
the wheels of his c., p. 29, (Jg. 5:28)
waters covered the c., p. 16, (Ex. 14:28)
Charity: c. shall cover the multitude of sins, p. 237, (I Pet. 4:8)
give c. secretly, p. 140, (Matt. 6:1–4)
Chastened: as c. and not killed, p. 212, (II Cor. 6:9)
Chasteneth: he that loveth him c., p. 71, (Prov. 13:24)
whom the father c. not?, p. 231, (Heb. 12:7)
whom the Lord loveth he c., p. 231, (Heb. 12:6)
Chebar: captives by the river of C., p. 105, (Ezek. 1:1)
Cheek: smite thee on thy right c., p. 140, (Matt. 5:39; Lk. 6:29)
Cheerful: God loveth a c. giver, p. 212, (II Cor. 9:7)
Cherith: hide by the brook C., p. 39, (I Kg. 17:3)
Cherubim: the vision of four c., p. 105, (Ezek. 1:4–14)
Cherubims: c. and a sapphire throne, p. 107, (Ezek. 10—11)

two c. overlaid with gold, p. 38, (I
Kg. 6:27, 28; II Chr. 3:10)

Chickens: as a hen gathereth her c.,
p. 172, (Matt. 23:37; Lk. 13:34)

Child: a c. is born, . . . a son is
given, p. 84, (Isa. 9:6)

a little c. shall lead them, p. 85, (Isa.
11:6)

behold the c. was dead, p. 42, (II Kg.
4:32)

better is a poor and a wise c., p. 75,
(Ec. 4:13)

c. shall play on the hole of the asp,
p. 85, (Isa. 11:8)

David sought God for the c., p. 36,
(II Sam. 12:16)

death of David's c., p. 36, (II Sam.
12:15–23)

divide the living c., p. 37, (I Kg.
3:25)

Elisha stretched himself upon the c.,
p. 42, (II Kg. 4:34)

even a c. is known by his doings, p.
72, (Prov. 20:11)

give her the living c., p. 37, (I Kg.
3:26)

humble himself as this little c., p.
162, (Matt. 18:4)

I am a little c., p. 37, (I Kg. 3:7)

Jesus set a c. in the midst, p. 162,
(Matt. 18:2; Mk. 9:36; Lk. 9:47)

Joseph, Mary and the c. returned, p.
134, (Matt. 2:21)

let this c.'s soul come into him again,
p. 40, (I Kg. 17:21)

Mary was found with c. of the Holy
Ghost, p. 132, (Matt. 1:18)

Mary who was great with c., p. 132,
(Lk. 2:5)

not see the death of the c., p. 9,
(Gen. 21:16)

say not I am a c., p. 99, (Jer. 1:7)

search for the young c., p. 134,
(Matt. 2:8)

the c. died, p. 36, (II Sam. 12:18)

the c. grew and waxed strong. . . ,
(Lk. 2:40)

the c. ministered unto the Lord, p.
31, (I Sam. 2:11)

the dead c. yours, p. 37, (I Kg. 3:22)

the living c. is mine, p. 37, (I Kg.
3:22)

train up a c. in the way, p. 72, (Prov.
22:6)

was a c., I spake as a c., p. 208, (I
Cor. 13:11)

while the c. was yet alive, p. 36, (II
Sam. 12:22)

Childish: I put away c. things, p. 208,
(I Cor. 13:11)

Children: be not c. in understanding,
p. 209, (I Cor. 14:20)

be the c. of light, p. 176, (Jn. 12:36)

brought young c. to him, p. 163,
(Matt. 19:13; Mk. 10:13; Lk.
18:15)

c. against their parents, p. 147,
(Matt. 10:21; Mk. 13:12)

c. also shall be dashed to pieces, p.
85, (Isa. 13:16)

c. are an heritage of the Lord, p. 67,
(Ps. 127:3)

c.'s bread and cast it to the dogs, p.
159, (Matt. 15:26; Mk. 7:27)

c. in the marketplace, p. 148, (Matt.
11:16; Lk. 7:32)

c., obey your parents, p. 217, (Eph.
6:1)

c. of Israel out of Egypt, p. 15, (Ex.
12:51)

c.'s teeth are set on edge, p. 102,
(Jer. 31:29; Ezek. 18:2)

c. that will not hear the law, p. 89,
(Isa. 30:9)

c., tossed to and fro, p. 217, (Eph.
4:14)

except ye become as little c., p. 162,
(Matt. 18:3)

Faithful c. not accused of riot or unruly, p. 227, (Tit. 1:6)

fathers, provoke not your c., p. 218,
(Eph. 6:4)

for the life of thy young c., p. 104,
(Lam. 2:19)

Herod slew all the c., p. 134, (Matt.
2:16)

I have . . . brought up c., p. 81,
(Isa. 1:2)

in sorrow shalt thou bring forth c., p.
5, (Gen. 3:16)

Jesus said: Suffer the little c. to
come, p. 163, (Matt. 19:14; Mk.
10:14; Lk. 18:16)

little c., yet a little while, p. 178, (Jn.
13:33)

not have mercy upon her c., p. 114,
(Hos. 2:4)

O c. of Israel, p. 118, (Amos 3:1)

Children: (continued)

Pharaoh pursued the c. of Israel, p. 16, (Ex. 14:8, 9)

Rachel weeping for her c., pp. 102, 134, (Jer. 31:15; Matt. 2:17–18)

return ye c. of men, p. 62, (Ps. 90:3)

Sarai bare Abram no c., p. 8, (Gen. 16:1)

teach them diligently unto thine c., p. 23, (Deut. 6:7)

the c. of God and if c., then heirs, p. 201, (Rom 8:16–17)

the c. of Israel are more, p. 13, (Ex. 1:9)

the c. of Israel were fruitful, p. 13, (Ex. 1:7)

the heart of the c. to their fathers, p. 127, (Mal. 4:6)

there were sealed . . . the c. of Israel, p. 243, (Rev. 7:4)

thy c. have forsaken me, p. 99, (Jer. 5:7)

walk as c. of light, p. 217, (Eph. 5:8)

when my c. were about me, p. 54, (Job 29:5)

woe to the rebellious c., p. 89, (Isa. 30:8–9)

would I have gathered thy c., p. 172, (Matt. 23:37; Lk. 13:34)

Chios: Paul travels via C., p. 196, (Acts 20:15)

Chosen: a c. generation, a royal priesthood, p. 236, (I Pet. 2:9)

I have c. thee, p. 92, (Isa. 41:9)

Lord hath not c. these, p. 33, (I Sam. 16:10)

many are called but few are c., p. 171, (Matt. 22:14)

to see the c. land, p. 20, (Num. 27:12)

you have not c. me, but I have c. you, p. 179, (Jn. 15:16)

Christ: are you the C., the Son of God?, p. 181, (Matt. 26:63; Mk. 14:61; Lk. 22:67, 70)

as C. also loved the church, p. 217, (Eph. 5:25)

believe on the Lord Jesus C., p. 195, (Acts 16:31)

both Lord and C., p. 190, (Acts 2:36)

by the revelation of Jesus C., p. 214, (Gal. 1:12)

C. also suffered for us, p. 236, (I Pet. 2:21)

C. being raised from the dead dieth no more, p. 201, (Rom. 6:9)

C. died for our sins, p. 209, (I Cor. 15:3)

C. glorified not himself, p. 229, (Heb. 5:5)

C. is all and in all, p. 220, (Col. 3:11)

C. Jesus came into the world. . . . , p. 223, (I Tim. 1:15)

C. may dwell in your hearts by faith, p. 216, (Eph. 3:17)

C. our passover is sacrificed, p. 206, (I Cor. 5:7)

C. should suffer, p. 197, (Acts 26:23)

C. the one foundation, p. 205, (I Cor. 3)

C. took the form of a servant, p. 218, (Phil. 2:7)

come in my name, saying, I am C., p. 173, (Matt. 24:5, 24; Mk. 13:6, 22; Lk. 21:8)

created in C. Jesus unto good works, p. 216, (Eph. 2:10)

crucified with C., p. 214, (Gal. 2:20)

God was in C., reconciling the world, p. 211, (II Cor. 5:19)

grace according to the gift of C., p. 216, (Eph. 4:7)

he preached C. in the synagogues, p. 193, (Acts 9:20)

heirs of God and joint heirs with C., p. 201, (Rom 8:17)

I am not the C. but am sent before, p. 166, (Jn. 3:28)

I can do all things through C., p. 219, (Phil. 4:13)

if C. be not raised, p. 209, (I Cor. 15:17)

if C. be not risen, p. 209, (I Cor. 15:14)

in C. shall all be made alive, p. 209, (I Cor. 15:22)

in the liberty wherewith C. hath made us free, p. 215, (Gal. 5:1)

not I, but C. liveth in me, p. 214, (Gal. 2:20)

now ye are the body of C., p. 208, (I Cor. 12:27)

quickened us together with C., p. 215, (Eph. 2:5)

reconciled us to himself by C., p. 211, (II Cor. 5:18)

separate us from the love of C., p. 202, (Rom. 8:35)

so C. was once offered, p. 231, (Heb. 9:28)

spoke to Felix of faith in C., p. 197, (Acts 24:24)

the Gospel of C., p. 199, (Rom. 1:16)

This is the C., p. 160, (Jn. 7:41)

this mind be in you which was in C. Jesus, p. 218, (Phil. 2:5)

thou art the C., p. 160, (Matt. 16:16; Mk. 8:29; Lk. 9:20; Jn. 6:69)

to live is C., to die is gain, p. 218, (Phil. 1:21)

to them which are in C. Jesus, p. 201, (Rom. 8:1)

walk in love as C. hath loved us, p. 217, (Eph. 5:2)

we, being many, are one body in C., p. 203, (Rom 12:5)

what think ye of C.?, p. 172, (Matt. 22:42; Mk. 12:35; Lk. 20:41)

which is C. the Lord, p. 133, (Lk. 2:11)

while we were yet sinners, C. died for us, p. 200, (Rom. 5:8)

would see C. before he died, p. 133, (Lk. 2:26)

you are all one in C. Jesus, p. 214, (Gal. 3:28)

you are C.'s and Christ is God's, p. 206, (I Cor. 3:23)

you are that C., the Son of . . . God, p. 167, (Jn. 6:69)

you may know the love of C., p. 216, (Eph. 3:19)

Christian: Agrippa: . . . persuadest me to be a C., p. 197, (Acts 26:28)

if any man suffer as a C., p. 237, (I Pet. 4:16)

called C. first at Antioch, p. 194, (Acts 11:26)

Church: as Christ also loved the c., p. 217, (Eph. 5:25)

early persecution of the c., p. 191, (Acts 8:1–8)

how shall he take care of the c.?, p. 224, (I Tim. 3:5)

persecution against the c., p. 191, (Acts 8:1)

Saul made havoc of the c., p. 191, (Acts 8:3)

to the c. of Ephesus, p. 240, (Rev. 2:1–7)

to the c. in Laodicea, p. 241, (Rev. 3:14–22)

to the c. in Pergamos, p. 241, (Rev. 2:12–17)

to the c. in Philadelphia, p. 241, (Rev. 3:7–13)

to the c. in Sardis, p. 241, (Rev. 3:1–6)

to the c. in Thyatira, p. 241, (Rev. 2:18–29)

to the c. of Smyrna, p. 241, (Rev. 2:8–11)

which is the c. of the living God, p. 224, (I Tim. 3:15)

Churches: send it to the seven c. of Asia, p. 240, (Rev. 1:11)

the care of all the c., p. 212, (II Cor. 11:28)

Cilicia: churches in Syria and C., p. 195, (Acts 15:36–41)

Circumcised: every man child . . . shall be c., p. 8, (Gen. 17:10)

except ye be c., p. 194, (Acts 15:1)

he was c. and called Jesus, p. 133, (Lk. 2:21)

Cities: until the c. be wasted, p. 83, (Isa. 6:11)

Citizen: a c. of no mean city, p. 97, (Acts 21:39)

City: a c. set on a hill, p. 138, (Matt. 5:14)

beheld the c. and wept, p. 169, (Lk. 19:41)

c. against c., p. 86, (Isa. 19:2)

glorious things are spoken of thee, O c. of God, p. 62, (Ps. 87:3)

how doth the c. sit solitary, p. 104, (Lam. 1:1)

Jerusalem—the c. of David, p. 35, (II Sam. 6; I Chr. 11:16)

make glad the c. of God, p. 60, (Ps. 46:4)

make thee a desolate c., p. 108, (Ezek. 26:19)

no continuing c. but we seek one to come, p. 232, (Heb. 13:14)

the ark into the c. of David, p. 35, (II Sam. 6:12)

the c. is smitten, p. 109, (Ezek. 33:21)

the c. of David, p. 35, (I Chr. 15:1)

the faithful c. become an harlot, p. 81, (Isa. 1:21)

City: (continued)
woe to the bloody c., p. 123, (Nahum 3:1)

Clap: let the floods c. their hands, p. 64, (Ps. 98:8)

Clay: as the c. is in the potter's hand, p. 101, (Jer. 18:6)

his feet part of iron, part of c., p. 110, (Dan. 2:33)

shall the c. say to him . . . , p. 93, (Isa. 45:9)

the potter power over the c. . . . ? p. 202, (Rom. 9:21)

Clean: be thou c., p. 143, (Matt. 8:3; Mk. 1:41; Lk. 5:13)

c. hands, and a pure heart, p. 57, (Ps. 24:4)

laws concerning c. and unclean, p. 19, (Lev. 11—18; Deut. 14:3–21)

make c. the outside of the cup, p. 172, (Matt. 23:25; Lk. 11:39)

thou canst make me c., p. 143, (Matt. 8:2; Mk. 1:40; Lk. 5:12)

Cleanse: c. the lepers, p. 146, (Matt. 10:8)

Cleansed: what God hath c., p. 193, (Acts 10:15)

Clearly: saw every man c., p. 160, (Mk. 8:25)

Cloak: let him have thy c. also, p. 140, (Matt. 5:40; cf. Lk. 6:29)

Closet: enter into thy c., p. 140, (Matt. 6:6)

Clothes: laid their c. at Saul's feet, p. 191, (Acts 7:58)

Cloud: a little c. out of the sea, p. 40, (I Kg. 18:44)

goodness is as a morning c., p. 115, (Hos. 6:4)

in a pillar of c., p. 16, (Ex. 13:21)

Lord rideth upon a swift c., p. 86, (Isa. 19:1)

Clouds: number the c. in wisdom, p. 55, (Job 38:37)

the c. are the dust of his feet, p. 122, (Nahum 1:3)

Coal: with a live c. in his hand, p. 83, (Isa. 6:6)

Coals: c. of fire upon his head, p. 73, (Prov. 25:22)

heap c. of fire on his head, p. 204, (Rom. 12:20)

Coat: a c. of many colors, p. 12, (Gen. 37:3)

if any man take away thy c., p. 140, (Matt. 5:40; cf. Lk. 6:29)

Cock: c. shall not crow till thou hast denied me, p. 179, (Matt. 26:34; Mk. 14:30; Lk. 22:34; Jn. 13:38)

while he was speaking, the c. crowed, p. 181, (Matt. 26:74; Mk. 14:68, 72; Lk. 22:60; Jn. 18:27)

Coin: the lost c., p. 152, (Lk. 15:8–10)

Cold: thou art neither c. nor hot, p. 241, (Rev. 3:15)

Colors: a coat of many c., p. 12, (Gen. 37:3)

Colossae: Paul's letter to C., p. 220, (Col.)

to the saints and faithful at C., p. 220, (Col. 1:2)

Colt: they brought the c., p. 169, (Matt. 21:7; Mk. 11:7; Lk. 19:35; Jn. 12:14)

you shall find a c., p. 169, (Matt. 21:2; Mk. 11:7; Lk. 19:30)

Come: art thou he that should c., p. 148, (Matt. 11:3; Lk. 7:19)

c., for all things are ready, p. 171, (Lk. 14:17)

c. out of him, p. 138, (Mk. 1:25; Lk. 4:35)

even so, c., Lord Jesus, p. 247, (Rev. 22:20)

I will c. again, p. 178, (Jn. 14:3)

let him c. unto me, p. 18, (Ex. 32:26)

let him that heareth say, c., p. 247, (Rev. 22:17)

Surely I c. quickly, p. 247, (Rev. 22:20)

which was and which is to c., p. 240, (Rev. 1:8)

Cometh: he that c. after me, p. 135, (Matt. 3:11; Mk. 1:7; Lk. 3:16; Jn. 1:15)

Comfort: c. all her waste places, p. 93, (Isa. 51:3)

c. all that mourn, p. 95, (Isa. 61:2)

c. me with apples, p. 77, (Song 2:5)

c. ye, c. ye, my people, p. 91, (Isa. 40:1)

c. your hearts, p. 223, (II Thess. 2:17)

she hath none to c. her, p. 104, (Lam. 1:2)

so will I c. you, p. 96, (Isa. 66:13)

the God of all c., p. 210, (II Cor. 1:3)

the Lord shall c. Zion, p. 93, (Isa. 51:3)

the Lord shall yet c. Zion, p. 125, (Zech. 1:17)

Comfortably: into the wilderness and speak c., p. 114, (Hos. 2:14)

speak ye c. to Jerusalem, p. 91, (Isa. 40:2)

Comforted: now he is c., you are tormented, p. 153, (Lk. 16:25)

Comforter: the Father shall give you another C., p. 178, (Jn. 14:16; 15:26)

Comforters: miserable c. are ye, p. 52, (Job 16:2)

Comforteth: c. us in all our tribulation, p. 210, (II Cor. 1:4)

Comfortless: I will not leave you c., p. 178, (Jn. 14:18)

Commanded: when ye shall have done all things which are c., p. 153, (Lk. 17:10)

Commandment: A new c. I give unto you, p. 178, (Jn. 13:34)

Commandments: fear God and keep his c., p. 76, (Ec. 12:13)

he kept the Lord's c., p. 44, (II Kg. 18:6)

if thou wilt enter into life, keep the c., p. 163, (Matt. 19:17; cf. Mk. 10:19; Lk. 18:20)

if ye love me, keep my c., p. 178, (Jn. 14:15)

if you do all his c., p. 22, (Deut. 28:1)

keep the c. of the Lord, p. 22, (Deut. 8:6)

O that thou hadst hearkened to my c., p. 93, (Isa. 48:18)

on these two c., p. 172, (Matt. 22:40)

the great c., p. 171, (Matt. 22:34–40; Mk. 12:28–34; Lk. 10:25–28)

the Lord wrote the c., p. 18, (Ex. 24:12, 31:18; 32:16)

the ten c., p. 17, (Ex. 20:1–17; Deut. 5:6–21)

Commit: into thine hand I c. my spirit, p. 58, (Ps. 31:5)

unto God would I c. my cause, p. 50, (Job 5:8)

Commitment: Moses called the nation to a new c., p. 22, (Deut. 27—30)

Common: not call any man common, p. 194, (Acts 10:28)

Communication: c. be: Yea, yea; Nay, nay, p. 140, (Matt. 5:37)

Companion: a c. to owls, p. 54, (Job 30:29)

Compassion: a Samaritan had c., p. 150, (Lk. 10:33)

and of some have c., p. 239, (Jude v. 22)

be of one mind having c. one of another, p. 236, (I Pet. 3:8)

c., according to the multitude of his mercies, p. 105, (Lam. 3:32)

I have c. on the multitude, p. 159, (Matt. 15:32; Mk. 8:2)

Jesus had c.: Young man arise, p. 155, (Lk. 7:13–14)

Jesus, moved with c., touched him, p. 143, (Mk. 1:41)

moved with c. and forgave the debt, p. 163, (Matt. 18:27)

saw the multitudes he was moved with c., p. 146, (Matt. 9:36; Mk. 6:34)

the Lord is gracious, full of c., p. 68, (Ps. 145:8)

who had c., and ran and kissed him, p. 152, (Lk. 15:20)

Compassions: his c. fail not, p. 105, (Lam. 3:22)

Complete: c. in him which is the head, p. 220, (Col. 2:10)

Conceived: Hagar c. a son, Ishmael, p. 8, (Gen. 16:4, 11)

she c. a child, p. 35, (II Sam. 11:3–5)

Conclusion: hear the c. of the whole matter, p. 76, (Ec. 12:13)

Condemn: do not c. me, p. 51, (Job 10:2)

neither do I c. thee, p. 167, (Jn. 8:11)

Condemnation: is therefore now no c., p. 201, (Rom. 8:1)

Condemned: woman, has no man c. you?, p. 167, (Jn. 8:10)

Condemnest: thou judgest another, thou c. thyself, p. 199, (Rom. 2:1)

Condemneth: own mouth c. thee, p. 52, (Job 15:6)

Conference: the c. at Jerusalem, p. 194, (Acts 15:1–35)

Confess: c. your faults one to another, p. 235, (Jas. 5:16)

Confess: (*continued*)

every tongue c. that Jesus Christ is Lord, p. 218, (Phil. 2:11)

if we c. our sins, he is faithful, p. 238, (I Jn. 1:9)

Confessed: Israel stood and c. their sins, p. 46, (Neh. 9:2)

Confessing: c. their sins, p. 135, (Matt. 3:6; Mk. 1:5; cf. Lk. 3:3)

Confidence: in quietness and in c., p. 89, (Isa. 30:15)

Confident: in this will I be c., p. 58, (Ps. 27:3)

Confusion: God is not the author of c., p. 209, (I Cor. 14:33)

I am full of c., p. 51, (Job 10:15)

Congregation: over the c., p. 20, (Num. 27:16)

you shall not bring this c. into the land, p. 17, (Num. 20:12)

Conquering: went forth c. and to conquer, p. 243, (Rev. 6:2)

Conquerors: we are more than c., p. 202, (Rom. 8:37)

Conscience: a c. void of offence, p. 197, (Acts 24:16)

c. seared with a hot iron, p. 225, (I Tim. 4:2)

convicted by their own c., p. 167, (Jn. 8:9)

Consecration: c. of Aaron and his sons, p. 19, (Lev. 8–10)

Consider: my people doth not c., p. 81, (Isa. 1:3)

Consolation: everlasting c. and good hope, p. 223, (I Th. 2:16)

so our c. also abounds, p. 210, (II Cor. 1:5)

Consume: shall c. the glory of his forest, p. 84, (Isa. 10:18)

Content: having food . . . let us be c., p. 225, (I Tim. 6:8)

in whatsoever state I am, to be c., p. 219, (Phil. 4:11)

Contrite: a broken and a c. heart, p. 60, (Ps. 51:17)

Convenient: when I have a c. season, p. 197, (Acts 24:25)

Conversation: be holy in all manner of c., p. 235, (I Pet. 1:15)

Conversion: the c. of Saul, p. 192, (Acts 9:1–9; cf. 22:6–11; 26:12–18)

Cord: a threefold c. is not quickly broken, p. 75, (Ec. 4:12)

let them down by a c. through the window, p. 27, (Josh. 2:15)

Cords: the c. became as flax, p. 30, (Jg. 15:14)

Coriander: it was like c., p. 17, (Ex. 16:31; Num. 11:7)

Corinth: Paul's letters to C., p. 205, (Cor.)

Paul visits C., p. 195, (Acts 18:1)

Corn: Joseph gathered c., p. 12, (Gen. 41:49)

pluck the ears of c. and to eat, p. 149, (Matt. 12:1; Mk. 2:23; Lk. 6:1)

seven ears of c., p. 12, (Gen. 41:5, 6)

the c. withered, p. 116, (Joel 1:17)

the full c. in the ear, p. 156, (Mk. 4:28)

to Egypt to buy c., p. 12, (Gen. 42:3)

Cornelius: An angel of God came to C., p. 193, (Acts 10:3)

C. fell down and worshipped him, p. 193, (Acts 10:25)

C. the centurion, p. 193, (Acts 10:1–33)

Corner: a c. of the housetop, p. 72, (Prov. 21:9; 25:24)

Jesus Christ the chief c. stone, p. 216, (Eph. 2:20)

Corpses: they stumble upon their c., p. 123, (Nahum 3:3)

Correction: she received not c., p. 124, (Zeph. 3:2)

Corruption: c.: Thou art my father, p. 52, (Job 17:14)

The body is sown in c., p. 209, (I Cor. 15:42)

Cos: Paul travels via C., p. 196, (Acts 21:1)

Cost: does not count the c., p. 151, (Lk. 14:28)

Counsel: darkeneth c. by words without knowledge, p. 54, (Job 38:2)

his own c. shall cast him down, p. 52, (Job 18:7)

we took sweet c. together, p. 61, (Ps. 55:14)

Counselor: called Wonderful, C., The mighty God, p. 84, (Isa. 9:6)

Counsels: c. of old are faithfulness and truth, p. 87, (Isa. 25:1)

Countenance: a king of fierce c., p. 113, (Dan. 8:23)

Jesus' c. was altered, p. 161, (Matt. 17:2; Mk. 9:2–3; Lk. 9:29) lift up the light of thy c., p. 56, (Ps. 4:6)

merry heart maketh a cheerful c., p. 71, (Prov. 15:13)

the Lord lift up his c., p. 19, (Num. 6:26)

Countenances: their c. were fairer and fatter, p. 110, (Dan. 1:15)

Country: go unto my c., to my kindred, p. 9, (Gen. 24:4)

Courage: be strong and of a good c., p. 27, (Josh. 1:6, 9)

Courageous: the c. shall flee away naked, p. 118, (Amos 2:16)

Courts: a day in thy c. is better than a thousand, p. 62, (Ps. 84:10)

Covenant: a new c. with . . . Israel, p. 102, (Jer. 31:31)

Abram's vision and c., p. 8, (Gen. 15)

ark of the c. was brought to the temple, p. 38, (I Kg. 8:1–13; II Chr. 5:2—6:11)

behold the ark of the c., p. 27, (Josh. 3:11)

c. . . . with the house of Israel, p. 230, (Heb. 8:10)

give thee for a c., p. 93, (Isa. 42:6)

God's c. with Abram, p. 8, (Gen. 17:1–19)

God's c. with Noah, p. 7, (Gen. 8:21—9:17)

God shall keep . . . the c., p. 22, (Deut. 7:12)

he made a c. with God, p. 45, (II Kg. 23:21–23; II Chr. 34:31; 35:1)

I establish my c., p. 7, (Gen. 9:11)

I will establish my c. with him, p. 8, (Gen. 17:19)

if you keep my c., p. 17, (Ex. 19:5–6)

made a c. with the Lord, p. 43, (II Kg. 11:17; II Chr. 23:16)

the renewal of the c., p. 46, (Neh. 8—10)

we have made a c. with death, p. 88, (Isa. 28:15)

Cover: c. thee with my hand, p. 18, (Ex. 33:22)

Covet: thou shalt not c., p. 18, (Ex. 20:17)

Cows: dreamed of seven fat c., p. 12, (Gen. 41:2)

Craftiness: the wise in their own c., p. 50, (Job 5:13)

Crashing: a great c. from the hills, p. 124, (Zeph. 1:10)

Create: I c. new heavens, p. 96, (Isa. 65:17)

Created: behold who hath c. these things, p. 92, (Isa. 40:26)

by him were all things c., p. 220, (Col. 1:16)

for thou hast c. all things, p. 242, (Rev. 4:11)

God c. great whales, p. 3, (Gen. 1:21)

God c. man in his own image, p. 4, (Gen. 1:27)

God c. the earth and the seas, p. 3, (Gen. 1:9–10)

God c. the heaven and the earth, p. 3, (Gen. 1:1)

Creation: Second account of c., p. 3, (Gen. 2:4–25)

Second account of the c. of Adam and Eve, p. 4, (Gen. 2:7–25)

the c. of Adam and Eve, p. 4, (Gen. 1:26–31)

The c. of the world, p. 3, (Gen. 1—2:3)

the whole c. groaneth and travaileth, p. 202, (Rom. 8:22)

Creator: the creature more than the C., p. 199, (Rom. 1:25)

Creature: the c. more than the Creator, p. 199, (Rom. 1:25)

Creatures: waters bring forth living c., p. 3, (Gen. 1:20)

with the likeness of four living c., p. 105, (Ezek. 1:5)

Creeping: cattle and c. things, p. 4, (Gen. 1:24)

Cripple: a c. from his mother's womb, p. 194, (Acts 14:8)

Crooked: c. cannot be made straight, p. 74, (Ec. 1:15)

the c. shall be made straight, p. 91, (Isa. 40:4)

Cross: compelled Simon of Cyrene to bear his c., p. 182, (Matt. 27:32; Mk. 15:21; Lk. 23:26)

save in the c. of Christ, p. 215, (Gal. 6:14)

take up your c., p. 147, (Matt. 10:38–40; 16:24, 25; Mk. 8:34, 35; Lk. 9:23, 24; 14:27)

takes not his c. to follow after me, p. 147, (Matt. 10:38; 16:24; Mk. 8:34; Lk. 9:23; 14:27)

who for the joy . . . endured the c., p. 231, (Heb. 12:2)

Crossing: c. the Jordan, p. 27, (Josh. 3:9–17)

c. the Red Sea., p. 16, (Ex. 14)

Crowd: because of the c., p. 144, (Mk. 2:4; Lk. 5:19)

Crown: an Amelekite took Saul's c. to David, p. 34, (II Sam. 1:10)

and plaited a c. of thorns, p. 182, (Matt. 27:29; Mk. 15:17; Jn. 19.2)

he shall receive the c. of life, p. 233, (Jas. 1:12)

hoary head is a c. of glory, p. 71, (Prov. 16:31)

I will give thee a c. of life, p. 241, (Rev. 2:10)

royal c. upon her head, p. 46, (Est. 2:17)

you shall receive a c. of glory, p. 237, (I Pet. 5:4)

Crownest: c. the year with thy goodness, p. 61, (Ps. 65:11)

Crucified: betrayed to be c., p. 176, (Matt. 26:2)

c. with Christ, p. 214, (Gal. 2:20)

let him be c.!, p. 182, (Matt. 27:22; Mk. 15:13–14; Lk. 23:21, 23; Jn. 19:15)

they c. him and parted his garments, p. 182, (Matt. 27:35; Mk. 15:24; Lk. 23:33–34; Jn. 19:18, 23–24)

two thieves c. with him, p. 183, (Matt. 27:38; Mk. 15:27; Lk. 23:33; Jn. 19:18)

we preach Christ c., p. 205, (I Cor. 1:23)

Crucifixion: the c., p. 182, (Matt. 27:32–44; Mk. 15:21–32; Lk. 23:26–43; Jn. 19:17–29)

Crucify: and led him away to c. him, p. 182, (Matt. 27:31; Mk. 15:20)

c. . . . the Son of God afresh, p. 230, (Heb. 6:6)

Cruel: c. with wrath and fierce anger, p. 85, (Isa. 13:9)

Crumbs: to be fed with c. from the table, p. 153, (Lk. 16:21)

Cry: a c. from the fish gate, p. 124, (Zeph. 1:10)

c. and thou wilt not hear!, p. 123, (Hab. 1:2)

c. day and night, p. 154, (Lk. 18:7)

c. out in the night, p. 104, (Lam. 2:19)

c. ye out and cry, p. 89, (Isa. 29:9)

for righteousness, but behold a c., p. 83, (Isa. 5:7)

Crying: I am weary of my c., p. 61, (Ps. 69:3)

Cucumbers: a lodge in a garden of c., p. 81, (Isa. 1:8)

Cup: after the same manner he took the c., p. 208, (I Cor. 11:25)

dregs of the c. of my fury, p. 94, (Isa. 51:22)

he took the c. and gave thanks, p. 177, (Matt. 26:27; Mk. 14:23; Lk. 22:17, 20; I Cor. 11:25)

I will take the c. of salvation, p. 66, (Ps. 116:13)

if it be possible let this c. pass from me, p. 180, (Matt. 26:39; Mk. 14:35–36; Lk. 22:42)

make clean the outside of the c., p. 172, (Matt. 23:25; Lk. 11:39)

only those that c. their hand, p. 29, (Jg. 7:6)

the c. of the Lord and the c. of devils, p. 207, (I Cor. 10:21)

the c. of trembling, p. 94, (Isa. 51:22)

this c. is the new testament, p. 208, (I Cor. 11:25)

Cures: I cast out devils and do c., p. 169, (Lk. 13:32)

Curse: bless them that c. you, p. 140, (Matt. 5:44; Lk. 6:28)

c. God and die, p. 49, (Job 2:9)

he will c. you, p. 49, (Job 2:5)

touch his possessions and he will c. you, p. 49, (Job 1:11)

Cursed: c. be the man that trusteth in man, p. 101, (Jer. 17:5)

c. shalt thou be, p. 22, (Deut. 28:15, 16)

Cursing: life and death, blessing and c., p. 23, (Deut. 30:19)

Custody: in c. in Caesarea, p. 197, (Acts 23:15–35; 24)

Cut: c. it down, p. 150, (Lk. 13:7)

c. off from thee the righteous and the wicked, p. 108, (Ezek. 21:3)

Cyprus: Paul and Barnabus visit C., p. 194, (Acts 13:4)

Cyrus: proclamation of C., King of Persia, p. 45, (II Chr. 36:22; Ezra 1:1)

Damascus: D. shall be a ruinous heap, p. 86, (Isa. 17:1)

he came near D., p. 192, (Acts 9:3)

on the road to D., p. 192, (Acts 9:1–
9; cf. 22:6–11; 26:12–18)

Dan: from D. even to Beersheba, p.
30, (Jg. 20:1)

Dance: with the timbrel and d., p. 69,
(Ps. 150:4)

Danced: d. and pleased Herod, p.
158, (Matt. 14:6; Mk. 6:22)

David d. before the Lord, p. 35, (II
Sam. 6:14)

piped and ye have not d., p. 148,
(Matt. 11:17; Lk. 7:32)

Dances: with timbrels and d., p. 16,
(Ex. 15:20)

Daniel: D. and cast him into the den
of lions, p. 112, (Dan. 6:16)

D., Hananiah, Mishael and Azariah,
p. 110, (Dan. 1:6)

D., I am come to give thee skill, p.
113, (Dan. 9:22)

D. saw a ram with two horns, p. 112,
(Dan. 8:3)

D.'s vision of the four beasts, p. 112,
(Dan. 7)

D. was found making supplication to
God, p. 112, (Dan. 6:11)

D. would not defile himself, p. 110,
(Dan. 1:8)

let D. show the interpretation, p.
111, (Dan. 5:12)

O D., greatly beloved, understand, p.
113, (Dan. 10:11)

O D. is thy God able to deliver thee?,
p. 112, (Dan. 6:20)

the dream was revealed to D., p. 110,
(Dan. 2:19)

Darius: Belshazzar was slain and D.
became king, p. 112, (Dan. 5:30,
31)

D. decreed that the work resume, p.
46, (Ezra 6:3, 14)

D. . . . no man should petition, p.
112, (Dan. 6:7, 9)

Dark: understanding d. sentences, p.
113, (Dan. 8:23)

Darkeneth: d. counsel by words without knowledge, p. 54, (Job 38:2)

Darkness: a d. over all the earth, p.
183, (Matt. 27:45; Mk. 15:33;
Lk. 23:44)

against principalities, powers, rulers
of the d., p. 218, (Eph. 6:12)

before he cause d., p. 100, (Jer.
13:16)

cast into outer d., p. 171, (Matt.
22:13)

cast off the works of d., p. 204,
(Rom. 13:12)

d. was upon the face of the deep, p.
3, (Gen. 1:2)

d. which may be felt, p. 15, (Ex.
10:21)

deep things out of d., p. 51, (Job
12:22)

how great is that d., p. 141, (Matt.
6:23; cf. Lk. 11:34)

if the light . . . be d., p. 141, (Matt.
6:23; cf. Lk. 11:35)

lest d. come upon you, p. 176, (Jn.
12:35)

no fellowship with the works of d., p.
217, (Eph. 5:11)

shall not walk in d., p. 168, (Jn. 8:12)

such as sit in d., p. 65, (Ps. 107:10)

the d. has not overcome it, p. 131,
(Jn. 1:5)

the d. he called Night, p. 3, (Gen.
1:5)

the people that walked in d., p. 84,
(Isa. 9:2)

thy d. be as the noonday, p. 95, (Isa,
58:10)

what I tell you in d., p. 147, (Matt.
10:27; cf. Lk. 12:3)

when I sit in d., p. 122, (Micah 7:8)

you brethren are not in d., p. 222, (I
Th. 5:4)

Daughter: as is the mother, so is her
d., p. 107, (Ezek. 16:44)

d. is vexed with a devil, p. 159,
(Matt. 15:22; Mk. 7:26)

her d. was made whole, p. 159,
(Matt. 15:28; Mk. 7:29–30)

Jairus' d., p. 145, (Matt. 9:18–26;
Mk. 5:21–43; Lk. 8:40–56)

my d. is even now dead, p. 145,
(Matt. 9:18; Mk. 5:23; Lk. 8:42)

rejoice greatly, O d. of Zion, p. 126,
(Zech. 9:9)

shout O d. of Jerusalem, p. 126,
(Zech. 9:9)

the d. of Herodias danced, p. 158,
(Matt. 14:6; Mk. 6:22)

the Greek woman's d., p. 159, (Matt.
15:21–28; Mk. 7:24–30)

Daughters: the d. of Zion are
haughty, p. 82, (Isa. 3:16)

David: concerning D.'s son, p. 172, (Matt. 22:41–46; Mk. 12:35–37; Lk. 20:41–44)

D. and all Israel, p. 35, (I Chr. 11:4)

D. and Bathsheba, p. 35, (II Sam. 11)

D. and Goliath, p. 33, (I Sam. 17)

D. besought God for the child, p. 36, (II Sam. 12:16)

D. brought the ark of God into the city, p. 35, (II Sam. 6:12)

D.'s charge to Solomon, p. 37, (I Chr. 22, 28, 29:1–19)

D. danced before the Lord, p. 35, (II Sam. 6:14)

D. gave to Solomon the pattern, p. 37, (I Chr. 28:11–12)

D. his ten thousands, p. 34, (I Sam. 18:7)

D.'s lament . . . Saul and Jonathan, p. 34, (II Sam. 1:17–27)

D. made king over all Israel, p. 35, (II Sam. 5:1–5; I Chr. 11:1–3)

D.'s music helped Saul, p. 33, (I Sam. 16:23)

D. prevailed over the Philistine, p. 33, (I Sam. 17:50)

D.'s psalm of thanksgiving, p. 35, (I Chr. 16:8–36)

D. said I have sinned, p. 35, (II Sam. 12:13)

D. said to Bathsheba, Solomon, thy son shall reign, p. 37, (I Kg. 1:30)

D. slept with his fathers, p. 37, (I Kg. 2:10)

D. the outlaw, p. 34, (I Sam. 21–26)

D. the son of Jesse, p. 36, (II Sam. 23:1)

D. took Bathsheba, wife of Uriah, p. 35, (II Sam. 11:3–5)

D.'s victory song, p. 36, (II Sam. 22)

D. was forced to fight Absalom, p. 36, (II Sam. 15:13—19:8)

death of D.'s child, p. 36, (II Sam. 12:15–23)

friendship between D. and Jonathan, p. 33, (I Sam. 18:1–5)

if D. then call him Lord, p. 172, (Matt. 22:45; Mk. 12:37; Lk. 20:44)

Jerusalem—the city of D., p. 35, (II Sam. 6; I Chr. 11—16)

knit with the soul of D., p. 33, (I Sam. 18:1)

Nathan told D. a parable, p. 35, (II Sam. 12:1–14)

Obed, father of Jesse, father of D., p. 31, (Ruth 4:17)

Pharisees said: the son of D., p. 172, (Matt. 22:42; Mk. 12:35; Lk. 20:41)

Samuel anointed D., p. 33, (I Sam. 16:13)

Saul, jealous of D., p. 34, (I Sam. 18–23)

saved D. from Saul's anger, p. 34, (I Sam. 19–20)

spirit of the Lord came upon D., p. 33, (I Sam. 16:13)

the ark into the city of D., p. 35, (II Sam. 6:12)

the city of D., p. 35, (I Chr. 15:1)

the house of D., p. 35, (II Sam. 7; I Chr. 17)

the Lord hath sworn unto D., p. 67, (Ps. 132:11)

the Lord's sign to the house of D., p. 83, (Isa. 7:13, 14)

took Saul's crown and armlet to D., p. 34, (II Sam. 1:10)

what D. had done displeased the Lord, p. 35, (II Sam. 11:27)

will raise unto D. a righteous branch, p. 101, (Jer. 23:5)

Day: a d. in thy courts is better than a thousand, p. 62, (Ps. 84:10)

behold the d., behold, it is come, p. 107, (Ezek. 7:10)

behold the d. cometh, p. 127, (Mal. 4:1)

d. of the Lord cometh, p. 85, (Isa. 13:9)

d. of the Lord is at hand, p. 124, (Zeph. 1:7)

d. unto d. uttereth speech, p. 56, (Ps. 19:2)

God called the light D., p. 3, (Gen. 1:5)

great d. of his wrath has come, p. 243, (Rev. 6:17)

the d. of atonement, p. 19, (Lev. 23:27)

the d. of the Lord cometh, p. 116, (Joel 2:1)

the d. of the Lord is a d. of wrath, p. 124, (Zeph. 1:14–15)

the d. of the Lord is near, p. 117,
(Joel 3:14)

the d. of the Lord is near, p. 119,
(Obad. v. 15)

the d. of the Lord's vengeance, p. 90,
(Isa. 34:8)

the d. of the Lord will come as a
thief, p. 237, (II Pet. 3:10)

the d. which the Lord hath made, p.
66, (Ps. 118:24)

the great and dreadful d. of the
Lord, p. 127, (Mal. 4:5)

this d. in which ye came out from
Egypt, p. 16, (Ex. 13:3)

until the d. break, p. 77, (Song 2:17)

who may abide the d. of his coming,
p. 127, (Mal. 3:2)

Days: all the d. of my life, p. 57, (Ps.
23:6)

as thy d. so shall thy strength be, p.
21, (Deut. 33:25)

d. on the earth are as a shadow, p.
37, (I Chr. 29:15)

my d. are consumed like smoke, p.
64, (Ps. 102:3)

my d. are past, p. 52, (Job 17:11)

my d. are vanity, p. 50, (Job 7:16)

our d. upon earth are a shadow,
p. 51, (Job 8:9)

Dayspring: the d. from on high, p.
132, (Lk. 1:78)

Deacons: the d. be grave, not given
to much wine, p. 224, (I Tim.
3:8)

the first d., p. 191, (Acts 6:1–8)

Dead: a living dog is better than a d.
lion, p. 76, (Ec. 9:4)

am d. to the law, p. 214, (Gal. 2:19)

behold the child was d., p. 42, (II
Kg. 4:32)

blessed are the d. which die in the
Lord, p. 245, (Rev. 14:13)

daughter is even now d., p. 145,
(Matt. 9:18; Mk. 5:23; Lk. 8:42)

d. bury their d., p. 144, (Matt. 8:22;
Lk. 9:60)

d. in Christ shall rise first, p. 222, (I
Th. 4:16)

d. to the law, p. 214, (Gal. 2:19–20)

d. with him we shall also live with
him, p. 226, (II Tim. 2:11)

full of d. men's bones and uncleanness, p. 172, (Matt. 23:27)

God is not the God of the d., p. 171,

(Matt. 22:32; Mk. 12:27; Lk.
20:38)

he that was d. sat up, p. 155, (Lk.
7:15)

how are the d. raised up, p. 209, (I
Cor. 15:35)

I am forgotten as a d. man, p. 58,
(Ps. 31:12)

I saw the d. stand before God, p.
247, (Rev. 20:12)

if you are d. with Christ, p. 220,
(Col. 2:20)

in dark places as they that be d., p.
104, (Lam. 3:6)

now he is d. can I bring him back?,
p. 36, (II Sam. 12:23)

raise the d., p. 146, (Matt. 10:8)

the d. know not anything, p. 76, (Ec.
9:5)

the d. which are already d., p. 74,
(Ec. 4:2)

the d. which he slew at his death, p.
30, (Jg. 16:30)

the maid is not d. but sleepeth, p.
145, (Matt. 9:24; Mk. 5:39; Lk.
8:52)

there was a d. man carried out, p.
155, (Lk. 7:12)

though he were d., yet shall he live,
p. 169, (Jn. 11:25)

trumpet sound and the d. be raised,
p. 210, (I Cor. 15:52)

what advantage is the d. rise not?, p.
209, (I Cor. 15:32)

Deaf: brought to Jesus one who was
d., p. 159, (Mk. 7:32)

healing of a d. and dumb man, p.
159, (Mk. 7:31–37)

the d. adder that stoppeth her ear, p.
61, (Ps. 58:4)

the d. to hear and the dumb to
speak, p. 159, (Mk. 7:37)

Death: a pale horse: His rider was d.,
p. 243, (Rev. 6:8)

Absalom's treachery and d., p. 36, (II
Sam. 15:13—19:8)

became obedient unto d. even of the
cross, p. 218, (Phil. 2:8)

d. hath no more dominion over him,
p. 201, (Rom. 6:9)

d. is swallowed up in victory, p. 210,
(I Cor. 15:54)

d. of David's child, p. 36, (II Sam.
12:15–23)

Death: (continued)

die the d. of the righteous, p. 20, (Num. 23:10)

he was at the point of d., p. 166, (Jn. 4:47)

in the land of the shadow of d., p. 84, (Isa. 9:2)

in the shadow of d., p. 65, (Ps. 107:10)

in their d. they were not divided, p. 34, (II Sam. 1:23)

life and d., blessing and cursing, p. 23, (Deut. 30:19)

love is strong as d., p. 78, (Song 8:6)

neither d., nor life, nor angels, nor principalities . . . , p. 202, (Rom. 8:38)

not see the d. of the child, p. 9, (Gen. 21:16)

O d., I will be thy plagues, p. 116, (Hos. 13:14)

O d. where is thy sting?, p. 210, (I Cor. 15:55)

ready to go with thee into prison and to d., p. 179, (Lk. 22:33)

should taste d. for every man, p. 229, (Heb. 2:9)

so d. passed upon all men, p. 200, (Rom. 5:12)

swallow up d. in victory, p. 87, (Isa. 25:8)

that they might put him to d., p. 181, (Matt. 26:59; Mk. 14:55)

the dead which he slew at his d., p. 30, (Jg. 16:30)

the d. of Aaron, p. 20, (Num. 20:22–29)

the d. of his saints, p. 66, (Ps. 116:15)

the d. of King Saul, p. 34, (I Sam. 31; II Sam. 1; I Chr. 10)

the last enemy . . . is d., p. 209, (I Cor. 15:26)

the shadow of d., p. 51, (Job 10:21)

the sorrows of d. compassed me, p. 56, (Ps. 18:4)

the valley of the shadow of d., p. 57, (Ps. 23:4)

the way of life and the way of d., p. 101, (Jer. 21:8)

there is d. in the pot, p. 42, (II Kg. 4:40)

. . . there must be the d. of the testator, p. 230, (Heb. 9:16)

there shall be no more d., p. 247, (Rev. 21:4)

to light the shadow of d., p. 51, (Job 12:22)

turneth the shadow of d. into morning, p. 119, (Amos 5:8)

until the d. of Herod, p. 134, (Matt. 2:15)

waves of d. compassed me, p. 36, (II Sam. 22:5)

we have made a covenant with d., p. 88, (Isa. 28:15)

Deborah: D., a prophetess, was judge, p. 28, (Jg. 4:4)

D. and Barak, p. 28, (Jg. 4)

I D. arose a mother in Israel, p. 29, (Jg. 5:7)

song of D., p. 29, (Jg. 5)

Debt: moved with compassion and forgave the d., p. 163, (Matt. 18:27)

Deceit: the d. of their own heart, p. 101, (Jer. 23:26)

thine habitation is in the midst of d., p. 100, (Jer. 9:6)

Deceitful: heart is d. . . . who can know it?, p. 101, (Jer. 17:9)

Deceiveth: d. them that dwell on earth, p. 245, (Rev. 13:14)

Deceiving: d. your own selves, p. 233, (Jas. 1:22)

Decently: all things be done d. and in order, p. 209, (I Cor. 14:40)

Deep: d. calleth unto d., p. 59, (Ps. 42:7)

Defile: to eat with unwashed hands does not d., p. 159, (Matt. 15:20)

Defiles: not what goes into the mouth d., p. 159, (Matt. 15:22; Mk. 7:15, 18)

Delight: his d. is in the law of the Lord, p. 55, (Ps. 1:2)

no d. in your solemn rituals, p. 119, (Amos 5:21)

Delilah: Samson and D., p. 30, (Jg. 16)

Deliver: d. thee from the king of Assyria, p. 91, (Isa. 38:6)

d. thee from the snare of the fowler, p. 63, (Ps. 91:3)

d. us from the fiery furnace, p. 111, (Dan. 3:17)

d. you up to be afflicted, p. 173, (Matt. 24:9; Mk. 13:9; Lk. 21:12)

I am come to d. them, p. 14, (Ex. 3:8)

neither shall the mighty d. himself, p. 118, (Amos 2:14)

O Daniel is thy God able to d. thee?, p. 112, (Dan. 6:20)

they will d. you to the councils, p. 146, (Matt. 10:17; Mk. 13:9; Lk. 12:11; 21:12)

thy God whom thou servest will d. thee, p. 112, (Dan. 6:16)

who shall d. me from this body of death?, p. 201, (Rom. 7:24)

Delivered: at that time thy people shall be d., p. 114, (Dan. 12:1)

d. me from them that hate, p. 36, (II Sam. 22:18)

d. us from the power of darkness, p. 220, (Col. 1:13)

Deliverer: my fortress, and my d., p. 36, (II Sam. 22:2)

Demands: in answer to persistent d., p. 150, (Lk. 11:8)

Den: a d. of dragons, p. 100, (Jer. 9:11)

become a d. of robbers, p. 100, (Jer. 7:11)

Daniel and cast him into the d. of lions, p. 112, (Dan. 6:16)

the king went unto the d. of lions, p. 112, (Dan. 6:19)

Denied: till thou hast d. me thrice, p. 179, (Matt. 26:34; Mk. 14:30; Lk. 22:34; Jn. 13:38)

Deny: if we d. him, he also will d. us, p. 226, (II Tim. 2:12)

Depart: d. from me, p. 137, (Lk. 5:8)

d. from me ye that work iniquity, p. 142, (Matt. 7:23; Lk. 13:27)

he will not d., p. 72, (Prov. 22:6)

Depths: out of the d. have I cried unto thee, p. 67, (Ps. 130:1)

Derbe: Paul and Barnabus visit D., p. 194, (Acts 14:6, 20)

Descend: d. from heaven with a shout, p. 222, (I Th. 4:16)

Desert: her d. like the garden, p. 93, (Isa. 51:3)

make straight in the d., p. 91, (Isa. 40:3)

the d. shall rejoice, p. 90, (Isa. 35:1)

Desire: d. shall fail, p. 76, (Ec. 12:5)

his d. is toward me, p. 78, (Song 7:10)

the d. accomplished, p. 71, (Prov. 13:19)

the d. of our soul, p. 88, (Isa. 26:8)

Desolate: and make the land d., p. 106, (Ezek. 6:14)

I will lay the land most d., p. 109, (Ezek. 33:28)

in their d. houses, p. 85, (Isa. 13:22)

the land utterly d., p. 83, (Isa. 6:11)

Desolation: how is she become a d., p. 124, (Zeph. 2:15)

Despise: I d. your feast days, p. 119, (Amos 5:21)

let no man d. thee, p. 227, (Tit. 2:15)

let no man d. thy youth, p. 225, (I Tim. 4:12)

Despised: d. and rejected of men, p. 94, (Isa. 53:3)

hath d. the day of small things, p. 126, (Zech. 4:10)

Destroy: d. the righteous with the wicked, p. 9, (Gen. 18:23)

for the sake of ten I will not d., p. 9, (Gen. 18:32)

he will d. the mighty and the holy, p. 113, (Dan. 8:24)

not come to d. but to fulfill, p. 139, (Matt. 5:17)

not hurt nor d. in all my holy mountain, p. 85, (Isa. 11:9)

the Lord said: I will d. man, p. 6, (Gen. 6:7)

the owner will d. the workers, p. 170, (Matt. 21:41; Mk. 12:9; Lk. 20:16)

to d. both soul and body, p. 147, (Matt. 10:28; cf. Lk. 12:5)

Destroyed: d. all that was in the city, p. 27, (Josh. 6:21)

he hath d. his strongholds, p. 104, (Lam. 2:5)

Jerusalem d. by Babylon, p. 103, (Jer. 39–40)

Destruction: prediction of the d. of Jerusalem, p. 169, (Lk. 19:41–44)

prediction of the d. of the temple, p. 172, (Matt. 24:1–2; Mk. 13:1–2; Lk. 21:5–6)

pride goeth before d., p. 71, (Prov. 16:18)

the d. of Jericho, p. 27, (Josh. 6)

thou turnest man to d., p. 62, (Ps. 90:3)

whose end is d., p. 219, (Phil. 3:19)

Devil: Jesus rebuked the d., p. 161, (Matt. 17:18; cf. Mk. 9:25; Lk. 9:42)

laid hold of the d. and bound him, p. 246, (Rev. 20:2)

Devil: (continued)

resist the d. and he will flee, p. 234, (Jas. 4:7)

stand against the wiles of the d., p. 218, (Eph. 6:11)

that old serpent called the d., p. 244, (Rev. 12:9)

the d. offered Jesus the kingdoms, p. 136, (Matt. 4:8–9; Lk. 4:5–7)

the d. set him on a pinnacle of the temple, p. 136, (Matt. 4:5; Lk. 4:9)

your adversary the d. as a roaring lion, p. 237, (I Pet. 5:8)

Devils: by the prince of d., p. 145, (Matt. 9:34)

d. went into a herd of swine, p. 144, (Matt. 8:32; Mk. 5:13; Lk. 8:33)

I cast out d. and do cures, p. 169, (Lk. 13:32)

the Pharisees said he casts out d., p. 145, (Matt. 9:34)

Devour: seeking whom he may d., p. 237, (I Pet. 5:8)

Devoured: be d. with the sword, p. 81, (Isa. 1:20)

Dew: as the early d. it goeth away, p. 115, (Hos. 6:4)

begotten the drops of d.?, p. 54, (Job 38:28)

thou hast the d. of thy youth, p. 65, (Ps. 110:3)

Diana: D. of the Ephesians, p. 196, (Acts 19:28)

Die: a time to d., p. 74, (Ec. 3:2)

believeth in me shall never d., p. 169, (Jn. 11:26)

come down ere my child d., p. 166, (Jn. 4:49)

curse God and d., p. 49, (Job 2:9)

eat and drink for tomorrow we d., p. 209, (I Cor. 15:32)

fall into the ground and d., p. 175, (Jn. 12:24)

firstborn of Egypt shall d., p. 15, (Ex. 12:12)

for tomorrow we shall d., p. 87, (Isa. 22:13)

if a man d. shall he live again?, p. 51, (Job 14:14)

if it d. it bringeth forth . . . , p. 175, (Jn. 12:24)

it is better for me to d., p. 121, (Jonah 4:3)

ready to d. at Jerusalem, p. 197, (Acts 21:13)

the dead which d. in the Lord, p. 245, (Rev. 14:13)

the living know that they shall d., p. 76, (Ec. 9:5)

to live is Christ, to d. is gain, p. 218, (Phil. 1:21)

we must needs d., p. 36, (II Sam. 14:14)

whether we live or d. we are the Lord's, p. 204, (Rom. 14:8)

wisdom will d. with you, p. 51, (Job 12:2)

Died: Christ d. for our sins, p. 209, (I Cor. 15:3)

he d. in a good old age, p. 37, (II Chr. 29:28)

he d. unto sin once, p. 201, (Rom. 6:10)

Jesus d. and rose again, p. 222, (I Th. 4:14)

Moses d. in the land of Moab, p. 21, (Deut. 34:5)

the child d., p. 36, (II Sam. 12:18)

why d. I not from the womb?, p. 50, (Job 3:11)

would God I had d. for thee, p. 36, (II Sam. 18:33)

would God that we had d., p. 19, (Num. 14:2)

would to God we had d., p. 16, (Ex. 16:3)

Difference: God put no d. between us, p. 195, (Acts 15:9)

Diligence: thy heart with all d., p. 69, (Prov. 4:23)

Diligently: looking d. lest any man fail, p. 231, (Heb. 12:15)

teach them d. unto thine children, p. 23, (Deut. 6:7)

Dinner: better is a d. of herbs, p. 71, (Prov. 15:17)

when you give a d., p. 151, (Lk. 14:12)

Direct: he shall d. thy paths, p. 69, (Prov. 3:6)

Discerner: a d. of the thoughts, p. 229, (Heb. 4:12)

Disciple: (See also Apostle)

the d. is not above his master, p. 147, (Matt. 10:24; Lk. 6:40)

his mother and the d. he loved, p. 183, (Jn. 19:26)

the d. whom Jesus loved, p. 185, (Jn. 21:7)

who does not forsake all cannot be my d., p. 151, (Lk. 14:33)

Disciples: all men know that ye are my d., p. 178, (Jn. 13:35)

all the d. forsook him and fled, p. 180, (Matt. 26:56; Mk. 14:50)

call of the first d., p. 136, (Matt. 4:18–22; Mk. 1:16–20; Lk. 5:1–11)

came to the d. and found them asleep, p. 180, (Matt. 26:40; Mk. 14:37; Lk. 22:45)

d. disobey the tradition, p. 158, (Matt. 15:2; Mk. 7:5)

d. rebuked those that brought them, p. 163, (Matt. 19:13; Mk. 10:13; Lk. 18:15)

d. went unto a mountain in Galilee, p. 185, (Matt. 28:16)

his d. were indignant, p. 176, (Matt. 26:8; Mk. 14:4)

Jesus' appearance to the d., p. 184, (Mk. 16:14–18; Lk. 24:36–49; Jn. 20:19–23)

Saul and the d. in Jerusalem, p. 193, (Acts 9:26–31)

the d. sent forth, p. 146, (Matt. 10:5–16; Mk. 6:7–11; Lk. 9:1–6)

the d. took him by night, p. 193, (Acts 9:25)

the d. were called Christians, p. 194, (Acts 11:26)

the suffering of the d., p. 173, (Matt. 24:9–14; Mk. 13:9–13; Lk. 21:12–19; Jn. 16:2–6)

the twelve d., p. 146, (Matt. 9:35–38; 10:1–4; Mk. 3:13–19; 6:34; Lk. 6:13–16)

thy d. could not cure him, p. 161, (Matt. 17:16; Mk. 9:18; Lk. 9:40)

told the d. she had seen the Lord, p. 184, (Mk. 16:10–11; Jn. 20:18)

when he called his twelve d., p. 146, (Matt. 10:1; Mk. 3:14, 15)

your d. not fast, p. 145, (Matt. 9:14; Mk. 2:18; Lk. 5:33)

Discipleship: the nature of d., p. 144, (Matt. 8:18–22; Lk. 9:57–62)

Dismayed: be not d. for I am thy God, p. 92, (Isa. 41:10)

Disobedience: by one man's d. many

were made sinners, p. 200, (Rom. 5:19)

Disobedient: held out my hands to a d. people, p. 202, (Rom. 10:21)

Displeased: d. with your fathers, p. 125, (Zech. 1:2)

it d. Jonah and he was angry, p. 121, (Jonah 4:1)

Distress: I will bring d. upon men, p. 124, (Zeph. 1:17)

Ditch: both shall fall into the d., p. 159, (Matt. 15:14)

Divide: d. the living child, p. 37, (I Kg. 3:25)

lift up thy rod and d. the sea, p. 16, (Ex. 14:16)

Divided: if a house be d. against itself, p. 146, (Matt. 12:25; Mk. 3:25; Lk. 11:17)

Division: the d. of the land, p. 28, (Josh. 13:22)

Divisions: that there be no d. among you, p. 205, (I Cor. 1:10)

Divorce: d., p. 139, (Matt. 5:31–32; 19:9; Mk. 10:11–12; Lk. 16:18)

Do: as ye would that men should d., p. 142, (Matt. 7:12; Lk. 6:31)

d. not the things which I say, p. 142, (Lk. 6:46)

Doctrine: make to understand d., p. 88, (Isa. 28:9)

my d. is not mine, p. 160, (Jn. 7:16)

Doers: d. of the word not hearers only, p. 233, (Jas. 1:22)

Dog: a living d. is better than a dead lion, p. 76, (Ec. 9:4)

d. is turned to his own vomit, p. 237, (II Pet. 2:22)

d. returneth to his vomit, p. 73, (Prov. 26:11)

is thy servant a d.?, p. 43, (II Kg. 8:13)

that lap the water as a d., p. 29, (Jg. 7:5)

Dogs: children's bread and cast it to the d., p. 159, (Matt. 15:26; Mk. 7:27)

d. shall lick thy blood, p. 41, (I Kg. 21:19)

the d. shall eat Jezebel, p. 41, (I Kg. 21:23)

yet the d. eat of the crumbs, p. 159, (Matt. 15:27; Mk. 7:28)

Doings: known by his d., p. 72, (Prov. 20:11)

Dominion: d. over all the earth, p. 4, (Gen. 1:28)

his d. is an everlasting d., p. 112, (Dan. 7:14)

Done: as thou hast d., it shall be d. unto thee, p. 119, (Obad. v. 15)

what could have been d. more, p. 82, (Isa. 5:4)

Door: he that enters by the d. is the shepherd, p. 168, (Jn. 10:2)

I am the d., p. 168, (Jn. 10:7, 9)

I beheld a d. and he said: Go in, p. 107, (Ezek. 8:8–9)

lintels and d. posts, p. 15, (Ex. 12:7)

set before thee an open d., p. 241, (Rev. 3:8)

Doorkeeper: a d. in the house of my God, p. 62, (Ps. 84:10)

Dorcas: Tabitha (D.) restored to life, p. 193, (Acts 9:36–42)

Dothan: cast him into a pit in D., p. 12, (Gen. 37:17, 24)

Double: a d. minded man is unstable, p. 233, (Jas. 1:8)

a d. portion of thy spirit be upon me, p. 42, (II Kg. 2:9)

Dove: d. brought an olive leaf, p. 6, (Gen. 8:11)

Noah sent forth a d., p. 6, (Gen. 8:8)

the spirit of God descending like a d., p. 135, (Matt. 3:16; Mk. 1:10; Lk. 3:21–22; Jn. 1:32)

Doves: thou hast d.' eyes, p. 77, (Song 4:1)

wise as serpents, harmless as d., p. 146, (Matt. 10:16)

Downfall: the d. of the Assyrians, 86, (Isa. 14:25)

Downsitting: my d. and mine uprising, p. 67, (Ps. 139:2)

Dragon: a great red d. having seven heads, p. 244, (Rev. 12:3)

Michael and his angels fought the d., p. 244, (Rev. 12:7)

the great d. was cast out, p. 244, (Rev. 12:9)

Dragons: a brother to d., p. 54, (Job 30:29)

a den of d., p. 100, (Jer. 9:11)

a dwelling place for d., p. 103, (Jer. 51:37)

a wailing like the d., p. 121, (Micah 1:8)

d. in their pleasant palaces, p. 85, (Isa. 13:22)

habitation of d. and a court for owls, p. 90, (Isa. 34:13)

ye d., and all deeps, p. 68, (Ps. 148:7)

Dream: appeared to Joseph in a d., p. 134, (Matt. 2:13)

being warned in d., p. 134, (Matt. 2:12)

I will interpret his d., p. 110, (Dan. 2:24)

old men shall d. dreams, p. 117, (Joel 2:28)

the d. was revealed to Daniel, p. 110, (Dan. 2:19)

Dreamed: Jacob d. of a ladder, p. 10, (Gen. 28:12)

Dreamer: a d. of dreams, p. 22, (Deut. 13:1)

Dreams: a dreamer of d., p. 22, (Deut. 13:1)

Joseph interpreted Pharaoh's d., p. 12, (Gen. 41:1–36)

Joseph interpreted the d. of butler and baker, p. 12, (Gen. 40)

Nebuchadnezzar dreamed d., p. 110, (Dan. 2:1)

old men dream d., p. 189, (Acts 2:17)

Dregs: d. of the cup of my fury, p. 94, (Isa. 51:22)

Drink: are ye able to d. of the cup . . . ?, p. 164, (Matt. 20:22; Mk. 10:38)

d. ye all of it, p. 177, (Matt. 26:27; Mk. 14:23; Lk. 22:17, 20)

early in the morning to follow strong d., p. 83, (Isa. 5:11)

I will not d. henceforth . . . , p. 177, (Matt. 26:29; Mk. 14:25; cf. Lk. 22:16, 18)

Jesus said: Give me to d., p. 166, (Jn. 4:7)

stagger but not with strong d., p. 89, (Isa. 29:9)

strong d. is raging, p. 72, (Prov. 20:1)

this do ye, as oft as ye d. it, p. 208, (I Cor. 11:25)

thou shalt no more d. it again, p. 94, (Isa. 51:22)

until I d. it new with you, p. 177, (Matt. 26:29; Mk. 14:25; cf. Lk. 22:16, 18)

Drinking: came eating and d., p. 148, (Matt. 11:19; Lk. 7:34)

neither eating nor d., p. 148, (Matt. 11:18; Lk. 7:33)

Drinks: whosoever d. of the water I shall give, p. 166, (Jn. 4:14)

Driving: the d. is like the d. of Jehu, p. 43, (II Kg. 9:20)

Drops: begotten the d. of dew?, p. 54, (Job 38:28)

Dropsy: the healing of a man with d., p. 151, (Lk. 14:1–6)

Drunk: Eli, . . . , thought she was d., p. 31, (I Sam. 1:13)

Drunken: not d. as ye suppose, p. 189, (Acts 2:15)

d. but not with wine, p. 89, (Isa. 29:9)

stagger like a d. man, p. 65, (Ps. 107:27)

Dry: in a d. and thirsty land, p. 61, (Ps. 63:1)

let the d. land appear, p. 3, (Gen. 1:9)

rivers of water in a d. place, p. 89, (Isa. 32:2)

through walls of water on d. ground, p. 16, (Ex. 14:22)

ye d. bones hear the word of the Lord, p. 109, (Ezek. 37:4)

Dues: render therefore to all their d., p. 204, (Rom. 13:7)

Dumb: healing of a deaf and d. man, p. 159, (Mk. 7:31–37)

makes the d. to speak, p. 145, (Matt. 9:32–34)

the deaf to hear and the d. to speak, p. 159, (Mk. 7:37)

Dust: d. you are and to d. you shall return, p. 5, (Gen. 3:19)

the d. of the earth, p. 10, (Gen. 28:14)

the d. of your feet, p. 146, (Matt. 10:14; Mk. 6:11; Lk. 9:5)

God formed man of the d., p., 4, (Gen. 2:7)

he remembereth that we are d., p. 64, (Ps. 103:14)

the d. of the land became lice, p. 15, (Ex. 8:16)

the d. thereof into brimstone, p. 90, (Isa. 34:9)

ye that dwell in d., p. 88, (Isa. 26:19)

your seed as the d. of the earth, p. 8, (Gen. 13:16)

Duty: the whole d. of man, p. 76, (Ec. 12:13)

we have done our d., p. 153, (Lk. 17:10)

Dwell: d. in a corner of the housetop, p. 72, (Prov. 21:9; 25:24)

I will d. in the midst of thee, p. 126, (Zech. 2:10)

who shall d. in thy holy hill, p. 56, (Ps. 15:1)

ye that d. in dust, p. 88, (Isa. 26:19)

Dwelt: was made flesh and d. among us, p. 131, (Jn. 1:14)

Dying: d., behold we live, p. 212, (II Cor. 6:9)

Eagle: a lion, an ox and an e., p. 195, (Ezek. 1:10)

a second e. and the vine did bend, p. 108, (Ezek. 17:7)

the fourth was like an e., p. 242, (Rev. 4:7)

e. with great wings . . . came unto Lebanon, p. 107, (Ezek. 17:3)

Eagles: mount up with wings as e., p. 92, (Isa. 40:31)

swifter than e., p. 34, (II Sam. 1:23)

Ear: by the hearing of the e., p. 55, (Job 42:5)

cut off the e. of a servant, p. 180, (Matt. 26:51; Mk. 14:47; Lk. 22:50; Jn. 18:10)

first the blade, then the e., p. 156, (Mk. 4:28)

he touched his e. and healed him, p. 180, (Lk. 22:51)

incline thine e., O Lord, p. 90, (Isa. 37:17)

Jesus put his fingers into his e., p. 159, (Mk. 7:33)

nor the e. with hearing, p. 74, (Ec. 1:8)

the deaf adder that stoppeth her e., p. 61, (Ps. 58:4)

Ears: e. shall hear a word behind thee, p. 89, (Isa. 30:21)

e. to hear, let him hear, p. 156, (Matt. 13:9; Mk. 4:9; Lk. 8:8)

have e., but they hear not, p. 66, (Ps. 115:6; 135:17)

his e. were opened, p. 159, (Mk. 7:35)

my cry did enter his e., p. 36, (II Sam. 22:7)

Earth: dominion over all the e., p. 4, (Gen. 1:28)

e. is utterly broken down, p. 87, (Isa. 24:19)

e. shall be full of the knowledge, p. 85, (Isa. 11:9)

easier for heaven and e. to pass away, p. 139, (Lk. 16:17; cf. Matt. 5:18)

foundations of the e., p. 54, (Job 38:4)

God called the dry land, E., p. 3, (Gen. 1:10)

God created the e. and the seas, p. 3, (Gen. 1:9–10)

God created the heaven and the e., p. 3, (Gen. 1:1)

he hath made the e. by his power, p. 103, (Jer. 51:15)

let the e. rejoice, p. 64, (Ps. 97:1)

O e., earth, earth, p. 101, (Jer. 22:29)

sing unto the Lord all the e., p. 63, (Ps. 96:1)

swear not . . . nor by the e., p. 139, (Matt. 5:35)

the dust of the e., p. 10, (Gen. 28:14)

the e. is full of thy riches, p. 65, (Ps. 104:24)

the e. is the Lord's, p. 57, (Ps. 24:1)

the e. is the Lord's and the fulness thereof, p. 208, (I Cor. 10:26)

the e. mourneth, p. 87, (Isa. 24:4)

the e. shall quake, p. 116, (Joel 2:10)

the e. sitteth still and is at rest, p. 125, (Zech. 1:11)

the e. was without form, p. 3, (Gen. 1:2)

the heavens are higher than the e., p. 94, (Isa. 55:9)

the Lord maketh the e. empty, p. 87, (Isa. 24:1)

thou hadst formed the e., p. 62, (Ps. 90:2)

though the e. be removed, p. 60, (Ps. 46:2)

upon the circle of the e., p. 92, (Isa. 40:22)

while the e. remaineth, p. 7, (Gen. 8:22)

Earthquake: after the wind an e., p. 41, (I Kg. 19:11)

e. freed the prisoners, p. 195, (Acts 16:26)

the Lord was not in the e., p. 41, (I Kg. 19:11)

East: as far as the e. is from the west, p. 64, (Ps. 103:12)

Eat: and e. the fruit of them, p. 96, (Isa. 65:21)

did all e. and were filled, p. 159, (Matt. 15:37; Mk. 8:8)

ears of corn and to e., p. 149, (Matt. 12:1; Lk. 6:1)

e. and drink for tomorrow we die, p. 209, (I Cor. 15:32)

e. with unwashed hands, p. 159, (Matt. 15:20)

God told them not to e., p. 5, (Gen. 3:3)

let us e. and drink, p. 87, (Isa. 22:13)

not plant and another e., p. 96, (Isa. 65:22)

rise, Peter; kill, and e., p. 193, (Acts 10:13)

take, e.. This is my body, p. 177, (Matt. 26:26; Mk. 14:22; I Cor. 11:24; cf. Lk. 22:19)

the multitude did e. and were filled, p. 158, (Matt. 14:20; Mk. 6:42; Lk. 9:17; Jn. 6:12)

to e., drink and be merry, p. 76, (Ec. 8:15)

when you e. you will be like gods, p. 5, (Gen. 3:5)

you may freely e., p. 4, (Gen. 2:16)

you shall not e., p. 4, (Gen. 2:17)

Eater: out of the e. came forth meat, p. 30, (Jg. 14:14)

Eateth: e. your master with sinners, p. 145, (Matt. 9:10–13; Mk. 2:15–17; Lk. 5:29–32)

Eating: came e. and drinking, p. 148, (Matt. 11:19; Lk. 7:34)

neither e. nor drinking, p. 148, (Matt. 11:18; Lk. 7:33)

Eden: a garden eastward in E., p. 4, (Gen. 2:8)

make her wilderness like E., p. 93, (Isa. 51:3)

Eggs: the partridge sitteth on e., p. 101, (Jer. 17:11)

Egypt: a new king over E., p. 13, (Ex. 1:8)

Abram went down into E., p. 7, (Gen. 12:10)

brought you up from the land of E., p. 118, (Amos 2:10)

children of Israel out of E., p. 15, (Ex. 12:51)

deliver them out of E., p. 14, (Ex. 3:8)

died in the land of E., p. 16, (Ex. 16:3)

firstborn of E. shall die, p. 15, (Ex. 12:12)

flee into E., p. 134, (Matt. 2:13)

flight of the holy family into E., p. 134, (Matt. 2:13–15; 19–23)

in E. there was bread, p. 12, (Gen. 41:54)

I will pass through E., p. 15, (Ex. 12:12)

over all the land of E., p. 12, (Gen. 41:41)

rivers of E. turned to blood, p. 15, (Ex. 7:20)

sold into E., p. 12, (Gen. 45:4)

spirit of E. shall fail, p. 86, (Isa. 19:3)

the burden of E., p. 86, (Isa. 19:1)

the cattle of E. died, p. 15, (Ex. 9:6)

the land of E. shall be desolate, p. 108, (Ezek. 29:9)

this day in which ye came out from E., p. 16, (Ex. 13:3)

to E. to buy corn, p. 12, (Gen. 42:3)

with chains unto the land of E., p. 108, (Ezek. 19:4)

Egyptian: and slew the E., p. 14, (Ex. 2:12)

E. beating an Hebrew, p. 14, (Ex. 2:11)

Egyptians: E. against the E., p. 86, (Isa. 19:2)

Elder: e. shall serve the younger, p. 10, (Gen. 25:23)

rebuke not an e., p. 225, (I Tim. 5:1)

the e. son was angry, p. 152, (Lk. 15:28)

Elders: concerning bishops (e.), p. 224, (I Tim. 3:1–7; Tit. 1:5–9)

e. sitting around the throne, p. 242, (Rev. 4:4)

in the midst of the e. stood a Lamb, p. 242, (Rev. 5:6)

ordain e. in every city, p. 224, (Tit. 1:5)

the apostles and e. came together, p. 194, (Acts 15:6)

the apostles and e. sent letters, p. 195, (Acts 15:23)

Elect: gather his e. from the four

winds, p. 173, (Matt. 24:31; Mk. 13:27)

Eli: E. and Samuel, p. 31, (I Sam. 2:11–26; 3:1–20)

E. . . . thought she was drunk, p. 31, (I Sam. 1:13)

ministered unto the Lord before E., p. 31, (I Sam. 2:11)

she took him to E. in the temple, p. 31, (I Sam. 1:24–25)

Elihu: E.'s wrath kindled against Job, p. 54, (Job 32:2)

Elijah: E. and the prophets of Baal, p. 40, (I Kg. 18:17–40)

E. cast his mantle upon Elisha, p. 41, (I Kg. 19:19)

E. cried unto the Lord, p. 40, (I Kg. 17:21)

E. dwelt with a widow, p. 40, (I Kg. 17:8–24)

E. fed by ravens, p. 39, (I Kg. 17:2–7)

E. fled from Jezebel, p. 41, (I Kg. 19:2–3)

E. prayed for rain, p. 40, (I Kg. 18:41–46)

E. prophesied drought, p. 39, (I Kg. 17:1)

E. prophesies to Ahab, p. 41, (I Kg. 21:17–25)

E. went up by a whirlwind into heaven, p. 42, (II Kg. 2:11)

E. went up . . . Mount Carmel, p. 40, (I Kg. 18:42)

Elisha inherited E.'s mantle, p. 42, (II Kg. 2:12–15)

he took the mantle of E., p. 42, (II Kg. 2:14)

I will send you E. the prophet, p. 127, (Mal. 4:5)

Moses and E. appeared in glory, p. 161, (Matt. 17:3; Mk. 9:4; Lk. 9:30–31)

scribes say E. must come first?, p. 161, (Matt. 17:10; Mk. 9:11)

the Lord commanded E. to flee, p. 39, (I Kg. 17:2–3)

Eliphaz: E., Bildad, and Zophar, p. 49, (Job 2:11)

E. reproved Job, p. 52, (Job 15)

E. speaks of confidence in God, p. 50, (Job 4—5)

E.'s speech, p. 53, (Job 22)

Elisabeth: Mary visited her cousin E., p. 132, (Lk. 1:39–40)

E., shall bear thee a son, p. 131, (Lk. 1:13)

Elisha: Elijah cast his mantle upon E., p. 41, (I Kg. 19:19)

E. and the Shunammite woman, p. 42, (II Kg. 4:8–37)

E. and the widow's oil, p. 42, (II Kg. 4:1–7)

E. cast a stick in, p. 43, (II Kg. 6:6)

E. inherited Elijah's mantle, p. 42, (II Kg. 2:12–15)

E. prayed unto the Lord, p. 42, (II Kg. 4:33)

E. stretched himself upon the child, p. 42, (II Kg. 4:34)

E. was come into the house, p. 42, (II Kg. 4:32)

E. was fallen sick, p. 44, (II Kg. 13:14)

Naaman cured of leprosy by E., p. 42, (II Kg. 5)

the call of E., p. 41, (I Kg. 19)

the death of E., p. 44, (II Kg. 13:14–21)

Eloquent: an e. man, p. 196, (Acts 18:24)

Emmanuel (See also Immanuel)

call him E., meaning God with us, p. 132, (Matt. 1:23)

Emmaus: went to a village called E., p. 184, (Lk. 24:13)

Empty: she is e., and void, and waste, p. 123, (Nahum 2:10)

Enclosed (See Inclosed)

End: an e. is come upon the four corners . . . , p. 107, (Ezek. 7:2)

better is the e. . . . than the beginning, p. 75, (Ec. 7:8)

even unto the e. of the world, p. 185, (Matt. 28:20)

harvest is the e. of the world, p. 156, (Matt. 13:39)

how long shall it be to the e.?, p. 114, (Dan. 12:6)

I not make a full e., p. 99, (Jer. 4:27)

make me to know mine e., p. 59, (Ps. 39:4)

sealed till the time of the e., p. 114, (Dan. 12:9)

then shall the e. come, p. 173, (Matt. 24:14)

Endor: Saul and the witch of E., p. 34, (I Sam. 28)

Ends: e. of the world shall remember, p. 57, (Ps. 22:27)

Endure: e. unto the end shall be saved, p. 173, (Matt. 24:13; Mk. 13:13)

Endureth: he that e. to the end, p. 147, (Matt. 10:22; Mk. 13:13)

the word of the Lord e. for ever, p. 235, (I Pet. 1:25)

Enemies: avenged themselves against their e., p. 28, (Josh. 10:13)

I make thine e. thy footstool, p. 65, (Ps. 110:1)

in the presence of mine e., p. 57, (Ps. 23:5)

love your e., p. 140, (Matt. 5:44; Lk. 6:17, 35)

the Jews smote all their e., p. 46, (Est. 9:5)

Enemy: am I become your e.?, p. 215, (Gal. 4:16)

an e. sowed weeds, p. 156, (Matt. 13:25)

hast thou found me, O mine e.?, p. 41, (I Kg. 21:20)

if thine e. hunger, feed him, p. 203, (Rom. 12:20)

rejoice not against me, O mine e., p. 122, (Micah 7:8)

the Lord was as an e., p. 104, (Lam. 2:5)

Ensign: an e. for the nations, p. 85, (Isa. 11:12)

Entice: if sinners e. thee, p. 69, (Prov. 1:10)

Entreat: e. me not to leave thee, p. 31, (Ruth 1:16)

Envying: not in strife and e., p. 204, (Rom. 13:13)

Ephesians: Diana of the E., p. 196, (Acts 19:28)

Ephesus: fought with beasts at E., p. 209, (I Cor. 15:32)

Paul at E., p. 196, (Acts 19)

Paul's letters to E., p. 215, (Eph.)

Paul travels from E., p. 196, (Acts 19—21:15)

the saints which are at E., p. 215, (Eph. 1:1)

to the church of E., p. 240, (Rev. 2:1–7)

Epileptic: the healing of an e. boy, p. 161, (Matt. 17:14–21; Mk. 9:14–29; Lk. 9:37–43; cf. 17:6)

Esau: birth of Jacob and E., p. 10, (Gen. 25:21–26)

E. cried, bless me, p. 10, (Gen. 27:34)

E. had skin like a hairy garment, p. 10, (Gen. 25:25)

E. hated Jacob, p. 10, (Gen. 27:41)

E. ran to meet him, p. 11, (Gen. 33:4)

E. sells his birthright to Jacob, p. 10, (Gen. 25:27–34)

from the hand of my brother E., p. 11, (Gen. 32:11)

Jacob flees from E., p. 10, (Gen. 27:41—28:10)

Jacob took hold of E.'s heel, p. 10, (Gen. 25:26)

Jacob's and E.'s reconciliation, p. 11, (Gen. 32:3–21; 33:1–20)

steals E.'s blessing from Isaac, p. 10, (Gen. 27:1–40)

the hands are E.'s, p. 10, (Gen. 27:22)

Escape: the e. from prison, p. 191, (Acts 5:19–42)

Escaped: e. all safe to land, p. 198, (Acts 27:44)

Esther: E.: a Jewish Queen of Persia, p. 46, (Est. 1—2:1—18)

E. interceded with the king, p. 46, (Est. 7:3)

he loved E. and laid the crown upon her head, p. 46, (Est. 2:17)

Ethiopian: can the E. change his skin, p. 100, (Jer. 13:23)

the E. eunuch, p. 192, (Acts 8:26–40)

Eternal: the gift of God is e. life, p. 201, (Rom. 6:23)

things which are not seen are e., p. 211, (II Cor. 4:18)

what shall I do to have e. life?, p. 163, (Matt. 19:16; Mk. 10:17; Lk. 18:18)

you think you have e. life, p. 167, (Jn. 5:39)

Eunuch: Philip baptized the e., p. 192, (Acts 8:38)

the Ethiopian e., p. 192, (Acts 8:26–40)

the e. said: I believe, p. 192, (Acts 8:37)

Eutychus: E. fell asleep, p. 196, (Acts 20:9)

Evangelist: do the work of an e., p. 227, (II Tim. 4:5)

Eve: E. ate the forbidden fruit, p. 5, (Gen. 3:6)

second account of the creation of Adam and E., p. 4, (Gen. 2:7–25)

temptation and disobedience of Adam and E., p. 5, (Gen. 3:1–6)

the creation of Adam and E., p. 4, (Gen. 1:26–31)

Even: would God it were e., p. 23, (Deut. 28:67)

Evening: her judges are e. wolves, p. 124, (Zeph. 3:3)

in the e. it is cut down, p. 62, (Ps. 90:6)

Everlasting: an e. sign, p. 94, (Isa. 55:13)

but have e. life, p. 165, (Jn. 3:16)

he that believes . . . e. life, p. 167, (Jn. 6:47)

some to e. life, p. 114, (Dan. 12:2)

the e. arms, p. 21, (Deut. 33:27)

water springing up into e. life, p. 166, (Jn. 4:14)

Evidence: the e. of things not seen, p. 231, (Heb. 11:1)

Evil: abhor that which is e., p. 203, (Rom. 12:9)

and Lazarus [received] e. things, p. 153, (Lk. 16:25)

an unruly e., full of poison, p. 234, (Jas. 3:8)

by e. report and good report, p. 211, (II Cor. 6:8)

call e. good and good e., p. 83, (Isa. 5:20)

cease to do e., p. 81, (Isa. 1:16)

depart from e., and do good, p. 58, (Ps. 34:14)

God repented of the e., p. 121, (Jonah 3:10)

God saw that they turned from their e., p. 121, (Jonah 3:10)

imagine e. against his brother, p. 126, (Zech. 7:10)

is the e. thereof, p. 141, (Matt. 6:34)

Job feared God and shunned e., p. 49, (Job 1:1)

my hope in the day of e., p. 101, (Jer. 17:17)

neither . . . help the e. doers, p. 51, (Job 8:20)

overcome e. with good, p. 204, (Rom. 12:21)

Evil: (continued)

not rendering e. for e., p. 236, (I Pet. 3:9)

recompense to no man e. for e., p. 203, (Rom. 12:17)

repenteth him the e., p. 117, (Joel 2:13)

resist not e., p. 140, (Matt. 5:39)

see that none render e. for e., p. 222, (I Th. 5:15)

the e. which I would not, that I do, p. 201, (Rom. 7:19)

to depart from e. is understanding, p. 53, (Job 28:28)

tree of knowledge of good and e., p. 4, (Gen. 2:17)

Ewe: save one little e. lamb, p. 35, (II Sam. 12:3)

Exalted: lest I should be e. above measure, p. 213, (II Cor. 12:7)

Exalts: who e. himself will be humbled, p. 151, (Lk. 14:11)

Excuse: began to make e., p. 171, (Lk. 14:18)

Executioner: e. brought his head on a platter, p. 158, (Matt. 14:11; Mk. 6:27–28)

Exile: carried Israel away into e., p. 44, (II Kg. 17:6)

Expedient: all things are not e., p. 206, (I Cor. 6:12; 10:23)

it is e. that I go away, p. 179, (Jn. 16:7)

Extortion: full of e. and wickedness, p. 172, (Matt. 23:25; Lk. 11:39)

Eye: an e. for an e., p. 140, (Matt. 5:38)

e. for e., p. 18, (Ex. 21:24; Matt. 5:38)

e. hath not seen, nor ear heard, p. 205, (I Cor. 2:9)

e. is not satisfied with seeing, p. 74, (Ec. 1:8)

if thine e. be single, p. 141, (Matt. 6:22; Lk. 11:34)

light of the body is the e., p. 141, (Matt. 6:22; Lk. 11:34)

mine e. shall not spare thee, p. 107, (Ezek. 7:4)

now mine e. seeth thee, p. 55, (Job 42:5)

shall see e. to e., p. 94, (Isa. 52:8)

the apple of his e., p. 21, (Deut. 32:10)

the beam that is in thine own e., p. 142, (Matt. 7:3; Lk. 6:41)

the mote that is in thy brother's e., p. 142, (Matt. 7:3; Lk. 6:41)

the sound e., p. 141, (Matt. 6:22–23; Lk. 11:34–36)

Eyelids: or slumber to mine e., p. 67, (Ps. 132:4)

Eyes: e. have they, but they see not, p. 66, (Ps. 115:5; 135:16)

e. of the blind shall be opened, p. 90, (Isa. 35:5)

e. to the blind, p. 54, (Job 29:15)

he put out Zedekiah's e., p. 103, (Jer. 39:7)

his e. were dim, p. 10, (Gen. 27:1)

lift up mine e. unto the hills, p. 66, (Ps. 121:1)

open thine e., O Lord, and see, p. 90, (Isa. 37:17)

their e. were opened, p. 5, (Gen. 3:7)

their e. were opened and they knew him, p. 184, (Lk. 24:31)

their rings were full of e., p. 105, (Ezek. 1:18)

the Philistines put out his e., p. 30, (Jg. 16:21)

thine e. shall see thy teacher, p. 89, (Isa. 30:20)

which have e. and see not, p. 99, (Jer. 5:21)

Ezekiel: a hand gave E. a book, p. 106, (Ezek. 2:9)

E. prophesies to those in captivity, p. 107, (Ezek. 12)

Ezra: E. read the book of the law, p. 46, (Neh. 8:1–3)

Face: but then f. to f., p. 208, (I Cor. 13:12)

canst not see my f., p. 18, (Ex. 33:20)

cause his f. to shine upon us, p. 61, (Ps. 67:1)

each with the f. of a man . . . , p. 105, (Ezek. 1:10)

Hezekiah turned his f. toward the wall, p. 91, (Isa. 38:2)

his f. had the appearance of lightning, p. 113, (Dan. 10:6)

I fell upon my f., p. 106, (Ezek. 1:28)

make his f. shine upon thee, p. 19, (Num. 6:25)

why hidest thou thy f. from me?, p. 62, (Ps. 88:14)

Faces: f. shall gather blackness, p. 116, (Joel 2:6)

the f. gather blackness, p. 123, (Nahum 2:10)

Fade: we all do f. as a leaf, p. 96, (Isa. 64:6)

Faint: the whole heart f., p. 81, (Isa. 1:5)

walk, and not f., p. 92, (Isa. 40:31)

Fair: behold thou art f., my love, p. 77, (Song 4:1)

f. as the moon, p. 78, (Song 6:10)

f. weather cometh out of the north, p. 54, (Job 37:22)

how f. and how pleasant art thou, O love, p. 78, (Song 7:6)

rise up, my love, my f. one, p. 77, (Song 2:10)

thou art all f., my love, p. 78, (Song 4:7)

Faith: according to your f. be it done, p. 145, (Matt. 9:29)

by grace are ye saved through f., p. 215, (Eph. 2:8)

by the hearing of f.?, p. 214, (Gal. 3:2)

Christ may dwell in your hearts by f., p. 216, (Eph. 3:17)

f. as a grain of mustard seed, p. 161, (Matt. 17:20; Lk. 17:6)

f. but not works, can faith save him?, p. 233, (Jas. 2:14)

f. hath made three whole, p. 145, (Matt. 9:22; Mk. 5:34; Lk. 8:48)

f. is the substance of things hoped for, p. 231, (Heb. 11:1)

f. not be in the wisdom of men, p. 205, (I Cor. 2:5)

f. without works is dead, p. 234, (Jas. 2:26)

I have kept the f., p. 227, (II Tim. 4:7)

I have not found so great f., p. 143, (Matt. 8:10; Lk. 7:9)

just shall live by f., p. 214, (Gal. 3:11)

justification by f., p. 200, (Rom 3:9—5:11)

justified by f. without the deeds of the law, p. 200, (Rom. 3:28)

now abideth f., hope, love, p. 209, (I Cor. 13:13)

O thou of little f., p. 158, (Matt. 14:31)

O woman, great is thy f., p. 159, (Matt. 15:28)

O ye of little f., p. 144, (Matt. 8:26; cf. Mk. 4:40; Lk. 8:25)

one Lord, one f., one baptism, p. 216, (Eph. 4:5)

spoke to Felix of f. in Christ, p. 197, (Acts 24:24)

the just shall live by f., pp. 199, 231, (Rom. 1:17; Heb. 10:38)

thy f. hath made thee whole, p. 153, (Lk. 17:19)

thy f. hath saved thee, p. 155, (Lk. 7:50)

to another f. by the same Spirit, p. 208, (I Cor. 12;9)

walk by f. not by sight, p. 211, (II Cor. 5:7)

Faithful: be thou f. unto death, p. 241, (Rev. 2:10)

called F. and True, p. 246, (Rev. 19:11)

he who is f. in very little, p. 141, (Lk. 16:10)

it is required . . . a man be found f., p. 206, (I Cor. 4:2)

Faithfulness: betroth thee unto me in f., p. 114, (Hos. 2:20)

counsels of old are f. and truth, p. 87, (Isa. 25:1)

Faithless: f. wife restored, p. 114, (Hos. 2:14–23)

Israel the f. wife, p. 114, (Hos. 2:1–13)

O f. and perverse generation, p. 161, (Matt. 17:17; Mk. 9:19; Lk. 9:41)

Fall: a thousand shall f. at thy side, p. 63, (Ps. 91:7)

shall not f. on the ground, p. 147, (Matt. 10:29)

take heed lest he f., p. 207, (I Cor. 10:12)

when I f., I shall arise, p. 122, (Micah, 7:8)

Fallen: a prince f. this day in Israel, p. 34, (II Sam. 3:38)

how are the mighty f., p. 34, (II Sam. 1:25)

False: against f. prophets, p. 101, (Jer. 23)

beware of f. prophets, p. 142, (Matt. 7:15)

f. Christs and false prophets, p. 173, (Matt. 24:24; Mk. 13:22)

False: (*continued*)

many f. prophets shall arise, p. 173, (Matt. 24:11)

set up f. witnesses, p. 191, (Acts 6:13)

sought f. witness against Jesus, p. 181, (Matt. 26:59; Mk. 14:55–56)

thou shalt not bear f. witness, p. 18, (Ex. 20:16)

Falsehood: under f. have we hid, p. 88, (Isa. 28:15)

Fame: exceedeth the f. which I heard, p. 38, (I Kg. 10:7; II Chr. 9:6)

his f. was noised, p. 27, (Josh. 6:27)

the f. of Jesus, p. 138, (Mk. 1:28; Lk. 4:37)

Families: God setteth the solitary in f., p. 61, (Ps. 68:6)

of all the f. of the earth, p. 118, (Amos 3:2)

Famine: f. was over all the earth, p. 12, (Gen. 41:54–56)

into Egypt for there was a f., p. 7, (Gen. 12:10)

seven years of f., p. 12, (Gen. 41:30)

there arose a f. and he tended swine, p. 152, (Lk. 15:14–15)

Far: a brother f. off, p. 73, (Prov. 27:10)

Fast: Nineveh believed God and proclaimed a f., p. 121, (Jonah 3:5)

sanctify a f. call a solemn assembly, p. 116, (Joel 1:14)

the f. that I have chosen, p. 95, (Isa. 58:6)

when ye f., p. 141, (Matt. 6:16)

your disciples not f., p. 145, (Matt. 9:14; Mk. 2:18; Lk. 5:33)

Fasted: he had f. forty days, p. 135, (Matt. 4:2; Lk. 4:2)

I f. and wept. p. 36, (II Sam. 12:22)

Fasting: not send them away f., p. 159, (Matt. 15:32; Mk. 8:3)

so as not to appear f., p. 141, (Matt. 6:18)

Fat: the f. of the land, p. 13, (Gen. 45:18)

Father: a man leave his f. and mother, p. 217, (Eph. 5:31)

a man shall leave f. and mother, p. 163, (Matt. 19:5; Mk. 10:7)

Abraham, f. of many nations, p. 8, (Gen. 17:5)

all things are delivered unto me of my F., p. 148, (Matt. 11:27; Lk. 10:22)

be about my F.'s business, p. 134, (Lk. 2:49)

crying Abba, F., p. 214, (Gal. 4:6)

did the will of his f., p. 170, (Matt. 21:31)

everlasting F., the Prince of Peace, p. 84, (Isa. 9:6)

F. save me from this hour, p. 176, (Jn 12:27)

F., Word and Spirit these three are one, p. 239, (I John 5:7)

glorify your F., p. 138, (Matt. 5:16)

hath seen me hath seen the F., p. 149, (Jn. 14:9)

hath the rain a f.?, p. 54, (Job 38:28)

have we not all one f., p. 127, (Mal. 2:10)

he arose and came to his f., p. 152, (Lk. 15:20)

he that hath seen me hath seen the F., p. 178, (Jn. 14:9)

he that loveth f. or mother, p. 147, (Matt. 10:37; cf. Lk. 14:26)

honor thy f. and thy mother, p. 217, (Eph. 6:2)

honor thy f. and thy mother, p. 18, (Ex. 20:12)

I am in the F., p. 178, (Jn. 14:11)

in my F.'s house are many mansions, p. 178, (Jn. 14:2)

my f., my f., the chariot of Israel!, p. 44, (II Kg. 13:14)

my f.'s servants have bread, p. 152, (Lk. 15:17)

No one comes to the F. but by me, p. 178, (Jn. 14:6)

our F. (The Lord's Prayer), p. 140, (Matt. 6:9; Lk. 11:2; cf. Mk. 11:25–26)

so shall my heavenly F. do to you, p. 163, (Matt. 18:35)

the F. and I are one, p. 148, (Jn. 10:30)

the F. had given all things, p. 177, (Jn. 13:3)

the F. loves the son, p. 166, (Jn. 3:35)

the F. shall give you another Comforter, p. 178, (Jn. 14:16; 15:26)

the F., the Son and the Holy Ghost, p. 185, (Matt. 28:19)

thy F. which seeth in secret, p. 140, (Matt. 6:4)

wise son maketh a glad f., p. 70, (Prov. 10:1)

your F. knoweth what things ye have need of, p. 140, (Matt. 6:8)

Fatherless: oppress not the widow and the f., p. 126, (Zech. 7:10)

pure religion is to visit the f., p. 233, (Jas. 1:27)

Fathers: f. have eaten a sour grape, p. 102, (Jer. 31:29; Ezek. 18:2)

f., provoke not your children, p. 218, (Eph. 6:4)

the heart of the children to their f., p. 127, (Mal. 4:6)

the land of your f., p. 13, (Gen. 48:21)

turn the heart of the f., p. 127, (Mal. 4:6)

your f., where are they?, p. 125, (Zech. 1:5)

Fatted: bring the f. calf, p. 152, (Lk. 15:23)

Fault: I find in him no f. at all, p. 182, (Jn. 18:38)

Faults: cleanse thou me from secret f., p. 57, (Ps. 19:12)

what glory if you are beaten for your f., p. 236, (I Pet. 2:20)

Favor: in f. with God and man, p. 135, (Lk. 2:52)

thou hast found f. with God, p. 131, (Lk. 1:30)

Fear: be strong, f. not, p. 90, (Isa. 35:4)

Doth Job f. God, . . . ?, p. 49, (Job 1:9)

f. came upon me and trembling, p. 50, (Job 4:14)

f. God and give glory to him, p. 245, (Rev. 14:7)

f. God and keep his commandments, p. 76, (Ec. 12:13)

f. God. Honor the king, p. 236, (I Pet. 2:17)

f. not, I am the first and the last, p. 240, (Rev. 1:17)

f. not . . . , I bring you good tidings, p. 133, (Lk. 2:10)

f. not, Mary, p. 131, (Lk. 1:30)

f. not O land, p. 117, (Joel 2:21)

f. not, peace be unto thee . . . , p. 113, (Dan. 10:19)

f. not . . . the Lord will be with you, p. 42, (II Chr. 20:17)

f. not them which kill, p. 147, (Matt. 10:28; Lk. 12:4)

f. of the Lord is the beginning of wisdom, p. 65, (Ps. 111:10)

f. of the Lord, that is wisdom, p. 53, (Job 28:28)

f. thou not for I am with thee, p. 92, (Isa. 41:10)

f. ye not, ye are of more value, p. 147, (Matt. 10:31; Lk. 12:7)

God hath not given us . . . f., p. 226, (II Tim. 1:7)

I know you f. the Lord, p. 9, (Gen. 22:12)

I will not f. what man shall do unto me, p. 232, (Heb. 13:6)

in weakness and in much f. and trembling, p. 205, (I Cor. 2:3)

men's hearts failing them for f., p. 173, (Lk. 21:26)

perfect love casteth our f., p. 239, (I John 4:18)

who through f. of death were in bondage, p. 229, (Heb. 2:15)

whom shall I f.?, p. 58, (Ps. 27:1)

will not we f., though the earth be removed, p. 60, (Ps. 46:2)

with f. and trembling, p. 219, (Phil. 2:12)

Feared: Job f. God and shunned evil, p. 49, (Job 1:1)

Fearful: to them that are of a f. heart, p. 90, (Isa. 35:4)

Fearfully: I am f. and wonderfully made, p. 68, (Ps. 139:14)

Feast: a f. is made for laughter, p. 76, (Ec. 10:19)

a f. of fat things, p. 87, (Isa. 25:6)

a f. of wines on the lees, p. 87, (Isa. 25:6)

a king who gave a marriage f., p. 171, (Matt. 22:2)

assembled . . . much people to keep the f., p. 44, (II Chr. 30:13)

Belshazzar the king made a great f., p. 111, (Dan. 5:1)

bidden . . . to a wedding f., p. 151, (Lk. 14:8)

I despise your f. days, p. 119, (Amos 5:21)

the f. of harvest, p. 21, (Ex. 23:16)

the f. of Purim, p. 46, (Est. 9)

the f. of tabernacles, p. 22, (Lev. 23:34; Deut. 16:13)

Feast: (continued)

the f. of unleavened bread, p. 21, (Ex. 23:15; Lev. 23:6)

the f. of weeks, p. 21, (Ex. 23:16; Lev. 23:9–22; Deut. 16:9–12)

therefore let us keep the f., p. 206, (I Cor. 5:8)

unto the governor of the f., p. 137, (Jn. 2:8)

Feasting: two days of f. and gladness, p. 46, (Est. 9:17)

Feasts: your new moons and your f., p. 81, (Isa. 1:14)

Feeble: confirm the f. knees, p. 90, (Isa. 35:3)

Feed: f. my sheep, p. 186, (Jn. 21:16)

Jesus said: F. my lambs, p. 185, (Jn. 21:15)

Feeding: f. of the five thousand, p. 158, (Matt. 14:14–21; Mk. 6:30–44; Lk. 9:10–17; Jn. 6:1–14)

Feet: f. was I to the lame, p. 54, (Job 29:15)

his f. like fine brass, p. 240, (Rev. 1:15)

how beautiful are the f. of him . . . , p. 94, (Isa. 52:7)

not my f. only, but also my hands . . . , p. 177, (Jn. 13:9)

the dust of your f., p. 146, (Matt. 10:14; Mk. 6:11; Lk. 9:5)

washed his f. with tears, p. 155, (Lk. 7:38)

Felix: F. trembled, p. 197, (Acts 24:25)

Paul told F. the governor, p. 197, (Acts 23:26; 24:10)

spoke to F. of faith in Christ, p. 197, (Acts 24:24)

Fell: I f. at his feet as dead, p. 240, (Rev. 1:17)

Fellow: this f. also was with him, p. 181, (Matt. 26:73; Mk. 14:70; Lk. 22:59; Jn. 18:26)

Fellowship: hands of f., p. 214, (Gal. 2:9)

if we walk in the light we have f., p. 238, (I John 1:7)

Female: [neither] male nor f., p. 214, (Gal. 3:28)

Field: a treasure hid in a f., p. 157, (Matt. 13:44)

him in the f. not turn back, p. 173, (Matt. 24:18; Mk. 13:16)

two men will be in the f., one is taken . . . , p. 174, (Matt. 24:40; Lk. 17:36)

Fiery: deliver us from the f. furnace, p. 111, (Dan. 3:17)

shall be cast into a f. furnace, p. 111, (Dan 3:6)

Fig: a f. tree planted in his vineyard, p. 150, (Lk. 13:6)

the f. tree without figs, p. 150, (Lk. 13:6–9)

the leaves of the f. tree, p. 174, (Matt. 24:32–33; Mk. 13:28–29; Lk. 21:29–31)

they sewed f. leaves together, p. 5, (Gen. 3:7)

Fight: f. everyone against his brother, p. 86, (Isa. 19:2)

f. the good fight of faith, p. 225, (I Tim. 6:12)

f. with the sword of my mouth, p. 241, (Rev. 2:16)

I have fought a good f., p. 227, (II Tim. 4:7)

Filled: f. with all the fulness of God, p. 216, (Eph. 3:19)

Filthy: not greedy of f. lucre, p. 224, (I Tim. 3:3, 8)

Find: seek and ye shall f., p. 142, (Matt. 7:7; Lk. 11:9)

where I might f. him, p. 53, (Job 23:3)

Finished: Jesus said: It is f., p. 183, (Jn. 19:30)

the heavens and the earth were f., p. 4, (Gen. 2:1)

Fingers: f. of a man's hand wrote upon the wall, p, 111, (Dan. 5:5)

Fir: shall come up the f. tree, p. 94, (Isa. 55:13)

Fire: a pillar of f., p. 16, (Ex. 13:21)

cast their gods into the f., p. 90, (Isa. 37:19)

depart from me into everlasting f., p. 175, (Matt. 25:41)

f., and hail; snow, and vapors, p. 68, (Ps. 148:8)

God is a consuming f., p. 232, (Heb. 12:29)

his ministers a flaming f., p. 65, (Ps. 104:4)

how great a matter a little f. Kindleth!, p. 234, (Jas. 3:5)

I will kindle a f. in thee, p. 108, (Ezek. 20:47)

man's work . . . f. shall try it, p. 205, (I Cor. 3:13)

on Sodom and Gomorrah brimstone and f., p. 9, (Gen. 19:24)

take f. in his bosom, p. 70, (Prov. 6:27)

the appearance of f. round about within it, p. 106, (Ezek. 1:27)

the God that answereth by f., p. 40, (I Kg. 18:24)

the Lord descended . . . in f., p. 17, (Ex. 19:18)

then the f. of the Lord fell, p. 40, (I Kg. 18:38)

they saw a f. of coals, p. 185, (Jn. 21:9)

through f. and through water, p. 61, (Ps. 66:12)

tongues like as of f., p. 189, (Acts 2:3)

Firmament: f. sheweth his handiwork, p. 56, (Ps. 19:1)

First: fear not, I am the f. and the last, p. 240, (Rev. 1:17)

sanctify all the f., p. 16, (Ex. 13:2)

the f. and the last, p. 247, (Rev. 22:13)

Firstborn: brought forth her f. son, p. 132, (Lk. 2:7)

f. of Egypt shall die, p. 15, (Ex. 12:12)

smite the f., p. 15, (Ex. 12:12)

Firstfruits: being the f. unto God, p. 245, (Rev. 14:4)

f. of thy labors, p. 21, (Ex. 23:16)

Fish: a great f. to swallow up Jonah, p. 120, (Jonah 1:17)

a net which gathered all kinds of f., p. 157, (Matt. 13:47)

Jonah was in the belly of the f., p. 120, (Jonah 1:17)

not able to draw it in for the multitude of f., p. 185, (Jn. 21:6)

the Lord spake unto the f., p. 120, (Jonah 2:10)

took bread and gave it to them with the f., p. 186, (Jn. 21:13)

Fish gate: a cry from the f., p. 124, (Zeph. 1:10)

Fishermen: they were f., p. 136, (Matt. 4:18; Mk. 1:16)

Fishers: make you f. of men, p. 136, (Matt. 4:19; Mk. 1:17; cf. Lk. 5:10)

Fishes: five loaves and two f., p. 158, (Matt. 14:17; Mk. 6:38; Lk. 9:13; Jn. 6:9)

he took the loaves and f., p. 159, (Matt. 15:36; Mk. 8:6–7)

multitude of f. in their nets, p. 136, (Lk. 5:6)

Fishing: f. all night but caught nothing, p. 185, (Jn. 21:3)

Five: feeding of the f. thousand, p. 158, (Matt. 14:14–21; Mk. 6:30–44; Lk. 9:10–17; Jn. 6:1–14)

Flagons: stay me with f., p. 77, (Song 2:5)

Flame: his Holy One for a f., p. 84, (Isa. 10:17)

Flattereth: that f. with his lips, p. 72, (Prov. 20:19)

Flax: a line of f. and a measuring reed, p. 109, (Ezek. 40:3)

as f. that was burnt, p. 30, (Jg. 15:14)

Fled: the host ran and cried and f., p. 29, (Jg. 7:21)

Flee: courageous shall f. away naked, p. 118, (Amos 2:16)

f. also youthful lusts, p. 226, (II Tim. 2:22)

f. into Egypt, p. 134, (Matt. 2:13)

f. to her brother Laban, p. 10, (Gen. 27:42, 43)

f. to the mountains, p. 173, (Matt. 24:16; Mk. 13:14; Lk. 21:21)

no, we will f. upon horses, p. 89, (Isa. 30:16)

O man of God, f. these things, p. 225, (I Tim. 6:11)

resist the devil and he will f., p. 234, (Jas. 4:7)

they shall f. far off, p. 86, (Isa. 17:13)

whither shall I f.?, p. 68, (Ps. 139:7)

Fleece: dew on a f. of wool as a sign, p. 29, (Jg. 6:37)

Flees: Jacob f. from Esau, p. 10, (Gen. 27:41—28:10)

Flesh: all f. is grass, p. 91, (Isa. 40:6)

f. and blood cannot inherit, p. 210, (I Cor. 15:50)

f. of my f., p. 4, (Gen. 2:23)

in my f. shall I see God, p. 52, (Job 19:26)

Flesh: (continued)
manifest in the f., justified in the
Spirit, p. 225, (I Tim. 3:16)
no man ever yet hated his own f., p.
217, (Eph. 5:29)
not fulfill the lust of the f., p. 215,
(Gal. 5:16)
shall be one f., p. 4, (Gen. 2:24)
that which is born of the f., p. 165,
(Jn. 3:6)
the f. lusteth against the Spirit, p.
215, (Gal. 5:17)
the word was made f., p. 131, (Jn.
1:14)
their f. as the dung, p. 124, (Zeph.
1:17)
they are no longer two but one f., p.
163, (Matt. 19:6; Mk. 10:8)
they two shall be one f., p. 217,
(Eph. 5:31)
ye shall eat f., p. 17, (Ex. 16:12)
Fleshly: f. lusts which war against the
soul, p. 236, (I Pet. 2:11)
Fleshpots: sat by the f., p. 16, (Ex.
16:3)
Flies: a grievous swarm of f., p. 15,
(Ex. 8:24)
Flight: f. of the holy family into
Egypt, p. 134, (Matt. 2:13–15;
19–23)
Floating: the f. axe-head, p. 43, (II
Kg. 6)
Flock: feed his f. like a shepherd, p.
92, (Isa. 40:11)
I will feed my f., p. 109, (Ezek.
34:15)
keeping watch over their f., p. 132,
(Lk. 2:8)
Flood: the f., p. 6, (Gen. 7:4–24)
the f. recedes, p. 6, (Gen. 8:1–20)
Floods: let the f. clap their hands, p.
64, (Ps. 98:8)
the f. came and it fell, p. 143, (Matt.
7:27; Lk. 6:49)
the f. came and it fell not, p. 143,
(Matt. 7:25; Lk. 6:48)
the f. compassed me about, p. 120,
(Jonah 2:3)
Flower: as a f. of the field . . . , p.
64, (Ps. 103:15)
as the f. of the field, p. 91, (Isa. 40:6)
in the f. of their age, p. 31, (I Sam.
2:33)
the f. fadeth, p. 91, (Isa. 40:7)

the glory of man as the f. of grass, p.
235, (I Pet. 1:24)
Flowers: f. appear on the earth, p.
77, (Song 2:12)
Foes: f. . . . . of his own household, p.
147, (Matt. 10:36; cf. Lk. 12:53)
Fold: other sheep . . . not of this f.,
p. 168, (Jn. 10:16)
Follow: f. after the things which
make for peace, p. 204, (Rom.
14:19)
Jesus said: f. me, pp. 136, 144, 145,
(Matt. 4:19; 8:22; Mk. 1:17;
2:14; Lk. 5:27; 9:59)
Master, I will f. thee, p. 144, (Matt.
8:19; Lk. 9:57)
thou shalt f. me afterwards, p. 179,
(Jn. 13:36)
whither I go thou canst not f., p.
179, (Jn. 13:36)
Followed: left their nets and f. him,
p. 136, (Matt. 4:20; Mk. 1:18)
they left and f. him, p. 136, (Matt.
4:21–22; Mk. 1:20; Lk. 5:11)
Folly: a fool returneth to his f., p. 73,
(Prov. 26:11)
wisdom excelleth f., p. 74, (Ec. 2:13)
Food: Take with you every sort of f.,
p. 6, (Gen. 6:21)
Fool: a f. returneth to his folly, p. 73,
(Prov. 26:11)
a f., when he holdeth his peace, p.
72, (Prov. 17:28)
F.! This night thy soul . . . , p. 150,
(Lk. 12:20)
I have played the f., p. 34, (I Sam.
26:21)
I speak as a f., p. 212, (II Cor.
11:23)
the f. hath said in his heart . . . , p.
56, (Ps. 14:1; 53:1)
the parable of the rich f., p. 150,
(Lk. 12:13–21)
the way of a f., p. 70, (Prov. 12:15)
whosoever shall say, Thou f., p. 139,
(Matt. 5:22)
Foolish: a f. son is the heaviness of
his mother, p. 70, (Prov. 10:1)
an old and f. king, p. 75, (Ec. 4:13)
for my people is f., p. 99, (Jer. 4:22)
God has chosen the f. things, p. 205,
(I Cor. 1:27)
O f. Galatian, p. 214, (Gal. 3:1)
shall be like a f. man, p. 143, (Matt.
7:26; cf. Lk. 6:49)

Fools: f. make a mock at sin, p. 71, (Prov. 14:9)

for ye suffer f. gladly, p. 212, (II Cor. 11:19)

they became f., p. 199, (Rom. 1:22)

we are f. for Christ's sake, p. 206, (I Cor. 4:10)

Foot: he set his right f. on the sea, p. 244, (Rev. 10:2)

not suffer thy f. to be moved, p. 66, (Ps. 121:3)

Footstool: I make thine enemies thy f., p. 65, (Ps. 110:1)

it [earth] is his f., p. 139, (Matt. 5:35)

Forbidden: Eve ate the f. fruit, p. 5, (Gen. 3:6)

Forbidding: no man f. him, p. 198, (Acts 28:31)

Forehead: upon her f. was a name, p. 246, (Rev. 17:5)

Forest: say to the f. of the south, p. 108, (Ezek. 20:47)

shall consume the glory of his f., p. 84, (Isa. 10:18)

Forget: f. not all his benefits, p. 64, (Ps. 103:2)

how long wilt thou f. me?, p. 56, (Ps. 13:1)

Forgetting: f. those things which are behind, p. 219, (Phil 3:13)

Forgive: f. and ye shall be forgiven, p. 142, (Lk. 6:37)

f. them for they know not what they do, p. 182, (Lk. 23:34)

how often shall I f. my brother?, p. 162, (Matt. 18:21; cf. Lk. 17:4)

if you f. anyone's sins, p. 184, (Jn. 20:23)

if you f. not your brother's trespasses, p. 163, (Matt. 18:35)

who can f. sins, but God?, p. 144, (Mk. 2:7; Lk. 5:21)

Forgiven: forgive and ye shall be f., p. 142, (Lk. 6:37)

sins . . . are f.; for she loved much, p. 155, (Lk. 7:47)

they [sins] shall be f. him, p. 235, (Jas. 5:15)

thy sins are f., p. 144, (Matt. 9:2; Mk. 2:5; Lk. 5:20)

to whom little is f., p. 155, (Lk. 7:47)

Forgiving: f. one another even as Christ . . . , p. 221, (Col. 3:13)

Forgotten: I am f. as a dead man, p. 58, (Ps. 31:12)

Form: a f. of godliness but denying the power, p. 226, (II Tim. 3:5)

Former: the f. things are passed away, p. 247, (Rev. 21:4)

Forsake: who does not f. all, p. 151, (Lk. 14:33)

Forsaken: my God, my God, why hast thou f. me?, p. 57, (Ps. 22:1)

Peter said: We have f. all, p. 164, (Matt. 19:27; Mk. 10:28; Lk. 18:28)

that hath f. houses, or brethren . . . , p. 164, (Matt. 19:29; Mk. 10:29; Lk. 18:29)

why hast thou f. me?, p. 183, (Matt. 27:46; Mk. 15:34)

Fortress: my f., and my deliverer, p. 36, (II Sam. 22:2)

Fortresses: nettles and brambles in the f., p. 90, (Isa. 34:13)

Fortune: restores Job's f., p. 55, (Job 42:7–17)

Forty: f. days and forty nights, p. 6, (Gen. 7:12)

he had fasted f. days, p. 135, (Matt. 4:2; Lk. 4:2)

in the wilderness f. days, p. 135, (Matt. 4:1–2; Mk. 1:13; Lk. 4:2)

in the wilderness f. year, p. 19, (Num. 14:33)

Forum: Paul stops at F. of Appius, p. 198, (Acts 28:15)

Found: f. the piece which I had lost, p. 152, (Lk. 15:9)

I have f. my sheep which was lost, p. 162, (Lk. 15:6; cf. Matt. 18:13)

we have f. him, p. 137, (Jn. 1:45)

Foundation: built upon the f. of the apostles . . . , p. 216, (Eph. 2:20)

Christ the one f., p. 205, (I Cor. 3)

for other f. can no man lay, p. 205, (I Cor. 3:11)

f. of the house of the Lord, p. 46, (Ezra 3:11)

I have laid the f., p. 205, (I Cor. 3:10)

stones to lay the f., p. 38, (I Kg. 5:17)

Foundations: f. of the earth, p. 54, (Job 38:4)

Fountains: f. of the great deep, p. 6, (Gen. 7:11)

Four: as the f. winds of the heaven, p. 126, (Zech. 2:6)

Four: (continued)

f. angels on the f. corners, p. 243, (Rev. 7:1)

f. horsemen of the apocalypse, p. 243, (Rev. 6)

holding the f. winds, p. 243, (Rev. 7:1)

Fox: tell that f., p. 169, (Lk. 13:32)

Foxes: f. have holes, p. 144, (Matt. 8:20; Lk. 9:58)

little f., that spoil the vines, p. 77, (Song 2:15)

Fragments: gather the f., p. 158, (Jn. 6:12; cf. Matt. 14:20; Mk. 6:43; Lk. 9:17)

Frankincense: gifts of gold, f., and myrrh, p. 134, (Matt. 2:11)

Free: I was f. born, p. 197, (Acts 22:28)

neither bond nor f., p. 214, (Gal. 3:28)

Freedom: with a great sum obtained I this f., p. 197, (Acts 22:28)

Friend: a f. loveth at all times, p. 71, (Prov. 17:17)

a f. of mine is come, p. 150, (Lk. 11:6)

a f. of publicans and sinners, p. 148, (Matt. 11:19; Lk. 7:34)

f. that sticketh closer than a brother, p. 72, (Prov. 18:24)

he will not rise because he is a f., p. 150, (Lk. 11:8)

Friends: call not your f. or rich neighbors, p. 151, (Lk. 14:12)

God rebukes the f., p. 55, (Job 42:7–17)

Job's three silent f., p. 49, (Job 2:11–13)

lay down his life for his f., p. 179, (Jn. 15:13)

wealth maketh many f., p. 72, (Prov. 19:4)

wounded in the house of my f., p. 127, (Zech. 13:6)

Friendship: f. between David and Jonathan, p. 33, (I Sam. 18:1–5)

Frogs: f. came up and covered the land, p. 15, (Ex. 8:6)

Fruit: fill the face of the world with f., p. 88, (Isa. 27:6)

f. of the Spirit is love, joy, peace, p. 215, (Gal. 5:22)

f. of thy body . . . upon thy throne, p. 67, (Ps. 132:11)

f. tree yielding fruit, p. 3, (Gen. 1:11)

he sought f. and found none, p. 150, (Lk. 13:6)

it bringeth forth much f., p. 175, (Jn. 12:24)

Fruitful: a vineyard in a f. hill, p. 82, (Isa. 5:1)

be f. and multiply, p. 4, (Gen. 1:28)

thy wife shall be as a f. vine, p. 67, (Ps. 128:3)

Fruits: by their f. ye shall know, p. 142, (Matt. 7:16, 20; Lk. 6:44)

Fugitive: You shall be a f., p. 5, (Gen. 4:12)

Fulfill: not come to destroy but to f., p. 139, (Matt. 5:17)

Full: in a f. age, p. 50, (Job 5:26)

Furnace: Shadrach . . . into the f., p. 111, (Dan. 3:23)

shall be cast into a fiery f., p. 111, (Dan. 3:6)

Fury: dregs of the cup of my f., p. 94, (Isa. 51:22)

until thy brother's f. turn, p. 10, (Gen. 27:44)

Future: the course of f. history, p. 113, (Dan. 11)

Gabriel: G. appeared to Zacharias, p. 131, (Lk. 1:11, 19)

G., make this man understand the vision, p. 112, (Dan. 8:16)

G. was sent from God, p. 131, (Lk. 1:26)

the gift of G., p. 113, (Dan. 9:20–27)

Gadarene: the G. swine, p. 144, (Matt. 8:28–34; Mk. 5:1–20; Lk. 8:26–39)

Gain: if he g. the whole world, p. 147, (Matt. 16:26; Mk. 8:36; Lk. 9:25)

what things were g. to me . . . , p. 219, (Phil. 3:7)

Galatia: Paul's letter to G., p. 213, (Gal.)

unto the churches of G., grace, p. 213, (Gal. 1:2–3)

Galatians: O foolish G., p. 214, (Gal. 3:1)

Galilee: departure from G., p. 169, (Lk. 13:31–33)

disciples went unto a mountain in G., p. 185, (Matt. 28:16)

go before you to G., p. 179, (Matt. 26:32; Mk. 14:28)

he went about all G., p. 137, (Matt. 4:23; Mk. 1:39; Lk. 4:44)

Jesus, walking by the Sea of G., p. 136, (Matt. 4:18; Mk. 1:16)

Gall: in the g. of bitterness, p. 192, (Acts 8:23)

they gave me g. for my meat, p. 61, (Ps. 69:21)

Gallows: the g. prepared for Mordecai, p. 46, (Est. 7:10)

Gamaliel: G.: If this idea be of men, p. 191, (Acts 5:38)

Garden: a g. eastward in Eden, p. 4, (Gen. 2:8)

a g. inclosed is my sister, my spouse, p. 78, (Song 4:12)

God put man in the g., p. 4, (Gen. 2: 15)

her desert like the g., p. 93, (Isa. 51:3)

in the g. of Gethsemane, p. 180, (Matt. 26:36–46; Mk. 14:32–42; Lk. 22:40–46)

the g. of the Lord, p. 93, (Isa. 51:3)

Garment: the g. of praise, p. 95, (Isa. 61:3)

Garments: part my g. among them, p. 57, (Ps. 22:18)

Gate: enter the narrow g., p. 142, (Matt. 7:13; Lk. 13:24)

for wide is the g., p. 142, (Matt. 7: 13)

rich man's g., p. 153, (Lk. 16:20)

strait is the g., p. 142, (Matt. 7:14)

Gates: all her g. are desolate, p. 104, (Lam. 1:4)

g. thereof are burned with fire, p. 45, (Neh. 2:3)

her high g. shall be burned with fire, p. 103, (Jer. 51:58)

into his g. with thanksgiving, p. 64, (Ps. 100:4)

lift up your heads, O ye g., p. 57, (Ps. 24:7)

Gath: tell it not in G., p. 34, (II Sam. 1:20)

Gather: scattered Israel will g., p. 102, (Jer. 31:10)

Gathered: g. unto thy people, p. 20, (Num. 27:13)

Gave: the Lord g., p. 49, (Job 1:21)

Genealogies: fables and endless g., p. 223, (I Tim. 1:4)

Generation: a stubborn and rebellious g., p. 62, (Ps. 78:8)

g. to g. it shall lie waste, p. 90, (Isa. 34:10)

g. who did not know the Lord, p. 28, (Jg. 2:10)

O faithless and perverse g., p. 161, (Matt. 17:17; Mk. 9:19; Lk. 9:41)

one g. passeth away . . . , p. 74, (Ec. 1:4)

Generations: our dwelling place in all g., p. 62, (Ps. 90:1)

Gentile: to the Jew first and to the G., p. 199, (Rom. 2:10)

Gentiles: a light of the G., p. 93, (Isa. 42:6)

great among the G., p. 127, (Mal. 1:11)

I will go unto the G., p. 196, (Acts 18:6)

letters to the G., p. 195, (Acts 15:23)

seen of angels, preached unto G., p. 225, (I Tim. 3:16)

Gently: deal g. . . . with Absalom, p. 36, (II Sam. 18:5)

Gethsemane: in the garden of G., p. 180, (Matt. 26:36–46; Mk. 14:32–42; Lk. 22:40–46)

Ghost: (See also Holy Ghost, Holy Spirit, Spirit)

I had given up the g., p. 51, (Job 10:18)

in the name of the Father, the Son and the Holy G., p. 185, (Matt. 28:19)

man giveth up the g., p. 51, (Job 14:10)

the Holy G. shall come upon thee, p. 131, (Lk. 1:35)

Gibeonites: the deceit of the G., p. 28, (Josh. 9)

Gideon: angel of the Lord came to G., p. 29, (Jg. 6:11)

G. and the Midianites, p. 29, (Jg. 7)

G. asked for a sign, p. 29, (Jg. 6:36)

G. destroyed the altar of Baal, p. 29, (Jg. 6:25, 27)

G. put a trumpet in every man's hand, p. 29, (Jg. 7:16)

sword of the Lord, and of G., p. 29, (Jg. 7:18)

Gift: according to the g. of the grace of God, p. 216, (Eph. 3:7)

every good g. every perfect g., p. 233, (Jas. 1:17)

Gift: (*continued*)

grace according to the g. of Christ, p. 216, (Eph. 4:7)

leave thy g. before the altar, p. 139, (Matt. 5:24)

the g. of God is eternal life, p. 201, (Rom. 6:23)

the g. that is in thee, p. 225, (I Tim. 4:14)

thought the g. of God may be purchased, p. 192, (Acts 8:20)

Gifts: diversities of g. but the same Spirit, p. 208, (I Cor. 12:4)

g. differing according to the grace that is given, p. 203, (Rom. 12:6)

g. of gold, frankincense and myrrh, p. 134, (Matt. 2:11)

Gilead: no balm in G., p. 100, (Jer. 8:22)

Gilgal: twelve stones from the Jordan in G., p. 27, (Josh. 4:20)

Gird: g. up thy loins like a man, p. 54, (Job 38:3)

wherefore g. up your mind, p. 235, (I Pet. 1:13)

Give: as he purposeth in his heart, so let him g., p. 212, (II Cor. 9:7)

freely g., p. 146, (Matt. 10:8)

g. charity secretly, p. 140, (Matt. 6:1–4)

g. half my goods to the poor, p. 154, (Lk. 19:8)

I will g. a tenth unto thee, p. 11, (Gen. 28:22)

more blessed to g., p. 197, (Acts 20:35)

Given: ask and it shall be g. you, p. 142, (Matt. 7:7; Lk. 11:9)

g. all things into his hand, p. 166, (Jn. 3:35)

g. the horse strength, p. 55, (Job 39:19)

of thine own have we g. thee, p. 37, (I Chr. 29:14)

to whom much is g., p. 150, (Lk. 12:48)

unto every one that hath shall be g., p. 175, (Matt. 25:29; Lk. 19:26)

Giver: God loveth a cheerful g., p. 212, (II Cor. 9:7)

Glad: hast made me g. through thy work, p. 63, (Ps. 92:4)

I was g. when they said unto me, p. 66, (Ps. 122:1)

make g. the city of God, p. 60, (Ps. 46:4)

Gladness: serve the Lord with g., p. 64, (Ps. 100:2)

Glass: now we see through a g., darkly, p. 208, (I Cor. 13:12)

Glean: g. the remnant of Israel, p. 99, (Jer. 6:9)

Gleaned: Ruth g. in the field of Boaz, p. 31, (Ruth 2:3)

Glorified: Christ g. not himself, p. 229, (Heb. 5:5)

they g. him not as God, p. 199, (Rom. 1:21)

Glorify: g. God in your body . . . , p. 206, (I Cor. 6:20)

g. your Father, p. 138, (Matt. 5:16)

Glorifying: and departed g. God, p. 144, (Lk. 5:25; cf. Matt. 9:7; Mk. 2:12)

Glorious: g. things are spoken of thee, p. 62, (Ps. 87:3)

Glory: change their g. unto shame, p. 115, (Hos. 4:7)

crownedst him with g. and honor, p. 228, (Ps. 8:7)

do all to the g. of God, p. 208, (I Cor. 10:31)

earth is full of his g., p. 83, (Isa. 6:3)

even Solomon in all his g., p. 141, (Matt. 6:29; Lk. 12:27)

fear God and give g. to him, p. 245, (Rev. 14:7)

give g. to the Lord your God, p. 100, (Jer. 13:16)

give unto the Lord the g., p. 63, (Ps. 96:8)

g. of the Lord shall be revealed, p. 91, (Isa. 40:5)

g. to God in the highest, p. 133, (Lk. 2:14)

God forbid that I should g., p. 215, (Gal. 6:14)

he is the King of g., p. 57, (Ps. 24:10)

heavens declare the g. of God, p. 56, (Ps. 19:1)

if I must g., p. 213, (II Cor. 11:30)

likeness of the g. of the Lord, p. 106, (Ezek. 1:28)

our light affliction worketh . . . g., p. 211, (II Cor. 4:17)

shall consume the g. of his forest, p. 84, (Isa. 10:18)

Son of man shall come in his g., p. 175, (Matt. 25:31)

the g. is departed from Israel, p. 32, (I Sam. 4:22)

the g. of man as the flower of grass, p. 235, (I Pet. 1:24)

the g. which shall be revealed in us, p. 202, (Rom. 8:18)

what g. if you are beaten for your faults, p. 236, (I Pet. 2:20)

who is this King of g.?, p. 57, (Ps. 24:8, 10)

Will I rather g. in my infirmities, p. 213, (II Cor. 12:9)

worthy O Lord to receive g. and . . . , p. 242, (Rev. 4:11)

Glutton: a g. and winebibber, p. 148, (Matt. 11:19; Lk. 7:34)

Gnashing: weeping and g. of teeth, p. 171, (Matt. 22:13)

Go: g. and the Lord be with thee, p. 33, (I Sam. 17:37)

I shall g. to him, p. 36, (II Sam. 12:23)

Goat: behold, and the g. ran unto him, p. 112, (Dan. 8:5, 6)

the g. the king of Greece, p. 112, (Dan. 8:21)

the vision of the ram and the g., p. 112, (Dan. 8)

Goats: as a shepherd divideth sheep from g., p. 175, (Matt. 25:32)

Goblet: navel is like a round g., p. 78, (Song 7:2)

God: (See also Christ, Jesus, Lord)

a G. of truth, p. 21, (Deut. 32:4)

a G. ready to pardon, p. 46, (Neh. 9: 17)

and I will be their G., p. 230, (Heb. 8:10)

and thy G. my God, p. 31, (Ruth 1:16)

be my people and I will be your G., p. 102, (Jer. 30:22)

be still, and know that I am G., p. 60, (Ps. 46:10)

because there is not a G. in Israel, p. 42, (II Kg. 1:6)

but G. shall set up a kingdom . . . , p. 111, (Dan. 2:44)

call him Emmanuel, meaning G. with us, p. 132, (Matt. 1:23)

called Wonderful, Counselor, The mighty G., p. 84, (Isa. 9:6)

cans't thou by searching find out G.?, p. 51, (Job 11:7)

come from G. and went to G., p. 177, (Jn. 13:3)

David brought the ark of G. into the city, p. 35, (II Sam. 6:12)

draw nigh to G., p. 234, (Jas. 4:8)

far be it from G . . . do wickedness, p. 54, (Job 34:10)

filled with all the fulness of G., p. 216, (Eph. 3:19)

for G. is love, p. 238, (I John 4:8)

for G. so loved the world, p. 165, (Jn. 3:16)

for the Lord is a great G., p. 63, (Ps. 95:3)

G.'s anger was kindled, p. 20, (Num. 22:22)

G. answers Job out of the whirlwind, p. 54, (Job 38:1)

G. appeared to Moses, p. 17, (Ex. 19–31)

G. be merciful unto us, and bless us, p. 61, (Ps. 67:1)

G. be true but every man a liar, p. 200, (Rom. 3:4)

G. blessed the seventh day, p. 4, (Gen. 2:3)

G. called to Moses, p. 14, (Ex. 3:4)

G.'s concern for us, p. 147, (Matt. 10: 29–31; Lk. 12:6, 7)

G. created man in his own image, p. 4, (Gen. 1:1)

G. created the heaven and the earth, p. 3, (Gen. 1:27)

G. did rest the seventh day, p. 229, (Heb. 4:4)

G. did send me before you, p. 13, (Gen. 45:5)

G. discovereth deep things, p. 51, (Job 12:22)

G. fainteth not, p. 92, (Isa. 40:28)

G. formed man of the dust, p. 4, (Gen. 2:7)

G. has sent forth the Spirit of his Son, p. 214, (Gal. 4:6)

G. hath made man upright, p. 75, (Ec. 7:29)

G. hath made that same Jesus both Lord and Christ, p. 190, (Acts 2:36)

G. hath overthrown me, p. 52, (Job 19:6)

God: (continued)

G. heard the voice of the lad, p. 9, (Gen. 21:17)

G. himself shall be with them, p. 247, (Rev. 21:3)

G. is a consuming fire, p. 232. (Heb. 12:29)

G. is in heaven and thou on earth, p. 75, (Ec. 5:2)

G. is in the midst of her, p. 60, (Ps. 46:5)

G. is light and in him is no darkness, p. 237, (I John 1:5)

G. is not a man, that he should lie, p. 20, (Num. 23:19)

G. is not mocked, p. 215, (Gal. 6:7)

G. is not the author of confusion, p. 209, (I Cor. 14:33)

G. is not the God of the dead, p. 171, (Matt. 22:32; Mk. 12:27; Lk. 20:38)

G. is our refuge and strength, p. 60, (Ps. 46:1)

G. is Spirit, p. 166, (Jn. 4:24)

G. . . . neither is weary, p. 92, (Isa. 40:28)

G.'s promise of Israel's return, p. 102, (Jer. 29–30)

G. promised to teach Moses, p. 14, (Ex. 4:12)

G. put man in the garden, p. 4, (Gen. 2:15)

G. put no difference between us, p. 195, (Acts 15:9)

G. rebukes the friends, p. 55, (Job 42:7–17)

G. repented of the evil, p. 121, (Jonah 3:10)

G. resisteth the proud, p. 234, (Jas. 4:6)

G. rested on the seventh day, p. 4, (Gen. 2:2)

G. save the king, p. 32, (I Sam. 10:24)

G. saw everything he had made, p. 4, (Gen. 1:31)

G. saw that is was good, p. 3, (Gen. 1:4, 10, 12, 18, 21, 25, 31)

G. saw that they turned from their evil, p. 121, (Jonah 3:10)

G. saw the wickedness, p. 6, (Gen. 6:5)

G. sent him forth from the garden, p. 5, (Gen. 3:23)

G. shall bring you, p. 13, (Gen. 48:21)

G. shall keep . . . the covenant, p. 22, (Deut. 7:12)

G. that made the world, p. 196, (Acts 17:24)

G. told Moses to go to Mount Abarim, p. 20, (Num. 27:12)

G. was in Christ, reconciling the world, p. 211, (II Cor. 5:19)

G. was manifest in the flesh, p. 225, (I Tim. 3:16)

G. will bless you, p. 22, (Deut. 28:2)

G. will cast them away, p. 116, (Hos. 9:17)

G. will not cast away, p. 51, (Job 8:20)

G. will prosper us, p. 45, (Neh. 2:20)

G. will provide a lamb, p. 9, (Gen. 22:8)

G. will render . . . according to his deeds, p. 199, (Rom. 2:6)

G. wrought special miracles, p. 196, (Acts 19:11)

he that built all things is G., p. 229, (Heb. 3:4)

he that is of G. heareth God's words, p. 168, (Jn. 8:47)

heavens declare the glory of G., p. 56, (Ps. 19:1)

heirs of G. and joint heirs with Christ, p. 201, (Rom. 8:17)

I am the Lord your G., p. 17, (Ex. 20:1)

I am thy G., p. 92, (Isa. 41:10)

I the Lord will be their G., p. 109, (Ezek. 34:24)

I will joy in the G. of my salvation, p. 124, (Hab. 3:18)

if G. for use . . . , p. 202, (Rom. 8:31)

if it be of G., p. 191, (Acts 5:39)

in my flesh shall I see G., p. 52, (Job 19:26)

in the beginning G. created, p. 3, (Gen. 1:1)

in the sight of G., p. 192, (Acts 8:21)

it is G. which worketh in you, p. 219, (Phil. 2:13)

Job answers G. in humility, p. 55, (Job 40)

Job feared G. and shunned evil, p. 49, (Job 1:1)

know that I am the Lord your G., p. 17, (Ex. 16:12)

know ye that the Lord he is G., p. 64, (Ps. 100:3)

Lord G. will wipe away tears, p. 87, (Isa. 25:8)

love the Lord your G., p. 23, (Deut. 6:5; Mk. 12:33)

MENE: G. hath numbered thy kingdom, p. 111, (Dan. 5:26)

Moses argued with G., p. 14, (Ex. 3:11; 4:1–17)

Moses asked G.'s name, p. 14, (Ex. 3:13–17)

Moses went up unto G., p. 17, (Ex. 19:3)

my G. hath sent his angel . . . , p. 112, (Dan. 6:22)

my G., my God, why hast thou forsaken me?, p. 183, (Matt. 27:46; Mk. 15:34)

no man hath seen G., p. 148, (Jn. 1:18)

no respect of persons with G., p. 200, (Rom. 2:11)

none is good, save one . . . G., p. 163, (Matt. 19:17; Mk. 10:18; Lk. 18:19)

O Daniel is thy G. able to deliver thee?, p. 112, (Dan. 6:20)

O Lord, thou art my G., p. 87, (Isa. 25:1)

obey my voice and I will be your G., p. 100, (Jer. 7:23)

one G. and father of all, p. 216, (Eph. 4:6)

one G. created us, p. 127, (Mal. 2:10)

our G. whom we serve is able to deliver us, p. 111, (Dan. 3:17)

peace from G. the Father, p. 213, (Gal. 1:3)

prepare to meet thy G., p. 118, (Amos 4:12)

present before G. to hear all things, p. 194, (Acts 10:33)

promise made by G. to our fathers, p. 197, (Acts 26:6)

shall any teach G. knowledge, p. 53, (Job 21:22)

shall be called the Son of G., p. 131, (Lk. 1:35)

shall not G. likewise avenge, p. 154, (Lk. 18:7)

the G. of Abraham, Isaac and Jacob, p. 171, (Matt. 22:32; Mk. 12:26; Lk. 20:37)

the G. of all comfort, p. 210, (II Cor. 1:3)

the G. of Jacob is our refuge, p. 60, (Ps. 46:11)

the G. that answereth by fire, p. 40, (I Kg. 18:24)

the judgment of G., p. 5, (Gen. 3:14–24)

the judgment of G. is according to truth, p. 199, (Rom. 2:2)

the Lord, the G. of hosts, is his name, p. 118, (Amos 4:13)

the Lord G. omnipotent reigneth!, p. 246, (Rev. 19:6)

the Lord our G. is one Lord, pp. 23, 171, (Deut. 6:4; cf. Mk. 12:29)

the spirit of G. descending like a dove, p. 135, (Matt. 3:16; Mk. 1:10; Lk. 3:21–22; Jn. 1:32)

there is no G. . . . but in Israel, p. 43, (II Kg. 5:15)

the Word was G., p. 131, (Jn. 1:1)

the Word was with G., p. 131, (Jn. 1:1)

the wrath of G. against all ungodliness, p. 199, (Rom. 1:18)

they shall say: Thou are my G., p. 115, (Hos. 2:23)

this Jesus hath G. raised up, p. 190, (Acts 2:32)

this work was wrought of our G., p. 46, (Neh. 6:16)

thou shalt love the Lord thy G., p. 171, (Matt. 22:37; Mk. 12:30; Lk. 10:27; Deut. 6:5)

thou shalt worship the Lord thy G., p. 136, (Matt. 4:10; Lk. 4:8)

thy G. whom thou servest will deliver thee, p. 112, (Dan. 6:16)

to appear in the presence of G. for us, p. 230, (Heb. 9:24)

to fall into the hands of the living G., p. 231, (Heb. 10:31)

to obey G. not men, p. 191, (Acts 5:29)

to the unkown G., p. 196, (Acts 17:23)

to whom will ye liken G.?, p. 92, (Isa. 40:18)

unto G. the things that are God's, p. 171. (Matt. 22:21; Mk. 12:17; Lk. 20:25)

God: *(continued)*

we have heard that G. is with you, p. 126, (Zech. 8:23)

what G. hath joined together, p. 163, (Matt. 19:6; Mk. 10:9)

what hath G. wrought, p. 20, (Num. 23:23)

whatsoever thou wilt ask of G., p. 168, (Jn. 11:22)

which G. hath prepared for them that love him, p. 205, (I Cor. 2:9)

will think he does G. a service, p. 173, (Jn. 16:2)

with G. all things are possible, p. 164, (Matt. 19:26; Mk. 10:27; Lk. 18:27)

ye believe in G., believe also in me, p. 178, (Jn. 14:1)

you cannot serve G. and mammon, p. 141, (Matt. 6:24; Lk. 16:13)

Gods: cast their g. into the fire, p. 90, (Isa. 37:19)

his heart after other g., p. 39. (I Kg. 11:4)

no g., but the work of men's hands, p. 90, (Isa. 37:19)

no other g. before me, p. 17, (Ex. 20:3)

the g. are come down to us, p. 194, (Acts 14:11)

Gog: thy face against G. the land of Magog, p. 109, (Ezek. 38:2)

Gold: gifts of g., frankincense and myrrh, p. 134, (Matt. 2:11)

g. and silver, brass, iron, wood and stone, p. 111, (Dan. 5:4)

I shall come forth as g., p. 53, (Job 23:10)

like apples of g., p. 73, (Prov. 25:11)

more to be desired than g., p. 57, (Ps. 19:10)

overlaid the temple with g., p. 38, (I Kg. 6:21, 22; II Chr. 3:8)

silver and g. have I none, p. 190, (Acts 3:6)

two cherubims overlaid with g., p. 38, (I Kg. 6:27, 28; II Chr. 3:10)

Golden: Aaron made a g. calf, p. 18, (Ex. 32:3–4)

do not ye worship the g. image?, p. 111, (Dan. 3:14)

Nebuchadnezzar set up a g. image, p. 111, (Dan. 3:1)

the g. rule, p. 142, (Matt. 7:12; Lk. 6:31)

Golgotha: brought him to a place called G., p. 182, (Matt. 27:33; Mk. 15:22; Jn. 19:17)

Goliath: a champion, G., p. 33, (I Sam. 17:4)

David and G., p. 33, (I Sam. 17)

Gomer: he went and took G., p. 114, (Hos. 1:3)

Gomorrah: have been as Sodom and G., p. 81, (Isa. 1:9)

on Sodom and G. brimstone and fire, p. 9, (Gen. 19:24)

Good: all things work together for g., p. 202, (Rom. 8:28)

bringeth thee into a g. land, p. 22, (Deut. 8:7)

call evil g. and good evil, p. 83, (Isa. 5:20)

created in Christ Jesus unto g. works, (p. 216, (Eph. 2:10)

depart from evil, and do g., p. 58, (Ps. 34:14)

every creature of God is g., p. 225, (I Tim. 4:4)

for the g. that I would I do not, p. 201, (Rom. 7:19)

for the Lord is g., p. 64, (Ps. 100:5)

God saw that it was g., p. 3, (Gen. 1: 4, 10, 12, 18, 21, 25, 31)

g. and acceptable in the sight of God, p. 224, (I Tim. 2:3)

g. for nothing but to be cast out, p. 138, (Matt. 5:13)

g. news from a far country, p. 73, (Prov. 25:25)

g. tidings of great joy, p. 133, (Lk. 2:10)

g. to them that hate you, p. 140, (Matt. 5:44; Lk. 6:27)

have done that which is g., p. 91, (Isa. 38:3)

he that doeth g. is of God, p. 239, (III John v. 11)

him that bringeth g. tidings, p. 94, (Isa. 52:7)

hold fast that which is g., p. 222, (I Th. 5:21)

I held my peace even from g., p. 59, (Ps. 39:2)

in life you received g. things, p. 153, (Lk. 16:25)

let us do g. unto all men, p. 215, (Gal. 6:10)

Lord will not do g. nor evil, p. 124, (Zeph. 1:12)

Mary hath chosen the g. part, p. 150, (Lk. 10:42)

none is g., save one . . . God, p. 163, (Matt. 19:17; Mk. 10:18; Lk. 18:19)

none that doeth g., no, not one, pp. 56, 200, (Ps. 14:3; 53:3; Rom. 3:12)

overcome evil with g., p. 204, (Rom. 12:21)

. . . peace to every man that worketh g., p. 199, (Rom. 2:10)

some [fell] . . . on g. ground, p. 156, (Matt. 13:8; Mk. 4:8; Lk. 8:8)

stablish you in every g. word and work, p. 223, (II Th. 2:17)

taste and see that the Lord is g., p. 58, (Ps. 34:8)

that they see your g. works, p. 138, (Matt. 5:16)

the g. Samaritan, p. 149, (Lk. 10:29–37)

to do g. . . . , forget not, p. 232, (Heb. 13:16)

to do g. they have no knowledge, p. 99, (Jer. 4:22)

tree of knowledge of g. and evil, p. 4, (Gen. 2:17)

why callest thou me g.?, p. 163, (Matt. 19:17; Mk. 10:18, Lk. 18:19)

Goodness: crownest the year with thy g., p. 61, (Ps. 65:11)

g. is as a morning cloud, p. 115, (Hos. 6:4)

surely g. and mercy shall follow me, p. 57, (Ps. 23:6)

Gopher: an ark of g. wood, p. 6, (Gen. 6:14)

Goshen: bring my father to the land of G., p. 13, (Gen. 45:9–10)

Gospel: g. which was preached not after man, p. 214, (Gal. 1:11)

I am ready to preach the g., p. 199, (Rom. 1:15)

Paul takes the g. to Europe, p. 195, (Acts 16:6—18:28)

preach the g. to every creature, p. 184, (Mk. 16:15; cf. Lk. 24:47)

the G. of Christ, p. 199. (Rom. 1:16)

the g. shall be preached, p. 173, (Matt. 24:14; Mk. 13:10)

the spread of the g., p. 191, (Acts 8:1–8)

the true g., p. 214, (Gal. 1:9–12)

Gourd: a g. to come over Jonah to shade him, p. 121, (Jonah 4:6)

a worm smote the g. which withered, p. 121, (Jonah 4:7)

thou hast had pity on the g., p. 121, (Jonah 4:10)

Government: g. shall be upon his shoulder, p. 84, (Isa. 9:6)

of the increase of his g. and peace, p. 84, (Isa. 9:7)

Governor: Paul told Felix the g., p. 197, (Acts 23:26; 24:10)

Grace: according to the gift of the g. of God, p. 216, (Eph. 3:7)

all g. abound toward you, p. 212, (II Cor. 9:8)

by g. are ye saved through faith, p. 215, (Eph. 2:8)

by the g. of God I am what I am, p. 209, (I Cor. 15:10)

find g. to help in time of need, p. 229, (Heb. 4:16)

gifts differing according to the g. that is given, p. 203, (Rom. 12:6)

g. according to the gift of Christ, p. 216, (Eph. 4:7)

G. be unto you and peace, p. 221, (I Th. 1:1)

g. to you and peace from God . . . , p. 199, (Rom. 1:7)

g. was upon them all, p. 190, (Acts 4:33)

my g. is sufficient for thee, p. 213, (II Cor. 12:9)

receive not the g. of God in vain, p. 211, (II Cor. 6:1)

that g. may abound?, p. 200, (Rom. 6:1)

the g. of the Lord Jesus Christ, . . . , p. 213. (II Cor. 13:14)

unto the churches of Galatia, g., p. 213, (Gal. 1:2–3)

yet not I, but the g. of God, p. 209, (I Cor. 15:10)

Gracious: g. and merciful, slow to anger, pp. 46, 117, (Neh. 9:17; Joel 2:13)

the Lord is g., full of compassion, p. 68, (Ps. 145:8)

Grain: a g. of wheat fall into the ground, p. 175, (Jn. 12:24)

Grape: fathers have eaten a sour g., p. 102, (Jer. 31:29; Ezek. 18:2)

Grapes: it brought forth wild g., p. 82, (Isa. 5:2)

Grass: all flesh is as g., p. 235, (I Pet. 1:24)

all flesh is g., p. 91, (Isa. 40:6)

as for man, his days are as g., p. 64, (Ps. 103:15)

eateth g. like an ox, p. 55, (Job 40:15)

let the earth bring forth g., p. 3, (Gen. 1:11)

like g. which groweth up, p. 62, (Ps. 90:5)

Nebuchadnezzar . . . did eat g. as oxen, p. 111, (Dan. 4:33)

the g. withereth, p. 91, (Isa. 40:7)

the g. withereth and the flower falleth, p. 235, (I Pet. 1:24)

Grasshopper: the g. shall be a burden, p. 76, (Ec. 12:5)

Grave: O g., I will be thy destruction, p. 116, (Hos. 13:14)

O g., where is thy victory?, p. 210, (I Cor. 15:55)

thou shalt come to thy g., p. 50, (Job 5:26)

Graven: g. upon the table of their heart, p. 101, (Jer. 17:1)

g. with an iron pen, p. 52, (Job 19:24)

not make any g. image, p. 17, (Ex. 20:4–5)

Great: g. men are not always wise, p. 54, (Job 32:9)

Greece: the goat the king of G., p. 112, (Dan. 8:21)

Greedy: not g. of filthy lucre, p. 224, (I Tim. 3:3, 8)

Greek: neither Jew nor G., p. 214, (Gal. 3:28)

the G. woman's daughter, p. 159, (Matt. 15:21–28; Mk. 7:24–30)

there is neither G. nor Jew, p. 220, (Col. 3:11)

to the Jew first and to the G., p. 199. (Rom. 1:16)

Greeks: unto the G. foolishness, p. 205, (I Cor. 1:23)

Grief: and acquainted with g., p. 94, (Isa. 53:3)

his g. was very great, p. 49, (Job 2:13)

in much wisdom is much g., p. 74, (Ec. 1:18)

that my g. were thoroughly weighted, p. 50, (Job 6:2)

Griefs: he hath borne our g., p. 94, (Isa. 53:4)

Grieve: nor g. the children of men, p. 105, (Lam. 3:33)

Grind: g. the faces of the poor, p. 82, (Isa. 3:15)

Groanings: g. that cannot be uttered, p. 202, (Rom. 8:26)

Guest: the g. of a sinner, p. 154, (Lk. 19:7)

Guests: none of the g. came, p. 171, (Matt. 22:5)

Guide: the Lord shall g. thee continually, p. 95, (Isa. 58:11)

Guile: an Israelite in whom is no g., p. 137, (Jn. 1:47)

Gulf: between us there is a great g., p. 153, (Lk. 16:26)

Habakkuk: H.'s prophecy, p. 123, (Hab. 2:2–12)

prayer of H., p. 124, (Hab. 3)

Habitation: bring Israel again to his h., p. 103, (Jer. 50:19)

I have loved the h. of thy house, p. 58, (Ps. 26:8)

thine h. is in the midst of deceit, p. 100, (Jer. 9:6)

Hagar: Abraham sent H. and Ishmael away, p. 9, (Gen. 21:9–21)

H. conceived a son, Ishmael, p. 8, (Gen. 16:4, 11)

Sarai gave H. her maid to Abram, p. 8, (Gen. 16:1–2)

Haggai: word of the Lord to H., p. 125, (Hagg. 1–2)

Hail: fire, and h.; snow, and vapors, p. 68, (Ps. 148:8)

the Lord rained h., p. 15, (Ex. 9:23)

Hair: not a h. of their head was singed, p. 111, (Dan. 3:27)

Hairs: h. of your head are all numbered, p. 147, (Matt. 10:30; Lk. 12:7)

Hairy: Esau had skin like a h. garment, p. 10, (Gen. 25:25)

Ham: Shem, H. and Japheth, p. 6, (Gen. 6:10)

Haman: H. sought to destroy the Jews, p. 46, (Est. 3:6)

they hanged H., p. 46, (Est. 7:10)

Hananiah: Daniel, H., Mishael and Azariah, p. 110, (Dan. 1:6)

Hand: a man with a withered h., p. 149, (Matt. 12:9–13; Mk. 3:1–5; Lk. 6:6–10)

as the clay is in the potter's h., p. 101, (Jer. 18:6)

fingers of a man's h. wrote upon the wall, p. 111, (Dan. 5:5)

his h. is stretched out still, p. 84, (Isa. 9:12, 17, 21; 10:4)

his h. will be against every man, p. 8, (Gen. 16:12)

if thy right h. offend thee, p. 139, (Matt. 5:30; 18:8; Mk. 9:43)

in the hollow of his h., p. 92, (Isa. 40:12)

let not thy left h. know, p. 140, (Matt. 6:3)

only those that cup their h., p. 29, (Jg. 7:6)

stretched forth his h. and it was whole, p. 149, (Matt. 12:13; Mk. 3:5; Lk. 6:10)

stretcheth out his h. against God, p. 52, (Job 15:25)

the h. of the Lord was strong upon me, p. 106, (Ezek. 3:14)

thy h. findeth to do, do it with thy might, p. 76, (Ec. 9:10)

thy right h. . . . is become glorious, p. 16, (Ex. 15:6)

will hold thine h., p. 93, (Isa. 42:6)

Handiwork: firmament sheweth his h., p. 56, (Ps. 19:1)

Handmaid: behold the h. of the Lord, p. 132, (Lk. 1:38)

Handmaiden: the low estate of his h., p. 132, (Lk. 1:48)

Hands: behold my h. and my feet, p. 184, (Lk. 24:39; cf. Jn. 20:20)

by the putting on of my h., p. 226, (II Tim. 1:6–7)

h. are full of blood, p. 81, (Isa. 1:15)

h. of fellowship, p. 214, (Gal. 2:9)

let the floods clap their h., p. 64, (Ps. 98:8)

not in temples made with h., p. 196, (Acts 17:24)

Paul laid his h. upon them, p. 196, (Acts 19:6)

pierced my h. and my feet, p. 57, (Ps. 22:16)

skins of goats upon his h., p. 10, (Gen. 27:16)

spread forth your h., p. 81, (Isa. 1:15)

the h. are Esau's, p. 10, (Gen. 27:22)

these wounds in thy h., p. 127, (Zech. 13:6)

Hanged: they h. Haman, p. 46, (Est. 7:10)

threw down the silver and h. himself, p. 181, (Matt. 27:5)

Hannah: H. prayed for a son, p. 31, (I Sam. 1:11)

H.'s song of thanksgiving, p. 31, (I Sam. 2:1–10)

Harlot: a h. named Rahab, p. 27, (Josh. 2:1)

Joshua saved Rahab, the h., p. 27, (Josh. 6:25)

the faithful city become an h., p. 81, (Isa. 1:21)

thou, Israel, play the h., p. 115, (Hos. 4:15)

Harmless: wise as serpents, h. as doves, p. 146, (Matt. 10:16)

Harp: those who play the h., p. 6, (Gen. 4:21)

Harps: hanged our h. upon the willows, p. 67, (Ps. 137:2)

Hart: the h. panteth after the water brooks, p. 59, (Ps. 42:1)

the lame man leap as an h., p. 90, (Isa. 35:6)

Harvest: grain is ripe . . . the h. has come, p. 156, (Mk. 4:29)

let both grow until the h., p. 156, (Matt. 13:30)

the feast of h., p. 21, (Ex. 23:16)

the fields are white to h., p. 166, (Jn. 4:35)

the h. is past the summer is ended, p. 100, (Jer. 8:20)

the h. is plenteous, p. 146, (Matt. 9:37; Lk. 10:2)

the h. is the end of the world, p. 156, (Matt. 13:39)

Haste: make h., my beloved, p. 78, (Song 8:14)

maketh h. to be rich, p. 73, (Prov. 28:20)

Hate: a time to h., p. 74, (Ec. 3:8)

Hate: (continued)

delivered me from them that h., p. 36, (II Sam. 22:18)

good to them that h. you, p. 140, (Matt. 5:44; Lk. 6:27)

h. the one and love the other, p. 141, (Matt. 6:24; Lk. 16:13)

marvel not . . . if the world h. you, p. 238, (I John 3:13)

Hated: Esau h. Jacob, p. 10, (Gen. 27:41)

no man ever yet h. his own flesh, p. 217, (Eph. 5:29)

ye shall be h., p. 147, (Matt. 10:22; Mk. 13:13; Lk. 21:17)

ye shall be h. of all nations, p. 173, (Matt. 24:9)

Hateth: spareth his rod h. his son, p. 71, (Prov. 13:24)

Hatred: h. stirreth up strifes, p. 70, (Prov. 10:12)

than a stalled ox and h., p. 71, (Prov. 15:17)

Haughty: h. spirit before a fall, p. 71, (Prov. 16:18)

the daughters of Zion are h. p. 82, (Isa. 3:16)

Head: Absalom's h. caught fast in an oak, p. 36, (II Sam. 18:9)

and poured it on his h., p. 176, (Matt. 26:7; Mk. 14:3)

become the h. of the corner, p. 170, (Matt. 21:42; Mk. 12:10; Lk. 20:17)

brought his h. on a platter, p. 158, (Matt. 14:11; Mk. 6:27–28)

the h. of John the Baptist, p. 158, (Matt. 14:8; Mk. 6:25)

the whole h. is sick, p. 81, (Isa. 1:5)

Headstone: become the h. of the corner, p. 66, (Ps. 118:22)

Heal: centurion asked Jesus to h., p. 143, (Matt. 8:5, 6; Lk. 7:2, 3)

he besought Jesus to h. his son, p. 166, (Jn. 4:47)

he hath torn and he will h., p. 115, (Hos. 6:1)

h. the sick, p. 146, (Matt. 10:8; Lk. 9:1, 2)

h. thee of thy wounds, p. 102, (Jer. 30:17)

I will come and h. him, p. 143, (Matt. 8:7)

Healed: a leper is h., p. 143, (Matt. 8:1–4; Mk. 1:40–45; Lk. 5:12–16)

my servant shall be h., p. 143, (Matt. 8:8; Lk. 7:7)

Healing: a h. in Lystra, p. 194, (Acts 14:8–18)

h. all manner of sickness, p. 137, (Matt. 4:23; cf. Mk. 1:39)

h. of a deaf and dumb man, p. 159, (Mk. 7:31–37)

h. of two blind men, p. 145, (Matt. 9:27–31)

the h. of a man born blind, p. 168, (Jn. 9)

the h. of a man with dropsy, p. 151, (Lk. 14:1–6)

the h. of an epileptic boy, p. 161, (Matt. 17:14–21; Mk. 9:14–29; Lk. 9:37–42)

the h. of ten lepers, p. 153, (Lk. 17:11–19)

the h. of the lame man, p. 190, (Acts 3)

with h. in his wings, p. 127, (Mal. 4:2)

Health: thine h. shall spring forth, p. 95, (Isa. 58:8)

thy saving h. among all nations, p. 61, (Ps. 67:2)

Heap: shall be a ruinous h., p. 86, (Isa. 17:1)

Heaps: Babylon shall become h., p. 103, (Jer. 51:37)

I will make Jerusalem h., p. 100, (Jer. 9:11)

Hear: cry and thou wilt not h.!, p. 123, (Hab. 1:2)

ears to h., let him h., p. 156, (Matt. 13:9; Mk. 4:9; Lk. 8:8)

h., O heaven, p. 81, (Isa. 1:2)

h. O Israel, p. 23, (Deut. 6:4; cf. Mk. 12:32)

H. O Israel: The Lord our God, p. 171, (Mk. 12:29; Deut. 6:4)

he that heareth let him h., p. 106, (Ezek. 3:27)

h. the word of the Lord, p. 101, (Jer. 22:29)

my God will h. me, p. 122, (Micah 7:7)

O my God incline thine ear and h., p. 113, (Dan. 9:18)

the deaf to h. and the dumb to speak, p. 159, (Mk. 7:37)

whether they h. or forbear, p. 106, (Ezek. 2:5)

while they are yet speaking, I will h., p. 96, (Isa. 65:24)

Heard: believe in him of whom they have not h.?, p. 202, (Rom. 10:14)

God h. the voice of the lad, p. 9, (Gen. 21:17)

have ye not h.?, p. 92, (Isa. 40:21)

we have h. that God is with you, p. 126, (Zech. 8:23)

Hearers: not the h. of the law, p. 200, (Rom. 2:13)

Heareth: thy servant h., p. 31, (I Sam. 3:9)

whosoever h. these sayings, p. 143, (Matt. 7:24; Lk. 6:47)

Hearing: by the h. of the ear, p. 55, (Job 42:5)

Heart: a broken and a contrite h., p. 60, (Ps. 51:17)

a new h. and a new spirit, p. 108, (Ezek. 18:31)

a revolting and a rebellious h., p. 99, (Jer. 5:23)

a wise and an understanding h., p. 37, (I Kg. 3:9; II Chr. 1:10)

as he thinketh in his h., p. 73, (Prov. 23:7)

create in me a clean h., O God, p. 60, (Ps. 51:10)

graven upon the table of their h., p. 101, (Jer. 17:1)

his h. was lifted up in the ways of the Lord, p. 42, (II Chr. 17:6)

hope deferred maketh the h. sick, p. 71, (Prov. 13:12)

I the Lord search the h., p. 101, (Jer. 17:10)

keep thy h. with all diligence, p. 69, (Prov. 4:23)

let no man's h. fail, p. 33, (I Sam. 17:32)

let not your h. be troubled, p. 178, (Jn. 14:1, 27)

let us lift up our h., p. 105, (Lam. 3:41)

on pages of the human h., p. 210, (II Cor. 3:3)

pour out thine h., p. 104, (Lam. 2:19)

rend your h. and not your garments, p. 117, (Joel 2:13)

the h. is deceitful . . . who can know it?, p. 101, (Jer. 17:9)

the h. melteth and the knees smite together, p. 123, (Nahum 2:10)

the h. of the children to their fathers, p. 127, (Mal. 4:6)

the Lord looks on the h., p. 33, (I Sam. 16:7)

the whole h. faint, p. 81, (Isa. 1:5)

their h. is far from me, p. 158, (Matt. 15:8; Mk. 7:6)

there will your h. be also, p. 141, (Matt. 6:21; Lk. 12:34)

these words shall be in thine h., p. 23, (Deut. 6:6)

thy h. is not right, p. 192, (Acts 8:21)

trust in the Lord with all thine h., p. 69, (Prov. 3:5)

turn the h. of the fathers, p. 127, (Mal. 4:6)

understanding to the h., p. 54, (Job 38:36)

wash thine h. from wickedness, p. 99, (Jer. 4:14)

whose h. departeth from the Lord, p. 101, (Jer. 17:5)

with all your h., p. 23, (Deut. 6:5; Mk. 12:33)

with my whole h., p. 102, (Jer. 32:41)

Hearts: Absalom stole the h., p. 36, (II Sam. 15:13)

direct your h. into the love of God, p. 223, (II Th. 3:5)

make manifest the counsels of the h., p. 206, (I Cor. 4:5)

shall keep your h. and minds, p. 219, (Phil. 4:7)

write it in their h., p. 102, (Jer. 31:33)

write them in their h., p. 230, (Heb. 8:10)

you are written in our h., p. 210, (II Cor. 3:2)

Heathen: made thee small among the h., p. 119, (Obad. v. 2)

speak peace unto the h., p. 126, (Zech. 9:10)

why do the h. rage, p. 55, (Ps. 2:1)

Heaven: a great wonder in h., p. 244, (Rev. 12:1)

and hath stretched out the h. by his understanding, p. 103, (Jer. 51:15)

Heaven: (*continued*)

easier for h. and earth to pass away, p. 139, (Lk. 16:17; cf. Matt. 5:18)

from h. or of men?, p. 170, (Matt. 21:25; Mk. 11:30; Lk. 20:4)

he was carried up into h., p. 186, (Mk. 16:19; Lk. 24:51; Acts 1:9–11)

h. and earth shall pass away, p. 174, (Matt. 24:35; Mk. 13:31; Lk. 21:33)

h. opened and behold a white horse, p. 246, (Rev. 19:11)

her sins have reached h., p. 246, (Rev. 18:5)

I will ascend into h., p. 86, (Isa. 14:13)

I will rain bread from h., p. 17, (Ex. 16:4)

into h., thou art there, p. 68, (Ps. 139:8)

neither by h. for it is God's throne, p. 139, (Matt. 5:34)

Heavenly: the h. Jerusalem, p. 232, (Heb. 12:22)

Heavens: hear, O h., p. 81, (Isa. 1:2)

h. declare the glory of God, p. 56, (Ps. 19:1)

the h. are higher than the earth, p. 94, (Isa. 55:9)

the h. as a curtain, p. 92, (Isa. 40:22)

Heaviness: the spirit of h., p. 95, (Isa. 61:3)

Heber: Jael, H.'s wife, killed Sisera, p. 28, (Jg. 4:21)

Hebrew: decreed the death of all H. sons, p. 13, (Ex. 1:15–16)

Egyptian beating an H., p. 14, (Ex. 2:11)

Hebrews: a letter to the H., p. 228, (Heb.)

one of the H.' children, p. 13, (Ex. 2:6)

Paul's letter to H., p. 228, (Heb.)

Hebron: oaks of Mamre at H., p. 8, (Gen. 13:18)

Hedge: h. up her way with thorns, p. 114, (Hos. 2:6)

Heel: Jacob took hold of Esau's h., p. 10, (Gen. 25:26)

Height: nor h., nor depth, nor any other creature, p. 202, (Rom. 8:39)

Heirs: h. of God and joint h. with Christ, p. 201, (Rom. 8:17)

Hell: in danger of h. fire, p. 139, (Matt. 5:22)

out of the belly of h. cried I, p. 120, (Jonah 2:2)

shalt be brought down to h., p. 86, (Isa. 14:15)

the keys of h. and of death, p. 240, (Rev. 1:18)

the rich man . . . from h. saw Lazarus, p. 153, (Lk. 16:23)

with h. are we at agreement, p. 88, (Isa. 28:15)

Helmet: the h. of salvation, p. 218, (Eph. 6:17)

Help: from whence cometh my h., p. 66, (Ps. 121:1)

Helper: the Lord is my h., p. 232, (Heb. 13:6)

Hem: the h. of his garment, p. 145, (Matt. 9:20; Mk. 5:27; Lk. 8:44)

Hemorrhage: a woman with a h., p. 145, (Matt. 9:20; Mk. 5:25; Lk. 8:43)

Hen: as a h. gathereth her chickens, p. 172, (Matt. 23:37; Lk. 13:34)

Herb: h. yielding seed, p. 3, (Gen. 1:11)

Herbs: better is a dinner of h., p. 71, (Prov. 15:17)

Here: h. am I., p. 31, (I Sam. 3:4)

Heritage: made mine h. an abomination, p. 99, (Jer. 2:7)

Herod: danced and pleased H., p. 158, (Matt. 14:6; Mk. 6:22)

depart for H. will kill thee, p. 169, (Lk. 13:31)

H. had bound John in prison, p.158, (Matt. 14:3; Mk. 6:17)

H. slew all the children, p. 134, (Matt. 2:16)

H. was king, p. 134, (Matt. 2:1)

Jesus before H., p. 182, (Lk. 23:6–16)

until the death of H., p. 134, (Matt. 2:15)

Herodias: John in prison for H.' sake, p. 158, (Matt. 14:3; Mk. 6:17)

the daughter of H. danced, p. 158, (Matt. 14:6; Mk. 6:22)

Hewers: h. of wood and drawers of water, p. 28, (Josh. 9:21, 27)

Hezekiah: and H. wept, p. 91, (Isa. 38:3)

H.'s passover, p. 44, (II Chr. 30)

H.'s reign, p. 44, (II Kg. 18—20; II Chr. 29—32)

H. sick unto death, p. 91, (Isa. 38:1)

H. turned his face toward the wall, p. 91, (Isa. 38:2)

Hid: heard the voice of the Lord and h., p. 5, (Gen. 3:8)

h. these things from the wise, p. 148, (Matt. 11:25; Lk. 10:21)

your life is h. with Christ in God, p. 220, (Col. 3:3)

Hide: h. by the brook Cherith, p. 39, (I Kg. 17:3)

h. me under thy wings, p. 56, (Ps. 17:8)

h. thee in the dust, p. 82, (Isa. 2:10)

h. thyself as it were, p. 88, (Isa. 26:20)

I will h. mine eyes, p. 81, (Isa. 1:15)

Hidest: why h. thou thy face from me?, p. 62, (Ps. 88:14)

Hiding: an h. place from the wind, p. 89, (Isa. 32:2)

High: be like the most H., p. 86, (Isa. 14:14)

we have a great h. priest, Jesus, p. 229, (Heb. 4:14)

Highly: not to think of himself more h. than he ought, p. 203, (Rom. 12:3)

Highway: a h. for our God, p. 91, (Isa. 40:3)

Highways: go to the h. and hedges, p. 171, (Lk. 14:23)

Hill: ascend into the h. of the Lord, p. 57, (Ps. 24:3)

Hills: and all the h. shall melt, p. 119, (Amos 9:13)

lift up mine eyes unto the h., p. 66, (Ps. 121:1)

shall be exalted above the h., p. 121, (Micah 4:1)

the h. in a balance, p. 92, (Isa. 40:12)

the little h. like lambs, p. 65, (Ps. 114:4)

Himself: none of us liveth to h., p. 204, (Rom. 14:7)

Hip: smote them h. and thigh with a great slaughter, p. 30, (Jg. 15:8)

Hiram: King H. of Tyre to hew ce-dars, p. 38, (I Kg. 5:1–10; II Chr. 2:3–16)

Hired: he h. other laborers, p. 164, (Matt. 20:3–7)

h. laborers for his vineyard, p. 164, (Matt. 20:1)

Hiss: everyone that passeth by shall h., p. 124, (Zeph. 2:15)

Hoary: h. head is a crown of glory, p. 71, (Prov. 16:31)

Hold: h. fast that which thou hast, p. 241, (Rev. 3:11)

Holier: I am h. than thou, p. 96, (Isa. 65:5)

Holiness: created in righteousness and h., p. 217, (Eph. 4:24)

in the beauty of h., p. 58, (Ps. 29:2)

not called us unto uncleanness but unto h., p. 222, (I Th. 4:7)

worship the Lord in the beauty of h., p. 63, (Ps. 96:9)

Holy: a h. nation, p. 17, (Ex. 19:5–6)

be h. in all manner of conversation, p. 235, (I Pet. 1:15)

be ye h. for I am h., p. 235, (I Pet. 1:16)

flight of the h. family into Egypt, p. 134, (Matt. 2:13–15; 19–23)

his H. One for a flame, p. 84, (Isa. 10:17)

h., h., h., is the Lord of hosts, p. 83, (Isa. 6:3)

in my h. mountain, p. 116, (Joel 2:1)

into the h. places made with hands, p. 230, (Heb. 9:24)

not hurt nor destroy in all my h. mountain, p. 85, (Isa. 11:9)

rest not day and night: say H., h., h., p. 242, (Rev. 4:8)

take not thy h. Spirit from me, p. 60, (Ps. 51:11)

the place on which you stand is h. ground, p. 14, (Ex. 3:5)

who shall dwell in thy h. hill, p. 56, (Ps. 15:1)

Holy Ghost and *Holy Spirit:* see Ghost and Spirit

Honestly: let us walk h. as in the day, p. 204, (Rom. 13:13)

Honey: flowing with milk and h., p. 14, (Ex. 3:8)

his food was locusts and wild h., p. 135, (Matt. 3:4; Mk. 1:6)

Honey: (*continued*)

it floweth with milk and h., p. 19, (Num. 13:27)

lips of a loose woman drip h., p. 69, (Prov. 5:3)

sweeter than h., p. 57, (Ps. 19:10)

Honeycomb: Jonathan and the h., p. 32, (I Sam 14:24–33)

Honor: before h. is humility, p. 71, (Prov. 15:33; 18:12)

h. all men, p. 236, (I Pet. 2:17)

h. thy father, p. 18, (Ex. 20:12)

in a place of h., p. 151, (Lk. 14:8)

in h., and understandeth not, p. 60, (Ps. 49:20)

Honors: h. me with their lips, p. 158, (Matt. 15:8; Mk. 7:6)

Hook: draw out leviathan with an h., p. 55, (Job 41:1)

Hope: against h. believed in h., p. 200, (Rom. 4:18)

am judged for the h., p. 197, (Acts 26:6)

h. deferred maketh the heart sick, p. 71, (Prov. 13:12)

h. that is seen is not h., p. 202, (Rom. 8:24)

h. was taken away, p. 198, (Acts 27:20)

now abideth faith, h., love, p. 209, (I Cor. 13:13)

therefore will I h. in him, p. 105, (Lam. 3:24)

thou art my h. in the day of evil, p. 101, (Jer. 17:17)

what is my strength that I should h.?, p. 50, (Job 6:11)

ye prisoners of h., p. 126, (Zech. 9:12)

Horse: a pale h.: His rider was death, p. 243, (Rev. 6:8)

came out another h. that was red, p. 243, (Rev. 6:4)

given the h. strength, p. 55, (Job 39:19)

heaven opened and behold a white h., p. 246, (Rev. 19:11)

I beheld a black h., p. 243, (Rev. 6:5)

I saw a white h., p. 243, (Rev. 6:2)

man riding upon a red h., p. 125, (Zech 1:8)

the h. and his rider, p. 16, (Ex. 15:1)

Horses: as fed h. in the morning, p. 99, (Jer. 5:8)

forty thousand stalls of h., p. 38, (I Kg. 4:26)

no, we will flee upon h., p. 89, (Isa. 30:16)

prancing h. and jumping chariots, p. 123, (Nahum 3:2)

red h., speckled and white, p. 125, (Zech. 1:8)

Hosanna: H.! Blessed is he that comes, p. 169, (Matt. 21:9; Mk. 11:9; Lk. 19:38; Jn. 12:13)

Hosea: the Lord said to H., p. 114, (Hos. 1:2)

Hospitality: a love of h., p. 227, (Tit. 1:8)

Host: an h. should encamp against me, p. 58, (Ps. 27:3)

the h. ran and cried and fled, p. 29, (Jg. 7:21)

Hot: thou art neither cold nor h., p. 241, (Rev. 3:15)

Hour: h. is not yet come, p. 137, (Jn. 2:4)

House: an h. not made with hands, p. 211, (II Cor. 5:1)

blessed are they that dwell in thy h., p. 62, (Ps. 84:4)

built his h. on the sand, p. 143, (Matt. 7:26; cf. Lk. 6:49)

burnt the h. of the Lord, p. 45, (II Kg. 25:9; II Chr. 36:19)

called the h. of prayer, p. 170, (Matt. 21:13; Mk. 11:17; Lk. 19:46)

except the Lord build the h., p. 67, (Ps. 127:1)

foundation of the h. of the Lord, p. 46, (Ezra 3:11)

he who hath builded the h. hath more honor, p. 229, (Heb. 3:3)

his h. upon a rock, p. 143, (Matt. 7:24; Lk. 6:48)

I have loved the habitation of thy h., p. 58, (Ps. 26:8)

if a h. be divided against itself, p. 146, (Matt. 12:25; Mk. 3:25; Lk. 11:17)

let us go into the h. of the Lord, p. 66, (Ps. 122:1)

let him on the h. top not come down, p. 173, (Matt. 27:17; Mk. 13:15; cf. Lk. 21:21)

Lord God . . . build him an h. in Jerusalem, p. 45, (II Chr. 36:23; Ezra 1:2; Isa. 44:28) my h. shall be built in it, p. 125, (Zech. 1:16)

repaired the h. of the Lord, p. 44, (II Kg. 12:14; II Chr. 24:13)

ruleth well his own h., p. 224, (I Tim. 3:4)

set thine h. in order, p. 44, (II Kg. 20:1)

set thine h. in order, p. 91, (Isa. 38:1)

show the h. to the h. of Israel, p. 109, (Ezek. 43:10)

that join h. to house, p. 83, (Isa. 5:8)

the h. of David, p. 35, (II Sam. 7; I Chr. 17)

the Lord's sign to the h. of David, p. 83, (Isa. 7:13, 14)

the pattern of the h. of the Lord, p. 37, (I Chr. 28:11–12)

the zeal of thine h. hath eaten me up, p. 61, (Ps. 69:9)

they came and worked in the h. of the Lord, p. 125, (Hagg. 1:14)

today I must abide at thy h., p. 154, (Lk. 19:5)

unclean spirit will return to an empty h., p. 155, (Matt. 12:43–44; Lk. 11:24)

work on the h. of God ceased, p. 46, (Ezra 4:24)

Household: foes . . . of his own h., p. 147, (Matt. 10:36; cf. Lk. 12:53)

Houses: build h. and inhabit them, p. 96, (Isa. 65:21)

he built h. in the city, p. 35, (I Chr. 15:1)

in their desolate h., p. 85, (Isa. 13:22)

the great h. shall have an end, p. 118, (Amos 3:15)

Housetop: a corner of the h., p. 72, (Prov. 21:9; 25:24)

How: h. can these things be?, p. 165, (Jn. 3:9)

Howl: h., ye ships of Tarshish, p. 87, (Isa. 23:14)

Howling: h. from the second quarter, p. 124, (Zeph. 1:10)

Humble: h. himself as this little child, p. 162, (Matt. 18:4)

h. yourselves in the sight of the Lord, p. 234, (Jas. 4:10)

Humbly: to walk h. with thy God, p. 122, (Micah 6:8)

Humbles: who h. himself will be exalted, p. 151, (Lk. 14:11)

Humbleth: he that h. himself shall be exalted, p. 154, (Lk. 18:14)

Humility: before honor is h., p. 71, (Prov. 15:33; 18:12)

Job answers God in h., p. 55, (Job 40)

parable on h., p. 151, (Lk. 14:7–11)

Hunger: he that comes to me shall never h., p. 167, (Jn. 6:35)

I perish with h., p. 152, (Lk. 15:17)

shall h. no more neither thirst, p. 243, (Rev. 7:16)

that faint for h., p. 104, (Lam. 2:19)

to kill us with h., p. 16, (Ex. 16:3)

Hungry: deal thy bread to the h., p. 95, (Isa. 58:7)

for I was h. and you gave me meat, p. 175, (Matt. 25:35)

to the h. soul, p. 73, (Prov. 27:7)

when did we see you h.?, p. 175, (Matt. 25:37)

Hur: Aaron and H. held up Moses' hands, p. 17, (Ex. 17:11, 12)

Hurt: h. not the earth, p. 243, (Rev. 7:3)

not h. nor destroy in all my holy mountain, p. 85, (Isa. 11:9)

Husband: every woman her own h., p. 207, (I Cor. 7:2)

let not the h. put away his wife, p. 207, (I Cor. 7:11)

let not the wife depart from her h., p. 207, (I Cor. 7:10)

the h. of one wife, p. 227, (Tit. 1:6)

the wife reverence her h., p. 217, (Eph. 5:33)

h., love your wives, p. 217, (Eph. 5:25)

Husks: willingly have eaten the h., p. 152, (Lk. 15:16)

Hymn: after they had sung an h., p. 179, (Matt. 26:30; Mk. 14:26)

h. to wisdom, p. 53, (Job 28)

Hymns: in psalms and h. and spiritual songs, p. 217, (Eph. 5:19)

Hypocrisy: leaven of the Pharisees is h., p. 160, (Lk. 12:1)

Hypocrites: be not as the h., p. 141, (Matt. 6:16)

Jesus said: You h., p. 158, (Matt. 15:7; Mk. 7:6)

Hypocrites: (*continued*)
scribes and Pharisees, h., p. 172, (Matt. 23:25)
Hypocritical: send him against an h. nation, p. 84, (Isa. 10:6)
Hyssop: purge me with h., p. 60, (Ps. 51:7)

I: I am that I am, p. 14, (Ex. 3:14)
I am the Lord your God, p. 17, (Ex. 20:1)
before Abraham was, I am, p. 168, (Jn. 8:58)
by the grace of God I am what I am, p. 209, (I Cor. 15:10)
I, even I, am against thee, p. 106, (Ezek. 5:8)
here am I, p. 31, (I Sam. 3:4)
there am I in the midst, p. 162, (Matt. 18:20)
yet not I, but the grace of God, p. 209, (I Cor. 15:10)
Iconium: Paul and Barnabus visit I., p. 194, (Acts 13:51)
Idea: Gamaliel: If this i. be of men, p. 191, (Acts 5:38)
Idols: abominable beasts and all the i. of Israel, p. 107, (Ezek. 8:10)
Image: do not ye worship the golden i.?, p. 111, (Dan. 3:14)
God created man in his own i., p. 4, (Gen. 1:27)
Nebuchadnezzar set up a golden i., p. 111, (Dan. 3:1)
not make any graven i., p. 17, (Ex. 20:4–5)
thou, O king, sawest a great i., p. 110, (Dan. 2:31)
who is the i. of the invisible God, p. 220, (Col. 1:15)
Imagine: i. evil against his brother, p. 126, (Zech. 7:10)
Immanuel: See also Emmanuel shall call his name I., p. 83, (Isa. 7:14)
Impossible: nothing shall be i. unto you, p. 162, (Matt. 17:20; cf. Mk. 11:23)
nothing they propose will be i., p. 7, (Gen. 11:6)
Imprisonment: i. and beheading of John the Baptist, p. 158, (Matt. 14:1–12; Mk. 6:14–29)
Impudent: i. children and stiff-hearted, p. 106, (Ezek. 2:4)

Incense: i. is an abomination, p. 81, (Isa. 1:13)
my prayer be set forth as i., p. 68, (Ps. 141:2)
Inclosed: he hath i. my ways, p. 104, (Lam. 3:9)
Incorruption: raised in i., p. 209, (I Cor. 15:42)
Increase: he must i. but I must decrease, p. 166, (Jn. 3:30)
Indignation: until the i. be overpast, p. 88, (Isa. 26:20)
who can stand before his i.?, p. 122, (Nahum 1:6)
Inexcusable: thou art i., O man, p. 199, (Rom. 2:1)
Infirmities: I will glory . . . which concern my i., p. 213, (II Cor. 11:30)
to bear the i. of the weak, p. 204, (Rom. 15:1)
will I rather glory in my i., p. 213, (II Cor. 12:9)
Infirmity: had had an i. thirty-eight years, p. 166, (Jn. 5:5)
the woman with a spirit of i., p. 151, (Lk. 13:10–17)
Inhabit: not build and another i., p. 96, (Isa. 65:22)
Inhabitants: the i. of the land tremble, p. 116, (Joel 2:1)
Inherit: he that overcometh shall i., p. 247, (Rev. 21:7)
i. the kingdom of God, p. 210, (I Cor. 15:50)
i. the kingdom prepared for you, p. 175, (Matt. 25:34)
the meek shall i. the earth, p. 59, (Ps. 37:11)
Inheritance: this land shall fall unto you for i., p. 109, (Ezek. 47:14)
Iniquity: depart from me ye that work i., p. 142, (Matt. 7:23; Lk. 13:27)
I was shapen in i., p. 60, (Ps. 51:5)
if i. be in thine hand, p. 51, (Job 11:14)
in the bond of i., p. 192, (Acts 8:23)
i. is taken away, thy sin purged, p. 83, (Isa. 6:7)
that draw i. with cords of vanity, p. 83, (Isa. 5:18)
the Lord hath laid on him the i., p. 94, (Isa. 53:6)

ye have reaped i., p. 116, (Hos. 10:13)

Inn: no room for them in the i., p. 132, (Lk. 2:7)

Innocent: make haste to shed i. blood, p. 95, (Isa. 59:7)

shall not be i., p. 73, (Prov. 28:20)

who ever perished being i.?, p. 50, (Job 4:7)

Innocents: the slaughter of the i., p. 134, (Matt. 2:1–8; 16–18)

Instrument: upon an i. of ten strings, p. 63, (Ps. 92:3)

Intercession: Spirit itself maketh i., p. 202, (Rom. 8:26)

Interpret: . . . came to i. the dream, p. 110, (Dan. 2:2)

I will i. his dream, p. 110, (Dan. 2:24)

Invite: i. the poor, the maimed, p. 151, (Lk. 14:13)

i. those in need, p. 151, (Lk. 14:12–14)

Iron: an i. pen and lead in the rock, p. 52, (Job 19:24)

and the i. did swim, p. 43, (II Kg. 6:6)

his feet part of i., part of clay, p. 110, (Dan. 2:33)

Isaac: I. blessed Jacob, p. 10, (Gen. 27:23)

I. took Rebekah, she became his wife, p. 9, (Gen. 24:67)

I. was old, p. 10, (Gen. 27:1)

Sarah shall bear thee a son . . . I., p. 8, (Gen. 17:19)

steals Esau's blessing from I., p. 10, (Gen. 27:1–40)

the birth of I., p. 9, (Gen. 21:1–7)

the God of Abraham, I. and Jacob, p. 171, (Matt. 22:32; Mk. 12:26; Lk. 20:37)

the sacrifice of I., p. 9, (Gen. 22:1–18)

to find a wife for I., p. 9, (Gen. 24)

Ishmael: Abraham sent Hagar and I. away, p. 9, (Gen. 21:9–21)

Hagar conceived a son, I., p. 8, (Gen. 16:4, 11)

Island: i. was called Melita, p. 198, (Acts 28:1)

Israel: See also Jacob

a new covenant with . . . I., p. 102, (Jer. 31:31)

a plumbline in the midst of I., p. 119, (Amos 7:8)

a watchman unto I., p. 106, (Ezek. 3:14–27)

abominable beasts and all the idols of I., p. 107, (Ezek. 8:10)

all I. scattered upon the hills, p. 41, (I Kg. 22:17; II Chr. 18:16)

and I. dwell safely, p. 101, (Jer. 23:6)

assemble the outcasts of I., p. 85, (Isa. 11:12)

atonement for the iniquities of I., p. 19, (Lev. 16:10, 21)

because there is not a God in I., p. 42, (II Kg. 1:6)

Bethlehem out of thee . . . one who is to be the ruler in I., p. 122, (Micah 5:2)

bring I. again to his habitation, p. 103, (Jer. 50:19)

called no more Jacob, but I., p. 11, (Gen. 32:28; 35:10)

carried I. away into exile, p. 44, (II Kg. 17:6)

children of I. out of Egypt, p. 15, (Ex. 12:51)

come up against my people of I., p. 109, (Ezek. 38:16)

David made king over all I., p. 35, (II Sam. 5:1–5; I Chr. 11:1–3)

declare . . . to I. his sin, p. 121, (Micah 3:8)

glean the remnant of I., p. 99, (Jer. 6:9)

God's promise of I.'s return, p. 102, (Jer. 29–30)

he hath swallowed up I., p. 104, (Lam. 2:5)

he that scattered I., p. 102, (Jer. 31:10)

hear O I., p. 23, (Deut. 6:4; cf. Mk. 12:32)

hear O I.: The Lord our God, p. 171, (Mk. 12:29; Deut. 6:4)

hearken, ye house of I., p. 115, (Hos. 5:1)

I send thee to the children of I., p. 106, (Ezek. 2:3)

in those days there was no king in I., p. 31, (Jg. 21:25)

I., art my servant, p. 92, (Isa. 41:8)

I. asked Samuel for a king, p. 32, (I Sam. 8)

Israel: **(continued)**
I. blessed Joseph's sons, p. 13, (Gen. 48)
I. did secretly, things that were not right, p. 44, (II Kg. 17:9)
I. doth not know, p. 81, (Isa. 1:3)
I. forsook the Lord, p. 28, (Jg. 2:13)
I. is a scattered sheep, p. 103, (Jer. 50:17)
I. loved Joseph more, p. 12, (Gen. 37:3)
I. passed through walls of water, p. 16, (Ex. 14:22)
I. prevailed, p. 17, (Ex. 17:11, 12)
I. shall blossom, p. 88, (Isa. 27:6)
I. stood and confessed their sins, p. 46, (Neh. 9:2)
I. the faithless wife, p. 114, (Hos. 2:1–13)
Joshua became the leader of I., p. 27, (Deut. 34—Josh. 1)
Judah and I. dwelt safely, p. 38, (I Kg. 4:25)
light of I. shall be for a fire, p. 84, (Isa. 10:17)
Pharaoh pursued the children of I., p. 16, (Ex. 14:8, 9)
returned the ark to I., p. 32, (I Sam. 6:21)
returned to I. and dwelt in Nazareth, p. 134, (Matt. 2:21, 23)
Samuel judged I., p. 32, (I Sam. 7:15)
save I. from the hand of the Midianites, p. 29, (Jg. 6:14)
sent I. and the prophets of Baal to Mount Carmel, p. 40, (I Kg. 18:20)
show the house to the house of I., p. 109, (Ezek. 43:10)
the children of I. are more, p. 13, (Ex. 1:9)
the children of I. were fruitful, p. 13, (Ex. 1:7)
the glory is departed from I., p. 32, (I Sam. 4:22)
the kings of I. and Judah, p. 43, (II Kg. 8:16—17:41)
the lost sheep of the house of I., p. 146, (Matt. 10:6)
the remnant of I., p. 102, (Jer. 31:7)
the restoration of I., p. 102, (Jer. 31:1–30)
the tribes of I., p. 28, (Josh. 13—22)
the twelve tribes of I., p. 13, (Gen. 49)
these bones are the whole house of I., p. 109, (Ezek. 37:11)
thou, I., play the harlot, p. 115, (Hos. 4:15)
to both the houses of I., p. 84, (Isa. 8:14)
to the lost sheep of I., p. 159, (Matt. 15:24)
to your tents, O I., p. 39, (I Kg. 12:16)
vineyard of the Lord is the house of I., p. 83, (Isa. 5:7)
woe be to the shepherds of I., p. 109, (Ezek. 34:2)
word of Samuel came to all I., p. 32, (I Sam. 4:1)
Israelite: an I. in whom is no guile, p. 137, (Jn. 1:47)
I. conquered the kingdom of Ai, p. 28, (Josh. 7—8)
I. solemnly repented, p. 32, (I Sam. 7:6)
the I. passed over on dry ground, p. 27, (Josh. 3:17)
Ivory: i., apes and peacocks, p. 38, (I Kg. 10:22; II Chr. 9:21)
neck is as a tower of i., p. 78, (Song 7:4)

Jacob: Also see Israel
birth of J. and Esau, p. 10, (Gen. 25:21–26)
called no more J., but Israel, p. 11, (Gen. 32:28; 35:10)
Esau hated J., p. 10, (Gen. 27:41)
I will slay my brother J., p. 10, (Gen. 27:41)
Isaac blessed J., p. 10, (Gen. 27:23)
J. abode with him, p. 11, (Gen. 29:14)
J.'s and Esau's reconciliation, p. 11, (Gen. 32:3–21; 33:1–20)
J. built . . . booths, p. 11, (Gen. 33:17)
J. called the place Bethel, p. 11, (Gen. 28:19)
J. dreamed of a ladder, p. 10, (Gen. 28:12)
J. flees from Esau, p. 10, (Gen. 27:41—28:10)
J.'s ladder, p. 10, (Gen. 28:10–22)

J. loved Rachel and served seven years, p. 11, (Gen. 29:18, 20)

J. moved the stone from the well, p. 11, (Gen. 29:10)

J. steals Esau's blessing, p. 10, (Gen. 27:1–40)

J. told Rachel he was Rebekah's son, p. 11, (Gen. 29:12)

J. took hold of Esau's heel, p. 10, (Gen. 25:26)

J. wrestles with an angel, p. 11, (Gen. 32:24)

Laban took Leah to J., p. 11, (Gen. 29:23)

Rebekah disguised J., p. 10, (Gen. 27:15)

Rebekah told J. to flee, p. 10, (Gen. 27:42, 43)

the God of Abraham, Isaac and J., p. 171, (Matt. 22:32; Mk. 12:26; Lk. 20:37)

the voice is J.'s, p. 10, (Gen. 27:22)

to declare to J. his transgression, p. 121, (Micah 3:8)

to J. for pottage, p. 10, (Gen. 25:27–34)

thy tents, O J., p. 20, (Num. 24:5)

Jael: H., Heber's wife, killed Sisera, p. 28, (Jg. 4:21)

Jailkeeper: the j., trembling, p. 195, (Acts 16:29)

Jairus: a ruler named J., p. 145, (Matt. 9:18; Mk. 5:22; Lk. 8:41)

J.' daughter, p. 145, (Matt. 9:18–26; Mk. 5:21–43; Lk. 8:40–56)

James: a letter from J., p. 232, (Jas.)

J., Cephas and John gave to me and Barnabus, p. 214, (Gal. 2:9)

Jesus, . . . J. went up a mountain to pray, p. 161, (Matt. 17:1; Mk. 9:2; Lk. 9:28)

the mother of J. and John, p. 164, (Matt. 20:20–28; cf. Mk. 10:35–45)

two other brothers, J. and John, p. 136, (Matt. 4:21; Mk. 1:19; Lk. 5:10)

Japheth: Shem, Ham and J., p. 6, (Gen. 6:10)

Jawbone: with the j. of an ass, p. 30, (Jg. 15:16)

Jealous: Saul, j. of David, p. 34, (I Sam. 18—23)

Jealousy: j. is cruel as the grave, p. 78, (Song 8:6)

Jehoiada: J., the priest, anointed Joash, p. 43, (II Kg. 11:12; II Chr. 23:11)

Jehoiakim: J. shall have none upon the throne of David, p. 103, (Jer. 36:30)

King J. cast it in the fire, p. 103, (Jer. 36:22–23)

King J. cut it with his penknife, p. 102, (Jer. 36:23)

the Lord gave J. into his hand, p. 110, (Dan. 1:2)

the reign of J. king of Judah, p. 110, (Dan. 1:1)

Jehoshaphat: J. made peace with Israel, p. 42, (I Kg. 22:44)

reign of J. of Judah, p. 42, (I Kg. 22:41–50; II Chr. 17—20)

the Ammonites came against J., p. 42, (II Chr. 20:1)

Jehovah: in the Lord J. is . . . strength, p. 88, (Isa. 26:4)

Jehu: J. conspired against Joram of Judah, p. 43, (II Kg. 9:14)

J. smote Joram dead, p. 43, (II Kg. 9:24)

J. was anointed King of Israel, p. 43, (II Kg. 9—10)

the driving is like the driving of J., p. 43, (II Kg. 9:20)

Jeopardy: in j. of their lives, p. 37, (II Sam. 23:17)

Jeremiah: Baruch wrote from the mouth of J., p. 102, (Jer. 36:4)

J. commanded Baruch to read, p. 102, (Jer. 36:8)

J. prophesies to Zedekiah, p. 101, (Jer. 21)

J.'s call to be God's prophet, p. 99, (Jer. 1)

Jericho: as Jesus was leaving J., p. 165, (Mk. 10:46; cf. Matt. 20:29; Lk. 18:35)

Jesus entered J., p. 154, (Lk. 19:1)

the destruction of J., p. 27, (Josh. 6)

to view the land, especially J., p. 27, (Josh 2:1)

Jeroboam: J. ruled as King of Israel, p. 39, (I Kg. 12:20)

Jerusalem: a man in J. named Simeon, p. 133, (Lk. 2:25)

Jerusalem: *(continued)*

a prophet perish out of J., p. 169, (Lk. 13:33)

a vision of J.'s idolatry, p. 107, (Ezek. 8)

carried away all J. to Babylon, p. 45, (II Kg. 24:14–15; Jer. 39:9)

condemnation of J., p. 124, (Zeph. 3:1–7)

I will make J. heaps, p. 100, (Jer. 9:11)

J. destroyed by Babylon, p. 103, (Jer. 39—40)

J. lieth waste, p. 45, (Neh. 2:3)

J.—the city of David, p. 35, (II Sam. 6; I Chr. 11—16)

Jesus as a boy in J. at passover, p. 134, (Lk. 2:40–52)

Jesus tarried behind in J., p. 134, (Lk. 2:43)

kings of Judah to the fall of J., p. 44, (II Kg. 18—25; II Chr. 10—36)

Lord God . . . build him an house in J., p. 45, (II Chr. 36:23; Ezra 1:2; Isa. 44:28)

Nebuchadnezzar beseiged J., p. 110, (Dan. 1:1)

Nebuchadnezzar came up against J., p. 45, (II Kg. 24:10–11; II Chr. 36:7; Jer. 39:1)

O J., Jerusalem, p. 172, (Matt. 23:37; Lk. 13:34)

O J., wash thine heart, p. 99, (Jer. 4:14)

out of J. . . . . a remnant, p. 44, (II Kg. 19:31)

Paul in J., p. 197, (Acts 21:13–40; 22; 23:1–22)

Paul sails from J. to Rome, p. 198, (Acts 27—28)

Paul travels to J., p. 196, (Acts 19—21:15)

prediction of the destruction of J., p. 169. (Lk. 19:41–44)

ready to die at J., p. 197, (Acts 21:13)

rebuilding the walls of J., p. 46, (Neh. 3—6; 12:27–47)

return to J., p. 45, (Ezra 1, 2, 7—10; Neh. 1, 2, 7:6–73)

returned to J. with mercies, p. 125, (Zech. 1:16)

Saul and the disciples in J., p. 193, (Acts 9:26–31)

search J. with candles, p. 124, (Zeph. 1:12)

shout O daughter of J., p. 126, (Zech. 9:9)

speak ye comfortably to J., p. 91, (Isa. 40:2)

swear not . . . neither by J., p. 140, (Matt. 5:35)

temple in J. on Mount Moriah, p. 38, (II Chr. 3:1)

the conference at J., p. 194, (Acts 15:1–35)

the entry into J., p. 169, (Matt. 21:1–11; Mk. 11:1–10; Lk. 19:28–38; Jn. 12:12–19)

the fall of J., p. 109, (Ezek. 33:21–33)

the fate of J., p. 104, (Lam. 1)

the holy city, new J., p. 247, (Rev. 21:2)

there was great joy in J., p. 44, (II Chr. 30:26)

they returned to J., p. 189, (Acts 1:12)

this is J. in the midst of the nations, p. 106, (Ezek. 5:5)

thy fury be turned away from J., p. 113, (Dan. 9:16)

went to J. for the feast, p. 134, (Lk. 2:42)

wipe J. as a man wipeth a dish, p. 45, (II Kg. 21:13)

wise men from the east to J., p. 134, (Matt. 2:1)

Jesse: a rod out of the stem of J., p. 84, (Isa. 11:1)

David the son of J., p. 36, (II Sam. 23:1)

he sent Samuel to J., p. 33, (I Sam. 16:1)

I am the son of J., p. 33, (I Sam. 17:58)

J. made seven sons pass before, p. 33, (I Sam. 16:10)

Obed, father of J., father of David, p. 31, (Ruth 4:17)

Jesus: Also see Christ
after J.' ascension, p. 189, (Acts 1:12–14)

as J. sat with them he took bread, p. 184, (Lk. 24:30)

as J. was leaving Jericho, p. 165, (Mk. 10:46; cf. Matt. 20:29; Lk. 18:35)

begged the body of J., p. 183, (Matt.

27:58; Mk. 15:43; Lk. 23:52; Jn. 19:38)

brought to J. one who was deaf, p. 159, (Mk. 7:32)

by the revelation of J. Christ, p. 214, (Gal. 1:12)

call his name J., p. 131, (Lk. 1:31)

devil offered J. the kingdoms, p. 136, (Matt. 4:8-9; Lk. 4:5-7)

every tongue confess that J. Christ is Lord, p. 218, (Phil. 2:11)

fame of J. . . . throughout Galilee, p. 138, (Mk. 1:28; cf. Lk. 4:37)

he besought J. to heal his son, p. 166, (Jn. 4:47)

he took J. up in his arms, p. 133, (Lk. 2:28)

he was circumcised and called J., p. 133, (Lk. 2:21)

in the name of J. Christ, p. 190, (Acts 3:6)

J. and his disciples went through the corn, p. 149, (Matt. 12:1; Mk. 2:23; Lk. 6:1)

J. and Nicodemus, p. 165, (Jn. 3:1-15)

J. and the Samaritan woman, p. 166, (Jn. 4:5-42)

J.'s appearance to the disciples, p. 184, (Mk. 16:14-18; Lk. 24:36-49; Jn. 20:19-23)

J. appeared to Mary Magdalene, p. 184, (Mk. 16:9; Jn. 20:14)

J. as a boy in Jerusalem at passover, p. 134, (Lk. 2:40-52)

J. before Herod, p. 182, (Lk. 23:6-16)

J. before Pilate, p. 181, (Matt. 27:11-14; Mk. 15:2-5; Lk. 23:2-5; Jn. 18:33-38; 19:8-12)

J. . . . began to wash the disciples' feet, p. 177, (Jn. 13:4-5)

J. blessed them and gave, p. 158, (Matt. 14:19; Mk. 6:41; Lk. 9:16; Jn. 6:11)

J. came from Nazareth and was baptized, p. 135, (Matt. 3:13; Mk. 1:9; Lk. 3:21)

J. cast out all them that sold . . . , p. 170, (Matt. 21:12; Mk. 11:15; Lk. 19:45; Jn. 2:14-15)

J. Christ the chief corner stone, p. 216, (Eph. 2:20)

J.' countenance was altered, p. 161, (Matt. 17:2; Mk. 9:2-3; Lk. 9:29)

J. delivered to Pilate, p. 181, (Matt. 27:1-2; Mk. 15:1; Lk. 23:1; Jn. 18:28-32)

J. died and rose again, p. 222, (I Th. 4:14)

J. entered Jericho, p. 154, (Lk. 19:1)

J. had compassion: Young man arise, p. 155, (Lk. 7:13-14)

J. in the synagogue, p. 137, (Matt. 7:28-29; Mk. 1:21-28; Lk. 4:31-37)

J. increased in wisdom and stature, p. 135, (Lk. 2:52)

J.' mother and brothers, p. 156, (Matt. 12:46-50; Mk. 3:31-35; Lk. 8:19-21)

J., moved with compassion, touched him, p. 143, (Mk. 1:41)

J. put his fingers into his ear, p. 159, (Mk. 7:33)

J. read in the synagogue, p. 157, (Lk. 4:16)

J. rebuked the devil, p. 161, (Matt. 17:18; Mk. 9:25; Lk. 9:42)

J. said: Feed my lambs, p. 186, (Jn. 21:15)

J. said: If you answer one thing, p. 170, (Matt. 21:24; Mk. 11:29; Lk. 20:3)

J. said: Lovest thou me?, p. 186, (Jn. 21:16)

J. said: Thou hast said, p. 181, (Matt. 26:64; cf. Mk. 14:62; Lk. 22:67, 70)

J. said to Peter: Come, p. 158, (Matt. 14:29)

J. said to Thomas: Behold my hands, p. 185, (Jn. 20:27)

J. set a child in the midst, p. 162, (Matt. 18:2; Mk. 9:36; Lk. 9:47)

J., son of David, have mercy, p. 165, (Mk. 10:47; cf. Matt. 20:30; Lk. 18:38)

J. stood in the midst of them, p. 184, (Lk. 24:36; Jn. 20:19)

J. stood on the shore but they knew him not, p. 185, (Jn. 21:4)

J. tarried behind in Jerusalem, p. 134, (Lk. 2:43)

J. taught them from a boat, p. 156, (Matt. 13:2-3; Mk. 4:1-2)

Jesus: (continued)

J. the night he was betrayed took bread, p. 208, (I Cor. 11:23)

J. took bread and blessed it, p. 177, (Matt. 26:26; Mk. 14:22; Lk. 22:19; I Cor. 11:23–24)

J., walking by the Sea of Galilee, p. 136, (Matt. 4:18; Mk. 1:16)

J. was led by the Spirit, p. 135, (Matt. 4:1; Mk. 1:12; Lk. 4:1)

J. went into a ship, p. 144, (Matt. 8:23; Mk. 4:36; Lk. 8:22)

J. went into the Pharisee's house, p. 155, (Lk. 7:36)

J. went to them walking on the water, p. 158, (Matt. 14:25; Mk. 6:48; Jn. 6:19)

J., . . . went up a mountain to pray, p. 161, (Matt. 17:1; Mk. 9:2; Lk. 9:28)

J. went up into the temple, p. 160, (Jn. 7:14)

J. went with them but they knew him not, p. 184, (Lk. 24:15–16)

J. wept, p. 169, (Jn. 11:35)

J. whom thou persecutest, p. 192, (Acts 9:5)

J. . . . worthy of more glory than Moses, p. 229, (Heb. 3:3)

John speaks of J., p. 135, (Matt. 3:11–12; Mk. 1:7–8; Lk. 3:15–18; Jn. 1:15–28)

John the Baptist speaks of J., p. 166, (Jn. 3:25–36)

Lord J., receive my spirit, p. 191, (Acts 7:59)

made that same J. both Lord and Christ, p. 190, (Acts 2:36)

Mary and Martha, sent for J., p. 168, (Jn. 11:3)

not to teach in the name of J., p. 190, (Acts 4:18)

presentation of J. in the temple, p. 133, (Lk. 2:22–39)

sought false witness against J., p. 181, (Matt. 26:59; Mk. 14:55–56)

teaching those things which concern J. Christ, p. 198, (Acts 18:31)

that at the name of J., p. 218, (Phil. 2:10)

the angel said: . . . I know you seek J., p. 183, (Matt. 28:5; Mk. 16:6)

the arrest of J., p. 180, (Matt. 26:47–56; Mk. 14:43–52; Lk. 22:47–53; Jn. 18:2–11)

the authority of J., p. 170, (Matt. 21:23–27; Mk. 11:27–33; Lk. 20:1–8)

the baptism of J., p. 135, (Matt. 3:13–17; Mk. 1:9–11; Lk. 3:21–22; cf. Jn. 1:29–34)

the birth of J., p. 132, (Lk. 2:1–7)

the burial of J., p. 183, (Matt. 27:57–61; Mk. 15:42–47; Lk. 23:50–56; Jn. 19:38–42)

the disciple whom J. loved, p. 185, (Jn. 21:7)

the mocking of J., p. 182, (Matt. 27:27–31; Mk. 15:16–20; Jn. 19:2–5)

the name of J. Christ of Nazareth, p. 190, (Acts 4:10)

the name of the Lord J., p. 197, (Acts 21:13)

THIS IS J. THE KING OF THE JEWS, p. 183, (Matt. 27:37; Mk. 15:26; Lk. 23:38; Jn. 19:19–22)

this J. hath God raised up, p. 190, (Acts 2:32)

to slay J. for healing on the sabbath, p. 167, (Jn. 5:16)

we have a great high priest, J., p. 229, (Heb. 4:14)

what shall I do then with J.?, p. 182, (Matt. 27:22; cf. Mk. 15:12)

when he had scourged J., p. 182, (Matt. 27:26; Mk. 15:15; Jn. 19:1)

when J. was born in Bethlehem, p. 134, (Matt. 2:1)

when they saw J. they worshipped him, p. 185, (Matt. 28:17)

Jethro: J.'s counsel to Moses, p. 17, (Ex. 18)

Jew: I am a J. of Tarsus, p. 197, (Acts 21:39)

neither J. nor Greek, p. 214, (Gal. 3:28)

to the J. first and to the Gentile, p. 199, (Rom. 2:10)

to the J. first and to the Greek, p. 199, (Rom. 1:16)

Jews: a plot against the J., p. 46, (Est. 2:19–7)

confounded the J. of Damascus, p. 193, (Acts 9:22)

devout J. of every nation asked, p. 189, (Acts 2:5)

the J. of Asia, p. 197, (Acts 21:27)

the J. smote all their enemies, p. 46, (Est. 9:5)

the J. sought to kill him, p. 160, (Jn. 7:1)

unto the J. a stumblingblock, p. 205, (I Cor. 1:23)

unto the J. I became as a Jew, p. 207, (I Cor. 9:20)

unto the J. . . . no wrong, p. 197, (Acts 25:10)

where is he that is born King of the J.?, p. 134, (Matt. 2:2)

Jezebel: Ahab and J. worshipped Baal, p. 39, (I Kg. 16:31)

Elijah fled from J., p. 41, (I Kg. 19:2-3)

J. had Naboth stoned to death, p. 41, (I Kg. 21:8, 13)

J. painted her face, p. 43, (II Kg. 9:30)

J. slew the prophets, p. 40, (I Kg. 18:4)

Obadiah against J., p. 40, (I Kg. 18:1-16)

the dogs shall eat J., p. 41, (I Kg. 21:23)

Joab: J. . . . slew Absalom, p. 36, (II Sam. 18:14-15)

Joash: Jehoiada, the priest, anointed J., p. 43, (II Kg. 11:12; II Chr. 23:11)

J. came down and wept, p. 44, (II Kg. 13:14)

J. ruled over Judah, p. 43, (II Kg. 11:21; II Chr. 24:1)

J., son of Ahaziah, was saved, p. 43, (II Kg. 11:2; II Chr. 22:11)

the reign of J. of Judah, p. 44, (II Kg. 11:21—12:21; II Chr. 24)

Job: doth J. fear God . . . ?, p. 49, (Job 1:9)

Elihu's wrath kindled against J., p. 54, (Job 32:2)

Eliphaz reproved J., p. 52, (Job 15)

God answers J. out of the whirlwind, p. 54, (Job 38:1)

have you considered my servant, J.?, p. 49, (Job 1:8)

heard of the patience of J., p. 235, (Jas. 5:11)

J. answers God in humility, p. 55, (Job 40)

J. blessed the name, p. 49, (Job 1:21)

J. did not sin, p. 49, (Job 2:10)

J. feared God, p. 49, (Job 1:1)

J. lost all, p. 49, (Job 1:13-22)

J.'s three silent friends, p. 49, (Job 2:11-13)

Lord blessed the latter end of J., p. 55, (Job 42:12)

restores J.'s fortune, p. 55, (Job 42:7-17)

Satan smote J. with sore boils, p. 49, (Job 2:7)

Satan tests J., p. 49, (Job 2:1-10)

Joel: spoken by the prophet J., p. 189, (Acts 2:16)

the word of the Lord to J., p. 116, (Joel 1:1)

John: a letter from J., p. 237, (Jn.)

baptism of J., was it from heaven, p. 170, (Matt. 21:25; Mk. 11:30; Lk. 20:4)

baptized by J. in the Jordan, p. 135, (Matt 3:13; Mk. 1:9)

call his name J., p. 131, (Lk. 1:13)

entered the temple with Peter and J., p. 190, (Acts 3:8)

he spoke of J. the Baptist, p. 161, (Matt. 17:13)

Herod had bound J. in prison, p. 158, (Matt. 14:3; Mk. 6:17)

imprisonment and beheading of J. the Baptist, p. 158, (Matt. 14:1-12; Mk. 6:14-29)

James, Cephas and J. gave to me and Barnabus, p. 214, (Gal. 2:9)

Jesus, Peter, J. . . . went up a mountain to pray, p. 161, (Matt. 17:1; Mk. 9:2; Lk. 9:28)

J. bare witness unto the truth, p. 167, (Jn. 5:33)

J. came neither eating nor drinking, p. 148, (Matt. 11:18; Lk. 7:33)

J. in prison, p. 148, (Matt. 11:2-6: Lk. 7:18-23)

J. on Patmos, p. 240, (Rev. 1:9-11)

J. sent . . . disciples to Jesus, p. 148, (Matt. 11:2; Lk. 7:19)

J. speaks of Jesus, p. 135, (Matt. 3: 11-12; Mk. 1:7-8; Lk. 3:15-18; Jn. 1:15-28)

J. the Baptist speaks of Jesus, p. 166, (Jn. 3:25-36)

J. wore camel's hair, p. 135, (Matt. 3:4; Mk. 1:6)

J.'s vision of the Son of man, p. 240, (Rev. 1:12-20)

letters from J., p. 237, (John)

John: *(continued)*

one who heard J. speak was Andrew, p. 136, (Jn. 1:40)

tell J. what you hear and see, p. 148, (Matt. 11:4; Lk. 7:22)

the birth of J., p. 132, (Lk. 1:67–79)

the head of J. the Baptist, p. 158, (Matt. 14:8; Mk. 6:25)

the ministry of J. the Baptist, p. 135, (Matt. 3:1–6; Mk. 1:1–6; Lk. 3:1–6; Jn. 1:6–7)

the mother of James and J., p. 164, (Matt. 20:20–28; cf. Mk. 10:35–45)

two other brothers, James and J., p. 136, (Matt. 4:21; Mk. 1:19; Lk. 5:10)

whose name was J., p. 135, (Jn. 1:6)

Joined: shall be j. unto his wife, p. 217, (Eph. 5:31)

what God hath j. together, p. 163, (Matt. 19:6; Mk. 10:9)

Jonah: a gourd to come over J. to shade him, p. 121, (Jonah 4:6)

a great fish to swallow up J., p. 120, (Jonah 1:17)

and the lot fell upon J., p. 120, (Jonah 1:7)

it displeased J. and he was angry, p. 121, (Jonah 4:1)

it vomited out J, on dry land, p. 120, (Jonah 2:10)

J. and the whale, p. 120, (Jonah 1:17–2)

J. prayed out of the fish's belly, p. 120, (Jonah 2:1)

J. rose to flee from the Lord, p. 120, (Jonah 1:3)

J. . . . sat in a booth, p. 121, (Jonah 4:5)

J. was in the belly of the fish, p. 120, (Jonah 1:17)

the Lord said to J.: go unto Nineveh, p. 120, (Jonah 3:1–2)

took up J. and cast him into the sea, p. 120, (Jonah 1:15)

Jonas: the sign of J., p. 155, (Matt. 12:39; 16:4; Lk. 11:29)

Jonathan: David's lament . . . Saul and J., p. 34, (II Sam. 1:17–27)

friendship between David and J., p. 33, (I Sam. 18:1–5)

J. and the honeycomb, p. 32, (I Sam. 14:24–33)

J. saved David from Saul's anger, p. 34, (I Sam. 19—20)

J. loved him, p. 33, (I Sam. 18:1)

the soul of J. was knit with . . . David, p. 33, (I Sam. 18:1)

Joppa: send men to J. to Simon . . . Peter, p. 193, (Acts 10:5)

to J. and found a ship going to Tarshish, p. 120, (Jonah 1:3)

Joram: Jehu conspired against J. of Judah, p. 43, (II Kg. 9:14)

Jehu smote J. dead, p. 43, (II Kg. 9:24)

Jordan: baptized by John in the J., p. 135, (Matt. 3:13, Mk. 1:9)

cross the J. into Canaan, p. 27, (Josh. 1:2)

crossing the J., p. 27, (Josh. 3:9–4)

go and wash in J. seven times, p. 43, (II Kg. 5:10)

Lot chose the plain of J., p. 8, (Gen. 13:11)

many were baptized in the J., p. 135, (Matt. 3:6; Mk. 1:5; cf. Lk. 3:3)

passed clean over J., p. 27, (Josh. 3:17)

passeth over before you into J., p. 27, (Josh. 3:11)

twelve stones from the J. in Gilgal, p. 27, (Josh. 4:20)

Joseph: I am J. your brother, p. 12, (Gen. 45:4)

Israel blessed J.'s sons, p. 13, (Gen. 48)

Israel loved J. more, p. 12, (Gen. 37:3)

J. and Mary knew not of it, p. 134, (Lk. 2:43))

J. did not want to shame her, p. 132, (Matt. 1:19)

J., fear not to take Mary, p. 132, (Matt. 1:20)

J. gathered corn, p. 12, (Gen. 41:49)

J. interpreted Pharaoh's dreams, p. 12, (Gen. 41:1–36)

J. interpreted the dreams, p. 12, (Gen. 40)

J. knew his brothers, p. 12, (Gen. 42:8)

J. laid up food, p. 12, (Gen. 41:48)

J., Mary and the child returned, p. 134, (Mat. 2:21)

J. of Arimathea went to Pilate, p.

183, (Matt. 27:57–58; Mk. 15:43; Lk. 23: 50–52; Jn. 19:38)

J. took Mary as his wife, p. 132, (Matt. 1:24)

J. turned away and wept, p. 12, (Gen. 42:24)

J. was put into prison, p. 12, (Gen. 39:20)

J. was sold to Potiphar, p. 12, (Gen. 37:36)

J. went from Nazareth to Bethlehem, p. 132, (Lk. 2:4)

J.'s brothers came to Egypt, p. 12, (Gen. 42:3)

Pharaoh set J. over all, p. 12, (Gen. 41:41)

Potiphar's wife cast her eyes upon J., p. 12, (Gen. 39:7)

the angel appeared to J. in a dream, p. 134, (Matt. 2:13)

they found Mary, J., and the babe, p. 133, (Lk. 2:16)

who knew not J., p. 13, (Ex. 1:8)

Joshua: J. became the leader of Israel, p. 27, (Deut. 34—Josh. 1)

J. fought with Amalek, p. 17, (Ex. 17:8–16)

J. . . . in whom is the spirit, p. 20, (Num 27:18)

J. said to the people: Shout, p. 27, (Josh. 6:16)

J. saved Rahab, the harlot, p. 27, (Josh. 6:25)

J. sent spies to view the land, p. 27, (Josh. 2:1)

J. was old and stricken in years, p. 28, (Josh. 13:1)

J. was tricked into a treaty, p. 28, (Josh. 9:15–16, 22)

the calling of J., p. 20, (Num. 27:12–23)

Josiah: J. did that which was right, p. 45, (II Kg. 22:2; II Chr. 34:2)

J., King of Judah, p. 45, (I Kg. 13:1–3; II Kg. 22—23:28; II Chr. 34—35)

J. purged the land of pagan worhsip, p. 45, (II Kg. 23:4–20; II Chr. 34:3–7)

Jot: one j. or title of the law, p. 139, (Matt. 5:18; Lk. 16:17)

Journey: take nothing for your j., p. 146, (Matt. 10:9, 10; Mk. 6: 8; Lk. 9:3)

Journeys: j. of Barnabus and Paul, p. 194, (Acts 13—14)

Joy: all j. is darkened, p, 87, (Isa. 24:11)

I will j. in the God of my salvation, p. 124, (Hab. 3:18)

j. and gladness shall be found, p. 93, (Isa. 51:3)

j. cometh in the morning, p. 58, (Ps. 30:5)

j. follows sorrow, p. 179, (Jn. 16:6–33)

likewise j. shall be in heaven, p. 162, (Lk. 15:7)

shall reap in j., p. 66, (Ps. 126:5)

that your j. may be full, p. 237, (I John 1:4)

the oil of j. for mourning, p. 95, (Isa. 61:3)

there was great j. in Jerusalem, p. 44, (II Chr. 30:26)

turn their mourning into j., p. 102, (Jer. 31:13)

with j. unspeakable, p. 235, (I Pet. 1:8)

ye shall go out with j., p. 94, (Isa. 55:12)

your sorrow shall be turned into j., p. 179, (Jn. 16:20)

Joyful: make a j. noise unto God, p. 61, (Ps. 66:1)

Jubal: J. . . . those who play the harp, p. 6, (Gen. 4:21)

Judah: J. and Israel dwelt safely, p. 38, (I. Kg. 4:25)

gather J. from the four corners, p. 85, (Isa. 11:12)

in his days J. shall be saved, p. 101, (Jer. 23:6)

in the daughter of J. mourning and lamentation, p. 104, (Lam. 2:5)

Joash ruled over J., p. 43, (II Kg. 11:21; II Chr. 24:1)

J. is a lion's whelp, p. 13, (Gen. 49:9)

kings of J. to the fall of Jerusalem, p. 44, (II Kg. 18—25; II Chr. 10—36)

men of J. his pleasant plant, p. 83, (Isa. 5:7)

prophesies to Zedekiah of J., p. 101, (Jer. 21)

the kings of Israel and J., p. 43, (II Kg. 8:16—17:41)

Judah: (*continued*)

the men of J. bound him, p. 30, (Jg. 15:13)

the reign of Joash of J., p. 44, (II Kg. 11:21—12:21; II Chr. 24)

the reign of Jehoiakim king of J., p. 110, (Dan. 1:1)

the sin of J. is written, p. 101, (Jer. 17:1)

unto the cities of J., p. 92, (Isa. 40:9)

warning to J., p. 115, (Hos. 4)

Judas: J.' betrayal, p. 177, (Matt. 26:14–25; Mk. 14:10–21; Lk. 22:3–13; 21–23; Jn. 13:21–30)

J. came with a band with swords, p. 180, (Matt. 26:47; Mk. 14:43; Lk. 22:47; Jn. 18:3)

J. said: Master, is it I?, p. 177, (Matt. 26:25)

the death of J., p. 181, (Matt. 27:3–10; Acts 1:18–19)

Jude: a letter from J., p. 237, (Jude)

J., the servant of Jesus Christ, p. 239, (Jude v. 1)

Judge: a j. which feared not God, p. 153, (Lk. 18:2)

I j. no man, yet if I j., my judgment is true, p. 168, (Jn. 8:15–16)

I will j. you, O house of Israel, p. 108, (Ezek. 18:30)

j. among the nations, p. 82, (Isa. 2:4)

j. not according to appearance, p. 160, (Jn. 7:24)

j. not that ye be not judged, p. 142, (Matt. 7:1; Lk. 6:37)

j. nothing . . . until the Lord come, p. 206, (I Cor. 4:5)

parable of the unjust j., p. 153, (Lk. 18:1–8)

with righteousness shall he j. the poor, p. 85, (Isa. 11:4)

Judged: am j. for the hope, p. 197, (Acts 26:6)

were j. out of those books, p. 247, (Rev. 20:12)

Judges: as rulers and j., p. 17, (Ex. 18:21–22)

Lord raised up j., p. 28, (Jg. 2:16)

Judgest: thou j. another, thou condemnest thyself, p. 199, (Rom. 2:1)

Judgment: doth God pervert j.?, p. 51, (Job 8:3)

for j. is toward you, p. 115, (Hos. 5:1)

God's j. agianst Babylon, p. 103, (Jer. 51:16–64)

his ways are j., p. 21, (Deut. 32:4)

in danger of j., p. 139, (Matt. 5:22)

let j. run down as waters, p. 119, (Amos 5:24)

princes shall rule in j., p. 89, (Isa. 32:1)

looked for j., but behold oppression, p. 83, (Isa. 5:7)

remove violence . . . and execute j., p. 109, (Ezek. 45:9)

the hour of j. is come!, p. 245, (Rev. 14:7)

the j. of God, p. 5, (Gen. 3:14–24)

the j. of God is according to truth, p. 199, (Rom. 2:2)

the last j., p. 175, (Matt. 25:31–46)

with what j. ye judge, p. 142, (Matt. 7:2; cf. Lk. 6:38)

Judgments: changed my j. into wickedness, p. 106, (Ezek. 5:6)

in the way of thy j., p. 88, (Isa. 26:8)

unsearchable are his j., p. 203, (Rom. 11:33)

Jupiter: they called Barnabus, J., p. 194, (Acts 14:12)

Just: is not a j. man that . . . sinneth not, p. 75, (Ec. 7:20)

more j. than God?, p. 50, (Job 4:17)

rain on the j. and on the unjust, p. 140, (Matt. 5:45)

spirits of j. men made perfect, p. 232, (Heb. 12:23)

the j. shall live by faith, pp. 199, 214, (Rom. 1:17; Gal. 3:11)

Justice: doth the Almighty pervert j.?, p. 51, (Job 8:3)

Justification: j. by faith, p. 200, (Rom. 3:9—5:11)

Justified: he j. himself rather than God, p. 54, (Job 32:2)

j. by faith without the deeds of the law, p. 200, (Rom. 3:28)

no man is j. by law, p. 214, (Gal. 3:11)

this man went down to his house j., p. 154, (Lk. 18:14)

whosoever are j. by the law, p. 215, (Gal. 5:4)

Justly: but to do j., to love mercy, p. 122, (Micah 6:8)

Keepers: when the k. of the house tremble, p. 76, (Ec. 12:3)

Key: with the k. of the bottomless pit, p. 246, (Rev. 20:1)

Keys: give unto thee the k. of the kingdom, p. 160, (Matt. 16:19)

the k. of hell and of death, p. 240, (Rev. 1:18)

Kid: leopard shall lie down with the k., p. 85, (Isa. 11:6)

thou never gavest me a k., p. 152, (Lk. 15:29)

Kill: depart for Herod will k. thee, p. 169, (Lk. 13:31)

never again will I k., p. 7, (Gen. 8:21)

Saul, jealous of David, sought to k. him, p. 34, (I Sam. 18—23)

thou shalt not k., p. 18, (Ex. 20:13)

the Jews sought to k. him, p. 160, (Jn. 7:1)

which k. the body, p. 147, (Matt. 10:28; Lk. 12:4)

who took counsel to k. him, p. 193, (Acts 9:22)

ye have heard: Thou shalt not k., p. 139, (Matt. 5:21)

Killed: Cain . . . k. him, p. 5, (Gen. 4:8)

his son who was also k., p. 170, (Matt. 21:37–39; Mk. 12:6–8; Lk. 20:13–15)

thou k. the fatted calf, p. 152, (Lk. 15:30)

Kills: whoever k. you will think he does God a service, p. 173, (Jn. 16:2)

Kind: be ye k. one to another, . . . , p. 217, (Eph. 4:32)

Kindness: according to thy loving k., p. 60, (Ps. 51:1)

put on k., . . . meekness, long suffering, p. 221, (Col. 3:12)

thy loving k. in the morning, p. 63, (Ps. 92:2)

Kindred: go unto my country, to my k., p. 9, (Gen. 24:4)

King: a great K. above all gods, p. 63, (Ps. 95:3)

a k. of fierce countenance, p. 113, (Dan. 8:23)

a k. shall reign in righteousness, p. 89, (Isa. 32:1)

a k. who gave a marriage feast, p. 171, (Matt. 22:2)

a new k. over Egypt, p. 13, (Ex. 1:8)

Ahab K. of Israel, p. 39, (I Kg. 16:28—17:1)

an old and foolish k., p. 75, (Ec. 4:13)

art thou the K. of the Jews?, p. 181, (Matt. 27:11; Mk. 15:2; Lk. 23:3; Jn. 18:33)

behold, thy K. cometh, p. 126, (Zech. 9:9)

Belshazzar the k. made a great feast, p. 111, (Dan. 5:1)

Belshazzar was slain and Darius became k., p. 112, (Dan. 5:30, 31)

defile himself with the k.'s meat, p. 110, (Dan. 1:8)

Esther interceded with the k., p. 46, (Est. 7:3)

evil spirit troubled K. Saul, p. 33, (I Sam. 16:14–23)

give ye ear, O house of the k., p. 115, (Hos. 5:1)

God save the k., p. 32, (I Sam. 10:24)

hail, K. of the Jews!, p. 182, (Matt. 27:29; Mk. 15:18; Jn. 19:3)

he is the K. of glory, p. 57, (Ps. 24:10)

Herod was k., p. 134, (Matt. 2:1)

I have provided me a k., p. 33, (I Sam. 16:1)

I will punish the k. of Babylon, p. 103, (Jer. 50:18)

in those days there was no k. in Israel, p. 31, (Jg. 21:25)

Israel asked Samuel for a k., p. 32, (I Sam. 8)

Jehu was anointed K. of Israel, p. 43, (II Kg. 9—10)

Jeroboam ruled as K. of Israel, p. 39, (I Kg. 12:20)

Josiah, K. of Judah, p. 45, (I Kg. 13:1–3; II Kg. 22—23:28; II Chr. 34—35)

K. Hiram of Tyre to hew cedars, p. 38, (I Kg. 5:1–10; II Chr. 2:3–16)

k. Jehoiakim cast it in the fire, p. 103, (Jer. 36:22–23)

K. of kings and Lord of lords, p. 246, (Rev. 19:16; cf. Rev. 17:14)

K. of Kings, Lord of Lords, p. 225, (I Tim. 6:15)

King: (continued)

Lord repented making Saul k., p. 33, (I Sam. 16:1–13)

Mordecai . . . the k. delighted to honor, p. 46, (Est. 6:11)

Nebuchadnezzar k. of Babylon, p. 110, (Dan. 1:1)

proclamation of Cyrus, K. of Persia, p. 45, (II Chr. 36:22; Ezra 1:1)

punished the k. of Assyria, p. 103, (Jer. 50:18)

Rehoboam succeeded Solomon as k., p. 39, (I Kg. 12:1, 17; II Chr. 10:17)

Saul anointed k. by Samuel, p. 32, (I Sam. 9—10)

the death of K. Saul, p. 34, (I Sam. 31; II Sam. 1; I Chr. 10)

the goat the k. of Greece, p. 112, (Dan. 8:21)

the k. dethroned Queen Vashti, p. 46, (Est. 1:19–21)

the K. eternal, immortal, invisible . . . , p. 223, (I Tim. 1:17)

the k. of Assyria hath devoured him, p. 103, (Jer. 50:17)

the k. was furious, p. 110, (Dan. 2:12)

the k. went unto the den of lions, p. 112, (Dan. 6:19)

the reign of Jehoiakim k. of Judah, p. 110, (Dan. 1:1)

the year that K. Uzziah died, p. 83, (Isa. 6:1)

THIS IS JESUS THE K. OF THE JEWS, p. 183, (Matt. 27:37; Mk. 15:26; Lk. 23:38; Jn. 19:19–22)

this Nebuchadrezzar k. of Babylon, p. 103, (Jer. 50:17)

thou, O k., art a king of kings, p. 111, (Dan. 2:37)

thou, O k., sawest a great image, p. 110, (Dan. 2:31)

to the k. of terrors, p. 52, (Job 18:14)

Uzziah (Azariah) the leper k., p. 44, (II Kg. 15:1–7; II Chr. 26)

what k. . . . does not plan his strategy?, p. 151, (Lk. 14:31)

where is he that is born K. of the Jews?, p. 134, (Matt. 2:2)

who is this K. of glory?, p. 57, (Ps. 24:8, 10)

Kingdom: but God shall set up a k. . . . , p. 111, (Dan. 2:44)

establish his k., p. 35, (II Sam. 7:12; I Chr. 17:11; Lk. 1:32)

for of such is the k. of God, p. 163, (Matt. 19:14; Mk. 10:14; Lk. 18:16)

good seed are the children of the k., p. 156, (Matt. 13:38)

greatest in the k. of heaven, p. 162, (Matt. 18:4)

inherit the k. of God, p. 210, (I Cor. 15:50)

inherit the k. prepared for you, p. 175, (Matt. 25:34)

in the latter time of their k., p. 113, (Dan. 8:23)

k. against kingdom, p. 86, (Isa. 19:2)

k. of heaven is like a householder, p. 164, (Matt. 20:1)

k. of heaven is like a king . . . , p. 162, (Matt. 18:23)

k. of heaven is like a merchant, p. 157, (Matt. 13:45)

k. of heaven is like a mustard seed, p. 157, (Matt. 13:31; Mk. 4:30–31; Lk. 13:8–19)

k. of heaven is like a treasure, p. 157, (Matt. 13:44)

k. of heaven is like leaven, p. 157, (Matt. 13:33; Lk. 13:20–21)

k. of heaven is like ten virgins, p. 174, (Matt. 25:1)

my k. is not of this world, p. 181, (Jn. 18:36)

preach: the k. of heaven, p. 146, (Matt. 10:7; Lk. 9:2)

preaching the k. of God, p. 198, (Acts 28:31)

remember me when you come in your k., p. 183, (Lk. 23:42)

rend the k. from thee, p. 39, (I Kg. 11:11)

repent ye for the k. of heaven is at hand, p. 135, (Matt. 3:2)

shall not enter the k. of heaven, p. 162, (Matt. 18:3)

the K. of God, p. 141, (Matt. 6:33; Lk. 12:31)

the k. of God and the power of Christ, p. 245, (Rev. 12:10)

the k. of God is near, p. 174, (Matt. 24:29; Mk. 13:25; Lk. 21:26) the k. of God is within you, p. 153, (Lk. 17:21)

the k. of heaven is like a king, p. 171, (Matt. 22:2)

the k. of heaven is like a net, p. 157, (Matt. 13:47)

the k. splits in two, p. 39, (I Kg. 12—14; II Chr. 10, 12)

the mysteries of the k. of heaven, p. 156, (Matt. 13:11; Mk. 4:11; Lk. 8:10)

the peaceable k., p. 85, (Isa. 11:6–9)

their's is the k. of heaven, p. 138, (Matt. 5:3; Lk. 6:20)

translated us into the k., p. 220, (Col. 1:13)

with you in my Father's k., p. 177, (Matt. 26:29; Mk. 14:25; cf. Lk. 22:16, 18)

Kingdoms: all the k. of the earth, p. 90, (Isa. 37:20)

the k. of the world, p. 136, (Matt. 4:8–9; Lk. 4:5–7)

the k. of this world, p. 244, (Rev. 11:15)

Kings: k. of Judah to the fall of Jerusalem, p. 44, (II Kg. 18—25; II Chr. 10—36)

the k. of Israel and Judah, p. 43, (II Kg. 8:16—17:41)

the horns of the ram are the k. of Media and Persia, p. 112, (Dan. 8:20)

visit of the K., p. 134, (Matt. 2:1–2; 9–11)

Kiss: salute one another with an holy k., p. 204, (Rom. 16:16)

Kissed: said: Hail, Master! And k. him, p. 180, (Matt. 26:49; Mk. 14:45)

Knee: every k. should bow, p. 218, (Phil. 2:10)

Knees: confirm the feeble k., p. 90, (Isa. 35:3)

k. shall be weak as water, p. 107, (Ezek. 7:17)

the heart melteth and the k. smite together, p. 123, (Nahum 2:10)

Knew: Jesus stood on the shore but they k. him not, p. 185, (Jn. 21:4)

their eyes were opened and they k. him, p. 184, (Lk. 24:31)

Knewest: k. not the time of thy visitation, p. 169, (Lk. 19:44)

Knock: k. and it shall be opened, p. 142, (Matt. 7:7; Lk. 11:9)

stand at the door and k., p. 242, (Rev. 3:20)

Know: all shall k. me from the least to the greatest, p. 230, (Heb. 8:11)

forgive them for they k. not what they do, p. 182, (Lk. 23:34)

how shall this be seeing I k. not a man?, p. 131, (Lk. 1:34)

I k. not how to go out or come in, p. 37, (I Kg. 3:7)

k. that I am the Lord your God, p. 117, (Joel 2:27)

k. in part and prophesy in part, p. 208, (I Cor. 13:9)

k. that thou art the Lord, p. 90, (Isa. 37:20)

search me, O God, and k. my heart, p. 68, (Ps. 139:23)

thou shalt k. the Lord, p. 114, (Hos. 2:20)

try me, and k. my thoughts, p. 68, (Ps. 139:23)

whither I go you k., p. 178, (Jn. 14:4)

woman, I k. him not, p. 180, (Matt. 26:70; Mk. 14:68; Lk. 22:57)

Knowest: k. not what a day may bring, p. 73, (Prov. 27:1)

Lord, thou k. all things . . . , p. 186, (Jn. 21:17)

Knoweth: the Lord k. them that are his, p. 226, (II Tim. 2:19)

Knowledge: a wise man utter vain k., p. 52, (Job 15:2)

and the k. of God, p. 116. (Hos. 6:6)

darkeneth counsel by words without k., p. 54, (Job 38:2)

full of the k. of the Lord, p. 85, (Isa. 11:9)

how has this man k . . . ?, p. 160, (Jn. 7:15)

k. puffs up but love instructs, p. 207, (I Cor. 8:1)

my people are destroyed for lack of k., p. 115, (Hos. 4:6)

no truth, mercy, nor k. of God, p. 115, (Hos. 4:1)

Knowledge: (**continued**)
shall any teach God k., p. 53, (Job 21:22)
the k. of the glory of the Lord, p. 123, (Hab. 2:14)
the tree of k., p. 4, (Gen. 2:9)
. . . the wisdom and k. of God!, p. 203, (Rom. 11:33)
to do good they have no k., p. 99, (Jer. 4:22)
to the young man k., p. 69, (Prov. 1:4)
whom shall he teach k., p. 88, (Isa. 28:9)
Known: have ye not k?, p. 92, (Isa. 40:21)
k. by his doings, p. 72, (Prov. 20:11)
k. of them in breaking of bread, p. 184, (Lk. 24:35)
they have not k. me, p. 99, (Jer. 4:22)
they made k. abroad . . . concerning this child, p. 133, (Lk. 2:17)
thou hast searched me, and k. me, p. 67, (Ps. 139:1)
who hath k. the mind of the Lord, p. 203, (Rom. 11:34)

Laban: flee to her brother, L., p. 10, (Gen. 27:42, 43)
L.: thou art my bone and flesh, p. 11, (Gen. 29:14)
L. took Leah to Jacob, p. 11, (Gen. 29:23)
Labor: all ye that l., p. 149, (Matt. 11:28)
in all l. is profit, p. 71, (Prov. 14:23)
l. to enter into that rest, p. 229, (Heb. 4:11)
lest our l. be in vain, p. 221, (I Th. 3:5)
to forget your work and l. of love, p. 230, (Heb. 6:10)
what profit hath a man of all his l., p. 74, (Ec. 1:3)
your work of faith and l. of love, p. 221, (I Th. 1:3)
Laborers: but the l. few, p. 146, (Matt. 9:37; Lk. 10:2)
l. together with God, p. 205, (I Cor. 3:9)
Labors: first fruits of thy l., p. 21, (Ex. 23:16)

in l. more abundant, p. 212, (II Cor. 11:23)
Ladder: Jacob dreamed of a l., p. 10, (Gen. 28:12)
Jacob's l., p. 10, (Gen. 28:10–22)
Laid: l. him in a manger, p. 132, (Lk. 2:7)
l. their hands on them, p. 191, (Acts 6:6)
no man l. hands on him, p. 160, (Jn. 7:44)
Paul l. his hands upon them, p. 196, (Acts 19:6)
Lamb: a L. stood on Mount Sion, p. 245, (Rev. 14:1)
as a l. to the slaughter, p. 94, (Isa. 53:7)
behold the L. of God, p. 135, 136, (Jn. 1:29, 36)
God will provide a l., p. 9, (Gen. 22:8)
in the midst of the elders stood a L., p. 242, (Rev. 5:6)
l. . . . without blemish, p. 15, (Ex. 12:5)
save one little ewe l., p. 35, (II Sam. 12:3)
the L. . . . shall feed them, p. 244, (Rev. 7:17)
the marriage of the L. is come, p. 246, (Rev. 19:7)
the wolf also shall dwell with the l., p. 85, (Isa. 11:6)
they which follow the L., p. 245, (Rev. 14:4)
Unto the l. for ever and ever, p. 243, (Rev. 5:13)
where is the l.?, p. 9, (Gen. 22:7)
worthy is the L. that was slain, p. 242, (Rev. 5:12)
Lambs: he shall gather the l., p. 92, (Isa. 40:11)
Jesus said: Feed my l., p. 186, (Jn. 21:15)
like l. to the slaughter, p. 103, (Jer. 51:40)
the little hills like l., p. 65, (Ps. 114:4)
Lame: feet was I to the l., p. 54, (Job 29:15)
the healing of the l. man, p. 190, (Acts 3)
the l. man leap as an hart, p. 90, (Isa. 35:6)

the l. walk, p. 148, (Matt. 11:5; Lk. 7:22)

Lament: David's l. . . . Saul and Jonathan, p. 34, (II Sam. 1:17–27)

Lamentation: l. for the princes of Israel, p. 108, (Ezek. 19:1)

Lamentations: written therein l. and mourning, p. 106, (Ezek. 2:10)

Lamp: a l. unto my feet, p. 66, (Ps. 119:105)

Lamps: five did not get oil for their l., p. 174, (Matt. 25:3)

seven l. which are the seven Spirits, p. 242, (Rev. 4:5)

Land: a l. I will show thee, p. 7, (Gen. 12:1)

bringeth thee into a good l., p. 22, (Deut. 8:7)

his hands formed the dry l., p. 63, (Ps. 95:5)

a l. I will show thee, p. 7, (Gen. 12:1)

in the l. of the shadow of death, p. 84, (Isa. 9:2)

l. of darkness, p. 51, (Job 10:21)

place you in your own l., p. 109, (Ezek. 37:14)

the division of the l., p. 28, (Josh. 13—22)

the l. of the living, p. 53, (Job 28:13)

the l. utterly desolate, p. 83, (Isa. 6:11)

the whole l. shall be desolate, p. 99, (Jer. 4:27)

this l. shall fall unto you for inheritance, p. 109, (Ezek. 47:14)

to see the chosen l., p. 20, (Num. 27:12)

will I give this l., p. 7, (Gen. 12:7)

ye defiled my l., p. 99, (Jer. 2:7)

Landmark: the ancient l., p. 72, (Prov. 22:28)

Language: earth was of one l., p. 7, (Gen. 11:1)

Lord did therefore confound the l., p. 7, (Gen. 11:7)

Laodicea: to the church in L., p. 241, (Rev. 3:14–22)

Lap: that l. the water as a dog, p. 29, (Jg. 7:5)

Lasea (Crete): Paul sails via L. (C.), p. 198, (Acts 27:8)

Last: in the l. days, p. 82, (Isa. 2:2)

in the l. days it shall come to pass, p. 121, (Micah 4:1)

the l. will be first, and the first l., p. 164, (Matt. 20:16)

these l. worked only one hour . . . , p. 164, (Matt. 20:12)

Latter: as the l. and the former rain, p. 115, (Hos. 6:3)

Lord blessed the l. end of Job, p. 55, (Job 42:12)

Laugh: l. me to scorn . . . , p. 57, (Ps. 22:7)

Laughed: Abraham l. for they were old, p. 8, (Gen. 17:17)

Sarah l. within herself, p. 8, (Gen. 18:12)

upright man is l. to scorn, p. 51, (Job 12:4)

Laughter: a feast is made for l., p. 76, (Ec. 10:19)

Law: a l. unto themselves, p. 200, (Rom. 2:14)

all the l. and the prophets, p. 172, (Matt. 22:40)

am dead to the l., p. 214, (Gal. 2:19)

an oath to walk in God's l., p. 46, (Neh. 10:29)

by works of the l., p. 214, (Gal. 3:2)

dead to the l., p. 214, (Gal. 2:19–20)

done violence to the l., p. 125, (Zeph. 3:4)

Ezra read the book of the l., p. 46, (Neh. 8:1–3)

his delight is in the l. of the Lord, p. 55, (Ps. 1:2)

I through the l., p. 214, (Gal. 2:19)

Jesus' words on the l., p. 139, (Matt. 5:17–20; Lk. 16:17)

l. is not made for a righteous man, p. 223, (I Tim. 1:9)

my l. in their inward parts, p. 102, (Jer. 31:33)

no man is justified by l., p. 214, (Gal. 3:11)

not the hearers of the l., p. 200, (Rom. 2:13)

one jot or tittle of the l., p. 139, (Matt. 5:18; Lk. 16:17)

the book of the l. was found, p. 45, (II Kg. 22:8; II Chr. 34:14)

the doers of the l. shall be justified, p. 200, (Rom. 2:13)

the l. is good, if a man use it lawfully, p. 223, (I Tim. 1:8)

the l. is no more, p. 104, (Lam. 2:9)

Law: *(continued)*

the l. is the knowledge of sin, p. 200, (Rom. 3:20)

the l. of the Lord is perfect, p. 57, (Ps. 19:7)

the l. of the Medes and the Persians, p. 112, (Dan. 6:12)

the l. shall go forth of Zion, p. 122, (Micah 4:2)

the summary of the l., p. 23, (Lev. 19:18; Deut. 6—7; Matt. 19:19; 22:39; Mk. 12:31–33; Rom 13:9; Gal. 5:14; Jas. 2:8)

to destroy the l. or the prophets, p. 139, (Matt. 5:17)

to redeem them that were under the l., p. 214, (Gal. 4:5)

where no l. is, there is no transgression, p. 200, (Rom. 4:15)

whosoever are justified by the l., p. 215, (Gal. 5:4)

Lawful: all things are l. for me, p. 206, (I Cor. 6:12; 10:23)

is it l. to heal on the sabbath?, p. 149, (Matt. 12:10; Mk. 3:4; Lk. 6:9)

is not lawful on the sabbath, p. 149, (Matt. 12:2; Mk. 2:24; Lk. 6:2)

not l. to have thy brother's wife, p. 158, (Matt. 14:4; Mk. 6:18)

Laws: l. concerning clean and unclean, p. 19, (Lev. 11—18; Deut. 14:3–21)

l. concerning sacrifice, p. 18, (Lev. 1—7)

put my l. into their minds, p. 230, (Heb. 8:10)

teach them ordinances and l., p. 17, (Ex. 18:20)

Lay: l. me down in peace, and sleep, p. 56, (Ps. 4:8)

l. not your hand upon the lad, p. 9, (Gen. 22:12)

l. your hand on her, p. 145, (Matt. 9:18; Mk. 5:23)

will not l. upon man more than is right, p. 54, (Job 34:23)

Lazarus: cried with a loud voice: L., come forth, p. 169, (Jn. 11:43)

L. and the rich man, p. 152, (Lk. 16:19–31)

L. had lain in the grave four days, p. 168, (Jn. 11:17)

L. of Bethany was sick, p. 168, (Jn. 11:1)

send L. to comfort me, p. 153, (Lk. 16:24)

the rich man from hell saw L., p. 153, (Lk. 16:23)

Lead: even there shall thy hand l. me, p. 68, (Ps. 139:10)

l. me in a plain path, p. 58, (Ps. 27:11)

Leaf: we all do fade as a l., p. 96, (Isa. 64:6)

Leah: Laban took L. to Jacob, p. 11, (Gen. 29:23)

Leaping: and he, l. up stood and walked, p. 190, (Acts 3:8)

Learn: and l. of me, p. 149, (Matt. 11:29)

l. to do well, p. 81, (Isa. 1:17)

l. war any more, p. 82, (Isa. 2:4)

Learning: l. doth make thee mad, p. 197, (Acts 26:24)

Least: done it unto one of the l. of these, p. 175, (Matt. 25:40)

l. among you shall be great, p. 162, (Lk. 9:48)

Leave: entreat me not to l. thee, p. 31, (Ruth 1:16)

Leaven: a little l. leavens the whole, p. 206, (I Cor. 5:6)

kingdom of heaven is like l., p. 157, (Matt. 13:33; Lk. 13:20–21)

l. of the Pharisees is hypocrisy, p. 160, (Lk. 12:1)

the parable of the l., p. 157, (Matt. 13:33; Lk. 13:20–21)

Leavened: till the whole was l., p. 157, (Matt. 13:33; Lk. 13:21)

Lebanon: cedars of L., p. 38, (I Kg. 5:1–10; II Chr. 2:3–16)

eagle with great wings . . . came unto L., p. 107, (Ezek. 17:3)

Left: thou take the l. hand, p. 7, (Gen. 13:9)

Legion: my name is L., p. 144, (Mk. 5:9; Lk. 8:30)

Lend: l. me three loaves, p. 150, (Lk. 11:5)

Lent: he shall be l. to the Lord, p. 31, (I Sam. 1:28)

Leopard: or the l. his spots, p. 100, (Jer. 13:23)

the l. shall lie down with the kid, p. 85, (Isa. 11:6)

Leper: a great man but a l., p. 42, (II Kg. 5:1)

a l. is healed, p. 143, (Matt. 8:1–4; Mk. 1:40–45; Lk. 5:12–16)

Uzziah (Azariah) the l. king, p. 44, (II Kg. 15:1–7; II Chr. 26)

Lepers: cleanse the l., p. 146, (Matt. 10:8)

the healing of ten l., p. 153, (Lk. 17:11–19)

Leprosy: his l. was cleansed, p. 143, (Matt. 8:3; Mk. 1:42; cf. Lk. 5:13)

Naaman cured of l. by Elisha, p. 42, (II Kg. 5)

Let: L. my people go, p. 15, (Ex. 5:1—7:10)

Letter: a l. to the Hebrews, p. 228, (Heb.)

l. killeth but the spirit giveth life, p. 210, (II Cor. 3:6)

not of the l. but of the spirit, p. 210, (II Cor. 3:6)

Levi: the calling of Matthew (L.), p. 145, (Matt. 9:9; Mk. 2:14; Lk. 5:27, 28)

Leviathan: draw out l. with an hook, p. 55, (Job 41:1)

l. that crooked serpent, p. 88, (Isa. 27:1)

there is that l., p. 65, (Ps. 104:26)

Levites: The service of the L., p. 19, (Num. 8:6–26; I Chr. 23:24–32)

Lewd: certain l. fellows, p. 196, (Acts 17:5)

Liars: said in my haste, All men are l., p. 66, (Ps. 116:11)

Lice: the dust of the land became l., p. 15, (Ex. 8:16)

Liberty: in the l. wherewith Christ hath made us free, p. 215, (Gal. 5:1)

looks into the perfect law of l., p. 233, (Jas. 1:25)

might have been set at l., p. 198, (Acts 26:32)

proclaim l. to the captives, p. 95, (Isa. 61:1)

where the Spirit of the Lord is, there is l., p. 210, (II Cor. 3:17)

ye have been called unto l., p. 215, (Gal. 5:13)

Lie: changed the truth of God into a l., p. 199, (Rom. 1:25)

God is not a man, that he should l., p. 20, (Num. 23:19)

Lies: speaking l. in hypocrisy, p. 225, (I Tim. 4:2)

we have made l. our refuge, p. 88, (Isa. 28:15)

Life: come that they might have l., p. 168, (Jn. 10:10)

he that loseth his l. for my sake, p. 147, (Matt. 10:39; 16:25; Mk. 8:35; Lk. 9:24)

I am the resurrection and the l., p. 169, (Jn. 11:25)

in him was l., p. 131, (Jn. 1:4)

lay down his l. for his friends, p. 179, (Jn. 15:13)

l. and death, blessing and cursing, p. 23, (Deut. 30:19)

l. unto the bitter in soul, p. 50, (Job 3:20)

loveth his l. shall lose it, p. 175, (Jn. 12:25)

the breath of l., p. 4, (Gen. 2:7)

the tree of l. in the midst of the garden, p. 4, (Gen. 2:9)

therefore choose l., p. 23, (Deut. 30:19)

the way of l. and the way of death, p. 101, (Jer. 21:8)

Lift: let us l. up our heart, p. 105, (Lam. 3:41)

l. up thy hands to the Lord, p. 104, (Lam. 2:19)

l. up thy voice, p. 92, (Isa. 40:9)

l. up your heads, O ye gates, p. 57, (Ps. 24:7)

Lifted: everyone that is lifted up, p. 82, (Isa. 2:12)

if I be l. up, p. 176, (Jn. 12:32)

Light: a burning and a shining l., p. 167, (Jn. 5:35)

a l. from heaven, p. 192, (Acts 9:3)

a l. of the Gentiles, p. 93, (Isa. 42:6)

a l. unto my path, p. 66, (Ps. 119:105)

a little while is the l. with you, p. 176, (Jn. 12:35)

be the children of l., p. 176, (Jn. 12:36)

believe in the l., p. 176, (Jn. 12:36)

give l. to them that sit in darkness, p. 132, (Lk. 1:79)

God called the l. Day, p. 3, (Gen. 1:5)

God divided the l. from the darkness, p. 3, (Gen. 1:4)

Light: (*continued*)

God is l. and in him is no darkness, p. 237, (I John 1:5)

God said: Let there be l., p. 3, (Gen. 1:3)

have seen a great l., p. 84, (Isa. 9:2)

he is the true l., p. 131, (Jn. 1:9)

I am the l. of the world, p. 168, (Jn. 9:5)

if the l. . . . be darkness, p. 141, (Matt. 6:23; cf. Lk. 11:35)

if we walk in the l. we have fellowship, p. 238, (I John 1:7)

let us put on the armor of l., p. 204, (Rom 13:12)

let your l. so shine before men, p. 138, (Matt. 5:16)

lift up the l. of thy countenance, p. 56, (Ps. 4:6)

l. given to him that is in misery, p. 50, (Job 3:30)

l. is come . . . and men loved darkness, p. 165, (Jn. 3:19)

l. of Israel shall be for a fire, p. 84, (Isa. 10:17)

l. of the body is the eye, p.141, (Matt. 6:22; Lk. 11:34)

send out thy l. and thy truth, p. 59, (Ps. 43:3)

that speak ye in l., p. 147, (Matt. 10:27; cf. Lk. 12:3)

the life was the l. of men, p. 131, (Jn. 1:4)

the l. shineth in darkness, p. 131, (Jn. 1:5)

the Lord God giveth l., p. 247, (Rev. 22:5)

the Lord is my l. and my salvation, p. 58, (Ps. 27:1)

the Lord shall be a l. unto me, p. 122, (Micah 7:8)

to bear witness of the L., p. 135, (Jn. 1:7)

to l. the shadow of death, p. 51, (Job 12:22)

thy l. break forth as the morning, p. 95, (Isa. 58:8)

thy l. shall rise in obscurity, p. 95, (Isa. 58:10)

upon them hath the l. shined, p. 84, (Isa. 9:2)

walk as children of l., p. 217, (Eph. 5:8)

walk while you have the l., p. 176, (Jn. 12:35)

while ye have l., p. 176, (Jn. 12:36)

whole body shall be full of l., p. 141, (Matt. 6:22; Lk. 11:34)

with l. as with a garment, p. 65, (Ps. 104:2)

ye are the l. of the world, p. 138, (Matt. 5:14)

Lightning: his face had the appearance of l., p. 113, (Dan. 10:6)

Likeness: what l. will ye compare unto him?, p. 92, (Isa. 40:18)

Lilies: consider the l., p. 141, (Matt. 6:28; Lk. 12:27)

he feedeth among the l., p. 77, (Song 2:16)

heap of wheat set about with l., p. 78, (Song 7:2)

Lily: the l. of the valleys, p. 77, (Song 2:1)

Line: precept upon precept, l. upon l., p. 88, (Isa. 28:10)

Linen: his wife is arrayed in the fine l., p. 246, (Rev. 19:8)

wrapped it in clean l., p. 183, (Matt. 27:59; Mk. 15:46; Lk. 23:53; Jn. 19:40)

Lintels: blood on the l., p. 15, (Ex. 12:7)

Lion: a l., an ox and an eagle, p. 105, (Ezek. 1:10)

delivered out of the mouth of the l., p. 227, (I Tim. 4:17)

in the carcase of the l., p. 30, (Jg. 14:8)

Judah is a l.'s whelp, p. 13, (Gen. 49:9)

l. shall eat straw like the ox, p. 85, (Isa. 11:7)

the first beast was like a l., p. 242, (Rev. 4:7)

tread upon the l. and adder, p. 63, (Ps. 91:13)

Lioness: what is thy mother? A l., p. 108, (Ezek. 19:2)

Lions: Daniel and cast him into the den of l., p. 112, (Dan. 6:16)

God . . . shut the l.' mouths, p. 112, (Dan. 6:22)

my darling from the l., p. 58, (Ps. 35:17)

stronger than l., p. 34, (II Sam. 1:23)

the king went unto the den of l., p. 112, (Dan. 6:19)

Lips: keep the door of my l., p. 68, (Ps. 141:3)

l. are like a thread of scarlet, p. 77, (Song 4:3)

open thou my l., p. 60, (Ps. 51:15)

thy l. from speaking guile, p. 58, (Ps. 34:13)

Little: here a l. and there a l., p. 88, (Isa. 28:10)

Live: a man die shall he l. again?, p. 51, (Job 14:14)

and she will l., p. 145, (Matt. 9:18; Mk. 5:23)

I would not l. alway, p. 50, (Job 7:16)

l. and move and have our being, p. 196, (Acts 17:28)

seek ye me, and ye shall l., p. 119, (Amos 5:4)

that I might l. unto God, p. 214, (Gal. 2:19)

the just shall l. by faith, p. 214, (Gal. 3:11)

though he were dead, yet shall he l., p. 169, (Jn. 11:25)

to l. is Christ, to die is gain, p. 218, (Phil. 1:21)

whether we l. or die we are the Lord's, p. 204, (Rom. 14:8)

Lived: they l. and stood up upon their feet, p. 109, (Ezek. 37:10)

Liveth: he that l. and was dead, p. 240, (Rev. 1:18)

in that he l., he l. unto God, p. 201, (Rom. 6:10)

Living: a l. dog is better than a dead lion, p. 76, (Ec. 9:4)

give her the l. child, p. 37, (I Kg. 3:26)

man became a l. soul, p. 4, (Gen. 2:7)

the land of the l., p. 53, (Job 28:13)

the l. know that they shall die, p. 76, (Ec. 9:5)

to fall into the hands of the l. God, p. 231, (Heb. 10:31)

to him that is joined to all the l., p. 76, (Ec. 9:4)

two of every l. thing, p. 6, (Gen. 6:19)

Loaves: five l. and two fishes, p. 158, (Matt. 14:17; Mk. 6:38; Lk. 9:13; Jn. 6:9)

he took the l. and fishes, p. 159, (Matt. 15:36; Mk. 8:6–7)

lend me three l., p. 150, (Lk. 11:5)

Locusts: his food was l. and wild honey, p. 135, (Matt. 3:4; Mk. 1:6)

l. . . . over all the land, p. 15, (Ex. 10:14)

Lodge: a l. in a garden of cucumbers, p. 81, (Isa. 1:8)

Lodging: a l. place of wayfaring men, p. 100, (Jer. 9:2)

Loftiness: the l. of man, p. 82, (Isa. 2:17)

Loins: gird up thy l. like a man, p. 54, (Job 38:3)

your l. girt about with truth, p. 218, (Eph. 6:14)

Long: the thing that I l. for, p. 50, (Job 6:8)

Look: l. not at the things which are seen, p. 211, (II Cor. 4:18)

l. not behind thee, p. 9, (Gen. 19:17)

Loose: the lips of a l. woman, p. 69, (Prov. 5:3)

Lord: believe on the L. Jesus Christ, p. 195, (Acts 16:31)

both L. and Christ, p. 190, (Acts 2:36)

call and the L. shall answer, p. 95, (Isa. 58:9)

call on the name of the L., p. 190, (Acts 2:21)

even so, come, L. Jesus, p. 247, (Rev. 22:20)

every tongue confess that Jesus Christ is L., p. 218, (Phil. 2:11)

every word . . . of the L., p. 22, (Deut. 8:3)

except the L. build the house, p. 67, (Ps. 127:1)

fear not . . . the L. will be with you, p. 42, (II Chr. 20:17)

fear of the L., that is wisdom, p. 53, (Job 28:28)

for great is the L., p. 35, (I Chr. 16:25)

for the L. is a great God, p. 63, (Ps. 95:3)

for the L. is good, p. 64, (Ps. 100:5)

go and the L. be with thee, p. 33, (I Sam. 17:37)

he shall be lent to the L., p. 31, (I Sam. 1:28)

his name . . . THE L. OUR RIGHTEOUSNESS, p. 101, (Jer. 23:6)

I am the L., I change not, p. 127, (Mal. 3:6)

Lord: *(continued)*

I am the L. your God, p. 17, (Ex. 20:1)

I the L. search the heart, p. 101, (Jer. 17:10)

I the L. will be their be their God, p. 109, (Ezek. 34:24)

if David then call him L., p. 172, (Matt. 22:45; Mk. 12:37; Lk. 20:44)

in the L. Jehovah is . . . strength, p. 88, (Isa. 26:4)

institution of the L.'s supper, p. 177, (Matt. 26:26–29; Mk. 14:22–25; Lk. 22:14–20; I Cor. 11:23–25)

know that I am the L. your God, p. 17, (Ex. 16:12)

know that thou art the L., p. 90, (Isa. 37:20)

know ye that the L. he is God, p. 64, (Ps. 100:3)

let the L. set a man over the congregation, p. 20, (Num. 27:16)

L. blessed the latter end of Job, p. 55, (Job 42:12)

L. did therefore confound the language, p. 7, Gen. 11:7)

L. God Almighty which was, and is . . . , p. 242, (Rev. 4:8)

L. God . . . build him an house in Jerusalem, p. 45, (II Chr. 36:23; Ezra 1:2; Isa. 44:28)

L. God will wipe away tears, p. 87, (Isa. 25:8)

L. is my strength and my shield, p. 58, (Ps. 28:7)

L. Jesus, receive my spirit, p. 191, (Acts 7:59)

L. now lettest thou thy servant, p. 133, (Lk. 2:29)

L. raised up judges, p. 28, (Jg. 2:16)

L. repented making Saul king, p. 33, (I Sam. 16:1–13)

L. rideth upon a swift cloud, p. 86, (Isa. 19:1)

L., save thy people, p. 102, (Jer. 31:7)

L., what wilt thou have me do?, p. 192, (Acts 9:6)

L.'s house shall be exalted, p. 82, (Isa. 2:2)

love the L. your God, p. 23, (Deut. 6:5; Mk. 12:33)

ministered unto the L. before Eli, p. 31, (I Sam. 2:11)

name of the L. in vain, p. 17, (Ex. 20:7)

not everyone that saith L., L., p. 142, (Matt. 7:21)

O L., thou art my God, p. 87, (Isa. 25:1)

on the L.'s side, p. 18, (Ex. 32:26)

one L., one faith, one baptism, p. 216, (Eph. 4:5)

our Father (The L.'s Prayer), p. 140, (Matt. 6:9; Lk. 11:2; cf. Mk. 11:25–26)

put ye on the L. Jesus Christ, p. 204, (Rom. 13:14)

shall know that I am the L., p. 107, (Ezek. 12:15)

spirit of the L. is upon me, p. 95, (Isa. 61:1)

taste and see that the L. is good, p. 58, (Ps. 34:8)

the grace of the L. Jesus Christ, . . . , p. 213, (II Cor. 13:14)

the L. bless thee and keep thee, p. 19, (Num. 6:24)

the L. called Samuel, p. 31, (I Sam. 3:4)

the L. called unto him, p. 17, (Ex. 19:3)

the L. commanded Elijah to flee, p. 39, (I Kg. 17:2–3)

the L. descended . . . in fire, p. 17, (Ex. 19:18)

the L. gave the L. hath taken away, p. 49, (Job 1:21)

the L. hardened Pharaoh's heart, p. 15, (Ex. 7:13)

the L. hath fulfilled his word, p. 104, (Lam. 2:17)

the L. hath not chosen these, p. 33, (I Sam. 16:10)

the L. instructed him to cross the Jordan, p. 27, (Josh. 1:2)

the L. is a man of war, p. 16, (Ex. 15:3)

the L. is in his holy temple, p. 123, (Hab. 2:20)

the L. is my light and my salvation, p. 58, (Ps. 27:1)

the L. is my portion, p. 105, (Lam. 3:24)

the L. is my rock, p. 36, (II Sam. 22:2)

the L. is my shepherd, p. 57, (Ps. 23:1)

the L. is my strength, p. 16, (Ex. 15:2)

the L. is risen indeed! p. 164, (Lk. 24:34)

the L. lift up his countenance, p. 19, (Num. 6:26)

the L. make his face to shine, p. 19, (Num. 6:25)

the L. maketh the earth empty, p. 87, (Isa. 24:1)

the L. of hosts, he is the King, p. 57, (Ps. 24:10)

the L. of hosts is with us, p. 60, (Ps. 46:11)

the L. opened the mouth of the ass, p. 20, (Num. 22:28)

the Lord our God is one L., p. 23, 171, (Deut. 6:4; Mk. 12:32)

the L. said: I will destroy man, p. 6, (Gen. 6:7)

the L. seeth not as man seeth, p. 33, (I Sam. 16:7)

the L. shall be a sanctuary, p. 84, (Isa. 8:14)

the L. shall comfort Zion, p. 93, (Isa. 51:3)

the L. shall guide thee continually, p. 95, (Isa. 58:11)

the L. sitting upon a throne, p. 83, (Isa. 6:1)

the L. spoke to Moses and Aaron, p. 20, (Num. 20:23)

the L., the God of hosts, is his name, p. 118, (Amos 4:13)

the L. thundered from heaven, p. 36, (II Sam. 22:14)

the L. thy God bringeth thee into a good land, p. 22, (Deut. 8:7)

the L. was as an enemy, p. 104, (Lam. 2:5)

the L. was not in the earthquake, p. 41, (I Kg. 19:11)

the L. watch between me and thee, p. 11, (Gen. 31:49)

the L. went before them, p. 16, (Ex. 13:21)

the L. will not do good nor evil, p. 124, (Zeph. 1:12)

the L. will roar from Zion, p. 118, (Amos 1:2)

the L. wrote the commandments, p. 18, (Ex. 24:12; 31:18; 32:16)

the L. your God has chosen you, p. 23, (Deut. 7:6)

the L.'s passover, p. 15, 21, (Ex. 12:11; Lev. 23:5)

therefore will the L. wait, p. 89, (Isa. 30:18)

thou shalt love the L. thy God, p. 171, (Matt. 22:37; Mk. 12:30; Lk. 10:27; Deut. 6:5)

thou shalt worship the L. thy God, p. 136, (Matt. 4:10; Lk. 4:8)

which is Christ the L., p. 133, (Lk. 2:11)

who art thou, L.?, p. 192, (Acts 9:5)

who is the L., that I should obey, p. 15, (Ex. 5:2)

whosoever shall call upon the name of the L., p. 202, (Rom 10:13)

worthy O L. to receive glory and . . . , p. 242, (Rev. 4:11)

why call ye me, L., p. 142, (Lk. 6:46)

you know not what hour your L. comes, p. 174, (Matt. 24:42; Mk. 13:35)

Lose: if she l. one piece, p. 152, (Lk. 15:8)

l. his own soul, p. 147, (Matt. 16:26, Mk. 8:36; Lk. 9:25)

loveth his life shall l. it, p. 175, (Jn. 12:25)

Lost: l. all that he had, p. 49, (Job 1:13–22)

found the piece which I had l., p. 152, (Lk. 15:9)

go after that which is l., p. 162, (Matt. 18:12; Lk. 15:4)

go to the l. sheep, p. 146, (Matt. 10:6)

I have found my sheep which was l., p. 162, (Lk. 15:6; cf. Matt. 18:13)

sent but to the l. sheep of Israel, p. 159, (Matt. 15:24)

the l. coin, p. 152, (Lk. 15:8–10)

the l. sheep, p. 162, (Matt. 18:12–14; Lk. 15:1–7)

to save that which was l., p. 154, (Lk. 19:10)

Lot: Abram and L., p. 7, (Gen. 13—14:20)

Abram rescued L., p. 8, (Gen. 14:16)

and the l. fell upon Jonah, p. 120, (Jonah 1:7)

Lot: *(continued)*

L. chose the plain of Jordan, p. 8, (Gen. 13:11)

L.'s wife looked back, p. 9, (Gen. 19:26)

Love: a dinner of herbs where l. is, p. 71, (Prov. 15:17)

a time to l., p. 74, (Ec. 3:8)

above all put on l., p. 221, (Col. 3:14)

and have not l., p. 208, (I Cor. 13:1)

being rooted and grounded in l., p. 216, (Eph. 3:17)

beloved, let us l. one another, p. 238, (I John 4:7)

but of power, and of l., p. 226, (II Tim. 1:7)

by l. to serve one another, p. 215, (Gal. 5:13)

direct your hearts into the l. of God, p. 223, (II Th. 3:5)

for God is l., p. 238, (I John 4:8)

fruit of the Spirit is l., joy, peace, p. 215, (Gal. 5:22)

greater l. hath no man than this, p. 179, (Jn. 15:13)

hate the one and l. the other, p. 141, (Matt. 6:24; Lk. 16:13)

having not seen, ye l., p. 235, (I Pet. 1:8)

he that dwells in l., p. 239, (I John 4:16)

his banner over me was l., p. 77, (Song 2:4)

how dwelleth the l. of God in him?, p. 238, (I John 3:17)

how fair and how pleasant art thou, O l., p. 78, (Song 7:6)

husbands, l. your wives, p. 217, (Eph. 5:25)

I am sick with l., p. 77, (Song 2:5)

I will l. thee, O Lord, p. 56, (Ps. 18:1)

if we l. one another God dwells in us, p. 239, (I John 4:12)

if ye l. me, p. 178, (Jn. 14:15)

keep yourselves in the l. of God, p. 239, (Jude v. 21)

knowledge puffs up but l. instructs, p. 207, (I Cor. 8:1)

let brotherly l. continue, p. 232, (Heb. 13:1)

let l. be without dissimulation, p. 203, (Rom. 12:9)

Lord thou knowest that I l. thee, p. 185, (Jn. 21:15)

l. covereth all sins, p. 70, (Prov. 10:12)

l. him because he first loved us, p. 239, (I John 4:19)

l. is better than wine, p. 77, (Song 1:2)

l. is strong as death, p. 78, (Song 8:6)

l. never faileth . . . , p. 208, (I Cor. 13:8)

l. not the things in the world, p. 238, (I John 2:15)

l. the brotherhood, p. 236, (I Pet. 2:17)

l. the Lord your God, p. 23, (Deut. 6:5; Mk. 12:33)

l. thy neighbor as thyself, pp. 23, 171, (Lev. 19:18; Matt. 19:19; 22:39; Mk. 12:31; 33; Rom. 13:9; Gal 5:14; Jas. 2:8)

l. your enemies, p. 140, (Matt 5:44; Lk. 6:27, 35)

many waters cannot quench l., p. 78, (Song 8:7)

not l. in word but in deed and truth, p. 238, (I John 3:18)

now abideth faith, hope, l., p. 209, (I Cor. 13:13)

our fill of l., p. 70, (Prov. 7:18)

passing the l. of women, p. 34, (II Sam. 1:26)

perfect l. casteth out fear, p. 239, (I John 4:18)

rise up, my l., my fair one, p. 77, (Song 2:10)

separate us from the l. of Christ, p. 202, (Rom. 8:35)

shall separate us from the l. of God . . . , p. 202, (Rom. 8:39)

that ye l. one another, p. 178, (Jn. 13:34)

the greatest of these is l., p. 209, (I Cor. 13:13)

the l. of Christ constrains us, p. 211, (II Cor. 5:14)

the l. of many shall wax cold, p. 173, (Matt. 24:12)

there is no fear in l., p. 239, (I John 4:18)

thou shalt l. the Lord thy God, p. 171, (Matt. 22:37; Mk. 12:30; Lk. 10:27; Deut. 6:5) thy l. to me was wonderful, p. 34, (II Sam. 1:26)

to increase and abound in l., p. 222, (I Th. 3:12)

walk in l. as Christ hath loved us, p. 217, (Eph. 5:2)

with bands of l., p. 116, (Hos. 11:4)

you may know the l. of Christ, p. 216, (Eph. 3:19)

Loved: as I have l. you, p. 178, (Jn. 13:34)

conquerors through him that l. us, p. 202, (Rom. 8:37)

for God so l. the world, p. 165, (Jn. 3:16)

he l. them unto the end, p. 177, (Jn. 13:1)

Jonathan l. him as he l. his own soul, p. 33, (I Sam. 18:1)

not that we l. God, but that he l. us, p. 238, (I John 4:10)

sins . . . are forgiven: for she l. much, p. 155, (Lk. 7:47)

the Father has l. me, so I have l. you, p. 178, (Jn. 15:9)

Lovers: among all her l., p. 104, (Lam. 1:2)

Lovest: Jesus said, L. thou me?, p. 186, (Jn. 21:16)

Loveth: a friend l. at all times, p. 71, (Prov. 17:17)

he that l. father or mother, p. 147, (Matt. 10:37; cf. Lk. 14:26)

he that l. him chasteneth, p. 71, (Prov. 13:24)

he that l. his wife loveth himself, p. 217, (Eph. 5:28)

he that l. not knoweth not God, p. 238, (I John 4:8)

l. his life shall lose it, p. 175, (Jn. 12:25)

Low: shall be brought l., p. 82, (Isa. 2:12)

the l. estate of his handmaiden, p. 132, (Lk. 1:48)

Lowly: l. and hiding upon an ass, p. 126, (Zech. 9:9)

Lucifer: fallen from heaven, O L., p. 85, (Isa. 14:12)

Luke: L., the beloved physician, p. 221, (Col. 4:14)

Lukewarm: because thou art l., p. 241, (Rev. 3:16)

Lust: looketh on a woman to l., p. 139, (Matt. 5:28)

not fulfill the l. of the flesh, p. 215, (Gal. 5:16)

Lusteth: the flesh l. against the Spirit, p. 215, (Gal. 5:17)

Lusts: flee also youthful l., p. 226, (II Tim. 2:22)

Lydia: he baptized L. a seller of purple, p. 195, (Acts 16:14, 15)

Lystra: a healing in L., p. 194, (Acts 14:8–18)

Paul and Barnabus visit L., p. 194, (Acts 14:6)

Macedonia: come over into M., p. 195, (Acts 16:9)

Mad: learning doth make thee mad, p. 197, (Acts 26:24)

Made: God saw everything he had m., p. 4, (Gen. 1:31)

Magi: visit of the M., p. 134, (Matt. 2:1–2; 9–11)

Magician: Simon the m., p. 192, (Acts 8:9–24)

Magnificat: the m., p. 132, (Lk. 1:39–56)

Magog: thy face against Gog the land of M., p. 109, (Ezek. 38:2)

Maid: as with the m., p. 87, (Isa. 24:2)

way of a man with a m., p. 73, (Prov. 30:19)

Malta: Paul sails via M., p. 198, (Acts 28:1)

Mammon: you cannot serve God and m., p. 141, (Matt. 6:24; Lk. 16:13)

Man: a m. after his own heart, p. 32, (I Sam. 13:14)

a m. of unclean lips, p. 83, (Isa. 6:5)

a m. shall be as an hiding place, p. 89, (Isa. 32:2)

a m. of sorrows, p. 94, (Isa. 53:3)

as for m., his days are as grass, p. 64, (Ps. 103:15)

as the m. is so is his strength, p. 29, (Jg. 8:21)

Behold the m., p. 32, (I Sam. 9:17)

each with the face of a m. . . . , p. 105, (Ezek. 1:10)

every m.'s sword was against his fellow, p. 32, (I Sam. 14:20)

Man: (*continued*)

every m. that cometh into the world, p. 131, (Jn. 1:9)

gird up thy loins like a m., p. 54, (Job 38:3)

God created m. in his own image, p. 4, (Gen. 1:27)

God formed m. of the dust, p. 4, (Gen. 2:7)

God hath made m. upright, p. 75, (Ec. 7:29)

God is not a m., that he should lie, p. 20, (Num. 23:19)

I myself also am a m., p. 194, (Acts 10:26)

m. became a living soul, p. 4, (Gen. 2:7)

m. doth not live by bread only, p. 22, (Deut. 8:3)

m. is born unto trouble, p. 50, (Job 5:7)

m. looks on outward appearance, p. 33, (I Sam. 16:7)

m. riding upon a red horse, p. 125, (Zech. 1:8)

m. shall not live by bread alone, p. 135, (Matt. 4:4; Lk. 4:4)

m. that is born of woman, p. 51, (Job 14:1)

m. which is a worm, p. 53, (Job 25:6)

never m. spake like this m., p. 160, (Jn. 7:46)

[neither] m. nor female, p. 214, (Gal. 3:28)

no m. ever yet hated his own flesh, p. 217, (Eph. 5:29)

Pilate said: Behold the m.!, p. 182, (Jn. 19:5)

set a m. against his father, p. 147, (Matt. 10:35; Lk. 12:53)

the third beast had a face as a m., p. 242, (Rev. 4:7)

the Lord said: I will destroy m., p. 6, (Gen. 6:7)

the Lord seeth not as m. seeth, p. 33, (I Sam. 16:7)

there was a m. sent from God, p. 135, (Jn. 1:6)

this m. also was with him, p. 180, (Matt. 26:69; Mk. 14:66–67; Lk. 22:56)

thou art the m., p. 35, (II Sam. 12:7)

way of a m. with a maid, p. 73, (Prov. 30:19)

what is m., that thou art mindful, pp. 56, 228, (Ps. 8:4; Heb. 2:6)

what manner of m. is this, p. 144, (Matt. 8:27; Mk. 4:41; Lk. 8:25)

when I became a m., p. 208, (I Cor. 13:11)

Manger: laid him in a m., p. 132, (Lk. 2:7)

the babe . . . lying in a m., p. 133, (Lk. 2:12, 16)

Manifold: how m. are thy works, p. 65, (Ps. 104:24)

Manna: m. covered the ground, p. 17, (Ex. 16:13–15; Num. 11:9)

m. in the wilderness, p. 16, (Ex. 16; Num. 11:6–9, 31)

our fathers did eat m., p. 167, (Jn. 6:31)

Manoah: angel appeared to M.'s wife, p. 30, (Jg. 13:2–3)

Mansions: in my Father's house are many m., p. 178, (Jn. 14:2)

Mantle: Elijah cast his m. upon Elisha, p. 41, (I Kg. 19:19)

he took the m. of Elijah, p. 42, (I Kg. 2:14)

Mark: I press toward the m., p. 219, (Phil. 3:14)

The Lord put a m. on Cain, p. 5, (Gen. 4:15)

Marketplace: children in the m., p. 148, (Matt. 11:16; Lk. 7:32)

Marriage: a king who gave a m. feast, p. 171, (Matt. 22:2)

Christian m., p. 217, (Eph. 5:21–33)

on m., p. 163, (Matt. 19:4–6; Mk. 10:6–9)

the m. of the Lamb is come, p. 246, (Rev. 19:7)

the m. in Cana, p. 137, (Jn. 2:1–11)

Marrieth: and m. another, p. 139, (Matt. 19:9; Mk. 10:11–12; Lk. 16:18)

Marry: better to m. than to burn, p. 207, (I Cor. 7:9)

Martha: M. cumbered with much serving, p. 150, (Lk. 10:40)

Mary and M., p. 150, (Lk. 10:38–42)

Mary and M., sent for Jesus, p. 168, (Jn. 11:3)

Martyrdom: the m. of Stephen, p. 191, (Acts 6:9—8:2)

Mary: fear not, M., p. 131, (Lk. 1:30)

Jesus appeared to M. Magdalene, p. 184, (Mk. 16:9; Jn. 20:14)

Jesus said: M., p. 184, (Jn. 20:16)

Joseph and M. knew not of it, p. 134, (Lk. 2:43)

Joseph, fear not to take M., p. 132, (Matt. 1:20)

Joseph, M. and the child returned, p. 134, (Matt. 2:21)

Joseph took M. as his wife, p. 132, (Matt. 1:24)

M. and Martha, p. 150, (Lk. 10:38–42)

M. and Martha, sent for Jesus, p. 168, (Jn. 11:3)

M. hath chosen the good part, p. 150, (Lk. 10:42)

M. Magdalene and the other Mary went to the tomb, p. 183, (Matt. 28:1; Mk. 16:1–2; cf. Lk. 24:1; Jn. 20:1)

M. Magdalene came and told the disciples, p. 184, (Mk. 16:10–11; Jn. 20:18)

M. pondered them in her heart, p. 133, (Lk. 2:19)

M. sat at Jesus' feet, p. 150, (Lk. 10:39)

M. who was great with child, p. 132, (Lk. 2:5)

M. was found with child of the Holy Ghost, p. 132, (Matt. 1:18)

M. visited her cousin Elisabeth, p. 132, (Lk. 1:39–40)

sent from God to M., p. 131, (Lk. 1:26, 27)

the song of M., p. 132, (Lk. 1:39–56)

they found M., Joseph, and the babe, p. 133, (Lk. 2:16)

Master: the m. and his servant, p. 153, (Lk. 17:7–10)

the m. will come unexpectedly, p. 174, (Matt. 24:50; Lk. 12:46)

Matthew: M. sitting in the tax office, p. 145, (Matt. 9:9; Mk. 2:14; Lk. 5:27)

the calling of M. (Levi), p. 145, (Matt. 9:9; Mk. 2:14; Lk. 5:27, 28)

Matthias: the calling of M., p. 189, (Acts 1:23–26)

Meal: an handful of m., p. 40, (I Kg. 17:12)

the barrel of m. wasted not, p. 40, (I Kg. 17:16)

woman hid it in three measures of m., p. 157, (Matt. 13:33; Lk. 13:21)

Measured: hath m. the waters, p. 92, (Isa. 40:12)

Measuring: a line of flax and a m. reed, p. 109, (Ezek. 40:3)

Meat: defile himself with the king's m., p. 110, (Dan. 1:8)

go and sit down to m., p. 153, (Lk. 17:7)

if m. makes my brother to offend, p. 207, (I Cor. 8:13)

out of the eater came forth m., p. 30, (Jg. 14:14)

strong m. . . . to them that are of full age, p. 230, (Heb. 5:14)

their m. in due season, p. 65, (Ps. 104:27)

Medes: the law of the M. and the Persians, p. 112, (Dan. 6:12)

Meddle: m. not with him that flattereth, p. 72, (Prov. 20:19)

Media: the ram are the kings of M. and Persia, p. 112, (Dan. 8:20)

Mediator: there is one God and one m., p. 224, (I Tim. 2:5)

Medicine: a merry heart . . . like a m., p. 72, (Prov. 17:22)

Meek: the m. shall inherit the earth, p. 59, (Ps. 37:11)

Meekness: put on kindness, . . . m., long suffering, p. 221, (Col. 3:12)

Melchizedek: a priest . . . after the order of M., p. 230, (Heb. 5:6)

M. . . . blessed Abram, p. 8, (Gen. 14:19)

Melita: island was called M., p. 198, (Acts 28:1)

Melody: making m. in your heart to the Lord, p. 217, (Eph. 5:19)

thanksgiving and the voice of m., p. 93, (Isa. 51:3)

Melt: and all the hills shall m., p. 119, (Amos 9:13)

Members: we are m. one of another, p. 217, (Eph. 4:25)

Memorial: this day shall be a m., p. 15, (Ex. 12:14)

Men: from heaven or of m.?, p. 170, (Matt. 21:25; Mk. 11:30; Lk. 20:4)

Mene: M.: God hath numbered thy kingdom, p. 111, (Dan. 5:26)

Merchant: kingdom of heaven is like a m., p. 157, (Matt. 13:45)

Mercies: according to the multitude of his m., p. 105, (Lam. 3:32)

blessed be God the Father of m., p. 210, (II Cor. 1:3)

of the Lord's m. that we are not consumed, p. 105, (Lam. 3:22)

returned to Jerusalem with m., p. 125, (Zech. 1:16)

to God belong m. and forgiveness, p. 113, (Dan. 9:9)

Merciful: God be m. to me, a sinner, p. 154, (Lk. 18:13)

God be m. unto us, and bless us, p. 61, (Ps. 67:1)

gracious and m., slow to anger, p. 46, (Neh. 9:17)

he is gracious and m., p. 117, (Joel 2:13)

m. and gracious, slow to anger, p. 64, (Ps. 103:8)

m. to their unrighteousness, p. 230, (Heb. 8:12)

Mercury: they called . . . Paul, M., p. 194, (Acts 14:12)

Mercy: but to do justly, to love m., p. 122, (Micah 6:8)

have m. upon me, O God, p. 60, (Ps. 51:1)

his m. endureth forever, pp. 35, 42, 67, (I Chr. 16:34; II Chr. 20:21; Ps. 136:1)

his m. is everlasting, p. 64, (Ps. 100:5)

I desired m. and not sacrifice, p. 115, (Hos. 6:6)

in wrath remember m., p. 124, (Hab. 3:2)

Jesus, son of David, have m., p. 165, (Mk. 10:47; cf. Matt. 20:30; Lk. 18:38)

m. and truth are met together, p. 62, (Ps. 83:10)

no truth, m., nor knowledge of God, p. 115, (Hos. 4:1)

show m. and compassion, p. 126, (Zech. 7:9)

surely goodness and m. shall follow me, p. 57, (Ps. 23:6)

Merry: a m. heart . . . a cheerful countenance, p. 71, (Prov. 15:13)

a m. heart . . . like a medicine, p. 72, (Prov. 17:22)

to make m. with my friends, p. 152, (Lk. 15:29)

Meshach: Belteshazzar and Shadrach, M. and Abednego, p. 110, (Dan. 1:7)

Messenger: behold I send my m., p. 148, (Matt. 11:10; Lk. 7:27)

I will send my m., p. 127, (Mal. 3:1)

Messiah: we have found the M., p. 136, (Jn. 1:41)

Messianic: the M. prophecy, p. 126, (Zech. 9:9–12)

Methuselah: the days of M., p. 6, (Gen. 5:27)

Micah: the word of the Lord to M., p. 121, (Micah 1:1)

Micaiah: M.'s prophecy, p. 41, (I Ig. 22:1–40; II Chr. 18)

Michael: M. and his angels fought the dragon, p. 244, (Rev. 12:7)

M., who guards thy people, p. 113, (Dan. 12:1)

Midian: fled to the land of M., p. 14, (Ex. 2:15)

Midianites: Gideon and the M., p. 29, (Jg. 7)

save Israel from the hand of the M., p. 29, (Jg. 6:14)

Midst: I will dwell in the m. of thee, p. 126, (Zech. 2:10)

Might: not by m., nor by power, p. 126, (Zech. 4:6)

thy hand findeth to do, do it with thy m., p. 76, (Ec. 9:10)

Mighty: how are the m. fallen, p. 34, (II Sam. 1:25)

m. men of valor, p. 27, (Josh. 6:2)

neither shall the m. deliver himself, p. 118, (Amos 2:14)

Mile: compel thee to go a m., p. 140, (Matt. 5:41)

Miletus: Paul travels via M., p. 196, (Acts 20:15)

Milk: flowing with m. and honey, p. 14, (Ex. 3:8)

I have fed you with m., p. 205, (I Cor. 3:2)

it floweth with m. and honey, p. 19, (Num. 13:27)

Millstone: a m. were hanged about his neck, p. 162, (Matt. 18:6; Mk. 9:42)

Mind: be of one m. having compassion one of another, p. 236, (I Pet. 3:8)

be of the same m. one toward another, p. 203, (Rom. 12:16)

of love, and of a sound m., p. 226, (II Tim. 1:7)

renewed in the spirit of your m., p. 217, (Eph. 4:23)

this m. be in you which was in Christ Jesus, p. 218, (Phil. 2:5)

we have the m. of Christ, p. 205, (I Cor. 2:16)

who hath known the m. of the Lord, pp. 203, 205, (Rom. 11:34; I Cor. 2:16)

whose m. is stayed on thee, p. 87, (Isa. 26:3)

Minister: not to be ministered unto but to m., p. 164, (Matt. 20:28; Mk. 10:45)

was made a m. according to . . . the grace of God, p. 216, (Eph. 3:7)

Ministered: the child m. unto the Lord, p. 31, (I Sam. 2:11)

Ministers: able m. of the new testament, p. 210, (II Cor. 3:6)

his m. a flaming fire, pp. 65, 228, (Ps. 104:4; Heb. 1:7)

m. of Christ and stewards of the mysteries, p. 206, (I Cor. 4:1)

Ministry: take heed to the m., p. 221, (Col. 4:17)

Miracles: m. by the hands of Paul, p. 196, (Acts 19:11)

Miriam: M. and all the women, p. 16, (Ex. 15:20)

Mire: I sink in deep m., p. 61, (Ps. 69:2)

tread them down like the m. of the streets, p. 84, (Isa. 10:6)

Mirth: cause all her m. to cease, p. 114, (Hos. 2:11)

m. of the land is gone, p. 87, (Isa. 24:11)

Miserable: m. comforters are ye, p. 52, (Job 16:2)

Misery: to him that is in m., p. 50, (Job 3:20)

Mishael: Daniel, Hananiah, M. and Azariah, p. 110, (Dan. 1:6)

Mistress: so with her m., p. 87, (Isa. 24:2)

Mite: the widow's m., p. 172, (Mk. 12:41–44; Lk. 21:1–4)

Mitylene (Lesbos): Paul travels via M. (L.), p. 196, (Acts 20:14)

Moab: Moses died in the land of M., p. 21, (Deut. 34:5)

Mock: and after, m. on, p. 53, (Job 21:3)

fools make a m. at sin, p. 71, (Prov. 14:9)

Mocked: God is not m., p. 215, (Gal. 6:7)

Mocker: wine is a m., p. 72, (Prov. 20:1)

Mocketh: whoso m. the poor, p. 71, (Prov. 17:5)

Mocking: the m. of Jesus, p. 182, (Matt. 27:27–31; Mk. 15:16–20; Jn. 19:2–5)

Moderation: let your m. be known, p. 219, (Phil. 4:5)

Money: love of m. is the root of all evil, p. 225, (I Tim. 6:10)

no staff, no bread, no m., p. 146, (Matt. 10:10; Mk. 6:8; Lk. 9:3)

Moneychangers: casting out the m., p. 170, (Matt. 21:12–13; Mk. 11:15–19; Lk. 29:45–48; Jn. 2:13–17)

the tables of the m., p. 170, (Matt. 21:12; Mk. 11:15; Jn. 2:15)

Moon: fair as the m., p. 78, (Song 6:10)

praise ye him, sun and m., p. 68, (Ps. 148:3)

the m. into blood, p. 190, (Acts 2:20)

the m. stayed, p. 28, (Josh. 10:13)

Moons: your new m. and your feasts, p. 81, (Isa. 1:14)

Mordecai: M. . . . the king delighted to honor, p. 46, (Est. 6:11)

the gallows prepared for M., p. 46, (Est. 7:10)

Moriah: temple in Jerusalem on Mount M., p. 38, (II Chr. 3:1)

Morning: I will give him the m. star, p. 241, (Rev. 2:28)

in the m. it flourisheth, p. 62, (Ps. 90:6)

in the m. thou shalt say, p. 23, (Deut. 28:67)

looketh forth as the m., p. 78, (Song 6:10)

more than they that watch for the m., p. 67, (Ps. 130:6)

Morning: (continued)

that maketh the m. darkness, p. 118, (Amos 4:13)

the m. stars sang, p. 54, (Job 38:7)

thy loving kindness in the m., p. 63, (Ps. 92:2)

Mortal: m. man be more just than God?, p. 50, (Job 4:17)

Moses: Aaron and Hur held up M.' hands, p. 17, (Ex. 17:11, 12)

God appeared to M., p. 17, (Ex. 19—31)

God called to M., p. 14, (Ex. 3:4)

God told M. to go to Mount Abarim, p. 20, (Num. 27:12)

had you believed M., p. 107, (Jn. 5:46)

Jesus . . . worthy of more glory than M., p. 229, (Heb. 3:3)

Jethro's counsel to M., p. 17, (Ex. 18)

M. and Aaron at Mount Hor, p. 20, (Num. 20:23)

M. and Elijah appeared in glory, p. 161, (Matt. 27:3; Mk. 9:4; Lk. 9:30–31)

M. and the burning bush, p. 14, (Ex. 3:1–10)

M.' anger waxed hot, p. 18, (Ex. 32:19)

M. argued with God, p. 14, (Ex. 3:11; 4:1–17)

M. asked God's name, p. 14, (Ex. 3:13–17)

M. called the nation to a new commitment, p. 22, (Deut. 27—30)

M. died in the land of Moab, p. 21, (Deut. 34:5)

M. fled to Midian, p. 14, (Ex. 2:15)

M. hid his face, p. 14, (Ex. 3:6)

M.' mother . . . an ark of bulrushes, p. 13, (Ex. 2:3)

not a prophet . . . like unto M., p. 21, (Deut. 34:10)

M. put the testimony into the ark, p. 18, (Ex. 40:20)

M. saw his brothers' burdens, p. 14, (Ex. 2:11)

M. sent them to spy, p. 19, (Num. 13:17)

M. smote the rock, p. 17, (Ex. 17:6; Num. 20:11)

M. song of victory, p. 16, (Ex. 15:1–21)

M. stretched forth his hand, p. 16, (Ex. 14:27)

M. went up unto God, p. 17, (Ex. 19:3)

she called him M., p. 14, (Ex. 2:10)

the birth of M., p. 13, (Ex. 1:15–22; 2:1–10)

the blessing of M., p. 21, (Deut. 33:25-27)

they have M. and the prophets, p. 153, (Lk. 16:29)

the song of M., p. 21, (Deut. 32:1–43)

while M. was on Sinai, p. 18, (Ex. 32:1)

Mote: the m. that is in thy brother's eye, p. 142, (Matt. 7:3; Lk. 6:41)

Moth: where m. and rust doth corrupt, p. 141, (Matt. 6:19; cf. Lk. 12:33)

Mother: as is the m., so is her daughter, p. 107, (Ezek. 16:44)

as one whom his m. comforteth, p. 96, (Isa. 66:13)

Babylon the Great, M. of Harlots, p. 246, (Rev. 17:5)

behold thy m.!, p. 183, (Jn. 19:27)

came forth of his m.'s womb, p. 75, (Ec. 5:15)

despise not thy m., p. 73, (Prov. 23:22)

his m. and the disciple he loved, p. 183, (Jn. 19:26)

his m. kept all . . . in her heart, p. 135, (Lk. 2:51)

honor thy father and thy m., pp. 18, 217, (Ex. 20:12; Eph. 6:2)

I arose a m. in Israel, p. 29, (Jg. 5:7)

in sin did my m. conceive me, p. 60, (Ps. 51:5)

my m. and brothers are those, p. 156, (Matt. 12:49–50; Mk. 3:34–35; Lk. 8:21)

shall be a m. of nations, p. 8, (Gen. 17:16)

she is its m., p. 37, (I Kg. 3:27)

the heaviness of his m., p. 70, (Prov. 10:1)

the m. of James and John, p. 164, (Matt. 20:20–28; cf. Mk. 10:35–45)

your m. and brothers are outside, p. 156, (Matt. 12:47; Mk. 3:32; Lk. 8:20)

what is thy m.? A lioness, p. 108, (Ezek. 19:2)

who are my m. and brothers, p. 156, (Matt. 12:48; Mk. 3:33)

Mother-in-law: Peter's mother-in-law healed, p. 138, (Matt. 8:14–15; (Mk. 1:29–31; Lk. 4:38–39)

Mount: Aaron died on top of M. Hor, p. 20, (Num. 20:28)

a Lamb stood on M. Sion, p. 245, (Rev. 14:1)

ark rested on M. Ararat, p. 6, (Gen. 8:4)

Elijah went . . . M. Carmel, p. 40, (I Kg. 18:42)

God told Moses to go to M. Abarim, p. 20, (Num. 27:12)

Moses and Aaron at M. Hor, p. 20, (Num. 20:23)

Moses on M. Sinai, p. 17, (Ex. 19—31)

M. Sinai was wrapped in smoke, p. 17, (Ex. 19:18)

on the M. of Olives, p. 179 (Matt. 26:30–35; Mk. 14:26–31; Lk. 22:31–34, 39)

sent the prophets of Baal to M. Carmel, p. 40, (I Kg. 18:20)

temple in Jerusalem on M. Moriah, p. 38, (II Chr. 3:1)

the m. called Olivet, p. 189, (Acts 1:12)

went out to the M. of Olives, p. 179, (Matt. 26:30; Mk. 14:26; Lk. 22:39)

were come to the M. of Olives, p. 169, (Matt. 21:1; Mk. 11:1; Lk. 19:29)

Mountain: every m. made low, p. 91, (Isa. 40:4)

go up to the m. and build the house, p. 125, (Hagg. 1:8)

he sent up into a m. to pray, p. 149, (Matt. 14:23; Mk. 6:46; Lk. 6:12)

let us go to the m. of the Lord, p. 122, (Micah 4:2)

say to this m.: Move hence to yonder place, p. 161, (Matt. 17:20; 21:21; Mk. 11:23)

the m. of the house of the Lord, p. 121, (Micah 4:1)

went up on the m., p. 138, (Matt. 5:1)

Mountains: before the m. were brought forth, p. 62, (Ps. 90:2)

he that forms the m. and creates the wind, p. 118, (Amos 4:13)

men said to the m., fall on us, p. 243, (Rev. 6:16)

the m. shall drop sweet wine, p. 119, (Amos 9:13)

the m. skipped like rams, p. 65, (Ps. 114:4)

the m. will melt as wax, p. 121, (Micah 1:4)

weighed the m. in scales, p. 92, (Isa. 40:12)

Mourn: can the wedding guests m., p. 145, (Matt. 9:15; Mk. 2:19; Lk. 5:34)

friends came to m. with him, p. 49, (Job 2:11)

comfort all that m., p. 95, (Isa. 61:2)

Mourned: m. and ye have not lamented, p. 148, (Matt. 11:17; cf. Lk. 7:32)

Mourneth: the earth m., p. 87, (Isa. 24:4)

Mourning: better to go to the house of m., p. 75, (Ec. 7:2)

in the daughter of Judah m. and lamentation, p. 104, (Lam. 2:5)

sorrow and m. shall flee, p. 93, (Isa. 51:11)

the oil of joy for m., p. 95, (Isa. 61:3)

turn their m. into joy, p. 102, (Jer. 31:13)

when the m. was past, p. 35, (II Sam. 11:27)

Mouth: be not rash with thy m., p. 75, (Ec. 5:2)

he laid it upon my m., p. 83, (Isa. 6:7)

keep my m. with a bridle, p. 59, (Ps. 39:1)

my m. shall show forth thy praise, p. 60, (Ps. 51:15)

not thine own m., p. 73, (Prov. 27:2)

not what goes into the m. defiles, p. 159, (Matt. 15:11; Mk. 7:15, 18)

out of the m. of babes, p. 56, (Ps. 8:2)

out of the same m. . . . . blessing and cursing, p. 234, (Jas. 3:10)

own m. condemneth thee, p. 52, (Job 15:6)

set a watch, O Lord, before my m., p. 68, (Ps. 141:3)

the words of my m. . . . . be acceptable, p. 57, (Ps. 19:14)

what comes out of the m., p. 159, (Matt. 15:11; Mk. 7:15, 20)

Mouths: have m., but they speak not, p. 66, (Ps. 115:5; 135:16)

Mysteries: the m. of the kingdom of heaven, p. 156, (Matt. 13:11; Mk. 4:11; Lk. 8:10)

Moved: I shall not be m., p. 56, (Ps. 16:8)

Much: to whom m. is given, p. 150, (Lk. 12:48)

Multiply: be fruitful and m., p. 4, (Gen. 1:28)

Multitude: a m. of all nations, p. 243, (Rev. 7:9)

great m. spread their garments, p. 169, (Matt. 21:8; Mk. 11:8; Lk. 19:36)

m. gathered on the shore, p. 156, (Matt. 13:2; Mk. 4:1)

I have compassion on the m., p. 159, (Matt. 15:32; Mk. 8:2)

in the m. of counsellors, p. 70, (Prov. 11:14; 15:22)

the m. did eat and were filled, p. 158, (Matt. 14:20; Mk. 6:42; Lk. 9:17; Jn. 6:12)

Multitudes: m., m. in the valley of decision, p. 117, (Joel 3:14)

seeing the m., p. 138, (Matt. 5:1)

sent the m. away, p. 149, (Matt. 14:23; Mk. 6:46)

when he saw the m., p. 146, (Matt. 9:36; Mk. 6:34)

Mustard: faith as a grain of m. seed, p. 161, (Matt. 17:20; Lk. 17:6)

the parable of the m. seed, p. 157, (Matt. 13:31–32; Mk. 4:30–32; Lk. 13:18–19)

Myra: Paul sails via M., p. 198, (Acts 27:5)

Myrrh: gifts of gold, frankincense and m., p. 134, (Matt. 2:11)

Myrtle: shall come up the m. tree, p. 95, (Isa. 55:13)

stood among the m. trees, p. 125, (Zech., 1:8)

Mystery: the m. of the faith in a pure conscience, p. 224, (I Tim. 3:9)

Naaman: N. cured of leprosy by Elisha, p. 42, (II Kg. 5)

Naboth: Jezebel had N. stoned to death, p. 41, (I Kg. 21:8, 13)

N.'s vineyard, p. 41, (I Kg. 21:1–16)

Nail: a n. in a sure place, p. 87, (Isa. 22:23)

Naked: both n. and unashamed, p. 4, (Gen. 2:25)

brother or sister be n. and destitute, p. 234, (Jas. 2:15)

I will go stripped and n., p. 121, (Micah 1:8)

n. came I., p. 49, (Job 1:21)

n. shall he return, p. 75, (Ec. 5:15)

the n., that thou cover him, p. 95, (Isa. 58:7)

they were n., p. 5, (Gen. 3:7)

who told you that you were n., p. 5, (Gen. 3:11)

Name: a good n. is better than precious ointment, p. 75, (Ec. 7:1)

a good n. . . . than great riches, p. 72, (Prov. 22:1)

by what power or by what n., p. 190, (Acts 4:7)

call on the n. of the Lord, p. 190, (Acts 2:21)

come in my n., saying, I am Christ, p. 173, (Matt. 24:5, 24; Mk. 13:6, 22; Lk. 21:8)

do all in the n. of the Lord, p. 221, (Col. 3:17)

gathered together in my n., p. 162, (Matt. 18:20)

given him a n. above every n., p. 218, (Phil. 2:9)

his n. is called The Word of God, p. 246, (Rev. 19:13)

his n. shall be called Wonderful, p. 84, (Isa. 9:6)

his n. . . . THE LORD OUR RIGHTEOUSNESS, p. 101, (Jer. 23:6)

how excellent is thy n., p. 56, (Ps. 8:9)

in the n. of Jesus Christ, p. 190, (Acts 3:6)

in the n. of the Lord, p. 169, (Matt. 21:9; Mk. 11:9; Lk. 19:38; Jn. 12:13)

let my n. be named, p. 13, (Gen. 48:16)

Lord, the God of hosts, is his n., p. 118, (Amos 4:13)

my n. shall be great, p. 127, (Mal. 1:11)

n. of the Lord in vain, p. 17, (Ex. 20:7)

not to teach in the n. of Jesus, p. 190, (Acts 4:18)

that at the n. of Jesus, p. 218, (Phil. 2:10)

that cometh in the n. of the Lord, p. 66, (Ps. 118:26)

the Lord of hosts is his n., p. 103, (Jer. 50:34)

the n. of Jesus Christ of Nazareth, p. 190, (Acts 4:10)

the n. of the Lord Jesus, p. 197, (Acts 21:13)

thy n. and remembrance of thee, p. 88, (Isa. 26:8)

what is thy n., p. 144, (Mk. 5:9; Lk. 8:30)

whatsoever ye ask in my n., p. 178, (Jn. 14:13–14)

whosoever shall call on the n. of the Lord, p. 117, (Joel 2:32)

whosoever shall call upon the n. of the Lord, p. 202, (Rom. 10:13)

Names: Adam gave n. to all the . . . beasts, p. 5, (Gen. 2:20)

the n. of the twelve apostles, p. 146, (Matt. 10:2–4; Mk. 3:16–19; Lk. 6:13–16)

Naomi: Ruth and N., p. 31, (Ruth)

Narrow: n. the way leading into life, p. 142, (Matt. 7:14)

Nathan: N. told David a parable, p. 35, (II Sam. 12:1–14)

Nathanael: N.: Can any good thing, p. 137, (Jn. 1:46)

Nation: a holy n., p. 17, (Ex. 19:5–6)

devout Jews of every n. asked, p. 189, (Acts 2:5)

for n. shall rise against n., p. 173, (Matt. 24:7; Mk. 13:8)

make of thee a great n., p. 7, (Gen. 12:2)

Moses called the n. to a new commitment, p. 22, (Deut. 27:30)

n. shall not lift up sword, p. 82, (Isa. 2:4)

send him against an hypocritical n., p. 84, (Isa. 10:6)

Nations: Abraham, father of many n., p. 8, (Gen. 17:5)

all n. of men, p. 196, (Acts 17:26)

an ensign for the n., p. 85, (Isa. 11:12)

judge among the n., p. 82, (Isa. 2:4)

n. are as a drop of a bucket, p. 92, (Isa. 40:15)

n. before him are as nothing, p. 92, (Isa. 40:17)

shall be a mother of n., p. 8, (Gen. 17:16)

n. shall flow unto it, p. 82, (Isa. 2:2)

shall be gathered all n., p. 175, (Matt. 25:32)

teach all n. and baptize them, p. 185, (Matt. 28:19; cf. Mk. 16:15–16)

that he should deceive the n. no more, p. 246, (Rev. 20:3)

the n. shall rush, p. 86, (Isa. 17:13)

thou hast spoiled many n., p. 123, (Hab. 2:8)

two n. are in thy womb, p. 10, (Gen. 25:23)

thy saving health among all n., p. 61, (Ps. 67:2)

upon the earth distress of n., p. 173, (Lk. 21:25)

Naughtiness: the n. of thine heart, p. 33, (I Sam. 17:28)

Navel: n. is like a round goblet, p. 78, (Song 7:2)

Navy: Solomon's n. brought gold, silver, p. 38, (I Kg. 10:22; II Chr. 9:21)

Nazarene: prophecy: He shall be called a N., p. 134, (Matt. 2:23)

Nazareth: any good thing come out of N., p. 137, (Jn. 1:43–51; cf. 7:41–42)

Joseph went from N. to Bethlehem, p. 132, (Lk. 2:4)

returned to Israel and dwelt in N., p. 134, (Matt. 2:21, 23)

Nazarite: the child shall be a N., p. 30, (Jg. 13:5)

Neapolis: Paul visits N., p. 195, (Acts 16:11)

via Samothrace and N., p. 195, (Acts 16:11)

Nebuchadnezzar: See also: Nebuchadrezzar

N. beseiged Jerusalem, p. 110, (Dan. 1:1)

N. called them forth, p. 111, (Dan. 3:26)

N. came up against Jerusalem, p. 45, (II Kg. 24:10–11; II Chr. 36:6; Jer. 39:1)

N. . . . . did eat grass as oxen, p. 111, (Dan. 4:33)

N. dreamed dreams, p. 110, (Dan. 2:1)

N. in rage called Shadrach . . . ., p. 111, (Dan. 3:13)

N. king of Babylon, p. 110, (Dan. 1:1)

Nebuchadnezzar: (continued)
N. set up a golden image, p. 111, (Dan. 3:1)

N. slew the sons of Zedekiah, p. 103, (Jer. 39:6)

Nebuchadrezzar: I will deliver Zedekiah to N., p. 101, (Jer. 21:7)

this N. king of Babylon, p. 103, (Jer. 50:17)

Neck: n. is as a tower of ivory, p. 78, (Song 7:4)

Necks: stretched forth n. and wanton eyes, p. 82, (Isa. 3:16)

Need: God shall supply all your n., p. 220, (Phil. 4:19)

sees his brother in n., p. 238, (I John 3:17)

your Father knoweth what things ye have n. of, p. 140, (Matt. 6:8)

Neglect: n. not the gift, p. 225, (I Tim. 4:14)

Neighbor: a n. that is near, p. 73, (Prov. 27:10)

love thy n., p. 23, (Lev. 19:18; Matt. 19:19; 22:39; Mk. 12:31, 33; Rom. 13:9; Gal. 5:14; Jas. 2:8)

love thy n. as thyself, p. 171, (Matt. 22:39; Mk. 12:31; Lk. 10:27; Lev. 19:18)

neighed after his n.'s wife, p. 99, (Jer. 5:8)

who is my n.?, p. 149, (Lk. 10:29)

Neighed: n. after his neighbor's wife, p. 99, (Jer. 5:8)

Net: a n. which gathered all kinds of fish, p. 157, (Matt. 13:47)

cast the n. on the right side of the ship, p. 185, (Jn. 21:6)

casting a n. into the sea, p. 136, (Matt. 4:18; Mk. 1:16)

Nets: left their n. and followed him, p. 136, (Matt. 4:20; Mk. 1:18)

let down your n., p. 136, (Lk. 5:4)

mending their n., p. 136, (Matt. 4:21; Mk. 1:19)

Nettles: n. and brambles in the fortresses, p. 90, (Isa. 34:13)

Never: n. again will I kill, p. 7, (Gen. 8:21)

New: a n. heart and a n. spirit, p. 108, (Ezek. 18:31)

a n. heaven and a n. earth, p. 247, (Rev. 21:1)

all things are become n., p. 211, (II Cor. 5:17)

full of n. wine, p. 189, (Acts 2:13)

n. heavens and a n. earth, p. 96, (Isa. 65:17)

I make all things n., p. 247, (Rev. 21:5)

in Christ he is a n. creature, p. 211, (II Cor. 5:17)

n. cloth on an old garment, p. 145, (Matt. 9:16; Mk. 2:21; Lk. 5:36)

n. wine into old bottles, p. 145, (Matt. 9:17; Mk. 2:22; Lk. 5:37)

no n. thing under the sun, p. 74, (Ec. 1:9)

put on the n. man, p. 217, (Eph. 4:24)

saw the holy city, n. Jerusalem, p. 247, (Rev. 21:2)

they are n. every morning, p. 105, (Lam. 3:23)

this cup is the n. testament, p. 208, (I Cor. 11:25)

this is my blood of the n. testament, p. 177, (Matt. 26:28; Mk. 14:24; Lk. 22:20; I Cor. 11:25)

Newness: we should serve in n. of spirit, p. 201, (Rom. 7:6)

News: good n. from a far country, p. 73, (Prov. 25:25)

Nicodemus: Jesus and N., p. 165, (Jn. 3:1–15)

Night: by n. on my bed I sought him, p. 77, (Song 3:1)

instruct me in the n. seasons, p. 56, (Ps. 16:7)

n. cometh, when no man can work, p. 168, (Jn. 9:4)

the darkness he called N., p. 3, (Gen. 1:5)

the n. is far spent . . . , p. 204, (Rom. 13:12)

there shall be no n. there, p. 247, (Rev. 22:5)

Ninety: leave the n. and nine in the wilderness, p. 162, (Matt. 18:12; Lk. 15:4)

Nineveh: arise, go to N., p. 120, (Jonah 1:2)

forty days and N. shall be overthrown, p. 120, (Jonah 3:4)

N. believed God and proclaimed a fast, p. 121, (Jonah 3:5)

N. is laid waste, p. 123, (Nahum 3:7)

should not I spare N.?, p. 121, (Jonah 4:11)

the fate of N., p. 124, (Zeph. 2:15)

the Lord said to Jonah: go unto N., p. 120, (Jonah 3:1–2)

Noah: N.'s ark, p. 6, (Gen. 6:14–22)

N. begat three sons, p. 6, (Gen. 6:10)

N. builded an altar, p. 6, (Gen. 8:20)

God's covenant with N., p. 7, (Gen. 8:21—9:17)

N. found favor, p. 6, (Gen. 6:8)

God tells N. he will destroy, p. 6, (Gen. 6:5–13)

N. sent forth a dove, p. 6, (Gen. 8:8)

thus did N. as God commanded, p. 6, (Gen. 6:22)

Noise: make a joyful n. unto God, p. 61, (Ps. 66:1)

make a joyful n. unto the Lord, p. 64, (Ps. 100:1)

take away the n. of your songs, p. 119, (Amos 5:23)

Noised: when this was n. abroad, p. 189, (Acts 2:6)

None: I am, and there is n. beside me, p. 124, (Zeph. 2:15)

Noonday: clearer than the n., p. 51, (Job 11:17)

thy darkness be as the n., p. 95, (Isa. 58:10)

North: fair weather cometh out of the n., p. 54, (Job 37:22)

Noses: n., but they smell not, p. 66, (Ps. 115:6; Ps. 135:17)

Nothing: and I have n. to set before him, p. 150, (Lk. 11:6)

brought n. into this world, p. 225, (I Tim. 6:7)

having n., yet possessing all things, p. 212, (II Cor. 6:10)

is it n. to you?, p. 104, (Lam. 1:12)

we can carry n. out, p. 225, (I Tim. 6:7)

Number: teach us to n. our days, p. 63, (Ps. 90:12)

Nurse: as a n. cherishes her children, p. 221, (I Th. 2:7)

Nurture: in the n. and admonition of the Lord, p. 218, (Eph. 6:4)

Oath: an o. to walk in God's law, p. 46, (Neh. 10:29)

Obadiah: O. against Jezebel, p. 40, (I Kg. 18:1–16)

O. hid them in a cave, p. 40, (I Kg. 18:4)

Obed: O., father of Jesse, father of David, p. 31, (Ruth 4:17)

Obedience: by the o. of one shall many be made righteous, p. 200. (Rom. 5:19)

thank . . . for his o., p. 153, (Lk. 17:9)

Obedient: became o. unto death even of the cross, p. 218, (Phil. 2:8)

if you be willing and o., p. 81, (Isa. 1:19)

Obey: children, o. your parents, p. 217, (Eph. 6:1)

o. my voice and I will be your God, p. 100, (Jer. 7:23)

to o. God not men, p. 191, (Acts 5:29)

who is the Lord, that I should o., p. 15, (Ex. 5:2)

Obeyed: she o. not the voice, p. 124, (Zeph. 3:2)

Oblations: no more vain o., p. 81, (Isa. 1:13)

Obscurity: thy light shall rise in o., p. 95, (Isa. 58:10)

Offence: till they acknowledge their o., p. 115, (Hos. 5:15)

Offend: if thy right hand o. thee, p. 139, (Matt. 5:30; 18:8; Mk. 9:43)

o. one of these little ones, p. 162, (Matt. 18:6; Mk. 9:42)

Offense: they took o. at him, p. 157, (Matt. 13:57; Mk. 6:3)

Offering: a sin o. to the Lord, p. 19, (Ex. 30:10; Lev. 16:5; Num. 29:11)

offer him as a burnt o., p. 9, (Gen. 22:2)

Oil: a little o. in a cruse, p. 40, (I Kg. 17:12)

five did not get o. for their lamps, p. 174, (Matt. 25:3)

neither did the o. . . . . fail, p. 40, (I Kg. 17:16)

the o. of joy for mourning, p. 95, (Isa. 61:3)

Ointment: alabaster box of o., p. 176, (Matt. 26:7; Mk. 14:3)

anointed them with o., p. 155, (Lk. 7:38)

with an alabaster box of o., p. 155, (Lk. 7:37)

Old: an o. and foolish king, p. 75, (Ec. 4:13)

in the time of o. age, p. 62, (Ps. 71:9)

o. men dream dreams, p. 189, (Acts 2:17)

Old: *(continued)*

o. men shall dream dreams, p. 117, (Joel 2:28)

o. things are passed away, p. 211, (II Cor. 5:17)

profane and o. wives' fables, p. 225, (I Tim. 4:7)

thy mother when she is o., p. 73, (Prov. 23:22)

when is is o., p. 72, (Prov. 22:6)

Olives: were come to the Mount of O., p. 169, (Matt. 21:1; Mk. 11:1; Lk. 19:29)

Olivet: the mount called O., p. 189, (Acts 1:12)

Omnipotent: the Lord God o. reigneth!, p. 246, (Rev. 19:6)

One: all the members of that o. body, p. 208, (I Cor. 12:12)

by o. Spirit are we all baptized, p. 208, (I Cor. 12:13)

o. among a thousand, p. 54, (Job 33:23)

o. Lord, o. faith, o. baptism, p. 216, (Eph. 4:5)

that they all may be o., p. 180, (Jn. 17:21)

the Father and I are o., p. 148, (Jn. 10:30)

the Lord our God is o. Lord, p. 23, (Deut. 6:4; cf. Mk. 12:32)

there is o. body, and o. Spirit, p. 216, (Eph. 4:4)

with o. accord in o. place, p. 189, (Acts 2:1)

you are all o. in Christ Jesus, p. 214, (Gal. 3:28)

Onesimus: for my son O., p. 228, (Philem. v. 10)

Opened: knock and it shall be o., p. 142, (Matt. 7:7; Lk. 11:9)

Opinions: halt ye between two o.?, p. 40, (I Kg. 18:21)

Oppress: o. not the widow, p. 126, (Zech. 7:10)

Oppressed: relieve the o., p. 81, (Isa. 1:17)

Oppression: looked for judgment, but behold o., p. 83, (Isa. 5:7)

Ordinance: submit yourselves to every o., p. 236, (I Pet. 2:13)

Ordinances: teach them o. and laws, p. 17, (Ex. 18:20)

Organ: play the harp and the o., p. 6, (Gen. 4:21)

Orion: that maketh the seven stars and O., p. 119, (Amos 5:8)

Ornament: o. of a meek and quiet spirit, p. 236, (I Pet. 3:4)

Ornaments: the bravery of their o., p. 82, (Isa. 3:18)

Our: o. Father which art in heaven, p. 140, (Matt. 6:9; Lk. 11:2)

Outcasts: assemble the o. of Israel, p. 85, (Isa. 11:12)

Outlaw: David the o., p. 34, (I Sam. 21—26)

Overcome: I have o. the world, p. 179, (Jn. 16:33)

Overcometh: he that o. shall inherit all things, p. 247, (Rev. 21:7)

Owe: o. no man anything, p. 204, (Rom. 13:8)

Owl: an o. of the desert, p. 64, (Ps. 102:6)

Owls: a companion to o., p. 54, (Job 30:29)

and mourning as the o., p. 121, (Micah 1:8)

habitation of dragons and a court for o., p. 90, (Isa. 34:13)

Ox: a lion, an o. and an eagle, p. 105, (Ezek. 1:10)

an o. goeth to the slaughter, p. 70, (Prov. 7:22)

eateth grass like an o., p. 55, (Job 40:15)

lion shall eat straw like the o., p. 85, (Isa. 11:7)

than a stalled o. and hatred, p. 71, (Prov. 15:17)

the o. knoweth his owner, p. 81, (Isa. 1:3)

Oxen: Nebuchadnezzar . . . did eat grass as o., p. 111, (Dan. 4:33)

Pagan: purged the land of p. worship, p. 45, (II Kg. 23:4–20; II Chr. 34:3–7)

Pain: much p. is in all loins, p. 123, (Nahum 2:10)

wicked man travaileth with p., p. 52, (Job 15:20)

Palace: the p. is . . . for the Lord God, p. 37, (I Chr. 29:1)

Palaces: dragons in their pleasant p., p. 85, (Isa. 13:22)

thorns shall come up in her p., p. 90, (Isa. 34:13)

thy p. shall be spoiled, p. 118, (Amos 3:11)

Palm: shall flourish like the p. tree, p. 63, (Ps. 92:12)

Parable: Nathan told David a p., p. 35, (II Sam. 12:1–14)

p. of a friend in need, p. 150, (Lk. 11:5–8)

p. of a net, p. 157, (Matt. 13:47–50)

p. of building a tower, p. 151, (Lk. 14:28–33)

p. of Lazarus, p. 153, (Lk. 16:19–31)

p. of new wine and new cloth, p. 145, (Matt. 9:14–17; Mk. 2:18–22; Lk. 5:33–39)

p. of the empty house and the wicked spirits, p. 155, (Matt. 12:43–45; Lk. 11:24–26)

p. of the faithful servant, p. 174, (Matt. 24:45–51; Lk. 12:42–48)

p. of the fig tree, p. 174, (Matt. 24:32–33; Mk. 13:28–29; Lk. 21:29–31)

p. of the fig tree without figs, p. 150, (Lk. 13:6–9)

p. of the good Samaritan, p. 149, (Lk. 10:29–37)

p. of the great banquet, p. 171, (Lk. 14:16–24; cf. Matt. 22:1–14)

p. of the houses on rock and on sand, p. 143, (Matt. 7:24–27; Lk. 6:47–49)

p. of the laborers in the vineyard, p. 164, (Matt. 20:1–16)

p. of the leaven, p. 157, (Matt. 13:33; Lk. 13:20–21)

p. of the lost coin, p. 152, (Lk. 15:8–10)

p. of the lost sheep, p. 162, (Matt. 18:12–14; Lk. 15:2–7)

p. of the marriage feast, p. 171, (Matt. 22:1–14; cf. Lk. 14:26–24)

p. of the mustard seed, p. 157, (Matt. 13:31–32; Mk. 4:30–32; Lk. 13:18–19)

p. of the pearl of great price, p. 157, (Matt. 13:45–46)

p. of the prodigal son, p.152, (Lk. 15:11–24)

p. of the publican and the Pharisee, p. 154, (Lk. 18:9–14)

p. of the rich fool, p. 150, (Lk. 12:3–21)

p. of the seed growing secretly, p. 156, (Mk. 4:26–29)

p. of the sower, p. 156, (Matt. 13:1–23; Mk. 4:1–20; Lk. 8:4–15)

p. of the talents, p. 174, (Matt. 25:14–30; Lk. 19:11–27)

p. of the treasure, p. 157, (Matt. 13:44)

p. of the two sons, p. 170, (Matt. 21:28–32)

p. of the unjust judge, p. 153, (Lk. 18:1–8)

p. of the unjust steward, p. 152, (Lk. 16:1–8)

p. of the unmerciful servant, p. 162, (Matt. 18:23–35)

p. of the weeds, p.156, (Matt. 13:24–30; 36–43)

p. of the wicked tenants, p. 170, (Matt. 21:33–41; Mk. 12:1–9; Lk. 20:9–16)

p. of the wise and foolish virgins, p. 174, (Matt. 25:1–13)

p. on humility, p. 151, (Lk. 14:7–11)

Paradise: today you will be with me in P., p. 183, (Lk. 23:43)

Paralyzed: brought a man who was p., p. 144, (Matt. 9:2; Mk. 2:3; Lk. 5:18)

Parched: p. ground shall become a pool, p. 90, (Isa. 35:7)

Pardon: a God ready to p., p. 46, (Neh. 9:17)

Pardoned: her iniquity p., p. 91, (Isa. 40:2)

Parents: children, obey your p., p. 217, (Eph. 6:1)

Partition: broken down the . . . p. between us, p. 216, (Eph. 2:14)

Partner: if thou count me a p., p. 228, (Philem. v. 17)

Partridge: the p. sitteth on eggs, p. 101, (Jer. 17:11)

Pass: cover thee with my hand while I p. by, p. 18, (Ex. 33:22)

I will p. over you, p. 21, (Ex. 12:13)

Passing: p. the love of women, p. 34, (II Sam. 1:26)

Passions: men of like p., p. 194, (Acts 14:15)

Passover: p. 21, (Ex. 12; 23:15; Lev. 23:5–8; Deut. 16:1–8)

after two days is the P., p. 176, (Matt. 26:2; Mk. 14:1; Lk. 22:1)

celebrated the p., p. 45, (II Kg. 23:21–23; II Chr. 34:31; 35:1)

Passover: *(continued)*

Christ our p. is sacrificed for us, p. 206, (I Cor. 5:7)

Hezekiah's p., p. 44, (II Chr. 30)

Jesus as a boy in Jerusalem at p., p. 134, (Lk. 2:40–52)

the Lord's p., pp. 15, 21, (Ex. 12:11; Lev. 23:5)

Pasture: we are the people of his p., p. 63, (Ps. 95:7)

Pastures: to lie down in green p., p. 57, (Ps. 23:2)

Patara: Paul travels via P., p. 196, (Acts 21:1)

Path: lead me in a plain p., p. 58, (Ps. 27:11)

Paths: all her p. are peace, p. 69, (Prov. 3:17)

ask for the old p., p. 99, (Jer. 6:16)

he shall direct thy p., p. 69, (Prov. 3:6)

made my p. crooked, p. 104, (Lam. 3:9)

make his p. straight, p. 135, (Matt. 3:3; Mk. 1:3; Lk. 3:4)

will walk in his p., p. 82, (Isa. 2:3)

Patience: have p. with me and I will pay, p. 163, (Matt. 18:26)

heard of the p. of Job, p. 235, (Jas. 5:11)

let p. have her perfect work, p. 232, (Jas. 1:4)

let us run with p., p. 231, (Heb. 12:1)

who also begged p., p. 163, (Matt. 18:29)

Patient: be p. in tribulation, p. 203, (Rom. 12:12)

but he would not be p., p. 163, (Matt. 18:30)

Patmos: John on P., p. 240, (Rev. 1:9–11)

Pattern: the p. of the house of the Lord, p. 37, (I Chr. 28:11–12)

Paul: a vision appeared to P., p. 195, (Acts 16:9)

journeys of Barnabus and P., p. 194, (Acts 13—14)

miracles by the hands of P., p. 196, (Acts 19:11)

P., a prisoner of Jesus Christ, p. 227, (Philem. v. 1)

P., an apostle not of men, p. 213, (Gal. 1:1)

P. and Barnabus argue, p. 195, (Acts 15:36–41)

P. and Barnabus had dissension with them, p. 194, (Acts 15:2)

P. and Silas in prison, p. 195, (Acts 16:19–40)

P. at Athens, p. 196, (Acts 17:16–34)

P. at Ephesus, p. 196, (Acts 19)

P.'s attitude toward women, p. 224, (I Tim. 2:9–15)

P.'s defense, p. 197, (Acts 25–26)

P. dwelt . . . in his own hired house, p. 198, (Acts 28:30)

P. gathered a bundle of sticks, p. 198, (Acts 28:3)

P. in Jerusalem, p. 197, (Acts 21:13–40; 22; 23:1–22)

P. in Rome, p. 198, (Acts 28:16–31)

P. laid his hands upon them, p. 196, (Acts 19:6)

P. revisits churches, p. 195, (Acts 15:36–41)

P. sails from Jerusalem to Rome, p. 198, (Acts 27—28)

P. takes the gospel to Europe, p. 195, (Acts 16:6—18:28)

P., the prisoner of Jesus Christ, p. 216, (Eph. 3:1)

P. went to Philippi, p. 195, (Acts 16:12)

they called . . . P., Mercury, p. 194, (Acts 14:12)

P., thou art beside thyself, p. 197, (Acts 26:24)

P. told Felix the governor, p. 197, (Acts 23:26; 24:10)

P. travels from Ephesus, p. 196, (Acts 19—21:15)

Timothy joins P., p. 195, (Acts 16:1–5)

the Romans beat P. and Silas, p. 195, (Acts 16:23)

with our beloved Barnabas and P., p. 195, (Acts 15:25)

Peace: a fool, when he holdeth his p., p. 72, (Prov. 17:28)

a time of p., p. 74, (Ec. 3:8)

acquaint thyself with him and be at p., p. 53, (Job 22:21)

all her paths are p., p. 69, (Prov. 3:17)

and give thee p., p. 19, (Num. 6:26)

be led forth with p., p. 94, (Isa. 55:12)

follow after the things which make for p., p. 204, (Rom. 14:19)

follow p. with all men, p. 231, (Heb. 12:14)

grace to you and p. from God . . . , p. 199, (Rom. 1:7)

I held my p. even from good, p. 59, (Ps. 39:2)

lay me down in p., and sleep, p. 56, (Ps. 4:8)

let the p. of God rule in your hearts, p. 221, (Col. 3:15)

no p. unto the wicked, p. 93, (Isa. 48:22)

not p. but a sword, p. 147, (Matt. 10:34–37; Lk. 12:51–53; 14:26)

of the increase of his government and p., p. 84, (Isa. 9:7)

on earth p., good will toward men, p. 133, (Lk. 2:14)

p. be to this house, p. 146, (Matt. 10:13; Lk. 10:5)

p. be unto you!, p. 184, (Lk. 24:36; Jn. 20:19)

p. from God the Father, p. 213, (Gal. 1:3)

p. I leave with you, p. 178, (Jn. 14:27)

p. to him that is far, p. 95, (Isa. 57:19)

power . . . to take p. from the earth, p. 243, (Rev. 6:4)

righteousness and p. have kissed, p. 62, (Ps. 85:10)

saying, P., peace when there is no p., p. 99, (Jer. 6:14)

seek p., and pursue it, p. 58, (Ps. 34:14)

speak p. unto the heathen, p. 126, (Zech. 9:10)

the p. of God which passeth all understanding, p. 219, (Phil. 4:7)

thou wilt keep him in perfect p., p. 87, (Isa. 26:3)

thou wilt ordain p. for us, p. 88, (Isa. 26:12)

to guide our feet in the way of p., p. 132, (Lk. 1:79)

thy p. been as a river, p. 93, (Isa. 48:18)

way of p. they know not, p. 95, (Isa. 59:8)

what hast thou to do with p.?, p. 43, (II Kg. 9:18)

Peaceable: the p. kingdom, p. 85, (Isa. 11:6–9)

Peaceably: live p. with all men, p. 203, (Rom. 12:18)

Peacocks: ivory, apes and p., p. 38, (I Kg. 10:22; II Chr. 9:21)

Pearl: parable of the p. of great price, p. 157, (Matt. 13:45–46)

Pearls: p. before swine, p. 142, (Matt. 7:6)

Pelican: like a p. of the wilderness, p. 64, (Ps. 102:6)

Pen: an iron p. and lead in the rock, p. 52, (Job 19:24)

written with a p. of iron, p. 101, (Jer. 17:1)

Penknife: King Jehoiakim cut it with his p., p. 102, (Jer. 36:23)

Penny: they all received a p., p. 164, (Matt. 20:9)

Pentecost: on the day of P., p. 189, (Acts 2:1–13)

People: a stiffnecked p., p. 18, (Ex. 32:9)

and they shall be his p., p. 247, (Rev. 21:3)

as with the p. so with the priest, p. 87, (Isa. 24:2)

be my p. and I will be your God, p. 102, (Jer. 30:22)

go and tell this p., p. 83, (Isa. 6:9)

let my p. go, p. 15, (Ex. 5:1—7:10)

like p., like priest, p. 115, (Hos. 4:9)

spare thy p., O Lord, p. 117, (Joel 2:17)

the p. are too many, p. 29, (Jg. 7:2)

the p. are yet too many, p. 29, (Jg. 7:4)

the p. arose as one man, p. 31, (Jg. 20:8)

the p. that walked in darkness, p. 84, (Isa. 9:2)

they shall be my p., p. 230, (Heb. 8:10)

thy p. shall be my p., p. 31, (Ruth 1:16)

to be a special p., p. 23, (Deut. 7:6)

to make ready a p., p. 131, (Lk. 1:17)

unto them that were not my p. thou art my p., p. 114, (Hos. 2:23)

we are the p. of his pasture, p. 63, (Ps. 95:7)

Peres: P.: Thy kingdom is divided, p. 112, (Dan. 5:28)

Perfect: be ye therefore p., p. 140, (Matt. 5:48; cf. Lk. 6:36)

he was a p. . . . man, p. 49, (Job 1:1)

if thou would be p., p. 163, (Matt. 19:21)

make you p. in every good work, p. 232, (Heb. 13:21)

not cast away a p. man, p. 51, (Job 8:20)

p. and entire, wanting nothing, p. 232, (Jas. 1:4)

Perfected: the third day . . . p., p. 169, (Lk. 13:32)

Perga: Paul and Barnabus visit P., p. 194, (Acts 13:13)

Pergamos: to the church in P., p. 241, (Rev. 2:12–17)

Pergamum: to the church in . . . P., p. 241, (Rev. 2:12–17)

Perils: in p. of waters, in p. of robbers, p. 212, (II Cor. 11:26)

Perish: carest thou not that we p., p. 144, (Matt. 8:25; Mk. 4:38; Lk. 8:24)

let the day p., p. 50, (Job 3:3)

the people p., p. 73, (Prov. 29:18)

Perished: who ever p. being innocent?, p. 50, (Job 4:7)

Persecute: bless them which p. you, p. 203, (Rom. 12:14)

despitefully use you and p. you, p. 140, (Matt. 5:44)

Persecutest: Saul, Saul, why p. thou me?, p. 192, (Acts 9:4)

Persecution: all . . . in Christ Jesus shall suffer p., p. 226, (II Tim. 3:12)

early p. of the church, p. 191, (Acts 8:1–8)

p. against the church, p. 191, (Acts 8:1)

Perseverance: watching with all p., p. 218, (Eph. 6:18)

Persia: proclamation of Cyrus, King of P., p. 45, (II Chr. 36:22; Ezra 1:1)

the horns of the ram are the kings of Media and P., p. 112, (Dan. 8:20)

Persians: the law of the Medes and the P., p. 112, (Dan. 6:12)

Persuaded: be fully p. in his own mind, p. 204, (Rom. 14:5)

Pervert: doth God p. judgment?, p. 51, (Job 8:3)

doth God p. justice?, p. 51, (Job 8:3)

Pestilence: the p. that walketh in darkness, p. 63, (Ps. 91:6)

will send into her p., p. 108, (Ezek. 28:23)

Peter: a letter from P., p. 235, (Pet.)

entered the temple with P. and John, p. 190, (Acts 3:8)

Jesus, P. . . . went up a mountain to pray, p. 161, (Matt. 17:1; Mk. 9:2; Lk. 9:28)

Jesus said to P.: Come, p. 158, (Matt. 14:29)

letters from P., p. 232, (Pet.)

P. and the other apostles, p. 191, (Acts 5:29)

P. came to Caesarea, p. 193, (Acts 10:24)

P. followed him afar off, p. 180, (Matt. 26:58; Mk. 14:54; Lk. 22:54; Jn. 18:15)

P. freed from prison by an angel, p. 194, (Acts 12:1–19)

P.'s mother-in-law healed, p. 138, (Matt. 8:14–15; Mk. 1:29–31; Lk. 4:38–39)

P. said: Depart from me, p. 136, (Lk. 5:8)

P. said: Man, I am not, p. 181, (Matt. 26:72; Mk. 14:70; Lk. 22:58; Jn. 18:25)

P. said: We have forsaken all, p. 164, (Matt. 19:27; Mk. 10:28; Lk. 18:28)

P.'s sermon, p. 189, (Acts 2:14–36)

P.: Thou shalt never wash my feet, p. 177, (Jn. 13:8)

P.: thy money perish with thee, p. 192, (Acts 8:20)

P. walked on the water, p. 158, (Matt. 14:29)

P. went up upon the house top to pray, p. 193, (Acts 10:9)

rise, P.; kill, and eat, p. 193, (Acts 10:13)

send men to Joppa to Simon . . . P., p. 193, (Acts 10:5)

Simon, called P., p. 136, (Matt. 4:18; cf. Mk. 1:16)

the shadow of P. might fall on them, p. 190, (Acts 5:15)

thou art P., and upon this rock, p. 160, (Matt. 16:18)

Pharaoh: an officer of P., p. 12, (Gen. 37:36)

and all the host of P., p. 16, (Ex. 14:28)

hardened P.'s heart, p. 15, (Ex. 7:13)

I will send thee unto P., p. 14, (Ex. 3:10)

Joseph interpreted P.'s dreams, p. 12, (Gen. 41:1–36)

one more plague on P., p. 15, (Ex. 11:1)

P.'s butler and baker, p. 12, (Gen. 40)

P. decreed the death of all Hebrew sons, p. 13, (Ex. 1:15–16)

P. dreamed of seven, p. 12, (Gen. 41:2, 3)

P. pursued the children of Israel, p. 16, (Ex. 14:8, 9)

P. set Joseph over all, p. 12, (Gen. 41:41)

P.: Why did you not tell me?, p. 7, (Gen. 12:18)

the daughter of P., p. 13, (Ex. 2:5)

they built for P., p. 13, (Ex. 1:11)

who am I that I should go unto P.?, p. 14, (Ex. 3:11)

Pharisee: I am a P. the son of a P., p. 197, (Acts 23:6)

Jesus went into the P.'s house, p. 155, (Lk. 7:36)

parable of the publican and the P., p. 154, (Lk. 18:9–14)

Pharisees: leaven of the P. is hypocrisy, p. 160, (Lk. 12:1)

scribes and P., hypocrites, p. 172, (Matt. 23:25)

the P. said he casts out devils, p. 145, (Matt. 9:34)

Philadelphia: to the church in P., p. 241, (Rev. 3:7–13)

Philemon: letter to P., p. 223, (Philem.)

Paul's letter to P., p. 227, (Philem.)

P., our dearly beloved, p. 227, (Philem. v. 1)

Philip: Jesus findeth P., p. 137, (Jn. 1:43)

P. baptized the eunuch, p. 192, (Acts 8:38)

P. . . . Come and see, p. 137, (Jn. 1:46)

P. . . . preached unto him Jesus, p. 192, (Acts 8:35)

Philippi: letters to P., p. 218, (Phil.)

Paul's letter to P., p. 218, (Phil. 1:21)

Paul travels via P., p. 196, (Acts 20:6)

Paul visits P., p. 195, (Acts 16:12)

Paul went to P., p. 195, (Acts 16:12)

Philistine: David prevailed over the P., p. 33, (I Sam. 17:50)

fight with this P., p. 33, (I Sam. 17:32)

out of the P.'s camp, p. 33, (I Sam. 17:4)

Philistines: ark . . . captured by the P., p. 32, (I Sam. 4—7)

corn and vineyards of the P., p. 30, (Jg. 15:5)

deliver him to the P., p. 30, (Jg. 15:12)

P. returned the ark, p. 32, (I Sam. 6:21)

Samson's revenge on the P., p. 30, (Jg. 15)

the P. be upon thee, Samson, p. 30, (Jg. 16:20)

the P. put out his eyes, p. 30, (Jg. 16:21)

Philosophy: beware lest any man spoil you through p., p. 220, (Col. 2:8)

Physician: have no need of a p., p. 145, (Matt. 9:12; Mk. 2:17; Lk. 5:31)

Luke, the beloved p., p. 221, (Col. 4:14)

Pierced: p. his side with a spear, p. 183, (Jn. 19:34)

p. my hands and my feet, p. 57, (Ps. 22:16)

Pilate: Jesus before P., p. 181, (Matt. 27:11–14; Mk. 15:2–5; Lk. 23:2–5; Jn. 18:33–38; 19:8–12)

Jesus delivered to P., p. 181, (Matt. 27:1–2; Mk. 15:1; Lk. 23:1; Jn. 18:28–32)

Joseph of Arimathea went to P., p. 183, (Matt. 27:57–58; Mk. 15:43; Lk. 23:50–52; Jn. 19:38)

P. asked: What is truth?, p. 182, (Jn. 18:38)

P. said: Behold the man!, p. 182, (Jn. 19:5)

P. washed his hands, p. 182, (Matt. 27:24)

Pillar: a p. in the temple of God, p. 241, (Rev. 3:12)

a p. of fire, p. 16, (Ex. 13:21)

became a p. of salt, p. 9, (Gen. 19:26)

in a p. of cloud, p. 16, (Ex. 13:21)

Pillars: Samson grasped the two p. of the house, p. 30, (Jg. 16:29–30)

Piped: p. and ye have not danced, p. 148, (Matt. 11:17; Lk. 7:32)

Pisidian Antioch: Paul and Barnabus visit P. A., p. 194, (Acts 13:14)

Pit: cast him into a p. in Dothan, p. 12, (Gen. 37:17, 24)

cast him into the bottomless p., p. 246, (Rev. 20:3)

he brought me out of an horrible p., p. 59, (Ps. 40:2)

he was taken in their p., p. 108, (Ezek. 19:4)

the bottomless p., p. 244, (Rev. 9:1)

with the key of the bottomless p., p. 246, (Rev. 20:1)

Pitch: streams shall be turned into p., p. 90, (Isa. 34:9)

Pithom: treasure cities, P. and Raamses, p. 13, (Ex. 1:11)

Pitied: he hath thrown down and hath not p., p. 104, (Lam. 2:17)

Pity: neither will I have p., p. 107, (Ezek. 8:18)

thou hast had p. on the gourd, p. 121, (Jonah 4:10)

Place: give your p. to this man, p. 151, (Lk. 14:9)

I find out a p. for the Lord, p. 67, (Ps. 132:5)

Plague: one more p. on Pharaoh, p. 15, (Ex. 11:1)

the p. shall not be upon you, p. 21, (Ex. 12:13)

Plagues: O death, I will be thy p., p. 116, (Hos. 13:14)

the p. of Egypt, p. 15, (Ex. 7—11)

Plan: does not p. his strategy, p. 151, (Lk. 14:31)

Plant: not p. and another eat, p. 96, (Isa. 65:22)

they shall p. vineyards, p. 96, (Isa. 65:21)

Planted: I have p., Apollos watered, p. 205, (I Cor. 3:6)

p. the seed of the land, p. 108, (Ezek. 17:5)

Platter: brought his head on a p., p. 158, (Matt. 14:11; Mk. 6:27–28)

Pleasant: men of Judah his p. plant, p. 83, (Isa. 5:7)

fallen unto me in p. places, p. 56, (Ps. 16:6)

Pleasantness: her ways are ways of p., p. 69, (Prov. 3:17)

Pleasure: any p. to the Almighty, p. 53, (Job 22:3)

I will take p. in it, saith the Lord, p. 125, (Hagg. 1:8)

lived in p. on the earth, p. 235, (Jas. 5:5)

Pleiades: bind the . . . P. . . . ?, p. 54, (Job 38:31)

Plenty: in the years of p., p. 12, (Gen. 41:48)

seven years of p., p. 12, (Gen. 41:29)

Plot: a p. against the Jews, p. 46, (Est. 2:19–7)

Plow: they that p. iniquity, p. 50, (Job 4:8)

Plowshares: beat their swords into p., p. 122, (Micah 4:3)

beat your p. into swords, p. 117, (Joel 3:10)

their swords into p., p. 82, (Isa. 2:4)

Plumbline: a p. in the midst of Israel, p. 119, (Amos 7:8)

a wall made by a p., p. 119, (Amos 7:7)

with a p. in his hand, p. 119, (Amos 7:7)

Pomp: the p. of her strength shall cease, p. 109, (Ezek. 33:28)

Pondered: Mary p. them in her heart, p. 133, (Lk. 2:19)

Pool: go, wash in the p. of Siloam, p. 168, (Jn. 9:7)

the p. of Bethesda, p. 166, (Jn. 5:1–16)

Poor: as p., yet making many rich, p. 212, (II Cor. 6:10)

been a strength to the p., p. 87, (Isa. 25:4)

better is a p. and a wise child, p. 75, (Ec. 4:13)

blessed are the p., p. 138, (Matt. 5:3; Lk. 6:20)

bring the p., maimed, halt and blind, p. 171, (Lk. 14:21)

give half my goods to the p., p. 154, (Lk. 19:8)

grind the faces of the p., p. 82, (Isa. 3:15)

hath not God chosen the p.?, p. 233, (Jas. 2:5)

sell what thou hast and give to the p., p. 163, (Matt. 19:21; Mk. 10:21; Lk. 18:22) sold for much and given to the p., p. 176, (Matt. 26:9; Mk. 14:5; Jn. 12:5)

the p. man's lamb, p. 35, (II Sam. 12:4)

the p. man had nothing, p. 35, (II Sam. 12:3)

the p. shall never cease, p. 22, (Deut. 15:11)

the p. were given vineyards, p. 103, (Jer. 39:10)

they sold the p. for a pair of shoes, p. 118, (Amos 2:6; cf. 8:6)

two men, one rich, one p., p. 35, (II Sam. 12:1)

whoso mocketh the p., p. 71, (Prov. 17:5)

with righteousness shall he judge the p., p. 85, (Isa. 11:4)

ye have despised the p., p. 233, (Jas. 2:6)

ye have the p. always with you, p. 176, (Matt. 26:11; Mk. 14:7; Jn. 12:8)

Possessions: for he had great p., p. 164, (Matt. 19:22; Mk. 10:22; Lk. 18:23)

touch his p. and he will curse you, p. 49, (Job 1:11)

Possible: are p. to him that believeth, p. 161, (Mk. 9:23)

with God all things are p., p. 164, (Matt. 19:26; Mk. 10:27; Lk. 18:27)

Potiphar: Joseph was sold to P., p. 12, (Gen. 37:36)

P.'s wife, p. 12, (Gen. 39:7)

Pottage: to Jacob for p., p. 10, (Gen. 25:27–34)

Potter: as the clay is in the p.'s hand, p. 101, (Jer. 18:6)

the p. power over the clay . . . ?, p. 202, (Rom. 9:21)

the p.'s field to bury strangers, p. 181, (Matt. 27:7)

Pour: p. out thine heart, p. 104, (Lam. 2:19)

Power: a form of godliness but denying the p., p. 226, (II Tim. 3:5)

all p. is given unto me, p. 185, (Matt. 28:18)

all that he has is in your p., p. 49, (Job 1:12)

but in the p. of God, p. 205, (I Cor. 2:5)

but of p., and of love, p. 226, (II Tim. 1:7)

by what p. or by what name, p. 190, (Acts 4:7)

delivered us from the p. of darkness, p. 220, (Col. 1:13)

full of p. by the spirit of the Lord, p. 121, (Micah 3:8)

he gave them p., p. 146, (Matt. 10:1; Mk. 3:14; 15; Lk. 9:1)

not by might, nor by p., p. 126, (Zech. 4:6)

p. to become sons of God, p. 131, (Jn. 1:12)

the wicked in great p., p. 59, (Ps. 37:35)

will I give p. over the nations, p. 241, (Rev. 2:26)

with great p. gave the apostles, p. 190, (Acts 4:33)

Powers: when the p. of heaven are shaken, p. 174, (Matt. 24:29; Mk. 13; 25; Lk. 21:26)

Praise: everything that hath breath p. the Lord, p. 69, (Ps. 150:6)

I will p. thy name, p. 87, (Isa. 25:1)

let another man p. thee, p. 73, (Prov. 27:2)

loved the p. of men, p. 176, (Jn. 12:43)

my mouth shall show forth thy p., p. 60, (Ps. 51:15)

p. him, all ye stars, p. 68, (Ps. 148:3)

p. him with the sound of the trumpet, p. 69, (Ps. 150:3)

p. ye him, all his angels, p. 68, (Ps. 148:2)

p. ye him, sun and moon, p. 68, (Ps. 148:3)

shall every man have p. of God, p. 206, (I Cor. 4:5)

the garment of p., p. 95, (Isa. 61:3)

Pray: any among you afflicted? Let him p., p. 235, (Jas. 5:13)

into the temple to p., p. 154, (Lk. 18:10)

Jesus, . . . went up to a mountain to p., p. 161, (Matt. 17:1; Mk. 9:2; Lk. 9:28)

neither p. I for these alone, p. 180, (Jn. 17:20)

Peter went up upon the house top to p., p. 193, (Acts 10:9)

p. one for another, p. 235, (Jas. 5:16)

Pray: (continued)

p. for them which despitefully use you, p. 140, (Matt. 5:44; Lk. 6:28)

p. to the Lord for me, p. 192, (Acts 8:24)

p. to thy Father which is in secret, p. 140, (Matt. 6:6)

p. without ceasing, p. 222, (I Th. 5:17)

teach us to p., p. 140, (Lk. 11:1)

went up into a mountain to p., p. 149, (Matt. 14:23; Mk. 6:46; Lk. 6:12)

Prayed: Elijah p. for rain, p. 40, (I Kg. 18:41–46)

Elisha p. unto the Lord, p. 42, (II Kg. 4:33)

Hannah p. for a son, p. 31, (I Sam. 1:11)

he fell on his face and p., p. 180, (Matt. 26:39; Mk. 14:35; Lk. 22:41)

Jonah p. out of the fish's belly, p. 120, (Jonah 2:1)

p. and sang praises to God, p. 195, (Acts 16:25)

that which thou hast p. to me I have heard, p. 44, (II Kg. 19:20)

Prayer: all continued in p., p. 189, (Acts 1:14)

be patient in tribulation, constant in p., p. 203, (Rom. 12:12)

called the house of p., p. 170, (Matt. 21:13; Mk. 11:17; Lk. 19:46)

I have heard thy p., p. 91, (Isa. 38:5)

in everything by p. and supplication, p. 219, (Phil. 4:6)

my p. be set forth as incense, p. 68, (Ps. 141:2)

our Father (The Lord's P.), p. 140, (Matt. 6:9; Lk. 11:2; cf. Mk. 11:25–26)

p. of faith shall save the sick, p. 235, (Jas. 5:15)

p. of Habakkuk, p. 124, (Hab. 3)

Solomon's p. of dedication, p. 38, (I Kg. 8:14–61; II Chr. 6:12–42)

the fervent p. of a righteous man, p. 235, (Jas. 5:16)

whatsoever ye ask in p., p. 162, (Matt. 21:22; Mk. 11:24)

Prayers: many p., I will not hear, p. 81, (Isa. 1:15)

mention of thee always in my p., p. 227, (Philem. v. 4)

p. . . . be made for all men, p. 224, (I Tim. 2:1)

Prayest: when thou p., p. 140, (Matt. 6:6)

Preach: he has sent me to p., p. 157, (Lk. 4:18; Isa. 61:2)

how shall they p. except they be sent?, p. 202, (Rom. 10:15)

I am ready to p. the gospel, p. 199, (Rom. 1:15)

I charge thee, p. the word, p. 227, (II Tim. 4:2)

p. the gospel to every creature, p. 184, (Mk. 16:15; cf. Lk. 24:47)

p.: the kingdom of heaven, p. 146, (Matt. 10:7; Lk. 9:2)

p. unto it the preaching I bid, p. 120, (Jonah 3:2)

we p. Christ crucified, p. 205, (I Cor. 1:23)

we p. not ourselved but Christ Jesus, p. 211, (II Cor. 4:5)

Preached: he p. Christ in the synagogues, p. 193, (Acts 9:20)

the gospel shall be p., p. 173, (Matt. 24:14; Mk. 13:10)

Preacher: how shall they hear without a p.?, p. 202, (Rom. 10:14)

Preaching: p. in their synagogues, p. 137, (Matt. 4:23; Mk. 1:39; Lk. 4:44)

p. the kingdom of God, p. 198, (Acts 28:31)

Saul's first p., p. 193, (Acts 9:20–25)

then is our p. vain, p. 209, (I Cor. 15:14)

went everywhere p. the word, p. 191, (Acts 8:4)

Precept: p. upon p., line upon line, p. 88, (Isa. 28:10)

Prediction: p. of the destruction of Jerusalem, p. 169, (Lk. 19:41–44)

p. of the destruction of the temple, p. 172, (Matt. 24:1–2; Mk. 13:1–2; Lk. 21:5–6)

Prepare: go before . . . to p. his ways, p. 132, (Lk. 1:76)

go to p. a place for you, p. 178, (Jn. 14:2)

he shall p. the way, p. 127, (Mal. 3:1)

p. to meet thy God, p. 118, (Amos 4:12)

p. ye the way, p. 91, (Isa. 40:3)

p. ye the way of the Lord, p. 135, (Matt. 3:3; Mk. 1:3; Lk. 3:4)

who shall p. thy way, p. 148, (Matt. 11:10; Lk. 7:27)

Presentation: p. of Jesus in the temple, p. 133, (Lk. 2:22–39)

Preserve: the Lord shall p. thy going out . . . , p. 66, (Ps. 121:8)

Price: her p. is far above rubies, p. 73, (Prov. 31:10)

weighed for my p. thirty pieces, p. 126, (Zech. 11:12)

Pride: I know thy p., p. 33, (I Sam. 17:28)

p. goeth before destruction, p. 71, (Prov. 16:18)

the p. of thine heart hath deceived thee, p. 119, (Obad. v. 3)

the rod hath blossomed, p. hath budded, p. 107, (Ezek. 7:10)

Priest: a p. . . . after the order of Melchizedek, p. 230, (Heb. 5:6)

like people, like p., p. 115, (Hos. 4:9)

the high p. and Sadducees, p. 190, (Acts 5:17)

so with the p., p. 87, (Isa. 24:2)

Priests: hear this O p., p. 115, (Hos. 5:1)

her p. have polluted the sanctuary, p. 125, (Zeph. 3:4)

let the p. weep between the porch and the altar, p. 117, (Joel 2:17)

p. and scribes sought how to kill him, p. 176, (Matt. 26:3–4; Mk. 14:1; Lk. 22:2)

Prince: a p. fallen this day in Israel, p. 34, (II Sam. 3:38)

by the p. of devils, p. 145, (Matt. 9:34)

everlasting Father, the P. of Peace, p. 84, (Isa. 9:6)

Princes: lamentation for the p. of Israel, p. 108, (Ezek. 19:1)

p. shall rule in judgment, p. 89, (Isa. 32:1)

Principalities: against p., powers, rulers of the darkness, p. 218, (Eph. 6:12)

nor angels, nor p. . . . , p. 202, (Rom. 8:38)

thrones, dominions, p. or powers, p. 220, (Col. 1:16)

Prison: committing men and women to p., p. 191, (Acts 8:3)

John in p., p. 148, (Matt. 11:2; Lk. 7:18–23)

John in p. for Herodias' sake, p. 158, (Matt. 14:3; Mk. 6:17)

Joseph was put into p., p. 12, (Gen. 39:20)

opened the p. doors, p. 191, (Acts 5:19)

Paul and Silas in p., p. 195, (Acts 16:19–40)

Peter freed from p. by an angel, p. 194, (Acts 12:1–19)

put them in the common p., p. 190, (Acts 5:18)

ready to go with thee into p. and to death, p. 179, (Lk. 22:33)

the apostles in p., p. 190, (Acts 5:12–18)

the escape from p., p. 191, (Acts 5:19–42)

the men you put in p. are teaching, p. 191, (Acts 5:25)

Prisoner: a notable p. called Barabbas, p. 182, (Matt. 27:16; Mk. 15:7)

Paul, a p. of Jesus Christ, p. 227, (Philem. v. 1)

Paul, the p. of Jesus Christ, p. 216, (Eph. 3:1)

the governor was wont to release a p., p. 182, (Matt. 27:15; Mk. 15:6; Lk. 23:16–17; Jn. 18:39)

Prisoners: to bring out p. from prison, p. 93, (Isa. 42:7)

ye p. of hope, p. 126, (Zech. 9:12)

Prize: but one receiveth the p., p. 207, (I Cor. 9:24)

Proclaim: p. liberty to the captives, p. 95, (Isa. 61:1)

p. the acceptable year, p. 95, (Isa. 61:2)

Prodigal: the p. son, p. 152, (Lk. 15:11–24)

the p. son's brother, p. 152, (Lk. 15:25–32)

Profane: p. and old wives' fables, p. 225, (I Tim. 4:7)

shun p. and vain babblings, p. 226, (II Tim. 2:16)

Profit: what p. hath a man of all his labor, p. 74, (Ec. 1:3)

what shall it p.?, p. 147, (Matt. 16:26; Mk. 8:36; Lk. 9:25)

Promise: p. of Israel's return, p. 102, (Jer. 29–30)

Promise: (continued)

p. made by God to our fathers, p. 197, (Acts 26:6)

the p. of the Spirit in our hearts, p. 210, (II Cor. 1:22)

Prophecies: Baruch reads the p., p. 102, (Jer. 36—38)

Prophecy: fulfilling the p.: Rachel weeping . . . , p. 134, (Matt. 2:17–18)

Habakkuk's p., p. 123, (Hab. 2:2–12)

Micaiah's p., p. 41, (I Kg. 22:1–40; II Chr. 18)

p.: He shall be called a Nazarene, p. 134, (Matt. 2:23)

the Messianic p., p. 126, (Zech. 9:9–12)

Prophesies: Elijah p. to Ahab, p. 41, (I Kg. 21:17–25)

he that p. speaks to men, p. 209, (I Cor. 14:3)

Jeremiah p. to Zedekiah, p. 101, (Jer. 21)

Prophesy: commanded the prophets saying: P. not, p., 118, (Amos 2:12)

know in part and p. in part, p. 208, (I Cor. 13:9)

P.! Who is it that struck you?, p. 181, (Matt. 26:68; Mk. 14:65; Lk. 22:64)

sons and daughters shall p., p. 117, (Joel 2:28)

your sons and your daughters shall p., p. 189, (Acts 2:17)

Prophet: a great p. has risen, p. 155, (Lk. 7:16)

a p. perish out of Jerusalem, p. 169, (Lk. 13:33)

a p. unto the nations, p. 99, (Jer. 1:5)

call to be God's p., p. 99, (Jer. 1)

I will send you Elijah the p., p. 127, (Mal. 4:5)

not a p. . . . like unto Moses, p. 21, (Deut. 34:10)

people said: This is the P., p. 160, (Jn. 7:40)

p. is not without honor, p. 157, (Matt. 13:57; Mk. 6:4; Lk. 4:24; Jn. 4:44)

shall be called the p. of the Highest, p. 132, (Lk. 1:76)

shall know a p. has been among them, p. 106, (Ezek. 2:5)

to see a p., p. 148, (Matt. 11:9; Lk. 7:26)

Prophetess: Anna, a p., gave thanks, p. 133, (Lk. 2:36, 38)

Deborah, a p., was judge, p. 28, (Jg. 4:4)

Prophets: against false p., p. 101, (Jer. 23)

all the law and the p., p. 172, (Matt. 22:40)

beware of false p., p. 142, (Matt. 7:15)

Elijah and the p. of Baal, p. 40, (I Kg. 18:17–40)

her p. also find no vision, p. 104, (Lam. 2:9)

her p. are light and treacherous, p. 125, (Zeph. 3:4)

I have not sent these p., p. 101, (Jer. 23:21)

is Saul also among the p.?, p. 32, (I Sam. 10:11)

Jezebel slew the p., p. 40, (I Kg. 18:4)

many false p. shall arise, p. 173, (Matt. 24:11)

neither have we hearkened unto the p., p. 113, (Dan. 9:6)

p. of the deceit, p. 101, (Jer. 23:26)

p. . . . that steal my words, p. 101, (Jer. 23:30)

raised up of your sons for p., p. 118, (Amos 2:11)

sent the p. of Baal to Mount Carmel, p. 40, (I Kg. 18:20)

some apostles, some p. . . . , p. 216, (Eph. 4:11)

spake . . . unto the fathers by the p., p. 228, (Heb. 1:1)

the p., do they live forever?, p. 125, (Zech. 1:5)

thou that killest the p., p. 172, (Matt. 23:37; Lk. 13:34)

to destroy the law or the p., p. 139, (Matt. 5:17)

Propitiation: the p. for our sins, p. 238, (I John 2:2)

Prosper: God will p. us, p. 45, (Neh. 2:20)

Prosperity: thy wisdom and p. exceedeth, p. 38, (I Kg. 10:7; II Chr. 9:6)

Protection: they promised p. to her, p. 27, (Josh. 2:18, 19)

370

Proud: God resisteth the p., p. 234, (Jas. 4:6)

Prove: p. thy servants I beseech thee, p. 110, (Dan. 1:12)

Proverb: a p. and a byword, p. 38, (I Kg. 9:7)

become an astonishment, a p., p. 23, (Deut. 28:37)

this p. shall cease, p. 107, (Ezek. 12:22)

Proverbs: three thousand p., p. 38, (I Kg. 4:32)

Provide: p. able men, p. 17, (Ex. 18:21–22)

Provoke: people p. me, p. 19, (Num. 14:11)

Pruninghooks: your p. into spears, p. 117, (Joel 3:10)

Psalm: David's p. of thanksgiving, p. 35, (I Chr. 16:8–36)

Psalmist: sweet p. of Israel, p. 36, (II Sam. 23:1)

Psalms: in p. and hymns and spiritual songs, p. 217, (Eph. 5:19)

Psaltery: and upon the p., p. 63, (Ps. 92:3)

Ptolemais: Paul travels via P., p. 196, (Acts 21:7)

Publican: parable of the p. and the Pharisee, p. 154, (Lk. 18:9–14)

Publicans: friend of p. and sinners, p. 148, (Matt. 11:19; Lk. 7:34)

Pulse: p. to eat and water to drink, p. 110, (Dan. 1:12)

Punish: I will p. the king of Babylon, p. 103, (Jer. 50:18)

p. the men that say in their heart, p. 124, (Zeph. 1:12)

p. you according to the fruit, p. 101, (Jer. 21:14)

therefore I will p. you, p. 118, (Amos 3:2)

Punished: p. the king of Assyria, p. 103, (Jer. 50:18)

Punishment: the p. is more than I can bear, p. 5, (Gen. 4:13)

Purchased: thought the gift of God may be p., p. 192, (Acts 8:20)

Pure: clean hands, and a p. heart, p. 57, (Ps. 24:4)

unto the p. all things are p., p. 227, (Tit. 1:15)

Pureness: by p., by knowledge, by long suffering, p. 211, (II Cor. 6:6)

Purge: p. me with hyssop, p. 60, (Ps. 51:7)

Purim: the feast of P., p. 46, (Est. 9)

these days of P. should not fail, p. 46, (Est. 9:28)

Purpose: to what p. are your sacrifices, p. 81, (Isa. 1:11)

Purposes: my p. are broken off, p. 52, (Job 17:11)

Pursuing: either he is talking, or he is p. . . . , p. 40, (I Kg. 18:27)

Puteoli: Paul sails via P. (Italy), p. 198, (Acts 28:13)

Quails: at even the q. came, p. 17, (Ex. 16:13; Num. 11:31)

Queen: Athaliah, Q. of Judah, p. 43, (II Kg. 11:1–20; II Chr. 22:10—23:21)

Esther: a Jewish Q. of Persia, p. 46, (Est. 1—2:1–18)

Q. Athaliah was slain, p. 43, (II Kg. 11:20; II Chr. 23:21)

Q. of Sheba came to test Solomon, p. 38, (Kg. 10:1; II Chr. 9:1)

Solomon and the Q. of Sheba, p. 38, (I Kg. 10:1–23; II Chr. 9:1–22)

the king dethroned Q. Vashti, p. 46, (Est. 1:19–21)

Quickened: q. us together with Christ, p. 215, (Eph. 2:5)

Quickly: that thou doest, do q., p. 177, (Jn. 13:27)

Quiet: a q. and peaceable life, p. 224, (I Tim. 2:2)

to be q. and to do your own business, p. 222, (I Th. 4:11)

Quietness: better is an handful with q., p. 74, (Ec. 4:6)

in q. and in confidence, p. 89, (Isa. 30:15)

Quit: q. yourselves like men, p. 32, (I Sam. 4:9)

Quiver: that hath his q. full of them, p. 67, (Ps. 127:5)

Raamses: treasure cities, Pithom and R., p. 13, (Ex. 1:11)

Rabbi: R., thou art the son of God, p. 137, (Jn. 1:49)

Rabboni: she turned and said: R!, p. 184, (Jn. 20:16)

Race: the r. is not to the swift, p. 76, (Ec. 9:11)

Race: (continued)

the r. that is set before us, p. 231, (Heb. 12:1)

Rachel: did I not serve for R?, p. 11, (Gen. 29:25)

Jacob loved R. and served seven years, p. 11, (Gen. 29:18, 20)

Jacob told R. he was Rebekah's son, p. 11, (Gen. 29:12)

R. came to the well, p. 11, (Gen. 29:6)

R. weeping for her children, pp. 102, 134, (Jer. 31:15; Matt. 2:17–18)

serve another seven years for R., p. 11, (Gen. 29:27, 28)

Rage: why do the heathen r., p. 55, (Ps. 2:1)

Rags: our righteousnesses are as filthy r., p. 96, (Isa. 64:6)

Rahab: a harlot named R., p. 27, (Josh. 2:1)

Joshua saved, R., the harlot, p. 27, (Josh. 6:25)

R. and the spies, p. 27, (Josh. 2)

Rain: and the r. descended, p. 143, (Matt. 7:27; cf. Lk. 6:49)

as the latter and the former r., p. 115, (Hos. 6:3)

Elijah prayed for r., p. 40, (I Kg. 18:41–46)

hath the r. a father?, p. 54, (Job 38:28)

r. on the just and on the unjust, p. 140, (Matt. 5:45)

r. was upon the earth, p. 6, (Gen. 7:12)

that the r. stop thee not, p. 40, (I Kg. 18:44)

the heaven was black and there was a great r., p. 40, (I Kg. 18:45)

the r. descended, p. 143, (Matt. 7:25; cf. Lk. 6:48)

the r. is over and gone, p. 77, (Song 2:11)

waited for me as for the r., p. 54, (Job 29:23)

Rainbow: a r. about the throne, p. 242, (Rev. 4:3)

The r.: God's covenant, p. 7, (Gen. 8:21–9:17)

Raise: in the third day he will r. us up, p. 115, (Hos. 6:2)

r. the dead, p. 146, (Matt. 10:8)

will r. unto David a righteous branch, p. 101, (Jer. 23:5)

Raised: how are the dead r. up., p. 209, (I Cor. 15:35)

if Christ be not r., p. 209, (I Cor. 15:17)

the third day he shall be r., p. 161, (Matt. 17:23; 20:19; Mk. 8:31; 9:31; 10:34; Lk. 9:22; 18:33)

this Jesus hath God r., p. 190, (Acts 2:32)

trumpet sound and the dead be r., p. 210, (I Cor. 15:52)

Ram: Abraham beheld a r. in the thicket, p. 9, (Gen. 22:13)

Daniel saw a r. with two horns, p. 112, (Dan. 8:3)

the r. are the kings of Media and Persia, p. 112, (Dan. 8:20)

the vision of the r. and the goat, p. 112, (Dan. 8)

Ramah: a voice was heard in R., p. 102, (Jer. 31:15)

Ramoth-gilead: shall I go against R?, p. 41, (I Kg. 22:6; II Chr. 18:5)

Rams: the mountains skipped like r., p. 65, (Ps. 114:4)

Ran: and r. before Ahab, p. 41, (I Kg. 18:46)

Ransom: r. them from the . . . grave, p. 116, (Hos. 13:14)

to give his life a r. for many, p. 165, (Matt. 20:28; Mk. 10:45)

who gave himself a r. for all, p. 224, (I Tim. 2:6)

Ransomed: r. of the Lord shall return, p. 90, (Isa. 35:10)

Rash: be not r. with thy mouth, p. 75, (Ec. 5:2)

Ravens: Elijah fed by r., p. 39, (I Kg. 17:2–7)

the r. to feed thee, p. 39, (I Kg. 17:4)

Read: the wise men could not r. the writing, p. 111, (Dan. 5:8)

Readeth: that he may run that r. it, p. 123, (Hab. 2:2)

Reads: Baruch r. the prophecies, p. 102, (Jer. 36—38)

Reason: let us r. together, p. 81, (Isa. 1:18)

Rebekah: found R. at the well, p. 9, (Gen. 24:15–16)

Isaac took R., she became his wife, p. 9, (Gen. 24:67)

Jacob told Rachel he was R.'s son, p. 11, (Gen. 29:12)

R. disguised Jacob, p. 10, (Gen. 27:15)

R. gives birth, p. 10, (Gen. 25:21–26)

R. told Jacob to flee, p. 10, (Gen. 27:42, 43)

Rebelled: they have r. against me, p. 81, (Isa. 1:2)

Rebellious: a revolting and a r. heart, p. 99, (Jer. 5:23)

a stubborn and r. generation, p. 62, (Ps. 78:8)

that this is a r. people, p. 89, (Isa. 30:9)

woe to the r. children, p. 89, (Isa. 30:8–9)

Rebuilding: r. of the temple, p. 46, (Ezra 3—6)

r. the walls of Jerusalem, p. 46, (Neh. 3—6; 12:27–47)

Rebuke: God shall r. them, p. 86, (Isa. 17:13)

Rebukes: God r. the friends, p. 55, (Job 42:7–17)

Receive: shall r. an hundredfold, p. 164, (Matt. 19:29; Mk. 10:30; Lk. 18:30)

Received: As ye have r. Christ Jesus, p. 220, (Col. 2:6)

freely ye have r., p. 146, (Matt. 10:8)

Receives: he that r. me, p. 147, (Matt. 10:40)

Recompense: r. thee according to thy ways, p. 107, (Ezek. 7:9)

Reconciled: be r. to thy brother, p. 139, (Matt. 5:24)

r. us to himself by Christ, p. 211, (II Cor. 5:18)

Reconciliation: anger and r., p. 139, (Matt. 5:21–26)

to make r. for the sins, p. 229, (Heb. 2:17)

Reconciling: God was in Christ, r. the world, p. 211, (II Cor. 5:19)

Red Sea: crossing the R. Sea, p. 16, (Ex. 14)

Redeem: to r. them that were under the law, p. 214, (Gal. 4:5)

will r. them from death, p. 116, (Hos. 13:14)

Redeemed: hast r. us to God, p. 242, (Rev. 5:9)

these were r. from among men, p. 245, (Rev. 14:4)

Redeemer: know that my r. liveth, p. 52, (Job 19:25)

their r. is strong, p. 103, (Jer. 50:34)

Reed: a bruised. r., p. 93, (Isa. 42:3)

a r. shaken with the wind, p. 148, (Matt. 11:7, Lk. 7:24)

trusteth in the staff of this broken r., p. 90, (Isa. 36:6)

Reeds: laid it in the r. by the river's brink, p. 13, (Ex. 2:3)

Reel: they r. to and fro, p. 65, (Ps. 107:27)

Refuge: a r. from the storm, p. 87, (Isa. 25:4)

God is our r. and strength, p. 60, (Ps. 46:1)

my r., my Savior, p. 36, (II Sam. 22:3)

the God of Jacob is our r., p. 60, (Ps. 46:11)

Rehoboam: R. succeeded Solomon as King of Judah, p. 39, (I Kg. 12:1, 17; II Chr. 10:17)

Reign: Solomon thy son shall r., p. 37, (I Kg. 1:30)

the r. of Joash of Judah, p. 44, (II Kg. 11:21—12:21; II Chr. 24)

Reins: r. instruct me in the night seasons, p. 56, (Ps. 16:7)

Rejected: despised and r. of men, p. 94, (Isa. 53:3)

Rejoice: be glad and r., p. 117, (Joel 2:21)

let the earth r., p. 64, (Ps. 97:1)

r. evermore, p. 222, (I Th. 5:16)

r. in the Lord alway, p. 219, (Phil 4:4)

r. not against me, O mine enemy, p. 122, (Micah 7:8)

r. with me for I have found the piece, p. 152, (Lk. 15:9)

r. with them that do r., p. 203, (Rom. 12:15)

Rejoiced: r. in God my Saviour, p. 132, (Lk. 1:47)

Rejoicing: shall doubtless come again r., p. 66, (Ps. 126:6)

the r. city that dwelt carelessly, p. 124, (Zeph. 2:15)

Release: Whom will ye that I r. unto you? p. 182, (Matt. 27:17; cf. Mk. 15:9; Lk. 23:20; Jn. 18:39)

Religion: pure r. is to visit the fatherless, p. 233, (Jas. 1:27)

Remember: r. and turn unto the Lord, p. 57, (Ps. 22:27)

Remember: (continued)

r. from whence thou art fallen, p. 240, (Rev. 2:5)

r. me when you come in your kingdom, p. 183, (Lk. 23:42)

r. this day, p. 16, (Ex. 13:3)

r. thy creator in . . . thy youth, p. 76, (Ec. 12:1)

Remembered: when my soul fainted I r. the Lord, p. 120, (Jonah 2:7)

Remembrance: as oft as ye drink it, in r. of me, p. 208, (I Cor. 11:25)

do this in r. of me, p. 177, (Lk. 22:19; I Cor. 11:24, 25)

no r. of former things, p. 74, (Ec. 1:11)

this do in r. of me, p. 208, (I Cor. 11:24)

thy name and r. of thee, p. 88, (Isa. 26:8)

Remnant: glean the r. of Israel, p. 99, (Jer. 6:9)

out of Jerusalem . . . a r., p. 44, (II Kg. 19:31)

r. of the people shall spoil thee, p. 123, (Hab. 2:8)

stirred up the spirit of the r., p. 125, (Hagg. 1:14)

the faithful r., p. 125, (Zeph. 3:12–13)

the Lord had left us a small r., p. 81, (Isa. 1:9)

the r. of Israel, p. 102, (Jer. 31:7)

the whole r. of thee will I scatter, p. 106, (Ezek. 5:10)

Renewal: the r. of the covenant, p. 46, (Neh. 8—10)

Rent: r. his clothes, p. 46, (Est. 4:1)

Repay: they cannot r. you, p. 151, (Lk. 14:14)

Repent: hath sworn, and will not r., p. 65, (Ps. 110:4)

r. ye for the kingdom of heaven, p. 135, (Matt. 3:2)

Repented: but afterwards he r., p. 170, (Matt. 21:29)

God r. of the evil, p. 121, (Jonah 3:10)

Israelites solemnly r., p. 32, (I Sam. 7:6)

It r. the Lord, p. 6, (Gen. 6:6)

Repenteth: one sinner that r., p. 162, (Lk. 15:7)

r. him the evil, p. 117, (Joel 12:13)

Repenting: I am weary with r., p. 100, (Jer. 15:6)

Require: what doth the Lord r. of thee? p. 122, (Micah 6:8)

Rescue: r. my soul from destructions, p. 58, (Ps. 35:17)

Resist: r. not evil, p. 140, (Matt. 5:39)

r. the devil and he will flee, p. 234, (Jas. 4:7)

Respect: no r. of persons with God, p. 200, (Rom. 2:11)

Rest: do enter into r., p. 229, (Heb. 4:3)

God did r. the seventh day, p. 229, (Heb. 4:4)

in returning and r. shall ye be saved, p. 89, (Isa. 30:15)

labor to enter into that r., p. 229, (Heb. 4:11)

may r. from their labors, p. 245, (Rev. 14:13)

r. in the Lord, p. 149, (Matt. 11:28–30)

the earth sitteth still and is at r., p. 125, (Zech. 1:11)

Rested: God r. on the seventh day, p. 4, (Gen. 2:2)

Restoration: the r. of Israel, p. 102, (Jer. 31:1–30)

Restores: r. Job's fortune, p. 55, (Job. 42:7–17)

Restoreth: he r. my soul, p. 57, (Ps. 23:3)

Resurrection: concerning r., p. 209, (I Cor. 15:1–26)

concerning the r., p. 171, (Matt. 22:23–33; Mk. 12:18–27; Lk. 20:27–40)

I am the r. and the life, p. 169, (Jn. 11:25)

witness of the r., p. 190, (Acts 4:33)

Return: he shall not r. to me, p. 36, (II Sam. 12:23)

let us r. unto the Lord, p. 115, (Hos. 6:1)

r., r., O Shulamite, p. 78, (Song 6:13)

r. to Jerusalem, p. 45, (Ezra 2, 7—10; Neh. 1, 2, 7:6–73)

Returned: r. to Israel and dwelt in Nazareth, p. 134, (Matt. 2:21, 23)

Returning: in r. and rest shall ye be saved, p. 89, (Isa. 30:15)

Reuben: R. . . . unstable as water, p. 13, (Gen. 49:3–4)

Revealed: r. them unto babes, p. 148, (Matt. 11:25; Lk. 10:21)

r. them unto us by his Spirit, p. 205, (I Cor. 2:10)

Revelation: by the r. of Jesus Christ, p. 214, (Gal. 1:12)

Revenge: Samson's r. on the Philistines, p. 30, (Jg. 15)

Revive: O Lord r. thy work, p. 124, (Hab. 3:2)

Revolting: a r. and a rebellious heart, p. 99, (Jer. 5:23)

Reward: great is your r. in heaven, p. 138, (Matt. 5:12; Lk. 6:23)

r. him according to his works, p. 227, (II Tim. 4:14)

thy r. shall return upon thine own head, p. 119, (Obad. v. 15)

Rhegium (Italy): Paul sails via R. (I.), p. 198, (Acts 28:13)

Rhodes: Paul travels via R., p. 196, (Acts 21:1)

Rich: a r. man had no room to store his crops, p. 150, (Lk. 12:16–17)

a r. tax collector named Zacchaeus, p. 154, (Lk. 19:2)

be r. in good works, p. 225, (I Tim. 6:18)

hard for a r. man to enter the kingdom, p. 164, (Matt. 19:23; Mk. 10:23–24; Lk. 18:24)

Lazarus and the r. man, p. 152, (Lk. 16:19–31)

maketh haste to be r., p. 73, (Prov. 28:20)

r. in family and possessions, p. 49, (Job 1:1–3)

the parable of the r. fool, p. 50, (Lk. 12:13–21)

the r. man took the poor man's lamb, p. 35, (II Sam. 12:4)

the r. young man, p. 163, (Matt. 19:16–22; Mk. 10:17–22; Lk. 18:18–24)

they that will be r. . . . , p. 225, (I Tim. 6:9)

two men, one r., one poor, p. 35, (II Sam. 12:1)

you r. men weep and howl, p. 235, (Jas. 5:1)

Riches: a good name . . . than great r., p. 72, (Prov. 22:1)

he heapeth up r. . . . , p. 59, (Ps. 39:6)

he that trusteth in his r., p. 70, (Prov. 11:28)

Solomon's r. and wisdom, p. 38, (I Kg. 4:25–34)

the earth is full of thy r., p. 65, (Ps. 104:24)

the unsearchable r. of Christ, p. 216, (Eph. 3:8)

your r. are corrupted, p. 235, (Jas. 5:2)

Riddle: Samson's r., p. 30, (Jg. 14:5–19)

Right: one on thy r. hand . . . , p. 164, (Matt. 20:21; Mk. 10:37)

sit thou at my r. hand, p. 65, (Ps. 110:1)

that which was r. in his own eyes, p. 31, (Jg. 21:25)

the r. hand of the Majesty on high, p. 228, (Heb. 1:3)

thy r. hand . . . is become glorious, p. 16, (Ex. 15:6)

Righteous: be not r. over much, p. 75, (Ec. 7:16)

destroy the r. with the wicked, p. 9, (Gen. 18:23)

die the death of the r., p. 20, (Num. 23:10)

not to call the r. but sinners, p. 145, (Matt. 9:13; Mk. 2:17; Lk. 5:32)

will raise unto David a r. branch, p. 101, (Jer. 23:5)

Righteousness: a king shall reign in r., p. 89, (Isa. 32:1)

called thee in r., p. 93, (Isa. 42:6)

created in r. and holiness, p. 217, (Eph. 4:24)

fine linen of the r. of saints, p. 246, (Rev. 19:8)

for r., but behold a cry, p. 83, (Isa. 5:7)

his name . . . THE LORD OUR R., p. 101, (Jer. 23:6)

r. and peace have kissed, p. 62, (Ps. 85:10)

r. as a mighty stream, p. 119, (Amos, 5:24)

r. as the waves of the sea, p. 93, (Isa. 48:18)

the Lord hath brought forth our r., p. 103, (Jer. 51:10)

Righteousness: *(continued)*

the Sun of r. shall arise, p. 127, (Mal. 4:2)

with r. shall he judge the poor, p. 85, (Isa. 11:4)

Righteousnesses: our r. are as filthy rags, p. 96, (Isa. 64:6)

Riotous: with r. living, p. 152, (Lk. 15:13)

Rise: dead in Christ shall r. first, p. 222, (I Th. 4:16)

r. from the dead, p. 197, (Acts 26:23)

thy brother shall r. again, p. 168, (Jn. 11:23)

Risen: after I am r., p. 179, (Matt. 26:32; Mk. 14:28)

if Christ be not r., p. 209, (I Cor. 15:14)

tell his disciples that he is r., p. 183, (Matt. 28:7; Mk. 16:6–7)

the Lord is r. indeed!, p. 184, (Lk. 24:34)

River: reeds by the r.'s brink, p. 13, (Ex. 2:3)

there is a r., the streams whereof, p. 60, (Ps. 46:4)

thy peace been as a r., p. 93, (Isa. 48:18)

Rivers: all the r. run into the sea, p. 74, (Ec. 1:7)

r. of Egypt turned to blood, p. 15, (Ex. 7:20)

r. of water in a dry place, p. 89, (Isa. 32:2)

Roaring: our adversary the devil as a r. lion, p. 237, (I Pet. 5:8)

Robbers: become a den of r., p. 100, (Jer. 7:11)

Robe: stripped him and put on a purple r., p. 182, (Mk. 15:17; Jn. 19:2; cf. Matt. 27:28)

Rock: a stone of stumbling and a r. of offence, p. 84, (Isa. 8:14)

enter into the r., p. 82, (Isa. 2:10)

he is the R., p. 21, (Deut. 32:4)

his house upon a r., p. 143, (Matt. 7:24; Lk. 6:48)

my r. and my salvation, p. 61, (Ps. 62:6)

put me in a crack of the r., p. 18, (Ex. 33:22)

set my feet upon a r., p. 59, (Ps. 40:2)

the r. that is higher than I, p. 61, (Ps. 61:2)

the shadow of a great r., p. 89, (Isa. 32:2)

upon this r. I will build my church, p. 160, (Matt. 16:18)

Rod: a r. out of the stem of Jesse, p. 84, (Isa. 11:1)

he that spareth his r., p. 71, (Prov. 13:24)

lift up thy r. and divide the sea, p. 16, (Ex. 14:16)

O Assyrian, the r. of mine anger, p. 84, (Isa. 10:5)

r. became a serpent, p. 15, (Ex. 7:10)

r. hath blossomed, pride hath budded, p. 107, (Ezek. 7:10)

Roe: be thou like to a r., p. 78, (Song 8:14)

Roes: two breasts are like two young r., p. 77, (Song 4:5)

Roll: take thee another r., p. 103, (Jer. 36:28)

Rolling: a r. thing before the whirlwind, p. 86, (Isa. 17:13)

Romans: the R. beat Paul and Silas, p. 195, (Acts 16:23)

Rome: Paul in R., p. 198, (Acts 28:16–31)

Paul's letter to R., p. 199, (Rom.)

Paul sails from Jerusalem to R., p. 198, (Acts 27—28)

to all that be in R., p. 199, (Rom. 1:7)

Roof: through the r. on his bed, p. 144, (Mk. 2:4; Lk. 5:19)

Room: no r. to store his crops, p. 150, (Lk. 12:16–17)

Root: the r. of the matter is found in me, p. 52, (Job 19:28)

Rooted: being r. and grounded in love, p. 216, (Eph. 3:17)

Rose: and blossom as the r., p. 90, (Isa. 35:1)

he r. again the third day, p. 209, (I Cor. 15:4)

I am the r. of Sharon, p. 77, (Song 2:1)

Jesus died and r. again, p. 222, (I Th. 4:14)

Rosh Hashanah: 21, (Lev. 23:23–25; Num. 29:1–6)

Royal: a chosen generation, a r. priesthood, p. 236, (I Pet. 2:9)

Rubies: her price is far above r., p. 73, (Prov. 31:10)

price of wisdom is above r., p. 53, (Job 28:18)

wisdom is better than r., p. 70, (Prov. 8:11)

Rude: though I be r. in speech, p. 212, (II Cor. 11:6)

Rule: a man know not how to r. his own house, p. 224, (I Tim. 3:5)

r. them with a rod of iron, p. 241, (Rev. 2:27)

Ruler: Bethlehem out of thee . . . one who is to be the r. in Israel, p. 122, (Micah 5:2)

Rulers: as r. and judges, p. 17, (Ex. 18:21–22)

Ruleth: r. well his own house, p. 224, (I Tim. 3:4)

Run: many shall r. to and fro, p. 114, (Dan. 12:4)

r. and not be weary, p. 92, (Isa. 40:31)

that he may r. that readeth it, p. 123, (Hab. 2:2)

they which r. in a race, run all, p. 207, (I Cor. 9:24)

Rushing: the r. of many waters, p. 86, (Isa. 17:13)

Ruth: Boaz took R., p. 31, (Ruth 4:13)

R. and Naomi, p. 31, (Ruth)

R. bore a son, Obed, p. 31, (Ruth 4:13, 17)

R. gleaned in the field of Boaz, p. 31, (Ruth 2:3)

Sabbath: ears of corn on the s., p. 149, (Matt. 12:1–8; Mk. 2:23–28; Lk. 6:1–5)

is it lawful to heal on the s., p. 149, (Matt. 12:10; Mk. 3:4; Lk. 6:9)

not lawful on the s., p. 149, (Matt. 12:2; Mk. 2:24; Lk. 6:2)

the s., p. 19, (Gen. 2:3; Ex. 20:8–11; 23:12; Lev. 23:3; Deut. 5:15)

the s., to keep it holy, p. 18, (Ex. 20:8–11)

the s. was made for man, p. 149, (Mk. 2:27)

to slay Jesus for healing on the s., p. 167, (Jn. 5:16)

Sackcloth: gird themselves with s., p. 107, (Ezek. 7:18)

put on s. with ashes, p. 46, (Est. 4:1)

Sacrifice: an offering and s. to God, p. 217, (Eph. 5:2)

I desired mercy and not s., p. 115, (Hos. 6:6)

laws concerning s., p. 18, (Lev. 1—7)

present your bodies a living s., p. 203, (Rom. 12:1)

the s. of Isaac, p. 9, (Gen. 22:1–18)

Sacrifices: to what purpose are your s., p. 81, (Isa. 1:11)

with such s. God is well pleased, p. 232, (Heb. 13:16)

Sadducees: the high priest and S., p. 190, (Acts 5:17)

Safely: Judah and Israel dwelt s., p. 38, (I Kg. 4:25)

Safety: multitude of counsellors there is s., p. 70, (Prov. 11:14)

Saints: beloved of God, called to be s., p. 199, (Rom. 1:7)

fine linen of the righteousness of s., p. 246, (Rev. 19:8)

power to make war with the s., p. 245, (Rev. 13:7)

the death of his s., p. 66, (Ps. 116:15)

the perfecting of the s., p. 216, (Eph. 4:12)

the s. which are at Ephesus, p. 215, (Eph. 1:1)

Salt: became a pillar of s., p. 9, (Gen. 19:26)

if the s. has lost its savor, p. 138, (Matt. 5:13; Mk. 9:50, Lk. 14:34)

the s. of the earth, p. 138, (Matt. 5:13)

Salvation: God has . . . chosen you to s., p. 222, (II Th. 2:13)

he is become my s., p. 16, (Ex. 15:2)

he is just and having s., p. 126, (Zech. 9:9)

how shall we escape if we neglect so great s., p. 228, (Heb. 2:3)

I will joy in the God of my s., p. 124, (Hab. 3:18)

I will take the cup of s., p. 66, (Ps. 116:13)

mine eyes have seen thy s., p. 133, (Lk. 2:30)

my rock and my s., p. 61, (Ps. 62:6)

now is come s. and strength, p. 245, (Rev. 12:10)

now is the day of s., p. 211, (II Cor. 6:2)

Salvation: *(continued)*

s. to every one that believeth, p. 199, (Rom. 1:16)

the Lord is my light and my s., p. 58, (Ps. 27:1)

this day is s. come to this house, p. 154, (Lk. 19:9)

wait for the God of my s., p. 122, (Micah 7:7)

work out your own s., p. 219, (Phil. 2:12)

Samaria: S. falls to Assyria, p. 44, (II Kg. 17)

Samaritan: a S. had compassion, p. 150, (Lk. 10:33)

Jesus and the S. woman, p. 166, (Jn. 4:5–42)

the good S., p. 149, (Lk. 10:29–37)

Same: the s. yesterday, today and for ever, p. 232, (Heb. 13:8)

Samos: Paul travels via S., p. 196, (Acts 20:15)

Samothrace: via S. and Neapolis, p. 195, (Acts 16:11)

Samson: S. and Delilah, p. 30, (Jg. 16)

S. burned the corn and vineyards, p. 30, (Jg. 15:5)

S. grasped the two pillars of the house, p. 30, (Jg. 16:29–30)

S.'s revenge on the Philistines, p. 30, (Jg. 15)

S.'s riddle, p. 30, (Jg. 14:5–19)

the birth of S., p. 30, (Jg. 13:2-25)

the Philistines be upon thee, S., p. 30, (Jg. 16:20)

Samuel: bore a son and named him S., p. 31, (I Sam. 1:20)

Eli and S., p. 31, (I Sam. 2:11–26; 3:1–20)

he sent S. to Jesse, p. 33, (I Sam. 16:1)

Israel asked S. for a king, p. 32, (I Sam. 8)

S. anointed David, p. 33, (I Sam. 16:13)

S. grew in the presence of the Lord, p. 31, (I Sam. 2:21)

S. judged Israel, p. 32, (I Sam. 7:15)

Saul anointed king by S., p. 32, (I Sam. 9—10)

seven sons pass before S., p. 33, (I Sam. 16:10)

the Lord called S., p. 31, (I Sam. 3:4)

word of S. came to all Israel, p. 32, (I Sam. 4:1)

Sanctification: through s. of the Spirit, p. 222, (II Th. 2:13)

Sanctified: s. through . . . the body of Christ, p. 231, (Heb. 10:10)

Sanctify: God of peace s. you wholly, p. 222, (I Th. 5:23)

s. . . . all the first-born, p. 16, (Ex. 13:2)

Sanctuary: her priests have polluted the s., p. 125, (Zeph. 3:4)

the Lord shall be a s., p. 84, (Isa. 8:14)

Sand: as the s. of the sea, p. 12, (Gen. 41:49)

built his house on the s., p. 143, (Matt. 7:26; cf. Lk. 6:49)

the s. which is by the sea, p. 38, (I Kg. 4:20)

Sapphira: Ananias and S., p. 190, (Acts 5:1–11)

Sarah: Also see Sarai

S. bare Abraham a son, p. 9, (Gen. 21:7)

S. laughed within herself, p. 8, (Gen. 18:12)

S. shall be her name, p. 8, (Gen. 17:15)

S. shall bear thee a son . . . Isaac, p. 8, (Gen. 17:19)

Sarai: Also see Sarah

Abram pretended S. was his sister, p. 7, (Gen. 12:13)

S. bare Abram no children, p. 8, (Gen. 16:1)

S. gave Hagar her maid to Abram, p. 8, (Gen. 16:1–2)

Sardis: to the church in S., p. 241, (Rev. 3:1–6)

Satan: forty days tempted by S., p. 135, (Matt. 4:1–2; Mk. 1:13; Lk. 4:2)

get thee behind me, S.!, p. 160, (Matt. 16:23; Mk. 8:33)

get thee hence, S., p. 136, (Matt. 4:20; Lk. 4:8)

if S. also is divided, p. 146, (Matt. 12:26; Mk. 3:26; Lk. 11:18)

S.'s challenge, p. 49, (Job 1:16–12)

S. smote Job with sore boils, p. 49, (Job 2:7)

S. tests Job, p. 49, (Job 2:1–10)

S. transformed into an angel, p. 212, (II Cor. 11:14)

S., Whence comest thou?, p. 49, (Job 1:7)

S. which deceiveth the whole world, p. 244, (Rev. 12:9)

Saul: an Amelekite took S.'s crown to David, p. 34, (II Sam. 1:10)

David's lament . . . S. and Jonathan, p. 34, (II Sam. 1:17–27)

David's music helped S., p. 33, (I Sam. 16:23)

evil spirit troubled King S., p. 33, (I Sam. 16:14–23)

is S. also among the prophets?, p. 32, (I Sam. 10:11)

laid their clothes at S.'s feet, p. 191, (Acts 7:58)

Lord repented making S. king, p. 33, (I Sam. 16:1–13)

one called S. to restore his sight, p. 192, (Acts 9:11, 12)

S. and Ananias, p. 192, (Acts 9:10–18)

S. and the disciples in Jerusalem, p. 192, (Acts 9:26–31)

S. and the witch of Endor, p. 34, (I Sam. 28)

S. anointed king by Samuel, p. 32, (I Sam. 9–10)

S.'s first preaching, p. 193, (Acts 9:20–25)

S. hath slain his thousands, p. 34, (I Sam. 18:7)

S., jealous of David, p. 34, (I Sam. 18—23)

S. made havoc of the church, p. 191, (Acts 8:3)

S. took a sword and fell on it, p. 34, (I Sam. 31:4; I Chr. 10:4)

S., S., why persecutest thou me?, p. 192, (Acts 9:4)

S., yet breathing out threatenings, p. 192, (Acts 9:1)

saved David from S.'s anger, p. 34, (I Sam. 19—20)

the conversion of S., p. 192, (Acts 9:1–9; cf. 22:6–11; 26:12–18)

the death of King S., p. 34, (I Sam. 31; II Sam. 1; I Chr. 10)

Save: Father s. me from this hour, p. 176, (Jn. 12:27)

Lord, s. thy people, p. 102, (Jer. 31:7)

O Lord our God, s. us from his hand, p. 90, (Isa. 37:20)

s. yourself and us, p. 183, (Lk. 23:39)

to s. that which was lost, p. 154, (Lk. 19:10)

Saved: by grace are ye s. through faith, p. 215, (Eph. 1:8)

endure unto the end shall be s., p. 173, (Matt. 24:13; Mk. 13:13)

harvest is past . . . and we are not s., p. 100, (Jer. 8:20)

in returning and rest shall ye be s., p. 89, (Isa. 30:15)

Joash, son of Ahaziah, was s., p. 43, (II Kg. 11:2; II Chr. 22:11)

mine own hand hath s. me, p. 29, (Jg. 7:2)

thy faith hath s. thee, p. 155, (Lk. 7:50)

what must I do to be s.?, p. 195, (Acts 16:30)

who then can be s.?, p. 164, (Matt. 19:25; Mk. 10:26; Lk. 18:26)

who will have all men to be s., p. 224, (I Tim. 2:4)

Savior: a S. is born, p. 133, (Lk. 2:11)

my refuge, my S., p. 36, (II Sam. 22:3)

rejoiced in God my S., p. 132, (Lk. 1:47)

Sea: a s. of glass like unto crystal, p. 242, (Rev. 4:6)

and the s. ceased from raging, p. 120, (Jonah 1:15)

as the waters cover the s., p. 85, (Isa. 11:9)

cast me forth into the s., p. 120, (Jonah 1:12)

down to the s. in ships, p. 65, (Ps. 107:23)

dwell in the uttermost parts of the s., p. 68, (Ps. 139:9)

great and wide s., p. 65, (Ps. 104:25)

great beasts came up from the s., p. 112, (Dan. 7:3)

into the s. and drowned, p. 144, (Matt. 8:32; Mk. 5:13; Lk. 8:33)

into the s.; yet the s. is not full, p. 74, (Ec. 1:7)

let the s. roar, p. 64, (Ps. 98:7)

look toward the s., p. 40, (I Kg. 18:43)

Sea: (*continued*)

the s. is his, and he made it, p. 63, (Ps. 95:5)

the springs of the s., p. 54, (Job 38:16)

took up Jonah and cast him into the s., p. 120, (Jonah 1:15)

what shall we do that the s. may be calm?, p. 120, (Jonah 1:11)

winds and s. obey him, p. 144, (Matt. 8:27; Mk. 4:41)

Seal: another angel having the s. of God, p. 243, (Rev. 7:2)

as a s. upon thine heart, p. 78, (Song 8:6)

has put his s. upon us, p. 210, (II Cor. 1:22)

Sealed: an hundred and forty four thousand were s., p. 243, (Rev. 7:4)

s. the servants of our God, p. 243, (Rev. 7:3)

s. till the time of the end, p. 114, (Dan. 12:9)

Seals: a book sealed with seven s., p. 242, (Rev. 5:1)

take the book and open the s., p. 242, (Rev. 5:9)

Search: s. me, O God, and know my heart, p. 68, (Ps. 139:23)

Searched: thou hast s. me, and known me, p. 67, (Ps. 139:1)

Searching: cans't thou by s. find out God?, p. 51, (Job 11:7)

Seas: God created the earth and the s., p. 3, (Gen. 1:9-10)

he hath founded it upon the s., p. 57, (Ps. 24:2)

the waters called he S., p. 3, (Gen. 1:10)

Season: be instant in s., out of s., p. 227, (II Tim. 4:2)

their meat in due s., p. 65, (Ps. 104:27)

to every thing there is a s., p. 74, (Ec. 3:1)

willing for a s. to rejoice, p. 167, (Jn. 5:35)

word spoken in due s., p. 71, (Prov. 15:23)

Secret: bread eaten in s., p. 70, (Prov. 9:17)

cleanse thou me from s. faults, p. 57, (Ps. 19:12)

pray to thy Father which is in s., p. 140, (Matt. 6:6)

the s. place of the most High, p. 63, (Ps. 91:1)

the s. things belong unto the Lord our God, p. 23, (Deut. 29:29)

thy Father which seeth in s., p. 140, (Matt. 6:4)

Secretly: Israel did s., things that were not right, p. 44, (II Kg. 17:9)

See: I will s. you again, p. 179, (Jn. 16:22)

s. me and live, p. 18, (Ex. 33:20)

Seed: bearing precious s., p. 66, (Ps. 126:6)

good s. are the children of the kingdom, p. 156, (Matt. 13:38)

planted the s. of the land, p. 108, (Ezek. 17:5)

s. time and harvest, p. 7, (Gen. 8:22)

the parable of the mustard s., p. 157, (Matt. 13:31–32; Mk. 4:30–32; Lk. 13:18–19)

the s. growing secretly, p. 156, (Mk. 4:26–29)

the s. is rotten under the clods, p. 116, (Joel 1:17)

thy s. shall be as the dust, p. 10, (Gen. 28:14)

unto thy s. have I given this land, p. 8, (Gen. 15:18)

unto thy s. will I give, p. 7, (Gen. 12:7)

who sows the good s. is the Son, p. 156, (Matt. 13:37)

your s. as the dust of the earth, p. 8, (Gen. 13:16)

Seeds: some s. fell upon a rock, p. 156, (Matt. 13:5: Mk. 4:5; Lk. 8:6)

the smallest of all s., p. 157, (Matt. 13:32; Mk. 4:31)

Seek: s. and ye shall find, p. 42, (Matt. 7:7; Lk. 11:9)

s. me and find me, p. 102, (Jer. 29:13)

s. those things which are above, p. 220, (Col. 3:1)

s. ye the living among the dead?, p. 183, (Lk. 24:5)

s. ye first the Kingdom, p. 141, (Matt. 6:33; Lk. 12:31)

s. ye me, and ye shall live, p. 119, (Amos 5:4)

s. ye the Lord while he may be found, p. 94, (Isa. 55:6)

to s. and to save, p. 154, (Lk. 19:10)

Seen: he that hath s. me, p. 149, (Jn. 14:9)

Seeth: the Lord s. not as man s., p. 33, (I Sam. 16:7)

Sell: s. what thou hast and give to the poor, p. 163, (Matt. 19:21; Mk. 10:21; Lk. 18:22)

Sells: s. all and buys the field, p. 157, (Matt. 13:44)

Send: here am I. S. me, p. 83, (Isa. 6:8)

whom shall I s. . . . , p. 83, (Isa. 6:8)

Separate: shall s. us from the love of God . . . , p. 202, (Rom. 8:39)

Sepulchre: Also see tomb

no man knows of his s., p. 21, (Deut. 34:6)

you are like whited s., p. 172, (Matt. 23:27; cf. Lk. 11:44)

Seraphims: above it stood the s., p. 83, (Isa. 6:2)

one of the s. flew unto me, p. 83, (Isa. 6:6)

Sermon: Peter's s., p. 189, (Acts 2:14–36)

Serpent: leviathan that crooked s., p. 88, (Isa. 27:1)

rod became a s., p. 15, (Ex. 7:10)

sharpened their tongues like a s., p. 68, (Ps. 140:3)

that old s. called the Devil, p. 244, (Rev. 12:9)

the s. beguiled me, p. 5, (Gen. 3:13)

the s. was more subtle, p. 5, (Gen. 3:1)

Serpents: wise as s., harmless as doves, p. 146, (Matt. 10:16)

Servant: and reward the faithful s., p. 174, (Matt. 24:47, 51; Lk. 12:44, 46–48)

centurion's s., p. 143, (Matt. 8:5–13; Lk. 7:1–10)

Christ took the form of a s., p. 218, (Phil. 2:7)

doth he thank that s.?, p. 153, (Lk. 17:9)

free from all men yet s. unto all, p. 207, (I Cor. 9:19)

have you considered my s., Job?, p. 49, (Job 1:8)

Israel, art my s., p. 92, (Isa. 41:8)

my s., mine elect, p. 93, (Isa. 42:1)

not as a s. but above a s., p. 228, (Philem. v. 16)

O thou wicked s., p. 163, (Matt. 18:32)

parable of the unmerciful s., p. 162, (Matt. 18:23–35)

s. is not greater than his lord, p. 177, (Jn. 13:16)

s. was owed money by a fellow s., p. 163, (Matt. 18:28)

the master and his s., p. 153, (Lk. 17:7–10)

the parable of the faithful s., p. 174, (Matt. 24:45–51; Lk. 12:42–48)

thou art no more a s., p. 214, (Gal. 4:7)

thou wicked and slothful s., p. 175, (Matt. 25:26; cf. Lk. 19:22)

thy s. depart in peace, p. 133, (Lk. 2:29)

thy s. heareth, p. 31, (I Sam. 3:9)

well done, good and faithful s. . . . , p. 175, (Matt. 25:21; cf. Lk. 19:17)

whosoever will be chief let him be your s., p. 165, (Matt. 20:27; Mk. 10:44)

Servants: entrusted his goods to his s., p. 174, (Matt. 25:14; cf. Lk. 19:13)

he sent his s. for the fruit, p. 170, (Matt. 21:34–35; Mk. 12:2–5; Lk. 20:10–12)

he sent his s. to find others, p. 171, (Matt. 22:9)

his s. will arise and build, p. 45, (Neh. 2:20)

my father's s. have bread. p. 152, (Lk. 15:17)

sealed the s. of our God, p. 243, (Rev. 7:3)

we are unprofitable s., p. 153, (Lk. 17:10)

Serve: care that I s. alone?, p. 150, (Lk. 10:40)

did I not s. for Rachel?, p. 11, (Gen. 29:25)

if any man s. me, p. 176, (Jn. 12:26)

s. another seven years for Rachel, p. 11, (Gen. 29:27, 28)

Serve: (*continued*)

s. me till I have eaten, p. 153, (Lk. 17:8)

s. the Lord with gladness, p. 64, (Ps. 100:2)

s. two masters, p. 141, (Matt. 6:24; Lk. 16:13)

you cannot s. God and mammon, p. 141, (Matt. 6:24; Lk. 16:13)

Served: many years have I s. thee, p. 152, (Lk. 15:29)

Serving: Martha cumbered with much s., p. 150, (Lk. 10:40)

Seven: dreamed of s. fat cows, p. 12, (Gen. 41:2)

send it to the s. churches of Asia, p. 240, (Rev. 1:11)

Jacob loved Rachel and served s. years, p. 11, (Gen. 29:18, 20)

serve another s. years for Rachel, p. 11, (Gen. 29:27, 28)

s. days shall you eat unleavened bread, p. 15, (Ex. 12:15; Lev. 23:6; Deut. 16:3)

s. ears of corn, p. 12, (Gen. 41:5, 6)

s. spirits more wicked than he, p. 155, (Matt. 12:45; Lk. 11:26)

s. years of famine, p. 12, (Gen. 41:30)

s. years of plenty, p. 12, (Gen. 41:29)

Seventh: God blessed the s. day, p. 4, (Gen. 2:3)

God blessed the s. day, p. 19, (Gen. 2:3; cf. Ex. 20:10; Deut. 5:14)

God rested on the s. day, p. 4, (Gen. 2:2)

opened the s. seal, p. 244, (Rev. 8:1)

the s. angel sounded the trumpet, p. 244, (Rev. 11:15)

Seventy: not seven times but s. times seven, p. 162, (Matt. 18:22)

Scales: the s. fell from his eyes, p. 193, (Acts 9:18)

Scapegoat: a s. into the wilderness, p. 19, (Lev. 16:10)

Scarlet: lips are like a thread of s., p. 77, (Song 4:3)

your sins be as s., p. 81, (Isa. 1:18)

Scatter: s. them abroad, p. 7, (Gen. 11:8)

Scattered: all Israel s. upon the hills, p. 41, (I Kg. 22:17; II Chr. 18:16)

he that s. Israel, p. 102, (Jer. 31:10)

Israel is a s. sheep, p. 103, (Jer. 50:17)

they that were s. abroad, p. 191, (Acts 8:4)

Scattereth: s. the inhabitants, p. 87, (Isa. 24:1)

Science: s. falsely so called, p. 225, (I Tim. 6:20)

Scorner: reprove not a s., p. 70, (Prov. 9:8)

Scorpions: chastised you with whips but I . . . with s., p. 39, (I Kg. 12:11)

Scourge: s. you in their synagogues, p. 146, (Matt. 10:17; Mk. 13:9)

Scourged: when he had s. Jesus, p. 182, (Matt. 27:26; Mk. 15:15; Jn. 19:1)

Scribes: priests and s. sought how to kill him, p. 176, (Matt. 26:3–4; Mk. 14:1; Lk. 22:2)

s. and Pharisees: Who can forgive sins . . . ?, p. 144, (Matt. 9:3; Mk. 2:6–7; Lk. 5:21)

woe to you, s. and Pharisees, p. 172, (Matt. 23:25)

Scripture: all s. is given by inspiration, p. 226, (II Tim. 3:16)

Scriptures: mighty in the s., p. 196, (Acts 18:24)

search the s., p. 167, (Jn. 5:39)

thou hast known the holy s., p. 226, (II Tim. 3:15)

Shadow: a s. from the heat, p. 87, (Isa. 25:4)

a s. of things to come, p. 220, (Col. 2:17)

days on the earth are as a s., p. 37, (I Chr. 29:15)

in the land of the s. of death, p. 84, (Isa. 9:2)

in the s. of death, p. 65, (Ps. 107:10)

no variableness, nor s. of turning, p. 233, (Jas. 1:17)

our days . . . are a s., p. 51, (Job 8:9)

the s. of a great rock, p. 89, (Isa. 32:2)

the s. of death, p. 51, (Job 10:21)

the s. of Peter might fall on them, p. 190, (Acts 5:15)

to light the s. of death, p. 51, (Job 12:22)

turneth the s. of death into morning, p. 119, (Amos 5:8)

Shadows: the s. flee away, p. 77, (Song 2:17)

Shadrach: Belteshazzar and S., Meshach and Abednego, p. 110, (Dan. 1:7)

Nebuchadnezzar in rage called S. . . . , p. 111, (Dan. 3:13)

S. . . . into the furnace, p. 111, (Dan. 3:23)

Shame: change their glory unto s., p. 115, (Hos. 4:7)

some to s. and contempt, p. 114, (Dan. 12:2)

Sharper: s. than any two-edged sword, p. 229, (Heb. 4:12)

Shaven: if I be s. my strength will go, p. 30, (Jg. 16:17)

Sheaves: bringing his s., p. 66, (Ps. 126:6)

Sheba: Queen of S. came to test Solomon, p. 38, (I Kg. 10:1; II Chr. 9:1)

Solomon and the Queen of S., p. 38, (I Kg. 10:1–23; II Chr. 9:1–22)

Sheep: all we like s. have gone astray, p. 94, (Isa. 53:6)

as a shepherd divideth s. from goats, p. 175, (Matt. 25:32)

as s. in the midst of wolves, p. 146, (Matt. 10:16; Lk. 10:3)

as s. without a shepherd, p. 41, (I Kg. 22:17; II Chr. 18:16)

counted as s. for the slaughter, p. 59, (Ps. 44:22)

come to you in s.'s clothing, p. 142, (Matt. 7:15)

having an hundred s. if he lose one, p. 162, (Matt. 18:12; Lk. 15:4)

I know my s., p. 168, (Jn. 10:14)

Israel is a scattered s., p. 103, (Jer. 50:17)

other s. . . . not of this fold, p. 168, (Jn. 10:16)

seek out my s. and deliver them, p. 109, (Ezek. 34:12)

s. having no shepherd, p. 146, (Matt. 9:36; Mk. 6:34)

the s. of his hand, p. 63, (Ps. 95:7)

you were as s. going astray, p. 236, (I Pet. 2:25)

Sheet: a great s. descending, p. 193, (Acts 10:11)

Shem: S., Ham and Japheth, p. 6, (Gen. 6:10)

Shepherd: as a s. divideth sheep from goats, p. 175, (Matt. 25:32)

as sheep without a s., p. 41, (I Kg. 22:17; II Chr. 18:16)

feed his flock like a s., p. 92, (Isa. 40:11)

he that enters by the door is the s., p. 168, (Jn. 10:2)

I will set up one s. over them, p. 109, (Ezek. 34:23)

S. and Bishop of your souls, p. 236, (I Pet. 2:25)

the good s. gives his life, p. 168, (Jn. 10:11)

the Lord is my s., p. 57, (Ps. 23:1)

Shepherds: s. abiding in the field, p. 133, (Lk. 2:8)

s. came with haste to Bethlehem, p. 133, (Lk. 2:15–16)

the habitations of the s. shall mourn, p. 118, (Amos 1:2)

woe be to the s. of Israel, p. 109, (Ezek. 34:2)

Shibboleth: S. and he said Sibboleth, p. 29, (Jg. 12:6)

Shield: fear not Abram, I am thy s., p. 8, (Gen. 15:1)

he is my s., p. 36, (II Sam. 22:3)

Lord is my strength and my s., p. 58, (Ps. 28:7)

take the s. of faith, p. 218, (Eph. 6:16)

Ship: Jesus went into a s., p. 144, (Matt. 8:23; Mk. 4:36; Lk. 8:22)

ran the s. aground, p. 198, (Acts 27:41)

Ships: all the s. of Tarshish, p. 82, (Isa. 2:16)

down to the sea in s., p. 65, (Ps. 107:23)

howl, ye s. of Tarshish, p. 87, (Isa. 23:14)

there go the s., p. 65, (Ps. 104:26)

Shipwrecked: s. on the way to Rome, p. 198, (Acts 27:14—28:1)

Shock: like a s. of corn, p. 50, (Job 5:26)

Shoes: they sold the poor for a pair of s., p. 118, (Amos 2:6; cf. 8:6)

whose s. I am not worthy to unloose, p. 135, (Matt. 3:11; Mk. 1:7; Lk. 3:16; Jn. 1:27)

Shore: multitude gathered on the s., p. 156, (Matt. 13:2; Mk. 4:1)

Short: being s. of stature, p. 154, (Lk. 19:3)

Shout: Joshua said to the people: S., p. 27, (Josh. 6:16)

the people raised a great s., p. 27, (Josh. 6:20)

Shulamite: return, return, O S., p. 78, (Song 6:13)

Shunammite: Elisha and the S. woman, p. 42, (II Kg. 4:8–37)

Sick: brought the s. into the streets, p. 190, (Acts 5:15)

Hezekiah s. unto death, p. 91, (Isa. 38:1)

prayer of faith shall save the s., p. 235, (Jas. 5:15)

the whole head is s., p. 81, (Isa. 1:5)

Side: thrust it thy hand into my s., p. 185, (Jn. 20:27)

Sidon: set thy face against S., p. 108, (Ezek. 28:21)

S., p. 198, (Acts 27:3)

Sign: a s. from heaven, p. 155, (Matt. 12:38–42; 16:1–4; Mk. 8:11–13; Lk. 11:16; 29–32; 12:54–56)

adulterous generation seeketh a s., p. 155, (Matt. 12:39; 16:4; Lk. 11:29)

an everlasting s., p. 94, (Isa. 55:13)

dew on a fleece of wool as a s., p. 29, (Jg. 6:37)

Gideon asked for a s., p. 29, (Jg. 6:36)

I have set thee for a s., p. 107, (Ezek. 12:6)

master we would seek a s., p. 155, (Matt. 12:38; 16:1; cf. Mk. 8:11; Lk. 11:16)

no s. given but the s. of Jonas, p. 155, (Matt. 12:39; 16:4; Mk. 8:12; Lk. 11:29)

the Lord's s. to the house of David, p. 83, (Isa. 7:13, 14)

what shall be the s. of thy coming?, p. 173, (Matt. 24:3; Mk. 13:4; Lk. 21:7)

Signs: discern the s. of the times, p. 155, (Matt. 16:3; Lk. 12:56)

except ye see s. and wonders, p. 166, (Jn. 4:48)

s. in the earth beneath, p. 189, (Acts 2:19)

were many s. and wonders wrought, p. 190, (Acts 5:12)

Sight: he received his s. and followed Jesus, p. 165, (Mk. 10:52; Lk. 18:43; cf. Matt. 20:34)

he was three days without s., p. 192, (Acts 9:9)

that thou mightest receive thy s., p. 193, (Acts 9:17)

Silas: Paul and S. in prison, p. 195, (Acts 16:19–40)

the Romans beat Paul and S., p. 195, (Acts 16:23)

Silence: all the earth keep s. before him, p. 123, (Hab. 2:20)

put to s. the ignorance of foolish men, p. 236, (I Pet. 2:15)

there was s. in heaven, p. 244, (Rev. 8:1)

Siloam: go, wash in the pool of S., p. 168, (Jn. 9:7)

Silver: pictures of s., p. 73, (Prov. 25:11)

s. and gold have I none, p. 190, (Acts 3:6)

what woman having ten pieces of s., p. 152, (Lk. 15:8)

Simeon: a man in Jerusalem named S., p. 133, (Lk. 2:25)

Simon: compelled S. of Cyrene to bear his cross, p. 182, (Matt. 27:32; Mk. 15:21; Lk. 23:26)

send men to Joppa to S. . . . Peter, p. 193, (Acts 10:5)

S., called Peter, p. 136, (Matt. 4:18; cf. Mk. 1:16)

S. offered to buy the power, p. 192, (Acts 8:18–19)

S. the magician, p. 192, (Acts 8:9–24)

Simple: give subtilty to the s., p. 69, (Prov. 1:4)

Sin: a s. offering to the Lord, p. 19, (Ex. 30:10; Lev. 16:5; Num. 29:11)

be ye angry and s. not, p. 217, (Eph. 4:26)

by one man s. entered into the world, p. 200, (Rom. 5:12)

. . . committeth s. is the servant of s., p. 168, (Jn. 8:34)

declare . . . to Israel his s., p. 121, (Micah 3:8)

fools make a mock at s., p. 71, (Prov. 14:9)

go and s. no more, p. 167, (Jn. 8:11)

he died unto s. once, p. 201, (Rom. 6:10)

he that is without s. among you, p. 167, (Jn. 8:7)

if any man s., we have an advocate, p. 238, (I John 2:1)

if we say we have no s., we deceive ourselves, p. 238, (I John 1:8)

iniquity is taken away, thy s. purged, p. 83, (Isa. 6:7)

in s. did my mother conceive me, p. 60, (Ps. 51:5)

Job did not s., p. 49, (Job 2:10)

lay aside every weight and s., p. 231, (Heb. 12:1)

made him to be s. for us . . . , p. 211, (II Cor. 5:21)

my s. is ever before me, p. 60, (Ps. 51:3)

shall we continue in s., p. 200, (Rom. 6:1)

s. as it were with a cart rope, p. 83, (Isa. 5:18)

s. shall not have dominion, p. 201, (Rom. 6:14)

tempted . . . yet without s., p. 229, (Heb. 4:15)

the law is the knowledge of s., p. 200, (Rom. 3:20)

the s. of Judah is written, p. 101, (Jer. 17:1)

the wages of s. is death, p. 201, (Rom. 6:23)

where s. abounded, p. 200, (Rom. 5:20)

your s. will find you out, p. 21, (Num. 32:23)

Sinai: Moses on Mount S., p. 17, (Ex. 19—31)

Mount S. was wrapped in smoke, p. 17, (Ex. 19:18)

while Moses was on S., p. 18, (Ex. 32:1)

Sinful: I am a s. man, O Lord, p. 137, (Lk. 5:8)

Sing: awake and s., p. 88, (Isa. 26:19)

how shall we s. the Lord's song, p. 67, (Ps. 137:4)

let us s. unto the Lord, p. 63, (Ps. 95:1)

s. unto the Lord a new song, p. 64, (Ps. 98:1)

s. unto the Lord all the earth, p. 63, (Ps. 96:1)

Sink: afraid and beginning to s., p. 158, (Matt. 14:30)

I s. in deep mire, p. 61, (Ps. 69:2)

Sinned: David said I have s., p. 35, (II Sam. 12:13)

I have s. against heaven, p. 152, (Lk. 15:21)

I have s. for I knew not, p. 20, (Num. 22:34)

s. and come short of the glory of God, p. 200, (Rom. 3:23)

s. in betraying innocent blood, p. 181, (Matt. 27:4)

they s. against me, p. 115, (Hos. 4:7)

we have s. and have committed iniquity, p. 113, (Dan. 9:5)

Sinner: a woman . . . who was a s., p. 155, (Lk. 7:37)

one s. that repenteth, p. 162, (Lk. 15:7)

the guest of a s., p. 154, (Lk. 19:7)

Sinners: by one man's disobedience many were made s., p. 200, (Rom. 5:19)

eateth your master with s., p. 145, (Matt. 9:10–13; Mk. 2:15–17; Lk. 5:29–32)

friend of publicans and s., p. 148, (Matt. 11:19; Lk. 7:34)

if s. entice thee, p. 69, (Prov. 1:10)

not to call the righteous but s., p. 145, (Matt. 9:13; Mk. 2:17; Lk. 5:32)

to save s. of whom I am the chief, p. 223, (I Tim. 1:15)

while we were yet s., Christ died for us, p. 200, (Rom. 5:8)

Sinneth: is not a just man that . . . s. not, p. 75, (Ec. 7:20)

Sins: also for the s. of the whole world, p. 238, (I John 2:2)

confessing their s., p. 135, (Matt. 3:6; Mk. 1:5; cf. Lk. 3:3)

her s. have reached heaven, p. 246, (Rev. 18:5)

her s., which are many, p. 155, (Lk. 7:47)

if you forgive anyone's s., p. 184, (Jn. 20:23)

Israel stood and confessed their s., p. 46, (Neh. 9:2)

Sins: (continued)

love covereth all s., p. 70, (Prov. 10:12)

the propitiation for our s., p. 238, (I John 2:2)

their s. . . . will I remember no more, p. 230, (Heb. 8:12)

to make reconciliation for the s., p. 229, (Heb. 2:17)

thy s. are forgiven, p. 144, (Matt. 9:2; Mk. 2:5; Lk. 5:20)

to bear the s. of many, p. 231, (Heb. 9:28)

your s. be as scarlet, p. 81, (Isa. 1:18)

Sion: Also see Zion

a Lamb stood on Mount S., p. 245, (Rev. 14:1)

come unto Mount S., p. 232, (Heb. 12:22)

Sisera: fought against S., p. 29, (Jg. 5:20)

killed S. with a tent peg, p. 28, (Jg. 4:21)

to subdue S., p. 28, (Jg. 4:14)

Sister: a garden inclosed is my s., my spouse, p. 78, (Song 4:12)

Sit: grant that my two sons may s., p. 164, (Matt. 20:21; cf. Mk. 10:37)

s. not down in a place of honor, p. 151, (Lk. 14:8)

to s. on my right hand . . . , p. 164, (Matt. 20:23; Mk. 10:40)

Skill: to give thee s. and understanding, p. 113, (Dan. 9:22)

Skin: can the Ethiopian change his s., p. 100, (Jer. 13:23)

my bone cleaveth to my s., p. 52, (Job 19:20)

with the s. of my teeth, p. 52, (Job 19:20)

Skins: s. of goats upon his hands, p. 10, (Gen. 27:16)

Slain: s. a thousand men, p. 30, (Jg. 15:16)

Saul hath s. his thousands, p. 34, (I Sam. 18:7)

there is a multitude of s., p. 123, (Nahum 3:3)

Slaughter: an ox goeth to the s., p. 70, (Prov. 7:22)

the s. of the innocents, p. 134, (Matt. 2:1–8; 16:18)

Slave: plea for a runaway s., p. 228, (Philem.)

Slay: I will s. my brother Jacob, p. 10, (Gen. 27:41)

Sleep: folding of the hands to s., p. 70, (Prov. 6:10)

he giveth his beloved s., p. 67, (Ps. 127:2)

lay me down in peace, and s., p. 56, (Ps. 4:8)

many that s. shall awake, p. 114, (Dan. 12:2)

s. of a laboring man is sweet, p. 75, (Ec. 5:12)

them which s. in Jesus, p. 222, (I Th. 4:14)

we shall not all s., p. 210, (I Cor. 15:51)

will not give s. to mine eyes, p. 67, (Ps. 132:4)

yet a little s., a little slumber, p. 70, (Prov. 6:10)

Sleeping: lest coming suddenly he find you s., p. 174, (Mk. 12:36)

Sling: with a s. and a stone, p. 33, (I Sam. 17:50)

Slothful: thou wicked and s. servant, p. 175, (Matt. 25:26)

Sluggard: go to the ant, thou s., p. 69, (Prov. 6:6)

Slumber: he that keepeth thee will not s., p. 66, (Ps. 121:3)

Small: hath despised the day of s. things, p. 126, (Zech. 4:10)

Smell: instead of sweet s., p. 82, (Isa. 3:24)

Smitten: he hath s. and he will bind, p. 115, (Hos. 6:1)

Smoke: my days are consumed like s., p. 64, (Ps. 102:3)

Smote: s. them hip and thigh, p. 30, (Jg. 15:8)

Smyrna: to the church of S., p. 241, (Rev. 2:8–11)

Snare: deliver thee from the s. of the fowler, p. 63, (Ps. 91:3)

Snow: fire, and hail; s., and vapors, p. 68, (Ps. 148:8)

I shall be whiter than s., p. 60, (Ps. 51:7)

Sober: be s., be vigilant, p. 237, (I Pet. 5:8)

Soberness: words of truth and s., p. 197, (Acts 26:25)

Sodom: have been as S. and Gomorrah, p. 81, (Isa. 1:9)

on S. and Gomorrah brimstone and fire, p. 9, (Gen. 19:24)

Soft: s. answer turneth away wrath, p. 71, (Prov. 15:1)

Softly: go s. in the bitterness of my soul, p. 91, (Isa. 38:15)

Sojourner: a stranger with thee and a s., p. 59, (Ps. 39:12)

Sold: Joseph was s. to Potiphar, p. 12, (Gen. 37:36)

s. all he had and bought it, p. 157, (Matt. 13:46)

they s. the poor for a pair of shoes, p. 118, (Amos 2:6; cf. 8:6)

Soldier: endure hardness as a good s., p. 226, (II Tim. 2:3)

Solitary: God setteth the s. in families, p. 61, (Ps. 68:6)

Solomon: David's charge to S., p. 37, (I Chr. 22, 28, 29:1–19)

David gave to S. the pattern, p. 37, (I Chr. 28:11–12)

even S. in all his glory, p. 141, (Matt. 6:29; Lk. 12:27)

Queen of Sheba came to test S., p. 38, (I Kg. 10:1; II Chr. 9:1)

Rehoboam succeeded S., p. 39, (I Kg. 12:1, 17; II Chr. 10:17)

since the time of S. there was not the like, p. 45, (II Chr. 30:26)

S. and the Queen of Sheba, p. 38, (I Kg. 10:1–23; II Chr. 9:1–22)

S. and the two mothers, p. 37, (I Kg. 3:16–28)

S.'s apostasy, p. 39, (I Kg. 11:1–13)

S. asked God for wisdom, p. 37, (I Kg. 3:3–15; II Chr. 1:7–12)

S. built the temple, p. 38, (II Chr. 3:1)

S. loved many strange women, p. 39, (I Kg. 11:1)

S.'s navy brought gold, silver, p. 38, (I Kg. 10:22; II Chr. 9:21)

S.'s prayer of dedication, p. 38, (I Kg. 8:14–61; II Chr. 6:12–42)

S.'s riches and wisdom, p. 38, (I Kg. 4:25–34)

S. thy son shall reign, p. 37, (I Kg. 1:30)

song of songs, which is S.'s, p. 77, (Song 1:1)

the anointing of S., p. 37, (I Kg. 1—2:12; I Chr. 29:22–25)

the wisdom of S., p. 38, (I Kg. 4:34)

Zadok the priest anointed S., p. 37, (I Kg. 1:39)

Son: a child is born, . . . a s. is given, p. 84, (Isa. 9:6)

a foolish s. is the heaviness of his mother, p. 70, (Prov. 10:1)

a virgin shall conceive and bear a s., p. 83, (Isa. 7:14)

Abraham bound his s., p. 9, (Gen. 22:9)

all men should honor the S., p. 148, (Jn. 5:23)

are you the Christ, the S. of God?, p. 181, (Matt. 26:63; Mk. 14:61; Lk. 22:67, 70)

brought forth her firstborn s., p. 132, (Lk. 2:7)

but for thy s. who devoured thy living, p. 152, (Lk. 15:30)

concerning David's s., p. 172, (Matt. 22:41–46; Mk. 12:35–37; Lk. 20:41–44)

crucify . . . the S. of God afresh, p. 230, (Heb. 6:6)

to thy way, thy s. liveth, p. 166, (Jn. 4:50)

he besought Jesus to heal his s., p. 166, (Jn. 4:47)

he that has the S. has life, p. 239, (I John 5:12)

his s. who was also killed, p. 170, (Matt. 21:37–39; Mk. 12:6–8; Lk. 20:13–15)

how is he his s.?, p. 172, (Matt. 22:45; Mk. 12:37; Lk. 20:44)

I will raise up your s. after you, p. 35, (II Sam. 7:12; I Chr. 17:11; Lk. 1:32)

John's vision of the S. of man, p. 240, (Rev. 1:12–20)

Lucifer, s. of the morning, p. 85, (Isa. 14:12)

my s. was dead and is alive, p. 152, (Lk. 15:24)

no man knoweth the S., p. 148, (Matt. 11:27; Lk. 10:22)

O Absalom, my s., my s., p. 36, (II Sam. 18:33)

one like the S. of man, p. 112, (Dan. 7:13)

one like unto the S. of man, p. 240, (Rev. 1:13)

out of the hand of thy s., p. 39, (I Kg. 11:12)

Son: *(continued)*

Rabbi, thou art the S. of God, p. 137, (Jn. 1:49)

see, thy s. liveth, p. 40, (I Kg. 17:23)

shall be called the S. of God, p. 131, (Lk. 1:35)

s. of man can these bones live?, p. 109, (Ezek. 37:3)

s. of man dig now in the wall, p. 107, (Ezek. 8:8)

S. of man has nowhere to lay his head, p. 144, (Matt. 8:20; Lk. 9:58)

s. of man hear what I say, p. 106, (Ezek. 2:8)

S. of man shall come in his glory, p. 175, (Matt. 25:31)

S. of man should be glorified, p. 175, (Jn. 12:23)

s. of man that thou visitest him?, p. 228, (Heb. 2:6)

s., thou art ever with me, p. 152, (Lk. 15:31)

S., why hast thou thus dealt with us?, p. 134, (Lk. 2:48)

spoken unto us by his S., p. 228, (Heb. 1:2)

take now thy s., thy only s., p. 9, (Gen. 22:2)

that he gave his only begotten S., p. 165, (Jn. 3:16)

the Father loves the S., p. 166, (Jn. 3:35)

the Father, the S., and the Holy Ghost, p. 185, (Matt. 28:19)

the prodigal s., p. 152, (Lk. 15:11–24)

the S. can do nothing of himself, p. 148, (Jn. 5:19; 14:10)

the S. hath declared him, p. 148, (Jn. 1:18)

the s. of David, p. 172, (Matt. 22:42; Mk. 12:35; Lk. 20:41)

the S. of man came eating and drinking, p. 148, (Matt. 11:19; Lk. 7:34)

the S. of man came not to be ministered unto, p. 164, (Matt. 20:28; Mk. 10:45)

the S. of man coming with power and glory, p. 173, (Matt. 24:30; Mk. 13:26; Lk. 21:27)

the S. of man is betrayed, p. 176, (Matt. 26:2)

the S. of man is come to seek and to save, p. 154, (Lk. 19:10)

the S. of man must suffer, p. 161, (Matt. 16:21; Mk. 8:31; Lk. 9:22)

the s. of the widow fell sick and died, p. 40, (I Kg. 17:17)

this is my beloved S., p. 135, (Matt. 3:17; 17:5; Mk. 1:11; 9:7; Lk. 3:22; 9:35)

thou art my S., p. 229, (Heb. 5:5)

thou art the S. of God, p. 158, (Matt. 14:33)

thou shalt bring forth a s., p. 131, (Lk. 1:31)

truly this was the S. of God, p. 183, (Matt. 27:54; Mk. 15:39)

unto us a s. is given, p. 84, (Isa. 9:6)

who sows the good seed is the S., p. 156, (Matt. 13:37)

wise s. maketh a glad father, p. 70, (Prov. 10:1)

woman, behold thy s.!, p. 183, (Jn. 19:26)

you are that Christ, the S. of . . . God, p. 167, (Jn. 6:69)

Song: and they sung a new s., p. 242, (Rev. 5:9)

David's victory s., p. 36, (II Sam. 22)

Hannah's s. of thanksgiving, p. 31, (I Sam. 2:1–10)

Moses' s. of victory, p. 16, (Ex. 15:1–21)

sing unto him a new s., p. 58, (Ps. 33:3)

sing unto the Lord a new s., p. 64, (Ps. 98:1)

s. of Deborah, p. 29, (Jg. 5)

s. of Mary, p. 132, (Lk. 1:39–56)

s. of Moses, p. 21, (Deut. 32:1–43)

s. of songs, which is Solomon's, p. 77, (Song 1:1)

s. of Zacharias, p. 132, (Lk. 1:67–79)

Songs: Take away the noise of your s., p. 119, (Amos 5:23)

Sons: parable of the two s., p. 170, (Matt. 21:28–32)

power to become s. of God, p. 131, (Jn. 1:12)

Sorrow: any s. like unto my s., p. 104, (Lam. 1:12)

in s. shalt thou bring forth children, p. 5, (Gen. 3:16)

joy follows s., p. 179, (Jn. 16:6–33)

s. and mourning shall flee, p. 93,
(Isa. 51:11)

s. and sighing shall flee away, p. 90,
(Isa. 35:10)

s. hath filled your heart, p. 179, (Jn.
16:6)

s. of the world worketh death, p.
212, (II Cor. 7:10)

your s. shall be turned into joy, p.
179, (Jn. 16:20)

Sorrowful: as s. yet alway rejoicing, p.
212, (II Cor. 6:10)

my soul is exceeding s., p. 180,
(Matt. 26:38; Mk. 14:34)

Sorrows: a man of s., p. 94, (Isa.
53:3)

and carried our s., p. 94, (Isa. 53:4)

the s. of death compassed me, p. 56,
(Ps. 18:4)

Soul: he restoreth my s., p. 57, (Ps.
23:3)

how long will ye vex my s., p. 52,
(Job 19:2)

man became a living s., p. 4, (Gen.
2:7)

my s. doth magnify the Lord, p. 132,
(Lk. 1:46)

my s. is exceeding sorrowful, p. 180,
(Matt. 26:38; Mk. 14:34)

now is my s. troubled, p. 175, (Jn.
12:27)

the desire of our s., p. 88, (Isa. 26:8)

the waters are come in unto my s., p.
61, (Ps. 69:1)

this night thy s. shall be required of
thee, p. 150, (Lk. 12:20)

the destroy both s. and body, p. 147,
(Matt. 10:28; cf. Lk. 12:5)

why art thou cast down, O my s.?, p.
59, (Ps. 42:5)

why castest thou off my s.?, p. 62,
(Ps. 88:14)

with my whole s., p. 102, (Jer. 32:41)

Sound: a s. from heaven, p. 189,
(Acts 2:2)

Sounding: I am become as s. brass, p.
208, (I Cor. 13:1)

Sow: a sower went forth to s., p. 156,
(Matt. 13:3; Mk. 4:3; Lk. 9:5)

s. wickedness, p. 50, (Job 4:8)

Sowed: s. weeds among the wheat, p.
156, (Matt. 13:25)

Sower: the parable of the s., p. 156,

(Matt. 13:1–23; Mk. 4:1–20; Lk.
9:4–15)

Soweth: he which s. sparingly, p. 212,
(II Cor. 9:6)

whatsoever a man s., p. 215, (Gal.
6:7)

Sows: who s. the good seed is the
Son, p. 156, (Matt. 13:37)

Spare: s. me, that I may recover
strength, p. 59, (Ps. 39:13)

Spareth: he that s. his rod, p. 71,
(Prov. 13:24)

Sparks: as the s. fly upward, p. 50,
(Job 5:7)

Sparrow: a s. alone upon the house
top, p. 64, (Ps. 102:7)

the s. hath found an house, p. 62,
(Ps. 84:3)

Sparrows: more value than many s.,
p. 147, (Matt. 10:31; Lk. 12:7)

two s. sold for a farthing, p. 147,
(Matt. 10:29; cf. Lk. 12:6)

Spat: they s. in his face, p. 181,
(Matt. 26:67; Mk. 14:65; Lk.
22:64)

they s. upon him and smote him, p.
182, (Matt. 27:30; Mk. 15:19)

Speak: have mouths, but they s. not,
p. 66, (Ps. 115:5; 135:16)

I cannot s. for I am a child, p. 99,
(Jer. 1:6)

men shall s. well of you, p. 154, (Lk.
6:26)

s., Lord, for thy servant heareth, p.
31, (I Sam. 3:9)

what ye shall s., p. 146, (Matt. 10:19;
Mk. 13:11; Lk. 12:11)

whatsoever I command thee thou
shalt s., p. 99, (Jer. 1:7)

Speaking: while they are yet s., I will
hear, p. 96, (Isa. 65:24)

Spears: your pruninghooks into s.,
p. 117, (Joel 3:10)

Special: to be a s. people, p. 23,
(Deut. 7:6)

Spectacle: made a s. unto the world,
p. 206, (I Cor. 4:9)

Speech: an impediment in s., p. 159,
(Mk. 7:32)

great plainness of s., p. 210, (II Cor.
3:12)

I am slow of s., p. 14, (Ex. 4:10)

let your s. be always with grace
. . . , p. 221, (Col. 4:6)

Speech: (*continued*)

though I be rude in s., p. 212, (II Cor. 11:6)

thy s. is comely, p. 77, (Song 4:3)

Spew: I will s. thee out of my mouth, p. 241, (Rev. 3:16)

Spies: Joshua sent s. to view the land, p. 27, (Josh. 2:1)

Rahab and the s., p. 27, (Josh. 2)

twelve s. sent to Canaan, p. 19, (Num. 13—14:37)

Spirit: a double portion of thy s. be upon me, p. 42, (II Kg. 2:9)

a man with an unclean s., p. 138, (Mk. 1:23; Lk. 4:33)

a new heart and a new s., p. 108, (Ezek. 18:31)

absent in body but present in s., p. 206, (I Cor. 5:3)

all filled with the Holy S., p. 189, (Acts 2:4)

as many as are led by the S. of God, p. 201, (Rom. 8:14)

be filled with the S., p. 217, (Eph. 5:18)

by his S. in the inner man, p. 216, (Eph. 3:16)

by one S. are we all baptized, p. 208, (I Cor. 12:13)

diversities of gifts but the same S., p. 208, (I Cor. 12:4)

even the S. of truth, p. 178, (Jn. 14:17; 15:26)

evil s. troubled King Saul, p. 33, (I Sam. 16:14–23)

Father, Word and S. these three are one, p. 239, (I John 5:7)

fruit of the S. is love, joy, peace, p. 215, (Gal. 5:22)

God has sent forth the S. of his Son, p. 214, (Gal. 4:6)

God is S., p. 166, (Jn. 4:24)

Holy S. came upon them, p. 196, (Acts 19:6)

I have put my s. upon him, p. 93, (Isa. 42:1)

I will pour out my s. upon all flesh, p. 117, (Joel 2:28)

in the S. and heard a great voice, p. 240, (Rev. 1:10)

into thine hand I commit my s., p. 58, (Ps. 31:5)

into thy hands I commend my s., p. 183, (Lk. 23:46)

Jesus was led by the S., p. 135, (Matt. 4:1; Mk. 1:12; Lk. 4:1)

Joshua . . . in whom is the s., p. 20, (Num. 27:18)

Lord Jesus, receive my s., p. 191, (Acts 7:59)

manifest in the flesh, justified in the S., p. 225, (I Tim. 3:16)

my s. be troubled, p. 53, (Job 21:4)

my s. hath rejoiced in God my Saviour, p. 131, (Lk. 1:47)

my S. upon all flesh, p. 189, (Acts 2:17)

nor by power, but by my s. saith the Lord, p. 126, (Zech. 4:6)

not of the letter but of the S., p. 210, (II Cor. 3:6)

not ye but the Holy S., p. 146, (Matt. 10:20; Mk. 13:11; Lk. 12:12; cf. 21:15)

receive the Holy S., p. 184, (Jn. 20:22)

received the Holy S., p. 196, (Acts 19:2)

received ye the S. by works of the law?, p. 214, (Gal. 3:2)

revealed them unto us by his S., p. 205, (I Cor. 2:10)

so is also the Holy S., p. 191, (Acts 5:32)

S. itself maketh intercession, p. 202, (Rom. 8:26)

s. of the Lord came upon David, p. 33, (I Sam. 16:13)

s. of the Lord is upon me, p. 95, (Isa. 61:1)

s. of the Lord shall rest upon him, p. 85, (Isa. 11:2)

take not thy Holy S. from me, p. 60, (Ps. 51:11)

that which is born of the S., p. 165, (Jn. 3:6)

the firstfruits of the S., p. 202, (Rom. 8:23)

the flesh lusteth against the S., p. 215, (Gal. 5:17)

. . . the Holy S. be with you all, p. 213, (II Cor. 13:14)

the Holy S. fell on all, p. 194, (Acts 10:44)

the promise of the S. in our hearts, p. 210, (II Cor. 1:22)

the S. and the bride say, Come, p. 247, (Rev. 22:17)

the S. gave them utterance, p. 189, (Acts 2:4)

the s. is willing, but the flesh is weak, p. 180, (Matt. 26:41; Mk. 14:38)

the S. lifted me up, p. 106, (Ezek. 3:14)

the S. lifted me up between earth and heaven, p. 107, (Ezek. 8:3)

the S. of God descending like a dove, p. 135, (Matt. 3:16; Mk. 1:10; Lk. 3:21–22; Jn. 1:32)

the S. of God dwelleth in you, p. 206, (I Cor. 3:16)

the S. of God moved, p. 3, (Gen. 1:2)

the s. of heaviness, p. 95, (Isa. 61:3)

the S. of the Lord is upon me, p. 157, (Lk. 4:18; Isa. 61:1)

the S. revealed to him he would see Christ, p. 133, (Lk. 2:26)

the S. shall teach you all things, p. 178, (Jn. 14:26)

the S. that quickens, p. 167, (Jn. 6:63)

there is one body, and one S., p. 216, (Eph. 4:4)

through sanctification of the S., p. 222, (II Th. 2:13)

to another faith by the same S., p. 208, (I Cor. 12:9)

to one is given by the S. the word of wisdom, p. 208, (I Cor. 12:8)

unclean s. will return to an empty house, p. 155, (Matt. 12:43–44; Lk. 11:24)

walk in the S., p. 215, (Gal. 5:16)

when the S. of truth is come, p. 179, (Jn. 16:13)

whither shall I go from thy S.?, p. 67, (Ps. 139:7)

who hath directed the s. of the Lord?, p. 92, (Isa. 40:13)

whosoever speaketh against the Holy S., p. 155, (Matt. 12:32; Mk. 3:29; Lk. 12:10)

with the Holy S. and with fire, p. 135, (Matt. 3:11; Lk. 3:16; Jn. 1:33)

yet am I with you in the s., p. 220, (Col. 2:5)

you have received the S. of adoption, p. 201, (Rom. 8:15)

Spirits: seven s. more wicked than he, p. 155, (Matt. 12:45; Lk. 11:26)

who maketh his angels s., p. 65, (Ps. 104:4)

Spiritual: and raised a s. body, p. 210, (I Cor. 15:44)

that I may impart unto you some s. gift, p. 199, (Rom. 1:11)

Spiritually: to be s. minded is life, p. 201, (Rom. 8:6)

Spit: s. and touched his tongue, p. 159, (Mk. 7:33)

Spoil: take the s. and to take the prey, p. 84, (Isa. 10:6)

Spoke: he s. clearly, p. 159, (Mk. 7:35)

Spot: there is no s. in thee, p. 78, (Song 4:7)

Spread: cut down branches . . . and s. them, p. 169, (Matt. 21:8; Mk. 11:8; cf. Jn. 12:13)

s. their garments in the way, p. 169, (Matt. 21:8; Mk. 11:8; Lk. 19:36)

Springs: the s. of the sea, p. 54, (Job. 38:16)

the thirsty land s. of water, p. 90, (Isa, 35:7)

Spy: Moses sent them to s., p. 19, (Num. 13:17)

Staff: no s., no bread, no money, p. 146, (Matt. 10:10; Lk. 9:3; cf. Mk. 6:8)

Stagger: s. but not with strong drink, p. 89, (Isa. 29:9)

s. like a drunken man, p. 65, (Ps. 107:27)

Stalls: forty thousand s. of horses, p. 38, (I Kg. 4:26)

Stamped: cast him to the ground and s. on him, p. 112, (Dan. 8:7)

Stand: s. at the door and knock, p. 242, Rev. 3:20)

s. upright on thy feet, p. 194, (Acts 14:10)

s. ye in the ways, p. 99, (Jer. 6:16)

who shall s. when he appeareth?, p. 127, (Mal. 3:2)

Star: a great s. fell from heaven, p. 244, (Rev. 8:10)

the day s. arise in your hearts, p. 237, (II Pet. 1:19)

the name of the s. was Wormwood, p. 244, (Rev. 8:11)

the s. went before them, p. 134, (Matt. 2:9)

Star: (*continued*)
we have seen his s., p. 134, (Matt. 2:2)

Stars: exalt my throne above the s. of God, p. 86, (Isa. 14:13)
he telleth the number of the s., p. 68, (Ps. 147:4)
in his right hand seven s., p. 240, (Rev. 1:16)
praise him, all ye s., p. 68, (Ps. 148:3)
s. are not pure in his sight, p. 53, (Job 25:5)
s. shall withdraw their shining, p. 117, (Joel 2:10)
that maketh the seven s. and Orion, p. 119, (Amos 5:8)
the morning s. sang, p. 54, (Job 38:7)
the s. in their courses, p. 29, (Jg. 5:20)

Steal: thou shalt not s., p. 18, (Ex. 20:15)

Stem: a rod out of the s. of Jesse, p. 84, (Isa. 11:1)

Stephen: disputed with S., p. 191, (Acts 6:9)
S. did great wonders, p. 191, (Acts 6:8)
the martyrdom of S., p. 191, (Acts 6:9–8:2)
they cast S. out, p. 191, (Acts 7:58)

Steward: the unjust s., p. 152, (Lk. 16:1–8)

Stiffhearted: impudent children and s., p. 106, (Ezek. 2:4)

Stiffnecked: a s. people, p. 18, (Ex. 32:9)

Still: a s. small voice, p. 41, (I Kg. 19:12)
be s., and know that I am God, p. 60, (Ps. 46:10)
their strength is to sit s., p. 89, (Isa. 30:7)

Stink: there shall be s., p. 82, (Isa. 3:24)

Stir: s. up the gift of God, p. 226, (II Tim. 1:6)

Stole: Absalom s. the hearts, p. 36, (II Sam. 15:13)

Stolen: s. waters are sweet, p. 70, (Prov. 9:17)

Stone: a s. of stumbling and a rock of offence, p. 84, (Isa. 8:14)

all the people will s. us, p. 170, (Lk. 20:6)
not leave one s. upon another, p. 169, (Lk. 19:44)
not one s. upon another, p. 172, (Matt. 24:2; Mk. 13:2; Lk. 21:6)
s. of stumbling and a rock of offence, p. 236, (I Pet. 2:8)
the s. shall cry out of the wall, p. 123, (Hab. 2:11)
the s. which the builders refused, p. 66, (Ps. 118:22)
the s. which the builders rejected, p. 170, (Matt. 21:42; Mk. 12:10; Lk. 20:17)
with a sling and a s., p. 33, (I Sam. 17:50)

Stoned: cast Stephen out and s. him, p. 191, (Acts 7:58)
Jezebel had Naboth s. to death, p. 41, (I Kg. 21:8, 13)

Stones: command these s. be made bread p. 135, (Matt. 4:3; Lk. 4:3)
he chose five smoooth s., p. 33, (I Sam. 17:40)
s. to lay the foundation, p. 38, (I Kg. 5:17)
the s. of the field, p. 50, (Job 5:23)

Storm: stilling the s., p. 144, (Matt. 8:23–27; Mk. 4:35–41; Lk. 8:22–25)
with his disciples and a s. arose, p. 144, (Matt. 8:23, 24; Mk. 4:37; Lk. 8:22, 23)

Straight: make s. in the desert, p. 91, (Isa. 40:3)
make s. paths for your feet, p. 231, (Heb. 12:13)
the street called S., p. 192, (Acts 9:11)

Strait: s. is the gate, p. 142, (Matt. 7:14)

Strange: a stranger in a s. land, p. 14, (Ex. 2:22)
the Lord's song in a s. land, p. 67, (Ps. 137:4)

Stranger: for I am a s. with thee, p. 59, (Ps. 39:12)
I have been a s., p. 14, (Ex. 2:22)
oppress not the s., p. 100, (Jer. 7:6)

Strangers: s. and pilgrims on the earth, p. 231, (Heb. 11:13)

Streams: s. shall be turned into pitch, p. 90, (Isa. 34:9)

Street: in the top of every s., p. 104, (Lam. 2:19)

the s. called Straight, p. 192, (Acts 9:11)

Streets: go into the s. and bring the poor, p. 171, (Lk. 14:21)

her voice in the s., p. 69, (Prov. 1:20)

tread them down like the mire of the s., p. 84, (Isa. 10:6)

Strength: as the man is so is his s., p. 29, (Jg. 8:21)

been a s. to the poor, p. 87, (Isa. 25:4)

given the horse s., p. 55, (Job 39:19)

go from s. to s., p. 62, (Ps. 84:7)

he shall bring down thy s., p. 118, (Amos 3:11)

if I be shaven my s. will go, p. 30, (Jg. 16:17)

. . . in confidence shall be your s., p. 89. (Isa. 30:15)

in the Lord Jehovah is . . . s., p. 88, (Isa. 26:4)

Lord is my s. and my shield, p. 58, (Ps. 28:7)

so shall thy s. be, p. 21, (Deut. 33:25)

spare me, that I may recover s., p. 59, (Ps. 39:13)

s. is laid waste, p. 87, (Isa. 23:14)

the Lord is my s., p. 16, (Ex. 15:2)

their s. is to sit still, p. 89, (Isa. 30:7)

wherein thy great s. lieth, p. 30, (Jg. 16:6)

Strengthen: I will s. thee, p. 92, (Isa. 41:10)

s. me, I pray thee, p. 30, (Jg. 16:28)

s. ye the weak hands, p. 90, (Isa. 35:3)

Strife: a man of s. and a man of contention, p. 100, (Jer. 15:10)

no s. between me and thee, p. 7, (Gen. 13:8)

not in s. and envying, p. 204, (Rom. 13:13)

Strifes: hatred stirreth up s., p. 70, (Prov. 10:12)

Stripes: in s., in imprisonments, in tumults, p. 211, (II Cor. 6:5)

Strong: be s. and of a good courage, p. 27, (Josh. 1:6, 9)

be s. and quit yourselves like men, p. 32, (I Sam. 4:9)

be s., fear not, p. 90, (Isa. 35:4)

be s. in the Lord, p. 218, (Eph. 6:10)

out of the s. came forth sweetness, p. 30, (Jg. 14:14)

s. in the grace that is in Christ, p. 226, (II Tim. 2:1)

Stronger: s. than lions, p. 34, (II Sam. 1:23)

they are s. than we, p. 19, (Num. 13:31)

Stronghold: a s. in the day of trouble, p. 122, (Nahum 1:7)

turn ye to the s., p. 126, (Zech. 9:12)

Struck: Prophesy! Who is it that s. you?, p. 181, (Matt. 26:68; Mk. 14:65; Lk. 22:64)

Stubble: wrath which consumed them as s., p. 16, (Ex. 15:7)

Stubborn: a s. and rebellious generation, p. 62, (Ps. 78:8)

Study: much s. is a weariness of the flesh, p. 76, (Ec. 12:12)

Stumbling: a stone of s. and a rock of offence, p. 84, (Isa. 8:14)

Stumblingblock: unto the Jews a s., p. 205, (I Cor. 1:23)

Subjection: all things in s. under his feet, p. 228, (Heb. 2:8)

Submit: s. yourselves therefore to God, p. 234, (Jas. 4:7)

Subtilty: give s. to the simple, p. 69, (Prov. 1:4)

Succoth: booths in S., p. 11, (Gen. 33:17)

Suffer: better that ye s. for well doing, p. 236, (I Pet. 3:17)

if any man s. as a Christian, p. 237, (I Pet. 4:16)

if we s., we shall also reign, p. 226, (II Tim. 2:12)

if you do well and s. for it, p. 236, (I Pet. 2:20)

the Son of man must s., p. 161, (Matt. 16:21)

Suffered: Christ also s. for us, p. 236, (I Pet. 2:21)

in that he hath s., being tempted, p. 229, (Heb. 2:18)

Suffering: the s. of the disciples, p. 173, (Matt. 24:9–14; Mk. 13:9–13; Lk. 21:12–19; Jn. 16:2–6)

Sufferings: the s. of Christ abound in us, p. 210, (II Cor. 1:5)

the s. of this present time, p. 202, (Rom. 8:18)

Sufficient: s. unto the day, p. 141, (Matt. 6:34)

Summary: the s. of the law, p. 23, (Lev. 19:18; Deut. 6—7; Matt. 19:19; 22:39; Mk. 12:31–33; Rom. 13:9; Gal. 5:14; Jas. 2:8)

Summer: smite the winter house with the s. house, p. 118, (Amos 3:15)

the branch puts forth leaves . . . s is near, p. 174, (Matt. 24:32; Mk. 13:28; Lk. 21:30)

the s. is ended, p. 100, (Jer. 8:20)

Sun: a tabernacle for the s., p. 57, (Ps. 19:4)

a woman clothed with the s., p. 244, (Rev. 12:1)

from the rising of the s., pp. 65, 127, (Ps. 113:3; Mal. 1:11)

her s. is gone down, p. 100, (Jer. 15:9)

no new thing under the s., p. 74, (Ec. 1:9)

praise ye him, s. and moon, p. 68, (Ps. 148:3)

s. and the moon shall be dark, p. 117, (Joel 2:10)

s. shall be turned into darkness, p. 190, (Acts 2:20)

s. shall not smite thee by day, p. 66, (Ps. 121:6)

the s. go down on your wrath, p. 217, (Eph. 4:26)

the S. of righteousness shall arise, p. 127, (Mal. 4:2)

the s. shall be darkened . . . , p. 173, (Matt. 24:29; Mk. 13:24; cf. Lk. 21:25)

the s. stood still, p. 28, (Josh. 10:13)

your Father maketh his s. to rise, p. 140, (Matt. 5:45)

Sundry: at s. times and in divers manners, p. 228, (Heb. 1:1)

Sup: I will come in and s. with him, p. 242, (Rev. 3:20)

Superstitious: ye are too s., p. 196, (Acts 17:22)

Supper: a man made a great s., p. 171, (Lk. 14:16)

institution of the Lord's s., p. 177, (Matt. 26:26–29; Mk. 14:22–25; Lk. 22:14–20; I Cor. 11:23–25)

Swaddling: wrapped him in s. clothes, p. 132, (Lk. 2:7)

you will find the babe wrapped in s. clothes, p. 133, (Lk. 2:12)

Swallow: and the s. a nest, p. 62, (Ps. 84:3)

s. up death in victory, p. 87, (Isa. 25:8)

Swarm: a s. of bees and honey, p. 30, (Jg. 14:8)

Swear: s. not at all, p. 139, (Matt. 5:34)

Swearing: s., p. 139, (Matt. 5:33–37)

Sweat: in the s. of your face, p. 5, (Gen. 3:19)

Sweep: light a candle and s. the house, p. 152, (Lk. 15:8)

Sweet: every bitter thing is s., p. 73, (Prov. 27:7)

we took s. counsel together, p. 61, (Ps. 55:14)

wickedness be s. in his mouth, p. 53, (Job 20:12)

Sweetness: out of the strong came forth s., p. 30, (Jg. 14:14)

Swift: s. to hear, slow to speak, p. 233, (Jas. 1:19)

the flight shall perish from the s., p. 118, (Amos 2:14)

the race is not to the s., p. 76, (Ec. 9:11)

Swifter: s. than a weaver's shuttle, p. 50, (Job 7:6)

s. than eagles, p. 34, (II Sam. 1:23)

Swine: devils went into a herd of s., p. 144, (Matt. 8:32; Mk. 5:13; Lk. 8:33)

husks that the s. ate, p. 152, (Lk. 15:16)

pearls before s., p. 142, (Matt. 7:6)

s. . . . is unclean, p. 19, (Lev. 11:7–8; Deut. 14:8)

the Gadarene s., p. 144, (Matt. 8:28–34; Mk. 5:1–20; Lk. 8:26–39)

there arose a famine and he tended s., p. 152, (Lk. 15:14–15)

Sword: be devoured with the s., p. 81, (Isa. 1:20)

bring me a s., p. 37, (I Kg. 3:24)

every man's s. against his brother, p. 109, (Ezek. 32:21)

fight with the s. of my mouth, p. 241, (Rev. 2:16)

I will draw forth my s. out of his sheath, p. 108, (Ezek. 21:3)

man's s. was against his fellow, p. 32, (I Sam. 14:20)

nation shall not lift up s., p. 82, (Isa. 2:4)

not peace but a s., p. 147, (Matt. 10:34–37; Lk. 12:51–53; 14:26)

sharp as a two-edged s., p. 69, (Prov. 5:4)

the s. of the Lord and of Gideon, p. 29, (Jg. 7:18)

the s. of the Spirit which is the word of God, p. 218, (Eph. 6:17)

took a s. and fell upon it, p. 34, (I Sam. 31:4; I Chr. 10:4)

who take the s. will perish by the s., p. 180, (Matt. 26:52)

Swords: beat their s. into plowshares, p. 122, (Micah 4:3)

beat your plowshares into s., p. 117, (Joel 3:10)

their s. into plowshares, p. 82, (Isa. 2:4)

Sworn: the Lord hath s., and will not repent, p. 65, (Ps. 110:4)

Sycamore: climbed a s. tree, p. 154, (Lk. 19:4)

Zacchaeus in the s. tree, p. 154, (Lk. 19:1–10)

Synagogue: certain of the s. disputed with Stephen, p. 191, (Acts 6:9)

Jesus read in the s., p. 157, (L. 4:16)

the s. at Capernaum, p. 137, (Matt. 7:28–29; Mk. 1:21–28; Lk. 4:31–37)

Synagogues: preaching in their s., p. 137. (Matt. 4:23; Mk. 1:39; Lk. 4:4)

scourge you in their s., p. 146, (Matt. 10:17; Mk. 13:9; Lk. 12:11; 21:12)

Syracuse (Sicily): Paul sails via S. (S.), p. 198, (Acts 28:12)

Syria: churches in S. and Cilcia, p. 195, Acts 15:36–41)

Tabernacle: a t. for the sun, p. 57, (Ps. 19:4)

constructed the ark and the t., p. 18, (Ex. 35:10–12)

put the ark into the t., p. 18, (Ex. 40:21)

the ark and the t., p. 18, (Ex. 35:4–40)

the t. of God is with men, p. 247, (Rev. 21:3)

who shall abide in thy t., p. 56, (Ps. 15:1)

Tabernacles: how amiable are thy t., p. 62, (Ps. 84:1)

let us make three t., p. 161, (Matt. 17:4; Mk. 9:5; Lk. 9:33)

the feast of t., p. 22, (Lev. 23:34; Deut. 16:13)

Tabitha: T. (Dorcas) restored to life, p. 193, (Acts 9:36–42)

Table: thou preparest a t. before me, p. 57, (Ps. 23:5)

Tables: commandments on two t. of stone, p. 18, (Ex. 24:12; 31:18; 32:16)

the t. of the moneychangers, p. 170, (Matt. 21:12; Mk. 11:15; Jn. 2:15)

Tablets: he cast the t. out, p. 18, (Ex. 32:19)

make it plain upon t., p. 123, (Hab. 2:2)

Taken: from him that hath not shall be t. away, p. 175, (Matt. 25:29; Lk. 19:26)

the Lord hath t. away, p. 49, (Job 1:21)

Tale: spend our years as a t. that is told, p. 62, (Ps. 90:9)

Talent: I was afraid, and hid my t., p. 175, (Matt. 25:25; cf. Lk. 19:20)

Talents: here are five t. and five t. more, p. 175, (Matt. 25:20; cf. Lk. 19:16)

the parable of the t., p. 174, (Matt. 25:14–30; lk. 19:11–27)

to one he gave five t. . . . , p. 174, (Matt. 25:15)

Talk: t. tends only to penury, p. 71, (Prov. 14:23)

Talking: either he is t., or he is pursuing . . . , p. 40, (I Kg. 18:27)

Tarshish: all the ships of T., p. 82, (Isa. 2:16)

howl, ye ships of T., p. 87, (Isa. 23:14)

to Joppa and found a ship going to T., p. 120, (Jonah 1:3)

Tarsus: I am a Jew of T., p. 197, (Acts 21:39)

Taste: should t. death for every man, p. 229, (Heb. 2:9)

t. and see that the Lord is good, p. 58, (Ps. 34:8)

touch not, t. not, handle not, p. 220, (Col. 2:21)

Taught: opened his mouth and t. them, p. 138, (Matt. 5:2)

Taught: (continued)

t. them as one that had authority, p. 137, (Matt. 7:29; Mk. 1:22; Lk. 4:32)

Tax: a rich t. collector, p. 154, (Lk. 19:2)

Matthew sitting in the t. office, p. 145, (Matt. 9:9; Mk. 2:14; Lk. 5:27)

Taxed: to Bethlehem to be t., p. 132, (Lk. 2:4, 5)

Teach: not to t. in the name of Jesus, p. 190, (Acts 4:18)

shall any t. God knowledge, p. 53, (Job 21:22)

t. all nations and baptize them, p. 185, (Matt. 28:19; cf. Mk. 16:15–16; Lk. 24:47)

t. me thy way, p. 58, (Ps. 27:11)

t. no other doctrine, p. 223, (I Tim. 1:3)

t. them diligently unto thine children, p. 23, (Deut. 6:7)

t. us to pray, p. 140, (Lk. 11:1)

will t. us of his ways, p. 82, (Isa. 2:3)

Teacher: thine eyes shall see thy t., p. 89, (Isa. 30:20)

Teachers: desiring to be t. of the law, p. 223, (I Tim. 1:7)

Teaching: astonished at his t., p. 137, (Matt. 7:28; Mk. 1:22; Lk. 4:32)

the men you put in prison are t., p. 191, (Acts 5:25)

t. those things which concern Jesus Christ, p. 198, (Acts 28:31)

Tears: God shall wipe away all t., p. 244, (Rev. 7:17)

poureth out t. unto God, p. 52, (Job 16:20)

t. have been my meat day and night, p. 59, (Ps. 42:3)

they that sow in t., p. 66, (Ps. 126:5)

washed his feet with t., p. 155, (Lk. 7:38)

wipe away all t. from their eyes, p. 247, (Rev. 21:4)

wipe away t. from all faces, p. 87, (Isa. 25:8)

Teeth: children's t. are set on edge, p. 102, (Jer. 31:29; Ezek. 18:2)

with the skin of my t., p. 52, (Job 19:20)

Tekel: T.: Thou art weighed and found wanting, p. 111, (Dan. 5:27)

Tell: see thou t. no man, p. 143, (Matt. 8:4; Mk. 1:44; Lk. 5:14)

t. it not in Gath, p. 34, (II Sam. 1:20)

t. me, I pray thee, p. 30, (Jg. 16:6)

Tempest: no small t., p. 198, (Acts 27:20)

the Lord sent out a mighty t., p. 120, (Jonah 1:4)

Temple: a pillar in the t. of God, p. 241, (Rev. 3:12)

ark of the covenant was brought to the t., p. 38, (I Kg. 8:1–13; II Chr. 5:2–6:11)

body is a t. of the Holy Spirit, p. 206, (I Cor. 6:19)

chosen you to build the t., p. 37, (I Chr. 28:10)

devil set him on a pinnacle of the t., p. 136, (Matt. 4:5; Lk. 4:9)

drank out of golden vessels from the t., p. 111, (Dan. 5:3)

entered the t. . . . praising God, p. 190, (Acts 3:8)

into the t. to pray, p. 154, (Lk. 18:10)

Jesus went up into the t., p. 160, (Jn. 7:14)

overlaid the t. with gold, p. 38, (I Kg. 6:21, 22; II Chr. 3:8)

prediction of the destruction of the t., p. 172, (Matt. 24:1–2; Mk. 13:1–2; Lk. 21:5–6)

presentation of Jesus in the t., p. 133, (Lk. 2:22–39)

rebuilding of the t., p. 46, (Ezra 3–6)

she took him to Eli in the t., p. 31, (I Sam. 1:24–25)

sold and bought in the t., p. 170, (Matt. 21:12; Mk. 11:15; Lk. 19:45; Jn. 2:14–15)

Solomon built the t., p. 38, (II Chr. 3:1)

the building of the t., p. 38, (I Kg. 5—7; II Chr. 2—4)

the Lord is in his holy t., p. 123, (Hab. 2:20)

the t. was finished, p. 46, (Ezra 6:3, 14)

the veil of the t. was rent, p. 183, (Matt. 27:51; Mk. 15:38; Lk. 23:45)

they found him in the t., p. 134, (Lk. 2:46)

to the t. and measured the posts, p. 109, (Ezek. 40:48)

you are the t. of God, p. 206, (I Cor. 3:16)

Temples: not in t. made with hands, p. 196, (Acts 17:24)

Temporal: things which are seen are t., p. 211, (II Cor. 4:18)

Tempt: not t. the Lord thy God, p. 136, (Matt. 4:7; Lk. 4:12)

Temptation: count it joy when ye fall into t., p. 232, (Jas. 1:2)

t. and disobedience of Adam and Eve, p. 5, (Gen. 3:1–6)

the man that endureth t., p. 233, (Jas. 1:12)

the t., p. 135, (Matt. 4:1–11; Mk. 1:12–13; Lk. 4:1–13)

with the t. make a way to escape, p. 207, (I Cor. 10:13)

Tempted: able to succor them that are t., p. 229, (Heb. 2:18)

be t. above that ye are able, p. 207, (I Cor. 10:13)

forty days t. by Satan, p. 135, (Matt. 4:1–2; Mk. 1:13; Lk. 4:2)

in that he hath suffered, being t., p. 229, (Heb. 2:18)

t. . . . yet without sin, p. 229, (Heb. 4:15)

Ten: for the sake of t. I will not destroy, p. 9, (Gen. 18:32)

the t. commandments, p. 17, (Ex. 20:1–17; Deut. 5:6–21)

were not t. cleansed?, p. 153, (Lk. 17:17)

Tenants: parable of the wicked t., p. 170, (Matt. 21:33–41; Mk. 12:1–9; Lk. 20:9–16)

Tent: as a t. to dwell in, p. 92, (Isa. 40:22)

killed Sisera with a t. peg, p. 28, (Jg. 4:21)

Tenth: I will give a t. unto thee, p. 11, (Gen. 28:22)

Tents: how goodly are thy t., p. 20, (Num. 24:5)

in the t. of wickedness, p. 62, (Ps. 84:10)

to your t., O Israel, p. 39, (I Kg. 12:16)

Terror: not be afraid for the t. by night, p. 63, (Ps. 91:5)

Terrors: to the king of t., p. 52, (Job 18:14)

Testament: this cup is the new t. in my blood, p. 208, (I Cor. 11:25)

Testator: . . . there must be the death of the t., p. 230, (Heb. 9:16)

Testify: they t. of me, p. 167, (Jn. 5:39)

Thank: I t. thee . . . not as other men, p. 154, (Lk. 18:11)

Thanks: a good thing to give t. unto the Lord, p. 63, (Ps. 92:1)

give t. unto the Lord, p. 35, (I Chr. 16:8)

giving t. always for all things, p. 217, (Eph. 5:20)

he took the cup and gave t., p. 177, (Matt. 26:27; Mk. 14:23; Lk. 22:17, 20)

in every thing give t., p. 222, (I Th. 5:18)

t. be to God for his unspeakable gift, p. 212, (II Cor. 9:15)

when he had given t., he brake it, p. 208, (I Cor. 11:24)

Thanksgiving: David's psalm of t., p. 35, (I Chr. 16:8–36)

Hannah's song of t., p. 31, (I Sam. 2:1–10)

into his gates with t., p. 64, (Ps. 100:4)

t. and the voice of melody, p. 93, (Isa. 51:3)

Thessalonians: to the church of the T., p. 221, (I Th. 1:1)

Thessalonica: Paul's letters to T., p. 221, (I Th., II Th.)

Paul visits T., p. 195, (Acts 17:1)

Thief: knew when the t. was coming, p. 174, (Matt. 24:43; Lk. 12:39)

like a t. in the night, p. 222, (I Th. 5:2)

the day of the Lord will come as a t., p. 237, (II Pet. 3:10)

Thieves: a man fell among t., p. 149, (Lk. 10:30)

made it a den of t., p. 170, (Matt. 21:13; Mk. 11:17; Lk. 19:46)

t. break through, p. 141, (Matt. 6:19; cf. Lk. 12:33)

two t. crucified with him, p. 183, (Matt. 27:38; Mk. 15:27; Lk. 23:33; Jn. 19:18)

Thigh: smote them hip and t. with a great slaughter, p. 30, (Jg. 15:8)

the hollow of his t., p. 11, (Gen. 32:25)

Third: caught up to the t. heaven, p. 213, (II Cor. 12:2)

in the t. day he will raise us up, p. 115, (Hos. 6:2)

the t. day he shall be raised, p. 161, (Matt. 17:23; 20:19; Mk. 8:31; 9:31; 10:34; Lk. 9:22; 18:33)

the t. day . . . perfected, p. 169, (Lk. 13:32)

Thirst: and in my t. . . . vinegar, p. 61, (Ps. 69:21)

He said: I t., p. 183, (Jn. 19:38)

he that believes . . . never t., p. 167, (Jn. 6:35)

if any man t. let him come . . . , p. 160, (Jn. 7:37)

shall never t., p. 166, (Jn. 4:14)

Thirsteth: everyone that t., p. 94, (Isa. 55:1)

my soul t. for God, p. 59, (Ps. 42:2)

Thirsty: as cold waters to a t. soul, p. 73, (Prov. 25:25)

in a dry and t. land, p. 61, (Ps. 63:1)

the t. land springs of water, p. 90, (Isa. 35:7)

Thirty: for t. pieces of silver, p. 177, (Matt. 26:15)

t. pieces of silver, p. 126, (Zech. 11:12)

Thomas: Jesus said to T.: Behold my hands, p. 185, (Jn. 20:27)

T. said: My Lord and my God!, p. 185, (Jn. 20:28)

Thorn: instead of the t., p. 94, (Isa. 55:13)

was given to me a t. in the flesh, p. 213, (II Cor. 12:7)

Thorns: as t. in your sides, p. 28, (Jg. 2:3)

some [fell] among t., p. 156, (Matt. 13:7; Mk. 4:7; Lk. 8:7)

t. shall come up in her palaces, p. 90, (Isa. 34:13)

Thought: declares to man his t., p. 118, (Amos 4:13)

take no t. about your life, p. 141, (Matt. 6:25; Lk. 12:22)

take no t. . . . what ye shall speak, p. 146, (Matt. 10:19; Mk. 13:11; Lk. 12:11; cf. 21:14)

Thoughts: my t. are not your t., p. 94, (Isa. 55:8)

Thousand: a t. shall fall at thy side, p. 63, (Ps. 91:7)

a t. years in thy sight, p. 62, (Ps. 90:4)

one among a t., p. 54, (Job 33:23)

one day . . . as a t. years . . . , p. 237, (II Pet. 3:8)

Thousands: David his ten t., p. 34, (I Sam. 18:7)

Saul hath slain his t., p. 34, (I Sam. 18:7)

Threatenings: t. and slaughter, p. 192, (Acts 9:1)

Three: by those t. hundred, p. 29, (Jg. 7:7)

Paul stops at T. Taverns, p. 198, (Acts 28:15)

Threefold: a t. cord is not quickly broken, p. 75, (Ec. 4:12)

Threescore: t. years and ten, p. 63, (Ps. 90:10)

Throne: a rainbow about the t., p. 242, (Rev. 4:3)

a t. was set in heaven, p. 242, (Rev. 4:2)

above . . . was the likeness of a t., p. 106, (Ezek. 1:26)

cherubims and a sappphire t., p. 107, (Ezek. 10—11)

elders sitting around the t., p. 242, (Rev. 4:4)

exalt my t. above the stars of God, p. 86, (Isa. 14:13)

fruit of thy body . . . upon thy t., p. 67, (Ps. 132:11)

Jehoiakim shall have none upon the t., p. 103, (Jer. 36:30)

on the t. was a likeness of a man, p. 106, (Ezek. 1:26)

the Lord sitting upon a t., p. 83, (Isa. 6:1)

thy t. shall be established, p. 35, (II Sam. 7:16; I Chr. 17:14; Lk. 1:33)

without fault before the t. of God, p. 245, (Rev. 14:5)

Thrones: t., dominions, principalities or powers, p. 220, (Col. 1:16)

ye shall sit upon twelve t., p. 164, (Matt. 19:28)

Thrust: every one . . . shall be t. through, p. 85, (Isa. 13:15)

Thundered: the Lord t. from heaven, p. 36, (II Sam. 22:14)

Thyatira: Paul visits T., p. 195, (Acts 16:14)

to the church in T., p. 241, (Rev. 2:18–29)

Tidings: him that bringeth good t., p. 94, (Isa. 52:7)

Timbrel: with the t. and dance, p. 69, (Ps. 150:4)

Timbrels: with t. and dances, p. 16, (Ex.15:20)

Time: a t. to every purpose, p. 74, (Ec. 3:1)

for the t. to come for ever and ever, p. 89, (Isa. 30:8)

my t. is not yet come, p. 160, (Jn. 7:6)

now is the accepted t., p. 211, (II Cor. 6:2)

t. of war, a t. of peace, p. 74, (Ec. 3:8)

t. to be born, a t. to die, p. 74, (Ec. 3:2)

t. to love, a t. to hate, p. 74, (Ec. 3:8)

Times: my t. are in thy hand, p. 58, (Ps. 31:15)

Timothy: letters to T., p. 223, (Tim.)

Paul's letters to T., p. 223, (Tim.)

T. joins Paul, p. 195, (Acts 16:1–5)

T., my own son in the faith, p. 223, (I Tim. 1:2)

Tinkling: a t. with their feet, p. 82, (Isa. 3:16)

or a t. cymbal, p. 208, (I Cor. 13:1)

Tittle: one jot or t. of the law, p. 139, (Matt. 5:18; Lk. 16:17)

Titus: letter to T., p. 223, (Tit.)

Paul's letter to T., p. 227, (Tit.)

to T. mine own son, p. 227, (Tit. 1:4)

Told: it shall be t. thee, p. 192, (Acts 9:6)

Tomb: laid it in his own new t., p. 183, (Matt. 27:60; Mk. 15:46; Lk. 23:53; Jn. 19:41–42)

Mary Magdalene and the other Mary went to the t., p. 183, (Matt. 28:1; Mk. 16:1–2; cf. Lk. 24:1; Jn. 20:1)

the empty t., p. 183, (Matt. 28:1–10; Mk. 16:1–8; Lk. 24:1–11; Jn. 20:1–13)

Tomorrow: boast not . . . of t., p. 73, (Prov. 27:1)

Tongue: every man in our own t., p. 189, (Acts 2:8)

he that speaks in an unknown t., p. 209, (I Cor. 14:2)

keep thy t. from evil, p. 58, (Ps. 34:13)

my t. is the pen of a ready writer, p. 60, (Ps. 45:1)

the t. is a fire, a world of iniquity, p. 234, (Jas. 3:6)

the t. is a little member, p. 234, (Jas. 3:5)

Tongues: he that speaks with t., p. 209, (I Cor. 14:5)

sharpened their t. like a serpent, p. 68, (Ps. 140:3)

speak with the t. of men and of angels, p. 208, (I Cor. 13:1)

speaking in t., p. 209, (I Cor. 14)

to speak with other t., p. 189, (Acts 2:4)

t. like as of fire, p. 189, (Acts 2:3)

Tooth: a t. for tooth, p. 18, (Ex. 21:24; Matt. 5:38)

Torn: he hath t. and he will heal, p. 115, (Hos. 6:1)

Touch: t. his bone and his flesh, p. 49, (Job 2:5)

to me not for I am not yet ascended, p. 184, (Jn. 20:17)

t. not, taste not, handle not, p. 220, (Col. 2:21)

Tower: a t. whose top will reach unto heaven, p. 7, (Gen. 11:4)

intending to build a t., p. 151, (Lk. 14:28)

my high t. my refuge, p. 36, (II Sam. 22:3)

the t. of Babel, p. 7, (Gen. 11:1–9)

Tradition: disciples disobey the t., p. 158, (Matt. 15:2; Mk. 7:5)

Traditions: stand fast and hold the t., p. 222, (II Th. 2:15)

Train: t. up a child in the way, p. 72, (Prov. 22:6)

Trance: he fell into a t., p. 193, (Acts 10:10)

Transfiguration: the t., p. 161, (Matt. 17:1–8; Mk. 9:2–8; Lk. 9:28–36)

Transgression: to declare to Jacob his t., p. 121, (Micah 3:8)

where no law is, there is no t., p. 200, (Rom. 4:15)

Transgressions: I acknowledge my t., p. 60, (Ps. 51:3)

removed our t. from us, p. 64, (Ps. 103:12)

Transgressions: *(continued)*
the multitude of her t., p. 104, (Lam. 1:5)

Treacherously: why do we deal t.?, p. 127, (Mal. 2:10)

Treachery: Absalom's t. and death, p. 36, (II Sam. 15:13—19:8)

Tread: and t. upon the high places, p. 121, (Micah 1:3)

t. him underfoot, p. 86, (Isa. 14:25)

t. them down like the mire of the streets, p. 84, (Isa. 10:6)

Treasure: a t. hid in a field, p. 157, (Matt. 13:44)

for where your t. is, p. 141, (Matt. 6:21; Lk. 12:34)

layeth up t. for himself, p. 150, (Lk. 12:21)

parable of the t., p. 157, (Matt. 13:44)

this t. in earthen vessels, p. 211, (II Cor. 4:7)

t. cities, Pithom and Raamses, p. 13, (Ex. 1:11)

you have heaped t. together, p. 235, (Jas. 5:3)

Treasures: lay not up t., p. 141, (Matt. 6:19)

lay up . . . t. in heaven, p. 141, (Matt. 6:20; Lk. 12:33)

Treaty: Joshua was tricked into a t., p. 38, (Josh. 9:15–16, 22)

Tree: climbed a sycamore t., p. 154, (Lk. 19:4)

devour every green t. and every dry t., p. 108, (Ezek. 20:47)

every t. that is pleasant, p. 4, (Gen. 2:9)

I give to eat of the t. of life, p. 240, (Rev. 2:7)

like a green bay t., p. 59, (Ps. 37:35)

like a t. planted by the rivers, p. 55, (Ps. 1:3)

on either side . . . was the t. of life, p. 247, (Rev. 22:2)

shall flourish like the palm t., p. 63, (Ps. 92:12)

the t. of knowledge, p. 4, (Gen. 2:9)

the t. of life in the midst of the garden, p. 4, (Gen. 2:9)

when it is grown it becomes a t., p. 157, (Matt. 13:32; Mk. 4:32; Lk. 13:19)

Zacchaeus in the sycamore t., p. 154, (Lk. 19:1–10)

Trees: among the t. of the wood, p. 77, (Song 2:3)

fruitful t., and all cedars, p. 68, (Ps. 148:9)

see men as t. walking, p. 160, (Mk. 8:24)

stood among the myrtle t., p. 125, (Zech. 1:8)

Tremble: that made the earth to t., p. 86, (Isa. 14:16)

the inhabitants of the land t., p. 116, (Joel 2:1)

when the keepers of the house t., p. 76, (Ec. 12:3)

Trembled: Felix t., p. 197, (Acts 24:25)

Trespasses: if you forgive not your brother's t., p. 163, (Matt. 18:35)

Tribes: the t. of Israel, p. 28, (Josh. 13—22)

Tribulation: be patient in t., p. 203, (Rom. 12:12)

which came out of great t., p. 243, (Rev. 7:14)

Tribute: lawful to give t. unto Caesar?, p. 171, (Matt. 22:17; Mk. 12:14; Lk. 20:22)

Tricked: Joshua was t. into a treaty, p. 28, (Josh. 9:15–16, 22)

Tried: when he hath t. me, p. 53, (Job 23:10)

Triumphing: t. of the wicked is short, p. 53, (Job 20:5)

Troas: Paul travels via T., p. 196, (Acts 20:6)

Paul visits T., p. 195, (Acts 16:8)

Trodden: t. the winepress alone, p. 96, (Isa. 63:3)

t. under foot of men, p. 138, (Matt. 5:13)

Trogylium: Paul travels via T., p. 196, (Acts 20:15)

Trouble: a stronghold in the day of t., p. 122, (Nahum 1:7)

a time of t. such as never was, p. 113, (Dan. 12:1)

few days and full of t., p. 51, (Job 14:1)

t. me not. I cannot rise, p. 150, (Lk. 11:7)

Troubled: my spirit be t., p. 53, (Job 21:4)

she was t. at his saying, p. 131, (Lk. 1:29)

t. about many things, p. 150, (Lk. 10:41)

t. on every side yet not distressed, p. 211, (II Cor. 4:8)

True: God be t. but every man a liar, p. 200, (Rom. 3:4)

the t. gospel, p. 214, (Gal. 1:9–12)

whatsoever things are t., p. 219, (Phil. 4:8)

Trump: all be changed . . . at the last t., p. 210, (I Cor. 15:52)

with the t. of God, p. 222, (I Th. 4:16)

Trumpet: a t. in every man's hand, p. 29, (Jg. 7:16)

angels with a great sound of a t., p. 173, (Matt. 24:31)

blow a t. in Zion, p. 116, (Joel 2:1)

do not sound a t., p. 140, (Matt. 6:2)

praise him with the sound of the t., p. 69, (Ps. 150:3)

the seventh angel sounded the t., p. 244, (Rev. 11:15)

t. sound and the dead be raised, p. 210, (I Cor. 15:52)

Trumpets: a day of blowing the t., p. 21, (Lev. 23:24; Num. 29:1)

circled the city blowing t., p. 27, (Josh. 6:13, 14)

seven angels sounding seven t., p. 244, (Rev. 8:6)

Trust: he knoweth them that t. in him, p. 122, (Nahum 1:7)

in him will I t., p. 36, (II Sam. 22:3)

put not your t. in princes, p. 68, (Ps. 146:3)

that put their t. in him, p. 56, (Ps. 2:12)

t. in the Lord with all thine heart, p. 69, (Prov. 3:5)

t. ye in the Lord for ever, p. 88, (Isa. 26:4)

Trusted: she t. not in the Lord, p. 124, (Zeph. 3:2)

Trusteth: because he t. in thee, p. 87, (Isa. 26:3)

blessed is the man that t. in the Lord, p. 101, (Jer. 17:7)

he that t. in his riches, p. 70, (Prov. 11:28)

t. in the staff of this broken reed, p. 90, (Isa. 36:6)

Truth: a God of t., p. 21, (Deut. 32:4)

and the t. is not in us, p. 238, (I John 1:8)

changed the t. of God into a lie, p. 199, (Rom. 1:25)

counsels of old are faithfulness and t., p. 87, (Isa. 25:1)

even the Spirit of t., p. 178, (Jn. 14:17)

for we can do nothing against the t., p. 213, (II Cor. 13:8)

he will guide you into all t., p. 179, (Jn. 16:13)

I have walked before thee in t., p. 91, (Isa. 38:3)

John bare witness unto the t., p. 167, (Jn. 5:33)

mercy and t. are met together, p. 62, (Ps. 85:10)

no t., mercy, nor knowledge of God, p. 115, (Hos. 4:1)

Pilate asked: What is t.?, p. 182, (Jn. 18:38)

send out thy light and thy t., p. 59, (Ps. 43:3)

speak every man the t., p. 126, (Zech. 8:16)

speaking the t. in love, p. 217, (Eph. 4:15)

the pillar and ground of the t., p. 224, (I Tim. 3:15)

the t. shall make you free, p. 168, (Jn. 8:32)

to bear witness to the t., p. 181, (Jn. 18:37)

t. is perished and is cut off, p. 100, (Jer. 7:28)

words of t. and soberness, p. 197, (Acts 26:25)

ye shall know the t., p. 168, (Jn. 8:32)

your loins girt about with t., p. 218, (Eph. 6:14)

Try: t. me, and know my thoughts, p. 68, (Ps. 139:23)

Turn: and t. again to the Lord, p. 105, (Lam. 3:40)

he shall t. the heart of the fathers, p. 127, (Mal. 4:6)

remember and t. unto the Lord, p. 57, (Ps. 22:27)

t. to me with all your heart, p. 117, (Joel 2:12)

Turn: (continued)

t. unto the Lord your God, p. 117, (Joel 2:13)

Turtle: the voice of the t., p. 77, (Song 2:12)

Twelve: set up t. stones from the Jordan in Gilgal, p. 27, (Josh. 4:20)

the t. tribes of Israel, p. 13, (Gen. 49)

Two: t. nations are in thy womb, p. 10, (Gen. 25:23)

t. of every living thing, p. 6, (Gen. 6:19)

t. or three are gathered together, p. 162, (Matt. 18:20)

Tyre: behold I am against thee O T., p. 108, (Ezek. 26:3)

King Hiram of T. to hew cedars, p. 38, (I Kg. 5:1–10; II Chr. 2:3–16)

Paul travels via T., p. 196, (Acts 21:3)

the fall of T., p. 87, (Isa. 23)

Unbelief: after the same example of u., p. 229, (Heb. 4:11)

Unchastity: except for u., p. 139, (Matt. 5:32; 19:9)

Unclean: a man of u. lips, p. 83, (Isa. 6:5)

a man with an u. spirit, p. 138, (Mk. 1:23; Lk. 4:33)

laws concerning clean and u., p. 19, (Lev. 11:18; Deut. 14:3–21)

never eaten any thing u., p. 193, (Acts 10:14)

swine . . . is u., p. 19, (Lev. 11:7–8; Deut. 14:8)

u. spirit cried with a loud voice, p. 138, (Mk. 1:26; cf. Lk. 4:35)

u. spirit will return to an empty house, p. 155, (Matt. 12:43–44; Lk. 11:24)

Uncleanness: not called unto u. but unto holiness, p. 222, (I Th. 4:7)

Understand: make to u. doctrine, p. 88, (Isa. 28:9)

Understandeth: in honor, and u. not, p. 60, (Ps. 49:20)

Understanding: a wise and an u. heart, p. 37, (I Kg. 3:9; II Chr. 1:10)

give thee u. in all things, p. 226, (II Tim. 2:7)

in length of days u., p. 52, (Job 12:12)

the way of u., p. 92, (Isa. 40:14)

to depart from evil is u., p. 53, (Job 28:28)

to give thee skill and u., p. 113, (Dan. 9:22)

u. dark sentences, p. 113, (Dan. 8:23)

u. neither what they say . . . , p. 223, (I Tim. 1:7)

u. to the heart, p. 54, (Job 38:36)

Ungodly: the u. are like the chaff, p. 55, (Ps. 1:4)

u. men made me afraid, p. 56, (Ps. 18:4)

walketh not in the counsel of the u., p. 55, (Ps. 1:1)

Unity: for brethren to dwell together in u., p. 67, (Ps. 133:1)

Unjust: parable of the u. judge, p. 153, (Lk. 18:1–8)

the u. steward, p. 152, (Lk. 16:1–8)

Unknown: to the u. God, p. 196, (Acts 17:23)

Unleavened: eat u. bread, p. 15, (Ex. 12:15; Lev. 23:6; Deut. 16:3)

feast of u. bread. p. 21. (Ex. 23:15; Lev. 23:6)

in haste with u. bread, p. 15, (Ex. 12:8, 11)

Unsearchable: the u. riches of Christ, p. 216, (Eph. 3:8)

u. are his judgments, p. 203, (Rom. 11:33)

Unspeakable: for his u. gift, p. 212, (II Cor. 9:15))

Unspotted: keep oneself u. from the world, p. 233, (Jas. 1:27)

Unstable: Reuben . . . u. as water, p. 13, (Gen. 49:3–4)

Upper: they went into an u. room, p. 189, (Acts 1:13)

Uriah: David took Bathsheba, wife of U., p. 35, (II Sam. 11:3–5)

set ye U. in the forefront, p. 35, (II Sam. 11:15)

Uzziah: the year that King U. died, p. 83, (Isa. 6:1)

U. (Azariah) the leper king, p. 44, (II Kg. 15:1–7; II Chr. 26)

Vain: a wise man utter v. knowledge, p. 52, (Job 15:2)

people imagine a v. thing, p. 55, (Ps. 2:1)

turned aside unto v. jangling, p. 223, (I Tim. 1:6)

402

Valley: every v. shall be exalted, p. 91, (Isa. 40:4)

in the v. of decision, p. 117, (Joel 3:14)

the v. of dry bones, p. 109, (Ezek. 37)

the v. of the shadow of death, p. 57, (Ps. 23:4)

Valor: might men of v., p. 27, (Josh. 6:2)

Value: more v. than many sparrows, p. 147, (Matt. 10:31; Lk. 12:7)

Vanity: man at his best is altogether v., p. 59, (Ps. 39:5)

my days are v., p. 50, (Job 7:16)

that draw iniquity with cords of v., p. 83, (Isa. 5:18)

v. of vanities, all is v., p. 74, (Ec. 1:2)

Vapor: a v. that appears a little time, p. 234, (Jas. 4:14)

Variableness: no v., nor shadow of turning, p. 233, (Jas. 1:17)

Vashti: the king dethroned Queen V., p. 46, (Est. 1:19–21)

Vengeance: the day of the Lord's v., p. 90, (Isa. 34:8)

v. is mine, p. 203, (Rom. 12:19)

Vex: how long will ye v. my soul, p. 52, (Job 19:2)

Vexation: a v. only to understand the report, p. 89, (Isa. 28:19)

than both hands full with v., p. 74, (Ec. 4:6)

Victory: David's v. song, p. 36, (II Sam. 22)

Moses' song of v., p. 16, (Ex. 15:1–21)

swallow up death in v., p. 87, (Isa. 25:8)

to God which giveth us the v., p. 210, (I Cor. 15:57)

Vile: behold I am v., p. 55, (Job 40:4)

Vine: a second eagle and the v. did bend, p. 108, (Ezek. 17:7)

became a spreading v., p. 108, (Ezek. 17:6)

every man under his v., p. 38, (I Kg. 4:25)

every man under his v. and under his fig tree, p. 122, (Micah 4:4)

I am the true v., p. 178, (Jn. 15:1)

I am the v., ye are the branches, p. 178, (Jn. 15:5)

Vinegar: and in my thirst . . . v., p. 61, (Ps. 69:21)

gave him v. to drink, p. 183, (Matt. 27:48; Mk. 15:36; Jn. 19:29)

Vines: destroy her v. and her fig trees, p. 114, (Hos. 2:12)

little foxes, that spoil the v., p. 77, (Song 2:15)

Vineyard: a man planted a v., p. 170, (Matt. 21:33; Mk. 12:1; Lk. 20:9)

a v. in a fruitful hill, p. 82, (Isa. 5:1)

Ahab: Give me thy v., p. 41, (I Kg. 21:2)

Ahab took possession of the v., p. 41, (I Kg. 21:16)

give the v. to others, p. 170, (Matt. 21:41; Mk. 12:9; Lk. 20:16)

go work in my v., p. 170, (Matt. 21:28)

hired laborers for his v., p. 164, (Matt. 20:1)

Naboth's v., p. 41, (I Kg. 21:1–16)

parable of the laborers in the v., p. 164, (Matt. 20:1–16)

the Lord's v., p. 82, (Isa. 5)

v. of the Lord is the house of Israel, p. 83, (Isa. 5:7)

Vineyards: the poor were given v., p. 103, (Jer. 39:10)

they shall plant v., p. 96, (Isa. 65:21)

Violence: remove v. . . . . and execute judgment, p. 109, (Ezek. 45:9)

v. is risen up, p. 107, (Ezek. 711)

Viper: a poisonous v., p. 198, (Acts 28:3–6)

Virgin: a v. shall conceive and bear a son, p. 83, (Isa. 7:14)

Virgins: kingdom of heaven is like ten v., p. 174, (Matt. 25:1)

the parable of the wise and foolish v., p. 174, (Matt. 25:1–13)

Virtuous: a v. woman is a crown, p. 70, (Prov. 12:4)

find a v. woman, p. 73, (Prov. 31:10)

Vision: a v. appeared to Paul, p. 195, (Acts 16:9)

a v. of Jerusalem's idolatry, p. 107, (Ezek. 8)

Abram's v. and covenant, p. 8, (Gen. 15)

and every v. faileth, p. 107, (Ezek. 12:22)

Daniel's v. of the four beasts, p. 112, (Dan. 7)

Vision: (continued)

Gabriel, make this man understand the v., p. 112, (Dan. 8:16)

the v. of four cherubim, p. 105, (Ezek. 1:4–14))

the v. of four wheels, p. 105, (Ezek. 1:15–25)

the v. of the ram and the goat, p. 112, (Dan. 8)

where there is no v., p. 73, (Prov. 29:18)

Zechariah's v., p. 125, (Zech. 1:8–21)

Visions: I saw v. of God, p. 105, (Ezek. 1:1)

young men see v., p. 117, (Joel 2:28)

young men shall see v., p. 189, (Acts 2:17)

Visitation: knewest not the time of thy v., p. 169, (Lk. 19:44)

Vocation: the v. wherewith ye are called, p. 216, (Eph. 4:1)

Voice: a v. was heard in Ramah, p. 102, (Jer. 31:15)

he fell to the earth and heard a v., p. 192, (Acts 9:4)

heard the v. of the Lord and hid, p. 5, (Gen. 3:8)

her v. in the streets, p. 69, (Prov. 1:20)

his v. as the sound of many waters, p. 240, (Rev. 1:15)

lift up thy v., p. 92, (Isa. 40:9)

not hearken to the v. of charmers, p. 61, (Ps. 58:5)

the v. is Jacob's, p. 10, (Gen. 27:22)

the v. of one crying in the wilderness, p. 135, (Matt. 3:3; Mk. 1:3; Lk. 3:4)

the v. of the turtle, p. 77, (Song 2:12)

Vomit dog is turned to his own v., p. 237, (II Pet. 2:22)

dog returneth to his v., p. 73, (Prov. 26:11)

Vomited: it v. out Jonah on dry land, p. 120, (Jonah 2:10)

Vow: better thou shouldst not v., p. 75, (Ec. 5:5)

Wages: the w. of sin is death, p. 201, (Rom. 6:23)

Wailing: a voice of wailing is heard out of Zion, p. 100, (Jer. 9:19)

Wait: blessed are all they that w., p. 89, (Isa. 30:18)

that w. upon the Lord, p. 92, (Isa. 40:31)

therefore will the Lord w., p. 89, (Isa. 30:18)

w. for the God of my salvation, p. 122, (Micah 7:7)

Waited: I w. patiently for the Lord, p. 59, (Ps. 40:1)

w. for me as for the rain, p. 54, (Job 29:23)

Waiteth: blessed is he that w., p. 114, (Dan. 12:12)

my soul w. for the Lord, p. 67, (Ps. 130:6)

Wake: w. up the mighty men, p. 117, (Joel 3:9)

Walk: can two w. together, except they be agreed?, p. 118, (Amos 3:3)

nevertheless I must w., p. 169, (Lk. 13:33)

rise up and w., p. 190, (Acts 3:6)

take up thy bed and w., p. 144, (Mk. 2:9, 11; cf. Lk. 5:24)

this is the way, w. ye in it, p. 89, (Isa. 30:21)

to w. humbly with thy God, p. 122, (Micah 6:8)

w. and not faint, p. 92, (Isa. 40:31)

w. while you have the light, p. 176, (Jn. 12:35)

we will not w. therein, p. 99, (Jer. 6:16)

will w. in his paths, p. 82, p. 122, (Isa. 2:32; Micah 4:2)

Walked: the people that w. in darkness, p. 84, (Isa. 9:2)

he leaped up and w., p. 194, (Acts 14:10)

we have w. to and fro, p. 125, (Zech. 1:11)

Walking: from w. up and down, p. 49, (Job 1:7)

Jesus went to them w. on the water, p. 158, (Matt. 14:25; Mk. 6:48; Jn. 6:19)

w. and mincing, p. 82, (Isa. 3:16)

Wall: a w. made by a plumbline, p. 119, (Amos 7:7)

every fenced w., p. 82, (Isa. 2:15)

fingers of a man's hand wrote upon the w., p. 111, (Dan. 5:5)

I will break down the w., p. 83, (Isa. 5:5)

so the w. was finished, p. 46, (Neh.
6:15)

son of man dig now in the w., p.
107, (Ezek. 8:8)

the w. fell down flat, p. 27, (Josh.
6:20)

Walls: rebuilding the w. of Jerusalem, p. 46, (Neh. 3—6; 12:27–
47)

the broad w. of Babylon, p. 103,
(Jer. 51:58)

Wanderer: a w. on the earth, p .5,
(Gen. 4:12)

Wanderers: w. among the nations, p.
116, (Hos. 9:17)

Wanton: stretched forth necks and w.
eyes, p. 82, (Isa. 3:16)

War: a time of w., p. 74, (Ec. 3:8)

civil w. throughout their reigns, p.
39, (I Kg. 14:30; II Chr. 12:15)

learn w. any more, p. 82, (Isa. 2:4)

neither shall they learn w. anymore,
p. 122, (Micah 4:3)

power to make w. with the saints, p.
245, (Rev. 13:7)

the Lord is a man of w., p. 16, (Ex.
15:3)

there was w. in heaven, p. 244, (Rev.
12:7)

Warfare: her w. is accomplished, p.
91, (Isa. 40:2)

Warn: to w. his brothers, p. 153, (Lk.
16:28)

Wars: shall hear of w. and rumors of
war, p. 173, (Matt. 24:6; Mk.
13:7)

Wash: anoint thine head and w. thy
face, p. 141, (Matt. 6:17)

go and w. in Jordan seven times, p.
43, II Kg. 5:10)

go w. in the pool of Siloam, p. 168,
(Jn. 9:7)

if I w. thee not, p. 177, (Jn. 13:8)

Jesus . . . began to w. the disciples'
feet, p. 177, (Jn. 13:4–5)

ought to w. one another's feet, p.
177, (Jn. 13:14)

Peter: Thou shalt never w. my feet,
p. 177, (Jn. 13:8)

w. their hands before they eat, p.
158, (Matt. 15:2; Mk. 7:2, 5)

Washed: Pilate w. his hands, p. 182,
(Matt. 27:24)

w. his feet with tears, p. 155, (Lk.
7:38)

w. their robes in the blood of the
Lamb, p. 243, (Rev. 7:14)

Watch: could ye not w. with me one
hour? p. 180, (Matt. 26:40; Mk.
14:37)

let us w. and be sober, p. 222, (I Th.
5:8)

tarry ye here and w. me, p. 180,
(Matt. 26:38; Mk. 14:34)

the Lord w. between me and thee, p.
11, (Gen. 31:49)

w. for you know neither the day
. . . , p. 174, (Matt. 25:13)

w. ye, stand fast in the faith, p. 210,
(I Cor. 16:13)

w. you know not what hour your
Lord comes, p. 174, (Matt.
24:42; Mk. 13:35)

Watching: w. with all perseverance,
p. 218 (Eph. 6:18)

Watchman: a w. unto Israel, p. 106,
(Ezek. 3:14–27)

w., what of the night, p. 86, (Isa.
21:11)

Water: a pure river of w. of life, p.
247, (Rev. 22:1)

as w. spilt on the ground, p. 36, (II
Sam. 14:14)

bread of adversity, and w. of
affliction, p. 89, (Isa. 30:20)

drink w. with trembling, p. 107,
(Ezek. 12:18)

fill the waterpots with w., p. 137, (Jn.
2:7)

give us w. that we may drink, p. 17,
(Ex. 17:2)

hewers of woods and drawers of w.,
p. 28, (Josh. 9:21, 27)

I have baptized you with w., p. 135,
(Matt. 3:11; Mk. 1:8; Lk. 3:16;
Jn. 1:26, 33)

Israel passed through walls of w., p.
16, (Ex. 14:22)

poured out like w., 57, (Ps. 22:14)

rebuked the wind and the raging w.,
p. 144, (Lk. 8:24)

take the w. of life freely, p. 247,
(Rev. 22:17)

through fire and through w., p. 61,
(Ps. 66:12)

w. came forth abundantly, p. 17, (Ex.
17:6; Num. 20:11)

w. springing up into everlasting life,
p. 166, (Jn. 4:14)

Water: (continued)

whosoever drinks of the w. I shall give, p. 160, (Jn. 4:14)

Waters: as the w. cover the sea, p. 123, (Hab. 2:14)

cold w. to a thirsty soul, p. 73, (Prov. 25:25)

come ye to the w., p. 94, (Isa. 55:1)

hath measured the w., p. 92, (Isa. 40:12)

let the w. be gathered together, p. 3, (Gen. 1:9)

let the w. bring forth, p. 3, (Gen. 1:20)

stolen w. are sweet, p. 70, (Prov. 9:17)

the face of the w., p. 3, (Gen. 1:2)

the rushing of many w., p. 86, (Isa. 17:13)

the w. are come in unto my soul, p. 61, (Ps. 69:1)

the w. called he Seas, p. 3, (Gen. 1:10)

the w. prevailed, p. 6, (Gen. 7:24)

w. covered the chariots, p. 16, (Ex. 14:28)

Waterspouts: at the noise of thy w., p. 59, (Ps. 42:7)

Waste: comfort all her w. places, p. 93, (Isa. 51:3)

generation to generation it shall lie w., p. 90, (Isa. 34:10)

the kings of Assyria have laid w., p. 90, (Isa. 37:18)

Wasted: w. his substance with riotous living, p. 152, (Lk. 15:13)

Waves: raging w. of the sea, p. 239, (Jude v. 13)

thy billows and thy w. passed over, p. 120, (Jonah 2:3)

Wax: the mountains will melt as w., p. 121, (Micah 1:4)

Way: and the w. you know, p. 178, (Jn. 14:4)

he shall prepare the w., p. 127, (Mal. 3:1)

hedge up her w. with thorns, p. 114, (Hos. 2:6)

how can we know the w.?, p. 178, (Jn. 14:5)

prepare ye the w., p. 91, (Isa. 40:3)

prepare ye the w. of the Lord, p. 135, (Matt. 3:3; Mk. 1:3; Lk. 3:4)

teach me thy w., p. 58, (Ps. 27:11)

the w. of all the earth, p. 28, (Josh. 23:14)

the w. of life and the w. of death, p. 101 (Jer. 21:8)

the w., the truth, and the life, p. 178, (Jn. 14:6)

this is the w., walk ye in it, p. 89, (Isa. 30:21)

who shall prepare thy w., p. 148, (Matt. 11:10; Lk. 7:27)

Ways: amend your w. and your doings, p. 100, (Jer. 7:3)

go before . . . to prepare his w., p. 132, (Lk. 1:76)

her w. are w. of pleasantness, p. 69, (Prov. 3:17)

his w. are judgment, p. 21, (Deut. 32:4)

his w. past finding out, p. 203, (Rom. 11:33)

let us search and try our w., p. 105, (Lam. 3:40)

my w. higher than your w., p. 94, (Isa. 55:9)

neither are your w. my w., p. 94, (Isa. 55:8)

stand ye in the w., p. 99, (Jer. 6:16)

Weak: knees shall be w. as water, p. 107, (Ezek. 7:17)

strengthen ye the w. hands, p. 90, (Isa. 35:3)

to bear the infirmities of the w., p. 204, (Rom. 15:1)

to the w. and beggarly elements?, p. 214, (Gal. 4:9)

when I am w., then am I strong, p. 213, (II Cor. 12:10)

who is w. and I am not w.?, p. 213, (II Cor. 11:29)

Weaker: unto the wife, as unto the w. vessel, p. 236, (I Pet. 3:7)

Weakness: strength is made perfect in w., p. 213, (II Cor. 12:9)

I was with you in w., p. 205, (I Cor. 2:3)

Wealth: w. maketh many friends, p. 72, (Prov. 19:4)

Weapons: wisdom is better than w., p. 76, (Ec. 9:18)

Weariness: in w. and painfulness . . . in hunger and thirst, p. 212, (II Cor. 11:27) much study is a w. of the flesh, p. 76, (Ec. 12:12)

Weary: be not w. in well doing, p. 223, (II Th. 3:13)

God . . . neither is w., p. 92, (Isa. 40:28)

I am w. of my crying, p. 61, (Ps. 69:3)

great rock in a w. land, p. 89, (Isa. 32:2)

I am w. with repenting, p. 100, (Jer. 15:6)

lest by her coming she w. me, p. 154, (Lk. 18:5)

not be w. in well doing, p. 215, (Gal. 6:9; II Thess. 3:13)

run and not be w., p. 92, (Isa. 40:31)

the w. be at rest, p. 50, (Job 3:17)

Weather: fair w. cometh out of the north, p. 54, (Job 37:22)

Weaver: swifter than a w.'s shuttle, p. 50, (Job 7:6)

Wedding: bidden . . . to a w. feast, p. 151, (Lk. 14:8)

without a w. garment, p. 171, (Matt. 22:11)

Weeds: w. are the children of the wicked one, p. 156, (Matt. 13:38)

burn the w. but gather the wheat, p. 156, (Matt. 13:30)

parable of the w., p. 156, (Matt. 13:24–30; 36–43)

sowed w. among the wheat, p. 156, (Matt. 13:25)

Weeks: feast of w., p. 21, (Ex. 23:16; Lev. 23:9–22; Deut. 16:9–12)

shall be the feast of w., p. 21, (Deut. 16:9–10)

Weepest: woman, why w. thou? whom seekest thou?, p. 184, (Jn. 20:15)

Weepeth: he that goeth forth and w., p. 66, (Ps. 126:6)

she w. sore in the night, p. 104, (Lam. 1:2)

Weeping: Rachel w. for her children, p. 134, (Matt: 2:17–18)

w. and knashing of teeth, p. 171, 174, (Matt. 22:13; 24:51)

w. may endure for a night, p. 58, (Ps. 30:5)

Weighed: TEKEL: Thou art w. and found wanting, p. 111, (Dan. 5:27)

Well: found Rebekah at the w., p. 9, (Gen. 24:15–16)

Rachel came to the w., p. 11, (Gen. 29:6)

Went: I go, sir, and w. not, p. 170, (Matt. 21:30)

Wept: and Hezekiah w., p. 91, (Isa. 38:3)

beheld the city and w., p. 169, (Lk. 19:41)

he went out and w. bitterly, p. 181, (Matt. 26:75; Mk. 14:72; Lk. 22:62)

Jesus w., p. 169, (Jn. 11:35)

Joash came down and w., p. 44, (II Kg. 13:14)

Joseph turned away and w., p. 12, (Gen. 42:24)

West: as far as the east is from the w., p. 64, (Ps. 103:12)

Whale: Jonah and the w., p. 120, (Jonah 1:17–2)

Whales: God created great w., p. 3, (Gen. 1:21)

Wheat: a grain of w. fall into the ground, p. 175, (Jn. 12:24)

burn the weeds but gather the w., p. 156, (Matt. 13:30)

thy belly is like an heap of w., p. 78, (Song 7:2)

Wheel: a w. beside each living creature, p. 105, (Ezek. 1:15)

a w. in the middle of a w., p. 105, (Ezek. 1:16)

Wheels: spirit of the living creature was in the w., p. 105, (Ezek. 1:20)

the rattling of the w., p. 123, (Nahum 3:2)

why tarry the w., p. 29, (Jg. 5:28)

Whelps: she brought up one of her w., p. 108, (Ezek. 19:3)

Where: w. hast thou laid him?, p. 184, (Jn. 20:15)

w. I might find him, p. 53, (Job 23:3)

Whip: the noise of a w. and the rattling of the wheels, p. 123, (Nahum 3:2)

Whips: chastised you with w. but I . . . with scorpions, p. 39, (I Kg. 12:11)

Whirlwind: a rolling thing before the w., p. 86, (Isa. 17:13)

Whirlwind: (*continued*)

a w. came out of the north, p. 105, (Ezek. 1:4)

Elijah went up by a w. into heaven, p. 42, (II Kg. 2:11)

God answers Job out of the w., p. 54, (Job 38:1)

the Lord hath his way in the w., p. 122, (Nahum 1:3)

they shall reap the w., p. 116, (Hos. 8:7)

White: and his raiment became w., p. 161 (Matt. 17:2; Mk. 9:2–3; Lk. 9:29)

be as w. as snow, p. 81, (Isa. 1:18)

his hairs were w. as snow, p. 240, (Rev. 1:14)

will be clothed in w. raiment, p. 241, (Rev. 3:5)

Whited: you are like w. sepulchres, p. 172, (Matt. 23:27; cf. Lk. 11:44)

Whiter: I shall be w. than snow, p. 60, (Ps. 51:7)

Whither: w. goest thou?, p. 179, (Jn. 13:36; 16:5)

w. I go, ye cannot come, p. 168, (Jn. 8:21)

w. thou goest, I will go, p. 31, (Ruth 1:16)

Whole: faith hath made thee w., p. 145, (Matt. 9:22; Mk. 5:34; Lk. 8:48)

stretched forth his hand and it was w., p. 149, (Matt. 12:13; Mk. 3:5; Lk. 6:10)

will thou be made w.?, p. 166, (Jn. 5:6)

Whom: w. do men say that I am?, p. 160, (Matt. 16:13; Mk. 8:27; Lk. 9:18)

Whoredom: hath committed great w., p. 114, (Hos. 1:2)

w. and wine, p. 115, (Hos. 4:11)

Woe: w. is me, p. 83, (Isa. 6:5)

w. to you, scribes and Pharisees, p. 172, (Matt. 23:25)

Wolf: the w. also shall dwell with the lamb, p. 85, (Isa. 11:6)

Wolves: as sheep in the midst of w., p. 146, (Matt. 10:16; Lk. 10:3)

her judges are evening w., p. 124, (Zeph. 3:3)

Womb: came forth of his mother's w., p. 75, (Ec. 5:15)

camest forth out of the w., p. 99, (Jer. 1:5)

out of my mother's w., p. 49, (Job 1:21)

two nations are in thy w., p. 10, (Gen. 25:23)

why died I not from the w.?, p. 50, (Job 3:11)

Woman: a virtuous w. is a crown, p. 70, (Prov. 12:4)

a w. clothed with the sun, p. 244, (Rev. 12:1)

a w. from Adam's rib, p. 4, (Gen. 2:22)

a w. of sorrowful spirit, p. 31, (I Sam. 1:15)

a w. sit upon a scarlet colored beast, p. 246, (Rev. 17:3)

a w. with a hemorrhage, p. 145, (Matt. 9:20; Mk. 5:25; Lk. 8:43)

a. w. . . . who was a sinner, p. 155, (Lk. 7:37)

find a virtuous w., p. 73, (Prov. 31:10)

man that is born of w., p. 51, (Job 14:1)

the w. gave me fruit, p. 5, (Gen. 3:12)

the w. taken in adultery, p. 167, (Jn. 8:3)

the w. with a spirit of infirmity, p. 151, (Lk. 13:10–17)

the w. whose heart is snares, p. 75, (Ec. 7:26)

w., behold thy son!, p. 183, (Jn. 19:26)

w. hid it in three measures of meal, p. 157, (Matt. 13:33; Lk. 13:21)

w. what have I to do, p. 137, (Jn. 2:4)

w. with an alabaster box, p. 176, (Matt. 26:7; Mk. 14:3)

w. with an issue of blood, p. 145, (Matt. 9:18–26; Mk. 5:21–43; Lk. 8:40–56)

Women: blessed art thou among w., p. 131, p. 132, (Lk. 1:28, 42)

let the w. learn in silence, p. 224, (I Tim. 2:11)

Paul's attitude toward w., p. 224, (I Tim. 2:9–15)

seven w. shall take hold of one man, p. 82, (Isa. 4:1)

Solomon loved many strange w., p. 39, (I Kg. 11:1)

Wonder: stay yourselves and w., p. 89, (Isa. 29:9)

Wondered: all that heard it w., p. 133, (Lk. 2:18)

Wonderful: called W., Counselor, The mighty God, p. 84, (Isa. 9:6)

for thou hast done w. things, p. 87, (Isa. 25:1)

Wonders: I will show w. in heaven, p. 189, (Acts 2:19)

Wood: hewers of w. and drawers of water, p. 28, (Josh. 9:21, 27)

Word: a w. fitly spoken, p. 73, (Prov. 25:11)

doers of the w. not hearers only, p. 233, (Jas. 1:22)

every w. . . . of the Lord, p. 22, (Deut. 8:3)

Father, W. and Spirit these three are one, p. 239, (I John 5:7)

hear the w. of the Lord, p. 101, (Jer. 22:29)

his name is called The W. of God, p. 246, (Rev. 19:13)

in the beginning was the W., p. 131, (Jn. 1:1)

mightily grew the w. of God, p. 196, (Acts 19:20)

none spake a w., p. 49, (Job 2:13)

speak the w. only, p. 143, (Matt. 8:8; Lk. 7:7)

the Lord hath fulfilled his w., p. 104, (Lam. 2:17)

the w. of our God shall stand, p. 91, (Isa. 40:8)

the w. of the Lord endureth for ever, p. 235, (I Pet. 1:25)

the w. of the Lord to Micah, p. 121, (Micah 1:1)

the W. was God, p. 131, (Jn. 1:1)

the W. was made flesh, p. 131, (Jn. 1:14)

the W. was with God, p. 131, (Jn. 1:1)

went everywhere preaching the w., p. 191, (Acts 8:4)

who hear the w. of god and do it, p. 156, (Matt. 12:50; Mk. 3:35; Lk. 8:21)

w. of God is quick and powerful, p. 229, (Heb. 4:12)

w. of God is not bound, p. 226, (II Tim. 2:9)

w. of the Lord to Zechariah, p. 125, (Zech. 1:1)

w. spoken in due season, p. 71, (Prov. 15:23)

Words: darkeneth counsel by w. without knowledge, p. 54, (Job 38:2)

go speak the w. of this life, p. 191, (Acts 5:20)

he that is of God heareth God's w., p. 168, (Jn. 8:47)

let thy w. be few, p. 75, (Ec. 5:2)

my w. in thy mouth, p. 99, (Jer. 1:9)

my w. shall not pass away, p. 174, (Matt. 24:35; Mk. 13:31; Lk. 21:33)

oh that my w. were now written!, p. 52, (Job 19:23)

prophets . . . that steal my w., p. 101, (Jer. 23:30)

these w. shall be in thine heart, p. 23, (Deut. 6:6)

w. . . . were smoother than butter, p. 61, (Ps. 55:21)

w. without knowledge, p. 54, (Job 35:16)

Work: abounding in the w. of the Lord, p. 210, (I Cor. 15:58)

be strong ye people and w., p. 125, (Hagg. 2:4)

his w. is perfect, p. 21, (Deut. 32:4)

man's w. . . . fire shall try it, p. 205, (I Cor. 3:13)

this w. was wrought of our God, p. 46, (Neh. 6:16)

w. the works of him that sent me, p. 168, (Jn. 9:4)

the w. of the ministry, p. 216, (Eph. 4:12)

you shall w. six days, p. 19, (Ex. 20:9; 23:12; Lev. 23:3; Deut. 5:13)

Workers: w. together with him, p. 211, (II Cor. 6:1)

Workman: w. that need not be ashamed, p. 226, (II Tim. 2:15)

Workmanship: we are his w. p. 216, (Eph. 2:10)

Works: faith without w. is dead, p. 234, (Jas. 2:26)

great and marvellous are thy w., p. 245, (Rev. 15:3)

how manifold are thy w., p. 65, (Ps. 104:24)

not of w., lest any man boast, p. 215, (Eph. 2:9)

Works: (continued)

received ye the Spirit by w. of the law?, p. 214, (Gal. 3:2)

set him over the w. of thy hands, p. 228, (Heb. 2:7)

thy w., thy labor and thy patience, p. 240, (Rev. 2:2)

wrought all our w. in us, p. 88, (Isa. 26:12)

Worm: a w. smote the gourd which withered, p. 121, (Jonah 4:7)

man which is a w., p. 53, (Job 25:6)

Wormwood: bitter as w., p. 69, (Prov. 5:4)

feed them . . . with w., p. 100, (Jer. 9:15; 23:15)

the name of the star was W., p. 244, (Rev. 8:11)

World: be not conformed to this w., p. 203, (Rom. 12:2)

established the w. by his wisdom, p. 103, (Jer. 51:15)

for God so loved the w., p. 165, (Jn. 3:16)

he was in the w., p. 131, (Jn. 1:10)

I am not of this w., p. 168, (Jn. 8:23)

the kingdoms of the w., p. 136, (Matt. 4:8–9; Lk. 4:5–7)

the w. knew him not, p. 131, (Jn. 1:10)

the w. passeth away and the lust, p. 238, (I Jn. 2:17)

thou has sent me into the w., p. 180, (Jn. 17:18)

Worship: are come to w. him, p. 134, (Matt. 2:2)

come, let us w. and bow down, p. 63, (Ps. 95:6)

do not ye w. the golden image?, p. 111, (Dan. 3:14)

that I may come and w. him also, p. 134, (Matt. 2:8)

the w. of the golden calf, p. 18, (Ex. 32)

thou shalt w. the Lord thy God, p. 136, (Matt. 4:10; Lk. 4:8)

to fall down and w. it, p. 111, (Dan. 3:5)

w. in spirit and in truth, p. 166, (Jn. 4:24)

w. the Lord in the beauty of holiness, p. 63, (Ps. 96:9)

Worshipped: when they saw Jesus they w. him, p. 185, (Matt. 28:17)

w. and served the creature, p. 199, (Rom. 1:25)

Worthy: more than me is not w., p. 147, (Matt. 10:37; cf. Lk. 14:26)

no man was found w. to open and read it, p. 242, (Rev. 5:4)

not w. of me, p. 147, (Matt. 10:38; cf. Lk. 14:27)

not w. that . . . come under my roof, p. 143, (Matt. 8:8; Lk. 7:6)

thou art w. to take the book, p. 242, (Rev. 5:9)

w. is the Lamb that was slain, p. 242, (Rev. 5:12)

Wounded: a w. spirit, p. 72, (Prov. 18:14)

w. in the house of my friends, p. 127, (Zech. 13:6)

Wounds: these w. in thine hands, p. 126, (Zech. 13:6)

Wicked: a w. and adulterous genera- tion, p. 155, (Matt. 16:4; cf. 12:39; Lk. 11:29)

breath of his lips shall he slay the w., p. 85, (Isa. 11:4)

no peace unto the w., p. 93, (Isa. 48:22)

O thou w. servant, p. 163, (Matt. 18:32)

parable of the w. tenants, p. 170, (Matt. 21:33–41; Mk. 12:1–19; Lk. 20:9–16)

the w. cease from troubling, p. 50, (Job 3:17)

the w. in great power, p. 59, (Ps. 37:35)

thou w. and slothful servant, p. 175, (Matt. 25:26; cf. Lk. 19:22)

triumphing of the w. is short, p. 53, (Job 20:5)

w. man travaileth with pain, p. 52, (Job 15:20)

wickedness proceedeth from the w., p. 34, (I Sam. 24:13)

will not at all acquit the w., p. 122, (Nahum 1:3)

Wickedness: far be it from God . . . do w., p. 54, (Job 34:10)

full of extortion and w., p. 172, (Matt. 23:25; Lk. 11:39)

in the tents of w., p. 62, (Ps. 84:10)

loose the bands of w., p. 95, (Isa. 58:6)

not like unto Ahab for w., p. 41, (I Kg. 21:25)

the w. of man was great, p. 6, (Gen. 6:5)

their w. is come up before me, p. 120, (Jonah 1:2)

w. be sweet in his mouth, p. 53, (Job 20:12)

w. proceedeth from the wicked, p. 34, (I Sam. 24:13)

ye have plowed w., p. 116, (Hos. 10:13)

Wide: a brawling woman in a w. house, p. 72, (Prov. 21:9; 25:24)

for w. is the gate, p. 142, (Matt. 7:13)

Widow: Elijah dwelt with a w., p. 40, (I Kg. 17:8–24)

Elisha and the w.'s oil, p. 42, (II Kg. 4:1–7)

oppress not the w., p. 126, (Zech. 7:10)

the son of the w. of Nain, p. 155, (Lk. 7:11–17)

the w.'s heart to sing, p. 54, (Job 29:13)

the w.'s mite, p. 172, (Mk. 12:41–44; Lk. 21:1–4)

Wife: a w. of whoredoms, p. 114, (Hos. 1:2)

and cleave to his w., p. 163, (Matt. 19:5; Mk. 10:7)

faithless w. restored, p. 114, (Hos. 2:14–23)

he that loveth his w. loveth himself, p. 217, (Eph. 5:28)

Israel the faithless w., p. 114, (Hos. 2:1–13)

Joseph took Mary as his w., p. 132, (Matt. 1:24)

let every man have his own w., p. 207, (I Cor. 7:2)

let not the husband put away his w., p. 207, (I Cor. 7:11)

let not the w. depart from her husband, p. 207, (I Cor. 7:10)

man cleaves to his w., p. 4, (Gen. 2:24)

neighed after his neighbor's w., p. 99, (Jer. 5:8)

not tell me she was your w., p. 7, (Gen. 12:18)

shall be joined unto his w., p. 217, (Eph. 5:31)

the w. of thy bosom, p. 22, (Deut. 13:6)

the w. reverence her husband, p. 217, (Eph. 5:33)

thy w. shall be as a fruitful vine, p. 67, (Ps. 128:3)

to find a w. for Isaac, p. 9, (Gen. 24)

unto the w., as unto the weaker vessel, p. 236, (I Pet. 3:7)

whoso findeth a w., p. 72, (Prov. 18:22)

Wild: he will be a w. man, p. 8, (Gen. 16:12)

Wilderness: forty years through the w., p. 118, (Amos 2:10)

in the w. forty days, p. 135, (Matt. 4:1–2; Mk. 1:13; Lk. 4:2)

led by the Spirit into the w., p. 135, (Matt. 4:1; Mk. 1:12; Lk. 4:1)

make her w. like Eden, p. 93, (Isa. 51:3)

manna in the w., p. 16, (Ex. 16; Num. 11:6–9, 31)

voice of one crying in the w., p. 135, (Matt. 3:3; Mk. 1:3; Lk. 3:4)

wander in the w., p. 19, (Num. 14:33)

what went ye into the w. to see, p. 148, (Matt. 11:7; Lk. 7:24)

Will: did the w. of his father, p. 170, (Matt. 21:31)

he that doeth the w. of God abideth, p. 238, (I Jn. 2:17)

if the Lord w., we shall live, p. 234, (Jas. 4:15)

nevertheless not my w., but thine, p. 180, (Matt. 26:39; Mk. 14:36; Lk. 22:42)

to do the w. of him that sent me, p. 166, (Jn. 4:34)

Willing: if you be w. and obedient, p. 81, (Isa. 1:19)

Willows: hanged our harps upon the w., p. 67, (Ps. 137:2)

Wine: a little w. for thy stomach's sake, p. 225, (I Tim. 5:23)

and w. take away the heart, p. 115, (Hos. 4:11)

drunken but not with w., p. 89, (Isa. 29:9)

full of new w., p. 189, (Acts 2:13)

kept the good w. until now, p. 137, (Jn. 2:10)

love is better than w., p. 77, (Song 1:2)

new w. into old bottles, p. 145, (Matt. 9:17; Mk. 2:22; Lk. 5:37)

the mountains shall drop sweet w., p. 119, (Amos 9:13)

Wine: (continued)

when they wanted more w., p. 137, (Jn. 2:3)

w. is a mocker, p. 72, (Prov. 20:1)

w. maketh merry, p. 76, (Ec. 10:19)

w. to gladden the heart, p. 65, (Ps. 104:15)

Winebibber: a glutton and w., p. 148, (Matt. 11:19; Lk. 7:34)

Winepress: trodden the w. alone, p. 96, (Isa. 63:3)

Wines: a feast of w. on the lees, p. 87, (Isa. 25:6)

Wind: a great w. rent the mountains, p. 41, (II Kg. 19:11)

a mighty w., p. 189, (Acts 2:2)

arose a tempestuous w., p. 198, (Acts 27:14)

he that forms the mountains and creates the w., p. 118, (Amos 4:13)

his belly with the east w., p. 52, (Job 15:2)

rebuked the w. and the raging water, p. 144, (Matt. 8:26; Mk. 4:39; Lk. 8:24)

the w. bloweth where it listeth, p. 165, (Jn 3:8)

the w. passeth over it, p. 64, (Ps. 103:16)

they have sown the w., p. 116, (Hos. 8:7)

with every w. of doctrine, p. 217, (Eph. 4:14)

Window: by a cord through the w., p. 27, (Josh. 2:15)

Windows: the w. of heaven, p. 6, (Gen. 7:11)

Winds: as the four w. of the heaven, p. 126, (Zech. 2:6)

holding the four w., p. 243, (Rev. 7:1)

w. and sea obey him, p. 144, (Matt. 8:27; Mk. 4:41; Lk. 8:25)

Wings: hide me under thy w., p. 56, (Ps. 17:8)

if I take the w. of the morning, p. 68, (Ps. 139:9)

mount up with w. as eagles, p. 92, (Isa. 40:31)

two w. of every one were joined, p. 105, (Ezek. 1:11)

Winter: lo, the w. is past, p. 77, (Song 2:11)

smite the w. house with the summer house, p. 118, (Amos 3:15)

Wipe: w. Jerusalem as a man wipeth a dish, p. 45, (II Kg. 21:13)

Wisdom: fear of the Lord is the beginning of w., p. 65, (Ps. 111:10)

fear of the Lord, that is w., p. 53, (Job 28:28)

hymn to w., p. 53, (Job 28)

if you lack w. ask of God, p. 233, (Jas. 1:5)

in much w. is much grief, p. 74, (Ec. 1:18)

number the clouds in w., p. 55, (Job 38:37)

price of w. is above rubies, p. 53, (Job 28:18)

Solomon asked God for w., p. 37, (I Kg. 3:3–15; II Chr. 1:7–12)

Solomon's riches and w., p. 38, (I Kg. 4:25–34)

. . . the w. and knowledge of God!, p. 203, (Rom. 11:33)

the w. of Solomon, p. 38, (I Kg. 4:34)

thy w. and prosperity exceedeth, p. 38, (K Kg. 10:7; II Chr. 9:6)

to one is given by the Spirit the word of w., p. 208, (I Cor. 12:8)

we speak the w. of God in a mystery, p. 205, (I Cor. 2:7)

where shall w. be found, p. 53, (Job 28:12)

w. crieth without, p. 69, (Prov. 1:20)

w. excelleth folly, p. 74, (Ec. 2:13)

w. is better than rubies, p. 70, (Prov. 8:11)

w. is better than weapons, p. 76, (Ec. 9:18)

w. is the principal thing, p. 69, (Prov. 4:7)

w. of this world is foolishness, p. 206, (I Cor. 3:19)

w. strengtheneth the wise, p. 75, (Ec. 7:19)

w. will die with you, p. 51, (Job 12:2)

with the ancient is w., p. 52, (Job 12:12)

Wise: a w. and an understanding heart, p. 37, (I Kg. 3:9; II Chr. 1:10)

a w. man utter vain knowledge, p. 52, (Job 15:2)

be not w. in your own conceits, p. 203, (Rom. 12:16)

better is a poor and a w. child, p. 75, (Ec. 4:13)

great men are not always w., p. 54, (Job 32:9)

he told the w. men: search for the child, p. 134, (Matt. 2:7)

hid these things from the w., p. 148, (Matt. 11:25; Lk. 10:21)

how dieth the wise man?, p. 74, (Ec. 2:16)

professing themselves to be w., p. 199, (Rom. 1:22)

rebuke a w. man, p. 70, (Prov. 9:8)

to confound the w., p. 205, (I Cor. 1:27)

the visit of the w. men, p. 134, (Matt. 2:1–2; 9–11)

which are able to make thee w., p. 226, (II Tim. 3:15)

the w. in their own craftiness, p. 50, (Job 5:13)

the w. men did not return, p. 134, (Matt. 2:12)

the w. men . . . worshipped him, p. 134, (Matt. 2:11)

w. as serpents, harmless as doves, p. 146, (Matt. 10:16)

w. men from the east to Jerusalem, p. 134, (Matt. 2:1)

w. son maketh a glad father, p. 70, (Prov. 10:1)

wisdom strengtheneth the w., p. 75, (Ec. 7:19)

Witch: Saul and the w. of Endor. p. 34, (I Sam. 28)

With: behold I am w. you, p. 10, (Gen. 28:15)

for I am w. you, saith the Lord, p. 125, (Hagg. 2:4)

he that is not w. me, p. 155, (Matt. 12:30; Lk. 11:23)

I am w. you always even unto the end of the world, p. 185, (Matt. 28:20)

woe to them that are w. child, p. 173, (Matt. 24:19; Mk. 13:17; Lk. 21:23)

Withered: a man with a w. hand, p. 149, (Matt. 12:9–13; Mk. 3:1–5; Lk. 6:6–10)

Witness: John bare w. unto the truth, p. 167, (Jn. 5:33)

to bear w. to the truth, p. 181, (Jn. 18:37)

w. of the resurrection, p. 190, (Acts 4:33)

Witnesses: we are his w. and . . . the Holy Spirit, p. 191, (Acts 5:32)

whereof we all are w., p. 190, (Acts 2:32)

so great a cloud of w., p. 231, (Heb. 12:1)

Wives: his w. turned away his heart, p. 39, (I Kg. 11:4)

husbands, love your w., p. 217, (Eph. 5:25)

Wrath: affliction by the rod of his w., p. 104, (Lam. 3:1)

cruel with w., and fierce anger, p. 85, (Isa. 13:9)

Elihu's w. kindled against Job, p. 54, (Job 32:2)

great day of his w. has come., p. 243, (Rev. 6:17)

in w. remember mercy, p. 124, (Hab. 3:2)

pour out my w. upon them like water, p. 115, (Hos. 5:10)

seven golden vials full of the w. of God., p. 245, (Rev. 15:7)

soft answer turneth away w., p. 71, (Prov. 15:1)

the day of the Lord is a day of w., p. 124, (Zeoh. 1:14–15)

the sun go down on your w., p. 217, (Eph. 4:26)

the w. of God against all ungodliness, p. 199, (Rom. 1:18)

w. of man worketh not the righteousness of God, p. 233, (Jas. 1:20)

w. which consumed them as stubble, p. 16, (Ex. 15:7)

Wrapped: w. him in swaddling clothes, p. 132, (Lk. 2:7)

Wrestles: Jacob w. with an angel, p. 11, (Gen. 32:24)

Wretched: O w. man that I am!, p. 201, (Rom. 7:24)

Wrestle: we w. not against flesh and blood, p. 218, (Eph. 6:12)

Write: what thou seest w. in a book, p. 240, (Rev. 1:11)

w. it before them in a table, p. 89, (Isa. 30:8)

w. it in their hearts, p. 102, (Jer. 31:33)

Written: he of whom it is w., p. 148, (Matt 11:10; Lk. 7:27)

oh that my words were now w.!, p. 52, (Job 19:23)

Written: (continued)

you are w. in our hearts, p. 210, (II Cor. 3:2)

Writer: my tongue is the pen of a ready w., p. 60, (Ps. 45:1)

Wrong: unto the Jews . . . no w., p. 197, (Acts 25:10)

Wronged: if he hath w. thee, p. 228, (Philem. v. 18)

Wrought: what hath God w., p. 20, (Num. 23:23)

Yea: communication be: Y., y.; Nay, nay, p. 140, (Matt. 5:37)

Year: the acceptable y. of the Lord, p. 95, (Isa. 61:2)

the acceptable y. of the Lord, p. 157, (Lk. 4:19; Isa. 61:2)

the y. that King Uzziah died, p. 83, (Isa. 6:1)

Yesterday: a thousand years . . . are but as y., p. 62, (Ps. 90:4)

the same y., today and for ever, p. 232, (Heb. 13:8)

we are but of y., p. 51, (Job 8:9)

Yoke: bear the y. in his youth, p. 105, (Lam. 3:27)

my y. is easy, p. 149, (Matt. 11:30)

take my y. upon you, p. 149, (Matt. 11:29)

Yom Kippur: p. 22, (Lev. 23:26–32; Num. 29:7–11)

Young: the y. man went away sorrowful, p. 164, (Matt. 19:22; Mk. 10:22; Lk. 18:23)

to the y. man knowledge, p. 69, (Prov. 1:4)

y. men see visions, p. 117, (Joel 2:28)

y. men shall see visions, p. 189, (Acts 2:17)

Younger: elder shall serve the y., p. 10, (Gen. 25:23)

Youth: bear the yoke in his y., p. 105, (Lam. 3:27)

in the days of my y., p. 54, (Job 29:4)

let no man despise thy y., p. 225, (I Tim. 4:12)

rejoice, young man, in thy y., p. 76, (Ec. 11:9)

remember thy creator in . . . thy y., p. 76, (Ec. 12:1)

these have I kept from my y. up, p. 163, (Matt. 19:20; Mk. 10:20; Lk. 18:21)

thou hast the dew of thy y., p. 65, (Ps. 110:3)

Zacchaeus: Z., come down, p. 154, (Lk. 19:5)

Z. in the sycamore tree, p. 154, (Lk. 19:1–10)

Z. sought to see him, p. 154, (Lk. 19:3)

Zacharias: Gabriel appeared to Z., p. 131, (Lk. 1:11, 19)

the song of Z., p. 132, (Lk. 1:67–79)

Zadok: Z. the priest anointed Solomon, p. 37, (I Kg. 1:39)

Zeal: the z. of thine house hath eaten me up, p. 61, (Ps. 69:9)

Zebedee: with Z. their father, p. 136, (Matt. 4:21; Mk. 1:19)

Zechariah: word of the Lord to Z., p. 125, (Zech. 1:1)

Z.'s vision, p. 125, (Zech. 1:8–21)

Zedekiah: he put out Z.'s eyes, p. 103, (Jer. 39:7)

I will deliver Z. to Nebuchadrezzar, p. 101, (Jer. 21:7)

Jeremiah prophesies to Z., p. 101, (Jer. 21)

Nebuchadnezzar slew the sons of Z., p. 103, (Jer. 39:6)

Zepheniah: the word of the Lord to Z., p. 124, (Zeph. 1:1)

Zion: a voice of wailing is heard out of Z., p. 100, (Jer. 9:19)

blow a trumpet in Z., p. 116, (Joel 2:1)

rejoice greatly, O daughter of Z., p. 126, (Zech. 9:9)

shall yet comfort Z., p. 125, (Zech. 1:17)

the daughters of Z. are haughty, p. 82, (Isa. 3:16)

the law shall go forth of Z., p. 122, (Micah 4:2)

the Lord shall comfort Z., p. 93, (Isa. 51:3)

the Lord will roar from Z., p. 118, (Amos 1:2)

Zophar: Eliphaz, Bildad, and Z., p. 49, (Job 2:11)

Z.'s response, p. 53, (Job 20)

Z.'s speech, p. 51, (Job 11)